Miss Manners'® Guide for the Turn-of-the-Millennium

Judith Martin

Illustrated by Gloria Kamen

 A FIRESIDE BOOK
Published by Simon & Schuster Inc.
New York London Toronto Sydney Tokyo Singapore

Fireside
Simon & Schuster Building
Rockefeller Center
1230 Avenue of the Americas
New York, New York 10020

Copyright © 1983, 1984, 1985, 1986, 1987, 1988,
1989 by United Feature Syndicate, Inc.

Illustrations copyright © 1989 by Gloria Kamen
First Fireside Edition, 1990
Published by arrangement with Pharos Books

FIRESIDE and colophon are registered trademarks
of Simon & Schuster Inc.

Manufactured in the United States of America

10 9 8 7 6 5 4 3 2 1 Pbk.

Library of Congress Cataloging in Publication Data

Martin, Judith, date.
Miss Manners' guide for the turn-of-the-millennium / Judith
Martin.—1st Fireside ed.
p.   cm.
"A Fireside book."
Includes index.
1. Etiquette.   I. Title.
[BJ1853.M2935   1990]
395—dc20
                                                                90-36329
                                                                    CIP

ISBN 0-671-72228-X Pbk.

Miss Manners is a registered trademark of United Feature Syndicate, Inc.

For Robert

Contents

Illustrations

Preface

When the late Clara Grace Perfect (née Proper) wished to insult her growing daughter (an urge even Perfect mothers have been known to feel under stress), she was far too polite to say anything so natural and spontaneous as "You rotten kid, why couldn't you have taken after my side of the family instead of your father's?" Instead she said, in her gentle voice, "I don't wish you any evil, dearest Daffodil Louise, but I do hope that one day you will have a child just like you. Then—when it is too late, of course—you will understand what I'm going through."

It was an unfortunate curse, not because it came true, but because Daffodil Right (née Perfect), now well into her blameless middle age, sometimes sighs and wishes it had. She could have understood and helped anyone who had had the same unruly experiences she did when she was growing up.

Instead, her three children by her first marriage and her three stepchildren from her second husband's first marriage turned out, after a bit of turmoil, to be like—why, Mrs. Perfect, of all people. Oh, there were a few false starts here and there, heaven knows, and their lives are hardly circumspect. However, they have now all developed an unmistakable interest, although each from a slightly different angle, in doing the Proper thing.

The most conventional are Daffodil's son, Gregory, and son not-quite-in-law, Lars Uhmm, by now a staid old couple. Daffodil's husband, Theodore Right, who grumbles mildly when he has to dress up to go to their Victorian town house for five-course dinners, says that even Gregory's late grandfather would (if he weren't terminally dizzy from spinning in his grave all these years) enjoy listening to them complain about the deterioration of the modern world and the absence of good, old-fashioned standards.

Daffodil's elder daughter, Victorine, who had lived with her Whatchamacallit for a decade without once missing an opportunity to inform her grandmother and her great-aunt, Mrs. Plue Perfect, that she couldn't love freely and ecstatically if

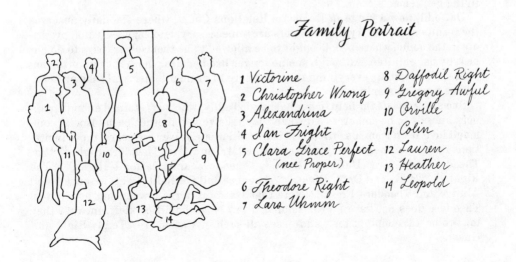

Family Portrait

1 Victorine
2 Christopher Wrong
3 Alexandrina
4 Ian Fright
5 Clara Grace Perfect (nee Proper)
6 Theodore Right
7 Lars Uhmm
8 Daffodil Right
9 Gregory Awful
10 Orville
11 Colin
12 Lauren
13 Heather
14 Leopold

bound by legal chains (a sentiment that they came to associate with their difficulty in digesting holiday dinners), now demanded a full-scale, formal wedding, which, she announced, she had dreamed of ever since she was a little girl.

The dream she described included a cathedral train with intertwined initials embroidered on it, eight bridesmaids dressed in black, a humorous master of ceremonies, and, in lieu of wedding presents, a guests' fund to pay off the happy couple's condo mortgage. At first, she wanted her son to toddle up the aisle with her to give her away (to his father), but then she thought of Jonathan Rhinehart Awful, whom she vaguely remembered to be her own father. When Victorine's stepfather graciously overlooked her overlooking him, he and Daffodil invited Rhino to come to tea to discuss the plans (which they had altered to taste).

After unfortunately mistaking Victorine for her married sister, to whom he directed a speech about how he couldn't stand to lose his baby to some beast of a man, Rhino asked if anybody expected him to pay for anything. Daffodil took this to be an acceptance. Mollified when they promised that there would be no charge for the role of father, Rhino dropped the demand that his current wife, Kimberly, being Victorine's age, should be a bridesmaid.

Daffodil and Rhino's other daughter, Alexandrina, had been married long ago in a wedding service she wrote herself, and before which Daffodil took the precaution of removing the batteries from her parents' hearing aids. After breast-feeding her new twins at office strategy sessions, Alexandrina finally decided to leave acquisitions and mergers to stay home with the nanny. Her hobby is telephoning her former colleagues when they are most harassed in order to ask whether they feel guilty about not doing the same. Alexandrina is also an active clubwoman; in fact, she is the only woman in the venerable Old Boys' (now Mature Persons') Club, which has, under her supervision, converted its Pinochle and Port Parlor into a splendid ladies' room complete with stage lighting. Out of fairness and a small extra assessment to the membership, she is having a babies' changing table installed in the gentlemen's room.

Daffodil, now a judge in Domestic Relations Court, where she daily observes the results of the theory that manners are unnecessary, and especially inappropriate in the home, where people ought to be allowed to be themselves, tries to do her best by her children. Although she no longer has her dear mother or aunt to consult, she remembers everything they took care to drum into her while she pretended she wasn't listening.

She also appeals for help to her husband, Teddy, who has retained enough manners himself to be embarrassed when they receive yet another pseudosocial command invitation from his office. (He is in solid waste.) Over the years, these invitations have been successively addressed to "Mr. and Mrs. Theodore Right," "Mr. Theodore and Mrs. Daffodil Right," "Theodore and Daffodil Right," "The Rights," "Teddy and Daffy Right," "Theodore and Daffodil Right, Esquire," and "Judge and Theodore Right." (Note that Daffodil is the lawyer and now judge; Theodore does not have a professional title.) Now the office staff, in what they take to be a triumph of tact, addresses all such invitations to "Teddy Right and Guest."

The Rights know wrongs when they see them, and are not intimidated into feeling that they must accept crude or callous behavior on the grounds that it is modern. However, they are unprepared for the questions they get from the elder children, who assume that they know the traditional answers for such questions as: Do you have to reciprocate when a corporation sends you a present? How often does a considerate person change the comic message on his or her answering machine? What is the difference between how you treat a cleaning service and how you treat a cleaning woman? What is the correct color to wear to a party given to celebrate the life of someone who has just died?

Then there are the problems concerning social behavior that Daffodil encounters from Heather, Lauren, and Orville, who are of school age. She feels that she did a better job in rearing them than her own children. For example, she successfully taught them not to be embarrassed when their friends find out that the family daily observes a strange ritual by which all of them eat the same dinner together around a table, instead of individually picking what they want from the refrigerator when they want it.

She also brought them up to answer birthday party invitations and send letters thanking their relatives for sending them presents. But she was at a loss when Lauren patiently explained that she couldn't answer a certain party invitation because she'd only "heard about the party" she was going to "from a friend who's a friend of the boy who's giving it, and he said she should round up some people." Even if she were allowed to attend such a function, to whom would she reciprocate—the unknown host or the message giver?

When Lauren's sister, Heather, confided that she didn't want to go out with a certain boy because she wasn't sure she liked him, Daffodil replied, "One evening won't kill you, dear, and you'll have a chance to meet other boys through him." She was unprepared when Heather looked at her, shocked, and explained that everyone would consider that she was "going out" with the original boy, not only for that evening but for the duration, and that no friend of his would dream of encroaching.

Although Daffodil had had a not uneventful youth, she was also embarrassed when she found out that she had granted Orville permission to spend the night at Chris's without knowing that Chris was a girl. The embarrassment occurred when she realized how deeply she had shocked Orville by presuming that "anything had happened." Reminding her indignantly that Natalie was his girlfriend and Chris their friend, Orville inquired how his stepmother could have had such a dirty mind as to imagine that he and Chris could have "done anything" just because they happened to spend the night together.

"Sometimes I feel as if I don't understand anything anymore," Daffodil often says to Teddy of an evening. "Everybody means well, but it's all so bewildering. What would Mother have done if she had had the prospect of living into the twenty-first century?"

It is to answer that question that this book is written.

Miss Manners'
Guide for the
Turn-of-the-Millennium

Introduction

Heavy Etiquette Theory

That etiquette actually does change over the years, to adapt to society's notions and technology's gadgets, is a fact with which Miss Manners does not trust anyone except her august self. Others who have guessed this fascinating secret have not immediately pondered how best to use it to improve the world. They were too busy falling all over themselves to see how quickly they could drop whatever duties they found irksome.

The odd thing is that they never seemed to get around to replacing courtesies they considered outmoded with modernized ones. The enlightened gentleman who has proudly given up yielding bus seats to ladies, refusing to compromise this principle no matter how desperately an individual lady hanging in front of him obviously needs to sit down before she falls, does not generally fight for egalitarianism on other fronts. Nor has he taught his daughter to yield her place to frail gentlemen. He can't even school himself to be civil when a polite young lady treats him with the deference due to age regardless of gender; that any lady should be able to think of him "regardless of gender" infuriates him into apoplexy.

So, to all those shouting "Oh, wow! Freedom!" Miss Manners responds, in her ladylike way: "Nice try. Now get a grip."

3

Miss Manners refuses to allow society to seek its own level. Having peered through her lorgnette into the abyss, she can guess how low that level would be. Throughout this book, you will find dreadful etiquette innovations suggested by amateurs and, she trusts, crushed by herself. Let us hear no more, after this, from people who have cunningly figured that their friends owe them presents at certain intervals and therefore that, rather than enduring the results of such people's taste and generosity, they could channel this resource by supplying shopping lists or demanding cash. Why they don't thoroughly modernize by having everyone run up charges (you owe me so much for getting married, I owe you so much for your graduation, we each owe for birthdays, but I get more because it was a significant one), and settling the difference with a bill at the end of the year, Miss Manners doesn't know. It can't be delicacy.

Human nature does not change. It still takes a while to get to know and trust people, and the phony use of the manners of friendship by strangers and mere acquaintances only misleads people into thinking that instant intimacy is pleasant and safe.

You will always have to write thank-you letters and answer invitations, admire new babies and pay condolence calls, and look after your guests at your own expense rather than theirs or your employer's.

Nevertheless, it is true that some things have changed since Miss Manners and Queen Victoria went to school together:

Most adults are in the work force, which means that ladies must practice, and must be treated with, good business manners. Social manners, by which one doesn't discuss money or insist upon recognition, do not apply in business, where it is inappropriate to treat colleagues as if they were dinner partners available for flirting or hostesses responsible for providing food and drink.

New customs must be developed for managing the domestic, social, and community realms that ladies used to run. The rule about not criticizing people for how they choose to live their lives is still in effect: It is as nasty for ladies to scorn other ladies for not taking pay for their work as the reverse was some years back. Everyone, in fact, seems to need a refresher course in the discipline known colloquially as Minding One's Own (insert an optional adjective here, as long as it is not a rude one) Business.

Divorce is widespread, so the old-fashioned luxury of maintaining lifelong public feuds, which involved dramatic scenes on the part of the former couple at their children's weddings, as well as the dissolution of all ties between the families, is no longer feasible. The manners of tolerance are required on a new scale. Miss Manners has also invented a new category called "relatives once removed" for those who choose to stay on good terms.

Servants have been largely replaced by household equipment—the butler is now an answering machine, for example—so the etiquette involving them is different. A new and dignified civility is required in the relationships between service people, whether they are doctors or house cleaners, and their clients.

Weddings are held at what we shall ever so gently call a later state of courtship, which means that the principals are apt to be older and their families geographically scattered. All of this requires adjustments in the ceremonial traditions designed for young people coming from the shelter of their parents' homes. Financial independence does not, however, buy control.

Society has learned to recognize social units short of marriage and needs rules for dealing with them. What we are going to call these relationships continues to baffle Miss Manners, who is still open to hearing a simple term suitable for public usage. The rest, as you will see, she has managed. To the thousands who have written Miss Manners asking how to address such a couple, the answer is: by their names, for goodness' sake. If it means squandering two whole lines on an envelope, so be it.

Even death has been subject to etiquette revision, sunglasses replacing veils to shield the immediately bereaved and friends, rather than clergy, providing the eulogies. Those who attempt to force more radical change, by abandoning ceremony (with the argument that it "can't help" the dead) and obliterating mourning (with the argument that people "feel better" by plunging back into normal life), are tragically wrong. Showing respect for the dead, and for the feelings of their survivors, is a basic tenet of civilization, not an old social fad to be left behind in these supposedly more sophisticated times.

Miss Manners has herein sorted out all this confusion to determine what from the past should be adapted for the future, what retained as is, and what abandoned. She has sorted through contemporary practices and decided which are acceptable and which must cease this instant. She has also slipped in a few futuristic inventions of her own, which are easier to get away with when one is a sweet little old-fashioned lady.

She is counting on you to learn all this so that we can have a nice, fresh, polite new millennium. As much fun as she has been having with the last millennium, she would like daily life in the next one to be just a shade more civilized.

❧ SOME PRINCIPLES

"Oh, all right. I suppose. If you must. Just this once." Every enterprising child is familiar with this pitiful form of parental permission and the insidious technique of extracting it. One chooses a request that, although known to be against the parent's wishes, is nevertheless non-life-threatening. Then one falsely promises that acquiescence will set no precedents and wheedles mercilessly until the parent can no longer stand to hear about it. For all its tone of exasperation and exhaustion, the resulting permission is as valid as an enthusiastic one. The most a parent can protest, if the permitted activity ends in disaster, is, "I knew I shouldn't have given in," which is, after all, only self-condemning.

Miss Manners brings this up not to tutor slow children in parental control but to explain the sort of pressure that has been brought to bear on august members of her own profession. We of the Etiquette Council are generally a tough lot, but there are those among us who have been weakened by relentless pummeling into sanctioning things that must be against their better judgment.

Thus it is now possible to cite some sort of authority for such obvious sins as:

Putting ketchup bottles on dining tables.

Handing out business cards at social events.

Using writing paper with the preprinted words "Thank you."

Cutting formality with cuteness, such as embellishing formal invitations with pictures, mottoes, nicknames, or strange wording; or gentlemen wearing evening clothes in patterns or colors that are supposed to denote originality or to match the ladies' dresses.

Organizing private occasions, such as weddings or anniversary parties, as fund-raising opportunities in which guests are given instructions for channeling their presumed generosity.

Miss Manners can picture—indeed, she has often been subjected to—the kind of pressure that has extracted these unfortunate concessions:

"It's only family dinner, and everybody's in a hurry."

"Nobody has social cards any more, and besides, I do a lot of important networking at parties."

"But I've got so many thank-yous to write! Besides, see how pretty it is, embossed in gold!"

"What's wrong with personalizing these things? I want it to express me."

"They'll only end up with a lot of junk they can't use, when they would really enjoy being able to take a nice vacation."

It becomes easier to understand why others in the etiquette profession give up and give in than it perhaps is to understand why Miss Manners objects. Whom do these compromises harm? Isn't the great battle cry of our day "Oh, why not?"

Miss Manners hardly knows which defense to make: that there are, in fact, people who are offended by these transgressions or that as the offenses are allowed to become increasingly common, there will soon be few people left who know the difference. Both are true. Miss Manners' Gentle Readers tell her that she is far from being the only crank who cringes when invited to do business while trying to relax or directed to sponsor the dreams of some far-from-indigent celebrant. In addition, she feels in charge of worrying about the general deterioration of the world (etiquette division). If necessary, she will stand guard alone against the sloppiness that results when people decide that nothing much is worth bothering about and the confusion that occurs when they grant themselves the right to ignore society's customs and invent their own.

Miss Manners' stance should not be interpreted as being against progress. Etiquette does, and must, grow and develop, as even the most stuffy-minded person will admit (and just did). Change that results from indifference to the feelings of others, refusal to recognize the need for tradition and grace, or the desire to gain a monetary advantage from one's social life is not acceptable. The idea that each person can develop his or her own language of behavior without worrying about its being comprehensible to others just doesn't work.

The Money Factor

It is astonishing to Miss Manners that so many people presume that the gentle art of manners is based on a preoccupation with money. Etiquette, it is widely believed, consists of forms of behavior requiring fortunes in silverware, evening clothing, and unwieldy vehicles. Most people feel they need etiquette only on occasions when they are spending a great deal of money—putting on a wedding, for example. Otherwise, they can apparently make do with rudeness. Dear, dear. You can imagine how upsetting Miss Manners finds this. She doesn't know which offends her more—people who seek to demonstrate their genuineness by eschewing manners or those who are scrambling to learn them to serve their social ambitions. They all end up rude. The truth is that there is very little relationship between manners and money. Certainly, Miss Manners has never noticed any preponderance of politeness on the part of the rich.

Good manners are, first of all, free. That is not generally true of status symbols. Second, they cover all forms of outward human behavior, from those needed for the most routine daily encounters in households or on highways, to special ones for special occasions. Third, the consequences of violating etiquette in ordinary life are more unpleasant than the effects of small technical errors on formal occasions, when it would be rude of other people present to notice. Fourth, the same people who disdain manners in the rich are outraged when they are treated rudely by those in their own circumstances.

Why, then, does etiquette's reputation for abetting snobbery persist? Miss Manners attributes it partly to the fact that one always thinks of familiar behavior as being simply natural, and strange behavior as etiquette. Everyday behavior is therefore classified as nice or mean, rather than good manners or bad, while the self-consciousness one has on rare occasions leads one to identify special practices as manners.

There is also a mistaken belief that knowledge and possession of expensive things is a demonstration of propriety. Propriety and impropriety have nothing to do with how much one can afford to spend. Etiquette's interest in taste, as that applies to consumer items, is chiefly in combatting ostentation. What is improper is the diamond bracelet worn for tennis, the car or house referred to as a "limousine" or "mansion," the visible designer label—any inappropriate display of wealth or preoccupation with the cost of one's own or other people's possessions.

Commercial hoity-toitiness, which is the deliberate policy of treating people contemptuously in order to make them spend money in the hope of buying better treatment, ought to be self-defeating. Why would anyone pay good money to be subjected to rudeness? Yet shops and restaurants and other public accommodations that systematically take the attitude that the customer has to fork over huge amounts of money—in overpriced goods or in bribes disguised as tips—to prove that he or she is acceptable to the help seem to thrive. Professional firms that require their receptionists to treat even expected visitors as intruders whose claims must be verified by the staff when they have the time continue to do business. Miss Manners is bewildered that this nastiness works. Why don't customers simply avoid places that treat them badly? Why don't they complain to management or to their professional hosts that they find this unpleasant?

She takes some pleasure in knowing that such businesses are particularly vulnerable to making mistakes about which potential customers are rich and demanding and which are not. Those with the most money to spend are least likely to feel that they have to dress up to go shopping or to advertise with their behavior that they don't care how much they spend on their entertainment. The less secure are more likely to go along with this test, hoping to pass muster with some disco doorman or to command the attention of a haughty salesman.

At the very least, hoity-toitiness should be recognized as the irritant it is, rather than the one it is meant to be. Just as graciousness to everyone is a true sign of superiority in an individual, giving excellent service to everyone is the best indication that a professional establishment is worth patronizing.

Evolution Not Revolution

"I suppose I'm being hopelessly old-fashioned," Miss Manners' Gentle Readers often begin when they are reporting other people's bad manners. Miss Manners knows immediately that the writers are confident of being exonerated. They feel not only right but positively charming. At worst, they figure, Miss Manners will confer on them an air of aristocratic conservatism because well-bred people never change.

Others introduce their complaints with "Am I senile to expect . . . ?" These people do not want Miss Manners' confirmation; they are not even confident that she will uphold their various positions. They plan to stand firm anyway, and the invocation of senility, far from suggesting that they are harmless, is meant to be threatening. While the "hopelessly old-fashioned" person wants to be pictured in superior isolation, the "senile" one represents him or herself as about to go on the rampage with a briar cane.

In her doddery way, Miss Manners has taken to pondering the true relationship of time to manners. She understands that people who use the word "nowadays" want exemption from decent behavior (as in "Nowadays, are you expected to answer invitations?") and those who say "any more" want to reestablish standards (as in "Are people expected to answer invitations any more?"). "This day and age" can go either way: to deplore a world without standards ("In this day and age, what do you expect?") or to deplore the world's being cluttered with obsolete requirements ("Surely, in this day and age, you don't expect . . .").

What is this all about? Miss Manners has a difficult time imagining that anyone could be so naive as to believe either that manners never change or that human behavior periodically changes so completely that the very premises of manners are subject to revision. Real etiquette changes happen slowly, usually to accommodate changes in philosophy or technology. For example, chivalry introduced the idea that the strong should yield to the weak, a reversal of the more natural and logical system of the weak yielding to the strong. We still accept the chivalrous order in private life (while the weak scurry to get out of the way of the strong in the marketplace), but the classification of women as weak has been challenged. We will probably soon settle on a version by which the young yield to the old.

These are not the sorts of change claimed by the gentle people Miss Manners has been quoting. Whether they are supporting or fighting particular developments, they all operate from the absurd notion that human nature itself has changed. What caused an entirely new world to appear is left vague. Perhaps there is somehow "less time" in the modern world than the old, or perhaps it was that troublesome recent invention, sex, that made the difference. The new etiquette they want or fear is based on the assumption that there is a new breed of human beings—people who no longer care to have their generosity acknowledged by gratitude, hosts who no longer need to know how many guests to expect, and so on.

Age is not a factor in being able to see the absurdity of this and of its crude weakness as an excuse for not respecting the eternal decencies of civilized life. The important factor is whether, young or old, you have the sense with which you were supposed to have been born.

The Grandparent Clause

"This is the way my generation was taught," pleaded the judge by way of asking for mercy. In the realm of courtesy, pleading for mercy is known as apologizing. In this instance, a federal judge in Pittsburgh was retreating from having insisted erroneously that a lawyer appearing in his court was legally required to style herself "Mrs." with her husband's surname, rather than following her preference of "Ms." with her birth name. Pennsylvania law, as it turned out, required no such thing.

That the judge's offense was made in an unmannerly way—he not only presumed to tell the lawyer what her own name was but intoned "What if I call you 'sweetie'?" and threatened her with jail—does not shock Miss Manners as much as it should. The emotional vehemence with which people react to etiquette changes is an old story to her.

She is, however, increasingly interested in the use of the generational excuse. When is it valid to plead custom and habit in retaining the etiquette one was brought up on, and when not?

This is not a simple issue. On the one side are people such as this judge who attempt to prevent the evolution of manners by bludgeoning others; but there are also people who simply want to do things the accustomed way without interference. On the other side are those who want to make sweeping reforms and force them on everyone, and those who simply invent their own forms and wonder why others do not understand, let alone employ, them.

All over the landscape, there are people who are puzzled and offended by the behavior of others because they are ignorant of old ways, or of new ones, or of who uses which. Somewhere in the middle, desperately trying to get everyone simmered down and make order out of it all, is poor Miss Manners.

Miss Manners acknowledges both the need for change and the difficulties change creates. Change should therefore come slowly. Pioneers will inevitably have a difficult time—hardship cannot be separated from the act of pioneering—as society weighs, judges, and either gets used to innovations or allows them to die. Miss Manners permits reformers zealous beliefs but not rude methods.

As a change gains hold, those who do not wish to go along may sometimes plead age. Miss Manners will recognize a Grandfather/Grandmother Clause as long as those forebears do not abuse it. This does not allow Grandpa to call the waitress "You purty thing you" or Grandma to address her granddaughter the doctor as "Mrs." when that young lady has made clear that she doesn't like it. By the same token, Dr. Granddaughter is not allowed to address Grandma as "Ms. Bella Wittingham-Purvis" when she has been known all her life as "Mrs. Hiram Purvis."

That previous generations had offensive habits, such as treating certain adults as children or all ladies as socially available, does not excuse doing so when this has been widely identified as insulting. Ignorance of society's reforms is no excuse unless you are in a line of work where you don't mind having it known that you are oblivious and insensitive—not a description of anyone who ought to be in a position to pass judgment.

The judge's apologetic statement to the contrary, his generation was taught not to contradict or insult ladies; and no generation was taught that it is polite to bully people. By threatening to call the lawyer "sweetie," he unfortunately lent credence to the argument that sexism, rather than merely custom, underlay his mistake.

Miss Manners is far from saying that all who cling to traditional ways are ill-motivated. There is grace and comfort in following the customs of one's youth, which should not be lightly abandoned. Miss Manners recognizes that the use of a husband's name by a wife is slowly becoming obsolete, as is the cumbersome use of separate abbreviations ("Miss" and "Mrs.") of the ancient respectable title of "Mistress," rather than one, "Ms." (which has been documented as far back as the seventeenth century), for all ladies to use with their own full names.

You will notice that Miss Manners herself does not abide by this. She also expects to be the last person on earth still using the full-service island at gasoline stations and acknowledges that she cries for help when her computer behaves peculiarly. This does not mean that Miss Manners would permit a young lady under her jurisdiction to operate an automobile or a computer without understanding how it works. Age has its privileges.

Where and When

One of the fine old weapons in the Etiquette Arsenal used to be the reprimand "There is a time and a place for that sort of thing." The words "and this isn't it" were understood. Delivered with something of a sniff (head tilted back, eyebrows slightly raised, nose pointed upward, features frozen except for a quivering of the nostrils and the minimum lip movement necessary to pronounce the words), this statement informed dependents that they had just demonstrated ignorance of a sense of the appropriate. What was most crushing about this enjoinder was that it quashed any hope the perpetrator might have had of shocking the elders. The time-and-place remark made it clear that it was not the action itself that was being condemned, but the arena in which it was performed.

Miss Manners wishes to reinstate this valuable tool. She finds that she must give lessons in its use, because while the young naturally have no sense of context unless they are taught, present-day grown-ups have lost confidence in the notion that proper behavior is not always an absolute but may vary with the circumstances. Mastering the ability to judge social context is one of the more sophisticated tools for the civilized life.

One is always hearing violators of the simplest social conventions—vocabulary, fit subject matter for conversation, clothing, the distinction between public and private behavior—arguing that what they are doing is appropriate somewhere and therefore could not be inappropriate anywhere. They will claim the right to use certain words, or to discuss certain matters in the drawing room, on the public airways, in institutional computer systems, or in any open forum on the grounds that the words appear in good literature or the topics are the object of scientific inquiry. Perhaps these people will reveal the fact that certain actions that are frowned upon when practiced in public are actually normal behavior. Revealing that it is natural for romantic couples to kiss or for a mother to breast-feed a child is supposed to establish that it is therefore unnatural to object to being required to view these actions.

All of this attempts to deny the importance of venue. The richness of civilized society depends on the ability to understand the subtleties of context, to manage more than one style of behavior, and to have a high sense of occasion. Knowing how to behave is only part of the struggle. One must also know when and where.

Obligations

Are social equality and independence finally being achieved? Miss Manners has heard a lot of talk by people who imagine they personify such an ideal. And highly unsavory talk it is, too:

"No, darling, we certainly cannot split the bill fifty-fifty. You had dessert and I didn't."

"What's the difference if they're related to us? I won't have them; they bore me."

"I presume they sent us a gift because they wanted to, not because they expected to be thanked."

"I'm perfectly capable of opening that door for myself; my arm's not broken."

"Why should I make allowances for the fact that she has children? That's her choice; I didn't ask her to have children."

When Miss Manners had wispy dreams of social equality, she never envisioned its meaning every man or woman for himself or herself, asking nothing and giving nothing. She rather thought that independence meant that we should all carry our full social weight, with nobody excused from the obligation to contribute to the general welfare.

There used to be a rough sort of reciprocity in automatically assigned roles. A lady was expected to offer an occasional home-cooked meal for a gentleman who took her out to dine. If things really steamed up and he lavished presents on her, she would needlepoint him a pair of slippers. (Yes, Miss Manners has heard about men whose idea of reciprocity was "What do you mean, you don't feel 'that way' about me? Do you know how much I spent on you this evening?" She was talking about gentlemen.) How much better things would be, Miss Manners and many others imagined, if they were more openly equalized.

Instead, they seemed to get worse. As the prescribed duties of gender, age, family, rank, and position were eroded, individual responsibility was seldom forthcoming to take their place. Too many people, Miss Manners has heard to her regret, act as if they don't owe anybody anything—and then brood that others are not doing enough for them. There are reports of both ladies and gentlemen who are perfectly content to be the objects of blatantly one-sided courtships if only they can get away with it. Where it used to be a point of pride with the young to grow up enough to make their own way and assist others instead of always being assisted, it is often now accepted that the elders should always provide the resources—money, hospitality, and responsibility. One hears people declare without embarrassment that they have decided to neglect or drop friends because their company is not immediately rewarding—they are absorbed in their children, or have troubles, or are falling behind socially. Even relatives have to pass such tests. There are those who feel so socially desirable that they consider themselves excused from any obligations to their entertainers, including answering invitations, dressing and arriving according to instructions, expressing gratitude, or reciprocating.

Miss Manners finds all this disillusioning. Having believed in the unfairness of rigidly assigned duties, she does not want to retreat and start barking out orders based on demographics. What she needs, then, is for everyone to volunteer to exhibit the sense of equality that makes receiving without giving intolerable and the real independence of being able to contribute to the welfare of others.

False Obligations

Perhaps there should be a warning: In Rare Cases, Etiquette Can Be Used Against You. Miss Manners is about as pleased to issue warnings with her product as a cigarette company. In her case, the obligation is self-inflicted, and she is prompted to do so not only by her relentlessly impeccable standards (such a nuisance) but by her satisfaction in being able to deliver the cure right after disclosing the complaint.

Etiquette danger occurs when one person knowingly depends on the good manners of another to allow the natural consequences of rudeness to pass unpunished.

Or rather, it occurs when the second person allows himself to be imposed upon rather than challenge the deliberate bad manners of the first because that in itself would be rude.

Mind you, Miss Manners said that such cases are rare. She has never subscribed to the notion that etiquette requires one to make others feel good when they are up to no good. This popular belief accounts for much of the unpopularity of the practice of etiquette. For all its nonnegotiable requirements, etiquette has never required anyone to be a patsy or, put more gently, a self-sacrificing social saint.

No polite person would fail to disturb the complacency of someone making a bigoted remark or omit to lodge a complaint when seeing the helpless bullied. Etiquette also recognizes the legitimacy of self-defense against ill treatment, provided that the defense is not itself rude. "How dare you?" is a proper retort to an insult; "Well, you're another" and/or the equivalent gesture is not.

When the polite person wavers, it is because the offender, far from being rude, seems to be engaged in an act of friendship. Geared toward being no less kind in return, the mannerly victim reacts to acceptable surface behavior rather than to the outrageous assumption underlying it.

For example:

A houseguest not only seems settled in indefinitely, but begins to feel at home enough to attempt to participate in family decisions and to offer suggestions as to how the household ought to be run.

The borrower of a book, a garden tool, or a chunk of money fails to return it; when the matter is discreetly hinted at, the borrower acts hurt and insulted.

Professional advice is sought or professional opportunities are offered under social circumstances, where they appear as favors, which it would be ungracious to refuse.

A perfect stranger uses compliments and other chatter to create an atmosphere in which allowing him or her the privileges of friendship—demands on time and privacy—seems appropriate.

In each of these cases, the burden of politeness seems to be on the innocent person. Accepting it can mean acquiring anything from a permanent addition to the family to a criminal attack, or losing anything from a favorite possession to control over one's own time. Child molesters are dependent on children's having been taught not to be rude to nice-talking adults. Even sophisticated grown-ups can be stymied when cornered by chatty strangers.

The solution requires recognizing the facts under that aura of politeness. One is under no obligation to share one's home, possessions, friendship, professional expertise, or time for the asking. Not even much explanation is required when stating one's rights: "I'm afraid I must have that money back," "Call me at my office if you really want my advice," even a nose-in-the air snub when one is familiarly addressed by a stranger. Miss Manners promises not only that this is not a violation of etiquette, but that it is a service to etiquette to defend it from evil usage.

The way to refuse to do something one is not obligated to do is to refuse: "No, thank you," "No, I'm so sorry," "No, I simply can't," "Thank you for asking, but no, I'm afraid it's impossible." These may be repeated as often as necessary to wear out the attacker. Politeness does not require one to enter into debatable excuses for not doing what one was not obligated to do in the first place. The proper feeling afterward is relief, not guilt.

One is under no social obligation (as distinct from a moral obligation to help someone in danger) to any stranger. You are not obligated to converse with every airplane seatmate, taxi driver, taxi passenger, or restaurateur who attempts to chat or lecture. You may if you wish, of course. It seems that there is hardly anything you may not do with a stranger, if you wish, except tell Miss Manners the details. The point is merely that you needn't if you don't want to. The stranger who makes improper conversation should be snubbed (or arrested); the one who makes unwelcome but respectable conversation may be politely answered in monosyllables and, if that doesn't stop the speaker, be told, "I'm sorry, but I planned to use this time to read" or sleep or think.

It is curious that false obligations exist at all in a society where observation of the real ones is so rare.

Miss Manners is not for a minute suggesting that you shirk your real duties. She said she had a touch of ennui, not that she was drunk.

Not Caring What Others Think

Some time back, when Miss Manners wasn't paying careful attention, Not Caring What Other People Think became an American social virtue.

"I don't care what the invitation says. I'm going to wear what I want. I dress to be comfortable, not because I care what other people think."

"I eat the way I please; what do I care what other people think?"

"I'm the one who's getting married, so it doesn't matter if they don't like rock music or think the food is weird. I don't care what other people think."

"I never go to funerals. It doesn't do any good for the person who counts, and it doesn't matter what anyone else thinks."

These are callous statements of the me-first and me-only variety. They broadcast defiance of the feelings of the speaker's hosts, fellow diners, guests, family, and friends. One would suppose that the reaction to be anticipated after such a stand is, "Oh, good for you, but then stay away from me." Those who elect to disregard the standards of others or of society itself should, at the very least, find that people refuse to invite them, eat with them, or attend their weddings or funerals. Persistent cases should even be prepared for attempts to hasten the last.

How is it, then, that such pronouncements are made with anticipation of being admired, rather than ostracized? Why are they meekly accepted more often than condemned?

That declarations of selfishness are unchallenged is, Miss Manners believes, a result of their being confused with the heroic defiance of a private conscience faced with evil or foolish social pressure. "I don't care what anyone else thinks!" can be a moral cry if hurled at the warning that one will be considered a prude for refusing to shoplift, a bad parent for not letting a child stay out half the night, or a failure for not having a new car. Using higher standards than one's peers or refusing to make private decisions by group consensus is indeed something that should be performed with pride.

What about when society is right? That does happen occasionally. Any civilized settlement of human beings develops nonprovocative ways of performing common tasks. Patterns are set for such simple matters as eating and dressing, so that people do not run the risk of upsetting or disgusting others over trivial matters. Complying serves as a demonstration that one respects the community.

Where important emotions are concerned, such as in the major milestones of life, traditions and conventions give order to erratic feelings. By following the time-honored routines of weddings or funerals, one smooths over the chaotic mix of emotion to make a dignified event. Individual nerves become encased in communal ritual.

The beauty of convention is that it is readable. If your looks and actions are within the accepted bounds of the society, you are conveying a basic agreement with the prevailing order. That is why rebels seldom confine their symbolism to questions of ideals, but seek to outrage through dress and behavior as well.

A great many people now behave as if they believe that such acts do not contain symbolism. Challenged that others will be offended if they go barefoot to church or spit back in their plates what they don't like, they claim that it is the reaction, not the action, that is inappropriate.

That is when the I Don't Care What People Think defense appears. Disguised as idealistic defiance of obtrusive and petty standards, it attacks the doctrine of Consideration for Others, which is the basic premise of civilization. If the society truly subscribed to the notion that pursuing individual natural impulses is a higher form of behavior than tempering them to show consideration for others, those others would not be offended by such behavior. A standard that offends a majority cannot work.

Not Caring What People Think is, at best, ignorance of the necessity for people to be able to read one another's behavior for signs of friendliness or hostility. At worst, it is a declaration of Not Caring How I Make Other People Feel.

Not Passing Judgment

"Any person who would behave the way he did is obviously sick."

"Poor soul—she must have been under a terrible strain to allow herself to do such a thing."

"I just feel so sorry for them; I think we should all close ranks and pretend it never happened."

Such charitable remarks have become commonplace whenever an outrage has been committed. You would think that kindly, peace-loving Miss Manners would be delighted. Civilized behavior requires sympathy, forgiveness, and refraining from running around condemning everybody else's behavior instead of looking to one's own. These statements are so much more gentle and tolerant than the remarks that people used to make on such occasions and that, Miss Manners dares say, still spring to mind but now have an old-fashioned ring:

"Any person who would behave the way he did is a disgrace to humanity."

"We always suspected she was a little crazy, but now she's gone totally out of control."

"No decent person would have anything to do with them."

Yet Miss Manners is not quite satisfied with the new tolerance. First, there is the question of etiquette: Are the new versions really the correct things to say when something dreadful has been purposely done? Second, there is the larger matter of articulating our social attitudes: Do these pronouncements accurately state our standards?

Miss Manners thinks not. She does not want to lose that novel tone of restraint and would be the last person to suggest that cries for vengeance are acceptable as being "more honest." But she would like to make some significant adjustments in the modern formula.

As a matter of etiquette, one must always express sympathy for the victim first, and more thoroughly, than one expresses understanding for a violator of social law. Curiously, this essential is often skipped in the haste to show that one believes that normal people do not have evil impulses, and that therefore anyone who would do anything bad is, by definition, himself a victim of illness or circumstances. (The victim of crime may, of course, express sympathy for the attacker if he is feeling up to it.)

The task of defending the standards of the society, in disrepute because it attracts unpleasant zealots, has been largely abandoned in polite society, where the greatest social crime of all has been identified as "passing judgment." Actually, the same people who announce this pass judgment all the time, and in the rudest possible ways—judgments about the eating habits, looks, possessions, clothing, and exercise habits of acquaintances or even strangers. It is only on questions of right and wrong, virtue and evil, that society has given up. When that happens, many people forget that some forms of behavior are actually worse than others, and children grow up believing that everything being excusable, striving for right is too confusing to attempt.

Miss Manners would like to hear just a bit more social outrage when the occasion demands: "What a dreadful thing to do," "How shocking that such things happen," "That was an intolerable breach," and so on. Then—after the standards of what polite society will tolerate have been reaffirmed, and the injured party offered sympathy and understanding—she will be happy to hear people commiserate with someone so unfortunate as to succumb, for whatever reasons, to uncivilized behavior.

Applying for Exemptions

"Don't take it personally. She acts like that to everyone."

"You just have to take me as I am."

"Oh, that's just his way."

"Don't be hurt. That's her idea of fun."

"You have to understand that I never—" write letters, visit the sick, wear a suit, associate with children, wait in line, invite people back.

Miss Manners does not grant indulgences. Nor can you be excused from civility or the performance of basic social duties if you bring a note from your mother. Yet many people—and, if not their mothers, then other apologists on their behalf—seem to believe that pleading eccentricity should get them a waiver on certain or all points of etiquette. They acknowledge that social conventions exist and have no objection to others' having to follow them—indeed, they may be glad to profit from the politeness of others— but they think of themselves as special cases, to whom such rules do not apply.

If an excuse is offered, it describes what seems to be a permanent condition: "Of course, he's my friend and I'm sorry for him, but you see, sick people upset me, so I just make it a rule never to go to hospitals." More often, the explanation is only that ordinary customs are simply not to one's taste: "Well, I don't know if I'm coming to your wedding. I like to be spontaneous, and I don't know how I'll feel then. Also, I never dress up." Either way, the argument for eccentricity is that one has decided to make one's own social laws.

It may not be stated that the eccentric is above the conventions and regulations that apply to ordinary people. Sometimes, it may even be cheerfully declared that he is below them—"Oh, I'm so terribly disorganized that you can't have expected me to remember a lunch date" or "He just makes it a point to be crude to everyone." You can hear that note of pride: You, my dear, it seems to say, lead a humdrum life in which you issue little invitations and expect people to be so pleased that they will feel bound by all the silly rules, but I am too free a spirit to be caught. Or: You, of course, must ingratiate yourself to others by polite and flattering talk, but I am so worthy that I can afford to disdain people.

None of this goes over with Miss Manners, who believes that duty increases with stature. It is no use wishing or imagining yourself so rich, famous, and successful that you can afford to be rude, because that's exactly when you get taxed highest—with *noblesse oblige*.

It is the apologists whom Miss Manners pities. Having decided to tolerate rudeness themselves, for whatever reason, they then make the argument that the perpetrators have special qualities that put them above mere consideration for others—in the hope that those others will join them as victims. It seems to Miss Manners a poor plea. If they truly believe that some people have the special right to be rude, then surely they should acknowledge the right of others to enjoy the privilege of shunning them.

Civil Disobedience

When Miss Manners mentions civil disobedience, she is careful to say the first word much more loudly than the second. Then she pauses in astonishment at herself for acknowledging that there can be such a thing as civilly performed civil disobedience. It is not the idea of deliberately disobeying authority when its strictures violate the individual conscience that troubles her. Miss Manners is aware that there are rare instances when a higher morality persuades good but desperate people to defy the law and take the consequences as a personal sacrifice for social change.

What sends her to her pocket vinaigrette box for a reviving sniff are attempts to extend this explosive technique to the holy laws of etiquette. Etiquette, with its folkloric, emotion-laden traditions, is not supposed to keep as up-to-date with pre-vailing social philosophy as law; it is allowed a graceful lag while people gradually adjust to new ways.

Miss Manners recognizes that there are forms of manners that are inherently rude because they are based on a low valuation of the dignity of certain people. These must be changed. So she would be failing her own conscience if she did not provide those who attempt civil disobedience with guidance on how to do it civilly.

True civil disobedience requires more thoughtfulness, not less, than does fol-lowing the rules. It means isolating a particular rule and educating others about why it is offensive—not promiscuously flouting established behavior and leaving others to guess why. The guess they will make is that the defier is contemptuous of their feelings and of society in general. By refusing to conform without a good rea-son, you alert those who do conform that you wish to dissociate yourself from them and from their dumb standards. That is no way to educate people about the need for change.

In civil disobedience, therefore, meticulous attention to etiquette is essential. By dressing, talking, and behaving like other members of the society in all ways but the one targeted for change, the protester demonstrates that he or she is seri-ously concerned with a particular injustice, not simply seizing it as an excuse to be—whoopee!—free from all civilized restraints. This goes double when a rule of etiquette is being defied. If you wish to be addressed more respectfully, you do not dress in a nonserious way; if it is clothing regulations you are attempting to change, you do not use provocative speech.

You can imagine, then, how frustrated and outraged Miss Manners is when she increasingly hears idealism cited as an excuse for poor manners. There is hardly a way of offending the sensibilities of others, from not wearing a necktie to necking in public, that is considered too trivial for a political defense. Those who are rude for the usual reasons, laziness and carelessness, are quick to devise explanations about opposing class oppression or defending individual rights against social evils.

Well, pooh. Rude is rude, and Miss Manners is not going to let every scoff-man-ners who fails to write a thank-you letter to his grandmother get away with posing as a champion of the masses.

Etiquette is generous with honorable exemptions—for children and strangers, until they learn what is expected; for those with medical or financial handicaps, who keep the spirit of rules they cannot exactly follow. It is tolerant of religious and cultural reasons for not practicing local custom—provided that these genu-inely arise from conflicting duties and loyalties, rather than from disrespect. But since disrespect is the catchall for other disobedience, the social reformer must demonstrate that his or her condemnation is not general.

"What Will Miss Manners Say?"

DEAR MISS MANNERS:

I am a collector of old etiquette books and have come across several references to a Mrs. Grundy, which have left me puzzled. For example (from *The Cyclopedia of Social Usage* by Helen L. Roberts, published in 1913): "By a special dispensation of Mrs. Grundy, one is allowed to lift the woody end of the boiled [asparagus] stalk in one's fingers to dip the head in the sauce on one's plate. . . . But even when deftly accomplished this is not a dainty sight." Please tell me, Miss Manners, if Mrs. Grundy was a real woman and an authority on correct deportment early in this century, a sort of precursor to yourself, or if she was some mythical creature whom our ancestors invoked as an excuse to relax the rules of etiquette?

GENTLE READER:

Mrs. Grundy, a character in Thomas Morton's rollicking 1798 hit play *Speed the Plough* (and thus roughly a contemporary of Mrs. Malaprop, the Richard Brinsley Sheridan character who has so much trouble with words), was a lady who disapproved of everything, usually because she found scandalous possibilities in innocent actions. It is a liberty to presume that she would have given out dispensations, which would have been quite against her nature. Thus Mrs. Grundy is quite unlike your own reasonable, warmhearted, tolerant Miss Manners. However, Miss Manners has noticed that the once popular expression "What would Mrs. Grundy say?" has been replaced in this era by a similar expression that modesty forbids her from repeating.

A Sampler of Problems
Mrs. Perfect Never Had to Face

Shocking Advice

DEAR MISS MANNERS:

I may or may not shock you. Our old college sorority has been meeting monthly for fifty years. We are mothers, grandmothers, and great-grandmothers and always have an annual mother/daughter luncheon. When a thirty-plus-year-old daughter of a member sighed and lamented, "I wish I had a baby," I said, "Well, why don't you?"

"I'm not married," she said, blushing.

"So," I said, "if you want a baby, have one. You're healthy, intelligent, financially able—you really don't have to be married. Nature gives us a time limit; love and marriage don't. Go for it!" Her mother was shocked, and so were the over-hearing near-bys. I am proud to have the most children, grandchildren, and great-grandchildren; I'm envied by some and disdained by the more sophisticated, and my remarks caused some eye rolling and shoulder shrugging.

I later dropped a note to the girl's mother, saying that I was sorry if I was too outspoken, and I realized that I might have upset her because of her straitlaced religious background and ideal marriage, with adopted children. I explained, "A child is a gift of love. How can a deep mother urge be denied because of convention and social principles? The overflowing joy and love for all children in spite of some worries and heartaches has kept me happy, healthy, well balanced, young-thinking, and grateful to God for my many blessings." Did I put too much weight on mother love, or am I out of sync with the world today?

GENTLE READER:

As you well know, you are extremely proud of being what you consider "in sync" with modernity by advocating that your sorority sister's child flout her family's morals. How chic you must find the role of wicked great-grandmother. Having successfully shocked your contemporaries, you are naturally venturing to "go for it" as you say, by attempting to shock the august Miss Manners.

Single motherhood at its best can be hard on both parent and child, although there are those who are heroically able to make a success of it. Nor is illegitimacy quite as easily accepted by modern society as you seem to believe. Miss Manners dares to say that your own children were not illegitimate. You are, from your own safe position, advocating a difficult life for this young woman and her child, along with the undisputed joys of motherhood.

However, as the young lady is over thirty, she is undoubtedly able to weigh your judgment, along with her own views and estimates of the situation. It may occur to her, as it has not to you, that being from an adoptive family herself, she could take special satisfaction in giving the happiness of family life to an existing child.

It would have been better if your apology—which ought to have been for butting into someone else's business, rather than for being outrageous—had not been used as an opportunity to restate your position. Miss Manners thinks you have done enough in attempting to shake up this family and ought now to leave them alone.

Ambiguous Flowers

DEAR MISS MANNERS:

Last summer, the florist delivered to me a lovely package containing a single red rose. When I opened the accompanying card, I was shocked to find that it was from my new dentist. It read, "Welcome to our dental practice." I am puzzled, because I had always thought that a single red rose was a symbol of romantic love. I am young, attractive, and married. At my next visit, neither he nor I said a word about the gift, and it was business as usual. Was I right not to mention it? Please explain this to me.

GENTLE READER:

A red rose accompanied by a card that says "I can't live without you" symbolizes romantic passion. A red rose accompanied by a card that says "Welcome to our dental practice" does not, no matter how young and attractive you are. Public relations gimmicks are not presents and need not be acknowledged, either with expressions of thanks or with romantic passion.

The Nude Wedding

DEAR MISS MANNERS:

Our twenty-six-year-old daughter plans to marry soon, inviting about one hundred guests to her grandmother's (father's side) place, near where we lived when she was growing up. She, her bridegroom, and all the attendants will be nude. The guests will be clothed. Can you believe? They say they got the idea from a television show. We think it is one of the stupidest ideas ever—and she's had some lulus.

Lisa has always been strong-willed. Arguments with her leave me drained for a week and leave her more determined. I have used every argument I can think of without effect. Her fiancé doesn't seem as determined as she is but is more than willing to go along with it. His parents are as upset as we are, blame everything on Lisa, but can do nothing about it. "Nana," the senile old biddy, doesn't seem to understand what's going on and just keeps saying, "If that's what Lisa wants." Lisa and Tom both have good jobs and a house. They have made it clear that they do not need our help and will proceed with this, with or without our blessing, but Lisa prefers us to be on good terms and wants me to be involved. I almost prefer that they simply live together.

She has suggested—and I have agreed—to handle the invitations. Is there a special etiquette here? Lisa is determined that everything be done "right." How does one word invitations to a wedding where the wedding party will be nude? I hope that I can use regular invitations and that she will change her mind. But what if she doesn't? I simply can't send out invitations as if everything will be normal. I have to let people know what to expect. Don't I? How do I explain that we approve of the marriage but not the costuming (or lack thereof)? Miss Manners, you get lots of letters. Have you ever heard of this situation before? How did it work out? What did they do about photographs? What did their friends and family think? Are they still together? Do they regret it now? Would they recommend it?

GENTLE READER:

Miss Manners hesitates to give out any prizes for Worst Original Idea, but no, she has not been confronted with this one before. It is her profound wish that she never will be again. She does not care to imagine their version of the moment of public affection after the couple is pronounced married. While etiquette has been spared the task of setting rules for whatever Lisa or some television show might dream up, there is, indeed, a general rule that one does not spring surprises on guests. The style of a wedding is declared from the gentlemen's clothing—white tie, black tie, or suit for evening, morning dress, sack coat, or suit for daytime—so what you have here is a nudist wedding.

To put it mildly, this must be classified as the least formal of weddings, and therefore a formality such as third-person invitations is incongruous. For an informal wedding, one invites guests by letter. Your letter might say, "Our daughter, Lisa, and Thomas Anvil, Junior, are being married on Saturday, December eleventh, at noon, at Pleasant Palms, the home of her grandmother, Mrs. Benford Lorton. It is to be a nudist ceremony, but guests are expected to dress. Although this is not our choice, we approve of the young man." (Speaking of approval, Miss Manners does not quite care for the way you characterize your mother-in-law. Unless that lady is really unable to understand the situation and must be protected from what she herself would normally find humiliating, she must be allowed to make her own decision.) You might consider insisting that you will skip the wedding itself—perhaps the bridegroom's parents would like to join you—which can then be held for whoever among the couple's friends finds the idea thrilling. You could give an ordinary reception in honor of the couple a week or two later, to which you invite your friends.

Officers' Beaux

DEAR MISS MANNERS:

I am a lieutenant in the U.S. Navy and a woman, unmarried. Military officers frequently have official functions to attend, which entail formal uniforms and many traditional toasts, and all officers present are expected to join in the toast.

One of these toasts is usually "To our charming ladies" and is directed by the masculine toaster to the wives and ladyfriends present.

Whether I attend these functions with a date or not, I am left in a quandary. Should I stand and toast my escort, should he stand and toast me, or should we both sit quietly?

If I don't join the toast, I'm not "taking part," and I don't feel it appropriate to allow myself to be classified as one of the charming escorts, since I am at the occasion in an official capacity.

Yet neither do I feel that I should toast my escort as a "charming lady." No one else at these functions seems to know what to do.

GENTLE READER:

Time for a major updating in the Navy. Miss Manners hopes that all personnel are paying attention.

Of course, this is an impossible situation for you. You are both an officer and a lady, and to pretend you are either one and not the other on an occasion when both are present would be ridiculous. This custom made sense only when all officers were gentlemen and their guests all ladies.

Henceforth, Miss Manners unilaterally declares that the toast should be "To our charming guests."

Chummy License Plates

DEAR MISS MANNERS:

A friend of mine, a middle-aged, married, and very respectable woman with small children, recently attached a plate to the front of her car bearing her first name only. I contend that it was improper, that it showed poor taste, that it could lead to situations which would prove unpleasant, and that it was a practice limited to single college students and people who were "on the make."

GENTLE READER:

Miss Manners doubts that your friend is on the lookout for social opportunities while driving the car pool but agrees with you that the practice of advertising one's name on one's car is silly and tasteless. It can only lead to shouts of "Okay, Betsy, move it!" and "Hey, Betsy! Where'd you learn to drive?"

Anniversary Entitlement

DEAR MISS MANNERS:

For many years as a widow, I gifted my friends at their multiple milestone anniversaries (ten, fifteen, twenty, etc.) and participated in the parties in honor of these occasions. Eventually, I remarried, and recently celebrated a twentieth anniversary. I guess compared to the fortieth and forty-fifth anniversaries that they are approaching, twenty years seems insignificant to our friends, because our anniversary passed without any festivities, only the usual greeting cards.

Since my husband and I are in our sixties, we look forward to having at least one more milestone anniversary, but realistically we can never hope to catch up with our friends. We feel that in a second marriage, caring friends and/or relatives who might be inclined to entertain for the anniversary couple should not wait for a twenty-fifth but should plan festivities for lesser years in a manner befitting a major anniversary. After all, it was not our fault that we had to start over at year one. What are your thoughts on the subject?

GENTLE READER:

Not your fault? And therefore you are entitled to fair compensation? Miss Manners' thoughts are not fit to be aired. She will only say that she cannot bear much more of this rampant sense of entitlement, replacing any feeling for the spirit of celebration, that many people now have. Sure, go ahead. Set up your account. Don't forget payments to your single friends in lieu of wedding presents. Make sure that you keep track of graduation presents so that each family collects the same monetary value, whether or not they have the same number of children. Just don't let Miss Manners hear about it. She would prefer to think of you and your husband as happily grateful that you found each other and are spending these years together—perhaps inviting your friends to rejoice with you on special occasions, but certainly not nursing together your grievance that others don't do enough for you.

Capitalizing on a Funeral

DEAR MISS MANNERS:

Our mother died recently, and her six grandsons were pallbearers. All comported themselves with dignity except our forty-six-year-old nephew (financially successful), who asked another aunt at the church if the funeral mass would last long enough for him to make a business call and get back in time to help carry out the casket. She was so appalled that she answered, "I don't know," and turned and left him. After the graveside services, we all adjourned to my sister's house. I walked into the dining room and was stunned to see that this same nephew had placed ten or twelve of his business brochures so that they covered a fourth of the dining-room table. As soon as I was able to move, I quickly gathered them and tucked them out of sight. Later, I noticed that he had replaced them on the dining table. I'm not sure there is any hope for a forty-six-year-old man who conducts himself in such a boorish manner. Should I, his aunt, explain to him that his actions were truly reprehensible, especially at a time that should have evoked his finest feelings?

GENTLE READER:

Miss Manners tries very hard to believe that no soul is truly lost to the possibility of redemption through etiquette, but she can't quite manage it in the case of a man who sees his grandmother's funeral as a business opportunity. In your place, she might only stipulate that he not be a pallbearer at her funeral and be carefully instructed that the top of her casket will not be available as a billboard. However, he is your nephew, and you might be more sanguine. The approach to take would be to say: "I don't know if you realized that you managed to associate the name of your company in everybody's mind with grief and loss."

New Technology

There is some new stuff around since the Etiquette Council held its last great congress, some time after the Congress of Vienna. Miss Manners is using the technical term "stuff" advisedly. These are things, most of them flashing tiny red lights at you in your home or office, that were not previously covered by rules of etiquette because they hadn't been invented. So here are some rules for stuff you can't exist without now that you know it exists.

You will forgive Miss Manners for speaking of it in old-fashioned terms. The fact is that while ways of doing things may be new, things to be done are generally not, and adaptation, rather than invention, is usually what is needed to cope.

Answering machine.   This is the modern equivalent of the butler, who makes peaceful domestic life possible by saying "Madam is not available; may I tell her who called?" when Madam is busy fighting a knot in her needlework or nursing a hangover. Miss Manners is tired of hearing that you hate it. Anyone who possesses one should make it behave in a dignified way (no funny messages), and callers may use it or not as they choose.

Beeper.   A butler without much judgment is apt to keep butting in with false emergencies. It must be made not to disturb other people (ones that alert by movement are more discreet than ones that bleep), and the user should exercise judgment about attending to its demands at the expense of other duties.

CD player.   It has always been rude to boast about one's possessions and to attempt to demonstrate to guests that these are better than whatever they have.

Call Waiting.   One of Miss Manners' least favorite devices, this is like a child screaming for attention while one is on the telephone. It is possible that the scream is "There's a fire in the kitchen," but demands to pay attention to a ringing telephone while you are already on the telephone constitute the rude policy of "Last come, first served."

Computer.   Contrary to what many people seem to hope, a computer file is not the same as a diary or private journal; there are too many ways it might be seen accidentally for it to have the sanctity of privacy. Computerized letters are neither better nor worse than typewritten ones, which is to say that while they cannot be condemned for their ease of production, "personalizing" devices do not make them adequate substitutes for handwritten letters or engraved announcements.

Cordless or otherwise portable telephone.   Yes, we all think it's wonderful that you are so important that you have to be on the telephone in your car, the health club swimming pool, and the movie theater. Nevertheless, the same rules apply as to corded telephones: You don't annoy other people with the noise or ignore those with you in favor of the disembodied voice.

Fax.   Once upon a time, the recipient of a letter had to pay the postage, so it was not considered nice to send more than you thought that person would be pleased to receive. The fax sender pays for the call, but the receiver supplies machine working time and paper. Junk fax material is even worse than junk mail. It is polite to send only what will be likely to be welcome. Social communications should look breathlessly slapdash; the level of formality is halfway between that of a telephone call and a letter.

Jacuzzi.   Guests must always be warned before attending any event at which people are going to take off their clothes. This problem is so old that its origins are lost in history.

Laptop computer.   Working at a laptop computer in a public setting, such as an airplane, is no different from doing paperwork in public. Workers should be allowed to work without being interrupted by curiosity about what they are doing.

Laser printer.   It is not the obligation of the possessor of fancy equipment to lend it out whenever the less endowed request. Doing so should be considered a favor.

Notebook.   Your-life-in-a-notebook systems, such as the Filofax, amount to an essential extension of the owner's memory. Those who fear that they have lost theirs should be treated with compassion, not scorn.

Photocopier. Disseminating material that its writer or owner does not want others to see is as bad for copies as for originals. A person who would photocopy another person's love letters qualifies as the modern basic definition of a cad.

Remote control. This is not to be used more dictatorially than regular controls. If more than one adult or peer is involved in a decision about what to watch or hear, having control of the controls does not absolve one from getting a consensus.

Money machine. This is not quite the same as a bank teller, because it always says thank you and occasionally eats your card. One need not say "please" to a machine, but one should try not to kick it when it makes a mistake. Courtesy requires those in line behind the bank customer not to stand too close.

Stereo. Although Miss Manners despises background music, she cannot actually label it rude unless it interferes with the conversation or audio health of guests. Subjecting strangers to one's taste in music, through whatever device, is unspeakable.

Tapes. Recording or video-recording your friends is like the old-fashioned custom—or plague, as many people consider it—of asking visitors to write in a guest book. While some welcome the opportunity to show off, those who loathe it should not be forced to participate simply in order to produce a souvenir.

VCR. The manners of watching a film at home, which can include talking, eating, and expressing affection (provided that all those present find this agreeable), are not to be confused with the manners of seeing a film in a theater, which permit none of these.

Walkman. Portable listening is like walking around while reading—rude only when it causes accidents or the snubbing of people with legitimate claims on the absorbed person's attention. Leaky earphones are the equivalent of humming.

1

Revised Conventions

Modern Ladies and Gentlemen

So many traditional opportunities for smutty giggles have disappeared from society. Young people today cannot imagine what fun was once had by the simple exercise of calculating the number of months between a first baby's birth and the date of the parents' wedding.

Miss Manners is therefore reluctant to subtract other such opportunities from modern life, which is grim enough. Nevertheless, it is high time that the traces of dirty humor be removed from friendships and business associations between ladies and gentlemen.

For some decades, we have been operating under a system naively assuming that the only possible relationship between ladies and gentlemen was you-know-what. Therefore, the only set of manners they knew how to use with each other was, shall we say, social gallantry. Businessmen kept trying to pick up the checks for business meals with female colleagues or even female superiors, because the only form of meal they knew how to have with ladies was the date, in which the gentleman traditionally paid. The only pleasant language they knew how to employ was the exaggerated personal compliment appropriate to courtship but jarring in professional situations. Spouses protested working arrangements that teamed their husbands or wives with partners of the other gender, because they could only think of one activity these people might do together.

Friendships were supposed to be segregated by gender, and opposite-gender people could see each other socially only if all spouses were present. Married couples did not accept dinner invitations unless both could attend. If someone you liked married someone you didn't, or your spouse didn't like the friend or the friend's spouse—and the statistical chance of finding four people who are crazy about one another is small—the tie was broken. The twentieth-century wedding is designed for the bride to have her close friends as bridesmaids, and the bridegroom to have his as groomsmen, with no role for her male or his female friends. The very term "just good friends" was popularly understood to refer to a clandestine romance.

Miss Manners hates to be the one to break the news that there is just not that much sex in the world. The fact is that such innovations as coeducational dormitories and equal employment opportunity have surprised society by leading to affable companionship as much as or more often than to unbridled lust. Nor is this strictly a modern phenomenon. Sophisticated society in past centuries not only assumed that respectable married people were capable of individual socializing without falling into sin but looked suspiciously at couples who were always seen in each other's company. There must be a reason, society figured, that they displayed so little trust.

As disappointing as it may be for salacious onlookers, we shall have to relearn the social forms of trust. It can no longer be safely assumed that ladies and gentlemen who are seen lunching or dining together are doing anything more exciting than talking or that people who take business trips in mixed groups are having a wonderful time. Gracious, you can't even be sure that people who are living together are—well, living together. These days they could simply be splitting the rent or pooling their Social Security payments. For such innocent circumstances, dignified but nonromantic manners are appropriate. The factor of gender is removed from such questions as who initiates meetings and who pays bills. In business, precedence is given to rank, and in comradeship, deference is paid to age.

Society must do its part by refraining from making smarmy assumptions: not teasing small children who play together about their "boyfriends" or "girlfriends" and not asking adults how they "feel" about a spouse's opposite-gender colleagues or friends. The truth is that such remarks were always in dreadful taste; they are also likely to be in error.

How, then, society wants to know, do we find out if something really racy is going on? If mere proximity and opportunity are no longer to constitute proof of sin, how on earth are we to be sure that people are not taking advantage of this license to disguise behavior that we are all dying to know about? Modern customs have taken care of this contingency. The answer is: They'll tell you.

Platonic Possibilities

DEAR MISS MANNERS:

How does a comfortably married person go about making friends (I mean what I say: friends) with an attractive member of the opposite sex? Is the answer simply "Very carefully," or are there rules? There must be rules, no doubt of the sort that are lost and recovered, only to be lost again. Let us say that one considers one's life to be enriched by the acquaintance and would be pleased to improve upon it. Adultery is out of the question. How can such a message be politely and convincingly delivered?

GENTLE READER:

Of course, there are proper ways for ladies and gentlemen to have innocent and rewarding friendships. Such relationships went on quite naturally in the eighteenth century (along with other interesting relationships) before the days when attempting a harmless friendship became simply not worth the scandal.

Only in the most rigid social systems is it possible to get ladies and gentlemen so aquiver from deprivation that anything at all from the opposite gender looks good to them. We are now, Miss Manners dearly hopes, emerging from such a period.

You must make it clear that although you and your spouse have individual activities and individual friendships, you are a permanent couple. Your friend should know that your spouse is aware of the friendship and that your life, as you will naturally speak of it in the course of the friendship, is happily shared. Your friend should also know that you do not keep secrets from your spouse, who trusts and approves of you. It is even understood that the confidences of the friendship—the promise-you-won't-tell-anyone confessions—do not restrict you from telling your spouse.

Occasionally, some effort should be made to include spouses. A two-person friendship between married people is usually pursued at lunchtime, which is the time of day when social engagements are not made in couples, but you might throw in an occasional dinner just to have people you care about get to know each other.

In spite of all these precautions, Miss Manners must warn you that some people will talk. Let them. If you lead a blameless life, it is ridiculous to curtail it simply for the purpose of avoiding the censure of nasty-minded people.

A Third-Party View

DEAR MISS MANNERS:

Is it proper for an unmarried man to call upon (about once a week), and occasionally take to dinner, the estranged wife of his nephew? The man is about sixty-five and the woman is about thirty. They both say that the relationship is platonic. I have been dating this man for several years, and while I realize that my complaints may sound like (and be) "sour grapes," I am also truly concerned about what friends and neighbors might think of the situation, not to mention what this woman's husband would think if he found out.

GENTLE READER:

There is hardly a social action on earth that is guaranteed to be gossip-proof, but Miss Manners does not consider it scandalous of a lady and gentleman, of whatever ages, simply to dine together. She herself has just invited to luncheon a gentleman considerably younger than herself—in fact, nine years old.

Your real question is: How should you deal politely with the fact that you feel left out? Not by attempting to squelch the gentleman's freedom through the threat of public disapproval. Even if you managed to do so, you would be establishing yourself as a social coward at best and probably a killjoy as well. The charming thing to do is to show interest, enthusiasm, and sympathy for the young woman. As your friend is fond of her, it should be easy to get him to talk about her, after which it is a natural step for you to tell him how much you would like to be friends with her, too, and perhaps you could join them at the next dinner.

Ladies' Rights

In the glorious names of etiquette and of feminism, a great deal of disreputable advice is being given out these days to people of Miss Manners' own gender. Ladies are being taught ruses and tricks to perform when they are in public places so as to create the impression that they are respectable. They are advised in detail of ways of dressing and behaving in restaurants, hotels, airplanes, trains, and business establishments so as to discourage unsolicited attention. There seems to be no end of answers to the presumed question: How can I prove that I am honest while I am out pursuing my normal business?

Miss Manners is deeply outraged at the premise of the question. She wants it clearly stated that a lady is presumed to be respectable unless proven otherwise. The burden of proof is not on the lady. If there are some who are eager to devote special attention to protecting womanhood from the transgressions of men who are not gentlemen, let them do it by restricting the men, and not their victims.

We have sadly regressed on this point in the last century or so. Back when all men felt that they had the right to oppress women, individual gentlemen did not permit the less well behaved of their gender to insult individual ladies in public. Ladies themselves were quick to take offense at the hint of such unpardonable behavior and to make their objections loud and clear.

Here, then, are Miss Manners' answers to modern questions of etiquette that ought never to be asked:

How does a lady by herself check into a hotel? By stating her name and the fact of her reservation to the room clerk. If she is expecting her husband (anyone of the opposite gender occupying a hotel room with the person registering is, by definition, a spouse), she signs her own name and informs the clerk that she is registering for a double. It is not necessary to give the name of anyone other than the person responsible for the bill.

How does a lady eat dinner alone in a restaurant? By asking for a table, sitting down when a satisfactory one is shown, selecting food from the menu, ordering it, and, when it appears, eating it.

Suppose someone assumes that a lady wants to be picked up and starts annoying her?   Any restaurant patron who is annoyed by any other patron should make an immediate, outraged complaint to the management. It is the restaurant's responsibility to see that indecent behavior, such as intruding on strangers in any way, is not permitted in the establishment.

Is it ever proper to address a lady traveling alone?   Whether introductory-level personal conversation between strangers is considered insulting depends on the length of the trip. On a crosstown bus, it is; on an ocean liner, it is not. Avoiding socializing on the latter requires the same sort of polite maneuvers one would use on land to avoid those to whom one has been properly introduced but whom one doesn't like. Trains and airplanes are in between: It is not rude to attempt conversation, but it is not rude to cut it off, either.

Suppose a lady is staying in a hotel and wants to go out for a drink? Oh, suppose. Suppose Miss Manners would like a drink herself after all this. Then woe betide the person who tried to interpret this as behavior unbecoming to a perfect lady.

Rebuffing Advances

DEAR MISS MANNERS:
   Let's face it. Polite is not always all it's cracked up to be. I received a call from a man of my acquaintance who said, "I'm coming over to your place now for a drink," and went on to imply that he was interested in more than social intercourse. I was polite. "No, John, I don't think you want to do that; it's not a good idea," etc. I've known John for years. He's a golf pro and has given me lessons. His wife is one of the partners in my firm, and I work for her on projects from time to time. The relationship with both has been purely professional until now.
   Well, about an hour after the first call, John called again to say that he was drunk (to which I said, "I thought so"); that he was sorry (I said, "It's forgotten"); and that since I knew a lot of his wife's friends, he was hoping I wouldn't say anything about the incident (of course, I said I wouldn't). Now I'm frightened, insulted, and furious, and dwelling on what I should have said. I don't want to be violated like that again.

GENTLE READER:
   Why are you picking on politeness? In fact, why are you stewing about all this now? It seems to Miss Manners that your reply worked just fine, extracting in short order the only kind of politeness—namely an abject apology and begging for mercy and forgiveness—that this man was in a position to offer.
   Miss Manners doubts that you will hear from him again in this fashion. If you do, you need only apply a bit more politeness, along the lines of, "John, your problem is obviously out of your control, and I do think that the kindest thing for me to do is to speak to your wife about it right away."

❧ TRADITIONAL CONFUSION

Ladies Where?

Let others prattle of unfulfilled dreams, graying hair, and shifting relationships. Miss Manners alone knows the true perils that beset the Woman of a Certain Age. A sensible woman is generally equipped to handle the normal vicissitudes of life, although a little gentle sighing is occasionally allowed in the privacy of her boudoir. What the modern mature lady did not expect was to be caught, in what ought to be the graceful years, smack in the middle of an etiquette revolution, with wild men going off in all directions around her.

The revolution, not yet completed, is the shift from a system of precedence based on gender to one that shows signs of eventually using age and business rank as the basis of precedence. We cannot all go through the door at the same time, as an astute diplomat once remarked, and general agreement on who should go first makes for a peaceful life.

But the change is by no means complete, and while most of the society is trying to squeeze through that door simultaneously, the lady is left standing there. Does she wait, as she was taught, for the gentleman to open the door for her? She may very well be left waiting while he saunters down the block. Does she plunge ahead and open it herself? She may leave behind a pouting gentleman who had been planning to get to the door handle, as he believes is proper, just as soon as he could figure out on which side it was.

Mind you, this lady was described by Miss Manners as a sensible lady, so she is only trying to go along with prevailing manners, not to enact her politics through symbolic behavior, any more than she wears her moral philosophy printed across her bodice. The problem is that she can't figure out what the prevailing manners are, since her acquaintance includes young gentlemen who were never taught ladies-first courtesy, older gentlemen who have renounced it, older gentlemen who practice it, and younger gentlemen who have recently taken it up because they have noticed how quaintly effective it can be. Ladies do not wish to imply disapproval of gentlemen's manners when the gentlemen plainly intend to be mannerly, so they must develop a few agile and ambiguous techniques.

At the door, for example, the lady can turn and smile at the gentleman just as she reaches the handle; she can observe then whether his hand is out. If it is a revolving door, she steps in, waits a split second (unless it is already going around, in which case she would be flattened like a fly with a fly swatter—but we were talking of sensible ladies), and then pushes with her arms unbent, so that her propelling hands are not visible to a gentleman who is gearing up his strength to push for her.

When walking down the street, she gains the inside on the pretense of looking into the shop windows, not because she seems to expect to be so placed. When about to alight from a car, she waits momentarily to see if the gentleman seems to

Conventions, Updated

The Household Buffer
(for regulating
spontaneous guests)

Flirtation Prop
(for giving strangers
a conversation opener)

The Mourner's Protection
(for shielding
swollen eyes)

be coming around to her side to open the door. The sight of his back entering the restaurant indicates that he is not, so she opens it herself. In the restaurant, she orders her meal with her eyes cast down on the menu and her face halfway between the gentleman's and the waiter's. If the gentleman wishes to repeat the order, he may; if not, the waiter has heard it.

You see the principle. It is troublesome, not to mention hazardous, and Miss Manners is not unsympathetic to the ladies who impatiently decide to adopt the new system for all, expecting no precedence—provided that they do not get unpleasant when it is offered. Nevertheless we are most charmed with what we knew in childhood, which is one reason for practicing the traditions among those who enjoy them. Another is that all this jumping about is good exercise for ladies of a certain age who do not care to jog.

Honks and and Whistles

DEAR MISS MANNERS:

As my wife and I walked to our car from a suburban theater, someone honked a horn. My wife turned around. I told my wife that no lady in the company of a gentleman turns her head when she hears a car's honk. The argument was on. Please advise me as to what a lady does when she hears a car's honk or a man's whistle.

G ENTLE R EADER:

A lady, married or unmarried, in the company of a gentleman or alone, ignores a car's honk or a man's whistle unless she is blocking traffic or unaware that she is on a construction site with building parts about to descend on her head. In either of those two cases, she moves fast. In any other case, she puts her nose in the air and continues at her normal pace.

An Acknowledgment of Differences

Are we ready yet to acknowledge that there are differences between ladies and gentlemen? An ardent feminist since she first noticed that she was a girl (which was some time ago and quite before the former idea became fashionable), Miss Manners would not for the world start any of those dreadful competitive discussions. It is only in the hope that we have firmly put behind us any question of differences in rights and abilities that she would dare to bring up the question of cultural distinctions.

It is true that some of these distinctions may have come, long ago, from unacceptable, not to mention foolishly inattentive, ideas of relative weaknesses and strengths. Even then, the male pattern is not necessarily the preferable one. Miss Manners happens to believe that one has more control over a horse by riding side-saddle than astride. Even distinctions that may seem to relate to real physical differences don't make much sense: An open-minded young lady of Miss Manners' acquaintance once suggested to her how much more suitable to gentlemen's bodies it would have been for them to develop the tradition of wearing skirts and, similarly, for ladies to wear pants.

None of these things matters once tradition has taken hold of the habit and heart. Then we do things because we were taught to do so, and therefore anything else seems wrong.

Here, then, are a few of the remaining differences that Miss Manners finds charming. You will note than none of them is connected with business life, which is properly genderless; and none has to do with such crucial matters as who gets the seat in the bus, pays the bill, or proposes marriage.

Ladies properly applaud differently from gentlemen.   While a gentleman bangs his vertically held palms together in front of him, a lady claps by holding her left palm upward without moving it, and hitting it with downward strokes by her right palm.

When wearing skirts, ladies sit differently from gentlemen, but not the way most of them seem to think.   Gentlemen either keep both feet on the floor, with the legs slightly parted, or, less formally, put the right ankle on the left knee. Females who are not ladies cross their knees. Ladies cross their ankles, keeping the knees together. This is actually very comfortable when you get used to it.

Ladies do not put their names above their return addresses in social correspondence.   As their social correspondence, as well as gentlemen's, is in their own handwriting, it is not generally necessary to expose their names to public view in order for them to recognize their own returned letters. (If they must include their names for practical reasons, Miss Manners will overlook it.) Those letters are written on double sheets of paper, while gentlemen's are on larger single sheets.

Ladies do not pour their own wine when gentlemen are present.   They hold their empty wine glasses casually in front of their noses while staring fixedly at the nearest gentleman, who then falls all over himself to do it for them.

Ladies go first through doors but last down steps.   This does not excuse ladies who sail through life letting doors slam in other people's faces or who fail to perform obvious courtesies for those who need them.

Ladies who are escorted by gentlemen begin carrying packages only when the gentlemen are fully loaded, so to speak.   Ladies who are out shopping with uniformed officers, who do not carry packages either, may insist that these gentlemen bring along their orderlies.

Ladies wear hats (except in their own houses) as a token of respect. Of course, ladies' buttons and belt buckles are on the left side of their clothing, while gentlemen's are on their right.

When they are walking outdoors, American ladies take the side away from the curb.   Never mind the old stories about that being so that gentlemen can take upon themselves the mud from the streets or garbage from upper-story windows or use their swords without slashing a lady's skirt. For a lady to grab a quick look at herself as she passes a reflecting window is perfectly acceptable and even endearing. For a gentleman to do so is vulgar.

Ladies Second

DEAR MISS MANNERS:

My husband states that the only time a woman precedes a man in a restaurant is when the host/hostess is leading the way to their table. At all other times, the man precedes the lady to the table, as well as to the dance floor and to the door when leaving. I disagree. What do you say?

GENTLE READER:

That your husband learned the complexities of the "ladies first" social rule, and not just the words. Indeed, he is correct that this particular protective code requires a gentleman to precede a lady when going through a crowd or in any other situation when he can be presumed to smooth the way for her. A gentleman precedes a lady down a staircase, for example, so that she can, if necessary, land comfortably on him when she falls.

The Driver's Seat

DEAR MISS MANNERS:

Is it just as proper for the gentleman to open and close the car door for the woman, assisting her into and out of the car, when she is the driver?

GENTLE READER:

Certainly. A lady's gender does not change when she takes the driver's seat.

Gentlemen Standing

DEAR MISS MANNERS:

Last evening, my girlfriend and I attended a charity ball. This was a black-tie affair, and we were seated at a table with three other couples whom we did not know. I rose each time a female at our table was seated or left. None of the other gentlemen rose, and it became apparent that they were anxious over my behavior. The gentleman to my left jokingly told me that I was making the other men nervous and that I should stop rising. Which is more proper, to continue to conduct oneself as a gentleman, if in fact mine was the proper behavior, or to forgo manners to avoid making the other gentlemen uncomfortable, which in itself is rude?

GENTLE READER:

Who says that a gentleman is obliged to make rude people feel comfortable about being rude? Certainly not Miss Manners. If everyone were obliged to conform to the lowest form of behavior present, we would have—well, pretty much the unfortunate world we have today. Do you really want to help it along, or do you want the ladies to see that you are the only gentleman left?

Ladies Rising

DEAR MISS MANNERS:

It often happens at dinner parties that a couple will arrive after those already at the party are seated in the living room having drinks and such. When the couple, man and woman, are brought to be introduced, the other men always stand. Sometimes women also stand. Is this proper?

GENTLE READER:

It depends on the relative ages and ranks of the various ladies. A lady stands for another lady who is of an older generation than hers or who holds considerably higher status, such as a government or church official. Ladies who rise for those three years older than themselves are considered to be practicing sarcastic manners.

Forms of Address

Nowadays, if someone said "Call me Ishmael," few people would. Strangers would say, "How y'doing, Ish?" Childhood friends would remember ancient and unpleasant nicknames. Even Miss Manners, in the course of holding the line for stuffiness, would be forced to reply, "How do you do, Mr. Ishmael?" to preclude reciprocal use of her first name (assuming he could find out what it is).

Miss Manners has a deskful of letters from people who cannot get themselves properly addressed by the names or honorifics they prefer. She has neatly sorted them by the likely causes:

Confusion—such as not understanding hyphenated names or not knowing how to address couples in which the lady uses a professional title socially;

Disapproval—deliberate misuse of someone else's choice, often accompanied by such tiresome cracks as that Mrs. "means her husband owns her" or Ms. "means I would be known as Manuscript Dorothy";

Malice—inequality in usage that seems to be connected with race or gender;

Misguided friendliness—unauthorized liberties such as using first names, making up nicknames, or inappropriate endearments;

Ignorance—unfamiliarity with the customs of a particular profession or even with standard usage;

Longing for uniformity and order—a feeling not unknown to Miss Manners herself, who one of these days will stop simpering about how people are entitled to be addressed as they wish and start issuing uniform regulations.

Forms of address are being adapted and invented at a great rate, and it is difficult to keep up with the variety of available choices. Miss Manners advises the misaddressed first to presume that mistakes are honest. A surprising number of people who are angry when their preferences are not respected are actually keeping the correct answer a secret. You must give others a fighting chance by telling them what your choice is at every opportunity—birth announcements, wedding correspondence, notes mentioning changes at the time of divorce, formal names on writing paper, introductions, and signatures. Those who have names that are difficult to pronounce or to spell, or who have changed their names or abandoned their nicknames, will have to resign themselves to going through life providing the correct information.

Misuses must politely be set straight:

"No, actually, I'm Daisy Higgenbottom-Drake, and my husband's name is Derek Drake."

"I'm sorry, I didn't realize you meant me. I've never been called Liz; my name is Elizabeth, and only people I've known from grammar school still call me Betsy."

"Yes, Caleb is my legal name, so I used it on the application, but I go by Michael Trilby."

"Since I'm not really prepared to call you Arthur, Mr. Merryman, perhaps you'd better call me Miss Jamison."

"I appreciate the courtesy, but actually 'The Reverend' is used only to address me on envelopes. Otherwise, it's plain Mr."

"I know that the members have always been listed under their husbands' names, but some of us would appreciate it if you would respect our preferences, too."

Finally, Miss Manners would like to prescribe a bit of perspective and the acknowledgment that there are times when the cause is hopeless. To the bride who claims that confusion about her hyphenated name "is frankly ruining my life" and the mother who threatens never again to take her toddler to visit his relatives if they keep calling him "Josh" instead of "Joshua," Miss Manners would like to suggest calming down. The time will come when the bride calls her husband by her brother's name (that is, if she's lucky in her lapses) and the mother says "Joshua" when she means his brother Nathaniel. It is well to develop a reputation for tolerance before that happens.

Impolite and Impolitic

DEAR MISS MANNERS:

I have not met either senator from my state. I have, as a constituent, written to them. Because previous letters from them addressed me by my first name, I habitually add a sentence to request the use of my honorific in their replies. The letters continue to arrive with the salutation "Dear William." What a waste of my time!

GENTLE READER:

And think what a waste of their resources it is to send out letters that only alienate a voter. What about the Williams who are always called Bill or Willy, or called by their initials or middle names, and who will be jarred by misusage? Miss Manners would be surprised to hear that any citizens are naive enough to be fooled by the ploy of pretended intimacy into glowing with affection for their senators— even the senators who don't bristle when others fail to give them the full dignity of their title.

Who Chooses the Form?

DEAR MISS MANNERS:

My husband and I have taught our children to address their elders as "Mr." or "Mrs." The children have no problem with this; it is our friends who have difficulty. The most common reply is, "Oh, no, Mrs. Jones is my mother-in-law; my name is Nancy." Who has the right of way in this situation? Do we, as parents, have the right to override our friends' wishes and have our children address them in what we feel is a more respectful manner? Or do our friends have the right to insist that our children call them by their first names? This has become a touchy situation.

GENTLE READER:

As irritated as Miss Manners is by people who sabotage parental lessons in manners, she must acknowledge that people do have a right to decide how they wish to be addressed. Please do not let that discourage you from bringing up your children to know what is right. Just add to the lesson that others must be indulged in their choice, no matter how foolish.

The Recommended Method

DEAR MISS MANNERS:

How do I know if I should call people by their first name or if I should call them by their titles?

GENTLE READER:

Recommended Method: Call the person by his or her title and surname. If you are told, "Oh, no, please call me Sam," then you will know to use the first name.

Not Recommended Method: Use the first name. If the person draws up stiffly and says "I am Dr. Smythers, if you please," you will know that you should have used the title and last name.

Under Difficult Circumstances

DEAR MISS MANNERS:

I was recently a suspect in the arson of my home. The accusation was unfounded, but while being questioned by the local authorities, I kept my wits about me enough to notice that the policemen invariably addressed me by my first name after introducing themselves as "Detective Bubblehead" or "Detective Slow." I found this familiarity offensive, but I was, understandably, a trifle timid about making my displeasure known at the time. Is it correct for the police to address adult suspects by their first names? Should I have asked their first names and used them? Or should I have told them I preferred the use of my surname to the informality of "Where were you at four-thirty, Jan?"

GENTLE READER:

As a matter of etiquette, the police were quite wrong to address you by your first name. As a practical matter, you were quite right to assume that it would not be a good idea for a suspected arsonist to correct the manners of the arresting officers. However, now that you are cleared, Miss Manners hopes you will take the trouble to lodge a complaint, for the good it may do to future suspects who feel the restraint that you did. The suspicion that you burned your house down does not entitle police to belittle your dignity.

Correcting Mistakes

DEAR MISS MANNERS:

My name is Tracey. Quite often, people make an innocent mistake and call me Stacey. For example, a co-worker at the same managerial level as I addressed me as Stacey in front of several other co-workers. Not wishing to embarrass her, I responded to her greeting but then felt embarrassed for having responded to the wrong name in the presence of others who knew better.

GENTLE READER:

There is hardly such a thing as being too tactful, but allowing others to change your name without protest probably qualifies. A smile, a slight shake of the head, and a gentle brief correction ("It's Tracey")—all done as if the mistake is a common one that rather amuses you—is called for. This generous stance (Miss Manners perfectly understands that there is nothing amusing in such an error) is continued, after the extracted apology, by your saying, "Don't worry about it—everyone does it."

Sharing a Name

Dear Miss Manners:

I have a distinctive name and a high-profile professional position. Two persons with the same last name have occasionally been the subject of news coverage of their pending criminal charges. Such media accounts always trigger the disagreeable question "Are you related to. . . . ?" This situation has been going on for several years and is likely to continue for several more. What does Miss Manners suggest?

Gentle Reader:

You don't have an etiquette problem. All you have to say, when asked if you are related to these people, is "No." The etiquette problem belongs to those whose answer is "Yes." Leave it to them to carry on about innocence until guilt is proven, hardships causing behavior that is symptomatic of illness and not evil, and forgiveness for those who make mistakes.

Addressing In-Laws

Dear Miss Manners:

My husband and I have been involved with each other for nine years but married for only a little over one year. When he first met my parents, I introduced them to him by their first names, as is customary in my family, and he has always referred to them this way. His parents are more formal and conservative than mine, and when I first met them he introduced them as "Mr. and Mrs." I have always called them that with their last name. When I married their son, they did not tell me to call them by other names, so I still call them "Mr. and Mrs." I really can't stand this situation, and I am embarrassed when other people hear me catching their attention when I am trying to be polite and not just say, "Hey, you." However, I am also timid about talking to them about it. My sister suggests referring to them by name whenever possible, so that they will get the message, but I am too chicken for even that.

Gentle Reader:

Perhaps you are too young to know that there can be kind, loving people in the world who nevertheless make a distinction between generations. Your parents-in-law's formality should not be interpreted as a reflection against you, but as a social tradition as normal to them as first-names-for-everybody is for you and your parents. Another social custom is that the elders decide how they wish to be addressed, not the children. If you think they might be agreeable to a change (and there are possibilities between "Mr. and Mrs." and "Joe and Betty," such as "Mother and Father Farthington"), ask your husband to ask them what they would like to be called. Haven't you discovered yet that one advantage of marriage is getting your spouse to do easily what might be difficult for you?

Insulting In-Laws

DEAR MISS MANNERS:

Is there any diplomatic way to stop calling one's mother-in-law "Mother" and begin calling her by her first name? My mother is still alive. My mother-in-law is so antithetical to anything I associate with motherhood that I feel it is an insult to my mother and all mothers to continue calling her "Mother." As far as I am concerned, calling her by her first name will do the relationship a lot of good. It will also knock her socks off, since I've perpetuated the farce for ten years. Is there some neat way to achieve my goal without horrifying anyone?

GENTLE READER:

As Miss Manners understands it, you wish to insult your mother-in-law without getting into trouble for it. That can only be done by being superpolite.

The title of "Mother" denotes both love and respect; but the use of first names (admittedly, hopelessly debased now) is intended to convey the intimacy and equality of friendship. People who call parents by their first names wish to (or are asked to) emphasize chumminess over the unique combination of love and inequality in the child-parent relationship. By calling her Thelma you suggest both closeness and, since it is unauthorized by the elder woman, cheekiness. That's the kind of thing that gets you in trouble. However, if you insist on addressing her as "Mrs. Delwaddy," you establish distance in an impeccably polite manner. Or, as you would put it, you knock her socks off.

Pet Names

DEAR MISS MANNERS:

In my family, we have had, for several generations, the custom of calling everyone by a pet name. For example, my great-grandfather was called Wozzy, although the name had no resemblance to any of his given names. The pet name is generally awarded to a child in toddlerhood by a sibling, a parent, or the child himself in an early attempt to say his name. My problem is that my brothers insist on using my private family pet name in social gatherings.

I have a fine given name and even a perfectly good nickname, but they have called me Bumpo at fraternity parties, sport events, and, most recently, in front of my major professor, whom I am trying to impress for a scholarship application. When asked how I got the name Bumpo, my elder brother said that it refers to a private part of my anatomy, which (he said) is hardly more than a bump. Miss Manners, I am desperate to stop this undignified, juvenile practice. I would leave town rather than be subject to my brothers' cruel behavior one more time.

GENTLE READER:

The follow-up to your brother's explanation should have been your giving him a meaningful smile and saying, "It's a family characteristic." But that is not the solution. Miss Manners regrets having lapsed from her policy against retaliating in kind.

127 Primrose Path

Ms. Alexandrina Perfect-Awful

Mr. Ian Fright

We are delighted to announce
the birth of our daughter
Bathsheba Annabel
Perfect-Awful-Fright
on June first

Ms. Victorine Right-Wrong

Mr. Christopher Wrong-Right

At Home

131 Primrose Path

Several more or less formal ways of telling people what your name is at different stages of life: Birth (and a mid-life change of parental names), marriage, and divorce.

Ms. Kristen Awful

I am no longer using the
surname of Awful-Mess, following
my divorce, but am resuming my
maiden name of Awful. My new
address is 133 Primrose Path
in Brookdale, Connecticut.

This birth announcement gives the baby's full name, because it's too hard to figure out from her parents' names. A hospital name and the weight could be included, but Bathsheba was born in the family multimedia room, and the Proper family thinks it questionable taste to mention a lady's poundage.

The "at home" card is enclosed with a formal marriage announcement (not shown), sent out immediately after a wedding and similar to the wedding invitation, except that the verb "announce," or the equally correct but smugger "have the honor of announcing," is substituted for "request the honor of your presence" and the hour is omitted.

A divorce is indirectly "announced." These "correspondence cards" are ideal for short news as well as informal invitations and answers to such, but not, repeat NOT, for thanking people for wedding presents, which requires a letter. With a monogram, they are less informative and slightly more informal, but make a snazzy substitute for a postcard or such atrocities as "from the desk of" paper.

The solution is a tough family council, with all offenders present and as many members of the elder generation as have developed sense and compassion. An overdue family tradition must be inaugurated to rule out embarrassing one another before outsiders. While making the argument for family loyalty, take care to mention some truly awful piece of information you know about each of the offenders but would never dream of telling anyone else. That is not a lapse; it is simple negotiating tactics.

❧ HONORIFICS

Is there no honorific left? Miss Manners is dismayed to find more and more people addressing envelopes with the names totally bald of any titles of courtesy: "Archibald Twimbal." Miss Manners always thinks that an exclamation point has been left out and it was intended as a ringing summons: "Archibald Twimbal!" Under this horrid system, a couple will be "Isabelle and Archibald Twimbal," or those additions so flattering to ladies, "Archibald Twimbal and Wife," or "and Guest."

That's just the formal social style. Should the gentleman or lady be distinguished for heroism or indicted for murder, rather than being so bluntly bidden to attend a wedding, the newspapers will call him or her merely "Twimbal."

If the couple accomplished one of these things together, each would be called "Twimbal" until the poor reader was totally confused as to who had done what.

Miss Manners must put a stop to this; no one is going to address her as "Manners." Her indignation is, however, tinged with sympathy because she knows how befuddled everyone is over correct usage. Many people figure that leaving off all such designations will eliminate the possibility of causing offense. Wrong. Stripping the language of honorifics makes us all sound like children. Surnames-only is a non-gender-specific prep school custom, as in "Hey, Twimbal! Can I borrow your notes the week before the exam?" Here, then, are the traditional rules with Miss Manners' authorized revisions:

A married couple is addressed as "Mr. and Mrs." unless it is known that there are other preferences, such as "Dr." or "Ms." In cases where that precludes the one-line formula, two lines are used, as in "Dr. Isabelle Smyth-Twimbal/Mr. Archibald Twimbal."

"Mrs." is not used with a lady's first name, but "Miss" and "Ms." are. Therefore, "Ms." is particularly useful for ladies who prefer their own full names after divorce to the traditional use of maiden and married surnames ("Mrs. Smyth Twimbal") and for married ladies in their professional lives, whether or not they choose to be "Mrs. Archibald Twimbal" socially.

When the addressee is not known, salutations are "Dear Madam or Sir" or "Ladies and Gentlemen," not "Dear Ace Laundry" or "Hi there."

Why are the boys in the back snickering? "Madam," gentlemen, is no longer funny. We are not going to lose this very proper term because of anybody's improper thoughts, the way we lost the once all-purpose and respectable title of "Mistress." It is really very simple. Whenever "Mr." is used for direct spoken address in combination with certain job titles (Mr. President, Mr. Vice President, Mr. Secretary, Mr. Ambassador, Mr. Speaker, Mr. Mayor), the female equivalent is "Madam." It is a solid-sounding word, unaffected by the office holder's marital status, and—in keeping with the American tradition of simplicity—as appropriate to a private citizen as to a woman of rank. (Well-brought-up southern children still call ladies "Ma'am," which is equally correct for addressing the Queen of England to her face.) When a lady is elected president of the United States, she will properly be addressed as "Madam President." Miss Manners is embarrassed for the Supreme Court justices who admitted publicly to an inability to figure out what the female equivalent would be to "Mr. Justice" and therefore had to drop the "Mr." altogether. It should be "Madam Justice," and the sooner they change their style back, the better.

They are, however, not the only people who are confused about themselves. The one remaining stronghold of titles, Miss Manners regrets to say, is self-misuse, as when people sign themselves as "Mrs. Archibald (or Mrs. Isabelle) Twimbal" or introduce themselves as "I'm Mr. Twimbal." This is incorrect. One never applies a title of courtesy to oneself. But Miss Manners (oh, dear—well, that's a special case, you see—ahem, can we go on a bit, and get to that later, perhaps next Turn of the Century?) understands that people who do this are desperately trying to avoid being promiscuously addressed by their first names. To inform correspondents how one is supposed to be addressed in return, it is correct to put one's own honorific in parentheses with one's signature: "(Ms.) Amantha Idlewild" or "Amantha Idlewild (Mrs. Anton Idlewild)."

Calling oneself by a title out loud nearly chokes Miss Manners, but with some regret, she now authorizes saying "Tell him Mrs. Idlewild is calling" in those impersonal transactions where the conventional "I'm Amantha Idlewild" would only invite a blithe "Okay, Manny, I'll tell him." This is a desperate measure, but cheeky people will be unable to call people by their first names if they aren't told what those names are.

"Ma'am" or "Miss"

DEAR MISS MANNERS:

My co-workers and I are bank tellers and must frequently refer to our customers as "Sir," "Miss," and "Ma'am." What is the proper way to refer to a woman? Do you refer to a married woman as "Ma'am" and a single woman as "Miss"? If you do not know the marital status of the woman, is an older woman called "Ma'am" and a younger woman called "Miss"? Is it insulting to call a young woman "Ma'am"?

GENTLE READER:

Any lady old enough to do her own banking business may be safely addressed as "Ma'am." No young gentleman would be insulted to be addressed as "Sir," would he? Oddly enough, "Miss" used without a name is not strictly proper in English, where it has a kind of slangy, cheeky connotation (which the equivalent in other languages does not have). Perhaps that is because it suggests that the lady's youth and marital status are being too carefully noted by people whose business this information is none of, so to speak.

A Lady No Longer Young

DEAR MISS MANNERS:

One of the few things that irritate me is to be called "young lady" by someone half my age. I am nearly seventy and feel that no young person can know or understand what I have experienced. Let us old persons be respected for our many years of living and surviving—of coping, working, pain, grief, loss, rejection, disappointment; of love, joy, fulfillment, fun, and laughter. It is only men who use this phrase, including doctors, salesmen, and waiters. I have never heard it from a woman. Please give me a courteous, effective reply to this discourteous, thoughtless form of address.

GENTLE READER:

It is an unfortunate general premise of this society that everyone wants to be young. Although you have well pointed out the advantages of long life, thoughtless people will continue to believe that you would rather be eighteen, insecure, and ignorant—and worse, that you will be flattered if they pretend to believe that you are. An advantage of age that you do not mention is the right to assume superiority of tone.

To those whom you see only once, such as salesmen or waiters, you may merely flinch visibly, or you can say coldly, "I beg your pardon." In the voice of a confident dowager, this phrase can be deadly. As you probably have a longer relationship with your doctor, you set him straight by saying, "My dear young man, have the kindness to indulge your elder and to call me by my proper name." It's the "young man" part that will make the idea hit home.

The Token Lady

"Gentlemen and"—the chairman bowed toward the newest member—"lady." He stood straighter and beamed with the confidence of the righteous. "Lady and gentlemen," he began again.

Not quite, sir. Although well meant and even well thought out, "lady and gentlemen" is not the correct formal salutation for a group indisputably composed of several gentlemen and a lady. (Yes, Miss Manners agrees that it is a shame that what makes sense is not always identical to what is correct, but she feels obliged to point out that in cases of conflict, the correct takes precedence.)

"Lady," when used to address an individual, is less than respectful usage, as in "Hey, lady, watch where you're going." Contrary to some congressional usage, there is no such thing as a "gentlelady." A lady is referred to in the third person as "the gentlewoman" or "the lady."

But don't be alarmed, gentlemen. Miss Manners is the last person in the world who would solve such a problem by doing away with traditional courtesies. She is not going to suggest a ringing "Women and men!" You may notice that she quaintly holds on to the practice of referring to her gentle readers as "ladies" and "gentlemen," in the hope that they may be encouraged to behave as such.

The solution is that useful word Miss Manners hopes she has succeeded in wresting from the hard times into which it fell—"madam." A collection of gentlemen with one lady among them is addressed as "Gentlemen and Madam." (A sole gentleman is addressed as "sir," not "gentleman," so a group of several ladies with one gentleman would be addressed as "Ladies and Sir.")

"Madam and gentlemen" is more gallant than the converse, of course, but gender gallantry is not required in polite business behavior. Miss Manners is assuming that the lady is the newcomer to the group, in which case it would be sufficiently polite to address her first the first time as a welcoming gesture. Subsequent usage could reflect that she is the member with the least seniority.

When she is in charge, well-meaning gentlemen often remember to call her "Chairperson." But since they don't remember to call themselves that, we have a peculiar usage that recognizes only the masculine and the neuter, "chairman" and "chairperson." Under the circumstances, Miss Manners believes, we might concede that calling a person "the Chair" isn't all that funny. "Madam Chairman" wouldn't bother her, either.

Another nicety the gentlemen should learn is not to turn and look at the lady whenever a subject arises that was traditionally the province of ladies or when another lady is mentioned.

A lady of Miss Manners' acquaintance reported an instance in which a gentleman, in an excess of what was intended to be courtesy, brought up an example of employee transgressions at a meeting and said to her, "I beg your pardon, but I am afraid that the offender in this particular case was a lady."

"I hardly knew whether to apologize on her behalf or to promise that I wouldn't get into such trouble myself," said the recipient of this remark.

The rudeness in this instance is the failure to conceal that the lady is not being considered a member of the group, but a representative of womanhood known, under such conditions, as the token.

Never mind that her presence was preceded by a great deal of soul searching about how "we really must have a woman here." Once she is there, she must be treated as an individual, free to speak up in representation of her gender when she thinks that appropriate, but otherwise presumed to be approaching business in as detached a fashion as everyone else.

This is the polite attitude to take to all sole or uncommon participants from racial, religious, or ethnic minorities in social as well as business situations. They may volunteer to speak as representatives of their kind, but they cannot be interrogated about or taxed with opinions based on these identifications. True courtesy consists of giving everyone the dignity of individuality.

The Use of Parentheses

DEAR MISS MANNERS:

We at Saint Mary's College are knowingly guilty of a social *faux pas,* but, after analyzing every possible way to correct it, find that we must continue with the offensive practice. The only way we have to keep accurate records of our alumnae is to file them by their maiden names. Name changes commonly occur in a woman's life because of marriage, divorce, or remarriage; a nickname is picked up or dropped; or part of a double name is dropped. The one constant throughout most of these changes is the maiden name.

We find that the only way we can easily recognize which is the maiden name is by putting "Mrs.," "Miss," or "Ms." in front of the woman's name. Therefore, we refer to Jane Carter Smith as "Mrs. Jane Carter Smith" or "Miss Jane Carter Smith" so that we can tell if "Carter" or "Smith" is the maiden name. We are well aware of the fact that, in the case of the married woman, we should call her either "Jane Carter Smith" or "Mrs. Robert F. Smith."

Our computer program, on which we keep our master alumnae list and generate mailing labels, will not highlight the maiden name or print it in all capital letters. Another computer could solve this problem, but unfortunately we are stuck with the one we have.

After every mailing, we receive letters of complaint from some of our alumnae, saying that they find this practice offensive. Are we justified in continuing a practice that we find to be the best way we can serve our alumnae? If so, how can we persuade them to bear with us in this necessary evil?

GENTLE READER:

Miss Manners analyzed your letter, looking for a parenthesis or two. She didn't find any, but she is nevertheless confident that your computer can manage a pair when needed. They are desperately needed here. Not only do you not want to continue offending your alumnae, but Miss Manners notes with satisfaction that the tone of your letter demonstrates a distaste for incorrect addresses on your own part.

Why don't you continue to address the unmarried ladies as "Miss Jane Carter Smith" but address the married ones as "Mrs. Robert F. Smith (Jane Carter)" or "Jane Carter (Mrs. Robert F.) Smith"?

Unintended Insults

DEAR MISS MANNERS:

My husband, a pastor, had a nervous breakdown eleven years ago. He has been supporting his family and leading a productive life for a long time. However, the relatives who were so hurt during his illness persist in writing to us as "Bill and Sue" or "The Smiths." He was not defrocked, and teaches and substitute preaches, but we don't even get the courtesy of a "Mr. and Mrs." on our mail, let alone "The Rev."! The greeting card or letter that arrives is totally wiped out, as far as I'm concerned, because of the put-down in the way it's addressed. What to do?

GENTLE READER:

Miss Manners promises you that the intolerable informality of which you justly complain has nothing whatsoever to do with the state of your husband's past health or present occupation. It is merely part of the increasing informality used as a misguided demonstration of friendliness.

The way to counteract this is not by assuming that people are sending you greeting cards for the purpose of insulting you but to inform them of your preference.

An easy way to get that across would be to have correspondence cards made with "The Reverend and Mrs. William Smith" at the top and to use them to write the sort of messages ("Happy birthday," "Thank you for the delightful evening") that less imaginative people buy greeting cards to convey.

The Clergy

DEAR MISS MANNERS:

Should a lady pastor be addressed as "Reverend Mary Jane Doe" or "The Reverend Mary Jane Doe"? As she is a doctor of divinity, should she be introduced as "Reverend Doctor," "The Reverend Doctor Mary Jane Doe," or just "Doctor Mary Jane Doe"? Is it correct to use her married name, as "Reverend" or "Doctor" (or both) and "Mrs. John Henry Doe"? How should she and her husband be introduced together when he is from a different profession? When there are two doctorates, should both be given after her name? Should her signature include her married name in parentheses under it? This is very confusing!

GENTLE READER:

Yes, but the answer is not nearly as confusing as the question. She is "The Reverend Mary Jane Doe, D.D." ("L.L. D.," too, if she has that) on the envelope, "Dr. Doe" to her face, and either "The Reverend Doctor Mary Jane Doe and Mr. John Henry Doe" socially or, if she prefers, "Mr. and Mrs. John Henry Doe."

Junior Honorifics

DEAR MISS MANNERS:

I am perplexed as to how I should address the invitations to my child's birthday party, with an age range from preschoolers to teenagers. I am not sure when to address the boys as "Master", nor am I sure of how to address the young ladies. Also, should the teenagers' names take precedence over the younger children's names, although it is for a five-year-old's party?

GENTLE READER:

Allow Miss Manners to remark that that is quite a project you are undertaking. She wishes you luck in simultaneously amusing such a variety of guests. When addressing siblings together, precedence goes by their age. The age of the host or guest of honor is irrelevant. If you want to do the sweet, old-fashioned thing (Miss Manners is judging by your interest in the term "Master," which is used for boys under ten), address the eldest daughter as "Miss Trister" and her sisters as "Miss Miranda Trister," "Miss Melissa Trister," and so on. But Miss Manners would like to point out how very much children enjoy receiving their own mail. Perhaps you could spare them each an envelope.

Anarchy in Address

DEAR MISS MANNERS:

I prefer informality at work. My loyal secretary has difficulty because traditionally the individual in my position is addressed by title. Often the manner of addressing individuals is associated with racism or sexism. During a meeting where I must, for these reasons, at the individual's request, address her or him more formally than the others, I am uncomfortable.

Pomposity regularly enters the situation. An attorney friend of mine enjoyed commenting that the demand of many physicians to be called "doctor," even in collegial or personal contact, annoyed him. He threatened to ask them to always address him as "Attorney So and So." Some academicians and retired military officers want present or past titles used.

Hidden or not-so-hidden agendas are often part of title preferences. Often when people inform me of their titles, they are implicitly asking for preferential treatment. On occasion, attempted intimidation is the motive.

GENTLE READER:

Miss Manners regrets to inform you that you are part of the problem, not of the solution. You mistake the opportunity to express preference, within a limited choice of titles ("Miss," "Ms.," "Mrs.," "Dr.," "Professor," "Colonel," etc.), for a state of anarchy, and you unilaterally condemn others by declaring evil motives for common usage.

Formality takes precedence over informality. That is, everyone should start at a respectful distance and advance toward intimacy as relationships progress. Miss Manners suggests that you get used to addressing everyone at work in a business-like way.

Then get it out of your mind that the inconsistency of tradition is deeply symbolic. Physicians and members of the military are addressed by titles because they are, not because they are better than lawyers (with their predilection for "esquire"). People who inform you of their honorifics are likely to be doing so only in the hope that you will address them correctly.

Professional Honorifics

DEAR MISS MANNERS:

Having only recently graduated from medical school, I still feel awkward when people refer to me as "Doctor." My fiancée states that it is improper to send out wedding invitations without referring to me this way. The guests are all close family members and friends who have known both of us since childhood. I can understand using my professional title on a business announcement, but I feel that using it on a wedding announcement is not only stuffy, but a bit pretentious and ostentatious. What does Miss Manners think?

GENTLE READER:

Miss Manners thinks you are a dear. Yours is the only such letter she has received, among hundreds from people who argue "Well, I earned it," as an excuse for flaunting their professional titles at every opportunity. American medical doctors, as opposed to other holders of the title, do use "Doctor" socially. There is no reason why they should, but it is customary.

Because of their wording, formal wedding invitations require an honorific for the bridegroom, but not the bride, when the parents are hosts, and they therefore refer to the bride only by her given names ("their daughter, Maria Louise"). There is nothing reasonable or fair about this. It is just the way things are done. But if Miss Manners felt moved to neaten it all up, she would call upon you, and abolish all professional titles socially, rather than allowing anyone to proclaim his or her job.

Honorable Relatives

DEAR MISS MANNERS:

Do I introduce my son as "Judge Harry" (not his real name) or just "Meet my son, Harry"?

GENTLE READER:

Just Harry. Miss Manners knows that this answer will disappoint you, but promises you that it will be all the more satisfying to have people then inquire, as they always do nowadays, what Harry "does."

❧ NAMES

The Conservative Lady's Solution

In Elizabethan times, a woman's title did not change upon marriage, any more than a man's does today. Mistress Nell Quickly became Mistress Nell Pistol. Our current tedious debate over "Miss" and "Mrs." dates from more recent, less enlightened, times when it was not considered necessary to have a form for a married businesswoman because there weren't supposed to be any. That left married businesswomen, who nevertheless exist, to wrestle with the difficulty individually.

Here is Miss Manners' recommended system for the conservative lady:

At work, she is known by her original surname, or the one under which she happened to make her professional reputation (which might be the name of a previous husband—conservativeness does not guarantee prudence), and is addressed as "Ms." This form meets Miss Manners' standard of old-fashioned propriety for married, single, or divorced ladies.

In her private life, the conservative lady is known as "Mrs." with her husband's name, so that elderly relatives, strangers, and their children's teachers and friends know that they are a couple. Having her own identity at work, she is able gracefully to accept, as well, the traditional designation as part of a family. She may even cherish this, as it will quickly separate her truly private friends from those whose interest in her is primarily professional.

When the children have grown, she advances her career to the point where it gives her an honorific suitable for both social and professional use, and becomes "Judge," "Admiral," or "Representative," with her own full name, while her husband takes his turn gracefully being "and Mr."

Complicated as all this is, it is the closest we have now to an intelligible standard of usage. If everyone followed this example, it would reduce the confusion and hurt feelings that are inevitable when everyone does something different and each person takes anyone's different preference as a symbolic affront.

The Progressive Solution

DEAR MISS MANNERS:

What is the solution to the problem of all those hyphenated kids getting married? Is the daughter of Matilda Snodgrass-Phleuvelhoffer and Robert Throckmorton-Bezzlehoff going to have to go through life as Carmella Snodgrass-Phleuvelhoffer-Throckmorton-Bezzlehoff?

The daughter could simplify things somewhat by dropping the names before her parents' hyphens and become Carmella Phleuvelhoffer-Bezzlehoff. But this use of the two fathers' names would rather miss the original point of hyphenating the names, i.e., to give the woman an equal share. She could, instead, use the prehyphen name of her mother and the posthyphen name of her father (Carmella Snodgrass-Bezzlehoff). But then she could never have dinner at the Phleuvelhoffers' or the Throckmortons'.

Also: While it makes perfect sense that a woman would want to have her maiden name as part of her married name, I do not know of a single case where a woman does this when her maiden name is less felicitous than her husband's name.

I know many traditional women who take the husband's name even though it is less felicitous, and many women who add their own names when these are more felicitous (i.e., Betty Robinson-Fruttlemeyer) and justify this as a way of maintaining their own identities. But I don't know of a single case of a woman who choses to be, say, Betty Fruttlemeyer-Robinson. Women with such maiden names always seem to drop the maiden name. This would seem to indicate that for the nontraditional woman, the "identity" explanation is really a rationalization for a name actually chosen for its felicitousness. Does this jibe with your observation?

GENTLE READER:

Miss Manners has certainly known ladies who were anxious to get rid of, or reluctant to assume, difficult surnames. (She assumes that names you consider infelicitous are those that have to be spelled twice to everyone who hears them and are still mispronounced.) She has known many ladies who changed or added to their names upon marriage, as well as many who did not, and often, although not always, the simpler name was chosen.

These observations do not lead Miss Manners to conclude that the "identity" factor in name keeping or changing is a sham. Rather, she concludes that more than one factor is involved when such a choice is made. The name borne when the lady became prominent professionally is often chosen in spite of how it sounds and who bestowed it on her.

These are all valid considerations. Furthermore, gentlemen are not always aware of what a traumatic experience it is for an adult to change her name. Brides have always commented on the peculiar feeling it gives them, regardless of their emotions about the father, husband, or what constitutes their identity.

Nevertheless, Miss Manners, along with practically everyone else, finds it difficult to live in a society where there is no standard system of names. She has long waffled about the problem by reciting the rule that people can call themselves whatever they wish, within reason, and expect others to respect their choices.

Isn't it about time, though, that something was done? People simply cannot carry around the names of all their ancestors. Someone is bound to be left out. Nor is the problem solved by having couples fashion their own names—from preexisting ones or from scratch—to be used only by them and their children. That only means that more people are left out.

Although a matriarchal system would seem to Miss Manners to be the most sensible one in a society where single custodial parents are nearly always the mothers, she cannot ignore the weight of patriarchal tradition.

She proposes that no one be allowed more than one hyphen. Earlier generations will have to be lopped off, much as law firms lop off the names of partners when they are not around to protest. Miss S.- P.- T.- B. therefore becomes Carmella Snodgrass-Bezzlehoff. The Phleuvelhoffers and the Throckmortons will just have to understand.

The Number of Names

DEAR MISS MANNERS:

What are your feelings about a bride keeping her maiden name before her new surname—for example, Anne Marie Smith becoming Anne Marie Smith Taylor, to be known as "Anne Taylor" or "Mrs. Whoever Taylor"? What about a mother's maiden name being placed within a newborn's name in that same "silent third" position? Finally, what are the rules concerning "surname stringing" when a woman is remarried, as in "Jacqueline Lee Bouvier Kennedy Onassis"?

GENTLE READER:

Miss Manners refuses to dictate to brides what they should call themselves or to parents what they should name their children. Nor will she allow anyone to consider four names laughable. (Five, yes.)

However, she cannot quite control herself to the extent of allowing the stringing of sequential husbands' names to pass without expressing her horror. Although a lady traditionally changed her name when she married, keeping her original middle name but dropping any previous surname in exchange for the current husband's, an excellent argument can be made for keeping it. But the idea of stringing along one's collection of married names, one after the other, as a mini-biography, is more than she can stand.

Names and Numbers

DEAR MISS MANNERS:

My friend's brother wants to name his first child after their father, Richard Stephen, who is deceased. My friend, named after his father, is Richard Stephen III. He's thirty-two and, because he's gay, isn't sure whether he's going to have children, but he says he might and would like to name his son Richard Stephen IV. He thinks of that name as his. The brother wants to use the name because he figures that my friend won't ever have a family. Can you discuss the circumstances in which a child is appropriately named III, IV, or Junior?

GENTLE READER:

In the first place, there is no such thing as having dibs on a name. One brother cannot prevent another from naming a child after their father. In the second place, except for royalty and other historical personages, names are traditionally numbered only among the living. The brother may have been Richard Stephen III when his grandfather and father were alive, but he is just Richard Stephen now, and his son would be Richard Stephen, junior. Whether or not that son ever materializes, the nephew, not being in the direct line of names, would be Richard Stephen II.

Miss Manners tells you this to clear up their problem, not to create problems among those who claim that their numbers are part of their names and do not change with the deaths of ancestors. People may call themselves what they wish: Henry Higgenbottom the Eighth, if that pleases them. The only stipulation is that they not pick on poor Miss Manners for knowing the rule.

Changing Back a Name

DEAR MISS MANNERS:

I was divorced after a brief marriage, but I chose to keep my married name. For some time now, I have been uncomfortable, feeling that this surname is not really mine. Therefore, I plan to change back to my maiden name. How do I make this known to the people I have various types of interactions with—friends, co-workers, acquaintances—in a proper manner?

GENTLE READER:

Although this information should be put in writing, so that people have a card to stick in their address books, please do not design a fancy announcement that looks like an invitation to a ceremony at which a champagne bottle will be broken over your head. Miss Manners has always wondered how people retain friends in such numbers that they must deal with them in mass mailings. A memo to colleagues, but brief, individual notes to friends (or parenthetically at the bottom of Christmas cards), with the simple statement "I am resuming my maiden name," with the old and new surnames, should do it. If you must have a printed announcement, use simple third-person wording such as "Ms. Laura Merton announces that she will resume her former name of Laura Nelwitter."

Losing a Name

DEAR MISS MANNERS:

I am the wife of a professor at a small but well-known fine arts college. My husband has been teaching at this school for more than two decades. It is a first marriage for us both, and we have been married thirteen years. For most of our married life, invitations from the institution have been addressed to "Mr. and Mrs. John Doe" or "John and Jane Doe," or sometimes "Professor and Mrs. John Doe." But recently, all our invitations have been sent to "Mr. John Doe and Guest."

At first, we thought this was a mistake. When my husband inquired, he was told that all invitations were so addressed. I suppose the college feels it is being tactful, since it is true that there are many single, separated, and divorced faculty members. But is there to be no acknowledgment of stable marriage anymore? Also, a faculty wife or spouse used to be accorded some dignity, prestige, and respect. Suddenly, we no longer exist.

I am afraid that I have taken this new address as an insult. At an institution where he has worked so long and contributed so much, and which does not have that large a faculty, shouldn't they take the time to find out if the marriage is on or off? For instance, couldn't they have sent a written inquiry asking each teacher what he would prefer? Do you think the president of the institution and his wife would accept an invitation to President Soandso and Guest?

GENTLE READER:

Before declaring herself on your side, which she intends to do, Miss Manners is forced to point out that the thinking that has led to this unfortunate solution has crept into your own attitude. "It is a first marriage for us both," you write. A first marriage? Time was when people talked simply of being married.

As we know, times have changed. Institutions and individuals have grown weary of trying to keep up with marriages, divorces, and all the possible states in between. Your idea, for the college to inquire periodically whether people's marriages are on or off is, if anything, more offensive than the solution they reached. What should be done instead is to send out a questionnaire at the beginning of the school year, when addresses and other information is being compiled anyway, asking how each professor wants his or her social invitations addressed. Should a person's marital status change during the school year, that person would have no right to complain about being misaddressed if he had not notified the central record-keeper of the change.

Conventional Gestures, Phrases, and Words

❧ GREETINGS

All right for you, Leo Buscaglia. Cut it out. Ladylike though she invariably may be, Miss Manners does not allow her reputation or her person to go undefended. This gentleman, who believes in freelance hugging for friend and stranger alike, reports, correctly, that Miss Manners is a dissenter from his doctrine for improving the world, but his account of their encounters must be corrected.

"Miss Manners," the gentleman writes in *Loving Each Other* (by which Miss Manners presumes he means "Loving One Another," but, then, what's grammar when the heart is involved?), "actually asked me not to touch her. She said she only allowed her husband and King Louis XIV to touch her. In the end I hugged her anyway, hoping that she received sufficient hugs from her husband, knowing that it was too late for Louis XIV."

Not exactly. In the first place, Miss Manners did not actually ask the gentleman not to touch her, although she certainly would have done so, possibly in Latin, if she had known he was contemplating it. On the one occasion that Miss Manners knowingly met him, he informed her that he had previously observed her in a foreign hotel elevator, and had contemplated hugging her but had been somehow warned off by her manner. (Miss Manners' elevator manner tends to be eyes-on-the-numbers, purely in the not always realized hope that she will disembark on the

62

correct floor.) Indeed, he was right to trust his instinct. Miss Manners would not have submitted willingly to the impromptu embraces of a stranger on an elevator, and anyone who wishes to interpret this as a symptom of emotional ill health is most welcome to do so. She even carries this frigidity to the point of believing that it is a respectable lady's fundamental privilege to decide who shall fondle her and who may not.

Even among acquaintances, the deterioration of the dignified and friendly American handshake into promiscuous social kissing annoys Miss Manners for its patently phony show of intimacy. However, being one to yield to acknowledged conventions, rather than to make scenes about abstaining, she did, on a later occasion, suffer without protest a public hugging from this gentleman, erroneously implying to onlookers that they were old friends, although they had in fact been introduced only a few minutes previously. (Miss Manners has been known to attempt warding off the more ridiculous instances of this, firmly putting out a hand on meeting people for the first time in the hope of giving would-be instant kissers a fist in the tummy, but it doesn't always succeed.) On the darker side is the idea that everyone is available as a target for whatever physical promptings others may have. The society has only recently become aware of a severe problem resulting from the failure to teach children the basic right of refusing to allow anyone to touch them.

At any rate, on the public occasion that Miss Manners and the hugging gentleman did formally meet, she explained to their mutual audience that he and she belonged to different schools of etiquette. "He believes in hugging on first sight," she said. "I, on the other hand, belong to the school of etiquette of the Queen Mother of England who after President Carter had taken the liberty of grabbing her and kissing her, commented frostily, 'Nobody but my late husband was allowed to do that.' Nobody," Miss Manners continued on her own behalf, "except my husband is allowed to do that. And, of course, her husband, George VI, and dear Prince Albert."

Therefore (speaking of unauthorized familiarity), Miss Manners is astonished to find her name linked with that of Louis XIV. Louis XIV? Oh, gross. Why, Miss Manners can't even bear his furniture.

The Social Kiss

DEAR MISS MANNERS:

Last year, my boss took me and a young female colleague out to lunch for Secretary's Day. The maitre d' was very attentive to all the tables with secretaries and bosses, and when we rose to leave, he came to our table, took my hand, and then the hand of my young colleague, and kissed each of us on the cheek. I was too surprised to say anything.

Last week, I thanked a gentleman whom I do not know for inviting me to a small reunion party for people who used to work in his office. He took my hand and then kissed me on the cheek.

I think men today feel that kissing a woman is the polite thing to do. I like to be kissed—by my husband, my son, my son-in-law, and all of my male relatives—but I do not like any man to take the privilege because he mistakenly feels it is polite. I wish they would wise up!

GENTLE READER:

Miss Manners heartily joins you in deploring the debasement of both the dignified American greeting of the handshake and the intimacy of the kiss. The cheek, as it were, of this being done by strangers and even those one meets in a nonsocial capacity, such as the restaurateur, borders on the insulting. It presumes that a lady is grateful for any attention at all that simulates the romantic.

The Hand Kiss

DEAR MISS MANNERS:

What does a woman say when a gentleman kisses her hand? While it is not an everyday occurrence, it has happened often enough for me to become uncomfortable with my lack of knowledge. Unfortunately, by the time the young man gets around to kissing my hand, I have already told him how nice it is to meet him or see him again and have inquired about his well-being. Thus, I've always ended up blushing like a fool and mumbling something like, "How sweet. Thank you!"

GENTLE READER:

Are you speaking of the gentleman who kisses the air above a matron's hand (never an unmarried girl's) in the European equivalent of a handshake or the gentleman who plants his kisses on an unmarried lady's fingers and palms as a prelude to heaven knows what?

Miss Manners just wondered. Actually, the answer is the same, although the response may be different. One never thanks a gentleman for either routine greetings or romantic gestures. In the former case, the lady merely nods her head pleasantly and smiles; in the latter—well, she must decide her own reaction. Miss Manners can't do everything, you know.

The Handshake

DEAR MISS MANNERS:

I am a professional woman in business, and lately I've found the handshake scenario to be rather awkward. I usually offer my hand to men, because otherwise I find that they're not sure what to do. However, many men only grasp my fingers lightly, rather than clasping my hand in a firm shake. I've asked a few male friends about this, and they all say that they were taught as youngsters to hold a woman's hand lightly when shaking it.

What is the proper way for a man to shake a woman's hand? Does the shake differ on business and social occasions? Who should offer the hand first? Should handshakes between men and women be exchanged as both a greeting and a farewell? In business, women shake my hand warmly and firmly. But on social occasions, women either give other women a superficial embrace or just stand there smiling and nodding.

GENTLE READER:

Gentlemen were taught to shake ladies' hands lightly because ladies, but not gentlemen, often wear rings on their right hands. A hearty grip on a hand on which a diamond is nestling between the fingers is a mistake. Other reasons for light shaking include arthritis, sweaty palms, and a hand frozen onto a cocktail glass. So, the game of judging a person's sincerity or worth by the firmness of his or her handshake is a silly one.

In spite of these hazards, Miss Manners thinks the handshake is a fine greeting, more dignified than promiscuous embracing and cheek kissing. The American custom is to shake hands upon introduction, and in greeting and taking leave of those whom one does not see often. Hands are not regularly shaken in offices, for example.

Socially, a lady should extend her hand to a gentleman; in business, the higher-ranking person or the person whose office it is should extend the hand. To refuse to shake a proffered hand is a much greater error—a full-fledged insult, in fact—than the error of extending the hand first when one should have waited.

The proper way to offer to shake hands is to extend one's own right hand, fingers together and thumb up. As the other person's hand approaches, you slide yours forward until the thumb joints meet, and then squeeze the hand together firmly but briefly. Isn't that fun enough for a working day?

Household Greetings

DEAR MISS MANNERS:

My roommate habitually leaves the apartment without saying goodbye to me. She also goes to bed without saying goodnight and enters the apartment without acknowledging my presence. Am I being overly sensitive, or am I correct in assuming that this is a breach of etiquette?

GENTLE READER:

Polite people are taught from babyhood to say "Good morning" and "Good night" to everyone in the household, and "Hello" (actually, it is more often "I'm home!") and "Goodbye" when they go in and out. So, this is a breach of etiquette.

Teaching manners to a roommate is also a breach of etiquette, but you are allowed to make requests—not because they are right, but because you like them. In other words, you may not say, "Decent people always greet one another," even though it is true, but rather, "Would you mind saying good morning and good night? The silence seems so cold."

Constituent Greetings

DEAR MISS MANNERS:

I jog in a park where the governor jogs. Is it okay for me to say hello, even though he doesn't know me?

GENTLE READER:

If it were someone in any field but politics, Miss Manners would give you her basic lecture about disguising your interest so as to allow others their privacy. However, there is no such thing as a voter who is unknown to a politician. There is only a voter he has not yet had the opportunity to meet. Don't go so far as to interrupt his jogging, but do call out hello. It will do him worlds of good.

❧ INTRODUCTIONS

It was on a crumbling page of a hundred-year-old etiquette book that Miss Manners came across the solution to that enduring problem of what to say when confronted with a person whose name you know you are expected to know but don't. The answer comes to us from an anonymous Victorian, apparently a Hero of Etiquette but described merely as "a good-natured eccentric." Beaming a jovial smile at a vaguely familiar face, he would inquire in a pleasant, oh-by-the-by tone, "You don't happen to remember your name, do you?"

Miss Manners is given to perusing aged volumes for just such forgotten devices to ease the difficulties of life. This example is admittedly a special one, for use when one can no longer get away with simply avoiding names, even in introductions ("Of course you know my wife"), and has learned through pain not to ask frank questions because they inspire frank answers ("Well, it almost was the same as yours—we used to be engaged"). Vintage etiquette holds up remarkably well. The human body may have changed, as anyone trying to squeeze into vintage clothing may discover, but the situations into which it manages to get itself are not all that different.

The Forgetful Spouse

DEAR MISS MANNERS:

Too many times, I have had to introduce myself socially when with my husband. I have brought this rudeness to his attention, but it still prevails. It can't be my appearance, because I am a former part-time model still complimented on my youthful good looks. We both are now fifty-five, but the years have been kinder to me. Can I bring this rudeness to an end in some way? Why do some husbands act this way?

GENTLE READER:

Perhaps it isn't just the years that have been unkind to them. Wives who point out that they are better preserved, or who hint that etiquette lapses suggest shame at a spouse's appearance, have an inhibiting effect. Miss Manners' guess is that your husband is merely uncertain about the correct forms of introduction. Tell him without rancor that he introduces gentlemen to you ("Gracie, this is Philip Merman; my wife, Grace") and you to other ladies ("Mrs. Purloin, this is my wife, Grace"). Failing that, you can at least teach him to say, "Oh, yes, yes, of course, I'm sorry," when you put out a hand and say, beaming with good will and youthful good looks, "I'm Brad's wife, Grace."

Identifying the Relationship

DEAR MISS MANNERS:

My brother is engaged to a lovely young woman, and my question concerns proper introductions during their engagement. Should the fact that she is my brother's fiancée be included in the introduction, or should she be allowed to stand on her own identity? Does this differ depending on the situation and who is doing the introducing?

GENTLE READER:

The irony of today's misguided search for conventionality never ceases to amuse Miss Manners. While you are kindly concerned that your future sister-in-law's identity may be compromised by the information that she is engaged to be married, thousands of unengaged couples are demanding the right to announce to everyone what it is that they privately mean or do to each other.

Marriage is a legal matter, legitimately of interest to society; other forms of romance are not. The ties of engagement or marriage are made known, but categories such as "lover" or "boyfriend (girlfriend)" are not. In business situations, a lady's marital status is irrelevant, but there is no social situation in which mentioning the engagement interferes with her "identity." Similarly, your brother would be introduced as her fiancé, and later as her husband.

Introducing Relations

DEAR MISS MANNERS:

I am a screenwriter and, for the most part, self-employed. The only "employer" I have would be the producer to whom I have sold a script. The rest of my contacts are other writers, producers, actors, and so on, with whom I have a casual or social acquaintance. What is the proper procedure for introducing such business colleagues to family members? Do I present my parents and siblings, boyfriends, friends, and others to my associates, or vice versa? It's not that my family hangs out on the set with me, but an encounter in a restaurant creates a predicament.

GENTLE READER:

In social life, unlike the movies, age gets you higher billing, especially where ladies are concerned, and intimacy, lower. Thus your relatives are introduced to your colleagues, except that gentlemen are introduced to ladies of their own or previous generations. In other words, you introduce the producer to your mother ("Mother, this is Cecil B. DeMille") but your father and teenage sister to him ("Mr. DeMille, may I present my sister, Natasha, and my father?").

Multiple Introductions

DEAR MISS MANNERS:

This is not a hypothetical situation: The hostess invited twelve people to a social evening in her home. Six of them, all of whom were well known to one another, were assembled in the living room. The remaining six guests all arrived at the same time. None of them had met the guests who were already present. How should the introductions have been handled?

GENTLE READER:

A group introduction is performed by reciting names in the order in which people are standing. A hostess who gets stage fright and finds her memory blank does not admit this, but gives a little laugh at the hopelessness of it all and asks the guests to recite their own names, looking around pleasantly and saying, "I'll let you introduce yourselves." Said charmingly, this suggests that she is forgoing a privilege in order to allow them the pleasure. Miss Manners knows perfectly well that it is impossible to learn names from mass introductions, but the formality will have been performed, and, all being equally in the dark, the guests may then split into smaller groups and tell one another, "I'm sorry, but I didn't catch your name. I'm——."

Self-Introductions

DEAR MISS MANNERS:

Why, oh why, do some people guard their identities like a state secret? I don't find it extremely easy to be the first to speak at a function at which many people don't know one another. However, I will approach a stranger, smile, and introduce myself. If appropriate, I'll add, "I am Mr. Drake's daughter-in-law"—or whatever fits the occasion. More often than not, the person smiles back and says, "Hello." End of conversation. Obvious rudeness is not the problem; I feel that ignorance is. I know this is not going to replace global warfare in importance, but it is a pet peeve that drives me wild.

GENTLE READER:

It is annoying; Miss Manners wants to be sure to catch this before it leads to global warfare. Your manners in introducing yourself are excellent, and you deserve a better response. The follow-up question you need to pry the information out is, "I don't believe I know your name?" The interrogative voice pattern is essential. If anyone replies, "No, I don't suppose you do," Miss Manners gives you leave to walk away and look for a better subject.

Introductions to Scoundrels

DEAR MISS MANNERS:

With my parents, I attended a large cocktail party, which was also attended by Reginald, the son of a friend of my mother's. Reginald and I graduated from the same university but had never met, so I introduced myself to him. We conversed for a few minutes; then Reginald abruptly turned to someone else and began a conversation from which I was excluded. Luckily, a charming older gentleman promptly engaged me in conversation, or I would have felt adrift.

Later, some ladies at a luncheon gleefully informed my mother that Reginald's mother reported that Reginald had thought it quite brazen of me to introduce myself to him and that he finds it quite a bother to be chased relentlessly by desperate young female professional-school graduates! Mother repeated Reginald's comments to me and added that she would have warned me not to introduce myself to Reginald, but that since I am such a headstrong young lady, I probably would not have heeded her. Miss Manners, I respectfully request your opinion. Is it improper for a young woman to introduce herself to a man? What should Mother have said to the ladies who reported Reginald's remarks? What, if anything, should Mother say to Reginald's mother the next time his name arises? Should Mother have spared my feelings and kept Reginald's remarks to herself?

GENTLE READER:

Although Miss Manners could discharge her duty merely by informing you that you have committed no rudeness and therefore have nothing further to do, she finds herself unwilling to spare the rude Reginald. This person has slandered you by interpreting an act of commonplace sociability as sexual aggression, and Miss Manners does not want to let him get away with it.

May we enlist your mother's help? She was right to tell you of the danger to your reputation, and indeed should have warned you beforehand. Surely she is willing to assist now. She should begin by telling Reginald's mother that she (your mother) is afraid that she committed a terrible *faux pas*. Having forgotten that Reginald has his own—shall we say, unusual—social ideas, she encouraged you to do the polite thing, and introduce yourself. Of course, it was a disaster—we all know that Reginald is so, ahem, sensitive—and now she wishes to convey her apologies to Reginald for having unwittingly distressed him instead of warning her daughter of his weakness. A version of this story may also be told to the other interested parties, your mother still all aflutter over having stirred up poor Reginald's strangeness.

You have nothing to do but to retain an air of bemused sympathy about Reginald's peculiarity. By the way, this is nothing more than the truth. A well brought up young lady would indeed be expected by her mother to be friendly at parties, and a young man who interprets such conventional politeness as lust for himself is decidedly peculiar.

Unwanted Introductions

DEAR MISS MANNERS:

As a houseguest of old friends of my parents, whom I don't know well but who have been very kind to me, I was introduced to a party guest who looked vaguely familiar. It was not until my hostess said the name that I recognized the individual as someone released on bail while making an appeal in a case that has received considerable publicity. I did not take his hand or say anything. I nodded slightly and quickly asked my hostess to introduce me to someone across the room. I do not approve of this individual, who has been convicted, and did not want to have any acquaintance with him, however slight. At the same time, I did not state my objections to my hostess for fear of seeming to criticize her. Was I correct in my behavior, or is there a better way of avoiding unwanted introductions?

GENTLE READER:

You were impeccable. Had the person not been proven guilty, Miss Manners would have had to give you a boring lecture on assuming innocence until. Had the meeting occurred in public, she would have allowed you the privilege of refusing the acquaintance more markedly by ignoring the person completely. Under the circumstances, however, you did a masterful job of satisfying your feelings while sparing those of your hostess, and Miss Manners congratulates you.

❧ CONVENTIONAL PHRASES

The Meaningless Exchange

Anyone can have a meaningful exchange. Tiresome people do it all the time, long past their and everybody else's bedtime. A meaningful exchange generally consists of one person's reciting all of his or her grievances against life from the time of birth on, for the benefit of someone who waits for a pause, quickly interjects, "Something like that happened to me, too," and starts his own recital. Or it can be one person's listing what he or she doesn't like about the other, who, under the pretext of listening because he is eager to receive constructive criticism, prepares a retaliatory list.

Meaningless exchanges, which are actually more comforting, are constantly being challenged. These are the little pleasant phrases one uses to greet or take leave of people, to signify a desire to converse, or simply to be agreeable. People keep analyzing these statements for meaning. They defy those who use them to justify themselves and thus discourage the distribution of innocent courtesies.

Miss Manners is becoming concerned. Any day now, people will begin complaining that "please" is subservient and that one should simply demand what one wants without it. Look at the reaction to that modern sign-off, "Have a nice day." Innocuous though this statement may be, there are those who hate it. Examining it for meaning, they demand to know why they should have to have a nice day, how dare anyone presume to tell them what kind of a day to have, and so on. With amazing penetration, they then declare that the remark is insincere. The person who says it doesn't really care about their day at all. Not deep down.

Is that so? Oh, my.

Is there really so much deeply felt good will being spread throughout this society that we have to rid ourselves of superficial amiability? Miss Manners is not prepared to argue in favor of "Have a nice day." She is perfectly satisfied with "Goodbye," which contains a similar kindly wish to speed one on one's way. She is just bored to tears by the literary and psychological analysis of simple conventions. Conventions work only when people understand their function and repeat the conventional response. All this overinterpreting has confused people, who then have to search their emotions for reactions.

A Gentle Reader inquires whether the salutation "My dear Helen" is more formal than "Dear Helen." "I feel it is somehow condescending or reprimanding," she says, "but maybe the writer doesn't mean it so."

"My dear" is traditionally more formal than "Dear" in America, for those few of us who remember it, and less formal in England, so you have to check your friend's age and nationality to be sure of why she used it. Nowhere is it intended as an insult. There is no conventional salutation intended to condescend or reprimand. People who wish to do that have to improvise ("Dear So-Called Executive," "Dear Spoil-Sport") and thus put themselves outside the bounds of etiquette.

"How are you?" is strictly a ritualistic utterance, intended to demonstrate polite benevolence. Unless exclaimed by a concerned friend rushing into one's sickroom, it is not an inquiry designed to determine whether the subject is healthy or happy. Therefore, it does not require more of an answer than the equally conventional "Fine, thank you, how are you?" "How do you do?" is an even simpler version, to which the reply is "How do you do?" It is the verbal equivalent of a handshake.

"Has the proper response to 'Thank you' changed from 'You're welcome' to 'Thank *you*'," another Gentle Reader inquires. No, people who overinterpret the simple and conventional "Thank you" are then overcome with embarrassment at receiving what they believe is boundless gratitude. "Thank *you*" is properly used as a response when someone thanks you when you should have thanked him, as in "Thank you for accepting a ride with me." "Oh, no, not at all, thank *you* for inviting me."

"Have a nice day" being a new entry, we need to establish a conventional answer for it. An English reader inquiring about American ways said that he found "Thank you" inadequate and "Why, thank you, I hope that you have an extremely pleasant day also" fulsome. Miss Manners hereby declares that the conventional answer should be "Thank you; you, too," sometimes shortened to a smile and "You, too." The Gentle Reader goes on to ask what the reply is to "You hurry back, you hear?" when said in a way which really means: "I hope never to see hide or hair of you again." Why, it's "Sure will," said in the same tone.

And thank you.

"May I Help You?"

DEAR MISS MANNERS:

Can you think of any phrase other than "May I help you?" to be used by persons who wait on the public? I don't mind being asked "May I help you?" if I step right up to a counter. However, if I'm fifth in line, say, and I am asked this when I finally reach the head of the line, my temptation to come up with a nasty retort is strong. I do so want to say "Oh, I thought this was a line for the restroom" or "No, thank you, I just enjoy standing in line." In other words, the query "May I help you?" is redundant. I am in line to be helped—right?

GENTLE READER:

Miss Manners can think of many phrases which would pass your test of meaning exactly what they say:

"Look, lady, we're closing in fifteen minutes, and I'm not about to get involved in your transaction."

"Can't you see we're having a good conversation behind the counter here and don't want you intruding with your stupid demands?"

"Why don't you just stand there and cool your heels while I fiddle with the stuff on my desk and hope that the phone rings before I have to talk to you?"

"I get paid by the hour, not on commission, so if you can't find what you want, don't come crying to me." And so on. "May I help you?" sounds pretty good to Miss Manners, and she will thank you for not discouraging people from using it by responding to their polite formula with your own rude originality.

"There You Go!"

DEAR MISS MANNERS:

Is there a proper reply to the increasingly used parting words of grocery clerks, etc., who are otherwise pleasant, well-meaning, and, I'm sure, well-mannered: the dreadful "There you go!" called "TYG." I am very distressed at this late development of the English language. How does one cope with it? How does one explain it to one's nephew from Norway? How does one effectively combat this outgrowth of store conversation? Has one, really, obediently to "go," as suggested by said clerk?

GENTLE READER:

Unfortunately, there is no conventional phrase to convey the idea of "There; I hope that takes care of your request satisfactorily."

"There you go" is an attempt to fill that blank. You can probably head it off by saying "Thank you," or you can make that your response.

Fighting Words

Swords and pistols being illegal now for settling differences of opinion or avenging insults, sharp words are generally the weapon of choice. Rude people use blunted ones. The few vulgarities with which the angry attack one another are so commonplace now as to be ineffective. Meanwhile, the language of strict formality is so rarely used as to be more compelling than ever.

The truth is that rude language is anything but direct. Obscenity, by using the language of what we shall euphemistically call romance, expresses the exact opposite of what is meant. Here, then, for those who have forgotten, are basic phrases that polite people use to insult one another:

"I beg your pardon."   This is the best all-purpose warning that the other person has transgressed. Different degrees of anger can be expressed by it. "I beg your pardon?" asked with raised eyebrows means "You'd better explain that you did not mean what you actually said." A loud "I beg your pardon!" means "Retreat this instant!"

"Pardon me."   Said as "Pardon me?" this means "You had better not suggest that I have stepped out of line," whereas "Pardon me!" means "You have just insulted me." (It should be noted that "pardon" is only used challengingly these days. The expression of true regret is "Excuse me" or "I'm sorry.")

"I believe you are gravely mistaken."   If the word "mistaken" is emphasized, this means "You don't know what you're talking about." With additional emphasis on "gravely," it means "You're lying."

"Perhaps you are unaware of the fact that . . ."   This raises the challenge. It means, "You're lying because you're trying to conceal a fraud."

"Perhaps I did not make myself clear."   Now we are really getting rough. This is positively the last warning to retreat before war is declared. By restating your position after this remark, you convey the meaning "If you challenge me on this again now, we will fight it out."

"How dare you?"   This is it, the declaration of war. It means "I will not give up until you surrender by apologizing or otherwise undoing whatever it is you did." Even then, politeness must be maintained. When an opponent finally declares

himself defeated by saying that his transgression "was not what I intended," the victor is obliged to confine himself to the polite expression of triumph: "Of course not; it was only a very unfortunate mistake." He may then add, but only in a gracious tone, "I'm sure it will never happen again." That means, "Watch yourself, because you may be sure that I'll be watching you."

"Did You Mind?"

DEAR MISS MANNERS:

Close friends commonly ask, "You didn't mind when I . . . did you?" If we are alone, I can honestly answer the question. The problem arises when I am asked this in a group, and did mind, and yet do not feel comfortable telling everyone that I did. For example, someone might ask me in a group meeting if I minded her making some important decision while I was on vacation and not waiting until I returned to the office. I might prefer to discuss the issue quietly and not make it a topic for office gossip. I usually either say nothing or lie and say that I didn't mind. Of course, it is clearly not sensible for good friends to bring up personal questions in front of others, but what does one do when it happens?

GENTLE READER:

The correct reply is "Let's talk about it later." Miss Manners is aware that this signifies to everyone present that you did in fact mind, and what is more, you mind its being brought up in public, but it is nevertheless the correct, polite alternative to a false "No, no, not at all."

The Magic Words

Where has the magic gone? No, Miss Manners is not complaining of a faded love affair. She is bemoaning the disappearing of magic in what the Etiquette Trade used to refer to, rather coyly, as the Magic Words.

One Magic Word was what you had to say before your mother would acknowledge any connection between her having sent the aroma of cookies into the air and any interest that this act may have aroused in you. Another was the phrase you had first to think of (generally to the accompaniment of great mental struggles, clearly visible in the strenuous play of young facial muscles) and then actually to utter clearly before she would let go of the cookie she was apparently offering you—but on which she was nevertheless retaining an iron grasp. These words were not "Gimme" (an expression that had no official existence at the time) or "I want——" nor even "Can I have——?"

Another magic phrase would occasionally elicit permission to leave the dinner table—temporarily, if one were under stress, or unconditionally, if the food service, but not the adult conversation, had concluded. This statement was neither "I don't want any more" nor "My favorite program is on now."

There were Magic Words for avoiding the consequences of unintentional infractions, such as stepping on another person's foot (where no previous animosity existed) or causing minor breakage (under reasonably no-fault circumstances). These were not "Well, why didn't you look where you were going?" or "I couldn't help it."

The Magic Words were "please," " thank you," " excuse me," and "I'm sorry." Ever since the nonsensical ideas began to get about that everything in this world should have a reasonable meaning, and that it is desirable to live life efficiently, people have lost faith in the Magic Words. It is true that they do not add to the clarity of a demand. They do not express any original thoughts. In fact, they often actually misrepresent the true feelings of the person who utters them because he is not really sorry for what he did, desirous of being excused, grateful for what is given, or feeling suppliant, rather than just plain greedy, when he wishes something.

The expression that springs to Miss Manners' mind, in answer to such a charge, is unfortunately far from magical, perhaps even inelegant. It is "So what?"

"Excuse Me"

DEAR MISS MANNERS:

I have been trained since childhood to utter a small "Excuse me" should I ever inadvertently burp in the presence of others. I was also trained never to burp in public. Both trainings made deep impressions on me with the following result: I never have the occasion to say "Excuse me" in public, but do in the privacy of my own home. My husband first chuckled at my "excuse mes" but has recently become annoyed. He claims that any such bodily function is only natural and needn't be apologized for. He has also been known to rail against my automatic response, calling me a victim of brainwashing, and also making me feel as if I were holding on to a nonsensical custom from the past.

GENTLE READER:

Which is it, "only natural" or optional? It seems to Miss Manners that you have a problem here, even aside from that of being married to a man of such charged emotions (or limited opportunities for excitement) that he can get first a laugh and then a grievance merely out of hearing you say "Excuse me."

Your husband's argument, as Miss Manners understands it, is that something that cannot be helped need not be excused. Etiquette does not admit such reasoning. You may not be able to help being sick on someone's rug, but you had better apologize for it.

According to your claim, burping can be helped. You say that burping in public has been perfectly trained out of you (a feat which commands Miss Manners' respect—which, by the way, the similar feat of simulated burping, especially by children, does not), so you must be choosing to do it at home. It's too late to try to slip in that little "inadvertently."

You are therefore really arguing that you may practice at home what you consider to be bad manners. Never mind that others who cannot control their burps may be excused; you can, so you are doing it voluntarily. By trying to get you to drop the "excuse me," your husband is abetting you in your own idea that you need not be polite at home. Miss Manners promises him that he will come to rue this.

"What's New?"

DEAR MISS MANNERS:
What am I expected to say when someone asks me, "What's new?" I realize that this is, for the most part, a greeting, but it also puts the person who is asked in the position of having to come up with a light response. I doubt that the asker expects me to start rattling off a list of everything that has gone on in my life since the last time we saw each other. On the other hand, I don't want to say only "Not much," which I have said for lack of anything better, because it sounds as if I haven't been up to anything at all. What is an appropriate response to this aggravating greeting? What do people expect to hear?

GENTLE READER:
Not much.

"I'm Fine"

DEAR MISS MANNERS:
When my son's college friends visit our home, their answer to "Would you like a Coke or something to eat or drink?" is "I'm fine." This is so strange to me. I was taught to say "No, thank you." I am not asking how they are. I'm asking if they would like something to drink, etc. If they would first say "No, thank you," and then "I'm fine," I would understand.
Is this a new form of etiquette? Is it just another shortcut to avoid wasting words? I will still insist that my son reply "No, thank you" unless I hear that it is correct to say "I'm fine" — but I don't believe I will.

GENTLE READER:
No, you won't, but Miss Manners would settle for this new cliché if she could just get a "thank you" into it. "I'm fine" is presumably a way of heading off a series of offers ("Would you like a lemonade?" "No, thank you"; "Would you like some coffee?" "No, thank you"; "Well, then, would you like some tea?" and so on). "No, thank you, I don't care for anything," would be just as preemptive without annoying you (and rankling Miss Manners just a little).

"I Don't Care"

DEAR MISS MANNERS:

I'm exposed to young children, including my own, whose irritating answer when they're asked if they want anything is often "I don't care." My response is always "I didn't ask if you cared. I asked if you would like something." Am I out of line in bringing this to their attention? My reasoning is that I would want my own children gently reminded to use good communication skills and the nicest manners while visiting others' homes.

GENTLE READER:

You don't expect Miss Manners to quarrel with your sentiments. However, she would like gently to point out that you should be especially sure that you do not embarrass a visiting child by making it clear that his manners are poor.

This would be poor manners. Fortunately, you can still make your point. The shade of difference is that you should seem to be puzzled by his remark, rather than disapproving. "Don't care about what, dear? I'm offering you some juice. Would you like some, or not?"

"You Shouldn't Have"

DEAR MISS MANNERS:

How am I to respond to the person who says, "You shouldn't have done it"? People who sit down to dinner at my table and see lighted candles or shrimp cocktail or whatever upon the table are apt to say, "You shouldn't have done it." People who upon the rather ordinary occasion of their marriage receive a rather ordinary wedding present from me are apt to say, "You shouldn't have done it." My impulse on these occasions is to say, "Ah, perhaps you are correct," and thereupon call off the dinner or ask for the return of the wedding present. No, no, that really won't do. These are basically good people who say this terrible thing. Somehow they have been deluded into thinking that they are saying something polite, when actually they are saying something insulting.

GENTLE READER:

Miss Manners agrees that "You shouldn't have done it" is a particularly silly remark. She understands that rather than pleasing the person to whom it is addressed, it has the effect of making him or her think that the kind effort was inappropriate. Nevertheless, we have to concede that it is meant well. What it awkwardly expresses is "I didn't deserve to have you go to that much trouble," rather than ingratitude. So Miss Manners asks your indulgence to take it as such and to reply, "Oh, but I enjoyed doing it."

"May I Use the Bathroom?"

DEAR MISS MANNERS:

When visiting friends or relatives, on not merely a drop-in-and-say-hello occasion, is it necessary, advisable, and proper to ask permission of the hostess to use the bathroom, especially when you know where it is located? When it cannot be done discreetly, asking permission seems like announcing to all present that you have to go. But I have seen an almost offended look on the face of a hostess when I returned from an "unauthorized" visit.

GENTLE READER:

"May I use the bathroom?" is an idiomatic expression, not to be taken literally. Miss Manners has never heard of a hostess' refusing permission. Surely you must be mistaken in assuming that yours wished to be consulted as to whether you could use her bathroom. Considering the consequences, this would be not only mean but foolish. The true meaning of the question is "Would you be so kind as to show me where the bathroom is?" Visitors who know where it is need only say, "Excuse me."

"Sex" and "Gender"

DEAR MISS MANNERS:

Is the use of incorrect grammar a breach of good manners? For example, I often hear people improperly use the word "gender" when they actually mean "sex." Ever since I first studied a foreign language, I have been aware of the difference between these two words, "gender" being a grammatical term and "sex" being a biological term pertaining to the distinction made between male and female. Would it be considered bad manners for me to explain the meaning of these two words to the perpetrator of this grammatical *faux pas?* I could, for instance, point out that words have gender and people have sex.

GENTLE READER:

Indeed, you could, and what a giggle you would get. However, you would also get some cold stares, the most freezing of them from Miss Manners. As devoted as she is to correctness in both manners and language, Miss Manners recognizes that using the word "sex" in discussions of discrimination and rights reinforces the idea that foremost and always, the female represents a romantic possibility. A lady of Miss Manners' acquaintance was not thrilled when, on promotion to a previously all-male professional group, she was congratulated by a well-meaning blunderer who said, "We're so happy finally to have sex in the office."

That argument aside, the answer to your question is: Yes, it is rude to correct other people's speech. You are supposed to be too interested in the content to notice the form.

"Okay!"

DEAR MISS MANNERS:

My name is Bill—okay? I am thirty-five years old—okay? My biggest gripe—okay?—is people who can't talk without saying "Okay?" I get the feeling that every time they say "Okay?" they are really saying, "Have you got sense enough to know what I am saying?" Please tell your readers that it is okay not to say "Okay?"

GENTLE READER:

Okay.

Conversation

❧ ESTABLISHING IDENTITY

"I don't feel that my job is really who I am."

"Why should I be defined by somebody I happen to be married to?"

"I don't take my identity from my children."

Miss Manners would not quarrel with any of these statements (indeed, she tries to avoid talking at all to people who take that belligerent tone), if not for some peculiar circumstances.

1. These declarations were not made in reply to demands about how the speakers wished to be known to society at large or remembered to posterity, but in reply to such casual social overtures as "What do you do?," "Congratulations on your wife's promotion," and "What are your children doing these days?"

2. They were made by people whose subsequent conversation revealed that they believe the choice of particular material objects—clothing, automobiles, beverages—represents calculated "statements" that serve as accurate clues to personality. Wonderful. We have now reached the point where personal and professional connections are considered irrelevant to one's identity, the real key to the soul being written on one's sneakers or consumed as a soft drink.

The very idea that anything at all can be read so as to sum up an entire person instantly offends Miss Manners. Never mind whether it is business or domestic af-filiations, or possessions. She even objects to voluntary statements of one's phi-losophy being used that way. If your deepest beliefs can be put into three words, so that they fit your bumper sticker, or your attitude toward life in one short word on your license plate, Miss Manners congratulates you and promises that she will not try to probe them further.

Yet the notion that one can get an immediate understanding of a new acquaint-ance is almost as widespread as the opposite suspicion that one is always in dan-ger of being unjustly pegged by others. The only issue under dispute seems to be which clues are truly revealing and which are not. This is where people who call themselves realistic argue that dress and other spending habits define one for oth-ers, so that a clever person should manipulate them to "say" what he or she means to say. Meanwhile, those who consider themselves sensitive are rebelling against offhand social inquiries as if they were invasions of privacy from hostile courts of inquiry.

We shall have to have a new consensus on what is nosy and what is not. There are indeed societies in which the facts of a person's life, such as age and income, are polite subjects for inquiry but asking for opinions on the news topics of the day is rude; and others in which any personal conversation at all is unacceptable until friendships are established. American manners traditionally have allowed super-ficial questions about jobs, family, and opinions on politics or the weather, but not specific personal statistics, especially in connection with money. Those guidelines still seem to Miss Manners to be a reasonable compromise between offensive nosi-ness and the American enjoyment of casual conversation.

Let us rid ourselves of the idea—and the resulting hurt feelings—that the pur-pose of asking opening questions is to define an individual. The fact is that it is im-possible to find out about a person all at once. One has to put some work into it. Placing the person in the general scheme of things is only a taking-off point to finding out about that person's attitudes, interests, nature, and disposition. Odd-ly enough, there is a way to impress people immediately. And that is by demon-strating that one considers them worth the investment of time and attention it takes to find out what they are all about.

Women's Work

DEAR MISS MANNERS:
Last night, a friend implied that I am insensitive, ignorant, and snobbish. My offense? I used the word "career" to refer to the pursuit of an occupation outside the home or for the benefit of others besides one's own family. My friend, a full-time mother, felt I thereby denigrated her status and responded with an indignant statement about motherhood's being a worthy career, too. I did not intend to im-ply that motherhood is less important or prestigious than other occupations, nor do I believe this. Indeed, I am delighted to have been the beneficiary of my own

mother's choice to assume this role. My usage of "career," however, is generally familiar, and I adopt it out of habit, not malice.

I am growing weary of being accused of making insults when none are intended and of receiving hostile responses to such questions as "What sort of work do you do?" I have now reached the point of being afraid to ask women I meet socially how they spend their days, which I suppose makes me vulnerable to accusations of self-absorption and a lack of interest in others' lives. This especially disturbs me because I would actually rather hear a nondefensive person discuss a child's development and activities than hear many people discuss such aspects of their jobs as sales reports or computer programs.

If I am wrong, I would appreciate some advice about language that would not be improper for meeting people and discussing their occupations.

GENTLE READER:

If we were to do battle over such terms, Miss Manners would question your usage of "full-time mother" as applying exclusively to mothers who do not have paying jobs. Surely all mothers are mothers all the time, even when they spend some of that time in offices or factories. But warfare over such terms is exactly what Miss Manners would like to see cease.

The emotional land mine you accidentally stepped on is set off by the insane idea that there is one correct pattern of life for all ladies and that anyone who doesn't follow the currently fashionable one must be held in disregard. Some years ago, there was a nasty edge to the term "career girl," which was used to describe a lady who had a paying job and therefore, it was implied, an unsatisfactory domestic setup. Now such a once revered term as "housewife" is perceived as an insult because a money-crazy society sees worth only in paid work. A general acknowledgment that the decision of each individual lady as to what she considers the best use of her time is equally worthy of respect would defuse this situation. You seem to understand that, but the ladies you meet are smarting from previous wounds, so you would do well to be careful.

At any rate, polite society never condoned the use of one's business identity socially. Miss Manners may well be the only person who remembers this, but asking people you meet socially what their jobs are used to be in questionable taste. You are far safer with some version of "What are your interests?" than any of the questions likely to be taken as inquiries into professional status.

The Noncommuting Worker

DEAR MISS MANNERS:

With disturbing frequency, I am asked by another woman, on a social occasion, "What do you do?" I reply that I work at home, taking care of my family and the clerical work and bookkeeping for my husband's business. Nine times out of ten, the woman will say something like, "Really? How interesting. I would love to be able to stay home" or "That must be nice. My job as a computer programmer (electronics engineer, stockbroker, department store manager, etc.) is so demanding that I rarely have time to relax."

The assumption, by members of my own sex especially, that I am a member of the soap opera and bonbon set because I do not commute to work simply renders me speechless while I do a slow burn. Some of these women do not bother me; they clearly do not mean to offend. The majority, however, whether they realize it or not, are snide and insulting.

The complete answer to their question would be that I rise at 5:45 A.M. to take care of my husband, three teenagers, three dogs, three cats, a 2,800-square-foot home (including all repairs and pool and yard maintenance), 1,800 pounds of laundry a month, at least 25 hours per week of desk and computer work for the business, and as much child transporting as can be managed, including children whose mothers are "at work." This reply is boring and argumentative, and would definitely not help the situation.

Could you recommend a few words that, while helping to salvage my pride, would be polite and intelligent? For those who are deliberately insulting, a vague reference to their ignorance and rudeness would be appreciated. As you can tell, I have completely lost my patience and perspective.

GENTLE READER:

Well, yes, you have gotten the thing somewhat out of perspective. The fantasy of what a holiday life outside of an office must be is a silly one, but then so is the fantasy, for those who are at home, that it must be all glamor and excitement at the office. Suppose you reply: "Why, that's just my problem. I rarely have time to relax, either. But I'm surprised you don't. I always thought how relaxing it must be to work in an office—all those coffee breaks and business lunches! When you work for yourself, your boss is always with you, so you never get to slack off."

What Follows "What Do You Do?"?

Miss Manners will admit that some of the deadliest conversations she knows follow the question "What do you do?" The evidence is piling up that all remarks following an honest answer to this question fall into one of four categories, each worse than the one before it.

There is the request for free labor, either advice or services. Everyone knows this is gauche, and yet people continue to make such demands. Miss Manners has heard a number of strategies from recipients to discourage this, beginning with her Great Uncle Simon's reply, when he was asked at parties for his medical opinion: "Certainly. Please take off your clothes."

Then there are the complaints. Miss Manners once saw the president of an international chain of household equipment stores furiously attacked at a black-tie party by a horde of well-dressed people whose vacuum cleaners didn't work. She would have been shocked if she had not been so anxious to explain that the tassels for her Austrian window shades had never arrived.

Artists of various kinds are among those plagued with the next sort of conversation, the one designed to find out how well one is actually doing in one's chosen profession. "Haven't you finished that book yet?" is apparently considered charming conversation to make to an author and "How many paintings did you sell?" to an artist.

Worst of all is the smart remark, based on a primitive understanding of what people in a particular field actually do and designed to twit them about it. A variation assumes that the other person goes about flaunting his expertise at the expense of everyone he meets. Thus a military person is asked whether he is yearning for war in order to destroy people; a teacher is told, "I suppose you're going to notice if I make any grammatical mistakes"; a psychiatrist is invited to guess who is normal and what they are thinking.

Miss Manners can only advise the targets to be tolerant and patient, knowing that the will to do so wears thin along about the 128th time a remark is repeated. If she cannot put a ban on clever comebacks, she makes a plea that they be reasonably good-natured. One of her favorites was developed by a geneticist who is often asked, as many scientists are, whether he is going to start making people.

"Oh, I already have," he replies. "A boy and a girl."

Etiquette advisers are not immune, and Miss Manners admits that her smile has grown very weak indeed when people say, "Oh, I guess I'd better watch myself or you'll catch me doing something wrong," as if she were in the habit of giving out traffic tickets for lunch-table violations.

The Overly Enthusiastic Response

DEAR MISS MANNERS:

I am a television reporter who daily goes out into the community, invading people's privacy, as any reporter does. But guilt is not my problem. Rather, from one to ten times on any given day, the following is shouted at me and the photographer I'm with: "Hey! Put me on TV!" or "C'mon, take my picture!" I have neither the time nor the patience to explain to all those would-be hams that there is no reason to put them on TV. Yet they are our viewing public, and I must be polite, though I am annoyed at the frequency with which the suggestion is made. Can you suggest a short but polite way to tell these people that they are being childish and annoying without offending them?

GENTLE READER:

There is no polite way to tell people that they are childish and annoying. If there were, it would come out sounding as if they were cute, and then they would really expect to be televised. One does not insult people for so thoughtless a practice, but one does not attempt to instruct them out of it, either. A weak smile will suffice. As a television reporter, you are doubtless familiar with such an expression.

The Opening Gambit

You are temporarily stranded at a large party and note with some satisfaction that a stranger is bearing down on you with a social gleam in his eye. You produce a modest smile, pleasant enough to be interpreted as a welcome but vacant enough—in case you mistook the stranger's goal—to be taken for a general air of imbecility.

"If you were to be hanged at noon tomorrow," says this candidate for friendship, "what three things would you try to do tonight?" A true opening gambit, requiring a thoughtful reply. Miss Manners' reply would undoubtedly be, "I'm so sorry, I was just on my way to find some sherry; please excuse me." Miss Manners detests opening gambits.

The problem remains of how to discover a topic of interest to a stranger on which real conversation may be based. It can be done, but it requires patience and cooperation. If you are not willing to make such investments, you will be forever at the mercy of the sort of hosts who push you toward a strange body and declare, "You'll love Samantha. She was just divorced, too!" Cooperation is necessary because there are two parts to be played; and patience is necessary, because it takes a few minutes, most of which are more utilitarian than interesting. Of course, you want to know whether the new person is married or has children, what he or she does by profession and for recreation, and generally how he or she prefers to live. Snobbery exists only when people decide beforehand what they find acceptable and avoid those who don't fit.

Direct questioning is awkward only because it restricts the probing to the subdivision selected by the questioner. Some people don't like to talk about their jobs because they think them not important enough, while others, satisfied with their success, feel exploited if asked to display their skills when out socially. The person who opens should therefore try a neutral question that can be answered in many ways. The opener must have the patience to withhold his own brilliance until the other person has had a chance to speak. Dare to be dull!

Unfortunately, people seem to be having the same trouble opening conversations these days as Miss Manners has opening anchovy cans. That is, they are afraid that even if they go about it in the prescribed way, they will not only hurt themselves but also make a mess. The traditional way of opening a conversation with a stranger is to utter a neutral comment or question that gives the person addressed the opportunity to choose a topic. If that topic does not suit, the first person tries another, and so on until they either find something to talk about or give up and go home.

What has ruined this perfectly workable routine? One thing is a new reluctance to engage in banal preliminaries for fear of losing a stranger's attention before real conversation can begin. The idea seems to be that one is allowed only a few seconds for an audition, and that if an opening line is dull or offensive, one will be dismissed.

The search is therefore on for that brilliant, all-purpose opening guaranteed to rivet anyone on the spot. Now and then, people apply to Miss Manners for such a line, imagining that there is one in the social lexicon, along with such successful gems as "My, don't you look lovely" and "Oh, I'm so sorry." If there were, it wouldn't be unused; don't look for originality in conventionality. Remarks about politics or segments of the society always turn out to be addressed to the people being criticized or their relatives. Jokes about other people's names are also strictly banned, even if they are funny.

The less snappy opening topics Miss Manners recommends include new books, plays, films, or other cultural activities, nonpolitical comments on the news, and complimentary remarks about the hosts. She assures you that any alert person will quickly be able to develop this into something more interesting. Personally, her idea of a truly welcome cocktail party line is, "May I freshen your drink?" What does the gambit player find out about Miss Manners? Only that she likes sherry. No—only that she prefers sherry to gambits.

What They Don't Teach at Harvard

DEAR MISS MANNERS:

I am afflicted with a peculiar social stigma due to attending a well-respected university. I may as well confess that the university is Harvard (if you will not hold it against me). The problem arises when I am outside Massachusetts and am introduced to someone at a social gathering, where the usual amenities include discussing one's occupation or school. I am truthful in answering the question "Where do you go to school?" only after at least one evasive reply (for example, "Back East"). When my Harvard affiliation has been revealed, however, I have several times received one of three reactions:

"You must be rich!"

"You must be a brain!"

"Wow, should I get on my knees and worship you?"

I have typically responded to the first two comments by protesting, truthfully, that I am neither rich nor especially brainy, but why should I have to rate my own wealth or intelligence? Silence would be worse, since it would look as if I were agreeing. Twice, I have tried a lighthearted response, such as "My (financial aid officer/professors) would disagree with you!" My only reaction to the last of the three responses has been "No, please, really."

In desperation, I have considered rude responses, such as, respectively, "Yes, I own your Senator" and "No, they won't let me rule the world until after I've graduated." For the next half-hour I bend over backward to prove I'm a "regular" guy: I use only monosyllabic words, never quote historical figures, avoid drinking wine, and so on—anything to avoid the stereotype of a Harvard man as a suave, rich, "ultraliterate" elitist. This problem has never been mentioned in any of Harvard's brochures or catalogs. What is the proper way to respond?

GENTLE READER:

You may be interested to know that your problem is about 350 years old. Miss Manners' colleague Cotton Mather told her that the response to members of the first few classes, when they admitted attending Harvard, was, "What's that?" From then on, however, it has been as you have described. Why, Miss Manners cannot say. With one exception, students at other colleges are asked "How do you like it?" or "What's your major?"

The reason help is not supplied by the administration is that Harvard students know instinctively how to respond, as you have demonstrated. One answers the first question geographically ("Back East," as you said, or "in Boston"; "in Cambridge" is too provocative) and mentions Harvard only when specifically asked for the name. There is no need to pretend to be less "ultraliterate" than you are. Harvard requires its students to take remedial writing for a reason.

You asked Miss Manners for other ways of handling this situation. One is to reply that you attend "Harvard-Radcliffe." For some reason, this throws people, to the extent that they forget to make the remarks that annoy you. It also happens to be the name of your school. The second method is to ignore the follow-up questions and merely repeat to your interlocutor his own questions and remarks: "Where do you go? Oh, you must be rich," and so on. This tactic is, at first, taken as an insult. Having assumed that you think your school to be the best—as, indeed, all loyal students think their own colleges are—he will then assume that you are making fun of his school. But all colleges train people to think. Therefore any educated student will realize, sooner or later, that if you use the same words he does, you cannot be insulting him any more or less than he is insulting you.

Life in Retirement

DEAR MISS MANNERS:

When one retires, it seems that many friends and co-workers have the impression that life suddenly becomes a ball. What do I reply to those polite, well-meaning people who seem to expect to be regaled with all sorts of wonderful tales about what has been happening in my "new life"—that is, without sounding like the most boring dullard around? I have never had more than a modest social life at best, and although I like to have a few interests outside the home, I'm not a person who has to be "going and doing" all the time to be content. Consequently, my life and activities are rather humdrum and not at all interesting to relate.

GENTLE READER:

Miss Manners doubts that these people are expecting to hear that you have taken up the harpsichord or are having an affair with the grocer's boy. Some of them may wish to hear that you are having a pleasant time or to be reassured that one does not atrophy when out of the workaday world. (Miss Manners remembers a more leisurely time when people assumed that that was what happened to the finer sensibilities when one was *in* the workaday world.) Most, she believes, are simply using their questions as a way of opening a conversation.

"I've become an avid gardener" or "I'm finally reading Proust," or "It's divine to sleep late" are perfectly acceptable answers, which enable the questioner to pursue that topic or to counter with another of his own.

Tuning Out

It is only right that you listen attentively to the dinner guests who remain after midnight, the school play, and Miss Manners when she is telling you to stop whatever it is that you like to do. However, the cunning will quickly demand to know how we know you are listening. This is where the art of Tuning Out comes in, so to speak.

We begin with ruthlessly excluding any signs that one has tuned out, all of which are, by nature, rude. (Yes, medical excuses cancel the offense, but only when made known. The person who charmingly says, "You'll have to forgive me; I'm hard of hearing and couldn't quite follow all your lecture," or the one who writes, "I knew that my drowsiness could not have been related to your charming party, and indeed, my doctor has now found the cause" is off free.)

For those who have everything properly functioning except the attention span, the first rule is not to do anything to alert others that you are not listening. Luckily, it is well known that many people concentrate better when they have their eyes closed and that some slumping is permitted when the brain is being taxed. Naturally, what cannot be seen in the dark doesn't count. (Don't abuse that last one; the lights are sometimes turned on suddenly.) Excessive fidgeting or indulgence in other activities is a giveaway. It is all very well to announce that you concentrate better when doing needlework or listening to music, but claiming that you are attentive while doing the tax returns or keeping an eye on the television set is stretching it. It is not wise to ask stupid questions. For a person who has not been listening, just about any question is stupid except "I'm sorry, I didn't quite get your last point."

The second rule is that one must occasionally check in. Mostly this is done by saying "Ummmmm" and "Is that so?" at proper intervals, but of course, that requires a good feel for the proper interval. It is too seldom if your interlocutor accuses you of not listening and too frequent if the accusation is of interrupting. The skilled tuner out will, of course, join any laughter or sympathetic murmurings from other, or rather real, listeners. Tuning *them* out can be disastrous. The facial expression should also follow smiles or looks of concern. The rest position for the face is that benign look into which people compose themselves for concerts.

Without these minimal talents, Tuning Out is not for you. But cheer up. If your face sinks into a stupor when others are talking, there is a whole other illicit social activity available to you. You are an ideal candidate for eavesdropping.

Eavesdropping

No nice person would ever eavesdrop, as Miss Manners trusts all of you know. The ears of a really fastidious person are too delicate even to receive words that were obviously not intended for them. As long as that is thoroughly understood, Miss Manners thought you might like to know how to eavesdrop politely.

Aside from natural curiosity about the ways of the world, the reason well-bred people might find this information interesting is that they may not want to listen to human behavior theory only from such professional observers as your very own Miss Manners but may occasionally care to tune in directly on the human drama in action.

That is voluntary eavesdropping, done for recreation. Ethics require that it be practiced only in plain view, on strangers, in public places. Deliberately listening in on the private conversation of people one knows in places where they think they are safe is called snooping. That is *really* never done by nice people. There is also involuntary eavesdropping, such as when one's desk at work is so close to another desk that one can't help overhearing telephone and other conversations, or when the apartment house walls are not thick enough to stop voices from visiting other apartments. Another instance occurs when an employee is privy to conversation obviously not intended to include him or her. Some service and supervisory jobs require the physical presence of workers among people who are otherwise in a social group and therefore believe themselves, in spite of the obvious evidence to the contrary, to be speaking strictly among friends.

The basic polite posture of the eavesdropper applies in all of these instances: head up, eyes vacant, mouth expressionless. If suddenly noticed, the eavesdropper gives a quick imitation of being in a trance and then says "What?" stupidly, as if just waking up. Staring, laughing, answering questions, or otherwise registering that one has overheard a conversation is rude, not to mention inhibiting to the speakers. Of course, when eavesdropping is involuntary, you may want to inhibit the speakers, especially if they are speaking while you are trying to work or sleep. Under no circumstances does one acknowledge comprehending what has been overheard. "I hope everything is all right. We heard some noises coming from your apartment and didn't know whether you were home" is acceptable; "I'm on your side; your husband is a rat" is not. "This place is an echo chamber. I wish we had some privacy," is all right; "Well, you sure botched that account" is not. Another politeness is to call the attention of someone to one's own presence; a loud cough can be a symptom of good manners rather than ill health.

Even in order to be helpful, one does not admit to acting upon overheard information. The waiter who overhears a complaint that no water was poured assumes a bland expression while pouring the water in order to shame the complainer into believing that he was prematurely angry, rather than satisfying him that his mutterings got results. A service person with a robot-like demeanor thus not only gets double credit for anticipating everyone's wishes, but establishes a cloak of invisibility that enables him to hear a lot of useful things. The point of etiquette is not to force the person overheard to deal with the fact that he has been overheard—at least until the servant's memoirs are published.

Mentioning No Names

DEAR MISS MANNERS:

Recently, my husband and I were dining out to celebrate my recent promotion at the company we both work for. The restaurant we chose is not one that is frequently patronized by our company's employees. (We live in a city of 250,000 people. Our company employs 150, most of whom know one another.) Our dinner conversation centered on work, as it often does. I mentioned the names of two fellow employees, one by first name only. I was holding forth animatedly about the criticisms one had made about the other's report. My husband stopped the conversation with a comment about the inappropriateness of mentioning names in a restaurant.

I was surprised and hurt, and it spoiled the evening for me. I feel that diners in a public restaurant can talk about anything, so long as they do not disturb the other patrons. I also feel that the chance of anyone near us hearing our conversation or knowing the people mentioned was slight. Also, the diners closest to us were a large family group enjoying their own conversation.

Is it bad manners to mention names in a public place? Is it good manners to bluntly interrupt another's conversation if one considers it to be inappropriate? I feel that my husband could have changed the subject in a much gentler way, such as "Let's not talk about work any more. I want to discuss our next vacation."

GENTLE READER:
Statistically, the chances of your being overheard by someone who knew the people you were talking about may have been small. Nevertheless, Miss Manners promises you that it was practically a certainty that such a coincidence would occur. That family group was about to have a sudden pause in its conversation, during which you would have made a remark about its closest friend, which every member of the family would have repeated back within the hour. None of them actually works at your company, but the children's baby-sitter, the mother's uncle, the father's brother-in-law, the cousin's fiancée, and all their neighbors do.

So you see, your husband stopped you just in time. Miss Manners hopes he said what he did kindly. Perhaps he could have been more subtle, but then that might not have worked. Anyway, the rule he invoked is not so much one of etiquette as of survival.

Talk-Show Conversation

It is with ghastly forebodings that Miss Manners will now compare the manners appropriate to participating in a television talk show with those practiced in the drawing room. Her intention is to illustrate to people who know how to make social conversation that it is possible to adapt the technique for being on television, a situation that can happen even to careful people. Suppose her words should be taken as a license for people to behave in houses the way many of them do on the screen? Horrors.

That has already happened, of course, without Miss Manners' assistance. Far too many people already take their manners from television, and just look at the way they behave.

Nevertheless, Miss Manners is going to attempt the comparison between talk shows and party talk in order to save people from assuming even less appropriate patterns for television appearances. Many media civilians who voluntarily go on television (as opposed to people who are assaulted when they are asked how they feel about having a relative murdered) imagine that the opportunity corresponds to:

- A lecture platform, from which they can, without interruption, say everything they have to say about the issue or viewpoint they are there to represent;
- A fantasy birthday party or lifetime achievement celebration, with the usual rules of decorum suspended in favor of oneself's being the center of attention and flatteringly informed praise; or
- A therapy session, where polite consideration is suspended in order to allow one to express oneself and attack others with unvarnished frankness.

What has been overlooked in all of these delusions is that egoism, unrestrained by a sense of what might interest other people and what form it might most pleasantly be presented to them, is not riveting television. Who really wants to watch someone blathering on, unrestrained, to unload, all at once, what even his or her intimates will not sit still for? The manners of conversation among friends do not allow this. Although one assumes that one's friends are interested in one's ideas, adventures, and causes, the polite person is careful to package these so that they do not become tiring.

The good talk-show guest remembers that he or she is expected to take responsibility for a share of the entertainment and not merely sit there, allowing the host to carry the entire burden, by only responding to questions. No well-bred person, however successful and celebrated, would take it for granted that others had made a study of his or her life and achievements; nor would this person condescend, as if these were too difficult for others to understand. The polite way of talking about yourself is to offer enough information to make what you are saying interesting, without either bragging blatantly ("Tell us what you've been doing" is intended as a limited invitation, not the prelude to one's autobiography) or taking offense at the need to supply the information to make one's statements self-contained. Stories about oneself are palatable only when they make a general point.

The person who lectures when out socially is always a bore, no matter how fascinating the topic may be in a classroom or book, when those who listen or read have made the commitment to ingest something long and complicated. A polite person talks in short bursts, allowing others to participate in the conversation. As in social talk, liveliness and interest—and the avoidance of silences—are more important than exhaustive thoroughness and logic. Good conversation does overlap a bit: One doesn't interrupt by taking the floor away, but a burst of enthusiasm, especially if preceded by "That's an interesting point but—" is permissible. Finally, it is well to remember that it is the charming person who is likely to be invited back.

Stuttering

DEAR MISS MANNERS:

What is the best way to converse with a colleague who has a severe stutter? Should one maintain eye contact when the person is having difficulty speaking, or should one discreetly look away?

GENTLE READER:

A stutterer does not require your help. When speaking with one, you behave normally. Normal conversation consists of waiting for a person who is speaking to finish what he or she is saying. You do not assist the speaker by supplying words, but neither do you emphasize the passage of time by pretending to be looking away.

A Simple Question

DEAR MISS MANNERS:

Would you please say what is the correct answer when you do not understand what is said to you or have not heard correctly?

GENTLE READER:
What?

Interruptions

DEAR MISS MANNERS:

I belong to a small community church where all of the members are quite close. After services, I often find it necessary to speak to several people before I leave, either to ask a question or to give them information they have requested. When I approach two people who are involved in a lengthy conversation, I usually stand a few feet away, so that it is obvious that I need to speak to them. I find it annoying when I am ignored and left awkwardly standing there. On occasion, I have resorted to "Excuse me, but I need to speak to you for just a moment," only to be answered with "Okay, just a minute," and they return to their conversation. Am I being rude by interrupting, or are they rude for leaving me standing when I need to speak to them?

GENTLE READER:

Your methods of interrupting are not rude, but they don't seem to be effective, either. Interrupters do not have the right of way. They must therefore offer those whom they wish to interrupt a choice, which may be accepted or refused.

The choice you are offering by standing politely to one side or saying "Excuse me" is "Would you like to drop what you're doing and talk to me?" The reply you are getting, which is "No, we'll just finish up and then get to you," is not rude. If you have either emergency information or answers to their own requests, you should offer them the choice between getting the information now or going on talking while you leave. This is done by flashing a hand to get attention and then saying, "Excuse me, I'm running off now. Do you have a minute for me to give you the directions you requested?" If you back up while you are talking, rather than standing obviously prepared to move forward, they will understand that both the opportunity and the interruption are fleeting.

Suffering Interruptions

DEAR MISS MANNERS:

How do you deal with a rude, boorish person who, while you are carrying on a civilized conversation with another person, comes barging up to your partner and, without acknowledging your presence on the planet Earth, starts a conversation or issues an invitation for a later date—which definitely does not include you? Do you stand there like the proverbial bump on a log, or do you wander off, apologizing for being born? I try to think of some witty thing Oscar Wilde might have said, but so far have had no luck penetrating their tough hides.

GENTLE READER:

Oscar Wilde was a man of many brilliant talents, but soothing over social differences was not one of them. As Miss Manners recalls, his method of going on the attack when he felt himself insulted got him into some rather serious trouble. Hers is less spectacular but works better. By all means, wander off with an apology—not for having been born but for "intruding."

Settlement Questions

DEAR MISS MANNERS:

I will soon be awarded a substantial settlement in a medical malpractice suit. In the years since litigation was initiated, a favorite inquiry of relatives, friends, and co-workers has been, "Is your lawsuit settled yet?" Hearing a negative response, they've asked, "How much do you think you'll get?" All along, I've played it down by answering, "Probably a few thousand."

My husband and I have decided that we will never divulge the true amount—which our attorney says will be many times more than a few thousand—to anyone, since we really don't think it's anyone else's business. One family member has already expressed his repugnance at my not being required to repay the insurance company for thousands of dollars in medical expenses. I don't want further arguments about the appropriateness of my settlement.

Soon people will be asking the final outcome—and I mean in dollars. We could spend the rest of our lives saying that the suit hasn't yet been settled, but we hate to lie. Or we could put people in their places by saying that it is none of their business. Or we could let them eat their hearts out by saying that it's quite a lot more than we anticipated.

GENTLE READER:

Or you could drive them properly crazy by saying, "It was a fair settlement, and we've agreed not to discuss the details."

Quizzing Trespassers

DEAR MISS MANNERS:

My husband and I own a hot air balloon, which we fly for sport. As you probably realize, one of the drawbacks of ballooning is that you cannot steer it, but must go wherever the wind takes you. This means that you are almost always trespassing whenever you land, so, of course, you must exercise great politeness to whoever meets you upon landing, since they may be the owners. Even if you land in a public park, you want to be pleasant and promote good will for the sake of the sport.

You are usually mobbed by people full of questions. Explaining how this or that works is just part of the fun of ballooning. But at least one person always rushes up and blurts out, "How much did this balloon cost?" I can't say I don't know, and I usually try to sidestep the rude question with "Oh, about the average price," or something else vague. But they just keep digging for the dollar amount. I know they are curious because they think you have to be rich to own a balloon, which we surely are not. So how do I kindly answer such questions?

GENTLE READER:

The principle that it is best not to be rude while trespassing is an extremely good one. You are also right about two other things: Asking prices is rude in a noncommercial situation; and this particular curiosity is not about whether you have a cheap balloon or an expensive one, but whether ballooning is a rich person's sport. There is no reason why you cannot answer the latter question without answering the former.

Miss Manners has no idea what balloons cost (except that the ones offered children in front of the zoo seem somewhat inflated) and would not dream of asking. If she were intrigued by yours enough to consider taking the sport up herself, she would want to know the general expense involved. It is not necessary to say what your particular balloon cost if you can hint at the general price range of the sport—is it like polo? shooting marbles? falconry? skate boarding? An answer such as "A lot less than your car; it's more like bicycling" or "Well, it's like horseback riding—you can spend a fortune, or you can manage to do it modestly" should be sufficient.

Checkout Curiosity

DEAR MISS MANNERS:

I have a small business and very often buy large quantities of food in the local supermarkets. I am a private person and do not like discussing my business with strangers. Please tell me how to handle the following questions:

From checkout cashiers:

"What are you going to do with all that x, y, or z?"

"Do you have twelve children?"

"You must be in the business. How are you doing in it?"

From customers standing in front of or behind me:

"What is a little girl like you going to do with all that food?"

"Wow, you must really like a, b, or c!"

"Can I come to your party?"

And so on. I cannot tell you the number of times I've pretended not to hear the question, only to have a cashier or customer ask it again in a louder voice. Two cashiers have told me twice that they are dying of curiosity to know what I do. I don't want to be a mystery woman, but how would you handle this invasion of privacy?

GENTLE READER:

A gentleman of Miss Manners' acquaintance found himself besieged with questions in a grocery store line because he was buying nothing but leeks. He admitted that they were for a production of *Henry V* and, in return for satisfying everyone's curiosity, extracted promises that they would buy tickets for the show, where they would be able to view the leeks again, and at greater advantage. This has almost nothing to do with your problem. Miss Manners must be getting rambly.

She really does sympathize with you, but the rude practice of translating curiosity directly into questions has become very widespread and is not easy to discourage. Try repeating in a monotone, "I'm just buying groceries" to every question, including successive ones from the same people. Eventually, they will either get bored and stop, or they will realize that it is late and they have to go home and cook whatever they have been buying.

❧ TRADITIONALLY FORBIDDEN TOPICS

Talking About Money

It's not that Miss Manners isn't flattered by admiration and interest. It's just that she can imagine more graceful compliments than "How much did those shoes set you back?" Time was when the only purchase polite people ever made was horses. Everything else—houses, clothes, jewelry, food—was just there, or wasn't there, as needed. If there was enough, it was because such things had been left lying around by the previous generation, which therefore made them unremarkable. If there wasn't enough, it was too grave a matter for casual discussion.

Miss Manners is not claiming that people made sensible conversation once upon a time. But at least they didn't tell their dinner guests how much the mushrooms cost a pound, inquire as to the designers' names of one another's garments, brag about the mortgage rates of their houses, or announce that they appreciated what other people's watches were worth. Nowadays, it seems, people hardly talk about anything else.

Such inquiries are equally embarrassing to rich and poor, putting them in a position where they must seem to be either showing off or asking for pity. Besides, it is not all that interesting. Miss Manners is not against people admitting that they occasionally make purchases and even thinks it quite sensible for them to seek advice. Here are some examples where it might be acceptable:

One shopper stops another, apologizes, and says, "I've been looking for a coat just like that one. I wonder if you might tell me where you got it."

Someone planning to rent a house inquires around the neighborhood (in that same "I wonder if" tone) what similar properties have been fetching.

A worker hoping for a raise asks around, not about his colleagues' actual salaries but about what policies seem to be, which techniques seem to be successful, and how much leeway the employer has to grant raises if he wishes.

A guest gets a host aside after a meal and says, "You always seem to have such marvelous foods. Would you mind awfully telling me where you shop?"

The common elements in these inquiries are that they have a clearly stated practical motivation, are made under confidential circumstances, and are put as requests for the favor of helping, rather than demands for information. But most of all, those asking the questions are under no illusion that they are conveying compliments, exercising their legitimate right to know, or making entertaining conversation.

Noticing One's Things

DEAR MISS MANNERS:

Is it considered vulgar to compliment a recent acquaintance on his or her possessions? In a televised episode of "Rumpole of the Bailey," Mrs. Rumpole, usually the soul of propriety, took great offense when a dinner guest admired her wine glasses, exclaiming (out of earshot, of course!), "The very idea! Noticing people's things!"

I can't imagine why one should object to having one's taste praised by a perceptive guest. Nevertheless, should I keep my mouth shut when my host of the evening proudly displays his crystal or china?

GENTLE READER:

Mrs. Rumpole must be the only creature on earth besides Miss Manners who remembers that rule. She probably also knows the one about never remarking on the food at a dinner party, even to compliment it. These attitudes date from a time when even comparatively modest households had inherited furniture and hired cooks. (Presumably what they saved by not buying furniture was used to pay the wages.) Any judgmental remark was therefore inappropriate, as the decor and food did not reflect the hosts' taste so much as their family background and their luck in servants.

Miss Manners does not recommend failing to compliment hosts who have spent the day slaving over a hot food processor or their lives decorating their houses. It is now expected. It's just that Miss Manners, and perhaps Mrs. Rumpole too, remembers fondly when there was something said at the dinner table besides how the meat was marinated or what the mortgage rate was on the house.

Theology

DEAR MISS MANNERS:

In the midst of a semiformal dinner, the conversation took a totally bizarre and unexpected turn. An ordinarily staid lady executive, after the second bottle of wine, began to speak passionately about angels in a company that included an agnostic, an atheist, a universal pantheist, and a fellow who identified himself as a "cultural Catholic" (as distinct, say, from a sacerdotal one). The lady became compulsive and highly animated in her defense of angels, and began badgering others at the table to determine whether they shared her faith. The atheist, alas, did not, and became assertively rational and argumentative, as did the pantheist. The agnostic simply didn't know, poor fellow. Oh, Miss Manners, the discussion got awkward when one person suggested that the angel lady was a closet romantic, which then led to the question of whether angels were sexless or merely divine spooks. Finally, heresy was broached when the lady confessed that she personally gave higher priority to angels than to the Deity Itself (for gender there is a problem, too). My question is merely this: Are obscure theological debates appropriate to polite after-dinner conversation? If not, how can one tactfully change the subject when others are given to public protestations of faith?

GENTLE READER:

Miss Manners' question is merely this: Why wasn't she invited to this dinner? Do you know how long it's been since she has heard a rousing debate on the nature of angels? It is true that debates involving personal religious beliefs are barred from the dinner table, and people who try to start them, whether they are motivated by fervor or wine, should simply be heard out without any attempt to argue them down, so that the matter drops. But if you can get up some theological speculation that doesn't insult anyone's faith—well, it sure beats comparing real estate prices at the dinner table.

Vulgarity

DEAR MISS MANNERS:

In late middle age, I find that more and more of my women friends (I hesitate to use the word "ladies")—people I enjoy and care about—are punctuating their conversations with vulgar four-letter words. How do I indicate that their language is most offensive to me? I would not like to appear prudish.

GENTLE READER:

Prudishness is such a charming novelty these days that Miss Manners is surprised that so few people are willing to admit to it. The way to avoid it, however, is to stick someone else with it: "If you people keep talking like that, I'm going to pick it up and I'll be in deep trouble with my children if I use those words. They're awfully straitlaced, you know."

Bluntness

DEAR MISS MANNERS:

Why do children always ask embarrassingly specific questions about sex when they are in public places (on the bus, etc.)? And how do I cope with this?

GENTLE READER:

Why? Now that is an example of a childish question that need not be answered at all. However, such questions as "What do 'soft core' and 'hard core' mean, and what's the difference?", asked in a clear voice by an alert child reading the signs while riding through the business district on a packed bus, do need to be answered. They are properly answered in two parts, only the second of which actually addresses the question. The first part consists of "I'll tell you later" and is designed to disappoint a suddenly silent and attentive busload of passengers.

Name Dropping

DEAR MISS MANNERS:

What should be done about name droppers? These people arrive at a gathering excited about having met some celebrity, implying that nobody present would ever have an opportunity to meet such an exalted person. Or they drop the name of a place that they imply is too exotic, expensive, or exclusive for us to hope to go visit.

What do I do if they are speaking about an old friend or a place I've often visited? If I speak up, they are irritated because I've taken the wind out of their sails. If I keep quiet, someone invariably brings out the fact later, and the situation seems worse. Since the primary obligation of any guest is to help the party be pleasant, what should I do?

Finally, what do I do when I am leaving a party and someone I never met before announces loudly, "I love you"? They can't possibly; they've just met me. I'm unwilling to tell a bald-faced lie and say I love them, too. I've tried things like "Aren't you a dear to say so," but it is such a feeble return that it sometimes sounds like a slap. I'm stumped.

GENTLE READER:

Whew—this was a close one. Miss Manners was just about to burst out herself with an announcement that she loves you for wanting to spare the feelings even of name droppers. Lest you either take her literally or believe that she is telling a bald-faced lie, she will control herself.

Do allow her to dismiss the last problem by explaining that the comment is merely an effusive way of saying, "I found you charming," and that your reply is perfectly adequate. Name droppers eventually get their comeuppance. The only choice is in how this is administered. By saying, "Yes, isn't he charming?" or "I'm so glad you like it—I have a small cottage there," you at least warn them against further excesses. Miss Manners tends to prefer the alternative of saying nothing and letting them find out later. She is aware that by admitting this, she reveals herself as less saintly than you.

A Prior Romance

DEAR MISS MANNERS:

At a dinner with the object of my affections, a female friend of his, and her male companion, the conversation was light and pleasant until this female friend brought up, out of the blue, the subject of a woman whom my companion had dated several years ago. They had discussed this woman on other occasions and had had a good laugh. I listened with good grace but several large knots in my stomach.

When my companion and I returned to our shared abode, I told him that I thought his friend's remarks were inappropriate. I said that she could not have known how I would react, and so should have saved reminiscences of that nature for their lunches together. My companion replied that no slight was intended, either to me or to our relationship, and I was being too sensitive. He said that once I got to know this friend better, as he fervently hoped I would, I could present my objections to her myself in a friendly and constructive manner. I replied that I thought it his responsibility, if not to train his friends, then to refrain from encouraging them by laughing along.

Am I being too sensitive? Should a person of the world be expected to take such gratuitous and uninvited remarks in stride? Or should a well-mannered person of the world be expected to know enough not to make such remarks in the first place?

GENTLE READER:

Those knots in your stomach worry Miss Manners. She could certainly make an etiquette case against two people discussing a third in front of a fourth who does not know the third. She most certainly believes that it is in bad taste to discuss with anyone at all the more romantic aspects of any intimacy in which one has participated. But she does not want to encourage you in believing that society must conspire to make you think that you are your companion's first love. You really do not want your beau, who has shown himself anxious to make his friend be your friend, to train others to censor their conversation by explaining how sensitive you are. How much better a figure you would cut if you gently defended this woman from their humor. Saying, with a tolerant smile, "Why, I think you're both awful; I'm sure she was a lovely woman, and you are just being wicked" will spoil this line of conversation for them much more effectively than showing discomfort.

Personal Questions and Remarks

Prying

Suppose you go around and find out how old everybody you meet is and how much they paid for their houses. Suppose each person with what you considered a physical oddity informed you in detail why he or she limped, was tall, had red hair, or was left-handed. Suppose all single people explained to you why they were single, all married people explained how they shared household chores, and every adult stated a rationale for the existence or nonexistence of his or her children. Suppose that upon greeting someone, you were able to find out immediately how old each piece of clothing he or she wore was, where it was bought, and for how much.

What would you have then? A full, rich, interesting life? Insights into the nature of humanity? Then why don't people quit asking such questions at every opportunity and go back to the system in which it was off-bounds to ferret information out of people and each person was allowed to volunteer topics he wished to discuss?

Nobody enjoys being grilled in this fashion. Miss Manners has yet to hear from someone who is pleased and flattered at the friendly interest implicit in a question such as "Why do you have so many children?" or "Did you retire voluntarily, or were you forced out, and aren't you getting bored?"

What she hears, instead is:

"When people find out (not from me) that I am sixty-eight years old, I get two responses that irritate me: 'You look wonderful. Did you have a face lift?' and 'Gee, when I'm your age, I hope I look as good as you do!' "

"We have an eleven-year-old daughter who is very obviously on the threshold of womanhood. She has begun to dread her grandmother's visits because she thinks the woman may ask her bald-faced, in mixed company, if she has yet begun to menstruate. My mother-in-law's dinner table conversation is appalling—including discussions of some very delicate gentleman's operations which several of her friends have needed—and this is a highly likely possibility."

"Ours is an adoptive family, and we are frequently asked, with no regard for how much information I have shared with my children or whether I wish to inform the world at large about my children's heritage, 'Why can't you have your own?' 'Who had the problem?' 'Where did you get the baby?' 'Was the birth mother young? Unwed? Was she having an affair?' 'Why didn't she want the baby?' 'Won't the parents come looking for you?' 'Is the adoption finalized yet?' Can you imagine what this line of questioning does to my children's feeling of security? If I overreact to these questions, my children will feel that there is something shameful going on. If I do not react, the questions will continue."

Why should such matters be considered so private? Why do so many well-intentioned or, at worst, thoughtless people ask, anyway?

People never consider themselves nosy. Miss Manners has heard from the questioners, who describe themselves as friendly and interested. "I would love to know how old each person is, how much they paid for their house or how much their rent is, how much they get paid, and how their chores are split up. Knowledge and ideas from others help one live a better life. If people wouldn't get so offended about what everyone thinks but won't speak about, life in general would be much better. I don't see why anyone would dislike such conversation instead of the usual mindless chatter. Is one not supposed to talk about anything that truly concerns one?"

One answer is that friendship must be earned, not assumed. The decision to give whatever information one's tradition deems personal must be voluntary. If you really want to help it along, look fascinated at any revelations, look sympathetic, ask general questions ("Tell me more about yourself"), and keep bringing up topics that lend themselves to personal illustration ("Have real estate values zoomed up in this neighborhood?") or your personal reasons for needing to know ("My sister has been trying to adopt children, and she's having a difficult time.") Miss Manners has always said that there is a polite way to do everything, even to pry.

Manners do not, however, require cheerful cooperation with determined prying. Those questioned often feel that their choice is between seeming oversensitive or accepting insensitivity. The answer is to ignore the question, whenever possible, and reply as if it had been an acceptable comment, such as "How are you?"

("Thank you, I'm fine") or "What lovely children" ("Yes, I'm very proud of them"). More direct interrogations should be met with a cool "I'm afraid that is a private matter" and totally outrageous ones with a firm "How dare you?"

Demurring

DEAR MISS MANNERS:

As an acquaintance was leaving our home, he said, "Well, you certainly have come a long way in the past few years. You're doing very well in your therapy." He was referring to the fact that I have been hospitalized for mental illness and am still having psychotherapy. Miss Manners, I deeply resented what he said. Even my therapist doesn't presume to pass judgment on my progress in therapy. I understand that he meant to compliment me. Nevertheless, I was upset for a long while afterward.

Is there some way I could have politely indicated that he was out of line? I merely murmured "Thank you" and saw him to the door. That left me struggling with feelings that, had we been in a therapy group, I would have been able to express in a more or less raw form.

GENTLE READER:

But it is exactly therapy group manners, which have unfortunately carried over into private social life, that created your problem. The concept that to refuse to discuss your problems is tantamount to announcing that you are ashamed of them has created this no-privacy policy in which ordinary, cheeky nosiness is mistakenly dignified.

You are quite right, however, that you cannot be rude to someone who meant well. For that matter, Miss Manners does not allow you to be rude to people who don't mean well. You are, however, allowed to embarrass both kinds when they overstep the boundaries of good taste, provided that you do it politely. What you should say under such circumstances is, "So-o-o-o kind of you to take an interest." The more "o's" in "So," the clearer it becomes that your meaning is the opposite of your words.

Confessions

Not even every close relationship requires telling all. Miss Manners' own mother was always the most devoted parent in the world, but she never for a moment thought that her age was any of her children's business. Your income is a good thing not to tell your children. First of all, they might tell it to others, perhaps with an unpleasant motive such as bragging or complaining; and second, you don't really want to give them the idea that they have anything to say about its use, so that they either decide that you are being stingy with them or they worry that the family will end up in the poorhouse.

Your medical problems should be told to those who are deeply worried either about your health or about their own similar symptoms. More care should be taken in comforting others with stories about having been through the same emotional problems, because the natural tendency is for you to point out that yours was worse and for them, once they are cured, to treat yours as mere gossip.

Your family secrets should be discussed only with other members of the family. Other people's family secrets should never be told them by outsiders.

Your scandalous past should be saved to entertain your great-grandchildren when they inform you that you lived in simpler and more innocent times than they.

Your scandalous present should be told to intimates who care about you enough to guard your interests, but not so much as to be hurt.

Your tricks for cheating on your expense account or taxes should never be told to anyone, because you should retain the proper shame until you have no alternative but to stop doing it.

Your dreams should be told to those who are there when you wake up.

In sum, your confidences should be made to those whose confidences you would receive as empathetically as you expect them to do yours. No fair telling your life story to someone you consider a bore because he only talks about himself.

Effective Innocence

DEAR MISS MANNERS:

I need the perfect squelch. My husband and I have been embarrassed so many times by a couple we've known for years. To make sure that we are aware of their active sex life, he always apprises us of the latest roll in the hay, with a remark such as "I gave her a present this morning before breakfast." This is said while he looks deeply into her eyes, and she blushes and coyly casts her eyes down. My husband and I feel like voyeurs of this couple's sex life. I really feel that this man wants us to know that he is virile and still as good a man as ever. All the phrases I think of to stop this embarrassment make me sound mean and petty and jealous. I might add that otherwise we enjoy their company.

GENTLE READER:

Miss Manners will not countenance your saying anything embarrassing or vulgar in response to these embarrassing and vulgar remarks. Innocence is so much more effective. Inquire gently, "What? I don't understand what you're talking about. Why are you telling me this? What does this have to do with us?"

The Proper Response

DEAR MISS MANNERS:

A young woman I have just met is expecting her fourth child. She mentions to all and sundry, frequently during the course of any conversation (her invariable topics are herself, her husband, and her family), that she is going to have her tubes tied after the baby is born. While speaking with another co-worker, she began a dissertation on her husband's impotence. What is an appropriate polite response?

GENTLE READER:

"How nice for you." This is properly pronounced with the emphasis on "for." It is accompanied by a so-what? smile (eyes fixed on the confessor, closed lips briefly moved upward and then down again), and followed by a change of subject.

The stance to assume when someone is telling you intimate details you don't want to hear is that of polite ennui. As the story unfolds, you maintain a glazed look, occasionally say listlessly, "Oh, really?" and at the first pause inquire, "Well, and what else have you been doing with yourself lately?"

Complaining

DEAR MISS MANNERS:

I sometimes stop at a certain store on my way to work. One morning, one of the people working there made a comment I found offensive and humiliating. There were about seven other people waiting along with me when she said, "Putting on a little weight, aren't you?" I am five feet four inches in height and weigh about 145 pounds. I tried not to let it bother me, but she made the same comment each time I went in there.

My mother and father always said, "If you can't say anything good to a person, you shouldn't say anything." I'm a good customer and dread going in there. I wonder how many other people she has offended. I considered writing a letter to her superiors but really don't like to handle things that way.

GENTLE READER:

Why don't you like to handle things that way? It is exactly the way to get results, and it is a kindness to those who run the shop to inform them why business may be dropping off.

Reluctance to complain is indeed a charming and rare quality. Miss Manners feels she has to curb it only when it means that innocent people are not only victimized but incorrectly put on the defensive. That you felt you had to tell Miss Manners your height and weight unfortunately suggests that you are not sufficiently indignant about having anyone else dare to appraise you.

Reprimanding

DEAR MISS MANNERS:

I'm twenty-nine, considered attractive, and have always been an active person. Three years ago, I was in a very bad accident. After three months in the hospital, I returned home with both my legs amputated at the hip, so now I'm in a wheelchair for life. This I can live with because I have to, and I refuse to let it ruin my life. I'm still an active person, and I take a lot of pride in my appearance. I get around by myself, I drive my own car, I work, I have my own apartment, and I've learned to do everything for myself so that I don't have to depend on anyone.

Appropriate Expressions for Inappropriate Questions

What I'm trying to say is that I'm still the same person I've always been, and I still like the same things I used to like. But the important thing is the way people treat me. Most of them are either very rude or sickeningly sweet. I don't want a perfect stranger to ask me what happened to my legs. I don't like being avoided by salespeople in the stores. I don't like, when I'm swimming, for everyone to get out of the water to watch me. I don't like people to stand and look at me and whisper. If men are going to make jokes, I want them at least to wait until they're far enough away that I can't hear them.

What happened to me can happen to anyone at any time. I've overcome the handicap as far as being able to do many things that I used to do before my legs were cut off. If people would just treat me like everyone else, my life would be complete. About the only way I can get my point across is through someone like you. Is it asking too much to want to be treated like everyone else?

GENTLE READER:

The standards of treatment for "everyone else" are extremely low now, and the rudeness you encounter is a particularly ugly and exaggerated form of offensiveness that just about everyone encounters at one time or another.

Miss Manners is afraid that you will have to learn to do one thing that you probably never did before, and that is to emphasize to people, by your reaction to their bad behavior, that you expect to be treated with dignity.

If a stranger asks "What happened?" or bystanders make remarks, stare at them and say in a firm voice, with no hint of a question at the end, "I beg your pardon!" Do not weaken and sympathize when you see that this causes them embarrassment. That is the idea. You want them to realize how their comments sound to you, become ashamed of themselves, and resolve never to behave this way again.

When salespeople ignore you, you must say in an indignant tone, "May I have some service, please?" This reminds them that what you are is a customer, not a curiosity. Similarly, if people stare at you while you are swimming, pause for a minute, stare at them, and say, "Is something the matter?" You do not mention the problem of friends or acquaintances who ask what happened, but that, too, is bound to happen. The solution, when you want to appear not unfriendly, is to smile weakly and say, "I get so bored telling the story over and over again. Some other time."

Miss Manners is sorry to put you to all this trouble when the fault belongs to others, but unless all of us attack this epidemic rudeness disguised as interest and sympathy, none of us are going to be able to go normally about our business.

❧ QUESTIONS AND COMMENTS
ABOUT . . .

Sexual Preferences

DEAR MISS MANNERS:

I have several gay friends. A few of my friends inquire about the sexual preference of every person I mention in the course of normal conversation. I find this very rude. It is none of their business and is usually irrelevant to the conversation. If I answer "It's none of your business," it is taken as "Yes."

GENTLE READER:

Surely the obvious answer here is a cold "Why, I have no idea. I wouldn't dream of asking about anything so extremely private." This is also the correct answer when one is asked why one's friends don't get married, divorced, or pregnant and how much they paid for their houses.

Surgery

DEAR MISS MANNERS:

I am a modern female, successful at my work, a good mother and wife, and in excellent physical shape. Recently, I had my breasts enlarged. Need I tell any woman what child bearing and the passage of time have done to my breasts? I'm happy with my decision but am in a dilemma about questions. How should I handle the inquiring looks and questions of my children? Should I announce my surgery or wait for questions from my friends? And what about the rude person who asks embarrassing questions in a group?

GENTLE READER:

Miss Manners has a feeling that she doesn't want to know exactly what these questions are that you are expecting. A lady does not, under any circumstances whatsoever, engage in a speculative discussion with casual acquaintances about her bosom.

Announcing the event suggests that you will then take questions.

Please try to confine your explanations to loyal intimates who care. Others who have a right to be concerned about you—your children, if they are too young to be confidants; your boss and co-workers; most of your relatives and friends—may, if necessary be told that you had "corrective" surgery. The proper reply to inquiries is a cold stare: immobile face with eyes popping out and unblinking until the offender dies of embarrassment.

DEAR MISS MANNERS:

My co-workers and I are in a sticky situation. A lady who works in our office had a "nose job" during her vacation and will be returning shortly. Should we comment on her surgery? And if so, how could we go about it in a tactful manner?

GENTLE READER:

If you found out accidentally, it would be rude to acknowledge that you noticed the specific change. In that case, you should reassure her that it was worthwhile by the general statement "You look wonderful," made while staring the lady straight in the eyes. If the lady announced the entire procedure before leaving, it would be rude not to notice. However, one should still emphasize the effect rather than the cause. "It makes you look so much more—you" is more charming than "They did a good job."

Beauty Aids

DEAR MISS MANNERS:

During a dinner party at our house for a few couples we have known for some time—we are all in our forties—the discussion got around to aging. I remarked that my friend Constance (who was there) and I help to maintain the illusion of youth by coloring our hair and wearing girdles. There were a few chuckles, and other people talked about some of their little ploys.

Yesterday, Constance chided me for my comments. A lady's hair coloring, and even more her girdle, she maintained, are subjects not mentioned in polite society. She claimed that I had humiliated her by giving away her secrets, especially in the presence of men. I told her that these taboos are long gone, and the fact that we color our hair is probably obvious anyway. As to girdles, I think a lady should be more embarrassed at having it thought that she does not wear one than that she does. Constance, however, is still miffed. Did I do something terribly wrong?

GENTLE READER:

You certainly did. You may decide on your own behalf that you no longer wish to observe the custom of reticence about your personal habits, but you may not do so on behalf of Constance or, as you presume, of the entire society. When taboos are abolished, Miss Manners will announce it, if you please. Until then, please allow others the courtesy of keeping or giving away their own secrets. You owe your friend an apology.

Marriage

DEAR MISS MANNERS:

I write on behalf of single people everywhere who, though they are educated, articulate, and at least reasonably socially adept, are flummoxed by the often asked and (ostensibly) well-meant question "Why aren't you married?" Sometimes the question appears as a statement: "So. You never married," sighed the mother of my college roommate, whom I hadn't seen in ten years. As I am thirty-six years old, I don't yet consider the case entirely closed, though she obviously does.

"I don't know" is the truthful answer, but it always sounds a trifle woebegone. "That's none of your business" is too rude, especially when the tormentor is an elderly uncle trying to make conversation at a family gathering—usually a wedding, of course.

While I am fairly content to remain single, I have not ruled out the possibility of marrying and deeply resent being put on the defensive by the frequent implication that my Ph.D. is some sort of consolation prize for a poor showing in the Big Contest of Life. My friends and I hope that you can offer an all-purpose reply that will take the sting out of the question and let the questioner know that he or she is causing considerable discomfort.

GENTLE READER:

Miss Manners does not believe you want to tell your questioner that he or she is causing discomfort. You could do that easily just by bursting into tears and saying, "I wish I knew." No, what you want to do is to cause that person enough discomfort to discourage the nosiness. Treat the statement as banter, which you then turn back on that person in such a way that the person knows you can't really mean it. The uncle should be told, "Oh, Uncle Nelson, I keep looking for someone as perfect as you, and every time I'm about to settle for something less, I find I just can't bring myself to do it." To the roommate's mother, you say, "Oh, Mrs. Pretzel, I've always thought you were probably the ideal wife, and I just know I'll never be as wonderful, so I guess I've put off trying."

Pregnancy

DEAR MISS MANNERS:

A group of recently married women agreed that the rudest question posed to newlyweds, besides "How's married life?", is "When are you going to have a baby?" What is the polite way to answer while discouraging the person from repeating the question at another time?

GENTLE READER:

In the annals of nosiness, there is a big difference between "How's married life?" and "When are you going to have a baby?" No one expects a real answer to the former, and it cannot therefore be classified as offensive. If you actually replied "I'm in such a state of ecstasy that I can hardly see straight" or "Kind of disappointing, actually," you would be the offender. The baby question is rude, however, and calls for the shocked expression or a cold "When the time comes, I suppose."

Parental Age

DEAR MISS MANNERS:

I had my only child when I was thirty-seven. He is now eight years old, and when we go places, someone will inevitably ask if he is my grandson. Although it doesn't bother me too much, when I go on to reply, "No, he is my son," I know that the person asking must feel like going through the floor. Is there a tactful way I can put these people back at ease?

GENTLE READER:

You might reply, "No, he's my mother's grandson." In the moment it takes people to figure that out, you can smile blandly in reassurance that you are not mortally wounded.

However, on behalf of those other forty-five-year-old mothers, Miss Manners requests that you keep enough restraint in that smile to show that you are not tickled by the mistake. Let us not put people so much at ease with the foolishness of hazarding unnecessary and possibly offensive guesses that they go on doing it.

Job Difficulties

DEAR MISS MANNERS:

My husband works for a large airline which has often been in the headlines because of severe financial losses, cutbacks, and merger rumors. We have learned to live with the uncertainty of his job situation, but I haven't yet found a way to deal with the cross-examinations we are subject to from friends, relatives, and casual acquaintances every time the media do a story on the subject. Although I understand that people are concerned, I find it annoying to be asked whether my husband will be laid off or if his salary has been cut.

GENTLE READER:

No doubt these people think they are showing sympathy for your plight and generously offering you a chance to unburden yourselves of your worries. Every busybody considers himself a volunteer therapist.

A firm "You are kind to take an interest, but we are hoping for the best" should do it. Persistent questioners may have to be told "It is nothing we wish to discuss" before you pointedly change the subject.

Career Changes

DEAR MISS MANNERS:

I decided to change careers a couple of years ago. Actually, I tired of my job in television. To this day, people constantly ask me why I'm not on television anymore and if I'm planning to return. They are very persistent and amazed that anyone would leave such a glamorous job (little do they know). How do I say "It's none of your business" without being rude or leaving the impression that I was fired? I don't want to discuss personal career plans with everyone in town.

GENTLE READER:

The answer to all job questions one does not wish to answer is "I enjoyed it when I did it, but eventually I needed a change—something more challenging." This is worded so as not to insult the job one has left, but merely to suggest that an active mind needs to keep learning. If, in your case, the answer is met with some stupefaction, that is not your fault. These people probably consider being on television to be the ultimate achievement in life and are actually stretching their imaginations to figure out why anyone would leave. Just keep repeating the answer until they grasp that the height of their ambition is something you have gone beyond. At that point, they will shut up.

Religion

DEAR MISS MANNERS:

How do people respond to statements about their religious or cultural background? My husband and I are both blond, fair-skinned, light-eyed Jews. Our last name is not necessarily an indication of our religion. When we meet people who do not know us well, we are sometimes subjected to unpleasant remarks about Jewish people. It is then difficult to announce that we are Jewish, as people say such things as "Really? You don't look Jewish." What was your mother's maiden name?" "Did you have your nose fixed?", and so on. This is very embarrassing and humiliating for everyone concerned.

At one time, I made a big joke of it by claiming that yes, I did have a "nose job," frosted my hair, and so on. Now that I'm older, married, and want children, I feel that it's important to hold tight to Jewish traditions and to take a more adult stand on the issue. It's sad for me to think that Judaism is associated more with the physical appearance than with the religious and traditional meaning of over 4,000 years. Whenever possible, I let it be known tactfully that I'm Jewish. My intention is not to be rude or insulting, but just to respect others and their beliefs and have my beliefs treated in the same manner. What is a kind, appropriate solution to this problem which does not entail a lecture on the history and background of Judaism?

GENTLE READER:

The jokes were a terrible idea, and Miss Manners is glad to hear that you have dropped them. This has nothing to do with age. If you have children, do not allow them to think that bigotry is a joking matter. Now drop the "tact" when responding to anti-Semitic remarks by informing people that you are Jewish. The correct way is to say it plainly in a challenging voice. If the person then says, "Oh, I hope you didn't think we meant . . ." and then denies the remark's meaning, you may— or may not—allow yourself to be mollified. In either case, you will find that you will not be insulted by that person again.

If the statement leads to such questions as you mention, do not attempt to answer them. That would be equivalent to conceding that you are exceptions to a stereotype. You may add, more in sadness at their ignorance than as a personal affront, "I'm afraid you don't know much about the Jews, or you wouldn't ask such questions."

There is an opportunity here for the decent person to be ashamed at what he or she has carelessly said and to apologize. Graciousness would consist of your accepting a truly remorseful apology. Only this could clear the air enough for you to resume friendly relations.

Dress

DEAR MISS MANNERS:

My appearance is, for the United States, somewhat singular. I adorn myself with the ornaments that are part of many Hindu women's wardrobes, namely, diverse bangles, a nose ring of gold, several smaller gold hoops in the earlobes, and a string of pearls between the nose and ear. In the winter, I don Western clothes, especially in foul weather, so there is mayhap some imbalance. Too bad!

First, I'm asked, "How do you blow your nose?" Thence on to "Do you make bracelets?", "Why do you wear so many?", "What do you do for a living?", "Why do you have on a fireman's coat?", "Do you want to sell it?", and "Why do you dress that way?" Women are usually attracted by the ornaments, and their questions, such as "How did you pierce your nose?" or " Didn't it hurt?", don't offend me. But how does one answer the questions of the men? They aren't really looking for answers but are just trying to be obnoxious.

GENTLE READER:

Miss Manners knows of no culture that requires ladies to discuss their dressing habits with strangers for the sake of politeness. The correct reply is no reply at all. At most, as in the case of ladies who you believe mean well, you could say, "I am sorry; it is not my custom to discuss my appearance."

Weight

DEAR MISS MANNERS:

Even people who would agree about the rudeness of pointing out a person's excess weight to her face feel that it is perfectly acceptable to "jokingly" tell a thin person how "disgusting" or "sickening" she is for being thin. I have been told this often for lo, these many years, especially since I don't diet. I have been good-natured about it all along, even when blatantly told that my figure is inadequate and that I should just wait until I'm over forty. This comes mostly from women, and my patience with their obvious jealousy is wearing thin.

GENTLE READER:

What these women are practicing is a particularly obnoxious modern social convention called the "compliment-insult." These are the kind of people who congratulate you on an achievement by saying, "I hate you," and thank you for a present by saying, "This is too good to use." They truly believe that they are expressing, in a humorous or original way, the politeness that such occasions demand.

There are two ways of dealing with this. Miss Manners will not let you use them unless you absolutely promise to do so naively, without any trace of sarcasm. She is willing to have you point out to these people what they are doing but will not have you humiliate them.

One is to take them at face value and, in your case, say in a flurried way, "Really? Is my appearance offensive? I had no idea I was so unattractive. Tell me your eating habits. Perhaps I could learn something. You look wonderful." The other is to take it as the compliment they intended and to reply, on being told that your figure is disgusting, "Oh, thank you."

Appearance

DEAR MISS MANNERS:

Whenever I'm with my friends or when I meet a stranger on the street, they comment on my beauty. Sometimes they say, "You are a very beautiful girl," to which I can answer a bland "thank you," but what do I reply when someone says, "Do you think you are pretty?" I am a very modest person and don't like to talk about my looks because I'm afraid to be thought conceited. I am fifteen years old.

GENTLE READER:

Miss Manners refuses to suggest, as many people would, that this is not a sympathetic problem. Comments on one's good fortune are often as difficult to handle as less pleasant remarks.

In this country, unlike many others, we accept compliments, rather than rejecting them with modest denials. You are right that only a simple "thank you" is required, or the more ambiguous "How kind of you to say so." It is graceful to accompany this with a look of surprised pleasure, as if one were hearing it for the first time. (Don't overdo this expression, however, or you will bring on an elaboration of the compliment.) The answer to "Do you think you are pretty?" is "Why, I never really thought about it." This, too, should be accompanied by a look of surprise. Skip the pleasure in the expression.

Miss Manners is disturbed by your reference to the compliments of strangers. Strangers have no business commenting on one's looks one way or the other. A truly harmless stranger—say, an old lady who says, "My, you're a pretty thing," before she thinks about it—may be acknowledged with a slight bow of the head and a distant smile. A strange man who makes such a comment should be pointedly ignored.

Advice

Unsolicited Cheer

"Lighten up!"

"Smile!"

"Things can't be that bad."

"Come on, cheer up."

To all those compassionate souls who issue such good-hearted injunctions to the obviously disheartened wherever they spot them, who thereby attempt to encourage high spirits whenever they seem to be failing, Miss Manners has a counter-exhortation: Please cut it out. If you don't understand the situation, don't try to fix it.

Miss Manners appreciates cheerfulness as much as anyone. Unlike the freelance emotional missionaries, of whom we seem to have quite a number now, she recognizes the legitimacy of somber moods and respects the privacy of strangers.

It is a noble undertaking to assist someone in grief by offering warmth, support, and understanding. This is a service that one owes everyone one cares about, and that gifted and committed people are sometimes able to offer to a wider circle. It requires both time and sensitivity.

Miss Manners once was traveling on an airplane when a fellow passenger, noticing that she was dressed in black from head to toe, probably with a facial expression to match, cheerily remarked, "Hey, it can't be that bad. You look as if you've lost your best friend." Possibly his motive was to spread good cheer. As Miss Manners happened to be traveling to a funeral, it did not accomplish the purpose. Not intruding her mood on anyone else, she was unpleasantly rattled to have anyone else intrude upon hers. An intrusion is exactly what this sort of thing is, however well meant. It is also uniformly ineffective.

There is no easy answer to tragedy. The damage that even close friends can do when they dispense ill-thought-out comfort to those with troubles is inestimable. People who attempt to assuage grief by announcing that "It was all for the best," or "You'll get over it," or one of those funeral favorites, "You'll marry again" or "You'll have other children," are heaping on additional pain. This is why we have conventional forms for offering consolation under nonintimate circumstances. These contain no advice, but only an expression of sympathy: "I'm so sorry," "I want you to know how much I feel for you," "You have my deepest sympathy."

Unsolicited Advice

We have a strong volunteer force, Miss Manners has observed. Everyone is already helping everyone else all the time, and generally without even waiting for the formality of a request.

Absolute strangers will offer help in the form of health advice, such as "Do you know that that stuff you're eating is poisoning your system?" Mere acquaintances will help out by recommending exercise programs, diets, and changes in hair style and wardrobe—all on the assumption that you couldn't really look the way you do on purpose. Friends and relations are especially helpful in evaluating your other intimate ties. "She's no good for you" and "You ought to know that everyone but you realizes he's a jerk" are only the surface remarks. Analyses are also available, such as "What you're really looking for is a mother" or "What you think is love is only unresolved guilt." The truly conscientious will not limit themselves to helping with the more exciting parts of one's life. They are also scrupulous about offering helpful suggestions regarding such mundane matters as your household arrangements, work habits, mannerisms, and use of the language. There is nothing like a good friend to help you out when you are not in trouble.

Life's little helpers reason that the first step toward improvement is the realization that things need to be improved. That is why they feel justified in approaching you when you are perfectly content in order to point out that everything you do, eat, and love is a dreadful mistake. Because they themselves are so full of good wishes for the rest of humanity, they do not expect their beneficiaries to be petty. They figure that upon being told how you have mismanaged your life, you will be grateful for the offer of assistance and reassured that others are watching out for you. It stands to reason that one who obviously does not know what is best for himself would be relieved to find that others are willing to take on that responsibility.

After all, they don't just stop after telling you what is wrong, but always go on to explain in detail how you can do things the way they do them. In other words, the right way.

Miss Manners would like gently to propose that everyone just cut out all this helpfulness right now. She suggests this first as a matter of manners. It is rude to call people's attention to their shortcomings, no matter how much you have their welfare at heart. It is rude to assume that anyone other than minors in your custody is less capable than you are of making minor and major decisions about how to live. No, it doesn't count if you prepare the way by attempting to convince people who didn't realize it just how badly in need of help they are. In the etiquette lexicon, the statements necessary to break down a person's self-satisfaction to the point where he admits that he was in worse shape than he had fondly imagined are still called "insults."

The following statements are all insults:

"You really ought to be going out more."

"Keep on smoking like that, and you'll be dead in five years, and you won't be able to say I didn't warn you."

"Why do you waste your time watching that trash?"

"How can you let anyone treat you like that? If you had any self respect, you'd tell him where to go."

"A good plastic surgeon could fix that."

"Now's the time for you to have children, while you're still young enough to cope with them."

"You just think you're in love."

"You ought to have your colors done."

Miss Manners might also point out that many matters commonly the subject of unsolicited help—such as looks and character evaluations—are purely subjective. Why should one person's estimation of what kind of haircut would flatter you be better than another's or than your own? On questions where there is generally conceded to be danger, the person who chooses to ignore the danger is bound to know that he is doing so at some risk. That smoking is bad for you, or that it is statistically perilous to marry someone who has had a dozen spouses who died mysteriously, has not escaped the awareness of the person who has decided to do this anyway. All that is added by helpful criticism in such a case is the information that others are standing by, expecting the worst.

The Computer Proselyte

DEAR MISS MANNERS:

The husband of one of my close friends is a computer buff. He asks me every time he sees me when I am going to get a word processor. (I am a freelance writer.) The first time, I didn't mind; many writers do use word processors, and I was happy to explain why I prefer not to. The problem is that he won't take no for an answer. He asks me the same question over and over. I lose patience quickly in situations like this, but I managed to be polite for several months. Finally, I told him not to mention the subject again. He seemed offended.

Nevertheless, the next time I saw him, he asked me whether I had decided yet to get a word processor. I know that this man doesn't mean any harm, but if he doesn't lay off, I am going to explode.

GENTLE READER:

Well, when are you going to get one? Miss Manners is a writer, too, you know, and let her tell you—Just kidding. Calm down. She didn't mean it. The polite way of saying "Mind your own business" is a firm "Don't bother to keep asking. I promise you that if I change my mind, I'll let you know."

Appraising Figures

DEAR MISS MANNERS:

Several prominent women in this city are suffering from anorexia, one so severely that she looks like a skeleton. As is so often the case with this illness, they refuse to get treatment, in spite of the urgings of family and friends. They continue to appear at charity balls and other social functions; in fact (another common feature), they are more active than ever.

Friends who see them at these events don't know how to treat the situation. Do they smile and kiss them as though everything were normal? Do they murmur a few words of concern? Or do they take more drastic action, such as calling an ambulance?

Nobody wants to be rude, but letting somebody die is bad manners, too, and anorexia kills.

GENTLE READER:

As you have been quick to point out to Miss Manners, the urgings of these ladies' own families and friends have not been successful. Do you seriously believe that rude murmurings at social occasions will be more effective?

If you are truly concerned about eating disorders, rather than enjoy making unpleasant assumptions about thin people (who might be suffering from other diseases they choose not to mention to you, or might be perfectly healthy and naturally thin), you could, in fact, do a great deal.

You could resolve not to take such an obvious interest in other people's weight and appearance. The society's preoccupation with these externals, which has set unrealistic national standards while ignoring the considerable normal variations, has surely contributed to the state of mind in which unfortunate people sacrifice their health to thinness.

Keeping America Beautiful

DEAR MISS MANNERS:

How do you politely tell strangers, acquaintances, or relatives that they need to brush their teeth or even have a dentist clean their teeth? I am interested in this subject from a public health standpoint and for beautification of the city. People with the problem of discolored teeth range from a college professor to clerks at the drug store to people in the local delicatessen.

GENTLE READER:

How public-spirited of you. What do you plan to do for people you consider too fat or too ugly? Find a polite way to mention to them that you really think they ought to do something to beautify the city? Move abroad, for example? There are plenty of legitimate outlets for people who are interested in working or contributing money in the areas of public health or civic beautification. Insulting people on the street is not one of them.

Avoiding Enlightenment

DEAR MISS MANNERS:

A business associate in my office has recently found enlightenment through an Est-like encounter group. He is so enthusiastic about his new passion that he is telling everybody—friends, colleagues, even clients. He has already told me that he "senses" that I would really benefit from taking this "training." Since I have to work with this man, I have always been polite and cordial, but I have absolutely no desire to have any kind of personal relationship with him. I am quite close to his ex-wife and know too much about his personal life from her perspective.

Now this man is repeatedly asking me (and others in the office) to lunch, and I'm sure he wants to proselytize. How can I refuse and continue to maintain a pleasant working relationship with him, and still continue to lunch with other associates? Can I accept on condition that he not discuss his new religion? Can I refuse to discuss certain topics at lunch? Can you come up with a more creative option? I don't think I could keep lunch down if I had to listen to his spiel.

GENTLE READER:

The best way to deal with bores is to avoid them. A good working relationship does not require socializing. You can declare that you already have a lunch date when he asks you or announce your intention to eat alone because you want to think.

Should you get stuck, the polite way to say "Shut up, you're boring me senseless" is "Yes, so you've already told me," accompanied by a vacant smile and followed by a change of subject. You are in a position to add, "You know, I've always put aside any personal information I happen to have heard about you from your ex-wife because we have such a nice professional relationship. Let's keep it that way." That is the polite method of blackmail.

Solicited Advice

"Tell me the truth: How do I look?"
"Like a polar bear. One whose fish got away."

Under what circumstances would Miss Manners permit such an exchange? Note that it is in direct violation of her admonitions that truth is no defense when delivering an insult, that one should never pose an unnecessary question to which one does not want to hear a likely answer, and that requests for reassurance should never be mistaken for the desire to hear the unvarnished truth, an urge that, so far as she knows, does not appear in nature. However, context is almost everything in etiquette, so let us consider the following situations.

1. Person who looks like polar bear (whoops; let's start again). Questioner is recovering from a long illness and wants to know if he is beginning to look normal.

2. Questioner confesses to going off a diet and is anxious about whether the additional poundage shows.

3. Questioner is going through an emotional ordeal and is trying to calculate, before going among outsiders, whether they will be able to detect this.

4. Questioner is about to leave for an important occasion and asks for a last-minute appearance evaluation.

5. Questioner is buying clothing for such an occasion and has brought a friend along on the shopping expedition.

6. Questioner appears before the family or close friends with a new haircut.

7. Questioner appears before the family or close friends with new makeup or a new way of wearing clothing.

8. Questioner is making nervous conversation with her bridesmaids, who have just helped her into her wedding dress.

Cruelly, Miss Manners has to point out that all these people do, in fact, look awful, at least in the opinions of their immediate beholders. Which of these people should have posed that question, and to which is the given answer within the bounds of courtesy?

The practical answer to the first part is that probably none of them should have posed the question. Even the bride can't assume that she is safe from being gone over by a committee of beauty, fashion, and health experts whose ethics do not permit them to consider the effect on the subject when delivering a certifiably impartial opinion. That is rather a shame, Miss Manners believes. Now and again, provided that they don't overdo it, people ought to have a way of asking their intimates to reassure them about their appearance.

Only questions 5 and 7 require visual judgment. In these cases, critical advice is being sought about something in the experimental stage. The Spinach on the Tooth Rule applies: You draw something unfavorable to a person's attention only if it can easily be fixed. Even then, you must be careful not to abuse the privilege. Fitting Room Etiquette requires that the critic confine himself to evaluating the item under consideration, not the figure on which it is displayed or the person's taste and style of dressing in general. Miss Manners' example of a snappy answer would be appropriate only among close friends who tease each other affectionately; the polite form is "I don't think it does anything for you."

The other questions require emotional judgment. The errant dieter might be told, "I don't know; it doesn't show in that outfit," or the person with the new haircut, "I can't tell; I'm sure I'll like it when I get used to it." You may be sure that these statements express quite as much negative opinion as any person can bear.

The others just want some emergency emotional bolstering, which ought to be generously given: "Nobody would ever guess what you'd been through," "You look sensational!", and so on. These are not lies; they are honest answers to the real question: "Do you think I'm all right?" How odd it is that in an age that recognizes that the soul needs occasional pampering, it is assumed that the body seeks only cold and aloof judgments.

Correcting Others

Rudenesses that violate the American concepts of fairness, honest trade, and individual dignity are the etiquette transgressions that people are least able to endure politely, Miss Manners recognizes. We believe in the principle of first come, first served—and then someone cuts into the line or abandons a palpable guest or customer in favor of one who cuts in by telephone. We believe in receiving value for money—and those who ought to be providing it argue unapologetically that they're not responsible, or are going on their lunch break, or it's the computer's fault. We believe in the autonomy of the individual—and find ourselves the targets of insults and advice.

Miss Manners shares these basic beliefs, but she cannot condone maniacal behavior on the grounds that such violations inspired it. She is sorely tried by would-be etiquetteers who report legitimate instances of other people's outrageous behavior and then triumphantly recount how they smashed 'em one in order to further the cause of good manners. The challenge of manners is not so much to be nice to someone whose favor and/or person you covet (although more people need to be reminded of that necessity than one would suppose) as to be exposed to the bad manners of others without imitating them.

That is not to say that one should not fight back. Miss Manners understands perfectly well that one reason retaliatory rudeness is popular is that the only alternative imagined is saintly (or wimpy) sufferance. Not at all. Polite fighting back requires discipline and often patience, but it actually works better. The first line of defense is to offer a face-saving way for the offender to retreat from the offense. "I beg your pardon, but the back of the line is over there," said in a loud, clear voice for the benefit of everyone present, is more effective than a push accompanied by "Hey, where do you think you're going?" Another use of politeness to counter rudeness is to say, with freezing correctness, "You are so kind to take an interest" when asked why you have so many children or offer a devastatingly simple "Thank you" in response to the information that you are overweight. Replying "You should talk!" does not have the same effect. Transgressions that cannot be allowed to pass so easily because of their consequences require more persistent politeness. "Well, then, I will be getting in touch with someone who can help me. What is your name?" No boss is going to listen sympathetically to the complaint of someone his own employee reported as shouting obscenities or threats.

Miss Manners does not lack enthusiasm for fighting rudeness just because she refuses to fight the enemy by joining its ranks. It is, however, impractical to do etiquette combat with everyone who behaves badly, however little it may affect you. A great many people wish to do that. They want to know what they can do about the rudeness of other drivers, fellow guests, and business and social acquaintances. Some of the transgressions are momentarily annoying—a driver has cut in out of turn or made a rude gesture. Others are simply observed—another guest doesn't eat properly. But even if correcting others' behavior unasked were not in itself a violation of etiquette, the sad fact is that you cannot give instant etiquette lessons that will casually change people's behavior for the better. Such engagements are only too likely to lead instead to a change of hostilities characterized by further rudeness.

Miss Manners would like to recommend a dignified, traditional response that has pretty much fallen out of use: Rising Above It. Let the driver or the guest go on his way without any recognition of the error except that inward satisfaction of knowing better than they how to behave. Let us save our energy for the major manners crusades.

Training the Young

DEAR MISS MANNERS:

Having reared five children of my own, I feel that I should be an expert on playground etiquette, but today I came across a new situation. My-two-and-a-half-year-old grandson was atop a climbing platform for a slide when a girl came up to the platform, and he proceeded to point his finger and say "Pow!" I immediately said, "No, no," to him. I could see that the girl's mother was not pleased (and I know my daughter does not allow her son to play with guns), so I made light of it and said, "I guess that's the way to get rid of girls." The mother said, "Is that the way to get rid of girls?" and took her daughter away. Later, I thought that maybe I should have tried to get my grandson to apologize, even though I'm not sure he would have. What should I have done?

GENTLE READER:

One teaches a child that young to apologize not only by explaining why and how but by doing it with him: taking him by the hand, announcing, "Timmy wants to apologize," and then saying, "Timmy?" pointedly until he mumbles something.

The fact is that you both needed to apologize. Your remark about getting rid of girls was offensive.

Now, Miss Manners knows that you didn't mean any insult. However, just as you probably did not question your children's playing with guns, you brought them up in an era when the idea that it is acceptable for boys to exhibit hostility toward girls was commonplace, even amusing. People look at both of these things more seriously now. If you recall how racial and other slurs were also once categorized as easy humor, you will understand that this change in playground etiquette is for the better, and you and your grandson can both learn from this experience.

Coming to Blows Over Compact Discs

DEAR MISS MANNERS:

I feel you should warn your readers that the list of subjects that cannot be safely discussed in polite society should be expanded to include compact-disc players. A few evenings ago, my lady friend and I invited a young couple we had known for years over to dinner. Knowing that the male was an audiophile like myself, I showed him my new compact-disc player and enthusiastically described the tremendous improvement it made in classical music reproduction.

To my surprise, he became quite agitated and excitedly lectured me on the theoretical faults of compact-disc players and digital music reproduction. I learned that he had never actually listened to a compact-disc player, and I insisted on demonstrating it, thinking that this would certainly put his objections to rest. He listened for a few seconds and then shouted at me over the music that the sound was artificial. I shouted back that all music reproduction is artificial. He yelled that if I had a decent system, I could get good music reproduction without resorting to this vile, newfangled gadget.

Can you believe it? The cad insulted my stereo system! A few claims and counterclaims later, he suddenly jumped up, slammed down his drink, and ordered his wife from the house. He himself paused long enough to challenge me to settle our differences outside. While I tried to evaluate my advantage in size and weight against his twenty-five-year age advantage, he contemptuously repeated the challenge. Since my manhood had been seriously questioned, I followed (wondering what the hell I was doing), and upon exiting the house was met by a karate kick to the groin. Fortunately, it was ineptly delivered. The rules have apparently changed in the decades since my last encounter. Always ready to try the new, I kicked my challenger in the posterior and propelled him to his car and out of my life. In the future, I plan to put a discreet cover over my compact-disc player before any social engagements, and I would strongly advise anyone who has one to do the same.

GENTLE READER:

One moment, sir. If you don't mind, Miss Manners will begin by warning her other Gentle Readers not to engage in duels with those who follow the new rules you describe for settling disagreements between gentlemen. Then she must inform you that this disreputable duel took place because you did, in fact, issue your former friend a challenge. You challenged both his judgment and his autonomy. Whether you struck him with gloves or a compact disc is irrelevant.

Many people are, like yourself, under the impression that it is either conversation or philanthropy to indicate that what one owns or believes is better than what others make do with. They are mistaken. It is, in fact, a particularly unpleasant form of showing off, in which as much emphasis is placed on the other person's lack as on one's own good fortune. There are decent ways to show off. You may simply play your music, perhaps make a few self-deprecating remarks about the difficulty of switching systems, and then modestly express your own satisfaction in the result, in the hope of attracting compliments. To announce that what you have is superior to what he has, insensitive to the possibility that he may not choose to replace expensive equipment and a record collection to which he may have also devoted a great deal of thought and effort—or that he may simply disagree with you—is a challenge.

It is not the compact-disc player that needs a discreet cover, sir; it is your pride.

Barroom Instruction

DEAR MISS MANNERS:

While out of town at a government training symposium, my father found himself so annoyed at someone's lack of manners that he almost became involved in a fight. As he tells it, he and three colleagues were enjoying drinks and munchies while watching the news in a bar, when suddenly a loud and boisterous man clad in a business suit flopped down at the table behind my father, nearly knocking over Pop's chair. My father ignored such rudeness until a scene followed at the happy hour buffet. Apparently the man was picking up food with his fingers and not using the appropriate utensils. Even this my father could tolerate; however, when the man bit into a bagel and then returned it to the serving tray, Pop could stand no more. He politely reproached the man for his unsanitary practice. The man denied having done anything wrong and stepped menacingly toward my father. If two of my dad's companions had not intervened and confirmed his complaint, there doubtless would have been fisticuffs.

The problem at hand is the propriety of my father's challenging the manners of this man. My mother, who is a pacifist and a lady, says that Pop should have quietly overlooked the uncouth actions. My father says that he was perfectly justified.

GENTLE READER:

So your father wishes to be one of Miss Manners' little helpers, does he? Going around bars teaching etiquette to the boisterous? How nice. But Miss Manners is not going to come and tend his wounds when he is finished. Politeness itself prevents one from giving freelance lessons in manners, if the instinct for survival does not. Your father would, however, have been justified in complaining to the bartender or proprietor that the unsanitary practices of other patrons prevented him from partaking of a buffet in which others had deposited their partly eaten food.

Rudeness for a Cause

Those who know, beyond any doubt, how to make the world right again (or for the first time in its history) tend to consider it a virtue not to be able to contain themselves, Miss Manners has observed. "Don't you think you've added enough to the population explosion?" they'll inquire of expectant parents, who were also expecting, among other things, to be congratulated. Or it might be a pithy shout to a passer-by on the street: "Hey, the animal looked better in that coat than you do!" Those with more time make surprise requests that other people confess their own complicity in countenancing some evil by having ignored it, or that they defend their politics or religion in the face of one with greater merit.

This is naturally followed by a burst of pride for having humiliated a citizen who was quietly going about his or her business. Lashing out, publicly or socially, is supposed to be a demonstration of the strength of one's convictions. It has been explained to Miss Manners that this behavior represents "being committed"—not to be confused with the other kinds of hostile and disruptive behavior.

Zealotry is no excuse for bad manners, whatever the cause. Even the feeling that the evil which one has spotted is fast dooming the society (as Miss Manners herself is given to musing) does not allow one to suspend decent behavior.

This is not to say that Miss Manners objects to demonstrations or declarations or debates on important topics. There are vigorous ways to attempt to enlighten others, or to get them to change their minds, which are fair. You won't get wily Miss Manners on the charge of stifling free speech or promoting bland conversation. It's only when the talk turns personal that it becomes rude.

Proselytizers, for whatever cause, can offer their opinions publicly in speeches, or by carrying or handing out printed statements. In private, they can propose their topics for discussion, and debate anyone who cares to take on the challenge. If people want to offer themselves as cases in point, they become fair game. Singling individuals out to embarrass them by using them as bad examples or otherwise challenging the way they choose to lead their lives, is not a fair way to offer one's ideas. The hostile surprise attack on people who are minding their own business, adapted from muggers by idealists, remains wrong.

Teaching Intimates

DEAR MISS MANNERS:

How does one teach an adult to say "thank you" and to give compliments as well as accept them? My boyfriend, whether from genetic imbalance or lack of proper training as a boy, has offended my mother by never thanking her for inviting him to dinner. I have done many nice things for him with nary a "thank you." The simplest task would be greatly rewarded if he would only acknowledge it verbally. He is also terrible about complimenting others. Is there any hope for him?

GENTLE READER:

Your only hope of teaching this gentleman manners is not to label them as such but to disguise them with popular jargon:

"I'm sure you don't realize it, but the people we visit often think I'm just dragging you along and you really hate to come." (He looks surprised and asks why anyone would imagine any such thing.) "Well, you know, they've all been brought up to say 'Thank you' automatically to hostesses, and so they think that you must have a deep reason for not doing so. My mother, for instance, is convinced that you don't like her."

"Do you resent my doing things for you? Oh, yes, you must. I know you don't want to hurt my feelings, but I can't help noticing that you never say anything when I try to please you, so I must be doing it all wrong."

"I wish I knew what you like to see me wear. I know it's foolish, but I would like so much to please you, and sometimes when I've taken a lot of care to get dressed up and you never say anything, I feel so deflated. I suppose you don't like it and avoid saying anything so that you won't hurt my feelings."

Personally, Miss Manners is made sick by this style of talking, but then, she does her reforming on a grand scale. Nevertheless, she admires you for undertaking to save a single soul under your jurisdiction and hopes this technique will be of use. It should at least tell you whether he is self-centered in addition to being rude.

Tolerating the Unteachable

DEAR MISS MANNERS:

At least once a day, I hear a snide remark from my dad about two "certain" kinds of people, because of their skin color or their size. This is always said jokingly, and I'm sure that he doesn't realize how prejudiced it sounds. He is in his eighties and senile. Because I respect my dad, I don't know how to approach the subject. He would think I was being too sensitive. But I still feel I should defend my views, even though I doubt that he will change.

GENTLE READER:

Obviously, you are not going to succeed in retraining, much less educating, your father. Attempting it will only annoy you both. However, you can register your disapproval, in order to make yourself feel better, without being disrespectful. Bigoted jokes depend on the assumption that certain traits are linked to certain groups, and failure to acknowledge the connection ("Really? That's not my experience") robs them of their alleged fun.

A Quick Fix

DEAR MISS MANNERS:

Last night, I was seated at dinner next to a gentleman who was generally well dressed, but with indications that it had been a while since his last all-over scrub, and his hair appeared to have been painstakingly coiffed at least several days back. The reason I mention his hair is that there was a small spider dangling behind his left ear, busily spinning a web. I swear, Miss Manners, that I am not making this up. He must have thought his conversation was brilliant because my attention was riveted to him. But I couldn't for the life of me think what to do. I was also apprehensive, I must admit, that the spider might not be the only fauna living in his hair, and that the disappearance of spider number one might be followed by the arrival of number two, and so on. I sat there and said nothing. The rest of the evening went along pleasantly enough, and when I said goodnight to him later on, the spider was still there. For all I know, he's still wearing the thing. Did I do the right thing by remaining silent?

GENTLE READER:

In eighteenth century France, hairstyles were so high and elaborate that, once done, they were left untended for weeks at a time, reputedly attracting not only spiders but mice. Unfortunately, Miss Manners' colleagues of that period neglected to leave instructions on whether or how to inform your dinner partner that he or she was harboring a perhaps unwelcome creature.

We are therefore on our own. Miss Manners trusts that you remember that one informs people of what is immediately correctable that they are likely to notice themselves too late, but not of errors that cannot be fixed or are unlikely to produce retrospective embarrassment.

A spider can clearly be removed on the spot, but its presence is so unthinkable that Miss Manners cannot imagine a gentleman's spotting one as he brushed his teeth that night and not consoling himself that it must have passed unobserved. (If the gentleman is not likely to be in the habit of brushing his teeth, it is even less likely that he will be so troubled.)

It is therefore your choice. Miss Manners would probably have chosen silence, as you did. If, however, you had wished to inform him, you were required to register both vagueness and alarm, an unusual combination. "There's something wrong with your hair; I'm afraid you'd better excuse yourself and go look" must be pronounced in a tone of alarm sufficient to get him moving; but you must also take care not to own up to knowing clearly what the problem is.

Mandated Criticism

DEAR MISS MANNERS:

A few months ago, I got a job at a wonderful company. I admire the pleasant group of people with whom I work, people who would never consider hurting others under normal circumstances. However, I have just discovered that every year, the members of my company go on a retreat where they are required to discuss what they really think about one another. I can't help but believe that this brand of honesty will hurt relationships in the long run, especially when the participants may not be genuinely interested in the others' opinions but feel forced to take part. How can I handle this horrible situation and avoid hurting others or getting my feelings hurt? Maybe I'm different, but I hold grudges and know that I would never feel the same about someone who pointed out my flaws publicly under the guise of doing me a favor.

GENTLE READER:

Miss Manners is opposed to the activity you describe. Having one's flaws pointed out publicly would be a trial even if there were agreement about what "flaws" are and if one needed only to know them to be able to change them. Any seriously offensive practices on the part of employees should be brought to their attention privately by a supervisor. The notion that everyone can and should change to accommodate everyone else's pet peeves also presumes that there is no need to tolerate an acceptable range of human behavior.

If you cannot be excused from these sessions, Miss Manners suggests that you set a standard by stating only that which you find pleasant about the others. People have a way of believing that only unpleasantness is honest, forgetting that appreciation can also be genuine.

A Different Method

DEAR MISS MANNERS:

I take exception to all this smarmy appeasement ("Oh, dear, I'm so sorry but I just can't"). There are times when it is well to stamp your foot, snarl, or even slap a face.

I remember that once when I had lost my job and was collecting unemployment compensation, I was having a friendly conversation with people I knew at a neighborhood bar. A male acquaintance came in and berated me for being out of work when I could easily get a job as a typist somewhere. He asked how I had the nerve to take a government check under the circumstances. I gritted my teeth, froze my face, and said out of the corner of my mouth, "Get lost, buster, or I'll throw this drink right in your face!" Believe me, he scuttled. A few weeks later, he dropped in again, settled safely at a distance, and called over pleasantly that he thought I owed him an apology. I responded that on the contrary, it was he who had insulted me. How would your way have been as effective?

GENTLE READER:

Well, it could hardly have been less effective, could it? The original offender has not apologized to you, and he has failed to be convinced that he did anything wrong. However, he and other witnesses now have an accurate and vivid memory of your being rude. So you only succeeded in shifting the cause of complaint from his rudeness to yours. Do you call that effective?

Let us now imagine Miss Manners in the same situation. At first she says nothing, but simply looks at the man, allowing his words to hang in the air. When the silence has commanded everyone's attention, she says quietly, "It's always a comfort, when things aren't going well, to know you can count on the sympathy of your fellow human beings." She would then have turned away. She dares say that the man would have scuttled away just as quickly as he did from you, if he didn't actually apologize. Nor would he have troubled her again, unless to make a shamefaced admission of understanding what he had done. At the very least, neither he nor anyone else would have had cause to complain of Miss Manners' being rude and vulgar, and thus, by implication, deserving of the same treatment.

Issues of politeness aside, Miss Manners asks you which of the two methods would be, in purely practical terms, more effective—the one that shamed the original wrong-doer or the one that wiped out his offense with the victim's own? And by the way, thank you for applying the word "smarmy" to Miss Manners' life work.

Fashionable Emotions

Nouveaux Riches Bashing

Far be it from Miss Manners to grudge the society a new sport, but the currently popular pastime of nouveaux riches bashing is growing increasingly vulgar. She would like to propose rules to make it more sporting.

Right now, there is altogether too much talk about "new money" and "old money" and how they are spent. The very terms are unseemly in America, where we are supposed to admire ingenuity and industry and to despise unearned assumptions of superiority. Never mind the fact that the most fervent users of these terms seem to be people who made it rich on Thursday and are anxious to heap scorn on those who got rich on Friday. For that matter, no American fortune is so antique as to have its often questionable sources decently obscured.

Freshly acquired riches, because they are in the possession of those who actually did the labor, ought to be the more esteemed. We do not admire an artist's indolent offspring more than the artist; why should heirs be more admired for their fortunes than the ancestors whose abilities amassed them? Miss Manners knows the answer, of course. It is that whatever our principles, earning is never as attractive to us as spending, and the former requires so much time and energy as rarely to leave one with the leisure to learn the fine points of the latter. That much has been going on throughout the history of civilization. Aristocracy, from the pedigreed variety to the fortunately haphazard American version, is merely one stage of a cycle in which the descendants of the newly rich acquire such subtle taste that they ridicule the next newly rich—right before they intermarry with them.

What Miss Manners sees that is different in the current American manifestation is that the subtle tastes and restrained habits that were the redeeming virtues of gently reared heirs have been eroded. Instead, we have a general agreement that admission to the higher ranks is based on prowess in purchasing. Knowing what to buy (or inherit, or pretend to inherit) is the sole test. It is understandable that the newly rich, with their fresh shopping lists and the excitement of being able to indulge themselves, should accept this standard. It seems simple enough, and fun, too. They will soon correct their excesses, but only to start bashing the even more newly rich.

Equally at fault are the many theorists who do not claim to be rich but who ruthlessly analyze people's belongings as if they were significant clues. Except among full-time status seekers, sentiment, availability, individual preference, and mere chance have a lot to do with these things. What you own is just not all that indicative of who you are.

Miss Manners may seem to be taking the sappily virtuous stand that one must refrain from making any judgment until appreciation of the inner soul is possible. Not at all. She just has a better superficial standard to suggest.

It is, of course, manners. How you choose to behave is, she submits, a pretty good basis for justifiable snobbery. She would tend to go easy, at first, on newcomers to the details of refined manners. The tricks of advanced etiquette must be learned by those who have not acquired them at home, but they are not that difficult. Besides, nobody seems to acquire them at home these days—the rich are as poorly brought up as anyone and as unlikely to be able to negotiate a formal dinner or proper evening clothes—so people are starting more or less even. Miss Manners would be ruthless about the more general manners of behaving decently to others, exhibiting consideration when there is a conflict of wishes, and exercising control when expressing dissatisfaction. That is something everyone can acquire and knows about.

Nouveaux Riches Defined

DEAR MISS MANNERS:

I need to know whether I am Old Money or still classifiable as Nouveau Riche. My mother thinks I am Old Money because I am three generations removed from the one who made the money. My boyfriend's mother thinks I am Nouveau Riche because the person who made the money is within recent memory and, worse, might show up at the wedding. The problem is my boyfriend's grandmother, an elderly matriarch who screens all prospective marriage candidates. She has made it clear that she does not wish to be introduced to Nouveau Riche girls. My boy-friend and his mother are flexible about these things, but we would all like to accommodate Granny, particularly since although Granny cannot remember who made their money, she has most of it.

GENTLE READER:

Miss Manners regrets to tell you that everybody mentioned in this letter is Nouveau Riche. Nouveau Riche is an attitude, rather than a date on the bank account. Only the Nouveaux Riches worry about the age of other people's money. Everybody else, including Old Money, merely worries about money.

Envy

There is such a thing, in Miss Manners' opinion, as bringing what is decently hidden too far out in the open. Husbands or wives who admit to being "threatened" by their spouses' successes, lonely people who voice their discomfort at having to witness the domestic pleasures of others, friends who examine everyone else's possessions in terms of their own chances of acquiring them—these are all members of the "What about me?" society. And an unattractive lot of spoilsports they are, too. Whatever happens to anyone else is, to them, an opportunity for unfavorable comparison with their own condition. The better anyone else's life is, the worse they feel. This does not do a lot to spread merriment in the world.

Wet blankets are flapping around in open air. There is no pleasure, however small, that they do not attempt to dampen with a dour announcement about how bad the happiness of others makes them feel. You got promoted? What about me? I've been stuck in the same job forever. You're having a baby? What about me? I can't even find a mate. You have a new house? What about me? I can barely afford to pay my rent.

The bolder members of the "What about me?" crowd even complain that it is rude of others to make them feel bad by the effrontery of being happy. If they had any consideration for me, they wouldn't indulge themselves. Wasn't that mean, they will complain, to invite me to their anniversary party when they know I have to live alone now? Imagine wishing me a happy summer! They know I'll be stuck at work while they're off vacationing. Never mind how it makes the person who was happy feel when he finds that those whom he assumed wished him well actually begrudge it to him.

Sometimes "What about me?" is barely disguised as the sharing of similar experiences. It is socially acceptable to offer limited relevant stories from one's own life upon hearing another person's news, provided that one does not attempt to top fresh news with reminiscences. However, if the moral of the tale is "Don't be so pleased now, because here's an example of how things can turn to disaster," it is not acceptable. You can tell a bride about your own wedding, but not about your divorce; you can tell a prospective parent about the pleasures of having children, but not about birth defects. One can learn to say "I'm so happy for you" with a cheerful smile. The smiling time can be used to swallow the words "Yes, but what about me?"

Vulnerability

Who was it who decreed that the most attractive personal characteristic a modern lady or gentleman can possibly have is vulnerability? Somehow word got out, and the society is now full of vulnerable people. You find them everywhere, those sensitive souls with their sad faces turned in remonstrance at obscure slights or in expectation of being hurt, constantly pleading for reassurance.

"You have to be nice to me," they say, as if we behave kindly only when directed to do so and as if we don't require kindness ourselves.

"You're just saying that to be nice, but you couldn't really mean it."

"I've been treated so badly (by parents, spouse, lover, life) that you have to be especially careful with me."

"You're probably tired of me, aren't you?"

Miss Manners has to muster all her training to stop herself from replying to that last question, "Why, yes, actually." She does find constant fishing for reassurance to be tiresome. An occasional request to an intimate—"Do I look all right?" or "How do you think the party went?"—is fine, but people who constantly plead for compliments, affection, and consideration are going to find their worst prophecies fulfilled.

Miss Manners disputes their claim to being considered sensitive. Claiming the right to special treatment on the grounds that one has been more deeply affected by life's ills, or that one has a more easily bruised soul than others, is simply arrogant.

It is insensitive to ask for more kindness than one is prepared to give, stating, in effect, a refusal to do one's full share of the obligations. The person who claims to be hurt because someone hasn't been in touch as often as desired should be told, "Well, if you wanted to talk to me, why didn't you call?" It is only too clear, in such cases, that the sullen one was not spending his time missing the other person, but counting up his grudges. Keeping careful count of how much each person does for the other is itself unfriendly, but doing so with the expectation that the count should come out unevenly, in one's own favor, is particularly unappealing.

Maintaining a civil relationship with people who go in for this sort of vulnerability is, Miss Manners admits, a strain. There is something about that pleading look such people maintain that sorely tempts one to give them what they expect. It brings out the desire to say, in effect, "If you must snivel, let me give you something to snivel about." Miss Manners will not, she is almost sorry to say, allow you to give in to this unpleasant impulse, but she does not require you to submit to emotional blackmail.

Mad and Not Mad

For all the talk about feelings in this society, people seem to recognize only two emotions in anyone other than themselves. These are Mad and Not Mad. Not Mad is the one you needn't do anything about.

Analyzing and expressing one's own infinitely varied and subtle feelings have been a national sport for some time now, and naturally it is a nuisance for anyone so engaged to be interrupted to deal with anyone else's. The common solution, Miss Manners has noticed, is to sort other people's feelings into these two rough categories and then to ignore the second group.

The first one cannot be safely ignored. Mad people do all sorts of unpleasant things, such as screaming, making scenes, slamming or breaking inanimate objects, and demanding to stay up all night talking things out. You must therefore placate the mad person, which is a lot of trouble. You have to find out why he is mad and what he expects you to do before he will agree to cease being mad. If you do not agree that the stipulated requirement is fair, you must bargain with the person, perhaps using anger of your own as a tool, until you establish mutually satisfactory terms for a truce.

The fear of bringing all this on is a powerful deterrent. So, if you know that something you do or fail to do will make another person mad, you will probably adjust your behavior accordingly. (If, on the contrary, it encourages you to get that anger going for the entertainment value, Miss Manners only asks you to find a partner who likes it, too, and stay out of the way of more peaceful souls, such as herself.)

What about that other category, Not Mad? What about those who, like Miss Manners, do not employ Going Over the Brink as a method of forcing their preferences to be treated seriously? Gentle souls have wishes and rights, too. They are not necessarily timid about stating these, either. They state them politely, however firmly, and therefore find themselves in the category of Not Mad. Does this mean that the requests of polite people are more apt to be ignored than those of people whose ordinary behavior includes Getting Mad? Yes, it does.

It is sadly but undoubtedly true that the world is full of spouses, lovers, friends, colleagues, employers, and even employees who feel it safe to ignore the reasonably stated requests of individuals who can be assumed not to go—or rather act—mad.

As a result, some disillusioned souls desert the ranks of the Not Mad and retrain their associates to treat them as carefully as they treat the Mad. Then there is so much less gentleness and sanity in the world. Others, who can't quite bear to do that, try an intermediate stage, Sad. In other words, they mope or cry when disappointed, hoping that pity for sadness will accomplish the same results as fear of madness. "Yes, I guess you did mention it once, but I didn't know you meant it." "How was I to know that you felt so strongly about it?"

Miss Manners hereby requests everyone to cooperate in lessening the anger level in this society. Getting mad, and failing to pay attention to the needs of others unless they get mad, only creates a world in which ever more stridency will be required to make oneself heard. She is only going to say this once, in her mild, ladylike voice. But she means it.

Future Nostalgia

When nostalgia first hit this country like a tidal wave a decade or two ago, Miss Manners was rather pleased. She dared to hope that she might never again have to hear the word "relevant" as a test of what was important.

A belated general recognition that the society has its traditions, including coherent and workable standards of behavior, could only do her cause good, Miss Manners thought.

Mind you, Miss Manners is not complaining, but people have now gone beyond respecting the past to anticipating it. Future nostalgia, as it were, is a conscious attempt to make history out of the present. What it is making out of the present is havoc.

Through the magic of video technology, birthday parties, too, are staged for future enjoyment, and so, for that matter, are births. Remember the time when the only way to embarrass a newly engaged son or daughter was to bring out a baby snapshot? Now only the state of the parents' technology limits their ability to humiliate the child. Vacations have long been opportunities to spoil everyone's fun so that the evidence of having gone away can be savored later.

What used to be dignified social events are scoured by the participants for artifacts. Miss Manners was shocked to read of a prominent dress designer that she was glad she had attended a White House dinner wearing a skirt "with big pockets," because "I had to take home the napkins, the matches, the menu, and the flags to remind myself that it really happened." The flags? Didn't she like the furniture?

What these people are forgetting, besides a sense of decorum, is that one has to spend time participating in an event if one hopes to get any memories out of it. There is a reason that these laboriously recorded pictures and carefully gathered artifacts are hardly ever brought out afterward and have a reputation for imposing massive boredom if they are.

Miss Manners is wary enough of a nostalgia that venerates old rubbish, as if everything had intrinsic value. Yesterday's junk is tomorrow's artifact, she supposes. But she draws the line at anticipatory nostalgia. That is memory building at the expense of living.

Dress

Fashion Statements

Two examples of big fashion stories are, in Miss Manners' authoritative opinion, the following:

A. The Prime Minister of Canada suggests that heads of government attending an economic summit conference in Toronto dress casually. The Prime Minister of Great Britain, having unilaterally escalated formality by wearing hats, shows up dressed in silk with pearls and high heels. She is quoted as having refused to participate in "a lowering of standards." The Prime Minister of Canada wears a suit.

B. A Washington messenger is barred from entering the Department of Justice while wearing a T-shirt referring to the then chief executive of that establishment as a pig. He responds by:

1. Unsuccessfully arguing the right of free speech.

2. Unsuccessfully offering to remove the T-shirt in return for access to the building, presumably shirtless.

3. Successfully arranging to have an acceptably dressed replacement sent from the messenger service in time to deliver the goods as promised.

4. Delivering his problem to the American Civil Liberties Union, which suc-

cessfully argues his right of free speech. The Department of Justice reverses its ruling after talk of the ACLU's filing a First Amendment lawsuit.

What do these two stories teach us? Quite a bit about politics, notably that it makes a lot of difference who is doing the talking. Also that anyone hoping to maintain a higher standard than the society generally recognizes has to be prepared to lend practical assistance. If the Department of Justice, like certain restaurants and clubs, kept articles of "proper attire" on hand to lend to those whom it deemed improperly dressed, solution 2 might have worked and there might not have been a need to escalate to solution 4.

The etiquette angle of all this is, naturally, more subtle. High symbolism, and some of the low kind as well, is involved. Social symbolism is not something in which modern people are skilled, and summer heat seems to rob them of any dexterity they might have. Each year, a number of otherwise relatively civilized gentlemen can be counted upon to raise a battle cry against the tyranny of the necktie. The quieter ones only rage about the extreme discomfort they claim to suffer from "a few inches of silk"; the more adventurous go on to suggest a full-scale clothing revolution so that each man (nonenthusiasts being stigmatized as "insecure") can express his true self.

Miss Manners hopes that sensible people can see the fallacy here. Clothing does express individual taste, but only within the context of the community. Who one "is" refers not only to the contents of the particular heart or mind but also to the age, gender, era, nationality, and specific activity in which one happens to be engaged at a given time. To choose clothing that violates those requirements is to broadcast that one is in conflict with them. The person who dresses much younger than he or she is draws ridicule; the one who wears sports clothes to a wedding or fancy clothes to a barbecue is perceived as wishing to show distance from, and by implication superiority to, the others present.

When the British Prime Minister refused to don clothes appropriate to relaxation, she was refusing to pretend that the economic summit was an informal gathering of friends rather than an occasion of serious international business. (Incidentally, by going in for feminine formality rather than attempting to adapt the male standard, she refused symbolically to concede that there is anything legitimate about associating the running of governments with masculinity.)

Miss Manners is less ready to cheer on the messenger, although she concedes that bumper sticker T-shirts seem to be the conventional uniform of the profession. Nevertheless, since they proclaim the wearer's presumed sentiments, it seems reasonable to hold the wearer as accountable for them as if he were uttering the statements publicly aloud or carrying them on a sign. In most situations, that would merely mean that the bearer should be prepared for counterattacks by people exercising the right of free speech. To those who have hardly noticed or have forgotten what their T-shirts that day happen to be proclaiming, this could be puzzling.

When the statement is likely to provoke immediate outrage in the location where it is displayed, the situation is more delicate. Miss Manners is extremely fond of the First Amendment, but she understands that it does not preclude certain restrictions (in regard to obscenity or even legitimate political protest) when the prospect of harm exists. Her idea of what is fair would be not to treat all T-shirts equally, but to treat a message-bearing shirt no differently than one would a picketer or public speaker delivering the same message. If this discouraged people from using themselves as billboards, she would not be sorry. The confinement of a necktie is not nearly as risky as offering one's innermost views to the chance reactions of strangers.

Protest Dress

DEAR MISS MANNERS:
I find myself quite caught up in litigation these days. What does a lady wear to her first felony trial? This is clearly a significant occasion. I do so want to do the Right Thing; even more, I want the jury to do the Right Thing. Surely, appropriate attire is integral to a speedy acquittal.

GENTLE READER:
Naturally, what one wears to a trial should have no bearing on the jury's finding. Naturally, what one wears to a trial has an influence on the jury. This is because in the complex process of determining what is just, juries take into consideration the view that the defendant has toward society and its laws. Is she, for example, someone who has been driven by conscience to violate a law or someone who routinely defies society, in big matters and small, out of lack of respect, a feeling of superiority, or simply for amusement?

By your small politenesses in the course of your action, you demonstrated that you subscribe to the idea that one follows the conventional gestures of one's society in order to reassure others that one means them no harm. Dressing in conformity with the most conservative standards of the community should not win you a speedy acquittal, but it should signal the jury that you respect society's standards.

General Appearance

DEAR MISS MANNERS:
A gentleman acquaintance of mine, a weekly guest for four years, has been barred from our house by my mother, who is displeased by the length of his hair. What exactly can a mother do about the hair length of someone else's child? After stating her opinion, how far can she go in enforcing it? She has offered to drive him to the barbershop of his choice. The objection is merely to the hair—and other than its length, he takes very good care of it—as the gentleman in question does not behave in the manner usually associated with long hair.

GENTLE READER:

When Miss Manners' dear late Aunt Grace was a girl, her father barred the door to one of her beaux because he wore a gold earring. He allowed another beau, conventional and shy, to continue calling. The first was Ezra Pound and the second D.H. Lawrence.

Aside from the fun of literary name dropping, Miss Manners recounts this story to alert parents that you never can tell. Had the vigilant papa but known how these two would turn out, he would still have pitched out the eccentric young man, of course, but he would have taken care to send the presentable-looking one sprawling after him.

Miss Manners does not deny that appearance is symptomatic of social attitude, only that it is difficult to read, especially in the young. In your case, the young man's supposed defiance of polite society in wearing long hair is extremely mild. One might even consider it nonexistent, as the current era admits a greater range of socially acceptable hair lengths than most earlier ones did.

Miss Manners disagrees with your mother about barring the door on such slight provocation. That is her privilege, however—but it is her only privilege. Even telling the caller that his hair is offensive is a violation of etiquette. One may only tell one's child and allow the child to pass on the explanation, presumably with her own disagreement. The mother's attempt to enforce her own standard is a really serious violation. For all she knows, the young man may only be dutifully copying the style of his father.

Mistaken Gender

DEAR MISS MANNERS:

I believe I have what could be considered a modern problem. It is that I am occasionally mistaken for a member of the opposite sex.

I am a college-age woman who strives to behave in a genteel manner. It may be my appearance by which I unintentionally deceive people. I dress in the uniform of youth: jeans, running shoes, oversized jacket. I wear no makeup, and my hair is cut short. Since I am not about to change my appearance, would Miss Manners please suggest a kind way to correct the people who make such mistakes? I know that the reply to "Are you a boy or a girl?" should be silence or, if one wants to be rude, "None of your business." But how does one correct a salesperson who says, "May I help you, young man?"

GENTLE READER:

Without questioning your predilection for wearing what you call the uniform of youth, Miss Manners would like to point out that you have omitted from your appearance any clues as to your gender. As strangers are often addressed in a gender-related form ("Sir," "Madam"), people who need to talk to you may well request the information or blunder in guessing. (People who don't need to talk to you, such as passing strangers calling out comments in the street, should indeed be ignored.) When there are no nonvisual clues provided, such as your name or your voice (although those are not always gender distinct, either) wouldn't it be possible for you either, to ignore a mistaken reference or to say, "Actually, I'm *not* a young man"?

Fear of Formality

A lady of Miss Manners' acquaintance was trying to persuade her fiancé to wear a tie.

"It's not that formal an occasion, is it?" he pleaded.

"Our wedding?" she replied.

Miss Manners is in favor of strewing life with special occasions when it is worth making an effort. Life is a drab affair if there is no sense of solemnity or festivity to relieve the ordinary routine—when "It's no big deal" describes every hand. Actually, a great many more people than admit to it secretly enjoy formality. They grumble when forced to comply with its regulations, but secretly they think they look rather cute dressed up—and so they do—and they come home pleased with their own behavior and conversation. Total relaxation does not seem to inspire creative flirtation or wit.

This is not to say that Miss Manners wants rent or tuition money to be diverted into a glove fund or that she tries to prod people of simple tastes into making a display of themselves. Formality is a relative concept, and she includes the effort of combing the hair and washing up for family dinner, so that there is something special about that daily event, as well as energies invested in more elaborate rites and traditions.

The attitude she finds disturbing is not that of genuine indifference —people who feel that way naturally go along with the requirements for other people's special occasions—but the attempt to sabotage formality. Miss Manners believes this to be motivated by a Fear of Formality that afflicts people who generally participate eagerly in the consumer crazes of the society.

One such fear is that dignity is pretentious and bespeaks a totalitarian attitude. There are adults who love expensive wines and audiovisual entertainment but who also love to denounce the trappings of formality as materialism. They congratulate themselves on their humanistic values in the act of snubbing others by refusing to participate appropriately in events those people deem important.

Formality is neither unfriendly nor pretentious. But it is merely an alternate style, appropriate to dignified occasions. A variation is that formality is appropriate only to certain age groups. It is one of those universally held individual secrets that nobody truly feels grown up. Miss Manners admits to being an exception to the rule about believing oneself to be a twelve-year-old in disguise. She happened to be born at full maturity and proceeded to an imperious and eccentric dotage while outwardly disguised as a toddler. Nevertheless, she understands that slightly comic fear that most people have of being caught impersonating adults. Every generation has had it, but former ones managed to enjoy the irony of that feeling without allowing it to cripple their period of command.

Then something strange happened. Big people not only started trying to pass themselves off publicly as youths on the grounds that it was more fun to be nubile and carefree than experienced and responsible, but grew wary of assuming any of the grand trappings of maturity, to which youth itself had traditionally aspired.

Formality was always considered the privilege of maturity. Little girls dreamed of being old enough to wear high heels and black strapless dresses long before women dreamed of looking young enough to wear children's clothes. Little boys tried to swagger like grown men before grown men tried to jog and act like boys.

There is now a renewed interest in the luxury and sheer swank of formality, but the current adult generation's fear of being unmasked has prevented the straightforward, confident assumption of this style. Instead, formality is being sabotaged by the very people who practice it. In the name of cordiality or humor or originality or unpretentiousness, they mangle tradition into an unattractive hybrid. With hilarious exaggeration, they don long black gloves and sequined stockings, or plaid dinner jackets and top hats, to parody conventionality. Unfortunately, Miss Manners is neither grateful nor amused by this tiresome joke.

Miss Manners has nothing against cordiality, humor, originality, and unpretentiousness. They are all valuable qualities to possess. She only claims that tradition is valuable as well. Obviously, as the legacy of a respected past, it is the very opposite of original. That alone should make it worthy of respect, not constantly to be satirized or otherwise undermined.

Coat and Tie

DEAR MISS MANNERS:

I am a rancher in South Texas. Despite the climate, some of us Texans still appear in public in a coat and tie or the equivalent, as our ancestors did (however inexpensive or worn the clothing may have been). I understand that this is still proper; it is certainly more private. One does not have to display defects in anatomy and skin, or show pocket items or perspiration.

Why the bigotry against people like us nowadays? Hosts insist on taking our coats and ties; even other guests nag. It seems that the only way to keep one's clothing is to claim that one has spilled food on his shirt and needs the coat to cover it. No one feels threatened around a slob with a dirty shirt. Are all Americans so insecure nowadays?

GENTLE READER:

Let us rather say naive. People who profess a belief in individuality always seem to try to tyrannize those of us whose choices are different from theirs.

In the name of comfort, they harass people who are most comfortable when properly dressed.

The idea that, deep down, everyone who is being honest about it would like to behave like a slob isn't true. Some of us put on a nonchalant air of informality only when necessary to meet the conventions of society. We really like formality, both aesthetically and for the way people tend to live up to it. Miss Manners urges you not to give in to this silly peer pressure, even to the extent of making any excuse. A firm "Thank you, but I prefer to keep my jacket" is enough.

The Ascot Tie

DEAR MISS MANNERS:

A few nights back, I was refused entrance to a restaurant. I was dressed in tailored slacks, sport coat, proper shirt, and ascot tie. The management claimed that it was necessary to have a buttoned shirt collar and tie, though a string tie would suffice. I have worn ascot ties off and on for years, and they have been fully acceptable in the best places.

GENTLE READER:

They are certainly acceptable at the races, which is where—from the races at Ascot, England—they take their name. Ascots have a funny social life. They are excellent at the most formal daytime situations (gray ascots with stiff shirts may be worn with the morning cutaway) or at rather spiffy informal occasions with open-necked shirts. But they do not qualify to take the place of a tie on those ordinary, boring occasions, such as business and nondressy but not sporty evening events, that constitute most of a modern gentleman's life.

Evening Dress

Formality requires a different type of ingenuity than does the sort of free-for-all open competition for originality that has so many people going about in broad daylight identically dressed in corporate-logo T shirts. It is conducted at a level of subtlety that saves you the trouble of dying your hair green or pasting sequins on your nose, only to make the discouraging discovery that everyone else at the party has done it, too. The idea is not to be funny. One can dress to stand out, but only if one is clever enough to do so while obeying the rules, so that a general visual homogeneity prevails.

That rules out dances at which the ladies are in evening dresses but the gentlemen are in daytime clothes. Or weddings at which the groomsmen are in white tie, the fathers in black tie, and the male guests in business suits. Or parties at which some ladies are in long dresses, some in short ones, and some in pants.

Not only should all the guests look as if they are attending the same event, but consistency is required from the top to the bottom of each person. Miss Manners does ask ladies not to spoil the effect of their pretty dresses with leather bags, leather shoes, or other daytime accessories. Evening gloves are white kid or doeskin, with any jewelry kept inside. Hats are not worn, but flowers, feathers, or jewels may be placed directly in the hair.

The point is to express individuality with small, pleasant shocks rather than knockout blows. Ladies have, of course, more leeway than gentlemen, for whom the competition is to see how close one can come to the ideal in tailoring and details, not how far one can stray from it. Black is the acceptable evening color for gentlemen, with midnight blue allowed those who must break with conformity and express their innermost souls. Any touches of red, plaid, or brocade should at least not be visible to the general company. Miss Manners considers it no compliment to a lady for a gentleman to wear a tie with her colors, as if she had had material left over from her dress and tied it on her pet.

Black tie and the more formal white tie seem to have gotten strangely mixed up. Wing-collared shirts belong with white tie only (never mind what the rental shop told you: the black band around the back of the neck looks like a major case of ring around the collar); black tie requires pleated shirts, not ruffled; and the choice of wearing a cummerbund, rather than a waistcoat, does not exist for white tie as it does for black tie. Miss Manners trusts that all this will not dampen anyone's festive spirits, and hastens to assure you that the joys of playing well according to the rules are as great as refusing to recognize that there are any.

Duplicate Dresses

DEAR MISS MANNERS:

What is the proper behavior for a lady who, after carefully selecting her attire, attends a formal or semiformal event, only to find another lady present wearing the same dress? On both occasions when this has happened to me, my attention was drawn to the problem, once by the other lady's escort and once by the other lady herself. This usually takes the form of a clever remark like "Nice dress," accompanied by a sneer. I feel that this is rude, and it serves only to increase my own discomfort and mortification.

I hope that I will not find myself in this situation again, but as I seem to have rather typical tastes, it is a possibility. Should I practice my hollow laugh (which I learned from you), effective in so many encounters with tactless people? Am I out of line by being offended? I do not wish to compound the error by behaving foolishly myself.

GENTLE READER:

The joke that ladies, being in constant and vicious sartorial competition, go to pieces when they see another lady wearing the same dress—while identically

dressed men stand around and laugh—is certainly one of the staple bores of obsolescent gender humor. Miss Manners hardly thinks it even worth one of her hollow
laughs—perhaps a hollow smile. This is done with an immobile face, except for the
closed lips being turned up at the corners without moving the center of the mouth.
It is directed at whoever makes the joke. The mouth is then opened to show the
teeth, in a social semismile, to the lady who is dressed like you, to whom you say,
"I admire your taste."

Hats and Gloves

The shops are full of hats and gloves. Miss Manners can hardly believe her eyes.
Is it possible that she will soon be able to walk around in broad daylight dressed
like a lady without making a spectacle of herself? It is now some decades since
Miss Manners was instructed in the use of these badges of ladyhood by her dear
mother. It is even some years since Miss Manners began to notice that such conventional—even banal—items as her little white gloves in summer or her hats at
teatime were being regarded as eccentricities. Although she enjoyed the thrill of
shocking society with her outrageous and original style, she is more than willing
to trade that distinction for company. She is aware that the new hats and gloves
are likely to be worn as humorous adjuncts to outfits for which they were never intended, in the spirit of Post-Modernist Dressing, but she wants, as a matter of historic record, to pass on the rules.

Only in very modern times (an era known to Miss Manners as Since Everything
Went to Pot) have either ladies or gentlemen habitually gone bareheaded. It was
not just that a lady or gentleman would not dream of going out without a hat; one
wouldn't go to bed without a nightcap. (On the head. Drinking habits are about the
same as they have always been.)

One was certainly not considered dressed without something on the head.
"Hairdressing" meant dressing the hair: An elaborate evening coiffure was not
complete without jewels, flowers, or feathers among the curls. Even informally
dressed ladies who were just hanging around the house wore flouncy caps.

In the twentieth century, evening head dressing shrank to the cocktail hat and
"headache band," and the at-home decoration to scarves done up in bundles of
various shapes. Then even these pretty much disappeared, leaving ladies only the
daytime going-out hat. (Gentlemen's daytime and evening hats remained nearly
the same for much longer.) No matter how fiercely fashion tried to blow away hats
entirely, many people hung on to them. Cowboys, taxi drivers, fishermen, baseball
players, and others still knew that a hat was part of one's identity and dignity.

The last coherent rules (the ones Miss Manners learned as a girl) were:

A lady always wears a hat when she goes out in the daytime, and without fail for
dress-up occasions such as weddings, funerals or other religious services, and formal luncheons and teas. She does not remove the hat until she reenters her house,
where she must never wear one, even when entertaining guests who are expected
to do so. For evening, what calls itself a hat should be only an anchor for miscella-

neous items from the notions department, the sorts of thing that used to be part of the hairdressing.

The gentleman's hat is, with certain religious exceptions, only a sign of respect in his gesture of removing it. (The swift-minded will realize that he must therefore be wearing one.) He wears it only outdoors or in large public indoor spaces (stadiums, but not elevators); even outdoors, he lifts it slightly upon greeting a lady.

Gloves are also never worn in one's own house, and hardly ever by gentlemen in anyone else's, opera and dancing gloves for men having disappeared heaven knows where. Ladies wear gloves when they are guests. They need not remove gloves for shaking hands or dancing, but if a lady so much as touches anything to eat or drink with a glove on, warts will grow all over the hand underneath.

Handbag Placement

DEAR MISS MANNERS:

Each time I dine out, I face a small predicament: where to put my purse. I use a clutch-style purse for formal to semiformal dinners, but even that can sometimes be a bit large. As many restaurants seat two guests at a tiny table, it is difficult to put it on the table and awkward for me, my escort, and the waiter to have to work around it. I've experienced the "Don't you know where to put that thing?" look, but unfortunately, the answer is "No."

It sometimes slips off the lap to the floor during conversation, and I won't even mention the loud "thump" when it hits the floor and my ever-so-essential articles come spilling out. Besides, the napkin goes there. If I'm in a chair with no arms, I can't very well slip it between my body and the arm of the chair. Even if I can, it might fall through the opening between the seat and the arm. And who wants to put a pretty purse on the floor?

I await your answer with purse in hand.

GENTLE READER:

Yes, it does properly go on the lap, and yes, it is a jolly nuisance there. You don't even mention the possibility of dancing, but clapping a metal minaudiere against a gentleman's back has an adverse affect on graceful twirling. You will find it easier to keep the purse from slipping off the lap if you fold the napkin around it. You may also request an extra chair to park it on. If enough ladies did so, perhaps restaurants would come up with a simpler solution to a problem that is theirs as well as their customers.

The Bottom Button

DEAR MISS MANNERS:

All my life, I have been adjured that the bottom button of a man's vest should *never* be buttoned. But I like to keep it buttoned. It covers a multitude of sins. How much of an iconoclast am I?

GENTLE READER:

You are certainly a rebel, but the personage against whom you are rebelling is King Edward VII, who invented that fashion for the accommodation of his personal girth. Perhaps you would be more comfortable considering yourself a loyalist, instead, to dear Prince Albert.

Ostentation

That does it. Miss Manners has seen one diamond watch too many with a dual-color metal band and one car too many so long that it can't turn corners. She is going to start proposing sumptuary laws. Sumptuary laws were generally hopeless attempts to prevent a society from indulging in so much ostentatious display that it made those with less money sick. No, that's not quite it. They were an ultimately vain attempt to control vanity.

Before attempting to bring in the law, Miss Manners will simply try appealing to people's better nature to exercise some restraint. Just in case that doesn't go over, she will also appeal to their worst nature. The better argument is that when display goes beyond the purchase of valuable things for aesthetic pleasure or practicality, to serving merely as signals to others of how much money you can afford to waste, it is intended as an offense. In a society where the rich establish the rule that you are what you purchase, they are deliberately stirring up envy and anger. A nastier, but no less true, argument is that ostentatious spenders are the objects of ridicule from those higher up—or longer established—on the scale of snobbery. Their judgment is that by spending conspicuously, you are only demonstrating that you haven't been rich long enough to inherit your valuables. This perhaps equally vulgar reasoning has the effect of disguising pride in money so that it presents a surface appearance of good taste. Miss Manners is always happy enough to see that not to argue about the motives.

Underwear

DEAR MISS MANNERS:

My son is a fully developed sixteen-year-old. From time to time, our next-door neighbor, Judy, has been in our home visiting us, and my son has walked around in his brief underwear. He feels there is nothing wrong with this, since he considers our neighbor as almost part of our family. My wife and he say that his non-see-throughable underwear is no different from my brief bathing suits, which I wear while working outside and around the house in summer. I see that similarity, but I still feel that there is a noticeable difference, and that it is wrong.

GENTLE READER:

Would you wear pajamas to the office, explaining that they cover as much as a business suit? Would your wife wear a strapless ball dress in the backyard, claiming that it exposes the same amount of skin as a bathing suit with a cover-up sarong skirt?

Wearing underwear in front of visitors is an insult. Not only does it imply that the visitor is not worth dressing for, but it suggests that a sexual relationship exists of a nature that does not require observing even minimum standards of formality.

Undress

DEAR MISS MANNERS:

Frequently, young women appear naked at the apartment pool where I like to have a daily swim. Oh, there's a wisp of fabric here and there, but essentially, they are naked. Though I am a man of mature years, I confess to a residual interest in what is exposed. But chiefly, I am embarrassed by and for the young women.

I am puzzled as to proper behavior. Consider the following: A friend and I, entering an office building, were startled to observe immediately ahead of us a young woman with her backside exposed from the waist down. I was dumbfounded; my friend, with more presence, immediately saw that the young woman's wraparound skirt had not been properly adjusted. He discreetly apprised her of the situation. She thanked him and adjusted her skirt.

Should I discreetly apprise them of the nakedness, assuming they don't know and would appreciate being told? My mind quavers and numbs at the thought that the nakedness is intentional. But assuming that it is, what is the proper response? Pretense, the-emperor-has no-clothes-style, that there is no breach of decorum?

GENTLE READER:

Please, sir. Miss Manners sympathizes with your state of shock, but get a grip on yourself. It is convention, not yardage, that determines decency in clothing, and the ladies at the pool, who are technically wearing bathing suits, are not indecent. When you calm down, you will acknowledge that there is a difference between accident and fashion, and that the poolside ladies, unlike the unwrapped one in the wraparound skirt, are not dressed as they are because they failed to notice that their muumuus fell off in the elevator. There is nothing for you to do except the one task that a gentleman must perform, no matter how difficult he finds it: pretending that he does not notice.

Standards of Undress

DEAR MISS MANNERS:

I have moved from the prudish Midwest to the laid-back West Coast, and along the way have acquired a hot tub. I still frequently see a number of friends of the

Wisconsin persuasion. I enjoy entertaining at my home, and am ever in a quandary regarding the appropriate approach to varying degrees of undress. Although I wouldn't think twice about stepping in with my friends and acquaintances, especially in my own house, should I:

1. tell my friends that dress/undress is up to the individual?

2. in a spirit of cautious empathy, wear a bathing suit, thereby setting the tone in this matter? or

3. announce that suits are not customary in my tub but will be tolerated if the wearer insists, and that those who would feel uncomfortable need not participate . . . or what?

P.S. How do I address my parents on this matter?

GENTLE READER:

The last one is easy. You say, "Mommy, Daddy, did you know that people generally go into these tubs naked together?" and, depending on whether they reply "Oh, boy!" or "WHAT?," you can either say, "Want to try it?" or "Of course, I was properly brought up."

The question about guests is more difficult, and solutions 1 and 3 are terrible. You do not embarrass guests by making them either declare themselves in a way that leaves them open to teasing or submerge their real feelings, as it were. Nor is it ever proper to have separate dress standards for guests at the same party.

One solution is simply to give bathing-suit parties for your friends from the Midwest. At worst, you will disappoint them until they make timid inquiries about local practices, and you can reply, "Well, we certainly can take these off if you want." Another is to ask them ahead of time whether they prefer "West Coast style" or bathing suits. While this has the same meaning as making them say whether they wish to bathe naked, the effect is different because you are making the difference sound regional rather than psychological.

Going Barefoot

DEAR MISS MANNERS:

I am most comfortable in decent weather when I wear no shoes. Unfortunately, some people find this unpleasant and offensive. If I were to wear sandals, the tops of my feet would show to the public, yet this is not offensive. When I am barefooted, the bottoms of my feet do not show. What, then, is so offensive about wearing no shoes?

GENTLE READER:

It's not your feet. Depending on local custom, you could just as easily offend people by keeping your shoes on—for example, when entering a Japanese home or temple—as by taking them off. In America, the wearing of shoes everywhere but the beach is considered minimal dress. People may speak of sanitary problems when complaining about barefootedness, but what is really bothering them is that failure to observe ordinary standards implies a lack of respect.

Seasonal Clothing

From Memorial Day to Labor Day, you may wear white shoes. Not before and not after. As a command, the White Shoe Edict should be clear and simple enough. Do not violate it. In a society in which everything else has become relative, a matter of how it makes you feel, a question between you and your conscience, and an opportunity for you to be really you, this is an absolute. Miss Manners not only doesn't want any argument about it, she doesn't even want any discussion. For goodness' sake, if you want to smash the conventions of your own heritage, find a rule that is more fun to break.

Considering that she had previously decreed this, once and for all, Miss Manners has been tossing letters she has received on the subject into a box marked "Oh, Stop It." However, it doesn't stop, and the time has come to clean out the box. Once and for all:

Memorial Day is Memorial Day, not Memorial Day Observed. It is on May 30. Confederate Memorial Day has nothing to do with shoes.

Yes, the rule applies to gentlemen as well as ladies. As a matter of fact, even in season, a gentleman never wears white shoes except with sports clothes and during the daytime.

No, sneakers don't count, except on the day they are purchased. After that, they're not white, anyway.

Yes, white shoes that are a part of certain set outfits worn for specific activities may be put on for the duration of that activity. Tennis players and brides and those taking first communion may wear white shoes, but they must change when the respective events are over. (Tennis players should also shower. Brides are always fresh. Miss Manners digresses.)

Comfort and heat have nothing to do with it, or we would all soon be wearing our bathing suits to the office. Weather is never an excuse. Dividing the calendar year into different seasons, one hot, one cold, one chilly, and one romantic, was one of nature's more charming ideas, but it was a vague one. Many perfectly agreeable places to live don't follow that system at all, and even regions that pretend to, enjoy upsetting people occasionally just for a laugh, and schedule heat waves and cold fronts (whatever they are) when they don't belong. Sensible people therefore adhere to the concept of seasons, without regard to whatever chaotic conditions may be prevailing outdoors. It is enough of a concession to the weather to allow it to dictate whether the clothes to be worn are light, heavy, or waterproof. By distinguishing between generally light summer clothes and darker fall and winter clothes, you acknowledge seasons without undue suffering.

Summer clothes include seersucker suits, patent leather shoes, white or very light cream blazers, white cotton gloves, and white dinner jackets (which Miss Manners despises). Velvet may be worn from October through March. White wool may be worn by a lady in the winter, but only with shoes and gloves that are dark enough to show that she is serious. Straw hats are supposed to be a sign of spring, but they look silly with warm clothes. Spring is the only season to have its own specific colors, like colleges. Spring's colors are Navy with Touches of White About the Face. It also has a sneaking fondness for babyish pastels. Unfortunately, spring was abolished by the clothing industry some years ago. (Miss Manners has the only authentic spring coat left in existence, because everybody else argues, with some reason, that they get more use out of their raincoats. Hers is a smashing pink mohair job that waits patiently for its annual airing at an April garden party. Before that, it is too cold out, and after that, it's too warm. Some years it is too warm at the garden party, but Miss Manners can't bear to disappoint her spring coat.)

Unfortunately, only the white shoes have their own entrance and exit days; the other seasons change by the pooled judgment of residents of a particular place. For example, spring is declared when everyone gets a good whiff of it in the air, even if it later turns cold; and summer is felt to have arrived when the children are underfoot. In spite of this potential for confusion, sensible people know that the human spirit requires some orderly variations, even from perfection, in order for one not to end up drinking suspicious-looking fruit drinks all day at the club and plotting schemes that will end in no good. People who find that everyone else has ceased to observe the amenities should be all the more careful to observe them themselves as their little contribution to preserve civilization.

Public Manners

❧ THE NEW SMOKING RULES

Are you going to behave yourselves, or do you want Miss Manners to call in the police? It is not Miss Manners' custom to resort to such harsh threats. She has always believed that courtesy, kindness, and an occasional deadly look with a raised eyebrow are weapons enough to regulate ordinary human behavior. But the issue of smoking has inspired such unacceptable manners in both smokers and non-smokers for so long that Miss Manners is almost relieved to have regulation of smoking made a matter of law, as many states are now doing.

She is, however, bothered by the idea that this might be a public acknowledgment of the failure of our society to observe elementary rules of etiquette in the interests of peace and harmony. Have we really sunk so low that we cannot practice simple toleration and consideration of others unless required by law? It would seem so. Miss Manners is hard put to say who is behaving worse, those who insist upon offending other people with their smoke or those who insist that only rudeness to and humiliation of smokers will clear the air.

It is true that the greater burden of consideration ought to be on smokers. Subjecting other people to the effects of one's pleasures is rude, and Miss Manners hopes that all those filling the air with noise are paying attention. Earphones are a marvelous solution for those who wish to enjoy their own taste in music privately in public, and there is no excuse at all for the broadcasting of foreground or background music in any public area. It is a great deal easier to settle conflicts on the superficial level of manners than to fight them out as matters of morals.

In more civilized times, it was always understood that smoking should not be done in the presence of nonsmokers. There were times and places to smoke, and even smoking jackets, so that smokers could go among nonsmokers afterward without bringing the smell of smoke with them. In those days, smokers were referred to as "gentlemen" and nonsmokers as "ladies." Gentlemen smoked in their smoking rooms or after the ladies had left the table. If one did wish to smoke in a lady's presence, he asked her permission politely, with the understanding that the permission could easily and politely be denied. No gentleman blew smoke into a lady's face, saying, "If you don't like it, tough." But then, no lady grabbed a cigarette out of a gentleman's mouth, shouting, "I don't care if you kill yourself, pig, but stop polluting my air." When ladies began smoking, too—or began smoking openly—all these manners were cast aside. Miss Manners suggests that we bring them back.

That means that smokers should generally smoke privately and that areas should be designated in which they can comfortably do so. It means that if they do want to smoke in front of a nonsmoker, they should ask, "Do you mind if I smoke?" and cheerfully accept a negative reply. But it also means that such a reply, or a request that an already lit cigarette be extinguished, be made politely. Rudeness is unacceptable, and it should not be necessary to claim an allergy. One should only need to say, "I'm so sorry, but smoke bothers me."

In Houses

DEAR MISS MANNERS:

My fiancé and I were invited to spend a weekend with some friends at their home. My fiancé smokes; I don't, nor do they. Some hours after our arrival, my fiancé smoked a cigarette on their patio. Their six-year-old son made a rather rude statement to the effect that "We don't like people to smoke in our house." Needless to say, my fiancé didn't smoke again that weekend, but we vowed never to go back to their house again.

This has happened to us before, and it's beginning to get on my nerves. No one dislikes smoking more than I; however, I would never dream of telling guests in my home not to smoke or make them feel uncomfortable about doing so. I don't think it's fair to invite people who you know are smokers and then, once they are there, embarrass them into not smoking by making them feel that you will be asphyxiated if they light up. Should I just stop accepting invitations to homes where there are "no smoking" rules? Should I tell the hostess why we cannot accept, so that she knows it isn't her cooking or personal hygiene that keeps us away? Help!

GENTLE READER:

If no one dislikes smoking more than you, and you are engaged to marry a smoker, Miss Manners can understand why your nerves are on edge. She deeply regrets that what she is about to say is apt to irritate them further.

Miss Manners hereby announces that all houses are nonsmoking houses unless proven otherwise. No host should have to resort to the ugly expedient of putting up signs or allowing the children to chastise guests. You smoke in someone's house if that person invites you to—as, indeed, you wait to be invited to eat, drink, or play Frisbee.

Miss Manners is not impressed with the argument that hosts may know someone to be a smoker. The guest is equally likely to know that the hosts are nonsmokers and can refuse the invitation accordingly. Miss Manners hopes that they would not have to. If smokers would have the courtesy to inquire if or where they may smoke, and if hosts would have the courtesy to help them find a place to smoke without sacrificing their own comfort, perhaps we could reach the standard of civilization that was common in this matter a century ago.

On the Street

A lady of Miss Manners' acquaintance has requested her permission to smoke on the street. Do not suppose that Miss Manners cannot hear the chorus of shocked stalwarts over there murmuring, "That is no lady." Smoking on the street is one of the traditional key signs by which one forfeits the claim to gentility meant by the term "lady." Never mind the fact that purity of heart is more important than trivial externals. Miss Manners never argues that point. She only maintains that it is possible, under some circumstances, for a lady to murder her husband; but that a woman who wears ankle-strap shoes and smokes on the street corner, though she may be a joy to all who know her and have devoted her life to charity, could never qualify as a lady.

Because there are ever more regulations, customs, and laws banning smoking from general-use areas such as offices, restaurants, and public transportation, and more individuals who do not permit smoking in their houses, there must be recognition, as well, of the fact that the many law-abiding citizens who smoke need unoffensive places to do so. Some of them may be ladies.

The advantage of outdoor smoking is that it removes the fumes from others, so it is not permitted in crowds or, indeed, when there is anyone nearby who objects. Miss Manners now pronounces outdoor smoking to be permitted to both ladies and gentlemen.

A lady still does not smoke while walking down the street, but she may pause discreetly at a park bench, balcony, garden, or other respectable stopping place and smoke. People may smoke alone in their own cars or with the consent of all passengers.

Flicking ashes into the air and discarding cigarette butts on the ground are almost as severe a source of complaint as the smoke itself. Two solutions have been offered: the institution of public ashtrays and the carrying of small portable ones by smokers.

🌹 DRIVING

A method for making short work of traffic annoyances came into practice one fine day on the southern California highways. Several people responded to what they considered pesky driving by shooting into the offending cars. Alleged offenses included failure to respond immediately to a signal requesting permission to pass, not moving past a stop sign, and pulling in front of another vehicle so that it had to slow down. When the psychologists appeared on the scene to explain why people had engaged in such behavior, they came up with: Broken homes. Television. Narcissism. Stress related to traffic congestion. Stress related to other problems, such as domestic disputes. A feeling of limitless power from being in command of an automobile.

No one mentioned manners, or rather the lack of them. And when Miss Manners began to do so, she was given those patronizing little smiles that mean "Yes, dear, I suppose it is bad manners to shoot people," signifying that they don't care to take the time to argue with her sweet but lightweight cause before they resume their serious discussions. There seems to be some trouble believing that manners can ever be a matter of life and death. They are frills for fancy occasions, it is widely assumed, and perhaps quite nice in their way if you go in for that sort of thing, but unnecessary if you don't.

Miss Manners begs to differ. It is true that the outward forms of etiquette particular to a time and place are, by definition, superficial. These arbitrary rules enable people to follow a workable pattern that they all know, rather than continually to engage in free-for-all contests of one person's wishes against another's. Following etiquette assumes and demonstrates commitment to the underlying idea that one belongs to a society and must therefore temper one's individual impulses according to its customs and needs. Etiquette anarchy—whether it is ignoring simple courtesies or the deepest obligations; whether one initiates it or practices it in response to the behavior of others—rejects the obligation to so control oneself and extolls the supremacy of one's personal desires.

This attitude was not uncommon on the road before law was introduced; it is also the premise of those who wish to punish other drivers by cursing or kicking. It comes of an even wider belief that manners—the habit of controlling individual behavior for the general harmony—are no longer necessary. However, it does not make a general case for individual freedom because it contains a firm belief in the obligation of others. Even the most lawless drivers realize that they would be threatened if everyone were allowed to make his or her own rules. Their real policy, therefore, is: You have to behave so that I can do whatever I want.

The odd but inevitable indignation when other people don't behave themselves creates a feeling of justification in punishing them, however unlawfully. Often one hears the latter practices referred to as "teaching them manners." Hardly. But the proof that manners are desperately needed is that the common alternative method used to deal with minor frustrations and infractions is violence.

Genteel Gestures

DEAR MISS MANNERS:

What is the proper response to people who make rude gestures while driving? Usually this is done after they've done something stupid. I presume it is to cover their embarrassment. I would deem it a great favor if you could advise me as to a proper response—preferably a contemptuous yet classy wordless response, since all concerned are in cars—without resorting to the same kind of action as the perpetrator.

GENTLE READER:

Drive on. Miss Manners regrets to say that there are no genteel hand gestures that say—no, there's no "classy" way of putting that into words, either. She suggests you bow your head sideways, with a wordless smile going up the right cheek only. What that says is "How charming of you." It is more effective than what you had in mind.

Sharing Costs

DEAR MISS MANNERS:

My husband and I do not own a car, but we often rent one to travel to other cities. Quite often, friends or relatives ask to travel with us. It is rare that someone offers to pay for a portion of the rental fee or even a portion of the gas. If they were to travel by public transportation, it would be quite expensive and I feel that some contribution should be made toward the expense. Do you consider it proper manners for one to offer money for this, and how much do you feel would be appropriate? Also, do you think it proper for the driver to ask, and how would one broach the subject?

GENTLE READER:

Your calculation is that they would otherwise have to pay for public transportation; their calculation is that you are going anyway and that their presence does not cost you extra. Put into manners terms, they consider that rides are favors, while you see them as services. Miss Manners is not against your bringing them around to your way of thinking, provided that you keep in mind that theirs is a legitimate way of considering the matter (if—and this if is crucial—they exhibit proper manners toward friends by doing return favors). Rather than treating them as deadbeats, you should take the approach that they are partners in the excursion. "Oh, great, we'd love to have you along. Do you want to split the rental fee, or should we take care of that and you get the gas bills?"

The Inept Favor

DEAR MISS MANNERS:

Have I got a new one for you! I was driving my car to a local shopping center in the rain when my windshield wiper came out of its binding and started flapping all over my windshield. The rain was not bad enough to obscure my vision, so I turned the wipers off and drove the rest of the way without them. When I arrived, I started to fix the wiper. A well-intentioned gentleman got out of his nearby car and said, "Having trouble with your wipers?" I got out of his way, figuring that he knew what he was doing. I had fixed it myself recently, so I knew how, but I thought he might be able to do it faster and better.

As I was watching, I noticed that he was trying to put it back the wrong way. I tried to tell him, but he said, "No," that it should fasten on the way he was trying. He continued to struggle, and again I tried to tell him the correct way, but he was sure he was right. Finally, he went to the other side of the car to check how the other wiper was attached. I casually slipped the broken one back on the correct way. Very easy.

I spent ten minutes in the rain and fell behind schedule because of this nonmechanically minded male. I could have done it in thirty seconds. How does a capable woman refuse the good but bumbling intentions of a man who wants to help but ends up hindering instead?

GENTLE READER:

Very likely you see this question as having to do with overthrowing the traditional male pretense to mechanical competence. It will therefore disappoint you to know that Miss Manners sees it merely as the ordinary etiquette problem of an inept favor. It seems silly to accept such an offer when one is sure of one's own competence. You apparently did so on the assumption that a gentleman would naturally do this better than yourself, a notion of which Miss Manners trusts you are now disabused. But having allowed him to help you, you were bound by etiquette to seem grateful and to repair his bungling as inconspicuously as you could. To refuse, you need only have smiled and said, "No, thank you, really, I've done this before and I'll have it done in a jiffy."

Car Pools

DEAR MISS MANNERS:

I am in my third car pool in less than two years. Each time, I've come across actions and habits that I find offensive or at least worthy of concern.

1. It's early morning. The passenger leans back to relax or nap a little. The driver, who is also sleepy, puts in a cassette tape and plays it at low volume. Just before reaching their destination, the passenger sits up and says, "I guess I didn't want to sleep, anyway," and comments on the selected music.

2. The driver has picked up the passenger, and they are a few miles from the passenger's home. The driver says, "By the way, I need to stop by such-and-such this afternoon to talk to someone about buying something."

3. The car poolers have driven together two or three times. They have agreed to meet at 6:30 A.M.. The driver waits until 7:00 one day, but the passenger doesn't show up or call. That evening, the driver calls the passenger, and the passenger says that he was out late the night before and decided to take the day off. He also

tells the driver not to wait past 6:30 for him. (The driver would have left at 5 A.M. to miss traffic had she known the passenger's plans.)

I could give you more scenarios, but your opinion on these will help me to determine if I am reading the situations fairly or not. From there, I can change my ways or look for a different car pool.

GENTLE READER:

No, no, don't look for a different car pool. We would only develop more scenarios, and 6:30 in the morning is too early for so much drama. What you need is explicit car pool etiquette. When there is no known standard, each person improvises, and the result is that they all end up finding the others either inconsiderate or inflexible. Sit down with this car pool—what is Miss Manners saying? Of course, you sit down with this car pool every day, twice a day. So all you need do is ask them to agree on such matters as what the waiting period should be when someone is late and when one is to call when not going at all; what errands, if any, should be permitted en route; and the use of the radio.

Car Radios

DEAR MISS MANNERS:

I have a friend who says that it is rude for me to play soft music in the car when she is a passenger. She even reaches over and switches it off. Soft music soothes my nerves when I drive, and I keep it low enough to have normal conversation. What do you say? Am I rude?

GENTLE READER:

Rude is a harsh word for what you claim is soft music. Nevertheless, Miss Manners shares your friend's feelings, although she would not dream of employing her rude method of expressing them. "Do you mind if we turn that off so that I can pay attention to what you're saying?" is more polite than switching off someone else's radio.

If you really can't drive safely without the radio on, your driver's license should state that, as those of others say that they cannot drive without wearing glasses. However, if you cannot bear a pleasant conversation without mechanical background, that is a dreadful affliction and perhaps your guests should be warned of it. Many people, Miss Manners foremost among them, find such conflicting noises distracting and an insult to both the conversation and the music.

🌹 DEALING WITH STRANGERS

It seems to Miss Manners that each of us has the same number of hours in every day and roughly equivalent claims on our attention. If the second requires more time than the first, you are in trouble. Under normal circumstances, it is not a problem for which you are allowed to impose upon the indulgence of other people.

Those who shove into crowds, shouting, "Let me through! I'm in a hurry!" do not, as it happens, inspire those elbowed out of the way to muse sympathetically, "Well, gee, I don't have anything special to do, so let me stand back." The fact is that everyone considers himself to be in a special hurry when performing the ordinary time-consuming chores of life. The person who claims urgency had better have a good reason, preferably to be borne out by the subsequent arrival on the scene of a team of paramedics. Otherwise, any behavior circumventing the natural system of crowds, in which precedence is accorded strictly on the basis of time put in waiting—sometimes known as "first come, first served"—is rude.

Miss Manners tries very hard to believe that people are not intentionally so selfish. They simply have a tendency to sympathize more with their own difficulties than they do with other people's. There is also a widespread illusion that things can be accomplished more efficiently than is really possible. If you run yellow lights, you will eventually hit a red one—if not anything more serious—and have to stop anyway; if you keep changing lanes constantly, breaking in ahead of one car after another, you will probably suffer the delays as well as the advances of them all. Trying to meet a dozen new people at a party, rather than troubling to talk at some length to one or two, is not likely to result in a dozen new friendships. Juggling three telephone calls simultaneously encourages being hung up on rather than additional communication.

Miss Manners is convinced that life will move just as fast, or as inevitably slowly, if you observe the basic decencies:

If there is a line, get on it and wait.

If there is a crowd with no formal line, such as at a bus stop—where the European system of queuing up is more sensible than ours—try to take your fair turn anyway.

When attempting to enter a place that a crowd is leaving, let people get out first and keep to the right.

And so on. Yes, Miss Manners is aware that impatience wells up in you until it amounts almost to fury. But pushing ahead is generally futile and always rude. For that reason, the well-bred person never goes about his business without either a book or some thoughts to keep him company, so that he may have a semblance of acceptance while enduring the inevitable waiting periods of life.

Waiting in Line

DEAR MISS MANNERS:

Often I find myself standing in line at the copy machine at the local print shop. When I have a large order, I avail myself of the services of the shop's employees; for just a few copies, I use the self-service copier. My time is as precious, in my estimation, as that of any other user. I always make an effort to allow enough time for waiting my turn and never ask to cut in.

Typically, I wait through three turns ahead of me, and invariably one is interminable—someone who is copying an article from a magazine and hasn't marked all the pages, or someone who keeps forgetting to copy the second side of two-sided documents and goes back to check several times. In any event, when I get to the machine with my three-page letter, or ten-page brief, or whatever it is, I am all too often asked by a newcomer, "Can I just make one copy? I'll only be a minute." It seems downright churlish to say no, but I feel that I have every right to, and no obligation to someone who has not waited on line. Yet I usually acquiesce.

Once, when I said no and went on to explain that I'd been waiting a long time and it just wasn't fair, I became far too emotional and aggravated and embarrassed myself, and put the line crasher at a distinct emotional advantage, which was doubly irritating. Miss Manners, please give me one of your snappy, tactful, correct responses.

GENTLE READER:

How about "no"? Oh, not quite a bald "no." More like, "No, I'm so sorry, I'm already running late." You say this while running the machine, so that it does not take extra time. Omit those tactless remarks about the unfairness of it all.

The etiquette of lines does not require someone with a large load to yield to someone with a smaller one, although it is nice to offer to do so when possible. Nor does it bar the person with the quick task from asking to go through, as long as it is understood that this is a favor and certainly need not be granted.

It is silly to acquiesce if you're in a hurry and even sillier to work yourself up to an emotional pitch over the request. But if you should happen to have an extra minute some day, why don't you use it to suggest to the copying shop that it have an express line as well as the regular one?

Switching Lines

DEAR MISS MANNERS:

I usually go to the grocery store twice a week. I'll be in line, patiently waiting my turn, when a new checker opens a line and says, "I can help someone over here." Without fail, the person in back of me runs over and is waited on immediately. I think that's rude. I'm the next one in line, and I should be the one waited on next. I think the checker should say, "I'll take the next person in line, please."

GENTLE READER:

This is the sort of provocation that leads to basket bashing in grocery stores, or at least to facial expressions that wilt the lettuce. Your solution is an excellent one, and Miss Manners commends you and recommends it to checkers and anyone else who deals with lines of people. She would also consider it proper for a customer who has missed out in the free-for-all run to the new checker to say, firmly but politely, "I believe I was next."

Improper Impatience

Rudeness has long since ceased to astonish Miss Manners, although it will never stop saddening her, as you can tell from the tiny pearl-like tear on her cheek (and the fire in her eye) when things get rough. But on two recent occasions, she observed public demonstrations of rudeness that utterly flabbergasted her. It is no small thing to flabbergast Miss Manners.

The first was in an airport, at the security entrance for an international flight. A passenger was loudly berating one of the guards for insisting that her husband produce whatever was setting off the alarm before he could be cleared to enter the boarding area.

"Can't you see he's an old man?" she demanded. "He's not bringing in anything contraband. Why don't you stop wasting time and let us through?"

Aha, thought Miss Manners, the old offense-as-camouflage maneuver. People assume that those who are up to no good want to be inconspicuous, and therefore the lady made a scene in order to mislead the guard into eliminating the possibility of her being a terrorist. Miss Manners threw a knowing smile to the guard, figuring that he was on to such tricks and grateful to him for having flushed out the troublemaker so easily. She fully expected him to extract a handgun from the husband and to lead them both away. What she saw was a very embarrassed-looking young man who stammered apologies to the offensive passenger but nevertheless insisted that regulations be followed. Miss Manners has occasionally encountered guards who use their authority belligerently, but this was not one of them. She was even more surprised when the gun that set off the alarm turned out to be a bunch of keys. The couple was allowed to board the airplane and, in fact, did nothing to impede its progress. That meant that these people were not terrorists. Evidently (here comes the flabbergasting part), ordinary, presumably honest people were making a rude fuss about following airport security procedures designed to protect them as passengers.

The second incident was at a city bus stop, where perhaps a dozen people were waiting, one of them in a wheelchair. The bus company had apparently gotten advance notice and had a car meet the bus, with someone to help run the apparatus for loading the wheelchair. Only it didn't work. Driver and supervisor gamely fooled with the steps for a considerable time before they flattened for the wheelchair and then folded again as steps, so that all the passengers were able to board. It was as cheerful a crowd as any group of commuters can be, and it was only later, when one person who had not been waiting outside in the cold made the mean but standard remark, "Why don't they give them taxi service? It would be quicker and cheaper," that Miss Manners was flabbergasted. Not surprised this time, but morally astounded. Witnessing the problems connected with a faulty bus, this person was suggesting that the solution was not to fix the bus to suit the passenger, but to alter the passenger's life so as not to trouble the bus!

In both of these cases, outrageous behavior was prompted by the inconvenience of a slight delay. Miss Manners is fortunately too polite to speculate on the value of the time of such callous people. What would they be doing with the few minutes saved—serving humanity? (Oh, dear, she just said that she wouldn't do that, didn't she?) She would like to point out that disabilities and the risk of crime are ordinary facts of life, and a decent society should not show impatience at whatever adjustments are necessary to transport people around safely and conveniently. We are all hoping that our flights will be uneventful and our lives long enough for us to need a little help getting around.

BUSES AND STREETS

In an age of stylistic simplicity, miniaturization, and electronic communication, why, Miss Manners occasionally wonders, is everyone trudging around carrying so much stuff? This reflection is apt to float idly into her mind when she is hit by the flying shoulder bag of someone marching obliviously down a bus aisle, or when a knapsack backs into her in a crowded elevator, or when an airplane seatmate pretends that he doesn't know how all the overhead and underfoot space in their row managed to get filled up before she arrived.

Everywhere she looks, she sees human pack animals. Ladies' purses have grown to the size of overnight bags. Briefcases have turned into portable desks. Devotees of exercise and those of magazine articles explaining how to change a "day look" into an evening one with "a few simple accessories" commute daily to work carrying extra wardrobes. Ever since it became fashionable to look natural, both ladies and gentlemen began carrying around hairbrushes and other major items of grooming equipment. Those who once hummed now have headphones and perhaps full-sized radios. People who used to scribble public addresses and private telephone numbers on the backs of envelopes carry looseleaf organizers.

Here are some beginning rules for the overburdened age:

1. Each person is responsible for knowing his or her own dimensions. We are generally only aware of our bodily outline and forget that the borders of the space we occupy include everything held, strapped on, or attached by a leash. (Even in the old days, ladies forgot to account for their hats in measuring their silhouettes at the theater, thus giving rise to a lot of resentment and bad cartoons.) One must be constantly as responsible for keeping that total bulk out of other people's way as one would in refraining from sticking an elbow or foot into someone else's territory.

2. A punitive attitude toward the burdened-down is not helpful. As far as possible, one must accept the legitimate presence of reasonable packages and help their owners to accommodate them.

3. We need to bring back professional assistance, including porters, shopping carts, curb depressions, and checking places. The callous theory that the world need be set up only for the able-bodied and strong is less appropriate than ever.

4. We need amateur assistance of two types:

a. Formal offers of help in carrying things—offers intended only as a courtesy, made to those who are able to handle their burdens as well as the person making the offer—apply to the social world only, not the business realm. A gentleman still offers to carry a lady's packages, and a young person an older one's. However, a gentleman does not offer to carry a lady's briefcase, or vice versa.

b. Functional offers are more necessary than ever. Door opening and holding, standing back to give others room, and package carrying should be generously offered on the basis of obvious need and treated graciously. A standing lady overloaded with groceries, law books, and a baby should not be ignored by those seated on the grounds that "You wanted equality, didn't you, lady?" That does not qualify as progress.

Assistance

DEAR MISS MANNERS:

What should a healthy, able-bodied young woman seated on a crowded train do when a physically handicapped man, in leg braces and crutches, in his mid-thirties or so, enters? Should she offer her seat and risk injuring his pride? Or should she remain seated and let him ride standing? I offered my seat and was politely refused, making me wonder if I should have said nothing.

GENTLE READER:

The rule about dealing with anyone who has any physical difficulty is: If you can't help, ignore it. By ignoring it, Miss Manners does not mean an elaborate pretending-not-to-notice, but a more positive approach of dealing with the person as a person, not as a patient.

Now, it *is* helpful to offer a person on crutches a seat. No question of pride need be involved if you do not make a grand gesture of it that emphasizes the sacrifice. Just vacate the seat as the person approaches it and keep walking. Miss Manners believes that the young man to whom you offered your seat could easily have accepted it with no loss of pride, but it was unnecessary even to force him to make the decision.

Kindness Rebuffed

DEAR MISS MANNERS:

On the bus yesterday, a nice young lady stood up and offered me her seat. I did not actually need it, but as an older person, I gratefully accepted it and said "Thank you." We smiled at each other a couple of times during the trip. A few minutes later, another older person entered the bus, and another nice young lady offered her the seat. This lady refused, saying that she might be gray-haired but was capable of standing. She said it in a nice way, and there was a bit of good-natured talking back and forth.

I had a feeling, however, that the young lady was a bit embarrassed. Both young ladies, who were between seventeen and twenty years of age, showed behavior above reproach and to be commended, it seemed to me. It is true that both older people responded with charm, smiles, and good humor, but which is Miss Manners' preferred response to such an offer?

GENTLE READER:

It is not, you may be sure, to teach the young that courtesy is inappropriate and unwelcome. To refuse an offer of politeness, and to bolster it with statements suggesting that the offerer has misjudged and insulted one is, however good-humoredly put, rude. You are undoubtedly right that the rebuffed young lady was embarrassed. If she was so much so as to resolve never to attempt such kindness again, Miss Manners hopes that her elderly (but still physically active) instructor will be satisfied.

Right of Way

DEAR MISS MANNERS:

Being a college professor, I frequently walk across campus, and many times I encounter three or more uncaring, free spirits walking toward me, taking up the entire walkway. I used to step on the grass to avoid them, but lately I have been lowering my shoulder, plunging straight ahead, and have startled—and smashed into—several inconsiderate students who were concentrating on their weekend activities rather than on who might be approaching them.

I have observed similar behavior in shopping malls, which I am convinced harbor the most moronic and ill-bred cretins in the Western Hemisphere. On any Saturday afternoon, go to your shopping mall and notice how long platoons of youths take up entire aisles, forcing people to walk around them. Once four or five males played a game of this until one person (yours truly) refused to get out of their way, and one was knocked to the floor (whereupon his necklace broke, one of his earrings fell off, and his bracelet was scratched). My wife thinks that my behavior is boorish, ill-mannered, and rude, and that I'm merely acting out my John Wayne fantasies. Maybe so, but how should the gentle people of the world handle a situation like this?

GENTLE READER:

If you don't mind, Miss Manners would like to subject your letter to a brief analysis—nothing more than you would expect your students to do in examining a specimen you might present to them from your own field. She finds it interesting that you are able to assess the mental capabilities of strangers as they approach you and to read their thoughts, even as you chortlingly smash them senseless.

What would happen if you find the path blocked by, let us say, the president of the university, who is too busy talking to one of its major donors for either of them to look where they are going, and the chairman of your department who is absently speculating on who might best be the recipient of the new chair that the other two are discussing? Or, say, your old mentor, now professor emeritus, who is thinking great thoughts? Or a colleague buried in a book, perhaps even your new book?

If you will be good enough to acknowledge that the age, looks, jewelry, brain capacity, and preoccupations of pedestrians have no bearing on the question of right of way on a thoroughfare, Miss Manners will refrain from inquiring about your attitudes toward the young. We will then be left with the simple etiquette problem of dealing with people who do not observe the convention of keeping to the right when others are advancing toward them, so that both can continue easily on their way.

The simplest solution is to go around them. If your pride will not allow that, you may politely command their attention to their oversight by calling out "Excuse me!" as you wait for them to step aside. If you really believe that a deliberate affront is being made, the simplest solution is still to go around them, and the way to defy them is still to issue a loud "Excuse me!" and stand firm while staring them down until they part.

If they then attack you physically, you have a different problem, one which has gone from being an etiquette problem to a legal one. As Miss Manners understands the shopping mall incident, you were the one who practiced assault. The gentle people of the world do not do that.

Talking to Strangers

DEAR MISS MANNERS:

I am twelve and in the sixth grade. I sometimes walk home alone from school, and a stranger passes by and says "hello." Do I say "hello" back, or do I keep on walking and say nothing? My parents have always taught me not to talk to strangers, but I don't want to be impolite. I feel really bad when people are being friendly and I snub them by not saying "hello" back.

GENTLE READER:

Your parents' rule is correct and sensible. Miss Manners assures you that you do not have an obligation, for the sake of politeness, to respond to strangers. However, this is not a simple rule. Few rules are. Part of growing up is learning how to comply with the intent of the rule, which is to prevent improper overtures from people you know nothing about, rather than adhering to it rigidly in situations where it might be inappropriate.

Can you safely call out hello to the lady sweeping her porch who says "Hi" as you go by on your bicycle? Sure. Should you respond to the friendly stranger who is new at your school this year? Of course. Ignoring a person who is walking down the street with you, and who shows signs of beginning a conversation if encouraged, is not impolite. It is merely a proper response to the rudeness of approaching a stranger—you—in the first place. The distinction is, first, whether the conversation is intended to lead anywhere (as the greeting to the lady on the porch is not), and second, whether there is a proper common meeting ground (as your school would be) for making new acquaintances.

Use of Territory

DEAR MISS MANNERS:

My husband and I were raised in opposite environments, he in New York City slums, while I had a middle-class upbringing. He has fought dearly to overcome his background and has finally achieved some respect and a good reputation in our town as a teacher.

The other night after a movie, my husband wanted to walk for a while. I had no objection, except that it was 11 P.M., and he wanted to walk down the main street. I suggested that we walk around the small shopping center and parking lot area near the theater, which was more pleasant and where we wouldn't be as conspicuous. He became very upset and told me that I was being ridiculous. I explained that it didn't seem quite proper for people with our reputation to be seen walking down the main street, where the low-lifes hung out, or teenagers cruised and sat on their cars along the boulevard.

I know that I would think it odd if I saw a respected, well-known person walking down that busy street at that hour. I would see nothing improper about walking a dog in a residential area. My husband said that I was wrong and insisted that it was no breach of etiquette. I told him that it was more a matter of feeling out of place than of being right or wrong. What is your feeling?

GENTLE READER:

Respectability is not a matter of geography. If it were, morality would be running rampant in the high-rent district, and such is not Miss Manners' experience.

Just as your husband's character was not damaged by growing up in the slums, it cannot be affected now by which street he walks on. Aside from safety considerations—which are another matter and could be even more important in a deserted residential area than in a crowded "low-life" district—honest people should walk where they wish. Who knows—perhaps some teenager will be inhibited from displaying poor behavior by the presence of a respected teacher. In any case, your husband seems to have made his way up in life without acquiring silly snobberies. Miss Manners requests you not to attempt to complete this part of his education.

❧ UNFORTUNATE HABITS

Offensive Others

Deep in a gloomy corner of Miss Manners' otherwise cheerful desk, away from the regular jolly war reports from the etiquette front—those daily skirmishes that make life so adventurous—is a file marked "Offensive Others." There are all the dossiers on people who produce odors and noises, accidentally or on purpose.

They burp; they spit; they chew gum dramatically; they crack their knuckles. They eat disgustingly and sneeze worse; sometimes they manage to combine the two. They give off evidence of being infrequent bathers. They hum tunelessly and jiggle their legs nervously. They clear their throats, and then they scrape their teeth. In a variety of ways Miss Manners never would have dreamed possible, they play with or work on their fingernails.

The one thing these people never seem to do is to entertain self-doubts. They did not get into Miss Manners' file by reporting themselves. Presumably, they are too busy having a good time, going about their business in perfect ignorance and happiness while disgusting everyone within range.

"The sounds send chills through my body, and the hair on my arms stands up!" pleads one victim. "Yuk!" says another. "Our stomachs turn, and we try to think of tactful ways to let this man know that his habit ruins our breakfasts and our mornings!" "What to do?" pleads still another. "Consider the source, as my dear mother used to say, and do nothing? Look fixedly out the window at the pigeons?"

Of course, Miss Manners is only taking the word of informants for this behavior. For all she knows, perfectly innocent and well-behaved people are being maligned—perhaps even by those who are obliviously doing something to make them gag in turn. Some of these pairs, the offender and the offendee, are married to each other. Others are locked together in office proximity. There are also utter strangers.

Miss Manners is sorry to say that there is no all-purpose way of complaining about, much less altering, the annoying personal habits of others. One adult cannot pounce on another, shouting, "Now you cut that out this minute before you drive me crazy!" If you want to do that, you should have children. However, her sympathies have been engaged by some of the more restrained descriptions. (The really vividly written ones she carefully pushes deeper into the corner of the desk. You don't want to see them.) So she will enumerate the permissible defenses while apologizing for their obvious weakness.

The grown-ups' version of "Cut that out," for use only on people with whom one has an otherwise warm relationship, is, "Darling, I wish you wouldn't do that." The usual response is "Do what?," to which one replies, "I don't know—whatever it is that makes that strange noise." The vaguer one is, and the more good-natured about retaliatory complaints, the more likely that the problem will be solved—at least after a few weeks of "Darling, I know you don't realize it, but you're doing it again."

More distant relationships require more distant allusions. One can offer a solution without mentioning the problem ("Do have a mint!"), or one can generalize the complaint ("We're going to have to ban eating lunch at the desks; nobody can concentrate"), even if it concerns only one person. One is not allowed to give instruction to strangers in the street. Even Miss Manners doesn't do that.

The last resort is to call in a third party to do the dirty work—an usher, a boss, a relative. This has the advantage of allowing the complainer to speak plainly— but passes on the etiquette burden to another. What does that other person say in order to be polite? That one is easy. "I beg your pardon, but there seem to be some complaints about knuckle cracking. I don't know anything about this, but if it applies to you, I'd appreciate your cooperation." The nice thing about waffling is that it hardly offends anyone.

Noise

DEAR MISS MANNERS:

I am totally fed up with that bad music that all the stores play. Why must they think that we like their type of music or need music at all? Even the drugstore plays loud music, and it makes me nervous. I would prefer having smoke than music, or what they call music. Why don't we make them turn it off? After all, we tell people they aren't allowed to smoke.

GENTLE READER:

Indeed, lead the charge and Miss Manners will follow, waving the etiquette flag. The comparison with smoke is a good one because it demonstrates that this is not a contest between two equal rights—the right to hear music and the right to silence—but rather a case of an intrusive preference against a nonintrusive one.

Portable Headphones

DEAR MISS MANNERS:

Please address the subject of portable stereo headsets that people are so fond of wearing everywhere these days. I work as a sales clerk, and sometimes a person will come up to the counter to buy something with the headphones in place and the radio on. I think it is very rude, and sometimes I feel like mouthing my words rather than speaking them.

GENTLE READER:

Actually, Miss Manners loves those headsets. She has never had a pair on in her life—they don't really go with chignons—but she thinks them a marvelously polite way for people who want to hear noise all the time to do so without intruding rudely on the right of others to listen to birds, silence, or their own thoughts.

That headsets engross the attention of those wearing them is often taken as an affront by people with little claim on that attention. Because she herself is treated with indulgent smiles for walking down the street or standing in lines reading a book, which is probably more absorbing and therefore potentially more dangerous, Miss Manners suspects some snobbery in the condemnation of headset wearers.

It would be rude to listen—or to read—while supposedly talking to someone. To do so when one wants someone to answer a question, as in the situation you describe, is merely foolish. If you want to point this out by mouthing your reply, Miss Manners deems that an acceptable and even amusing way to get the point across, provided that you do it with a polite smile.

Gum Chewing

DEAR MISS MANNERS:

Would you please inform my girlfriend when it is appropriate to chew gum and when it is not appropriate?

GENTLE READER:

Gum may be chewed in the presence of others only when it is safe to assume that they will not be offended. It is only safe to assume that others will not be offended if they are also chewing gum. It is safe for your girlfriend to assume that gum chewing offends you.

Spitting

DEAR MISS MANNERS:

Too many restaurant owners and theater managers (and even some barbers) are loath these days to provide spittoons for the use of their patrons, thus forcing one to consider expelling one's tobacco juice onto the floor. Would it be considered forward to offer, say, a paper cup to a stranger under these circumstances?

GENTLE READER:

Miss Manners would not hesitate to offer the nearest container to any person swishing tobacco juice in his mouth provocatively. However, that is a matter of self-defense rather than of etiquette. The fact is (and she hates to be the one to break the news to you) that spitting is not in the current lexicon of permissible public pleasures, except in rare areas that are especially consecrated to the purpose, such as old-fashioned porches among consenting cronies who are skilled enough to miss the porch railing and hit the ground. The etiquette error, therefore, is not that of the patron of a public accommodation, although he or she is the person most likely to suffer from the consequences.

Unmentionable Noises

DEAR MISS MANNERS:

Woe is me! Far too frequently, I am terribly embarrassed by having very audible gas. It surprises me with no warning, and I do hate it—but what shall I do? Fortunately, there is no smell, but the sound is terrible. I do sincerely apologize and am quite mortified. Have you a better way to handle this wretched situation?

GENTLE READER:

Woe are you, indeed. However, you do not have an etiquette problem. One says nothing on such occasions because there is a sensible social conspiracy to deny that anything happened. The danger of doing otherwise is illustrated in a story about Queen Elizabeth's apologizing, while reviewing troops on horseback with another chief of state, for her horse's having made such a noise. Allegedly, her host brushed off the apology, adding graciously that had she not mentioned it, he would have thought it was the horse. Miss Manners does not vouch for the veracity of this story. (It appears in *The Book of Royal Lists* by Craig Brown and Lesley Cunliffe.) She does vouch for the truthful point of etiquette it makes.

CRIME

Curiosity or Sympathy

DEAR MISS MANNERS:

Now that burglary, murder, and so on have become a way of life, don't you think that some protocol should be set up about how neighbors should behave? Suppose that our neighbors' house is burgled and their silver stolen. Should we:

1. Pretend that nothing has happened and just say "Have a nice day" when we meet them?

2. Keep peeping through the drapes to see what, if anything, is going on next door?

3. Go over and sympathize with them for having such a stupid dog that dirties our lawn and then sleeps while burglars burgle?

4. Send some silver and a bottle of champagne, or would a six-pack and some baloney do?

5. Just chain our own VCR to the table?

Or suppose that the neighbor's wife is murdered. Should we:

1. Condole with the husband even if, in our view, he is the prime suspect?

2. Inquire about how it was done?

GENTLE READER:

Satisfying one's curiosity about the neighbors' troubles is not strictly correct, but it may be done under the guise of sympathy. If the crime has been made public, or if the commotion connected with it was such as to make it obvious that it cannot be kept secret—if, for example, your street was cordoned off—you may say, "I'm so sorry about what happened. Please let me know if there is anything I can do to help." This gives the victim the choice of refusing to discuss his problems, which you must then respect, or of telling all. Miss Manners hopes that the satisfaction of hearing the neighbor tell you how he murdered his wife compensates you for the obligation you will then have to appear in court.

Suspicious Behavior

DEAR MISS MANNERS:

My sister, age eighteen, was home alone one night and answered the door, thinking that it was some friends, when she was startled to see a strange old man.

She tried to shut the door on him while he pushed from the other side, crying, "Let me in, sweetie." She finally managed to shut the door on him, catching his finger in the door. It turns out that this was our neighbors' elderly father, and he had made a mistake as to which home his daughter lived in. He had to go to the hospital and lost a nail. This tiff has caused a feud between us and the neighbors. The question is: Who should apologize?

GENTLE READER:
Both. This is a ghastly situation that is nobody's fault, but two apologies are better than none. Your sister's should be "I'm terribly sorry, but you see, I was terrified of a stranger's attempt to push his way in." That should elicit a second one, along the lines of "We are frightfully sorry, but Father was confused."

Interrogating the Victim

DEAR MISS MANNERS:
I am a counselor, and many of my clients are victims of physical or sexual child abuse, referred to me because of inappropriate feelings of guilt. The cause of this guilt, it seems to me, is usually the failure of nearly everyone involved to follow the rules of etiquette: The child is asked what he or she did to bring the abuse about and why he or she didn't report it immediately—usually with the implication that the child covertly enjoyed the abuse and is practically responsible for it.

I hold that there is a general rule here, which applies to all victims of crime. What we call "crime" is behavior sufficiently rude to warrant a legal prohibition against it. Since it is rude, there is no excuse for it, and it imposes obligations only upon the perpetrator. Unfortunately, it seems to be assumed that the perpetrators of criminal rudeness can guide their actions by self-interest, while the victims are bound by obligations. It seems to me that quite the converse is true. One cannot impose obligations upon people of any age by beating or raping them.

Surprisingly enough, few people agree with me that the rules of etiquette apply with the same force to criminally rude behavior as they do to more mundane breaches of correct behavior. Do you agree that criminal behavior which has a victim violates not only the law of the land but also the laws of etiquette, and should be held accountable to both?

GENTLE READER:
Could we sort out this request just a bit? Miss Manners is in great sympathy with you, but surely you do not expect her either to reclassify crime under the lesser charge of rudeness or to interfere with criminal investigations. She recognizes that there is an etiquette question there. We surely do not disagree on the heinousness of child abuse. You are welcome, if you wish, to point out that criminals are, by definition, rude.

What Miss Manners thinks you are really after is to establish etiquette rules for noncriminals (family, friends, acquaintances, perhaps police or medical workers, maybe even busybodies) in discussing the crime with the victim. Admittedly, some of these people have no right to mention it. Those who are truly close to the child or who are professionally involved will need to question the victim. It so happens that the effective way of doing this is also the polite way. That is to put things in a kind, low-key, nonprejudicial manner. Slanted questions tend to inspire skewed answers. "What happened just before that?" is a better question, both to gather information and to spare the child's feelings, than "Did you do anything to encourage this?" "Did you think of telling anyone?" is better than "Why didn't you report it sooner?" Miss Manners hasn't spent a lifetime as a journalist without understanding that the simple, polite question elicits the most revealing answer.

Consoling the Victim

DEAR MISS MANNERS:

I am the victim of a violent crime which included rape. After the event, police formalities, and so on, I was in a state of grief and shock. Although directed to psychotherapists, I would have appreciated more fully a display of manners by those around me. The pastor at my church seemed to feel that my family would be snubbed, even though the armed robber/rapist had given me no choice. So, our pastor forbade me to speak of the crime to anyone. Consequently, I found myself unable to explain my grief. It hurt more to have the pastor offer and ask for prayers for those who were ill or who had died, but skip our family. There is no formal color, like that of mourning, worn by a crime victim, so my sudden tears were interpreted as "psychological disturbance."

At the same time, relatives who were informed by my mother sometimes seemed to intrude, asking too many questions. It was just as if they had asked about the nature and duration of a disease that had caused death. I didn't want to be reminded of why I grieved. Also, relatives expected me to attend a wedding, and our church expected me to attend as usual. As being a victim of crime is nothing to feel dignified about, what should I have done?

GENTLE READER:

While Miss Manners thoroughly endorses your request for sympathetic understanding, she wishes to point out that widespread "sharing" of your experience is, by your own account, hardly more conducive to this than a general pretense that it didn't happen and that you should therefore behave normally. The curiosity that people display in hearing about a crime is not to be confused with what you want, which is comfort.

It is interesting that you compare this period with mourning. Since formal mourning practices have been abandoned, the bereaved have similar experiences both with insensitive prying and with prodding expectations to behave normally in circumstances for which their feelings are too fragile. Traditionally, people understood the necessity of withdrawing from the rough and tumble of life at such periods, as they were not up to it. You may not be able to get away altogether, but you should certainly eschew ordinary social life until you are recovered. This is the time to draw heavily on the sympathy of your intimates—not the world at large, but those people who are able to put aside their own busybodiness to offer you emotional sustenance in private. Incidentally, your pastor certainly ought to be one of them.

~2~

Home Life

Steprelations, Former Spouses, and Former In-Laws

In gentler days, etiquette arbiters were often asked to explain the difference between second cousins once removed and third cousins, whether one's brother-in-law's wife was one's sister-in-law, and the proper way to address in-laws when versions of "Mother" and "Father" stuck in the throat. It was not the highlight of the job, and we grand mavens were embarrassed if we had to take off our shoes to count up the number of times cousins had been removed from one another, but life can't all be fun and play.

Now the questions about nomenclature among relatives have taken on a different tone:

"How do I introduce my former daughter-in-law, who is now married to someone else but is still the mother of my grandchildren?"

"My father and his second wife are now divorced, but she was a mother to me for years and we're still friendly. What do I call her?"

"The man who's living with my aunt keeps calling himself my uncle; how do I make it clear that he's no such thing?"

"My former husband attends our son's school events, which my present husband also attends with me. How am I supposed to refer to them?"

"Do I have to call my stepfather 'Daddy'? I hate him."

"My elderly mother married a man whose first wife was my mother's first cousin. Consequently, my new stepfather's children, my cousins, have become my stepbrothers and stepsisters. When I introduce these people to someone, do I introduce them as cousins or stepbrothers and stepsisters?"

"How do we stop my new son-in-law's children from a previous marriage from calling us 'Grandpa' and 'Grandma,' the way they hear their younger sister, who really is our grandchild, do?"

Ah, the adventure of modern living! So many interesting questions. And you expect Miss Manners to supply the answers, do you?

Well, let's see. The children of siblings are first cousins. The children of those cousins are second cousins. The next generation down, provided that they move at the same rate, would be third cousins. However, when you proceed through the generations at different rates, that's when the element of removal enters. The relationship of the child of one of the original siblings (OS) to the grandchild of another of the OS's would be that of first cousin once removed. The same child and the great-grandchild of the other OS would be first cousins twice removed. Can Miss Manners go home now?

She supposes not, because that question probably long ago ceased to interest anyone. There's no use quibbling over what to call relatives when you can't even figure out who your relatives are. All right. Your relatives are the ones who are currently related to you, and if you can possibly extend to them the courtesy titles of their positions, you should. Exactitude is not always necessary. It is warmer to say "my brother" than "my half-brother" or "my stepbrother," and no one is going to accuse you of exaggeration.

A child who feels disloyal using a parental title for a stepparent or parent equivalent should be allowed to use the given name, and one who wants to give the exact relationship rather than the general one should be allowed to do so. It's high time we took the pejorative fairy tale shading out of the term "step" anyway.

Miss Manners does not allow adults the same privilege. To forbid a child who wants the right to call you by a parental or grandparental title is mean.

Relationships severed by divorce are described in the terms of the ties that are left: "Natasha is my grandchildren's mother" or "This is my husband, and this is Curt's father."

Miss Manners hereby declares a new category, Optional Relatives, for those with whom one never had blood ties and no longer has marriage ties. When a divorce occurs, the couple's relatives who have gotten fond of one another may continue to consider themselves related. If the friendly remains of these families want to go on calling one another courtesy relatives, Miss Manners is not the one to stop them. She even offers them the opportunity to refer to themselves as being relatives "once removed."

Always

DEAR MISS MANNERS:
My daughter passed away after thirty-four years of marriage. My son-in-law plans on getting married again. Will he still be my son-in-law, and will his new

wife be my daughter-in-law? He keeps saying he will always be my son-in-law, and she tells me she will be my daughter-in-law. Will this be? They are very good and dear to me and help me out in many ways, as I live alone and am eighty-five years old. They pick me up to visit them and bring me home again, and tell me I don't need an invitation to visit them.

GENTLE READER:

Yes, he will always be your son-in-law, and she will be your daughter-in-law. This does not necessarily apply to other people in a similar situation, and in fact rarely does. But if anyone tries to tell you that it doesn't apply to you, send them to Miss Manners, who will deal with them very severely.

Divorce "Announcements"

Miss Manners could not figure out how it was possible that more divorces were being announced than marriages. Even allowing for the fact that the current theme of romance is "Why shouldn't I have the best that's available on the market?", it seemed statistically impossible. Then she came to realize that while one marriage announcement serves for two people, there are two divorce announcements for every divorce.

How many should there be? None. No, no, Miss Manners has not revoked your right to be divorced as often as you choose. You may even tell people that you are being divorced—useful information for those who want to invite both of you to dinner or to court one of you. It may be told in person or by letter, with as many details and as much emotional coloration as you think fitting, although Miss Manners strongly advises unembellished statements (just sprinkled with kind words about the parting spouse to show that you are not a victim) on the grounds of dignity, privacy and the fact that bitterness and gloating are equally unattractive postures.

What you cannot do is to make a mass announcement. Miss Manners has seen a variety of ghastly ones: cutesy cards, pseudoformal ones, and even form letters, offshoots of the photocopied letters Miss Manners so despises, with a biographical sketch of the replacement and the notation that the change of address was occasioned by the former spouse's stipulation that the new couple get out of sight.

This is not quite tasteful, is it? Surely if you purport to tell the whole story, the quality of the original couple's intimate life should be included, too, along with the superior attractions of the newcomer. (Miss Manners shouldn't joke. It is probably only a matter of time until someone does that.)

Few of life's events, no matter how significant, are proper subjects of formal announcements. You do not send cards announcing pregnancies, engagements, or deaths, and Miss Manners does not really approve of them for births either. All these things may be told and written, and may slip into the newspapers with some help from the interested parties, but they do not get themselves done up in engraved announcements or the equivalent. The pretense is that you are telling individuals, individually.

The model that is being used for divorce announcements is, not surprisingly, the marriage announcement (as distinct from the invitation), Miss Manners has analyzed this incorrect impulse as part of the widespread yearning for the trappings of marriage that arose the minute that respectable society no longer insisted on a couple's entering and maintaining wedlock. One does not "announce" a divorce as if it were a joyous event (even if it is for the announcer). The forms of marriage, including the announcement, do not apply to other occasions, as there is nothing exactly like marriage. Divorcing people should know that.

Acceptable Announcements

DEAR MISS MANNERS:
My divorce will be final well ahead of the holidays, and I'd like to let my distant friends know about the situation to save all of us from embarrassment when I send my Christmas cards. Personal notes are out of the question. I have three children, one a toddler, and a full-time job. There are about seventy-five distant friends who aren't likely to hear of our divorce except through our annual Christmas correspondence. Would a simple printed letter with both new addresses and without any details be acceptable? Do you have other ideas?

GENTLE READER:
All right. Because you are resisting the temptation to put this in a single mailing—"Merry Christmas! Tim and I have split!"—and are limiting the information, Miss Manners will approve your slipping the idea into a simple change-of-address card.

Dividing Wedding Presents

DEAR MISS MANNERS:
My wife asked for, and I agreed to, "a simplified dissolution of marriage" after living together for eleven years. It was my second and her fourth marriage. Among our wedding presents was a Steuben vase given to us by the daughter of my previous wife. My wife claims that all of our wedding presents automatically go to her upon the dissolution of our marriage. Is she correct?

GENTLE READER:
Miss Manners hates to argue with someone who has had so much experience in the field, but no. The rule about wedding presents is that they are returned to the sender if the marriage does not take place. Once it does, they cease to be wedding presents and become the joint property of the couple, to be given to whoever can

make a better case for possession—such as your argument about the vase's coming from your side of the family—or has the better lawyer.

Meeting Replacements

DEAR MISS MANNERS:

Several months ago, I separated from my partner after ten happy, wonderful years. (We never married for reasons I shall not elaborate on.) When he informed me that he had found a more suitable person to spend his life with, I moved out and established a home, career, and life on my own, and I am proud to say that I am doing quite well.

Though the separation was initially difficult—I at first vowed not to speak to the man for all eternity—I have risen above that and look forward to whatever I might encounter in my future. I hold no animosity toward my former partner, but for reasons I cannot quite explain, I would very much like to meet his new love interest. Would it be proper to extend an invitation to dinner to the two of them? Which would be more comfortable for all—dining at my new home or finding a more neutral place?

GENTLE READER:

What exactly did you do in the lower realms before rising above it all? This undoubtedly has a strong bearing on how the gentleman and his new partner perceive your overtures. Will they believe that you hold no animosity?

Miss Manners understands why you want this meeting: You wish to take satisfaction in finding that he has done a lot worse for himself and in demonstrating to him that you are as well off or better without him. There is nothing wrong with these motivations unless you exhibit them to your guests, which would be rude. If you promise to maintain a neutrally friendly demeanor, in which they can only guess from your total absence of rancor that you hold no grudges, Miss Manners will help you arrange the meeting.

It will not be easy. Even if the other person has the same curiosity that you have, no gentleman in his right mind would sit still for such a confrontation. Some instinct ought to tell him that the fatuousness of enjoying the company of present and past loves at the same time would not be worth the risk he takes by sitting between you if anything should go wrong. He probably doesn't even imagine the risk if everything should go right. Suppose that you two hit it off and start exchanging confidences about his weaknesses?

Your best hope, therefore, is to form an excuse for seeing him—the need of advice, a request for some object you left behind, or, if it is plausible, merely the desire for a friendly talk. As he is reckoning how damaging a private visit with you would be to his present relationship, add, "Oh, and do bring Kim along. I wouldn't feel right about our meeting otherwise." Miss Manners promises you that he will relay the invitation reluctantly to Kim and that Kim will say, "You bet I'm coming along." You may then negotiate the circumstances. Your home is better for showing off how you live now, but a public place is regarded as a protection against emotional scenes.

The Subtle Gloat

DEAR MISS MANNERS:

How can I best congratulate my former husband on the birth of his first child? I divorced him three years ago for refusing to let me have children, and I was too honorable to trap him into a family. I've remarried and have a year-old baby despite medical difficulties. Last year, my ex met a divorcée with two children. They bought a house and she became "accidentally" pregnant, according to my former sister-in-law. The couple married in haste, and he recently mentioned the coming birth in a note accompanying a birthday card to my daughter. I have no idea how he feels about the baby.

The fact that they are creating a family when he would not do so with me annoys me, but I don't want them to suspect that. It also hurts because recent medical setbacks have forced us to postpone expansion of our own family, though I am approaching my mid-thirties and am longing to have two more children. On the other hand, I think it is poetic justice that this hussy snared him with a timeworn ploy that I disdained. Should I just act sweet and send a huge, atrocious-looking baby gift?

GENTLE READER:

It seems to Miss Manners that nature has settled this score by giving you a baby with a presumably proud father and giving your former husband, who has a pronounced dislike of children, custody of three of them. Surely that should satisfy you without tempting you to write or do something mean, which would, just as you fear, inform them of your continuing discontent. Well, if you promise to congratulate him straight (or almost straight, as in "I'm so happy for you; isn't parenthood marvelous?"), you may offer to send him your baby's outgrown clothes.

Casual Questions

DEAR MISS MANNERS:

The other day, I met an old friend whom I hadn't seen for a very long time. We went through the usual formalities, telling each other about our homes, families, and so on. When I inquired about the well-being of her husband, she replied, "Oh, we've been divorced for about two years now." I didn't know whether to say, "Oh, how nice for you," or "Oh, I'm so sorry." Being stunned, I simply replied, "Oh! . . . And how's your mother?" How should I have reacted?

GENTLE READER:

Exactly as you did. As congratulations on a divorce would be unseemly and commiseration may well be inappropriate, the tactful thing to do is to go on to the next pleasantry and hope that it will fare better.

Asking After Former Spouses

DEAR MISS MANNERS:

We have several friends who are divorcées and whose husbands we also knew as friends when they were still married. When we see these divorcées socially, is it proper to ask about their former husbands—where they are, how they are, and so on? One of us says yes; it is perfectly okay because the husbands are, after all, old acquaintances. The other says no; it is potentially embarrassing and/or distressing to the divorcée. What do you say?

GENTLE READER:

Does one of you want Miss Manners to decree that politeness requires inquiring after the health and welfare of former spouses? Is one of you mad?

The chances of getting more of an answer than you can stand are enormous. Besides, it is unreasonable to suppose that anyone is necessarily in constant touch with a former husband or wife, and that a question designed for members of the same household would apply after divorce. As a matter of fact, Miss Manners was toying with the idea of rescinding the old custom of inquiring after what is assumed to be a *present* spouse. A lot of people report being badly burned as a result of that pleasantry.

Dining with a Former Spouse

DEAR MISS MANNERS:

While in another city to visit her children, my wife went out to dinner (she paid for hers) with her former husband. Following dinner, they visited at his apartment. This came to my attention through a third party. My wife explained to me that she was without transportation at the time and was very hungry. It was a favor on his part to take her out, because he was not hungry at the time. I admit to not being too happy about it, but I have accepted it.

My wife and I will be in that city for a few days next month. I have met this man several times and wonder if it would be in order for me to invite him out to dinner with us, with no other reason than to return the favor. My wife doesn't think that this is necessary because she paid for her own meal.

GENTLE READER:

You are not seriously trying to tell Miss Manners that your motive is to reciprocate a favor that a gentleman showed to your wife, are you? Good. Because accompanying a lady to dinner is rather a minimal courtesy and, in any case, it was not extended to you. One could argue that she would be obliged to do the same for him under similar circumstances, but Miss Manners doesn't think you want to do that.

Let's address the real question, which is how you can properly discourage your wife from socializing with her former husband because, reasonable as it may be, you don't like it. You have already discovered that you do not have a good argument for objecting. Rather than claiming hunger, she could have mentioned the unassailable motive of wishing to discuss the children. You are also on the right track in guessing that the best way is therefore to join them. As you are both going to be in the city where he and the children live, you could voice an interest in being included in all visits—to the children because they are your stepchildren, and to him because he is their father or simply because (you must declare with a straight face) you like him. In doing this, you will show yourself to be friendly, rather than jealous, which is as unassailable as any reasons they might have for seeing each other. By the way, Miss Manners suggests that you sever relations with the third party who reported back to you. That person is really up to no good.

Split Family Holidays

DEAR MISS MANNERS:

My husband and I have been married for one year; it is the second marriage for both of us. Charlie has two grown sons in their twenties who live out of state. Both came to Thanksgiving dinner with us and brought their girlfriends. It was arranged ahead of time between Charlie and his former wife that we would host Thanksgiving dinner (they have their own plans for Christmas).

Wednesday night, after I had shopped for a fresh turkey and all the trimmings, we accidentally found out that the lady had prepared and served a full Thanksgiving feast. Unable to face the prospect of going through all that trouble only to duplicate a meal and set it in front of four already stuffed guests, I proposed to my husband that we serve something else. As it was past 9:00 P.M., we were lucky to find six good steaks in our freezer. Both he and I were very disappointed, and I must say that I took it hard, becoming furious and weepy in turns.

Needless to say, Thanksgiving was a subdued affair. Everyone was aware that there was something amiss. Little was said about the change in menu. Am I right in feeling that the former wife was thoughtless in her choice of menu? Should I have taken it so personally? Should I have served turkey anyway? Finally, should I call her and tell her about my feelings?

GENTLE READER:

The turkey is not the problem. Miss Manners never thought of turkey as a subtle bird, but that's not what caused the trouble. The problem is adjusting tradition to the nontraditional family. It is all very well to agree to split the holidays between the parties to a divorce the way you split the property, but it is even harder to do.

Miss Manners hopes that you are not going to condemn someone for trying to salvage a bit of family ceremony for her own consolation. Even if her motive was to undercut your party, she would be more pathetic than mean. Let it go. Redundancy is inevitable when the parents have separate households. Wherever the children dine on Christmas or their birthdays, you will each exchange presents with them and have your own little celebrations.

Everyone eats turkey at least two days in a row every Thanksgiving anyway. At least your stepsons would have gotten their seconds fresh and hot.

Delicate Disapproval

DEAR MISS MANNERS:

Everyone in our family was shocked when, after thirty-four years of marriage, my father-in-law suddenly divorced my mother-in law and almost immediately remarried. The children of the previous union felt bitter towards their father, and have all been emotionally and financially supportive of their mother.

However, in a recent desire to improve the relationship with his father, my husband suggested that we send anniversary cards and/or gifts to his father and the new wife. We remembered him at Christmas, Father's Day, and his birthday, and have invited Dad and his new spouse to our home for dinner. The message we are trying to convey is one of acceptance; however, I feel that to send congratulatory cards to celebrate their anniversaries is hypocritical, in that it would convey approval as well as acceptance, which is not the children's general attitude.

My husband and I recently celebrated an anniversary, for which we received no acknowledgment from his father, and my husband believes that a change in our policy toward the new marriage would effect one toward our own anniversary. Where does one draw the line?

GENTLE READER:

The line you wish to draw here is an extremely fine one. You want it to be all but invisible, so that your father-in-law cannot complain of rejection while you comfort yourself by withholding full acceptance. So far, you are succeeding in keeping on visiting terms in spite of what they evidently understand as the small slight of ignoring their anniversary; they are reacting to that only by ignoring yours.

Miss Manners sees nothing wrong with your continuing this policy, provided you pretend that you have not noticed the retaliatory action. If you try to have it both ways (recognition of your anniversary without that of your father-in-law's), you will be escalating a minor skirmish with tiny weapons into all-out warfare over your attitude towards his marriage—which is precisely what you have so far managed wisely to avoid.

Sending Thanks

DEAR MISS MANNERS:

Is it proper to write a letter to my mother in-law, prior to my divorce, telling her that I have enjoyed having her as a mother-in-law? My husband and I are recently separated. I will probably not see her or his two sisters again, except for weddings and/or funerals (they live in another state), and I feel that I would like to say that I've enjoyed being in their family.

GENTLE READER:

This is a charming idea, for which Miss Manners commends you. It is no small thing to make a daughter-in-law feel a part of one's family, and thanking someone for having done so seems highly appropriate.

Friends and Mothers

DEAR MISS MANNERS:

I am eighteen years old and have been away from home for nine months in the Air Force. Between the ages of sixteen and eighteen, I lived with my dad and his wife, Cathy, who is thirty. During that time, Cathy acted as a mother figure. But she's still trying to play the motherly role. She's too young for me to look at her as "Mom," but I like her as a friend. How do I tell her that I care for her as a friend but not as a mother? I don't want to hurt her feelings in any way.

GENTLE READER:

Miss Manners cannot help but wonder what motherly function Cathy is performing that you find objectionable. Offering to read you stories? Demanding that you clean up your room? Any parent or stepparent who performs parenting tasks that are no longer appropriate because of the child's age may be gently discouraged by an affectionate reminder that one is growing up. Do not object to parental caring, which is an intensified version of the partiality one hopes for from friends but is less likely to find. If Cathy exhibits this, good for her; it would be mean and purposeless to quibble about the relationship on the grounds of her age.

The Biological Father

DEAR MISS MANNERS:

I recently acquired the address of my biological father, with whom I have not had previous contact. What would be the proper salutation for a letter to him? Also, would it be rude for me to include in such a letter the fact that I grew up with a large, happy family, and inform him that my stepfather is putting me through college and probably law school? Is this a question of etiquette or simply personal judgment? Please don't suggest that I ask my mother.

GENTLE READER:

Etiquette decrees that you approach your father respectfully or not at all. To look him up simply for the purpose of pointing out how much better your stepfather has treated you, would be rude. Miss Manners suggests that you address him as "My dear father" to avoid the stiffness of using his name, as well as the perhaps startling effect of an unexpected letter beginning "Dear Daddykins." You should tell him that you are leading a happy family life, not only as a point of information but also to relieve him of any worry about the consequences of his action, but it is not necessary to single out your stepfather's contribution.

Grandparents

DEAR MISS MANNERS:

Two weeks ago, I had a small dinner party for my son's fourth birthday. I invited my mother and her fiancé, my brother and his family, my sister, and a cousin and her family. My husband and I have been separated for almost a year, and our divorce will be final in a month or two. I did not invite him to dinner, but I did tell him that he would be welcome to come and have birthday cake with us. He refused, but that is not the problem.

It seems that my soon-to-be former in-laws felt that they should have been invited. They have repeatedly ranted and raved to members of my family about what a terrible thing I did to them. I just felt that inviting them would be improper at this time, not to mention awkward. I didn't do it to be mean or rude. I just thought it was the correct thing to do.

How do I handle situations like this in the future? What happens if I remarry or even have a boyfriend I would like to invite? I can't see myself with a boyfriend and my former in-laws all at the same dinner table. I should add that my husband and his parents did have their own party the following week, so I can't understand why they are still screaming about mine. Please help!

GENTLE READER:

What bothers your former husband's parents is not that they were relegated to the status of former in-laws, which could explain leaving them out of many events in your life, but that they were being treated as former grandparents, which they are not. Your son will always be related to these people. When he is older, he may choose to be with them, rather than you, on special days if you establish the idea that one parent gets it all. (If you did not want to invite them, you could have made it possible for your son to spend part of the day with them; a party a week later may not mean the same thing. Or, if you think it does, you could have given your party on another day and let him spend the birthday with his grandparents.)

Stepparents

DEAR MISS MANNERS:

My husband's former wife developed the rather elaborate plan of having his mother and her mother accompany the two of them to their son's graduation. The impetus for this "equal" division of tickets became abundantly clear when my husband's mother declined to attend on the grounds that I, as the young man's stepmother and caretaker for many years of weekends, should be there for the celebration, and the former wife absolutely refused to give my husband a ticket for me. It's true that extra tickets are not available. Unfortunately, instead of listening to the urgings of my husband and his mother, she has now chosen to take both of her parents with her to the graduation. Her son has ratified her decision, but I say, pity the poor child put in the middle by his mother.

Are there any rules of etiquette which govern the division of places at graduation, or am I, along with other stepmothers, left with only common sense and common courtesy as grounds for my contention that this is a singularly vulgar display of pettiness and not a perfectly fitting disposition for four places at a graduation?

GENTLE READER:

Etiquette for stepmothers unfortunately requires forbearance under trying circumstances. Miss Manners is confident that if you thought it over, you would realize that inviting a child's grandparents to his graduation cannot be construed as an insult to his stepmother. Miss Manners believes that if you take the decision cheerfully and assure your stepson that you will be thinking of him with pride on that occasion, he will confide to you what a difficult choice it was.

One More Try

DEAR MISS MANNERS:

I was recently divorced from my wife of seven years. We have two children and have decided to give the marriage one more try. However, her mother is demanding an apology for the pain I caused her because of my weakness. (Another woman was involved in my departure, but I did not leave just for her. We had other problems, and that was simply the final act.) My mother-in-law never liked me or supported our marriage. I feel that the fact that my wife is coming back proves that she and the Lord have forgiven me.

GENTLE READER:

Perhaps, but the Lord does not necessarily offer an on-the-spot defense of this position at family gatherings. On the occasion of One More Try, it is customary to hand out abject apologies right and left, without counting how well deserved they are. (It is even particularly gracious for nonerring parties to say, "Well, I suppose in a way it was my fault," for the purpose of having this vigorously denied by the erring party.) One more apology won't hurt. After a while, you can enlist your wife's cooperation in declaring a cutoff, after which, if all goes well, no one can again bring up the subject of your sins.

The Child's Home

DEAR MISS MANNERS:

I share a house with my POSSLQ (Person of the Opposite Sex Sharing Living Quarters) and his fourteen-year-old son. The boy's mother lives in another city but comes here on business approximately one week out of every five or six. When they were married, she and my POSSLQ occupied the house that he and I now share.

She sees her son whenever possible, generally picking him up and taking him out to dinner, and we have no objection whatsoever to that. However, on several occasions, I have innocently bounded down the stairs of our home and, with no prior warning, found my POSSLQ's ex visiting and chatting with her son in our living room.

I contend that if she wishes to use our home, she should call and inquire if this is a convenient time to visit. Perhaps my POSSLQ's son should inform us that his mother wishes to visit him. (She usually calls him and just announces that she is coming.) My POSSLQ contends that she is the guest of his son and need only clear her visit with him. I feel that (1) she is in a special category of guest; (2) since these visits take place in the common living areas and not in the privacy of the boy's room (which is usually in a typical teenager's disheveled state), they affect us; and (3) it is uncomfortable for me to be caught completely unaware that my POSSLQ's ex is in our home.

I recognize the strong bond between mother and son, but do we not have any rights at all where our home is concerned?

GENTLE READER:

What do you mean, "we"? The two other Persons with whom you are Sharing Living Quarters seem to agree perfectly. Miss Manners also agrees that limiting the boy's privilege of entertaining his own mother in his own home would make it clear to him that this is no longer really his home. It is your home, too, and you have the right to ask the boy to check with you before scheduling visits and, if it is seriously inconvenient, to ask him to see her elsewhere. Miss Manners advises you against exercising this right beyond the formality of asking to be informed.

If the mother comes to town only once every five or six weeks and generally takes him out, we are talking about a home visit perhaps four times a year. There does not seem to be any question of her acting as if the house were still hers or of taking the opportunity to confront you. You don't even seem to know that she is there unless you happen to walk into the room. Miss Manners asks you, as an adult, to consider the inconvenience to you of having a quiet chat going on in your living room four times a year, as against the inconvenience to a child of having no private place where he can be with his mother. She believes that the two persons with whom you are sharing living quarters also expect an adult—not to mention compassionate—reaction from you.

Noncustodial Parental Duty

DEAR MISS MANNERS:

I have observed, at close hand, over the past two years, the relationship of a divorced father with his two out-of-state children. The father has sent the children $175 per month, not only on time but months ahead of time, so that no need would arise on their part. He has phoned his children weekly in a sincere attempt to have a positive influence on their lives. He has arranged and paid for plane fare for Christmas, Easter, and summer visits. When he lost his job, no one asked him how he was. He received threats of jail from the children's mother if payments stopped. Don't you think that at least a thank-you note should be sent in acknowledgment of the child support payments? I think that there is a definite lack of manners on the part of the receiving parties, to say the least.

GENTLE READER:

Why does Miss Manners think that you are in love with the divorced father? It comforts her to believe that he has someone close to him who appreciates his steadiness and commiserates with him in his troubles. She will go so far as to say that it is rude of the former wife to threaten him when he has always been faithful in meeting his obligations and unfeeling of the children to show no sympathy for him in his professional plight. But do not take that as agreement with you that the gentleman's children and former wife ought to be writing him thank-you letters for child support.

Financial and emotional support for one's children, whether one is married or divorced, is part of being a parent. Are the children in the habit of thanking their mother for rearing them, or, for that matter, does the father thank her for doing so? Miss Manners hopes that all grown children eventually reflect on the devotion of their parents and thank them for it. A youngster who did so would be making the pathetic assumption that the father is doing a favor rather than his natural duty.

The Changing Household

What Constitutes A Household

Along with the rest of her generation, Miss Manners is scandalized when she hears of unmarried couples who are living together without doing anything, uh, scandalous.

When a nice young lady explained placidly that her devoted fiancé was acquiring another nice young lady as a roommate while the fiancé was away finishing graduate school so that they could get married, Miss Manners had to reach for her smelling salts. She has been assured by a number of respectable young people that it is not uncommon to assume various living combinations, from dormitory life on, without any romantic goings-on at all. She believes it, but she will never understand it.

The shock has, however, determined Miss Manners not to get involved in the question of who should constitute a household. It's too bewildering. Genders and generations mean nothing anymore. Roommates, couples, noncouples, families, stepfamilies, friends—you are a unit if you declare yourself one.

But what constitutes a proper household, as opposed to who, is a topic Miss

Manners is not prepared to resign. In all this redesigning of living groups, household manners and traditions have been dangerously neglected.

Miss Manners does hear a great deal about what constitutes fair living arrangements. What troubles her is that it always centers on defending rights rather than building bonds.

Any household, even a collection of transient roommates who selected the house more carefully than another, needs rituals. A place where every inch and movement is the subject of jurisdictional decrees and jealously defended rights is not even a temporary home.

Certainly, those sharing a house need to know where they can count on having privacy and who will do which chores. Of course, things should be fair, although fairness in a household, as opposed to an impersonal organization, has less to do with sameness than with indulging everyone's individual differences. This requires a high sense of courtesy. Fooled by the fact that intimates can use informal manners among themselves, many people assume that this means abandoning politeness at the door. Why anyone would stay in a house where his or her feelings are treated more roughly than they are by strangers, Miss Manners cannot understand, and, judging from the divorce statistics, apparently they don't.

To forge a household, there must also be shared space and shared activities. The conventional method is to have several common rooms or areas—recreational and dining sites—and to meet daily for at least one meal.

Nothing that calls itself a family can afford to do without these basics, even if the common area is tiny and the meals are rushed. Regular gatherings, with their lack of a specific agenda, are what make people something more than just a collection of individuals delivering messages to one another.

Beyond the daily ritual are traditions—ways of celebrating holidays and birthdays and ways of spending weekends; shared fondness for possessions that no one else would want to have and jokes that outsiders wouldn't understand.

For those in looser arrangements, this may hardly seem worthwhile. Miss Manners wants to convince them that it is. Coming home to a warmthless hearth, with no apparatus for sharing the vicissitudes of life with others, is bound to have a depressing effect. A modified version for roommates might include keeping a table and chairs, or a futon area, where anyone at home can hang around and expect to find company, and having a regular Sunday brunch with everyone present.

Otherwise, what is going to happen when one of the householders gets into a shocking situation? How dreadful it would be to live amid people who wouldn't even know or care about it.

🌹 THE UNMARRIED COUPLE

Periodically, chiefly for the exercise, Miss Manners takes up the Great Insolvable Etiquette Problem. It is: What do you call the person you . . .? How do you introduce your son's . . .? What is the proper term for the man your mother . . .?

You see the problem. It isn't girlish innocence that prevents Miss Manners from finishing those descriptions. It's a vocabulary shortage. Once upon a time, when people were doing exactly what they are doing now, they didn't tell everybody about it, so they didn't need a word to describe the person whom they . . . . You see the trouble you can get into? Now that the relationship has gone public, we need a name for the participants. Miss Manners has long cherished the hope that once provided with a noun, these people will stop using all those verbs to explain what they are doing. But what noun, she asks her Gentle Readers?

The rules are:

1. No cute terms, overly descriptive of the private aspects of the relationship, are allowed; it should not sound too much like fun. The last requirement does not reflect moral disapproval, but only the impracticality of describing a complex bond only by its most recreational aspect. Not only is that not the public's business, but the public, far from being consumed with erotic envy, as the participants suppose, is revolted. A married person who regularly introduced a spouse by mentioning how much in love they are would find that society would kindly leave the two of them alone together forever. Besides, this shows a naiveté about the long-term household arrangement. Everyday life has its ups and downs, and there has to be a respectful but nonromantic term to describe the person who left wet towels on the bathroom floor and then forgot to stop for the groceries on the way home. The word must fit easily into this sentence: "Can you tell the jury in your own words why you shot your ——?"

2. One should not take ordinary, useful words that apply to other relationships and spray sexual innuendo all over them. "Friend" and "roommate" need to be kept free of romantic associations. Not only are they needed to describe the state of friendship and roommatehood, but they are useful to romantic couples who do not wish to share confidences with the public. There is little enough ambiguity left in the world as it is.

3. Minted words are extremely hard to get into circulation and should not be overly contrived. POSSLQ, for "people of the opposite sex sharing living quarters," is all very well, but does it have enough vowels in it?

Here are some readers' suggestions:

"May I suggest, when referred to together, a 'committed couple,' and, when referred to singly, 'committed partner.' "

" 'Householdmate.' It is a bit long, but I find that it indicates a commitment which 'housemate' does not —not just sharing a building, but sharing a decision to build a home or household—in other words, a family. We refer to each other's families, by the way, as 'un-laws.' "

"What do you think of 'bosom companions'—as a more literal term than 'friends,' that is?"

"I would like to suggest the word 'kimmering' as a solution both pleasant to the ear and of honorable pedigree. In the fictional society Ursula Le Guin describes in her novel *The Left Hand of Darkness,* citizens are biologically androgynous and marriage, as we understand it, does not exist. Rather there is the kimmering—

the union of two beings, two soul mates, who feel an enduring loyalty to each other regardless of other sexual liaisons."

"Tracing its etymology from Latin through Middle French and Middle English, one finds that the literal meaning of 'consort' is 'one who shares a common lot.' It is most appropriate when referring to the relationship between gods and goddesses, as well as modern cohabitors—who, in matters of love, recognize no authority higher than their own hearts."

" 'Virtual spouse,' while not as easy to say as 'paraspouse,' is a reasonable use of English. The humor comes from the IBM dictionary of computer terminology, which has four pages devoted to virtual this and virtual that. While I have a real, not a virtual, spouse, I do have a virtual sister-in-law: the mother of my husband's nephews."

"I send you an essay by Phillip Howard from his book *Words Fail Me*. While the end is a bit oblique, I take him to be recommending that we resurrect the medieval term 'leman.' "

"A local singles newspaper ran a contest and the winner was 'amourge,' a combination of the words 'amour' and 'merger.' "

' "Common-law wife' was good enough for the poor ladies of days gone by when their men didn't want to marry them, so it should be good enough for today's generation."

"The answer is so simple, Miss Manners. A gentleman who lives with a woman, entertains with her, sleeps with her, shops at K-Mart with her, and tends the dog with her calls her his 'wife.' Likewise, she tells the liquor delivery man that 'My husband will pay' and not 'My boyfriend, my lover, my concubine, my sweetie, or my sugar daddy will pay.' People who reject or cannot get legal sanction for their union are correctly called 'wife' and 'husband' so long as they are living the lives of wife and husband."

"A mother could proudly introduce the young man with whom her daughter has chosen to live without embarrassing her daughter, the young man, the third person, or herself, by saying, 'This is my daughter's sweetheart.' Doesn't that seem appropriate for public daytime usage? To me, it conveys the thought that the couple are indeed committed and in love. The implication of sexuality can be left to a shared address."

"I have suggested the French word 'habitant,' meaning dweller, occupier, or inmate of a house. After all, we got the word 'fiancé' from the French."

" 'Pliancé,' rhymes with 'fiancé,' and has a certain classy ring to it. The word is derived from: Persons Living In A Noncommitted Environment."

"When I was a young man just after World War II, soldiers who lived with native women without marriage were said to be 'shacked up,' presumably because they moved into shacks instead of living in the regular barracks. I believe the phrase still has some popularity as a mildly disapproving way of describing what used to be called 'living in sin.' So I propose that such persons be called 'shackmates.' "

"I suggest 'sweetmates.' "

"In her Darkover novels, Marion Zimmer Bradley uses the term 'freemate,' and I think it quite adequate."

Miss Manners is resisting the temptation to stamp objections 1, 2, or 3 on each of these. The problem has gone unsolved far too long, and she is weakened enough by it to be willing to accept anything that everybody else is prepared to go along with.

Telling

DEAR MISS MANNERS:

Having been involved in a long-distance romance for some time, I will move closer to my boyfriend this summer so that we can decide whether to marry some day. Though I would prefer to live in my own apartment, finances require that I accept his invitation to move into his spare bedroom, at least until I am settled into a new job. My parents understand the situation but have asked that I not tell my grandmother, who would disapprove of the arrangement. I am a terrible liar, and would prefer to answer my grandmother's questions truthfully and weather the storm of her disapproval. However, my parents would be the innocent targets of much of her raging. Should I create an acceptable fiction for my grandmother to spare my family these arguments?

GENTLE READER:

If you have convinced your mother that finances are the only reason for your moving into the gentleman's apartment, you are not as bad at fudging facts as you wish Miss Manners to believe. Were you ever so impoverished, Miss Manners dares say that you would find some way—doubling up with a female friend is the obvious one—to avoid sharing an apartment with a gentleman you found unappealing.

The issue that you present, of sparing your parents your grandmother's disapproval, is easily solved. As you say, you can take it on yourself, without attempting to cite parental approval, thus leaving your parents free to defend themselves with, "No, we don't like it, but she's grown up and makes her own decisions."

More difficult is the question of whether your grandmother needs sparing. If she is feisty enough to argue social questions with you, perhaps you should just tell her. If, however, she is frail and likely only to be distressed by the news—and unlikely to visit you—surely you can fudge a bit more. "I'm using Eric's address; after all, I'm over there practically all the time" is not exactly a lie.

Presumptuous Thanks

DEAR MISS MANNERS:

After my brother was hospitalized for surgery, his live-in girlfriend sent all family members thank-you notes for visiting him during his stay. His only daughter was totally outraged and is no longer speaking. I'm sure that the girlfriend meant no harm—in fact, meant well. Was she out of line?

GENTLE READER:

It is a novelty for Miss Manners to hear of someone who has managed to get seriously out of line by the act of writing thank-you letters, especially when it is entirely possible that the lady meant no harm. Allow Miss Manners to extend her congratulations. By demonstrating that she does the honors for the couple, your brother's friend has also, perhaps inadvertently, announced that she is his only intimate. Hospitals distinguish between family and other visitors, and she has attempted to put herself in the former category and the actual relatives in the latter. Even a wife would be presumptuous to write anything more than a "Jason asked me to let you know that he was grateful . . ." letter to other members of the family for gathering at the bedside of one of their own. Your brother's best hope for a peaceful recovery is to put out the word that she was merely expressing his own feelings when he didn't feel up to writing.

What We Need Not Know

DEAR MISS MANNERS:

My life partner is a man and my best friend. Even if marriage were legally obtainable between persons of the same sex, I seriously doubt that the two of us would seek to obtain such legal recognition. Our relationship does not include sharing sex, and we both prefer it that way. Aside from that, we relate to a great extent as a married couple. Therefore, I tend to assume that when I am invited anywhere and the invitation includes my "spouse," it is within the bounds of etiquette to take my friend and inform the host that I am doing so. I feel that society has no concern with anyone's private life. At the same time, I feel that I have the right to be as public about my sexual affiliations as heterosexual married couples are. People who also happen to be homosexual desire their meaningful, supportive, and loving relationships to be as recognized as those of people who happen to be heterosexual.

GENTLE READER:

Why did you feel obliged to explain to Miss Manners that your relationship does not include sharing sex? Did she ask you? If she invited you to dinner, do you suppose she would demand to know what you are likely to do when you go home? The fact is that there is altogether too much recognition being demanded nowadays concerning people's private lives. Miss Manners makes no distinction here between unmarried heterosexual and homosexual couples. Indeed, how could she, as she does not inquire into people's personal preferences when she sees them socially, unless it is to ask whether they are allergic to shellfish.

Nor does she approve of guests informing their hosts whom they will bring. It is courteous to invite two people together who are known to be a couple socially, regardless of the composition of the couple, but the hosts may not know of your arrangements. You can *ask,* "Do you mind if I bring Adam? We generally go about together." Miss Manners assures you that she would make no distinction in this matter between this and your saying, "Do you mind if I bring Eve?"

🥀 THE TRADITIONAL FAMILY

What are three things that you can safely say about people who habitually make the following statements?

"You never pay any attention to me."

"You've always got your head stuck in some old book instead of talking to me."

"You treat me like a piece of furniture."

"The minute you get me a drink at a party, you always disappear."

"Why is everything and everyone else so much more interesting than being with me?"

"You never talk to me anymore."

"I guess I bore you."

Well, let's see:

1. They're married.

2. They're right.

3. They are, nevertheless, too dreary to capture anyone's attention, so these pathetic pleas will never be satisfactorily answered.

Miss Manners realizes how harshly she is judging unhappy people whose only wish is the legitimate one of capturing the interest of their spouses. She promises that once she gets their attention, she will endeavor to help.

It is popularly believed, in these simplistic times, that the best way to get something one wants is to ask for it. Therefore, the more frankly, honestly, and clearly one states one's desires, the better the chance one has of achieving them.

The fact that this has never worked in the domain of emotions, not once since the world began, does not seem to discourage people from trying. By a perversity of nature, it just so happens that accusations such as "You don't love me" or "You don't love me enough" do not inspire great rushes of passion; they inspire a distaste only slightly tinged, in the case of well-meaning people, with regret.

What happens to those marital complaints of not being given attention? The spouse sighs, reluctantly stops whatever he or she was doing, denies the charge, and then, with visible effort, tries to fix attention on the person who asked for it. Good will and self-control stave off fidgeting for a while, but an air of being cornered is impossible to disguise. At the first decent excuse, the spouse's attention is off again. It is a second humiliation for the original complainer.

There is no greater believer than Miss Manners in observing pleasant forms, at least to disguise, and perhaps even to influence, unacceptable feelings. In the particular circumstances of marriage, however, excessive demands are often made for the forms of attention, without even minimum corresponding efforts being made to attract attention, as it were.

For example, it is not actually a required politeness that one "pay attention" to one's spouse at a social gathering, beyond the mechanics of disposing of coats, and acquiring first drinks, and making introductions. It can even be a rudeness. While we acknowledge that couples often wish to concentrate on each other, we assume that that is why they have a home together, and that when they emerge to go to parties, it is for the purpose of socializing with others.

Even in the home, certain social conditions prevail. One does not attempt to get someone's attention by depriving that person of other legitimate interests. Not only is it often rude, but it usually doesn't work. At the risk of dealing in substance rather than form, Miss Manners must reveal that satisfactory attention is the result of true interest rather than the demand for its semblance. While exclusive interest in one other human being, which is what we call courtship, is all very exciting in the stages of discovery, there is not enough substance in it for a lifetime, no matter how fascinating the people or passionate the romance.

The world, on the other hand, is chock-full of interesting and curious things. The point of the courtship—marriage—is to secure someone with whom you wish to go hand in hand through this source of entertainment, each making discoveries, and then sharing some and merely reporting others. Anyone who tries to compete with the entire world, demanding to be someone's sole source of interest and attention, is asking to be classified as a bore. "Why don't you ever want to talk to me?" will probably never start a satisfactory marital conversation. "Guess what?" will probably never fail.

Disguising Boredom

DEAR MISS MANNERS:

My husband and I were engaging in some after-dinner reading one recent evening. He sat down beside me and began to relate the details of an article he had just read on nuclear nonproliferation treaties. I wasn't at all interested in the topic (I know that everyone is supposed to be interested in nuclear warfare, but I am not interested *all* of the time) and showed my noninterest by my nonverbal behavior. I did not maintain eye contact, I did not look enthusiastic, I offered no verbal encouragement, and I even yawned a few times (unfeigned, I assure you). After about five minutes of nuclear nonproliferation details, my husband broke off and exclaimed angrily, "You're not listening! You're doing everything you can to discourage me from talking!" I replied, also angrily, "That's right! So why don't you take a hint?"

A quarrel ensued, with no resolution of the issue, which is: Was I rude to show a lack of interest, or should I have feigned attention? Was he rude to continue talking in the face of obvious lack of interest? Would your opinion of this be any different if the interchange occurred between friends, co-workers, or strangers rather than spouses? The last question bears on a larger issue of whether standards of civility ought to differ within families as opposed to outside them.

GENTLE READER:

They should, and you have violated them. There is hardly a more devastating insult that you can deliver to another human being than the judgment that he is boring you. This is not to say that we all have to allow others to talk us to death, even those to whom we are married, but only that you must offer some excuse other than ennui.

Here are some samples:

"Just a minute, dear, I'm in the middle of something. Can you tell me later?"

"My poor brain is too exhausted to follow what you're saying right now."

"That sounds interesting, but I can't quite follow it this way. Why don't you just give me the article when you're finished, and I'll read it myself as soon as I can."

"Darling, this is just not the day for me to worry about nuclear warfare. I know that everyone is supposed to be interested, and you know I am, but I just can't face it all the time." Notice that this one is taken from your own words, with just a little tact applied.

Incidentally, Miss Manners believes that exclaiming aloud about what one is reading is, when not abused, one of the basic rights of matrimony. If you discourage your husband from telling you what interests him, you will be making a serious mistake. Keeping alive the habit of sharing thoughts is certainly worth a few minutes of boredom cheerfully endured.

Miss Manners is not entirely without sympathy for you, however, so she will tell you how to discourage him from excesses, such as reading the newspaper or whatever magazines or books he is in the middle of, aloud to you every day. Jump up, say enthusiastically, "Let me see that!", and take the reading material away from him and start reading it yourself. He will learn to be more cautious about this particular subdivision of sharing, but without feeling that he bores you and should therefore control all desire to communicate.

Joined in Marriage, Not at the Hip

DEAR MISS MANNERS:

A good friend of my husband's from college days has asked my husband to be a member of his wedding party. I have met the groom several times and the bride once. We have learned that they intend to have a head table for the wedding party. I am to be seated by myself at another table with people I have met only at other weddings.

I have suggested that my husband call the groom and tell him that he appreciates the couple's desire to have a head table, but he would prefer to sit with his wife. My feeling is that if they are unable to accommodate his wish, I will simply not attend. My husband would then attend by himself and provide some (awkward?) excuse as to why I was unable to come. What is your opinion?

GENTLE READER:

That it's going to be a boring marriage—yours, that is—with no social life.

The best place for the two of you to sit together at dinner is at home. If you cannot exert yourself enough to make friends with your husband's old friends for the course of a meal, you certainly should not be going about socially.

Miss Manners hopes that you will not attempt to restrict your husband's social life as well. If it is not a serious embarrassment to him to have to declare that his wife cannot manage without his social support, it will be an increasing annoyance to have to entertain you in public, rather than being allowed to keep old friends and make new ones. Do not make the mistake of believing that insisting upon being together at all times will demonstrate how much in love you are. It will only suggest that at least one of you is afraid to let the other out of sight.

Controlling One's Spouse

DEAR MISS MANNERS:

How do I deal with a woman who always simpers, and engages my husband in very quiet and animated conversation, when we meet at social gatherings? She hangs on to him the whole time in a way that would be inappropriate if I did it! Her marriage is on the rocks. My husband is, of course, flattered and quite pathetic. I would dearly love to say something politely scathing but am at a loss. I really don't mind normal social chatter with other women, but this one is on her own!

GENTLE READER:

You would indeed be saying something scathing if you chose to show your disapproval of this lady's conduct. You would be saying to your husband, "Listen, you poor pathetic sap, don't you realize that you are not an independent human being, capable of making your own social decisions and free to do so? I will decide whom you will talk to, not you."

🌹 MARITAL COMMUNICATION

When Miss Manners hears people extolling the virtues of "communication" in marriage, she always wants to know what is being communicated. Certain types of marital communication, it seems to her, are best left uncommunicated.

"I had the wildest dream about a man at my office."

"There's something that's been bothering me for years that I'd like to get off my chest so I can forget it. Remember that time when I said I had to go to a convention in Mexico City?"

"Look what I found in your drawer."

"You want to know what I've resented all these years?"

"If you weren't married to me, what would you want to be doing now?"

"You know what I could have done with my life if I hadn't married you?"

"I suppose you know that you made a fool of yourself in front of everybody."

And so on. This is the sort of thing marital partners can't wait to communicate to each other, always to disastrous effect. If it can't be helped, Miss Manners believes, it needn't be stated. Yet she recognizes that there is a need for marital communication when things *can* be helped. Here are some thoughts that ought to be communicated:

"The story you're in the middle of telling was told to us by the person you're telling it to."

"Go ahead and invite these people for the weekend, but I think you should know that if they come, I'm going to move out."

"The reason nobody seems to be following your argument is that you have food on your chin."

"The woman you're talking to is the sister-in-law of the man you're talking about."

"If we don't go home in the next few minutes, I won't be responsible for my behavior."

One must be careful never to communicate these matters in words. That only adds to the unpleasantness the rather comic, pathetic touch of being reprimanded by one's spouse.

The following advice is for emergency use only. That lets out "No, dear, it didn't happen on Tuesday, it was Wednesday, and besides, you're spoiling the punchline." Nor should this service be confused with the common practice of offering after-the-fact unfavorable reviews of a partner's behavior. Any sentence after a gathering that begins "Why didn't you tell them that . . . ?" or "Why did you have to do . . . ?" should be outlawed. The idea that one of the advantages of being married is to have your own ever-present honest critic is a mistake.

Marital communication, performed in public to avert disaster, must be done in code. The most useful code is The Look—that facial expression, undecipherable to any outsider, that means "Watch out; something is very, very wrong."

Let us say, for example, that one person wants to go home from a gathering, while the other would prefer to stay longer. The first says, pleasantly enough, "I'm afraid it's late, darling," or "This is such fun, but I have to get up early." The second counters with a jovial, "Oh, let's just have one more drink," or "But tomorrow's Saturday." As stated, this is a toss-up. If the first statement is accompanied by The Look, it means "I can't stand this one more minute; get me out of here before I scream"; the second, with The Look added, is transformed into "Hold off; this is important to me." It should be a rule of marriage that the person with The Look should be obeyed, any disagreement to be conducted afterward.

The Look also means "Pay attention," so that a tiny accompanying gesture, such as dabbing one's chin with a napkin, should be enough to alert the partner that something is wrong with his own. A quick flash of The Look could accompany a seemingly irrelevant interruption, such as might stop someone's telling an unfortunate story. It is helpful then to give your partner a cue, such as, "Oh, yes, Bill, your brother-in-law—how is he?"

For the spoken code, every couple needs a Bunbury. Bunbury, you may recall, was the fictitious character whom dear Algernon Moncrieff in Oscar Wilde's play *The Importance of Being Earnest* used to claim he had to visit when he needed an excuse. Let us say that you have a fake Aunt Ida. While your spouse is extending or accepting what you consider appalling hospitality, you say, "Oh, darling, we can't that weekend. Remember, we promised Aunt Ida." Miss Manners prefers that you not make it an untruth by saying what you promised Aunt Ida.

However, there is one untruth that should follow all such communications. Miss Manners does not generally sanction lies (although she is often solidly in favor of withholding the whole damaging truth), but this one is the basis of any true relationship. It is: "Don't be silly, darling. Nobody noticed but me."

Confessing

DEAR MISS MANNERS:

I had an affair a few years ago with a married man. I'm now engaged to someone who I find is indirectly related to that man. At a family reunion coming up, and at other family gatherings, we will undoubtedly meet him and his wife. I've said nothing to my fiancé so far. I do not want any masquerade to flourish. Should I deny knowing the man, or simply say, "Hello, yes, we've met before, a few years ago," keeping it brief and civil. Also, I'd like to keep that man out of my life for obvious reasons. What can I do or say to my fiancé privately—that I don't want to be in that man's company and I don't feel comfortable with him? Or would it be easier just to admit the affair to my fiancé and trust that he will understand the predicament?

GENTLE READER:

Miss Manners dearly hopes that you are in a better position than she to know how your fiancé would react to such a confession. She can only tell you that it would result in making him—who had neither responsibility for, nor pleasure from, the affair—share in the discomfort you feel, and perhaps develop other painful feelings. Some people love to do this in the name of total openness, and that is a choice you must make. Why you would want to raise suspicion in his mind by announcing a desire to avoid the man, and then refuse to relieve the torture of doubt by providing the explanation, she cannot imagine. Destroying someone's innocent faith while refusing to take him into one's confidence doesn't sound like much fun for anyone.

Miss Manners' choice is merely to acknowledge the acquaintanceship while remaining as distant from the man as politely possible. She has a funny feeling that he will be only too happy to cooperate.

She has some reassurance to offer you. Only the affianced suppose that married life requires demonstrating an equal enthusiasm for all of one's new relations. A year from now, it will seem the most natural thing in the world to say to your husband, "Oh, dear, must we really see them?", not only about your former lover, but also about a variety of his (and your) cousins, classmates, and childhood companions.

Fighting

"Couples who don't fight couldn't have much of a relationship," a lady announced at dinner, and all the nearby guests turned automatically to look at her husband, who was obliviously out of earshot, blamelessly chewing his chicken.

"It's healthy to have a good knock-down, drag-out fight every once in a while," she persisted. "It makes for a good marriage; it clears the air." Her listeners, whose faces had all returned in her direction, reverted to him, tennis-fan style, in expectation of what he might hurtle through the air in order to clear it. But no plates came sailing across the table. Apparently the happy couple were not going to illustrate their formula for a successful marriage. The guests turned to their own plates.

Unsolicited information about how life should be lived is so generously distributed these days that no one remarked on this revelation. Sudden, involuntary insights into the intimate lives of acquaintances aren't that startling. There was the merest polite pause before the conversation shifted to something more riveting, such as the difficulty of getting good service on airlines.

Miss Manners, for one, was sorry to see the matter dropped without a fight, as it were. It seemed to her simply the perpetuation of another truism offering dangerous comfort to those who believe in therapeutic rudeness. Why should fighting be good for marriage or any other intimate relationship? Is bashing really that much more fun than making nice?

Miss Manners agrees that it would be odd for a couple to agree on everything. Not unhealthy, just odd. The fondest of couples may disagree on nearly everything.

The rules of airing marital disagreements require even more delicacy and politeness than do conflicts between those with less at stake emotionally. They start with a ban on unpleasant forms of expressing displeasure: Raising the voice, cursing, door slamming, and abusing property should be as thoroughly outlawed as hitting. So should the hurtful use of privileged information confided under happier circumstances. The word for "wrong," when used to describe the other's beliefs, factual accounts, attitudes, or practices, is "mistaken." Trespasses can only be announced after the phrase "I'm sure you didn't mean to, but. . . ."

In a proper marital dispute, issues are resolved by who is more strongly affected by them, rather than by recourse to anything resembling an outside standard. That you drive me crazy by humming tunelessly is more important than the fact that you have a right to do so, for example. The victor always absolves the conceder from blame. If an all-purpose "It wasn't your fault" isn't enough, he or she must supply the excuse: "I should have seen that you were exhausted," "It's the strange weather; it's driving us all crazy," or whatever will pass.

Miss Manners promises that it is as feasible to have a satisfying conflict under these rules as under the more pugnacious ones that believers in therapeutic rudeness often condone. What is more, it is an excellent achievement to be insufferable for the benefit of children, who are naturally interested in engaging in good, healthy, destructive, unbearable fights among themselves. "I don't care who did what, yelling is not permitted in this house," parents who have learned restraint are entitled to say. "You are not allowed to slam doors." Then, of course, they can graciously tell each other, "I know you didn't mean it, dear. It's the children being impossible that's getting to you."

❧ ROOMMATES

Privacy versus Opportunity

DEAR MISS MANNERS:

The most pressing problem our daughter and her friends face is what to do when a roommate brings a member of the opposite sex into the room and starts making love, pretending to believe that the other person present is asleep. Both male and female undergraduates are miserable about this situation, and none of them knows how to handle it. Leaving the premises is not always a practical solution. My suggestion is to throw open the windows, turn all the lights on, go for the vacuum, and start cleaning the room. I have never known anyone who could make love with the vacuum on.

If the misbehavers say that one has no right to clean one's room at 3:00 A.M., one has the right to say that otherwise one would be making a voyeur of oneself. (I had to put that in my letter to my daughter, because these young ones can think of nothing at all to say about why they object.) I felt that in short order the room would be available for such activities only by prearrangement. In any case, one would have a cleaner room.

GENTLE READER:

Miss Manners doesn't know, now that you mention it, whether anyone she knows is capable of making love with the vacuum running. She is so mesmerized by the question and, even more, by wondering how anyone could possibly have acquired such information about one's acquaintance, that she can hardly focus her attention on the chief problem.

Nevertheless, she is aware that what you describe has become a serious problem in college dormitories. That is what comes, she must say in her severest tsk-tsk tone, of abolishing parietal rules. The difficulty is that formal rules were changed, but not tacit ones. When institutions made romantic privacy rare, it was an un-written law that anyone who had such an opportunity must be given precedence over the lesser desires of roommates to study, sleep, or just live in their very own rooms. This law is still mistakenly observed, even though the privation that in-spired it has ceased to exist.

Your daughter and her friends should require neither excuses nor spring clean-ing to enjoy the privilege of using their own rooms. They must insist on setting firm rules about when the room may be used for private entertaining and enforce them by announcing to violators, preferably at the worst possible moments, "Okay—out! Social hour's over! Everybody who doesn't live here has to go home now!" Where this is not successful, written laws are being instituted forbidding any overnight guests.

Bathrooms

DEAR MISS MANNERS:

I am a concerned female college student who needs your help. One of the house-keeping staff is male. Therefore, before he enters the restroom to clean it, he knocks three times and announces, "Housekeeping." If I am inside, what is the appropriate reply?

GENTLE READER:

"I'll be out in a moment." This is an all-purpose bathroom statement which may be made in response to any knock and any announcement. No one has ever yet de-fined the length of time meant by the use of "a moment" in this context.

Nonromantic Roommates

DEAR MISS MANNERS:

I share an apartment with a very good friend who happens to be of the opposite sex. We share the apartment because we are both students (I am an undergradu-ate, he is a graduate), because we enjoy being with each other, and because our backgrounds and upbringings are similar and we are able to create a home-away-from-home atmosphere. The problem is that even if certain people are aware of our simply platonic relationship, they sometimes make comments about activities that might occur between my roommate and me when we are alone. How do I behave when someone makes such a comment? In the past, I have simply stated that we are just good friends or ignored it. Also, how do I convince my parents that there is no wedding to be planned?

GENTLE READER:

Miss Manners understands that shared living quarters do not necessarily indi-cate romantic involvement, and indeed may preclude its development. She does not expect such understanding of everyone brought up in racier times. You are living in a manner that must still be classified as unconventional, and therefore you must endure mistaken assumptions with good grace, correcting them politely. The mere statement that you and your roommate are friends is enough for most people, but you owe your parents an explanation of what they might better understand if you called it a brother-sister relationship.

Couple and Friend

DEAR MISS MANNERS:

My best friend and I share an apartment, along with my boyfriend. Every morning, when we are all up, she insists on parading around in a skimpy half-shirt and her underwear. She is now also making advances to my boyfriend while I am away at work. My boyfriend has just told me about this. I don't want to lose her friendship or my boyfriend. What should I do?

GENTLE READER:

Pick one roommate or the other. Miss Manners doesn't much care which one, but you can't tell a grown-up that she can't appear in a state of undress in her own home, or two roommates that you are supervising their behavior with each other.

The Semiresident Guest

DEAR MISS MANNERS:

My boyfriend has started sleeping over at my apartment three or four nights a week. The landlord has informed me that the visitor's section of the garage where he has been parking is strictly for occasional use and that I should rent a space for his car. I asked my boyfriend to pay for the space and he agreed, but I am now wondering if I was correct in asking him to pay all or part of the rent.

GENTLE READER:

Guests are not charged by hosts for the space they occupy. Residents usually share costs. Miss Manners will leave it up to you and the gentleman in question to define what he is doing in the apartment.

Family Matters

Who Reared These People?

Has your child written home yet from boarding school or college?

"Written?" (This is an echo Miss Manners is hearing.) "Is the woman mad? Why, we count ourselves lucky to get a collect telephone call asking for money."

What about the married children—do they write?

"Write?" (The echo in here is awful.) "No, my daughter only calls, and my son never writes because he expects his wife to do it for him."

Do they handle the question of your visiting satisfactorily?

"If they invite us at all, it's when they want us to look after their children. When we get there, they're always frightfully busy."

What about their visits to you?

"Then they expect us to wait on them. Don't even ask about thank-you letters."

Well, what about thank-you letters?

"Yes, what about them? We'd never even know if they received our gifts if we didn't ask. And of course, they don't teach their children to write letters. It's terribly embarrassing when our friends send them things and they never hear."

What about your birthdays and wedding anniversary?

"What about them? Sometimes they remember, and sometimes they don't.

Sometimes there's not even a card or a call. I don't mind for myself, of course, but . . ."

"You were a wonderful child when I was bringing you up," Miss Manners' dear grandmamma used to say to her dear mamma, "but then you started bringing yourself up." Actually, Miss Manners' mamma turned out just fine, as you can imagine from the fact that she brought up Miss Manners. The grand-matriarchal reference was to that awkward stage when a child has escaped parental supervision and feels the headiness of freedom from many things, including, regrettably, manners.

It is Miss Manners' (and no doubt the parents') fervent hope that well-reared children will, after a brief fling at irresponsibility in the name of independence, eventually revert to the behavior they were taught. In the meantime, parents who have otherwise completed their child rearing must protect themselves by setting explicit rules about how they expect to be treated. Leaving it to chance means setting up a test that equates the outward form of manners with the inner emotion: "If he cared, he'd remember," "She doesn't write because she hates the present or me or both." Why subject yourself to all that emotional wear and tear? The proper parental solution is simply to do a bit more child rearing for grown-up children:

"If we don't hear from you twice a week, we'll be so worried that we'll call the Dean of Students and inquire whether you're sick."

"If you don't send Uncle Digby a thank-you letter he's going to take it out on me, which is unfair; heaven knows, it wasn't my lack of teaching."

"As you know, your mother's birthday is next Tuesday; call early, because we're going out to dinner."

"This is still your home, but now that we have separate households, let's set some rules about visiting so that no one is inconvenienced."

"Of course, they're your children, dear, but I'm afraid you're going to have to teach them that their grandparents have certain expectations about manners. They'll appreciate all the more the freedom you allow them, won't they?"

Honoring Mother

One way to honor Mother is not to go around tattling on her. The four-year-old who is on the spot for something to contribute to Show and Tell, the teenager interested in exchanging information about the adult world, and the grown-up child who is after a laugh are all exposed to the temptation to report what is going on behind the scenes. However, much information about Mother to which the child is privy by virtue of his membership in the family, or the opportunities of observation around the house, should be considered sacred. This includes:

Statistics that Mother does not routinely give out herself, such as her age, her income, how many times she has been married, what organs she has had removed, and how much of a discount she got on the dress she is wearing.

What Mother does to make herself look good, including how she looks in a mud pack facial mask, whether she dyes her hair, what she looks like without her makeup, and how funny it is to see her struggle into her stretch-top pantyhose.

Mother's little failings, such as what she says or does when she loses her temper, what tricks she uses for cheating on her diet, humorous examples of how her memory, sight, and hearing seem to be going, and what her attempts to help with the homework demonstrate about her own education.

Another way of honoring Mother is for her children to pretend that her competence as a human being equals their own. It takes some doing even for a small child to act as if he presumes that Mother could manage her life reasonably without his critical advice, much of it retroactive, but the effort is a polite show of respect.

This means that the child does not explain to Mother that her appearance, conversation, values, opinions, politics, and choice of associates are sources of embarrassment and must be renovated to meet the child's tastes. He or she trusts her to make her own judgments in these matters, even if they differ from the child's, and acts as if proud of what Mother makes of herself.

The child does not inform her that she is always being measured against Everybody Else's Mother, as in "Everybody else's mother lets them stay up as long as they want," "Everybody else's mother gives them twenty dollars a week spending money," and "Everybody else's mother lets them have their noses pierced." Even if Everybody Else's Mother could be proven to exist, one honors one's own mother by pretending to respect her right to dissent. The retroactive part means that the child must assume that Mother has always done the best she could under whatever circumstances existed, and neither blame her for what the child considers failings in child rearing nor point out how much better he plans to be at the same tasks.

Finally, Mother can be honored by being treated as if she has a legitimate interest in the lives of her children. This does not preclude keeping secrets from Mother, especially those that would only cause her pain, such as one's rebellious thoughts or the gender of one's roommate. It does mean refraining from groaning when she shows concern and informing her about the major events in one's life before she finds out from the neighbors or the newspapers. And now Miss Manners has a request of her own to add to the duties of all good children. Would they please keep this list? She doesn't want to have to go through this all again for Father.

Grown-Up Grandchildren

DEAR MISS MANNERS:

My daughter (divorced) has three grown children, all in their twenties, living at home. As a widowed grandmother, when I ask them over for dinner or to celebrate something or other, I call and ask my daughter to bring them all over. She insists that as they are adults, each should be asked separately. I don't think they need special invitations to visit their grandmother. They never visit me on their own, although they drive.

GENTLE READER:

Evidently, they do need something more in the way of invitations, as they are not visiting you without them. Miss Manners would like to end this stand-off, which understandably pains you, but she requires you to give more thought than you have to what would make your grandchildren feel welcome.

Adult children, even those living in a family complex, maintain their own social and professional schedules. Their mother cannot simply produce them at any given time, as if they were under her jurisdiction. Even without the need to consult them individually about convenient times to hold family celebrations, it would be a great courtesy to show each one that you really wanted to see him or her, not just that you expect the family package to show up. If you would enjoy being dropped in on, say that, too. "You know, dear, I'm almost always home in the evenings, and any time you feel like a chat, or just some quiet visiting, I can produce a cup of tea. It would make me very happy to see you."

Note the tone. It is not "You are lapsing in your duty to me," which is chilling, but "I love you and am interested in you," which is warm. It may take some urging, and the understanding on your part that they may not have much time to spare. But Miss Manners assures you that once they see that you are offering them an affectionate haven, you will see more of them.

Bearing One's Parents

DEAR MISS MANNERS:

Soon, once again, I will be hostess for two of the most difficult guests imaginable. The problems? Here is a small sampling:

1. They ignore my request not to bring their pets. Once, when they brought a cat, we were obliged to rig up a cat box, which they resolutely kept outside their bedroom, while keeping the cat inside. After their departure, I was horrified to discover that the cat had voided on the carpet, leaving an unbearable stench. Then there was the time their dog defecated in my living room, but that's another story.

2. The wife becomes an instant invalid upon crossing my threshold. She petulantly and persistently demands constant attention and personal service. She demands to be served a bizarrely rigid diet (presumably doctor ordered), the likes of which I, as a professional nutritionist, have never encountered. She has, however, been observed to partake freely of all the forbidden foods elsewhere.

In spite of this and more, our entire family has always dealt with them with the greatest courtesy. My husband has been a marvel of cheerful patience, and our children are consistently respectful. Why do we continue to entertain such people? The reason, dear lady, is that they are my parents.

While they are now into their seventies, their peculiarities can't really be blamed on old age, as they have behaved this way for decades. My sister (a dear soul who has suffered much) and I have continued to maintain relations with our parents, in part from the habit of coping with them since our earliest days, and in part because they are so alone. They have no friends and have alienated everyone, including their clergyman. All they have is us.

I am now reaching my middle years, and the resultant changes, plus unhappy memories of past holiday visits, are causing me to lose some of my good-natured resilience. I dread what lies ahead. Is there some polite way to end this long-term victimization without creating an ugly family upheaval?

GENTLE READER:

A polite way to tell your parents, in their lonely old age, that you can't put up with them for another minute? Not really. You could develop a household crisis that necessitates putting them up in a nearby hotel, suggest that you all spend the holidays together in a resort, or schedule surgery for that week. Those are expensive and troublesome one-time solutions, however. The holidays will roll around again, and so will your parents.

You know that the right thing is to continue to bear it. There was a time when your own nutritional requirements and elimination practices needed their patience. The only comfort Miss Manners can offer you is the pride you should take in your husband's and children's kind tolerance.

Shared Stories

Who should have custody of the family stories? It is inevitable that people who live together will accumulate innumerable shared anecdotes. In addition to mutual experiences, each becomes so familiar with the oral heritage of the others as to acquire certain rights to the material. Who is properly in charge of this common property? Who decides which is the authorized version of a family story? Who gets to be narrator? Are there special rights associated with being the hero—or the victim—of the story? What supplementary contributions are acceptable during or after the narration?

This is one custody problem that does not exist among divorced couples, but Miss Manners does not believe it necessary to resort to smashing up families in order to solve the problem. As long as people are decently separated during the telling of a mutually owned story, there is no conflict if they tell it differently.

Children always develop their own versions of family adventures, often messing with the parental assignments of heroes, victims, villains, and the morals to be derived. As long as they confine the results to their own circles and don't publish their autobiographies during their parents' lifetimes, they are safe. The custom of separating couples at social events is also designed to avoid the shared-story fracas. Those sweethearts who protest that they cannot bear to be apart for the duration of a dinner party are challenging the chief hope of preserving their bond until such time as they are able to take their coffee and conversation to opposite ends of the drawing room.

For the best-regulated families, the moment of crisis will eventually arrive: Someone at a gathering inadvertently gives a cue suggesting to several members of a family that a particular family story would be appropriate. After an unseemly squabble over who will tell it, a full-fledged etiquette crisis evolves as (strictly in the interests of accuracy) the loser joins in by anticipating or correcting the winner. Because this is almost as great a strain on family life as it is on the patience of those forced to listen, Miss Manners would like to suggest a few family rules to be agreed upon in private in order to avoid such public debacles.

The first rule concerns which stories are to be told at all. Veto power should be granted to anyone claiming major embarrassment from appearing in a family anecdote. "Please don't tell the story about the time I was sick on the dance floor" is a request that should be honored. (Since children consider that their entire childhoods are, by definition, embarrassing, it requires some delicate negotiation on the part of parents to convince them that certain stories do not reflect upon them adversely. The word "cute" should be omitted from such an argument.)

A complementary rule is that you should never have to tell the stories of which the point is your own triumph. Other family members ought to be assigned to do that, leaving the hero or heroine free to protest that it is all fond exaggeration on the part of the relative-narrator.

There must be a ban on unnecessary factual corrections. It is notorious that no one in the audience cares whether an incident happened on Tuesday or Wednesday. Miss Manners does not expect relatives to be able to refrain from wincing at mistakes, but she asks them to save corrections for the ride home. At the same time, there must be an understanding that crucial corrections will be made and accepted gracefully. Noninterference is not an excuse for allowing a loved one to give away, or to forget, his or her own punch line. Whether such danger should be averted by murmured prompting, or requires the bungler to hand over the story to the person who knows it, should be the subject of prior agreement.

The understanding that entertainment has precedence over exactitude is the basis for the rule that whoever tells the story best becomes its custodian. The raw material of life requires some shaping to be presentable socially, so that it justifies the telling by having a point. The job of the relative, then, is to save the family honor by first joining in the general appreciation of the anecdote and then smilingly adding, "Well—that was more or less what happened."

Repeating Stories Again

DEAR MISS MANNERS:
Is there any method one can use to tell a friend that she has told a story previously and ask her to desist? Often we are told about the same incident several times during one meal. The person is not ill but simply forgets to whom she has related the item. We certainly would not wish to hurt her in any way. We just want to put our time to better use.

GENTLE READER:
Ah, yes. Miss Manners has heard this question before, possibly from you. There are different causes for the repetition of stories, and they require different de-

fenses. All of them should be tempered with knowledge of the frailty of the human memory.

If someone repeats himself only rarely, it is polite to let it pass. The person who says "Stop me if you've heard this one before" is really too wound up to stop comfortably, so you may as well let him finish. If it happens frequently, the hapless listener may break in at the beginning with "Ah, yes, so you told me. That's a wonderful story." If you let the story go until the middle, you can only say, "Oh, now I remember. Tell me the punch line again."

However, as your friend forgets several times during the course of one meal, it seems that she has serious memory problems. In that case, allow her to repeat herself without calling attention to her deficiency. Reminding her won't help, anyway, and informing someone suffering from memory loss that her handicap is also a social burden is therefore pointless as well as rude.

Greed

DEAR MISS MANNERS:

When younger relatives come to visit, they always seem to be looking enviously at my possessions. They will say things like "Would you want to sell that?" ("sell" being a euphemism for "give me") or "Would you want to part with that?" Why do they intimidate me and make me feel selfish? Just because I'm older than they are, it doesn't mean that I have no desire or use for my possessions. I could say "You can have that after I'm gone," but frankly, I don't plan on going anywhere any time soon.

GENTLE READER:

Why you should feel intimidated by greed, or selfish for enjoying your own possessions, Miss Manners cannot imagine. She would prefer that you put your emotional energy into gently teaching your relatives that their behavior is not acceptable. "I am so glad that you like my things" would be a proper response. "I hope you will continue to come here for many years and enjoy my home with me."

Respecting Eccentric Elders

DEAR MISS MANNERS:

How long does the arm of justice in the law of etiquette extend? Specifically, are eccentrics over the age of eighty to be excused their breaches of conduct? I recently had dinner with my grandmother, who is neither senile nor infirm but who is, and always has been, a confirmed eccentric. She is not always polite, to put it mildly. Nevertheless, she is loved by the whole family (including me). We generally shrug our shoulders and sigh, "Well, you know how Nana is sometimes."

Over dinner, she said to my husband loudly (she is always loud), "Don't you wish you weren't married so that you could be having dinner with that gorgeous blonde over there?" (pointing at gorgeous blonde). He mumbled something incoherent, and I let out a shocked "Nana! I can't believe what I'm hearing." She spent the rest of the night gloating aloud about how her remark had really gotten to me. I was annoyed, and she knew it; nothing could have thrilled her more.

My question is: What behavior do we overlook in the elderly—like the grandfather who eats peas with his knife, the ancient uncle who refers to one's spouse as "that gigolo," and my remorseless grandmother? Is everyone always responsible for his or her actions, barring the mentally ill, from four to ninety-four? I don't mean to pick nits—my grandmother has been forgiven gaffes that would have severed the most devoted friendships—but I'm curious.

GENTLE READER:

Being old does not excuse people from the need to be polite, but the requirement that one treat one's elders with respect means that sneaky and unscrupulous old people are often able to get away with rudeness. Your grandmother is counting on that. She figures, correctly, that if you chastise her, you will be guilty of such bad manners that her own transgression will look minor in comparison. Let us therefore see if we can spoil her fun without being disrespectful.

The first thing you must do, and train your husband to do, is to react respectfully to her outrageous remarks. Stop thrilling her. Instead of allowing her to see that she had succeeded in annoying you, you could have said blandly, "Oh, no, Nana, dear, we don't even know that lady." Similarly, the uncle who calls your husband "that gigolo" should be told, "Oh, no, Uncle Jack, that's Stephen. You remember! My husband." This method applies only to outrageous remarks. You do not correct the table manners of anyone but your own children. Fanny patters of any age are treated the same. One screams and then, when everybody's attention is drawn, explains, "You startled me."

Ill Persons

DEAR MISS MANNERS:

My mother is ill. She has a respiratory disorder and an acute case of depression. She looks frail and walks slowly. These problems have made her rude and impatient. How do I tell people that she is ill? Do I bother to tell them? How do I handle the inconsiderate people who gawk and stare?

GENTLE READER:

There are two problems here: how to treat the people who are rude to your mother and how to treat those to whom your mother is rude. People who stare rudely should be stared down, as it were. This is done by a fierce answering gaze, with a questioning look added by raising the eyebrows, as if to ask, "Do you have some business with us?" Only if your mother is directly hurtful to someone need you apologize for her. The dignified way to do so is to say, "I'm so sorry, but my mother isn't well."

Defending Others

DEAR MISS MANNERS:

I observed a bizarre lesson in "manners" while visiting a patient in a nursing home. As we sat chatting in the lounge, another patient, Mary, joined us. Mary is a confused but lovely lady. She likes to tell stories about her life when she was in the Marines during World War II. Some of the stories may be true and some fabricated. She repeats the stories many times in her confusion.

A young trainee on her break was also in the room. The trainee kept interrupting Mary in a deprecating way. This annoyed me, but Mary didn't seem to notice it. Mary indicated the dress she was wearing and said that she had made it. I said that the dress was very nice. Before Mary could say anything more, the trainee admonished her with "Where are your manners? Don't you know you should say 'thank you' when the lady says your dress is nice? You should be ashamed of yourself!" Taken aback by this, Mary said very solemnly, "I guess I'm getting a lesson in good manners; I do thank you." As the trainee was leaving the room, Mary thumbed her nose at her back. This gentle, confused lady knew all along that she was being put down, and I applauded her gesture. Was I wrong in not speaking up on Mary's behalf?

GENTLE READER:

Miss Manners has spent a lifetime admonishing people who make rude gestures in response to rudenesses, but she is going to grant Mary a pardon on this one. It is not so much the enormity of the provocation that has influenced Miss Manners as the fact that Mary had the grace to deal with the situation politely to the offender's face—an act that ought certainly to have made the trainee ashamed of herself—and only let her feelings go afterward. Yes, you should defend an injured lady, whether she was in the Marines or not. But Miss Manners' dispensation was only for Mary. You could have said, "I beg your pardon, but Mary and I understand each other perfectly, and I wonder if you would be kind enough to let us converse."

Repairing a Relationship

DEAR MISS MANNERS:

Several years ago, my stepdaughter and her boyfriend (whom she met in college, where they were dormmates) began to share an apartment. Although her roommate's parents live in the distant suburbs of our city, we made no effort to meet them, not wanting to encourage or in any way put our stamp of approval on this relationship. Although we had nothing against this particular young man, who is nice enough, we felt that they had little in common and that in time they would drift apart. The young couple have now moved to another, distant city, married, and had a baby. We have yet to meet his parents and feel that we are being rude. Whose responsibility is it to establish a relationship between his parents and us, or is it too late?

GENTLE READER:

It must have occurred to you, as it has to Miss Manners, that your lack of encouragement does not seem to have had any effect on this relationship, and that your choice now is to put that stamp of approval on the relationship or miss out on the opportunity to enjoy your stepdaughter's family life. It's not exactly too late, but it is high time. You were not obligated to have social ties with the parents of a mere boyfriend, but you are with a son-in-law's.

Technically, it is up to the young man's parents to call on the young lady's first. They may not have known this, but let us take advantage of it anyway. Write them a charming note, saying that your meeting is long overdue and proposing a visit. Then write an equally charming one to your stepdaughter, announcing this and saying that you have previously hesitated because you couldn't tell, from the other parents' silence, whether this would be welcome. We will not go so far as to blame them for not having called, but just far enough to erase the idea that your omission was due to any such nonsense as the hope that such a lovely young couple would drift apart. In the interests of family harmony, Miss Manners is willing to have etiquette itself take the blame.

Reforming a Mother-Out-of-Law

DEAR MISS MANNERS:

I am an unmarried parent living with my ten-month-old daughter. Keeping her best interests in mind, I have established a fairly good relationship with her natural father. He has unlimited visitation rights, as does his entire family. He lives at home with his divorced mother, and lately I've been going there twice a week with the baby.

His mother, when she's not working her day job, is constantly cleaning her house. She rarely takes time, when the baby and I are there, to just sit and relax and play with my daughter. As soon as the baby falls asleep, she cleans up her fingerprints. It has gotten to the point where I feel on edge and very uncomfortable there. I have confronted her on more than one occasion, being concerned about her blood pressure, and have suggested that she try to relax and enjoy her life. She becomes very defensive, suggests that I'm trying to reform her, and we get into an argument. It's hopeless to talk to her; she has a very closed mind. I tried to discuss the problem with her son, but he comes to her defense, stating that she's set in her ways and isn't going to change, and that I should either learn to live with the situation, or his mother and I won't get along.

I suggested that she should visit the baby at my home instead so that she wouldn't have to worry about her house being messed up. He said that she would be hurt if I didn't keep coming over and that she was too busy to come to my house. (Her idea of being busy is constantly cleaning the house, while I work full time and take care of a baby.)

Is it proper to ask someone to childproof their house? Otherwise, I feel that I have to constantly restrain my daughter from touching things, and "no" is the word I most often say to her.

GENTLE READER:

Under the best of circumstances, reforming a mother-in-law is extremely dangerous and difficult. Reforming a mother-out-of-law is, as you have noticed, hopeless. You will have to let others worry about her blood pressure and choice of recreation.

Your concern, as you also realize, is your daughter. No one could say that you have not been sufficiently gracious by inviting her grandmother to your house, but since she apparently will not come, this does not serve your purpose. Nor would it help if you went over the brink one day at the grudging hospitality she offers.

You should have the comfort of knowing that you are rising above this situation, unselfishly benefiting her as well as your child. As for your specific question about childproofing a house, the fact is that the burden is on the parent to ensure that the child does not destroy property. Even the warmest grandparents may not want to renovate for occasional visits. This is also in the eventual interest of your child. Although she is small, you must begin teaching her, not only for the sake of manners but for her safety, that there are limits to what she can touch.

Family Gatherings

DEAR MISS MANNERS:

Being an eldest daughter married to an eldest son, I take my position seriously as the one who brings the family together for the holidays. However, with the divorce rate as it is, emotions run high as to the most prestigious time slot, configuration of guests, and so on. My in-laws were divorced, with much hatred, after thirty-five years, and both remarried. My mother-in-law is very vocal about the "awful things that man did" to her. She is not a woman to argue with. She is not aware of the fact that my father-in-law is divorced again. This same mother-in-law refuses to be in the same room as my mother. My mother has similar feelings about her. There is a sister, a husband, and an "auntie" of my mother-in-law, and a younger sister who is everything but married, with a child and friend. My grandmother refuses to come if her daughter comes and brings her husband (of whom she disapproves on racial grounds).

In the past, I have cooked two Thanksgiving dinners and three Christmas dinners. No one else, for reasons of poverty, health, or inclination, offers to do anything. The expense and work don't bother me, but the mental hassle does. Should I continue to wear a "My Life Is a Soap Opera" T-shirt, keeping people separate, even if they complain that their arrangements are not fair? Or is there an easier way to handle this logically short of vacationing in the Bahamas in November and December? Should I give precedence to those of poor health and big mouths, and put those young and out of favor (with the family, not me) last? Or should I have one big dinner each holiday, inviting all and informing all of who is being invited, and let them decide whether to come? I fear that this will leave me with no one and a large amount of uneaten food. How do you politely ask someone to cease and desist from maligning someone you love dearly without hurting their feelings?

GENTLE READER:

Decent, cheerful, loving, tolerant behavior ought to be rewarded. You seem to have a great deal of that yourself, which has won you Miss Manners' admiration. Guile is also useful, she suggests.

Announce the family dinner, to which all have been invited. Then tell the I-won't-come-if-that-person-does crowd that you are terribly sorry they feel that way and will miss them. Tell them that you suspect that the objects of their wrath would be only too happy to end the feud if they would too. Make that the main meal. If ill will does keep away crucial relatives, such as your mother-in-law and grandmother, you might schedule a secondary dinner for them, but you needn't make it equal to the first. The point that hatred is out of place at the family celebrations should not be obscured.

Thanking Relatives

DEAR MISS MANNERS:

My mother believes that a formal thank-you note needs to be written after my children have spent a weekend at her second home, a ranch. I feel that the young adults, after warmly thanking their grandmother for asking them, as well as for different meals throughout the weekend, have shown the proper behavior.

GENTLE READER:

Besides teaching your children to please their grandmother, rather than themselves, in such a trifling matter, you should be grateful that they have such a grandmother. By holding them to a higher standard than yours, she is giving them practice in manners that will stand them in good stead should they visit anyone else. People who entertain houseguests do not weigh the enormous chore of writing a letter against that of cooking, cleaning, and entertaining people, and decide that it is too much to ask. On the contrary, they expect guests to be unable to restrain themselves from pouring out their grateful words on paper, as well as from their mouths.

No Rest for the Wicked

DEAR MISS MANNERS:

When I was visiting my sister, her youngest son and his wife came in to show the movies they had taken on their winter vacation. All they talked about was the wonderful couple they met skiing at Sun Valley and with whom they spent several weekends in California. The man in the movies is my son-in-law—and the woman is his secretary, whom he is passing off as his wife! What do I do? Consult a lawyer, confront my son-in-law, tell my daughter, or say nothing?

GENTLE READER:

Miss Manners has just resolved never again to doze quietly off in the dark while holiday home movies are being shown. She had no idea that they could be so interesting. The etiquette of such a situation is that one never disturbs the ignorance of the innocent.

Unnerving the guilty can, however, be quite satisfying. A private message expressing your astonishment over the coincidence of your son-in-law's having made the acquaintanceship of your nephew and niece, with a vague reference to their having recorded the occasion on film, ought to do it. Oddly, the less specific you make this statement, so that he is allowed a very small hope that you do not fully understand what happened, the more you will torture him.

Ending a Family Feud

DEAR MISS MANNERS:

When my wedding was planned, my dad wanted the woman he lives with to be in the lineup in the hall. My mother didn't, as she was the only one not family, and dad's sister could have walked in with him. I didn't care much, but to make my dad happy, I let her join the lineup, even though Mom said that if I did, I would be picking her over my own mother, and it would be good-bye. I thought she would forgive me, as any mother should. But when I came home from my honeymoon, my mom's phone number had been changed to a private line. She did exactly as she said. When she went to the hospital for a kidney operation, she did not want me there. She is going in again and still doesn't want me. She said that after what I put her through, she doesn't want me to cry over her when she dies. I miss her and would like to know what to do. I want her to love me and be my mother again, not an ex-mother.

GENTLE READER:

Miss Manners is heartbroken to recognize that what you have here is a full-fledged family feud, and a nasty one at that. Etiquette has only one tool for ending it, and that doesn't always work.

That tool is the apology. Never mind now that you didn't think the issue important at the time or take seriously your mother's warnings. Just keep writing her that you are sorry, and that you love her and miss her. Miss Manners dearly hopes that your mother will eventually recognize how tragic it is for you to be separated by a decision that was based merely on the desire for accommodation, not on malicious intent, and that is, in any case, irrevocably past.

Extra Guests

DEAR MISS MANNERS:

We have two daughters, one son-in-law by a second marriage, and one man who may soon become another son-in-law. Each daughter has two teenage children; one son-in-law has three teenage children, and the other man has three teenage children. For over thirty years, we have been hosts for family gatherings. We have a large home, and it has always been my pleasure to entertain the family. During the years before our children and my husband's sister married, when my husband's parents were still living, we seldom had more than ten people at gatherings, including close family friends.

Last time I invited the family, each teenager wanted to invite a boyfriend or girlfriend. Some called me on the day of the party and some didn't even ask. The total number of guests for the party was twenty-four. My husband was irate. I was exhausted from preparations and recriminations. "This cannot go on," he said. I agree. I have several options:

1. Ignore future celebrations.
2. Go out of town and avoid the issue.
3. Talk it over with the parents involved and limit the parties to family members.

Which choice shall I make? I am reluctant to break family ties or to hurt feelings.

GENTLE READER:

You are running a popular party. Don't you think it's rather charming that the teenagers want to bring their friends? That does not mean that you have to let them and allow this party to run you into the ground. Just let us not forget how much nicer a problem it is than the feuds and loneliness Miss Manners generally hears about.

Not liking any of your choices, she will make three of her own.

1. Turn the job of family entertaining over to your daughters, and tell them that you expect them to keep up the tradition of hospitality. You may or may not offer your house as the setting, but put them in charge of cooking and cleaning.

2. Limit the guest list to the family, but include obviously prospective members. Casual dates are out, but stepchildren and fiancés in.

3. Give the family party first, but ask your grandchildren and stepgrandchildren to help give an after-dinner party for their friends. Tell them how much you would enjoy meeting these people, but have them clean up after dinner and prepare refreshments for the evening party.

Cleaning Up

DEAR MISS MANNERS:

How does one deal with a mother-in-law who commands her dinner guests to perform as servants after the meal? My first experience with this took place at a small, informal dinner party my mother-in-law held in honor of my marriage. It proceeded pleasantly until the meal ended. My mother-in-law then rose from the table, announced, "I cooked it, you clean it!" and retired to the living room.

I was dumbfounded, to say the least. Everyone rose quietly and assembled in the kitchen. The catastrophe that awaited us makes me shudder to recall. Every dish, pan, and cooking utensil in the house had been used. Judging from the ceramic quality of the residue on several implements, much of the cooking had been done earlier in the day. The kitchen sink was stopped up and apparently had been for several days. It took four of us nearly two hours to clean the debris. I asked my sister-in-law if the evening's events were common practice, and she affirmed that they were.

Please understand, Miss Manners, that I am neither lazy nor disrespectful. I consistently offer my assistance to a host, and do so willingly, but I have never attended a function, particularly one in my honor, where the guests' assistance was commanded. Several years have passed, and nothing has changed. I have come to dread visiting my mother-in-law, but I have remained silent out of respect for my husband's feelings.

GENTLE READER:

Miss Manners was all puffed up with sympathy and vicarious resentment, coupled with wonder at how such a hostess could ever get any guests to return for a second meal and how your husband and his sister could allow guests to be so treated, when something brought her to a screeching halt. It was the four of you in the kitchen that night when you had the talk with your sister-in-law. The four people involved were, by Miss Manners' reckoning, the son and daughter of the hostess and their spouses.

This puts a strange cast on the terms "in my honor," "a function," and "dinner guests." What you are describing, it seems, is not a bizarre dinner party where unsuspecting guests are indentured, but an intimate family dinner following long-time family custom. Your mother-in-law is less a hostess who is shocking her guests by assigning them tasks than a matriarch who is reminding her brood that she expects them to pitch in. Certainly, it would be nicer if she did it more gracefully and if she were a more fastidious cook. It would have been charming if, at that first dinner when you were a bride, she had said, "The children do the cleaning up—but just this once, you come and sit with me instead." The division of labor itself is not unreasonable. When there is frequent entertaining in grown up families, the burden should not all fall on one person. If you don't like this method of sharing, perhaps you could hold more of the family dinners in your house instead.

After Death

DEAR MISS MANNERS:

If a man is divorced and remarried, and has not made his wishes known, should he be buried on the same cemetery lot as his former wife if his children desire this?

Parents and Children

To what extent should parents apologize to their children for earning a living? Miss Manners knows parents who believe in apologizing to their children for absolutely everything:

They apologize to the smallest toddlers if the foods they provide (or even the particular brands of packaged foods) meet with the displeasure of those discerning diners and rush to substitute something acceptable. They apologize to school children if homework or any other outside obligation interferes with such crucial recreation as television watching, and take care that no additional duties are imposed in the home. They apologize to teenagers for the embarrassment caused by their looking or thinking or behaving like parents, and acknowledge the paramount importance of the prevailing teenage standards, even if they can't always manage to live by these themselves.

Most of all, they apologize for working. Not in so many words, you understand. They just make separate apologies for each aspect of their jobs until they have covered everything. They apologize for not being available all day, for being tired in the evening, for needing quiet if they have work to do at home, for not being at home when doing overtime or taking business trips, and for not earning enough to allow the children to spend without limits. When possible, they bring the children presents that are clearly intended to supplement those apologies—small presents for coming home late, larger ones for business trips.

This is a relatively new phenomenon, begun by mothers who seemed to endorse a strange but widespread idea that their working at all on nondomestic tasks was a self-indulgence requiring formal expressions of regret. Miss Manners would have thought that the growing recognition that parents can be fathers as well as mothers—in fact, exactly as often are—might have put an end to this situation, but no, it only meant that fathers started apologizing, too.

Nobody is more in sympathy with the emotions that have led to all this groveling than is Miss Manners. She is keenly aware that the working world is set up as if having children were a hobby that the few who wish to practice must manage as best they can, without annoying a society that has no stake in future generations. Nor is she the one to complain about using kind words to soften the difficulties and disappointments that inevitably arise because parents must shoulder obligations other than child rearing.

It is the tone that bothers her. An apologetic tone is associated with having done wrong. A parent who has accused a child unjustly, snapped at one for something unrelated to the child, or knocked oatmeal onto a child's lap should apologize. Apologies are also called for when anything, including work, forces a parent to break a commitment to a child. But what amounts to routine apologizing for the fact of working suggests to the child that there is something amiss about doing it. In the same way, apologizing for a food, task, or way of living is an acknowledgment that child rearing and parental preferences can legitimately be considered impositions on the child.

Presumably, there are crucial reasons, involving the child's own benefit, that parents go out and earn money. It does not serve the purpose of harmony and sympathy in the household for the child to be led to believe that he or she is entitled to a permanent grudge because of a normal state of affairs.

The child who is gently led to understand that other people have obligations and feelings that must be taken into account, and that the general welfare of the family depends on balancing preferences and practicalities, will be the better for it. This is a basic way of teaching consideration for others: One does not need to apologize for the fact that the others may include oneself. The advanced lesson, for the child who is old enough to understand, is how life's little trade-offs are made. Why is the parent working overtime rather than going out with the child? Because that is his or her selfish desire, for which he shamefacedly apologizes? Or because he has to look at the overall benefit to the whole family?

Miss Manners considers the apology a staple of good manners and does not wish to abolish it in favor of explanations when wrong has been done. She is only pointing out its misuse when wrong has not been done. Those promiscuously given parental apologies should be saved to offer to children who have been wronged because their parents have spared them by not teaching them manners.

The Beginnings: Natural Child Rearing

DEAR MISS MANNERS:
Before I was born, my parents became disenchanted with the rigidity of society. They decided to bring me up "naturally," without the constrictions of their own childhoods, and they withdrew from all but a very few of their friends. I certainly had a happy, though somewhat lonely, childhood, but now I'm beginning to see that social skills—knowing how to dance, knowing how to dress appropriately for different occasions, and general poise—are as important as calculus and Moliere. They help one to live peacefully in a community and to express one's ideas.

Perhaps some lucky people don't need to be coached in etiquette, but I am awkward and self-conscious. I feel uncomfortable when I don't know how to respond to many everyday situations. Now that I am away from home—I am in my last year at a large boarding school—I can no longer hold my parents responsible for my behavior. I realize that one can't buy good manners, but is there any way I can help myself to gain poise and self-confidence in my dealings with others, both formal and informal?

GENTLE READER:

Miss Manners commends your generous understanding of your parents' kindly motives and your recognition of your own responsibility for your present behavior, as much as she does your sophisticated insight into the way life actually works. She dearly wishes that she could come up with a few quick rules that would see you through everything. People are always asking her to "boil down" etiquette to one or two pithy commands, as if one could ask the Chief Justice of the United States (point of etiquette: He is not called Chief Justice of the Supreme Court) to boil down American law to something law students could learn during a television commercial.

There are many forms of manners to be learned, which is why thorough child rearing takes as long as it does. Even beyond the forms, one needs practice to acquire the judgment to know how they apply in different contexts. If Miss Manners could compress it all, she would have written two bumper stickers and a T-shirt, instead of all those volumes and columns. She is, however, confident, because of the interest and alertness you show, that you will be able to compress the time necessary to master it. That may be done by reading, not only etiquette books but novels and plays where you can see the symbolism of social behavior, and how different ways of doing things affect people, and by observing the good and bad examples you will find all around you.

Miss Manners is pleased that she can immediately give you reasons for assuming the poise and self-confidence you desire. One is that many of your generation suffer from the same handicap of their parents' well-meaning naiveté, so your interest in pleasing others will have an immediate, dramatic effect, in contrast to the flounderings of others. Another is that practically everyone is preoccupied by his or her own behavior, judging that of others only as it affects the self. By focusing your interest on other people while you temper your behavior according to how you wish them to judge you, you will quickly gain a reputation for charm, even before you have acquired the specific manners to go with it.

❧ FOR PARENTS

Inexplicit Announcements

DEAR MISS MANNERS:

I am a single woman expecting a baby. Would it be improper for me to send out birth announcements? Since the father and I live together, would both of our names or just mine go on them?

GENTLE READER:

Miss Manners is always pleased to hear of a lady's wish to refrain from doing anything improper. Yes, certainly, you may announce the birth in the name of both parents. It is not, however, customary to use the occasion to explain the relationship between the parents.

Tasteless Remarks

DEAR MISS MANNERS:

I am thirty-seven, and my husband and I are expecting our fourth child. Although this addition is somewhat of a surprise, we are anticipating the blessed event with joy. Our relatives and friends do not seem to share our joy. I am at a loss to deal with some of their rude and thoughtless remarks, including condolences about our failure at birth control, questions about why we wish to "start over at our age," jokes that imply that we do not know how to prevent pregnancy, and warnings about the increased risk of birth defects. I would like to respond in such a manner as to let these people know that I do not care for their remarks and would not welcome more in that vein, but at the same time, I wish to maintain dignity.

GENTLE READER:

The correct reply for all is, "Thank you; we knew our friends would be happy for us." Accompanied by a cold smile and a deep stare, this is an impeccable way of conveying "How mean and tasteless of you to say that."

Inappropriate Questions

DEAR MISS MANNERS:

As a new mother, I daily encounter the question "Are you nursing?" Am I mistaken, or is this inappropriate? Strangers, such as grocery clerks, and acquaintances, such as my boss's wife, seem to think that this is their business, or at least acceptable conversation.

GENTLE READER:

It's amazing what people consider acceptable conversation. Miss Manners is sure that you didn't get to be a new mother without years of being asked whether you were pregnant and months of being asked whether you did it on purpose, whether you wanted a boy or a girl, and so on.

If you didn't learn before how to avoid answering a question, now is a good time to do so. It is excellent preparation for mothering. In this case, you need only say, "Thank you very much; the baby is being well fed. It is kind of you to worry about him." If the rude question is then repeated, you need only repeat the answer more firmly, with the loud declaration "I SAID" as a preface. This is a phrase that comes increasingly to the lips of parents anyway, so you might as well practice it.

Breast-feeding

DEAR MISS MANNERS:

When I was out of the office for a month with a new baby, my boss very kindly brought his small daughter to visit me at home. When the baby cried to be fed, I faced the dilemma of whether to breast-feed with my guests in attendance or leave them sitting alone while I retired to another room. (My husband was not at home.) I chose the former option, which I attempted to execute discreetly. My boss didn't bat an eyelash and his daughter hardly appeared traumatized, but it was awkward, and, I fear, unprofessional for me. What should I have done?

GENTLE READER:

Yes, it is neither formal nor professional-looking, however necessary it may be, to breast-feed a baby. This was an odd situation in that it had a pseudosocial aspect, although it was intended as a formal call in a professional relationship. Let us assume that your boss and his daughter are of the if-it's-natural-go-ahead school of thought, and no harm was done. Miss Manners must warn you that a great many people are not. In America, breast feeding is done only among intimates.

Didn't your boss call beforehand to check when it would be a good time for him to visit? Could you not then have fed the baby beforehand? In any case, such visits are not supposed to be of long duration. If your visitors had been with you for, say, fifteen minutes before the baby started to cry, you could have given them a helpless look, said, "Oh, do forgive me, I'm afraid it's her mealtime, and it will take me a while," which would have been the cue for them to make a graceful exit.

❧ FOR OTHERS

Prebirth Pictures

DEAR MISS MANNERS:

What is the correct response when your pregnant friends insist on showing you the photographs from their sonograms? This has happened to me three times, and I somehow feel that saying "Oh, how cute" is inappropriate. Any suggestions?

GENTLE READER:

None better than "Oh, how cute." Miss Manners presents her compliments to you.

Explicit Material

DEAR MISS MANNERS:

A proud father brought to our office an album containing photos recording the birth of his second child, including graphic delivery-room photos. Smiling, another female co-worker and I said that since we'd both had children, we knew what delivering a child involved. At the same time, one of us reached for the page to turn it past the delivery-room photos. The father prevented this by placing one hand on a page, and with the other, pointing out various photos, explaining in great detail why the child looked the way it did because of problems during the delivery process. When we finally were able to view the baby after it was cleaned up and clothed, we could exclaim how cute it was, along with all the other appropriate comments. What is the correct response in this situation?

GENTLE READER:

"Can't we skip this and see your baby? We're really so much more interested in him, than in seeing his delivery or conception."

Mixed Blessings

DEAR MISS MANNERS:

What is the proper thing to say to a new mother who has just given birth to a handicapped baby? "Congratulations" sounds as if I'm pleased that the baby has a handicap, and, of course, I am not. I realize that parents naturally hope for healthy babies. But "Oh, I'm so sorry" sounds as though there has been a death or as if I'm ignorant of the many blessings a very special child can bring. In this case, the baby has been diagnosed as mentally retarded, but would the phrasing change if the baby were born blind or crippled?

GENTLE READER:

A mixed blessing does not always require a mixed answer. Prenatal parental hopes are as nothing compared with the strength of parental love for the baby that exists. So, unless your commiseration is invited, you must respond to the pleasure the parents enjoy in having a new baby, rather than the distress about the baby's handicap. The correct statement, therefore, is "Congratulations."

🌹 SOCIAL LIFE WITH BABIES

You can imagine how shocked Miss Manners was to hear where babies come from. Babies, it seems, no longer appear from vegetable gardens or express deliveries by large birds (who refuse to leave them if you're not home to sign for them, even though they never tell you exactly when they will arrive). They don't even appear because Mamma and Papa, as they are fond of explaining, just couldn't live without their own little snookie one more minute. Babies appear, Miss Manners has been told, because their parents are making statements.

Making statements? With babies? Miss Manners has been known to make statements *to* babies, such as "But these are yummy-yummy apricots; you *know* you love yummy-yummy apricots." She has also been known to make deals with babies, such as "Give me five more minutes' sleep, just five minutes, and I promise you that I'll pick you up and bounce you around again," even though her experience with babies' integrity about fulfilling their sides of bargains has been disillusioning.

She had heard of a peculiar new form of the national sport of consumerism, whereby people claim that they "make statements" through their selection of dry goods. But she never paid much attention when people claimed that they were getting married, or not getting married, or living together, or breaking up together "to make a statement." As a rule, Miss Manners never listens when anyone attempts to justify the simple workings of nature with what are obviously intended to pass as reasons or principles. Nevertheless, the statement that a baby is a statement of its parent disturbs her, because it seems to go with some odd forms of behavior that are not, Miss Manners believes, in the interest of an infant who can't talk, much less issue its own statements of denial or clarification.

Parents whose babies are statements don't just pass the time playing with their babies' toes until they decide that they need a quick fix of adult conversation. They don't just prattle on to their friends about how far ahead of some written timetable their babies do amazing things. Instead, they take the babies with them to a lot of unsuitable places, and they babble to others not so much about their own babies as about the babies those people should have.

All this is highly offensive to these same babies, as well as to bigger people who can't figure out how to defend themselves. Miss Manners will therefore take their part and announce that babies are not status items to be used to argue the superiority of the lifestyle of their parents. (She is reminded of an advertisement she once saw for a Beverly Hills clothing store for children, which sought to attract parents with the announcement, "Your children are part of your image.") Having them is not a new fad, but something that has been going on for some generations now, so one gets no credit for having thought of it. For the same reason, one cannot assume that others need to be alerted to the possibility.

Babies do not belong at work or at adult social events. It is no pleasure to them to go to such things, as they are rarely interested in picking up financial tips or salacious gossip and have difficulty reading the subtitles on foreign movies. It is as unfair of the parents to take them as it is to subject others to the crankiness and boredom they quite naturally exhibit. Ostentatious family togetherness is even harder on the babies than it is on the audience to which it is directed.

That is not to say that Miss Manners is not sympathetic about two other reasons for bringing babies to inappropriate places: that one has no responsible person with whom to leave them and that one does not wish to be parted from one's own sweetums. The first of these serves as an excuse for bringing children along in an emergency, provided that one can give them enough attention to prevent them from disturbing others. Parties never qualify as emergencies. The second is an excellent reason for modifying one's social life when one's children are small. Parents who understandably regret being separated from their babies on nights and weekends should learn to give after-bedtime parties for adults only and multigenerational weekend parties where amusements are provided for their own and the guests' children.

There is all the more reason for doing this as the parents may be quite sure that the minute the children are old enough to receive their own social invitations, they will demonstrate quite clearly that they have no interest whatsoever in making a statement of family togetherness by asking to bring their parents along.

Priorities

DEAR MISS MANNERS:

I have been asked to be the best man for a lifelong friend—his second marriage and the first for his bride-to-be. Here is my dilemma: My wife and I are the proud parents of a ten-week-old daughter (five years in the making), and two days before the wedding, the bride telephoned me long-distance at work and requested that children not attend the ceremony or the reception. Children were not specifically mentioned on the invitation, nor was the topic discussed prior to my "two-day notice." My wife is breast-feeding, and we live two hours from the home of the bride and groom. Although we could leave the baby with my parents, and had planned to do so for the ceremony (to avoid potential interruptions), we felt that a party and reception were events that one would normally attend with a breast-fed baby.

We realize our relative lack of objectivity concerning our newborn, and we recognize that a wedding is an incredibly special event. Nonetheless, a formal ceremony, subsequent pictures, and a reception would likely last for several hours and would undoubtedly cause my wife considerable physical discomfort. My response in this case is clear. I need to attend the ceremony and other events, but what is a reasonable amount of time for me to be expected to stay and participate in the activities? As best man, I have several expected duties; should I ask that they be performed in a briefer than normal time frame? Also, what is the proper etiquette for the bride and groom?

GENTLE READER:

The bride and bridegroom do not have any etiquette problems that Miss Manners knows of, other than the ones you may cause. So, let us rather discuss etiquette for proud parents. Miss Manners congratulates you, both on your daughter and on your realization that parenthood does funny things to objectivity. It also does things to one's schedule. It is up to the parents to make the necessary compromises without passing the burden on to others.

Babies do not belong at wedding receptions. They are not mentioned on wedding invitations because they are not invited. Champagne is not good for them, and it does them no good to catch the bouquet. However, it is not fair to a lifelong friend to expect him to speed up his wedding for your family's convenience. Had you thought ahead, you would have not taken on such a duty at such a time; you did, and you must see it through. Your wife, however, is simply a guest, and as such can slip away early to feed the baby.

Babies as Guests

DEAR MISS MANNERS:

I do not entertain at home, except for intimates—you know, those you've been through a war with or can sleep in the same bed with—that sort of thing. We go to restaurants. They smoke and eat pork, I order fish and fresh vegetables; all the time is spent on good food and each other. They treat, I treat—wonderful. But my modus operandi has been sabotaged by a baby who has captured my heart. I have been entertained by his parents in their home while having a marvelous time playing with him. My dilemma: How can I reciprocate? I have to add that my social obligations are not a chore, but a pleasure.

GENTLE READER:

Allow Miss Manners to say that she finds your problem a pleasure. Falling promiscuously in love with friends' children is a weakness of her own. Moreover, she believes cross-generational friendships to be greatly beneficial to the society, and only too often has to listen instead to complaints from people who can't understand why their contemporary friends are wrapped up in their children to the extent of not wanting to abandon them for adult partying every chance they get.

Babies aren't generally any crazier about restaurants than restaurants are about babies. But you will find that asking a baby to dinner at home without its parents does not require elaborate cooking or a battle over who will clean up. Babies come with their own bottles, or can be more or less persuaded that a jar of pureed mush is dinner, and even the most doting parents who prefer not to go out and leave their babies have a slightly different attitude about their babies going out socially themselves on an evening when the parents might have another obligation.

❧ EARLY LESSONS

Training Fussbudgets

When Miss Manners deplores the absence of child rearing in this society, she is perhaps doing an injustice to parents who indeed put a great deal of love and effort into training their children, but unfortunately are training them to have bad manners. This requires just as much work as teaching children good manners; more, in fact.

Parents who have trained their children in bad manners usually try to retrain them in mid-childhood, which is twice as much work.

The success rate for retraining is pitiful. When the children themselves undertake the task of changing their manners, usually later in life and often as a result of the disappointment of alienating those they had hoped to enthrall, they do better at it. Nevertheless, it leaves them with some bitterness toward those who originally bungled the job, and family resentment is a sad reward for parents who spared no effort to teach their children to behave badly.

They surrender any chance they may have to enjoy their meals, or even digest them, by using mealtimes to force-feed defenseless children a diet of relentless questions:

"Don't you like your beans? Would you rather have potatoes? What do you feel like eating instead?"

"Would you rather have some gravy on that? Suppose we scrape off the sauce. Would you like it better?"

"Aren't you going to drink your milk? Shall I warm it? Let me put some chocolate sauce in it. Would you rather have juice? Apple juice, or orange, or cranberry? Oh, that's not the brand you like, is it? I'm sorry, that's all they had; Can you drink it this once? Okay, I'll get the other kind."

"You haven't touched your meat, and you've got to have something. How about a peanut butter sandwich? What kind of jelly do you want on it? You don't want the dark bread I know, but I've got some white. Don't worry, I'm not going to give you the crust; I know you don't like that. Do you want it toasted? Light or dark? Shall I cut it for you? Diagonally or straight across?"

Any self-respecting child is bored senseless by this routine. Children are more attentive to parental wishes than their elders suppose, and any alert child quickly learns from this exercise that the strong expression of likes and dislikes, whether one feels them or not, defines individuality, creates the amusing spectacle of anxious adults scurrying around to obey ever-changing commands and is usually the only claim a child can make on his share of mealtime attention and conversation.

Thus the parent has, with tremendous effort, turned a perfectly agreeable child into a food fuss, a tyrant, and a bore, whose idea of conversation is not sharing information or listening to others, but only expressing his own feelings. In comparison, the task of teaching a child to report what interesting things he has seen and to listen to the remarks of others, while incidentally being coached by rote to eat whatever food is placed in front of him and to use the proper tools to do so, is an easy one.

A Victim of Child Rearing

DEAR MISS MANNERS:

I don't like to clean the kitchen, but my mom got mad at me. I'd rather stay in my room watching television and listening to my radio. Also, I don't like to go to any parties, but my mom and dad make me go. I am mad at them. Please tell me about manners. Thank you very much.

GENTLE READER:

You are being brought up. Put another way, you are the victim of child rearing. Miss Manners sympathizes with you about the difficulty of this process and does not expect you to believe that it is your parents whom you will one day be thanking, but such is the case.

A Child's Share

DEAR MISS MANNERS:

We have a ten-year-old son who seems to be confused about the difference between a house and a home. His father and I have explained that we all share equally in taking care of the house. That is, we are responsible for keeping our rooms orderly, taking out the trash, and similar light housekeeping tasks. Our son argues that if this is our home and we share in everything, it belongs partly to him and he should have a role in the decision making. For example, if a repair or remodeling is needed, he complains. He doesn't want anything altered or changed.

No matter what we say to explain, he starts a tantrum. We recently had a small change made in the kitchen. After the usual tirade of complaints and obstructionist behavior, he appeared to have accepted the alteration. However, he now refuses to do assigned chores, since he says that it is not his house.

GENTLE READER:

The danger of oversimplifying matters so that a child can understand them is that he may understand them. What your child clearly understands is your gross oversimplification—in fact your unsettling distortion—of what you had meant to explain.

By telling him that he does an equal share of household management when he performs his chores, you have convinced him that he is naturally entitled to an equal share in running the place. You didn't mean either statement. Does he pay a third of the mortgage? Have you consulted him about insurance needs? Does he do a major part of the meal planning, grocery shopping, laundry, cleaning, or gardening?

What you actually meant is that he does a child's share. The adults' share is to make all the financial contributions, all decisions requiring knowledge and judgment, and all the planning. Adults are supposed to have more wisdom and experience—enough, for example, to remain unswayed by tantrums.

Miss Manners approves of your insisting that your son do his part by virtue of his membership in the family, rather than because you threaten him or pay him to do so. By exaggerating his contribution, you not only promote silly rebellion based on false expectations but very likely suggest that he is responsible for matters beyond his capabilities. That is no favor to a child. You really do not want him to have an equal share in the worries. It is "his house" in that he has a secure home there, complete with parents who are committed to looking after his interests, even, or perhaps especially, when he is unable to perceive what his true interests are.

Privileges

DEAR MISS MANNERS:

My daughter plays the piano. She's in the fourth grade, and this year she gets more homework than ever. She now wants to quit the piano. I don't know whether to let her quit or to make her practice so that she learns how to work for something.

GENTLE READER:

Then make her work for the privilege of music lessons. Even if she quits now, considering lessons a treat rather than an obligation is the only way ever to give her the incentive they require. Miss Manners' policy on the subject is that the proper business of children is schoolwork, about which they have no choice, but that lessons and other regular extracurricular activities—whether they are cultural or athletic—have to be earned by a demonstration of serious commitment. Oddly enough, it is the parent who grumbles about the expense and nuisance of music lessons and threatens to stop them if the child doesn't practice, rather than the parent who selflessly nags the child to practice and provides concert tickets and records, whose home is filled with music.

STEPPARENTS, TEACHERS, AND OTHERS

The Teacher's Pet

Perhaps because she is an outspoken champion of everyone's right to be treated courteously, regardless of age, height, weight, verbal dexterity, degree of cuteness, and condition of dependency, Miss Manners often has manners violations reported to her by children, usually in tones of high indignation. She is therefore well aware that the leading cause, perhaps the only cause, of poor academic achievement in lower schools is that the teacher is "mean," "picks favorites," or just "doesn't like me."

School systems are evidently well populated with people who don't much care for children in general and rarely, if ever, in particular. (If there is such a person as the child who does well by being the favorite of an unfair teacher, he or she has not yet checked in with Miss Manners.) That may be. Miss Manners listens judiciously to each of these charges before she asks a few discreet questions:

How is the meanness expressed? Is there any clue to what the teacher doesn't like about you? Do you have any idea how the favorite was chosen? What does the teacher seem to like about him or her?

So far, Miss Manners has always received the same answers: Meanness is expressed through poor grades and reprimands. Although these tastes are obviously arbitrary or based on unacceptable prejudices, teachers are wily enough to invent justification by finding fault with the child's schoolwork or attitude toward it. Teachers' favorites are also chosen arbitrarily, according to Miss Manners' informants, but they have in common an offensively craven form of behavior described as "being the teacher's pet." (There is a certain amount of circular nonreasoning going on here, but one must bear in mind that logic is not part of the lower school curriculum.) Forced to report the forms that this well-rewarded obsequiousness takes, those who are above indulging in it describe hypocritical and overdramatized enthusiasm in following rules and doing schoolwork.

Miss Manners always has to warn children that she is neither an arbiter of fairness nor the dispenser of justice; she deals in the humbler world of outward behavior. Her practical method of deflecting teachers from unfavorable actions is to employ those very underhanded tactics of demonstrating enthusiasm and diligence in regard to schoolwork. (Sorry about that.) Even if Miss Manners had not noticed the amazing correlation between pupils a teacher appears to "like" and pupils who appear to like the subject the teacher teaches, she would have serious questions about the necessity of that elusive emotional quality in education.

As serious students often discover, the teachers from whom they learn most may be too passionate about their fields to indulge in sociability in connection with teaching. Their very belief in a discipline's importance can make them enforce standards strictly, without that amiable tolerance students have generally come to expect in education. Even small children understand this when they share those feelings about the subject matter. Many of them thrive in ballet classes that are run like Siberian labor camps or strive to please coaches who are not known for their indulgence toward childish whims.

Miss Manners does not condone humiliation or other forms of cruelty as a teaching method. She understands the value of a teacher whose kind manner inspires trust and confidences. Nevertheless, she refuses to acknowledge that affability is required in the classroom, any more than it is in the workplace. It may be nice to have a friendly boss, but it is possible to find work rewarding with one who is personally distant but committed to having things done well.

By way of consolation, Miss Manners has noticed something very peculiar about all this. When the tough job is over or the course finished, an enormous retrospective liking has a way of sneaking up later on both teacher and pupil.

Remedial Teaching

DEAR MISS MANNERS:
I'm thirty-five, an elementary school teacher, and recently married to a man with three children, aged twelve, ten, and seven, from a previous marriage. They

use their fingers to eat, don't use a knife and fork properly, chew audibly, invariably get a "mustache" from drinking from a glass, and end up with almost as much food on themselves, the table, and the floor as they do in their mouths. On top of this, they are extremely picky eaters and strongly prefer junk food.

I always set a proper table and go to a lot of trouble to prepare well-balanced, attractive meals that I think they will enjoy. I have set my priorities of things to rectify and try to overlook the others for the present. I have shown them several times, in a calm way, how to use the cutlery and how to drink so that their mouths stay clean.

They go to their mother's home for two weeks, and when they come back, it's back to square one. They show no interest in self-improvement and tolerate me only because it's my house. My husband is not a disciplinarian, and is frustrated and embarrassed by his children, although he does not perceive the problem to be as great as I do. In the fifteen years of my teaching career, I have often taken children on week-long trips and am familiar with average table manners for the age group. I don't think that my expectations are out of line.

This is only one of many problems I have with the kids, but it's the one that wears me down the most. I'm embarrassed to have people over when they are here. I confess that I don't want to put myself out for them, as I once did, to please and teach them, and I feel guilty about my attitude.

GENTLE READER:
Heaven bless stepparents who undertake the remedial work made necessary by the non-child-rearing practices of the original parents. One day the children will thank you, but as that day may be a long time off, Miss Manners would like to do so now.

Do not give up. You are, after all, a teacher as well as a stepmother, and presumably dedicated to the idea of civilizing the young. It just so happens that eating is one of the mechanical skills most often used to place people in the society, and children who are not taught table manners early are put at a disadvantage all their lives by everyone from prospective lovers to prospective employers.

To keep you from discouragement, and from the even less productive feeling of guilt, Miss Manners would like to point out to your husband that he has a double duty here, to his children and to his wife. Disciplinarian or not, he must vehemently demand that your standards (no comparisons should be made to the mother's standards) be maintained in your and his household.

Nonparental Authority

DEAR MISS MANNERS:
I am a camp manager, and this year we have new junior counselors who are volunteering many hours and their talents. Some of their concerns are: how to deal with rude campers who barge into your room while you are dealing with a troubled, homesick child; how to deal with repeated questions when it is inappropriate to give the answer without violating someone's privacy; what to do with campers

who reply with extremely uncalled-for comments or refusals when asked to carry out the shared responsibilities of camp life, such as room sweeping or meal clean-up; and how to deal firmly with hysterical girls who overreact to power failures and bugs.

GENTLE READER:

This is all one question, but it is a difficult one: How do you establish authority over children while maintaining a warm and nonforbidding attitude? There is no simple trick. Your junior counselors will have to learn through practice that a self-confident air of being in command that discourages disobedience and rudeness is not incompatible with kindness and sensitivity. With that attitude, it is simple to tell the barger-in, "Excuse me, we're busy here; you'll have to come back later"; the questioner, "I'm sorry, but I'm not going to answer that"; the shirker, "You must do your share, as we all do"; and the hysteric, "Calm down, you have to learn to deal with these problems."

Insensitivity to Others

DEAR MISS MANNERS:

My mobility is severely limited as a result of multiple sclerosis, which I have had for several years. When I am out in my motorized wheelchair, shopping, or going to church or restaurants, children stare. (Adults do, too, but they try to hide it.) Some of the children smile sweetly, and to those I usually smile back and say, "Do you like my cart?" Then they give me a grin and feel better about me. When one child asked his father, "Why is she riding in that?" the father replied, "So that she can come out and see all the pretty things around." How nice! He made me feel better and did his child a world of good.

Other children laugh and giggle and point, thus creating a scene that makes me uncomfortable. While I was out shopping last week in the dress department, looking through the racks, some children laughed and followed me, looking through the racks and saying to one another, "Here she comes." The parents said nothing. I was so embarrassed that I left the department store. Children are naturally curious. But what has happened to parents who are supposed to teach them the courtesy to go with it? There are so many tragic implications in the public's attitude toward handicaps and the handicapped. People who are more self-conscious than I become prisoners and don't go out.

GENTLE READER:

Everyone is naturally curious, but that is no excuse for being rude. Miss Manners happens to think that society has created the underlying problem here by segregating the disabled to such an extent that they are an unusual sight, and hence the object of curiosity. If these children who annoyed you normally attended school with children in wheelchairs, they would not be so unpleasantly attentive to you. It is the responsibility of parents to teach their children to rise above the natural rudeness of curiosity. The father you mentioned did it particularly well by drawing his child's attention to the normality of going out and away from the detail of your method of mobility. Polite people are always more interested in the positive qualities of others than in their disabilities.

Tormenting Animals

DEAR MISS MANNERS:
   During a yard party, where the majority of the guests were members of a large family with their children (I was brought as a date by a family member), a young child was kicking and abusing a dog belonging to the host family, so that it yelped in pain. I waited several minutes for the parents, who were nearby, to correct the child, but they continued eating and laughing. I finally corrected the child myself, calling over to her as unobtrusively as possible to stop abusing the animal. I received an angry retort from the parents, to which I replied that I could not see them ignoring the situation any longer and did not intend to tolerate the abuse of the animal.
   During the afternoon, I was criticized by several guests, the consensus being that as a guest, I should have kept my mouth shut and left it up to the parents to correct the child or ignore the situation as they chose. They argued that if I could not bear to see the dog in pain, I had the option to get up and leave, but had no right to speak to the child.

GENTLE READER:
   Morally, you triumph in this story, with your sympathetic concern for the animal, compared with the parents' irresponsibility about making the child behave decently and the guests' callous suggestion of dealing with abuse by walking away from it. However, you do not triumph in the matter of manners. Miss Manners feels obliged to point out that you could have done so while being more effective, not less, in your rescue mission. If your object was to rescue the dog, why didn't you just do so? It would have been kinder to the animal simply to step quietly in and take it away from the child, rather than to let this abuse go on during the time you were reprimanding a child whose parents were present and abstaining from doing so (which is a transgression of manners). You could then have dealt with the other etiquette aspects by gently explaining, first to the child and then to the parents, that surely the child could not possibly have realized that she was inflicting pain, and that she must learn that she was.

Damaging Property

DEAR MISS MANNERS:
   What do I do about the children of guests who climb all over my furniture as if it were a jungle gym?

GENTLE READER:

Just shout, "No, no, get down—that's not safe!" Then flash a worried but apologetic smile to the parents, saying, "Oh, dear, I got so frightened. That sofa is really very fragile, and if it broke and one of your children got hurt, I would never forgive myself."

CHILD REARING SABOTAGED

Explanation and Example

DEAR MISS MANNERS:

We have taught our two-and-a-half-year-old to say "Please," "Thank you," and "You're welcome," but our guests commonly stare at him blankly or say "Oh, how cute" when he thanks them for a gift instead of saying "You're welcome." I've even had people accuse me of "teaching him to go through insincere rituals like a trained seal." I have no wish to raise my son to be pretentious, but had frankly not thought about teaching him these small courtesies until he started using them himself, in imitation of his father and me.

I could ignore this snubbing on the part of my guests, except that it teaches my son to be rude. None of these people would dream of leaving my thank-yous unacknowledged. How can I persuade them to use common courtesy with my children? Also, how can I get other people's children to be courteous, as I see no way to correct them without offending their parents?

GENTLE READER:

While congratulating you on the success of your use of example to teach manners to your son, Miss Manners feels obliged to warn you not to attempt to enlarge your instructional activities in the hope of bringing up your friend's and other people's children. Not only is such an enterprise doomed to failure, but it would provide your son with the unfortunate example of the rudeness of correcting anyone who is not, as he is, under your jurisdiction. You have to let their rude reactions pass and explain to your son the awful fact of life that not everyone knows how to behave properly. The disillusionment he may feel is nothing to the smugness of secretly knowing that he knows more than those big people.

However, when your friends question your premises, you may request them not to sabotage your parental authority. Any observations that being polite constitutes pretentiousness, insincerity, or mindlessness—as opposed to that wonderfully sincere, healthy, thoughtful rudeness that they so admire in other children—should be met with the contempt it deserves. That is not license to be rude yourself but merely to state, with freezing politeness, "I'm afraid I disagree with you, but in any case, you will, of course, allow me to bring up my child as I see fit."

This experience should teach you that example is not the only essential child-rearing tool. Many of the complexities of human behavior, including the fact that we should not allow the rudenesses of others to lower our own standards of manners, must be explained. You do not want your child to think, once he comes under less polite influences than yours, that prevailing behavior may be safely and uncritically followed.

Generous Strangers

DEAR MISS MANNERS:

My husband and I took our children to a public park to enjoy the beautiful day. After a lovely morning, we were meandering back to the car, seeing the remaining sights, and planning to go for lunch from there. We sat down on a bench because our daughter was tired and complaining that her legs hurt. The younger children began to complain that they were hungry. As I was explaining that we were on our way to get something to eat, a young woman who had been sitting nearby handed them candy sticks similar to the one she was eating. I allowed the children to have them after I quickly looked them over, but I felt terrible. I was trapped in a quandary. I have taught my children not to accept gifts from strangers, but I have also taught them that we do not hurt or embarrass other people. The young woman appeared to be only trying to be kind to my children. She obviously had no idea of the problem she had created for me. Since nothing happened, I think that my judgment of her intentions was correct, but I could have been wrong. My children's welfare is my highest priority, but how we treat others is important, too.

GENTLE READER:

It is essential to your children's welfare that you not allow them to believe that one must choose between doing whatever anyone happens to offer and insulting the offerer. Miss Manners shudders to think what could happen if they grow up believing that declining anything is rude. As you seem to be confused about this yourself, Miss Manners had better first teach the lesson to you.

Refusing an offer is never in itself rude; it is how the offer is refused that makes the difference between politeness and rudeness. Rudeness consists of snubbing a well-meant offer. As the young woman appeared to mean well, it would have been rude to turn away from her as if an insult had been intended. The polite refusal consists of a regretful look and the words "No, thank you, but it was kind of you to offer." You must teach the children this. As you had not, you as the mother could have said it, perhaps with some softening explanation, such as "I'd prefer that they didn't have sweets before lunch."

Their education would not be complete unless you also taught them to recognize the offer that is not well meant—the classic stranger offering candy or other enticements to children when the parents are not there to protect them. In that case, it is perfectly appropriate for the children to walk away, with or without a curt "No, thank you," refusing to be drawn into any discussion.

Softening Disappointment

DEAR MISS MANNERS:

My son got a new bike for his seventh birthday. He was told several times when he got it that it should be locked up in the shed when not in use. Well, it was not locked up, and six weeks later, it was stolen. My husband and I told him that we would get him a new bike when we got the insurance money. My mother thinks it is wrong to wait and wanted to get him a bike the day after it was taken, even after I told her no. She says that he's not responsible enough at age seven to put his bike away (which is not the real issue). I feel that she should respect our decision on the matter; after all, we are the parents. We feel that he may not be totally responsible, but waiting will help him be more responsible next time.

GENTLE READER:

Indeed, we have here two issues, the authority issue and the cruel world issue. As it happens, Miss Manners agrees with you on both. Nevertheless, she is full of sympathy for the erring grandmother. The instinct to protect one's progeny from cruel facts such as theft, creating a world where everything bad can be undone, is a strong one, motivated by nothing but love. Grandparents have the luxury of expressing emotional support without worrying about day-to-day child rearing.

You, as a parent, have the difficult job of gradually teaching the child about harsh reality and self-protection. By replacing the bicycle but explaining that there is a practical reason to delay, you are, Miss Manners believes, doing your duty to your child in a gentle but sensible way appropriate to his capacity to understand. All you need do now is to show the same gentleness, tolerance, and firmness toward your mother when you explain that you appreciate her warm offer but must act as you think best in educating your child.

⚘ ADOLESCENCE

The invention of the teenager was a mistake, in Miss Manners' opinion. She has nothing against people of that age; indeed, she is quite foolishly fond of some such individuals. It is not teenagers whom she wishes to abolish, but only the category.

Once you identify a period of life in which people have few restrictions and, at the same time, few responsibilities—they get to stay out late but don't have to pay taxes—naturally, nobody wants to live any other way. Thus we now have the equally unappetizing spectacles of small children and grown-ups unsuccessfully imitating teenage dress, speech, and social rites, while teenagers themselves have little motivation to learn the trappings of adulthood. We have, as a society, informed teenagers that not only are they entitled to have their own culture, but that we don't expect them to aspire to any other. Almost before they know their own tastes, teenagers are told that they like only junk food, primitive culture, and an unvarying standard of simplicity in clothes and manners. As such personal inclinations naturally vary more by individual than by age, this alerts teenagers who happen to like classical music or dressing up that they are weird. All that does not serve the cause of civilization. Nor does it promote the general happiness when something as universal and inevitable as getting older is perceived as a tragedy.

Under the old system, everyone was either an adult or a child. It was perfectly obvious which was which. Adults sentimentalized childhood as a time of carefree pleasure. They considered increased respect and dignity, not to mention more sophisticated pleasures, as compensation for leaving it. Children learned to talk dirty only in stages, making bathroom jokes long before they knew sexual terms. Their fantasy of adulthood as a time of untrammeled freedom led them to study the ways of adult life while pressing impatiently for its advantages.

Of course, the people who are now called teenagers have always tried to play both sides against the middle. They claimed adulthood when privileges were in question and childishness when it came to tasks. Basically, however, they used to strive rather than languish where they were. This had enormous practical benefits. By observing and imitating adult ways, apprentice adults/postchildren not only prepared themselves for the future but learned how to deal to advantage with grown-ups in their present lives.

Propriety and Privacy

DEAR MISS MANNERS:

The first time my boyfriend and I spent time in my bedroom, talking and nothing else, my mother said that I could never go into the bedroom with him again, simply saying that it wasn't right. Then she agreed that I could go into the bedroom with him as long as the door was kept completely open, but when he came over, she said she'd never agreed to anything of the sort. The next time, he and I were discussing a structural problem with a model helicopter in my bedroom. Everything was innocent. My mother came in and very rudely started telling us to leave. She's always rude to him, but when he's gone, she says that she likes him and denies that she's been rude.

Haven't I got the right to be in my own bedroom? I'll agree to keep the door wide open as long as she's not in there every five minutes checking up on us or asking me to wash the dishes when my friends are over. My friends have complained, and I can't blame them. Shouldn't she keep her word? There have been times I haven't kept my word, but I've paid the price.

GENTLE READER:

Without defending your mother, who should keep her word and not treat your friends rudely, Miss Manners feels sorry for her. Your mother is behaving the way she is because she has not thought the problem through. Like most grown-ups, she knows that appearances, as well as actual behavior, can be important. Instead of explaining that to you, she has tried to give in on the point of your entertaining in your bedroom. Then, because she has conceded something she cannot endorse, she falters.

Miss Manners does not doubt that your behavior is innocent, but for a couple to go off alone to a bedroom in a family dwelling is suggestive of something else. If it were a bed-sitting room in a dormitory, commonly used for social as well as sleeping purposes, that would not be the case. This is such a subtle argument that your mother doesn't attempt it because she is afraid that she would lose to a youthful declaration of rights and wrongs, in which mere appearances are discounted and issues of social custom dismissed as trivial, if not hypocritical, compared with actual moral behavior. Nevertheless, the violation of customs is offensive. Your mother can't stand it, and, Miss Manners assures you, your boyfriend's parents would also be swift to condemn you.

You are, however, right in wanting a private place in which to entertain. Surely there is some place in the house—the living room, a recreation or sitting room— that can be set aside at certain times for you and your guests. When conventionality is satisfied, your mother will be more ready to trust your moral behavior.

Standing Around Looking Stupid

What great fun it is for those of us old enough to appreciate nap time to imagine wild, free youth out there overflowing with exuberant emotions and happily struggling in vain to suppress the madcap ways they keep inventing to express them. Unfortunately, however, the real chief social problem of youth is the habit of standing around looking stupid.

Mind you, Miss Manners is not accusing anyone of actually being stupid. Tuning out of conversations that do not immediately concern one, responding minimally to banalities, and utterly relaxing the features whenever possible, short of allowing the tongue to loll outside the mouth, may be defended as rational behavior. Children who have been encouraged all their lives to act natural (although the admonishment does carry a certain curious contradiction) quite naturally turn to such expressionlessness once they have outgrown their bounciness.

Standing around looking stupid, however, is an extremely impractical social posture. Adults invariably interpret it as representing stupidity, or at least contempt for themselves, which they naturally believe to be the same thing. It is not a wise idea to leave this impression on adults, not so much because they have feelings but because they have beach houses, summer jobs to give out, places in schools to allot, and the ability and opportunity to air damaging opinions in front of their own children. Even adults who have a vested interest in believing these expressionless children to be miracles of cleverness react badly when they see it. A happy, active child is generally smiled upon by its parents; one who is hanging around looking stupid inspires them to request that he or she study, take out the trash, practice, or get a job. Standing around looking stupid is also a handicap for the young among people of their own age, however much these people may practice it themselves. The new kid in school or the neighborhood and the stranded person at a party or dance, who may well be standing around looking stupid because he or she quite properly feels stupid in such a difficult situation, nevertheless arouses scorn rather than pity. So you see, it is really a dreadful idea.

The alternative is to act something else: cheerful, attractive, amused, interested, absorbed, confident, or as if one knew what one were doing. Different expressions are appropriate for different occasions. The general idea is to anticipate the reaction you wish to get from the other person by simulating the feeling you want. In other words, you act interested if you hope that someone will find you interesting, confident if you want someone to give you an acceptance to a school or job that would build your confidence, and popular if you wish to win the friendship that would make you popular.

Miss Manners is not claiming that any of this is easy. Acting is a difficult profession, although an interesting one. Contrary to the popular notion that it just comes naturally to people born with talent, even the simple ability to observe, interpret, and reproduce the physical manifestations of emotions requires a great deal of intellect and work. And even the least stagestruck person must master a bit of this skill in order to dramatize his own real emotions, or the ones he wants to display, just enough to convey them to other people in his life.

The intelligent-looking face is therefore always alert when other people are around, as if capable of registering what its owner hears and sees. It need not be grimacing wildly, but the eyes should be in focus and the mouth in a state to be mobilized instantly for talk, laughter, frowning, or whatever. One should then learn basic responses, such as smiling upon greeting people, nodding occasionally when they talk, laughing when they look as if they have told jokes, appearing to be pleased when they show interest by asking silly questions, and so on.

The clever young person will understand that the fact that he has reason on his side for looking impassive at seeing these people, daydreaming while they talk, and remaining immobile at their humor and bored by their questions has nothing to do with it. One is not only being polite to them, regardless of their claim on such an effort, but practicing being charming. As the charming person has a marked advantage in life over all others, even those with decidedly more important virtues, it is a skill worth honing. And the first requirement of charm is that the bearer of it appear to be alive.

The College Registration Ritual

Every autumn the highways are clogged with what appear to be mobile yard sales. In addition to bulging with oddly assorted junk, these automobiles each have, squeezed in the back amid the pillows and records and cartons, one teenager. It is the annual rite by which parents deliver freshmen to college.

Invitations to skip this event, issued by the freshmen, should be ignored. They all believe that sophisticated classmates will arrive alone, and they will be the only ones exhibiting childish dependence by arriving encumbered with fond adults. They are all mistaken. Freshman registration is as necessary to parents as graduation. The very occasion that provides them with one last ritualistic fuss demonstrates to them the hopelessness of continuing their routine parental supervision at long distance.

It is true that the air will be filled with desperate, last-minute pleas:

"Promise me you won't skip breakfast."

"You know you need plenty of sleep. You'll just have to tell your roommates that, so they'll be quiet."

"You can't live on junk food and expect to be able to concentrate."

"You don't have to dress like a slob just because everybody else does."

"Remember, plan ahead: You don't want to be one of those people who doesn't even look at assignments until just before they're due."

"See? There's a washer and a dryer right here in the basement."

"I expect you to get a rounded education, not just pick courses you happen to like."

Listen to the tone. The parents know the futility of what they are saying. Any child who takes this as an opportunity to argue, who replies anything at all except a kindly "Don't worry about me, I'll be fine," is not mature enough for college. The entire event will, in fact, be an exercise in etiquette for the freshman; the most appreciative and loving child in the world will find it a trial. No matter how close the family is or how homesick the freshman may get the day after parents leave, he or she is going to be impatient for their departure. What is more, a freshman who actually succeeds in keeping his parents from attending, or one whose parents have their own good reasons not to go, is likely to come up with the blatantly unfair charge that they don't care.

It behooves the freshman to introduce his parents to everyone he meets and to show them, as much as he can, the places where he will be living, eating, and studying. He is obligated to listen to their advice and to their own reminiscences about school. Since it is his temporary home, he is the host and must do the honors, rather than rushing off while they are there to begin his new life.

They, in turn, should be ready to follow his suggestions about activities, behave politely but formally to others (that means not giving his roommates parental instructions, telling a proctor to take special care of him, or using a childhood nickname that its owner finally has hopes of living down), and spend some time chatting up the other parents to give the freshman an opportunity to talk to his classmates. It also means assuming the primary obligation of the guest, which is not to linger but to go home when it's time to go home. Arguments against doing so are to be taken no more seriously than arguments against going there.

Praise for the Parents

DEAR MISS MANNERS:

I am a twenty-one-year-old who decided to live in my hometown, albeit in my own apartment, after college. Thanks to my father and grandmother, I acquired a sense of social correctness. But it seems that every time I send a condolence note or thank-you-for-dinner flowers, the recipient rushes to the telephone and calls my father! They are so taken aback by common courtesy that they gush on and on. I realize that time will most likely take care of this, and I don't want to do anything ungracious, but would you, Miss Manners, without the burden of ungraciousness, say something about this? Please?

GENTLE READER:

No, because what springs to Miss Manners' mind is praise not only for you, but for your father and grandmother for doing such a good job in bringing you up. But Miss Manners will say no such thing, because she wouldn't want to offend such a well-bred young person.

Family Dinners

Good sport that she is, Miss Manners often gamely attacks modern questions about the etiquette of eating: What is the correct utensil for eating ice cream from a carton with the refrigerator door open? Answer: an ice cream scoop, so that if anyone discovers you, you can pretend that you were just licking off the drips before they hit the kitchen floor. The truth is that Miss Manners would rather be discussing the proper use of, say, ice cream forks. She cannot justify that by claiming that there is widespread anxiety on the subject, but will argue that there is a dearth of amusement in the world and that propriety always provokes merriment. However, she is aware that this does not relieve her from the duty of making modern eating methods as presentable as possible. She does not flinch from telling people not to crunch their empty beer cans and then try to fit them into their hosts' ashtrays.

There is some accommodation to modern living arrangements in Miss Manners' rules. Not much, but some. She once conceded that paper napkins are not incorrect at picnics, although she wouldn't dream of having them at her own four-course picnics. Modernity has taken advantage of her. While she was fussing over the details of mealtime manners, some sneaky people were working on abolishing the concept of mealtime altogether.

"Grazing" is the name she has heard applied to the increasingly popular habit of declaring all waking hours to be snack time and thus eliminating the sustenance motivation to have formal meals. Freed from the physical drive to show up at table, grazers have simply killed the ceremony of traditional communal eating. Grown-ups who live this way lay pretentious claim to being too busy for meals, and never mind the time they find to mope about the lack of fulfillment in their lives. More frightening, there are children who are actually being brought up that way. Some are permitted to wander away at will from family meals, and some are actually fed on demand all day long and then never required to attend a meal at all.

If this continues, such ritual statements as "Not now—it'll spoil your appetite for dinner" and "If you don't have room for spinach, you certainly won't have room for dessert—and guess what I baked?" will be incomprehensible to future generations.

Also, civilization will erode even more drastically than it has already. The dinner table is the center for the teaching and practicing not just of table manners but of conversation, consideration, tolerance, family feeling, and just about all the other accomplishments of polite society except the minuet.

We shall have to reestablish regular meals. Miss Manners promises not to nag you about what to eat at them (the world being too full already of those who will tell you, whether you ask them to or not, how to achieve salvation through nourishment) as long as you observe the ritual. Nor will she inquire how the food is cooked, or whether it is cooked at all, rather than unwrapped. That is, provided that it is unwrapped. If she catches you with a carton or a cooking pot on the table, you will be in trouble.

Mealtimes, for those who have already forgotten, consist of breakfast, luncheon, and dinner (tea optional). They take place at tables.

Participants time their eating so that changes of course occur at the same time for everyone. Except for performing the mechanics of meal serving and a certain emergency that is never discussed, no one is allowed to leave the table until the conclusion.

People who do not participate in such with some regularity are not leading a civilized life. Besides, they will forget or never learn the skills necessary for the one form of meal that the meal destroyers deem important: the one in the fancy restaurant on the company's expense account.

"What's For Dinner?"

DEAR MISS MANNERS:

When guests are visiting for dinner or an extended period, is it polite to ask the hostess "What's for dinner?" and then, after the answer is given, to walk away? As a child, I used to ask my mother "What's for dinner?" to see if I liked it and to prepare myself for the meal. Am I being critical to think that this is what they are doing as well? Would a polite way to ask be "Something smells good! What's cooking?" Then maybe they could ask if they could help with the preparations. Does this differ with relatives or close friends, as opposed to a client or a new acquaintance?

GENTLE READER:

There are only two possible reactions to being told what is for dinner: "Great!" and "Yuck!" They may be phrased as "You shouldn't go to all that trouble" or "Not again!" or "You know I'm on a diet," but that's what they boil down to, as it were. Members of the immediate family may indulge in such remarks in order to influence future menus, provided they know that the cook will take it in the same spirit, offering such traditional replies; as "Never mind, it's good for you" or

"That does it from now on, you do the cooking." Although compliments or adverse reactions may affect the cook, there is obviously no effect on that day's fare. (If the cook replies, "Okay, then, I'll throw it out and start again," duck.) So, Miss Manners doesn't know what you mean about needing preparation for dinner.

Guests have no business inquiring. Clients and new acquaintances don't even belong in the kitchen, and houseguests and other close friends who wander in should do so only for the purpose of offering to help. Any remarks they make about the food should be intended as compliments; your suggestion about asking what smells so good is fine because the emphasis is on the good, not the what.

The Importance of Ritual

It is with some trepidation that Miss Manners notes the passing of the tradition of bed making. Two innovations in interior decoration are making the very concept of bed making obsolete: the simple colored or patterned comforter, which serves as both blanket and spread, and is therefore more or less in place after the bed has been used; and the fancier lacy bed headed by a dozen little eyelet pillows in different shapes, intended to be exposed during the daytime as if always ready for use. In these states, beds can no longer be identified as either made or unmade, or people as the sort who do or do not make them.

You would think that Miss Manners would be grateful. She ought to be brimming with hope that those four saved matinal minutes will be applied to efforts that will assist, in more public and practical ways, the advance of civilization.

Perhaps it is that she knows they will not. Morning routines have steadily led the way to a deterioration of daily patterns of living. There are very good and serious excuses for each change. Mornings are frightfully rushed in all households where people have work to do or go to school, which accounts for just about everyone. It saves time not to pick up towels and nightclothes. Another second or two and some emotional energy can be squeezed by omitting ritual greetings to other members of the household. It is easier to put food on the table in the commercial containers in which the various items were bought, to leave off such useless objects as underliners for bowls, and to replace other items of tableware with disposable products. Breakfast can be eaten directly from the refrigerator or skipped entirely. Not saying good-bye not only saves time but distracts attention from the fact that one has grabbed other people's possessions because there wasn't time to find one's own.

Miss Manners would yield to the plea of necessity were she not familiar with the other end of the work and school day. Again, time is saved by not uttering civilities to other members of the household, by not following amenities in the serving of meals, or perhaps by giving up the idea of having a joint mealtime at all, allowing everyone to scrounge and to eat alone while performing other activities.

In other words, pleasant, orderly, civilized living is being sacrificed in an age when the work week is considerably shorter than it was when these practices were routine. The accompanying laments about lack of time are valid, and Miss Manners has no doubt that even without performing any niceties, people are dropping exhausted at the end of the day.

These are not, however, lives that are devoid of recreation. Athletics, including television watching and even more stimulating sports, are more widely practiced than ever. Miss Manners is forced to conclude that civilization is not being dropped as the last sacrifice of desperate people, but that a deliberate choice has been made that it is the most disposable luxury and therefore the first to go.

She finds that a tragic mistake. Mornings of jogging and evenings of television are all very well if one has the time, but no one will ever look back upon years spent that way with the fond reminiscences and satisfaction of family meals and tiny aesthetic rituals. It isn't bed making or the lack of it that bothers her so much as the worry that this is yet another contribution to the Why Bother School of Disappearing Domesticity that is turning homes into mere indoor parking places. She has an offer to make. Provided that you emerge from the bedroom in the morning willing to devote some effort to civilized living, she promises not to peek at whatever mess you left behind.

Table Manners

❧ EQUIPMENT AND HOW TO USE IT

Now and again, Miss Manners likes to frighten everyone by brandishing weird silverware. Lettuce forks. Ice cream knives. Bonbon spoons. She leaps out at kindly folk who say, "Etiquette is just simple consideration of others," and demands, "Oh, yes? Then what about THIS?"

It gets them every time. An astonishing number of people seem to harbor a deep fear of being helplessly confronted with such social weaponry. Strange configurations of metal appear in a standard American nightmare: Not Knowing Which One to Use.

Of course, Miss Manners is just having her bit of fun. In real life, it is unlikely that the proverbial five forks can make you the laughing stock of the social set immediately above yours. For those who are curious or horror-stricken, here is a small Inventory of Funny Silverware with which to eat things you never had trouble eating before.

Perhaps you thought sardines were so low-class that they wouldn't dare complain no matter how you attacked them. Actually, they were once used to grandeur, living in little silver boxes, where they were approached with sardine tongs. Any fool can recognize sardine tongs because they have sardines carved on them and are smaller than broad asparagus tongs or sandwich tongs, not big and narrow like steak tongs.

The favored instrument with which to attack ice cream is the human tongue. Nevertheless, ice cream served in molds is sliced with an ice cream knife (which looks like a cross between a crumber for the table—rectangular, higher on one side—and a fish slicer—a small version of the individual fish knife: flat, usually pointed, and engraved with sea motifs). It may then be eaten with ice cream forks (spoons whose bowls have rounded tines in an upward clutch), ice cream spoons (flattened in the center), or ice cream spades (square shovels with rounded or nipped-in sides, not to be confused with fat, triangular butter spades or pointed salt shovels). An accompanying candy is offered with a bonbon spoon (short, wide, and intricately decorated).

While we're uncharacteristically allowing choices, loose sugar may be served with sugar spoons (wider than teaspoons but not to be confused with the flatter jelly servers), sugar shells (shell motif on the bowl), or pierced-ladle sugar sifters (and well you may ask how you get the sugar over the food you want to sift it on). Cubed sugar is served to horses with the human hand and patronizing compliments, but people can use clawed tongs, also called "tea tongs," or sugar nippers (scissors action, but with flat blades).

Miss Manners is sorry to report that there is no banana spoon. You eat a banana with a fruit fork and fruit knife (don't you?). But there are long, triangular-bowled orange spoons, now often pressed into grapefruit service, berry spoons (the ones with the berries carved on the bowl), and strawberry forks, which look like lemon forks or lettuce forks with splayed tines.

The small salad knife has all but disappeared, unfortunately, because tough lettuce hasn't. Tomatoes are served on the tomato server (pierced and flat). Olives are speared with the prong end of the olive, or (sucket) fork, and eaten from the spoon end. These are not to be confused with mote spoons, where the pierced spoon is used for stirring tea and the tip at the other end for clearing the tea spout. Pickles are supposed to get themselves out of their barrels, but they have their own barbed forks. Butter pats are picked with butter picks (repeat fast three times), rather than butter knives, but not with the nut pick or the marrow scoop, which is not to be confused with the cheese scoop.

This is just the beginning. We haven't even gotten to the pudding spoon, horseradish spoon, snuff spoon, ice spoon, or caddy spoon. (No, it's not for eating caddies.) Miss Manners is not making these up. She is, in fact, on record as declaring that the age of silverware invention is over and opposing the coffee mug spoon. But not even to calm a hysterical population will she admit that it doesn't matter, go ahead, use any one for whatever you wish, scratch your back with the dessert fork if you feel like it. Neither does she tell people who own specialized hi-fi, computer, or sports equipment that they ought to allow people to play with it without regard to its intended function.

A Nightmare Service

Everyday Dinner Service

TABLE SETTINGS. *Although this nightmare dinner setting does not exist in real life—the rules of etiquette even for pig-outs prohibit putting this much silver on the table—many people claim to be frightened of it. At the extreme right is the oyster fork, nestling in the soup spoon; left of that is a marrow scoop. Then, in pairs on either side of the plate, from the outside in, are the fish knife and fork, the knife and fork for the entree (which does not mean the main course), the knife and fork for the main course, the salad knife and fork, and the fruit knife and fork. Above the plate are the dessert spoon and fork.*

Family meals are the only kind where a napkin ring is proper (guests don't need them because they get fresh napkins). The table is set for soup, bread and butter, the main course, and dessert.

Mismatched Silver

DEAR MISS MANNERS:

I paid no attention to silver and china at the time of my wedding, and I can hardly believe this of myself, but last year, ever since I inherited a set of sterling silver tableware, I have been hankering after additional pieces: demitasse spoons, iced-tea spoons, and the like. Luckily for me, the pattern is still available. Howev-

Formal Dinner Service

Mrs. Proper

Five course meals being as much as even gluttons can manage these days, this is as full a formal place setting as you are ever likely to face, no matter how grandly you dine. The soup spoon is at the right, followed, working from the outsides toward the plate, by the fish knife and fork, the meat knife and fork, and the salad knife and fork. A dessert spoon (large and oval—not a teaspoon) and fork are to be brought in on the dessert plate, but they could also be crossed (spoon facing left and fork facing right) above the plate, where the place card is shown here.

er, the pieces I have are all engraved with my great-aunt's last initial, which is an *H*. In fact, she left the silver to me partially because she knew I was going to marry a man whose last initial is *H* and assumed that mine soon would be as well. However, I have not changed my name, so my last initial is still a *B*.

It seems fraudulent to have the pieces I buy engraved with an *H,* as though I were misrepresenting the size of the set I inherited, but having a mismatched set of *H*'s and *B*'s seems odd, and no engraving would be the worst of all. I need a solution that is both elegant and correct because I am anxious to begin extending the set. It must be the sobering effect of married life.

GENTLE READER:

The solution is to relax. It is entirely proper, Miss Manners assures you, to have either unmarked silver or a variety of markings that don't match. One is supposed to inherit one's silver, getting most of it from one's grandmamma and odd pieces from this great aunt or that, rather than plunking down a huge wad for a chest of new stuff.

Therefore it is more suitable to have a mismatched set than a matched one. It is even chic to mix patterns at different courses —an odd set of fish or dessert knives and forks, for example, and certainly demitasse spoons, as they are not used at the table with the rest of the flatware anyway. This is convenient for those who round out their sets at thrift shop bins or who get it all there and have only to invent relatives to go with the initials. Not that Miss Manners is suggesting fraud. It is just silly to worry that you are "misrepresenting" your inheritance by augmenting it. Miss Manners' preference would be to leave the new pieces unmarked, or to mark them with your own initials, for the given names as well as the surname. Wedding silver is traditionally marked anyway with the bride's maiden initials (providing another unexpected convenience if the marriage does not last).

Setting the Table

DEAR MISS MANNERS:

I had always been taught that knives, forks, and spoons should be set on the table in the order in which they are to be used, starting on the outside, farthest from the plate. That is, if soup is the first course, the soup spoon is to the right of the teaspoon; the salad fork is to the left of the dinner fork if salad precedes the main course. What about the table knife and steak knife (cutting edges toward the plate, of course)? What about the seafood fork, butter knife, dessert forks and spoons? If coffee or tea is not served until dessert, are cups and saucers and teaspoons proper on the table at the beginning of the meal?

What does one do if the table is not set correctly? Suppose that the salad and dinner forks are interchanged. Does one eat salad with the dinner fork or use the salad fork anyway? Quite often the salad fork is the same one used for dessert, or at least looks the same. Is this correct? Of course, one would never be so crude as to call attention to the error, but one would wish not to err in the presentation of her own table.

GENTLE READER:

Certainly not. Unless you know the menu, it is safer to assume that the forks and knife, including the place or steak knife, are in the right order than to reach for an out-of-place salad fork, only to find out that it is the fish or dessert fork. Well-bred hosts never notice whether their guests err, and if they do, unobtrusively provide them with substitute correct implements. (Never mind the contradiction involved; social life is full of contradictions.)

Small forks may correctly be used as salad forks, luncheon forks, dessert forks, or fish forks. There is even a branch of snobbery that considers it vulgar to have too many specialized pieces.

Your outside-to-inside pattern of placing the flatware is correct. The exception is that the tiny seafood fork used for oysters goes on the right, nestling in the soup spoon. The butter knife goes on the bread-and-butter plate, the dessert fork and spoon go above the plate or arrive on the dessert plate; and teaspoons, cups, and saucers do not appear until coffee or tea is served.

The Unnecessary Spoon

DEAR MISS MANNERS:

My boyfriend and I have moved into an apartment together, and every time I set the table, I give each of us a fork, spoon, and knife. Well, my boyfriend has the idea that if we don't have a dessert, we don't need a spoon on the table. I tell him that it is the proper way of setting the table. This question has a bet going, so please tell us who is right.

GENTLE READER:

He is. Oh, dear. Miss Manners just hates to spread disharmony at the dinner table by taking sides, and is forced to do so only in the service of Truth in Etiquette. She hopes that the gentleman will be gracious in victory and take into consideration that you are disarmed, now that Miss Manners has taken your spoon away from you.

A Reply

DEAR MISS MANNERS:

I disagree with you about not needing a teaspoon at every table setting. A spoon may be needed for stirring coffee and cream and sugar, maybe for a vegetable or gravy, or for eating stew, and so on. I would feel rather nude at the table with only a fork and knife.

GENTLE READER:

Please put your clothes back on and let us discuss this rationally. At least, you be rational. Miss Manners has a hard time being so when people presume to disagree with edicts that are a clear matter of social tradition.

We agree, she supposes, that the soup spoon belongs on the table when soup is served and the dessert spoon for dessert. Our quarrel, then, is about the teaspoon and about the foods and drink for which you wish to use it. Miss Manners is sorry to have to inform you that vegetables and gravy are not properly eaten with any spoon at all, other than an infant feeding spoon. To mop up gravy, if that is what you have in mind, the sneaky way around the fact that the fork won't do the job alone is to drop a bit of bread on the plate and, when that is properly soaked, to eat it with the fork. Just barely allowable if inconspicuous, this maneuver is best performed with an absent-minded expression or a fixed gaze elsewhere, as if one is not responsible for the action.

Coffee is another matter. Miss Manners has been stern enough for one day, so she will not insist that coffee should be served after dinner, and not at the table. In return, she expects you to place the spoon on the coffee saucer. So you see, there really is no call for having a teaspoon lined up next to the knife.

Grandmother's Napkin

DEAR MISS MANNERS:

I am endowed with a size double-D cup bra, and this is part of a troubling problem. I am blessed with a granddaughter, now age thirteen. At twelve, she was compassionate and noncritical to a doting grandmother. Suddenly, her knowledge of proper etiquette is unbelievable. The following incident took place while she and I were having dinner at a local restaurant: During the soup course, I removed my napkin from my lap and placed it, bib style, on my chest. Lobster diners are permitted this; why not chesty grandmothers? My loving granddaughter requested that I write you about this. I have tried the upright method of eating, but my arms are too short. Isn't there some solution that would be acceptable to surrounding diners and a critical granddaughter?

GENTLE READER:

Miss Manners is rejoiced to hear of your granddaughter's interest in etiquette. Unfortunately, she seems to have neglected the most important knowledge when she learned the superficial part. Mind you, Miss Manners would be the last to minimize the importance of superficial behavior. Sloppy eating habits have probably ruined more relationships than evil hearts. You can, if you wish, eliminate the need for the protective napkin by taking smaller and neater spoonfuls of soup on that hazardous trip across your chest. The rule of etiquette that one does not criticize one's grandmother has precedence over all table rules. If your granddaughter is able to use her new knowledge to eat correctly herself, and remember her old compassion enough to accept her grandmother the way she is, she will have truly learned manners.

Snobbery

DEAR MISS MANNERS:

I have been confronted with a new kind of snob. A guest in my house demanded a paper napkin at lunch, refusing to use my immaculately laundered linen one. Since I never use paper ones, I was embarrassed. To my dismay, the other guests also quietly scorned my linen. Should I change my way of living? I feel that my guests and I rate the best. Or should I simply never invite these clods again for a meal?

GENTLE READER:

Miss Manners is delighted that you recognize this for what it is—sheer nasty snobbery. Her advice is exactly what it would be if a guest in a house where paper napkins were used indicated scorn and demanded a linen one. The host should reply, "I'm so sorry that I can't provide you with what you're used to. I wonder if you would be kind enough to try to make do with what I have."

Whether you wish to entertain again people who sneer at your household arrangements, Miss Manners will not presume to say. She cannot imagine that you are seriously entertaining the idea of redoing these arrangements to suit such people.

Napkins, Coasters, and Class

DEAR MISS MANNERS:

Are coasters under glasses *de rigueur?* Or, like napkin rings, are they just another middle-class convention? A brief history would be appreciated.

GENTLE READER:

A history of coasters? Both the East Coaster and the West Coaster? Miss Manners would be in the library for weeks. Perhaps you would settle for a brief history of the term "middle class" as used insultingly in a country where everyone claims to be middle class, lower, middle class, upper middle class, lower-lower middle, upper-upper middle, and so on. (Miss Manners has never heard an American yet claim to be plain upper or lower class.)

The middle class is usually spurned (by its own members) for being orderly and cautious. Miss Manners finds that curious. Yes, the mad, wild, devil-may-care thing to do is to toss all napkins in the wash after every meal (thus eliminating the need for napkin rings, which identify each family member's napkin for future reference) and to plop wet glasses smack down on furniture without regard to possible damage. Miss Manners has decidedly not noticed this being done in whatever class you call it that has antique furniture. Those who think it too middle class to have coasters may give out cocktail napkins with drinks. It is *de rigueur* in all classes to refrain from issuing napkin rings with those.

Soups

DEAR MISS MANNERS:

My questions have to do with serving soup as a first course for a party of eight or fewer.

1. Could a cold soup be at the place setting when the guests come to the table?
2. Must bouillon cups and saucers be on a service plate, and should the saucer be placed on a salad plate as well, making a total of four pieces of china at the place?
3. Where should the bouillon spoon be placed?
4. Can the dinner plate be on the table and left there when the soup course is removed?
5. Can hot soup be served from a tureen at the host's place, and then passed around the table by the other guests?
6. Can a large soup bowl be placed on the dinner plate at the place and removed before serving the main course, or must there be a service plate?

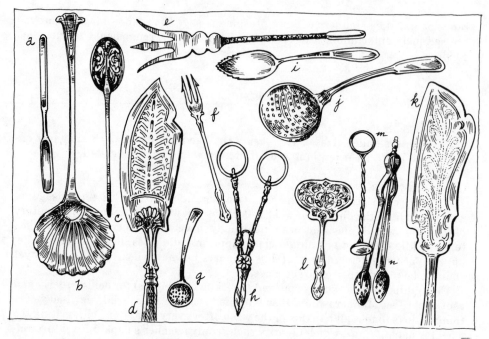

a. *marrow scoop* b. *soup ladle* c. *banana or nut spoon* d. *fish slice* e. *lettuce fork* f. *Pickle fork* g. *Gardinata spoon* h. *nut biscuit* i. *orange or Grapefruit spoon* j. *sugar sifter* k. *ice cream knife* l. *Bonbon spoon* m. *sugar spoon* n. *sugar nippers with spout stems*

GENTLE READER:

Service plates, which Miss Manners adores, are generally used when there is some sort of service, even if it is only the host's indentured children. Otherwise, the act of replacing service plates with dinner plates claims too much of the hosts' time and the dinner plates are used at the place setting, first as underliners for the bouillon cup and saucer or the rimmed soup plate. (What would the salad plate be doing in between—waiting for a radish to saunter in looking for a home?)

Miss Manners doesn't know who your friends are, but she would not risk passing a hot soup tureen around the table even in her own genteel circle. Only competent, grown-up help should even think about serving soup formally, with the waiter taking the tureen from guest to guest. In real life, soup is either brought to the table in individual servings, or served at the table by the host, or even, if it is intended to be cold, put out before guests appear. The soup spoon is placed to the right of the knives. One of the little-known thrills of formal dining is that one may scorn the bouillon spoon entirely, pick up the cup by its handles, and drink directly. It looks shocking, but it is proper.

Soup Spoon Placement

DEAR MISS MANNERS:

When one is served soup and the soup bowl is on a plate, where should one place the spoon after finishing the soup? I have noticed that when the soup bowl is a wide, shallow dish, people leave the spoon in the bowl. I always thought that it was supposed to be placed on the plate.

GENTLE READER:

It sometimes strikes Miss Manners that soup is like life itself—murky, delicious, contradictory. Such musing does not help her understand the mysteries of life, nor would it enhance her social desirability if she were not at least smart enough to keep this insight to herself. It does remind her that soup should not be approached simply, which is what you are discovering. You have, mastered the use of the soup bowl—but now, aha! You are confronted with a soup plate!

That's what that wide, shallow, broad-rimmed soup container is, and the plate underneath it is a service plate. After eating soup from a soup plate, one actually does leave the spoon in the bowl—plate—in the thing that had the soup in it. This nearly kills every well-brought up person who was correctly taught never, not even for a minute's pause, to allow a soup spoon to remain in a soup bowl. That rule is still in effect. It just doesn't apply to the soup plate. Such is soup.

Correct Techniques

DEAR MISS MANNERS:

As a religious brother, I live in community with twelve brothers in simple, yet tasteful, quarters. One of my dear brothers has provided for me a perplexing problem by virtue of his lack of manners. How one could grow to adulthood devoid of any sense of etiquette escapes me completely. Here are some examples of behavior: The consumption of a lovely dinner salad (with dressing) without the assistance of utensils. If my dear brother spies an enticing morsel on his neighbor's plate, he might at any moment take said morsel. The ability to blow bubbles of saliva simultaneously from each corner of his mouth. The use of his dinner plate as a dessert plate. An array of bodily noises that boggle the mind and sicken the stomach. And, at the close of the meal, one can be assured of hearing water noisily swishing around his mouth.

The brother in question is not a mental incompetent; indeed, he is extremely intelligent, but he views etiquette as superfluous, difficult as this is to believe. Outside of an untimely death, do you see any possible solution to this grave dilemma?

GENTLE READER:

Miss Manners is aware that there are those who might try to tell you to ignore etiquette violations in consideration of higher spiritual values. They would be wrong. Such etiquette assaults as you describe batter the soul until it is in no fit condition to contemplate anything more uplifting. As evidence, she need merely cite the example of you, who have dedicated your life to God, already contemplating with some relish the possibility of your brother's meeting an untimely death.

Miss Manners not only finds it hardly possible that anyone should consider etiquette superfluous, but she believes it totally impossible that this notion could be seriously entertained in a religious community if the meaning of etiquette is properly explained. The chances are that your brother has the common mistaken notion that manners are an affectation of the rich, and therefore inappropriate to his calling. He undoubtedly subscribes to the church's use of ritual and symbolic behavior. Miss Manners dares say that he follows, and even values, those gestures and patterns associated with worship.

Those, too, are manners. Any set way of doing things peculiar to a society or to a cohesive group within it constitutes etiquette. Miss Manners suggests that you explain to your superior that you find the affronts to commonly accepted ways of eating to be offensive and distracting to your peace of mind, and a poor precedent in the discipline and obedience of your community.

Originality

DEAR MISS MANNERS:

Since he was very small, our eleven-year-old son has been neat in his eating habits. He developed a way to scoop his food onto his fork or spoon by using another utensil as the backstop. He pushes the food into one area, uses a spoon on its end to keep the food from spilling onto the table, and his fork can easily be filled. I have seen some people use their fingers for this type of operation (ugh). Is the above process, using two hands and two utensils, proper? My husband does not think so. I feel that as long as he is neat (and this is a very effective way of eating), it causes no harm.

GENTLE READER:

As the distinguished anthropologist Claude Lévi-Strauss will tell you, table manners are not just more or less efficient ways to get food from plate to mouth. They are social customs rich in cultural associations, and the practice—or violation—of them produces effects on observers that are deeply emotional. Thus, while it is true that neatness counts, in judging eating methods, originality counts against you. Miss Manners will be happy to join you in admiring your son's cleverness, but she flunks him in table manners. He must eat in the accepted fashion in order not to be judged harshly by the society in which he lives. Fortunately, there are many other outlets for creative problem solving.

Respectful Silence

DEAR MISS MANNERS:

In our small lunchroom at work, the chairs are situated so that we are all facing one another. Recently, two co-workers have been inviting each other to pray aloud at the beginning of the meal. Though not offended by this practice, we wonder what is the polite behavior for the remainder of the group. Should we ignore them, continuing conversation, thereby granting them some privacy, or are we expected to withhold conversation in respect?

GENTLE READER:

Grace said before a meal does not require privacy, but it does require the respectful silence of others at the same table. Miss Manners trusts that your colleagues are not uttering private prayers, such as the hope for deliverance from intolerable working conditions, at the company lunch table.

Mopping Up Mistakes

DEAR MISS MANNERS:

My dear grandmother cooked lobster Newburg as the main course for the family. I was seated next to my aunt and across from my father. After a particularly witty remark, my aunt, who had some lobster in her mouth, laughed and accidentally spat a few particles in my direction. My aunt and my father saw it, but the others luckily failed to notice. My reaction was a slight laugh and smile, and then a quick wipe with my napkin to remove a particle from my cheek and tie. My aunt and I laughed again and did our best to forget what had happened.

As soon as we were on our way home, my father asked, "Did you have to make such a big deal about Aunt Martha spitting the food on your face?" He was hard put to give me a better way to react but argued that my actions served only to embarrass her needlessly. Miss Manners, I am not a sloppy eater. The thought of continuing with my dinner and engaging in lighthearted conversation with some of the main course hanging on my cheek makes my stomach turn.

Also, my aunt is in her thirties and aware of her action; if she were older and less alert or had poorer vision, perhaps I could have remedied the situation without her noticing. Was it improper to make light of the situation? Does it sound as if I made a scene—neither my mother nor brother knew what had happened—or was my father being unreasonable? What should my aunt have done?

GENTLE READER:

Nobody is suggesting that you sit there with lobster hanging on your face. Your father's and your methods of handling this situation are both correct. In his, you would say nothing and wipe your face inconspicuously. Had your aunt been unaware of her action, that would have been the better method. In this case, Miss Manners actually prefers your reaction. You didn't spread the knowledge to other diners, and you succeeded in making your aunt laugh about it. When humor works, that is a better catharsis for embarrassment than silent toleration.

Wine Tasting

DEAR MISS MANNERS:

My roommate recently learned that wine tasters, in order to appreciate the full flavor of a wine, aerate it: that is, they take a drink of a wine and hold it on the back of their tongues while sucking air over it. Unfortunately, he now takes every drink of wine this way, so that when we sit down to dinner, or when we're standing around entertaining friends, he drinks each glass of wine with loud slurping noises, which spoils my appreciation of the wine and greatly annoys me to boot. After several months, this has become a habit for him. When he began, he seemed so proud of his newly acquired knowledge and sophistication that I could not bring myself to tell him that it bothered me. I now fear that he may not be able to enjoy wine without this elaborate, if somewhat noxious, ritual. We live in a small apartment, and although we are friends, we're not close friends, and unless I can find a polite way to convey my feelings, it threatens to spoil our dinners together.

GENTLE READER:
It sounds as if your dinners are already spoiled, and as a matter of fact, the description of your roommate succeeded in spoiling Miss Manners' dinner. The society's preoccupation with wine has gotten terribly vulgar, and Miss Manners finds your friend's pretentiousness as unappetizing as his table manners. Far more to the point is his demonstration of utter selfishness in pursuing his own enjoyment while blithely sacrificing yours and that of your guests. Miss Manners hopes that you may simply call to his attention your assumption that he wishes others besides himself to enjoy their wine and that his methods, which were never designed for the table, preclude this. If he is really indifferent to your comfort, you may wish to make other living arrangements.

Scavengers

DEAR MISS MANNERS:
Twice during the past weekend, when I was in the company of close friends and family, the person seated to my left at the dinner table has used his or her own fork to sample food from my plate. This seems to be a common occurrence in restaurants these days; everyone wants to taste everyone else's dinner. On the first occasion, a friend who had already eaten from his own fork used it to reach for a piece of squid from my plate. He decided that the first piece he chose was too big, and so searched for a smaller one. In the second case, my own sister took the wafer from my ice cream, dipped it into the ice cream, took a bite, and replaced the wafer in my dish.

I find this behavior most objectionable but don't know how to handle it without causing hurt feelings. I generally say nothing but am unhappy with the situation. I am sure that I am not alone in this. Eating from a common bowl has long been the norm in many cultures. However, I would be forever grateful if you could suggest a delicate way of putting an end to it in my own social circle.

GENTLE READER:
Unfortunately, Miss Manners does not allow you to lean forward, elbows on the table and forearms encircling the plate, to protect your dinner from scavengers.

You are going to have to be on the alert. At the first gleam in a neighboring eye, say, "Let me give you a taste of this," and put some on your bread and butter plate. As for surprise attacks, you may be able to discourage them in the future by surrendering what you have at the time. Pass the entire plate to the attacker and say politely, "Oh, that's all right; you finish it." You may have to get your own dinner later, but it will establish the idea that you don't like involuntary sharing.

Passing the Salt

DEAR MISS MANNERS:
We have a disagreement over the correct way to pass a salt and pepper set to the person next to you when asked. One of us says, "Pick it up and pass it into the person's hands." Another says, "Pick it up and put it down next to that person on the table."

GENTLE READER:
The idea is to employ as many middle steps as possible. Because one cannot whip out a small tray, load on the salt and pepper, and pass that to the person, the next best thing is to set it down within that person's reach. Also, manners require passing both the salt and pepper together, even when only one is requested. They get lonely if separated.

❁ DIFFICULT FOODS

Finger Foods

DEAR MISS MANNERS:
I am a volunteer in the local school, where I lecture to a gifted class, bringing all kinds of information that they would not ordinarily get in school. One of the students asked for a list of the foods that may be eaten with the hand. All I know are corn, olives, bacon, and pickles. Are there others?

GENTLE READER:
Not so fast. You must teach those children judgment or you will have them eating creamed corn with their fingers and picking the bacon bits out of omelets. If you promise to do that, Miss Manners will help fill out your list: artichoke leaves, asparagus, bananas, bread, canapes, candy, cherries, cookies, deviled eggs, grapes, hot dogs, ice cream cones, potato chips, sandwiches. Under some circumstances, such as picnics and family gatherings, fried chicken, lobster from the shell, and pizza are eaten with the fingers. However, spaghetti, soft-boiled eggs, and soup never are.

Crudités

DEAR MISS MANNERS:

While dining with an eligible bachelor, I was reprimanded for my bad manners. Please explain the correct way to eat fresh vegetables (carrots, cauliflowers, cucumbers, etc.) from a salad bar display. I placed several vegetables and a spoonful of dip on my plate—and then committed the act. Using my left index finger and thumb, I picked up the cucumber and proceeded to eat, when my guest exclaimed, "Not with your hands!" I lost my appetite for lunch and for the bachelor. I think a true sophisticate would never make his company feel inferior, and if they did something improper would talk with them on the side or not take them out.

GENTLE READER:

"Crudités and Crudity," Miss Manners would call your tale if she were Jane Austen. It is true that salad must be eaten with the fork, even if it contains raw vegetables too big for one bite and too crisp to cut. Etiquette does occasionally have a way of blithely ignoring the practicalities. But was this really salad? The presence of a dip, rather than salad dressing, suggests that these vegetables were being presented as crudités. Crudités are *hors d'oeuvres* intended to be eaten with the fingers. They should be served on trays, to be taken and dipped one by one.

Sauces

DEAR MISS MANNERS:

My husband and I disagree about whether it is proper to eat spareribs and chicken with your fingers. I said that if the sauce gets all over your hands, you should just cut the meat off. It actually ruins my meal to watch him, and I'm not that particular about table manners.

GENTLE READER:

Miss Manners thought that she was particular, but even she considers it extreme to cut the meat off the man's hands just because he got sauce on them. The fact is that there is no way to eat sauce-drenched spareribs both effectively and genteelly, which is why one doesn't serve them at formal dinner parties. But the silly things are delicious, so one has them at barbecues or family-style dinners, with huge absorbent napkins and gobs of tolerance. The proper accompaniments for them are fingers, hot towels, old clothes, and old friends. You see, it's more complicated than merely matching the food with the procedure. How is the food cooked? Where is it being eaten? At what sort of event? In its softer forms, chicken can be a sophisticated dish at a formal dinner, in which case you would never dream of picking up a bone. It would be equally inappropriate to refrain from doing so with deep-fried chicken at a fast-food restaurant or picnic. Steak and prime ribs at a slow-food restaurant are not picked up. If you can't get the meat off with your knife and fork, ask for a sharper knife.

Half-Peeled Shrimp

Let us put a stop right now to that dreadful practice of serving half-peeled shrimp. Miss Manners has encountered these pink tricks a few times too many lately in restaurants, airplanes, and even privately served meals. There the sly creatures all are, snoozing cozily on beds of shredded lettuce, or perhaps getting their exercise by hanging from their tails on the edges of miniature bird baths filled with cocktail sauce. They are really just lying in wait, half naked and half encased in armor, ready to ambush the unwary diner.

Miss Manners can think of no motivation on the cook's part except pure meanness. There are a lot of strange people in the world, and perhaps some of them get their jollies by encouraging the hungry to anticipate happily devouring these oceanic treats and then frustrating or humiliating them. Fresh shrimp being a luxury item, they do not generally allow themselves to be caught in places where it is considered fair to attack them with the fingers. Therefore, many diners, who have very likely paid dearly for those shrimp, merely whack off the unpeeled part with the side of the fork and watch helplessly as the protected part is carted off as garbage. Others—and Miss Manners cannot find it in her heart to condemn them—decide to eat defensively. Even that is not satisfactory. You can pick up the unshelled part and squeeze the tail, but the chances of its then shooting the remaining meat into your mouth are not good.

Miss Manners' unaccustomed tolerance is born not only of a fondness for shellfish, but from the belief that fairness should prevail at the dining table. She expects people to use proper table manners, but she wants to give them a fighting chance. This means that food must be made reasonably accessible and that the proper tools for attacking it should be issued.

Shrimp must be entirely peeled, and lobster that has been scooped out should really be scooped out. No shellfish should be allowed to leave the kitchen under the cover of bouillabaisse unless all shells are open. Bite-sized seafood may be served with a mere oyster fork, but everything else from the sea requires a fish knife, as well as a fish fork, so that it may be cut without necessitating undue dry cleaning. Miss Manners does not know why fish knives are so rare in this country. No decent person would eat fish with a meat knife—it makes scales grow on the back of your hand—and the only proper alternative to a fish knife is the older method of eating fish with two forks.

While we are at it, where is the salad knife? Evil people are forever putting lettuce wedges and other booby traps into salads, and then demanding that they be eaten with the unaided fork. Is it all that funny to watch people squirt salad dressing into their eyes?

Another common dirty trick is to issue teaspoons to do jobs too big or too small for them. You can easily start the day by forcing a teaspoon, instead of a small egg spoon, into a boiled egg and watching it go off like a bomb, fallout dribbling down the side of the egg cup; and then end the day with a futile chase around the dessert plate, trying to catch some goody that can be cornered only with a larger dessert spoon and dessert fork.

Miss Manners is aware that many people think it snobbish to own or be able to use a place setting consisting of anything more than one fork and a toothpick. She will try, then, to appeal to their sense of fair play. It is right to pit a defenseless human being against an armed shrimp?

Oysters

DEAR MISS MANNERS:
Please tell us how to eat oysters correctly—fresh or stewed.

GENTLE READER:
It is difficult to eat anything correctly when you are stewed. Raw oysters are eaten whole with a teensy-weensy oyster fork, with which you rip them from their shells, which are gripped firmly in the left hand unless you are left-handed. Oysters encountered in soups are eaten whole on the soup spoon. Those found on plates, as opposed to shells or bowls, are eaten with a fork.

Bread

DEAR MISS MANNERS:
Please, what is the proper method of eating muffins, biscuits, and dinner rolls? I was taught that it was an insult to the baker to split such fresh breads with a knife; rather, one should break or tear them with one's bare hands. My husband has always mutilated his muffins, biscuits, and rolls with his knife. He says that it would be kinder always to cut such breads in order to spare possible embarrassment to those bakers whose goods may require more than bare-hands treatment. (And truthfully, having broken bread with his family, I must admit that he has a point!) Also, is there a separate rule covering day-old baked goods, or are there no such things in polite company? Last, could you please tell me if it is more correct to split one's muffin vertically than horizontally?

GENTLE READER:
What an exciting life you must lead, with moody bakers lurking near your breakfast table, ready to fly into high insult or embarrassment at your every move. Miss Manners imagines that this must do a lot to compensate you for having married into a family that serves tough bread.

At the table, bread is not cut, but is broken with, as you say, the bare hands. (Never gloved hands.) Polite society is certainly not above economies, such as day-old baked goods, but does not distress its company by announcing this to them. If the bread is too hard to be torn apart, one might consider what it will do to the teeth. Miss Manners knows of no humane reasons for all of this, etiquette not generally being based on consideration for the emotional welfare of those who prepare the food. She does know, however, that English muffins are split horizontally and other muffins vertically.

Cracker Crumbling

DEAR MISS MANNERS:

My family is embroiled in a ticklish controversy concerning cracker crumbs. Our question is: Does Miss Manners crumble crackers in her soup if she's dining with others? (We don't care what you do when you are eating alone, although Mother thinks one should always be consistent.)

GENTLE READER:

Mother ought also to have told you that what is more important than consistency is not getting caught. No, of course Miss Manners does not crumble crackers in her soup. That she doesn't happen to like flotsam in her soup is besides the point. If she did, she still wouldn't do it, but she might absently break off a corner of a cracker and accidentally drop it into the bowl.

Frogs' Legs

DEAR MISS MANNERS:

How should frogs' legs be eaten? Should one use fingers or a knife and fork? Should they be eaten at all in a public restaurant?

GENTLE READER:

Frogs love to defy systems of classification. That's their idea of being funny. Just when you place them neatly in one category, they leap unexpectedly into another. In the discipline of etiquette, as opposed to biology, frogs' legs are classified with small game birds. Those are first picked away at with knife and fork, then held in the fingers to get the clinging meat (except under the most formal circumstances, when one can only place the tiniest bones in the mouth, clean them internally with closed lips, and then remove the inedible—so most people just give up). However, the silly things look like skinny chicken drumsticks, which cannot be picked up in the moderately formal circumstances of a slow-food restaurant. Therefore you could properly pick up a frog's leg and still create the impression that you just didn't know how to eat chicken. Miss Manners hopes that this doesn't discourage you from ordering frogs' legs. Think of all the garlic butter you would miss.

Garnishes

DEAR MISS MANNERS:

My son insists that it is never correct to eat the garnish, such as fruit slices (specifically, orange slices), that sometimes decorate dinner plates or drinks in restaurants. I believe that if you wish to eat the garnish, you may do so, and, on occasion, I do. This causes great consternation on the part of my son, who claims to be "grossed out" by my actions. We have agreed to abide by your decision in this matter.

GENTLE READER:

You win. As your son was obviously not brought up with this odd notion, you must wonder where he picked it up. Well, it wasn't from Miss Manners. Short of munching on the centerpiece carnations or the ice sculpture, one may safely consume anything edible put in front of one, provided that one does it gracefully. If an orange slice is served on a duck, for example, one can cut the fruit free and eat it easily. The problem with an orange slice in a drink is that it comes with a narrow border of rind. If you can figure out how to eat the orange but not the rind without using your hands, you are welcome to it.

Ketchup and Mustard

DEAR MISS MANNERS:

My wife and I like to barbecue and usually have four or five gala outings during the summer. On a couple of occasions, we will just serve basic hot dogs or hamburgers, and not any of our exotic treats. I want to put out large bottles of ketchup and mustard, but my wife insists that this is highly improper and that we should have those little packets of condiments.

GENTLE READER:

Miss Manners admires your wife's delicacy and is sorry to have to say that it is misplaced. The distinction is between serving foodstuffs in commercial containers and decanting them, as it were, not between one type of wrapping and another. The proper way to serve ketchup and mustard is in small capped bowls, and were you having even a very informal meal indoors, Miss Manners would insist upon this. However, a backyard barbecue can be counted either as a dinner party in the garden, for which this rule would also apply, or as a picnic, in which case it wouldn't.

Croissants

DEAR MISS MANNERS:

We are at quite a loss as to the proper way of eating those delightful (but crumbly) French treats, croissants. When seated at table with dessert plate and accompanying silver, does one break away with one's hands a bite-sized piece, spread whatever is offered, and eat, repeating until the croissant is finished? Or may one tear the delicacy in half lengthwise (an authentic croissant is impossible to cut), spread both sides, and eat? Although one may have his or her heirloom linen napkin properly placed on the lap, what is to be done with the many flaky crumbs that invariably end up everywhere but on said linen?

GENTLE READER:

While only too aware that croissants are often made with sweet fillings, Miss Manners is confused by the mention of a dessert plate. Officially, there is no difference between croissants and other rolls, however much we know the truth in this instance of *vive la différence*. One must therefore break off a two-bite part, slather on the goodies, and then repeat the process. Officially, one has to leave the flakes, because they are impossible to pick up unless (come closer, Miss Manners is about to tell you a secret) you lick your finger while nonchalantly passing your hand near your face, and then transfer the flakes to your mouth in the same undetectable fashion. (If you get caught, you must deny that Miss Manners told you this.)

Cake and Ice Cream

DEAR MISS MANNERS:
What is the proper way to serve ice cream and cake?
If they are served in the same dish, does one eat the cake with a spoon?
Should the ice cream be served first and the cake distributed after all the ice cream has been served? Or should a slice of cake be added by the host before being served to the guest?

GENTLE READER:
This is one of the few matters of table etiquette (milk is another) in which the key factor is the age of the guests. People of all ages know that ice cream and cake are best eaten by mashing the ice cream down into the cake with the back end of a spoon, preferably while chanting rhythmically but tunelessly to oneself. Only people under the age of five can get away with it when Miss Manners isn't looking.

In order to allow adults to simulate this enjoyment, which is to say, to eat ice-cream-and-cake rather than two separate desserts, the items are put on a plate together, with the ice cream on top of the slice of cake or, more dangerously for the tablecloth, off to one side. The adults are issued both dessert spoons and forks. They may alternate using these, eating the ice cream with the spoon and the cake with the fork, or may keep the fork in the left hand and use it to push ice cream soaked cake into the spoon, which is held in the right hand. They are not allowed to hum.

Cake and Black Ooze

DEAR MISS MANNERS:
At a social gathering where cake is being served, and one discovers that there is black ooze on top of one's portion, what is one to do so as not to look rude?

GENTLE READER:
Black ooze? BLACK OOZE? Do not, repeat not, alert others by shouting "Eeew, gross!" Oil spills and other potentially harmful substances should be reported—first, quietly, to your host or a waiter, and then, only if necessary, to environmental authorities. However, if you just don't happen to like fudge sauce on your cake, don't call it nasty names; just don't eat it.

Household Help

🌹 THE REAL SERVANT PROBLEM

It has always been crass in America to speak of how impossible it is to find servants who are not shifty, lazy, impertinent, and immoral (before returning to gossip about one's own level of society, where people are only restless, indolent, outrageous, and wicked).

Miss Manners is aware that the low quality of the serving class was once a staple of conversation among certain American ladies. These were ladies, she noticed, who had considerable trouble grasping the ideals of equality. They thought, for example, that it would be nice to marry their daughters to foreign titles, without regard to the personal quality of the attached gentlemen.

In this more enlightened era, Miss Manners almost never hears snobbish talk about the servant problem. Perhaps the din is too great from those who are incessantly talking about the child care problem, the cleaning problem, the problem getting anything repaired, the laundry problem, the telephone-answering and message-taking problems, the car pool problem, the mealtime problem (cooking, shopping, and serving), and the problem with having things delivered when there's no one home. Such complaints are not improper. Not enthralling, either, perhaps, but at least they do not outrage the American conviction, which Miss Manners shares, that it is inappropriate, in a land of freedom, to expect anyone to be subservient to anyone else.

It does not follow that Miss Manners opposes applying the system of the division of labor to households or that she wants to go on hearing such grousing forever. She is not deluded into thinking that manners alone can now make domestic service an attractive way of earning a living. Prospective employees have a way of noticing what the wages and working conditions will be, no matter how much charm is applied. She does believe that a deep and unresolved question of courtesy is responsible for creating and prolonging the problem of household management by allowing domestic service to be equated with subservience.

For a little background here, she would like to call upon the Beecher sisters, Catharine E. and Harriet Stowe, as they described, in 1869, how domestic arrangements had deteriorated from those of "simpler, old-fashioned days." The trouble they identified was that America had never developed its own democratic pattern of household employer-employee relations to replace the inappropriate European one that presumed the existence of a permanent serving class or the unspeakable American one of slavery.

"Is it not mainly from the want of a definite idea of the true position of a servant under our democratic institutions that domestic service is so shunned and avoided in America, and that it is the very last thing which an intelligent young woman will look to for a living?" they asked in *American Woman's Home*. "It is more the want of personal respect toward those in that position than the labor incident to it which repels our people from it. Many would be willing to perform these labors, but they are not willing to place themselves in a situation where their self-respect is hourly wounded by the implication of a degree of inferiority, which does not follow any kind of labor or service in this country but that of the family."

The Beecher sisters went on to deplore both those who treated their servants haughtily and those who "made pets of them." They did not think it necessary for employers to presume to direct the servants' private lives, or for them to surrender their own privacy by including them in the family circle—at the dinner table, for example. They suggested a mutual demeanor of dignified and compassionate respect, as is appropriate to any other form of employment where labor is valued.

We have never managed to develop the manners to carry this out. The two styles of behavior between domestic employer and employee are still condescension and intrusiveness. This is particularly odd since it has been the American pattern increasingly to confer prestige on those who attend to our bodily needs and wants, from doctors to hairdressers. Domestic service, more needed now than ever, remains undesirable employment. That it is the stigma, rather than the labor, that is repellent is demonstrated by the willingness of enterprising people to perform the work under different conditions. House-cleaning services that work under contract, British-style nannies who intimidate their charges' families, food companies from caterers to fast-food deliverers to grocery stores that have cooked-food counters—all have found ways to protect themselves from the bad manners of those who use their services. Miss Manners suggests that anyone who would like to look beyond these to more personalized and steady household assistance should observe the treatment, as well as the fees, that are rightly expected.

Privacy with Servants

DEAR MISS MANNERS:

When our son was born, my mother-in-law gave us as a present the services, for a year, of the daughter of her long-time housekeeper, now dead. I admit that I was resentful at the idea, which seemed to indicate that my mother-in-law didn't think I could handle the baby and was putting in someone she could trust. Also, I am not used to having help, which is what my family used to call it. Is that an incorrect term? My husband's family always calls them servants. Anyway, Nora turned out to be a cheerful and helpful person, with a lot of experience of babies from having had lots of younger brothers and sisters. We get along quite well, and she is crazy about the baby. The year is almost up, but my husband says that we can keep her on if I want.

Now, let me tell you my problem. Nora was very strictly brought up, as I know from my husband's stories about her mother. She has a boyfriend who is in the army, but when he comes here on leave, she is always ordering him around, and once I came into the kitchen and saw her slap him. They both blushed and nobody said anything, but I'm sure he tried to get what she considered fresh, and she let him have it. You probably think I'm afraid that she'll be too strict with the baby. No—her mother didn't hurt my husband any, and I know that she's too kind-hearted to do anything mean.

My fear is that she disapproves of me! Not that I've ever done anything wrong, but naturally, our lifestyle is a bit more sophisticated than hers. For instance, we have tickets for a concert series, and when my husband is out of town, I go with a male friend and usually give him dinner here before. Sometimes my uncle, who is younger than I, spends the night, and once he brought friends when my husband was away. He is my uncle, after all, but Nora was looking at me oddly, even though she didn't say anything. My husband brushes it off—he doesn't think these things are wrong—and I'm afraid that I am betraying my origins to care what Nora thinks. But after all, she is almost like a friend to me. And even if she weren't, don't you think she might gossip about me if she left us? Should I talk it all out with her and explain how I feel and behave?

GENTLE READER:

Certainly, she will gossip about you. Do you know anyone, in any occupation whatsoever, who doesn't gossip about his or her boss? Besides, it seems to Miss Manners that you have been gossiping to her about Nora's personal life. That is no reason, however, for you to supply her with the details of yours. By ignoring your accidental intrusion and perhaps obvious curiosity, Nora has set you an excellent example.

Your incidental question about what to call domestic employees is a key to your problem. The term "help" is an early American one, based on a democratic aversion to the idea of one person serving another. Thus the euphemistic concept that everyone does his or her own work but that obliging people sometimes appear, out of the goodness of their hearts, to help. Miss Manners finds the objection to "servants" odd in a society where the most distinguished officials are proud to call themselves public servants. Besides, when the term "help" was invented, Americans also prided themselves on their disdain for the demeaning institution of tipping. Whatever happened to that?

Miss Manners' point here is to remind you that however much you and Nora like and appreciate each other, you are employer and employee, and the relationship should be given its full dignity. When you call her almost a friend, are you sure that you want a live-in friend, who would naturally offer her advice and opinions on the way you live? If you do, it would still seem that Nora doesn't.

Servants are entitled to privacy, and so are their employers (which is not to say that they can't speculate privately on one another's lives). Traditionally, the violations were more on the employer's side, with the ladies of the household always making rules intended to keep the servants to certain moral standards and the gentlemen of the household attempting to subvert this goal. Nowadays, the courteous person will allow her employer or her employee to enjoy the freedom of maintaining separate personal standards and habits, free from comment.

The Nanny

DEAR MISS MANNERS:

Could you please address yourself to the question of nanny etiquette?

I am a homemaker and mother, and am fortunate enough to be able to stay home with my children. Some of my friends have nannies, even though they also stay home.

More than once, I have run into a situation where, when I have invited the mother for coffee and the child to play, the mother has declined the invitation for herself but has wanted to send the child with the nanny. I have also invited the child over to play, and had the parent suggest that it would be such a burden that she would be sending their nanny along, too.

How do I gracefully decline this new, turned-about situation? I would feel more comfortable having their nannies if I had one of my own, I suppose, though it strikes me that changing an invitation to suit their own inclinations is not quite right in any case.

GENTLE READER:

That is true, but the dual invitation is a tricky one. You need to separate the elements. "Come over for coffee, Deirdre, and let's have a chat" is not going to leave you open to receiving a substitute, even if you add "and the children can play."

"Would Tiffany like to come play with Noah?" means that it doesn't matter who walks the child over. You should consider the advantages of accepting the offer of the nanny's supervision, which would give you some free time on your own.

However, the tone of your incidental remark about not having a nanny leads Miss Manners to draw your attention to the underlying elements of your question. The mommy-nanny problem is a delicate one because it seems to involve the issue of class—whether two people looking after children are socially equivalent, even though one is the lady of the house and the other a paid worker—and has thus confused and upset democracy-loving Americans. The difference is neither class nor respect, but being on or off duty.

However kindly meant, pretending that they are equivalent during working hours does neither any service. If your neighbor's husband were out tinkering with the the car, you might stand around and chat with him or even bring him a drink; you would not do so with a professional mechanic, although you might pass a pleasant word with him.

Those who would call these distinctions snobbery fail to perceive that they cut both ways. The element of choice is paramount in social relations, and a worker may not feel free to express personal preferences in rejecting overtures of friendship. The nanny may resent their interfering with her work. In other words, a visiting nanny would be offered courtesies but is there to look after her charge. You would not sit her down and begin gossiping with her, however entertaining you might find the conversation.

The "Au Pair"

DEAR MISS MANNERS:

We are expecting our first child. My wife hopes to return to work two months after the birth, and a young woman from Sweden will live with us for a year as a paid *au pair,* taking care of the baby during the day and doing some light housework. Despite the stringent requirements of the law, we have obtained the necessary authorizations. We do not know what kind of relationship to establish with this young woman. I grew up with a maid, but I do not think that the *au pair* relationship is supposed to be exactly like the one that prevailed between employers and maids in the South in the 1950s. We would appreciate your guidance.

GENTLE READER:

Like the poor governess who has been the heroine of so many romantic novels, the *au pair* girl is neither houseguest nor servant. If you treat her as a member of the family circle, you will lose your privacy; if you treat her as a servant, you will lose her. This ambiguity is awkward, and the traditional governess solved the problem—after a lot of hurt feelings and crying in her room—by marrying the young master of the house, or the widowed old one, and thus obtaining the clear-cut position of lady of the house.

As this solution is neither likely nor desirable in your case, you will have to be extra careful to preserve both privacy and dignity. You might take advantage of the fact that the *au pair* girl, unlike the traditional governess, is generally more interested in having an independent social life with her contemporaries than in participating in family events. If everyone presumes that she wants to give her intense attention to the baby while on duty (taking quick meals separately from the family, for example) because she has her social life off duty, you can eat privately without inequality. Because she is a young foreigner, you may need to do some friendly supervising—introducing her to people of her age, offering practical information, consoling her when she's homesick—but any exaggeration of this function will compromise her privacy, while leaving you with two children to look after instead of one.

The Butler

DEAR MISS MANNERS:

Is it still correct to address a man who acts as a butler for social occasions by his surname? I sometimes engage a man to help me with the serving when I have twelve to fourteen people at the table for dinner. I have always addressed him as "Mr. Jones," but one of my friends tells me that this is improper and that people who do this work prefer to be called "Jones." Although the relationship is strictly business, I do not wish at this stage to risk alienating him by having him think that I have suddenly become uppity. Were I to change my tactics, I'd hate to have him respond by calling me "Doe" or, worse yet, "John."

GENTLE READER:

No doubt there are people calling themselves butlers who have so little self-respect that they pretend to be the pals of their employers —pals who collect money for the favor of passing the drinks—and who might therefore address you chummily. A proper butler is too proud to do this and uses the traditional address of his calling, which is the surname only. He does not condescend to notice whether the employer is doing everything correctly—his only concern is that *he* is—and wastes no time speculating on such matters as whether the employer is getting uppity, a subject that provides giggles only to parlor maids and footmen.

Try calling him "Jones" and be ready, if he retaliates with "Doe," to say, "I prefer the formal address." You may also simply say to him, "I'm told that a proper butler prefers being called by his surname only," by way of announcement. It is more flattering to indicate that you believe him to be at the top of his profession than to pretend that he is only on a level with you and your friends.

The Guard

DEAR MISS MANNERS:

When your community of town houses has a security guard at the gate, is it correct to wait for the guard to call you when your guest arrives, or must you call in advance to tell him you are expecting this person? Most of the time, he checks anyway.

GENTLE READER:

A security guard is not a butler, who presumes that your guests are welcome and that his or her function is to announce them respectfully. The guard's job is to keep out the intruders. No matter how polite he may be, the tone of his inquiries to unexpected visitors is bound to reflect that responsibility.

Miss Manners doesn't know if you have ever shown up in a mood for fun, only to be asked what your business was, but it has a dampening effect. Forewarned with your list of guests, the guard may still feel obliged to check with you, but at least he will be acting with the presumption that your friends have been authorized.

Repair People

It is not often that Miss Manners puts down her teacup with a rattle and announces that society must be radically restructured. The present demand has to do with appointments for household repairs.

If you consider that of trivial import, you have not waited lately to have a dishwasher or heating unit fixed. The customer makes a request (after having listened for some time to the repair firm's choice of musical selections), and a day is agreed upon. The customer promises to be home then. Inquiring what time to expect the person who is to save him from floods, freezing, or whatever, the customer is told that it is impossible to determine the time. Perhaps he is told that it will be the morning or afternoon; perhaps not. On the appointed day, one of several things may happen:

The repairman does not arrive.

The customer decides to sneak out for a short errand, and returns to find that the repairman arrived and departed in his absence.

The repairman shows up as promised but cannot complete the job for some reason, and says that another appointment will be necessary.

In all of these cases, the customer, irritable anyway from hanging around waiting, starts shouting insults at the repairman or his or her employer, beginning with slurs on the individual's capabilities but working up to deploring the state of the country, once filled with honest craftsmen who had pride in their work but now populated with crooked morons. The repairman, whose experience is that every customer is nasty and crazy, might well also indulge in discouraging statements about the population. Out of a combination of ennui and pride, he generally does not shout back, but instead finds a way to sever the business connection. He goes on to another customer while this one tries to find another repairman, and the entire charade begins again.

There is no dearth of etiquette violations there. Miss Manners could occupy herself forever just listening to the claims of outrage on either side, but she believes that the troubles arise from the following erroneous and outdated assumptions on which these arrangements are still based:

1. That every house has a housewife who spends all day in it, and that her time is completely flexible.

2. That the services of an expert are more valuable than any occupation the person who needs them may have, and the urgency of his demand for them necessitates sacrificing other demands on his time. (Doctors are among the repairmen most guilty of making this assumption.)

If we do away with these mistaken premises, it becomes obvious that we need to establish a different system for making house-call appointments that will be as convenient to the customer as to the roving expert. Working out the details of this is trivial, and not a matter of etiquette, so Miss Manners will leave it to others.

NEIGHBORLINESS

What is the modern definition of neighborliness, that engaging trait on which we Americans have traditionally prided ourselves? Giving the people next door a warning to turn down the volume before you report them to the police, or to curb their dog before you poison it? Refraining from dumping your leaves and snow on their property, your extra trash in their cans, and your guests' cars in their parking places, and/or arguing that you had a right to do so? Welcoming newcomers with at least a nominal greeting before hitting them with a sales pitch?

American neighborliness was once such a renowned national characteristic that it was used effectively to counter foreign charges of etiquette failure. So what if we don't know every tiny rule, some Americans used to argue. At least we try to be friendly and helpful, which is more than a lot of you folks do who are so proud of your fine manners.

Miss Manners has never approved of etiquette bashing and did not understand why it was assumed that one had to choose between kind and correct behavior. Contrary to popular opinion, etiquette rules are designed to ease social activity, not test for social caste. When a choice must be made, kindly motivation counts a lot. Not everything but a lot.

Modern neighborliness should still be a careful balance of respect for others' peace, privacy, and property. This requires a lot of on-the-spot judgment. It is an invasion of privacy to drop in on neighbors unannounced, for example, but not conducive to their peace if you respect their privacy by not pointing out that someone else is dropping in unannounced through their bedroom window.

Neighbors are supposed to register their complaints with one another in a polite fashion. The standard form uses the fiction that they do not realize they are offending—"I suppose you're probably not aware how much the noise carries when you have band practice at your house, and we go to bed early. We would be very grateful if you could tone it down a bit." And yes, you can call the police if this doesn't work. Just keep that sad, forced-to-do-it expression. Open warfare is never a good idea unless you want to live in a war zone.

Petitions at Parties

DEAR MISS MANNERS:

At a social function, my hostess approached me with a petition concerning a neighborhood political issue unknown to me. When I explained to her that I was reluctant to sign petitions unless I was familiar with the issue and had a bona fide opinion of my own, she replied, "It's a good cause; trust me."

I told her that I would look it over and managed to abandon the document on a table a few moments later. I assume that you think as little of her behavior as I do, but my question is: How can one politely but firmly decline this kind of invitation in the face of such persistence?

GENTLE READER:

Never trust a hostess who tries to do business under social conditions. This one was probably trying to slip by you a petition requiring all neighbors to paint their porches annually and to chain up their toddlers. You seem to have managed very well. You got out of the house without signing the petition or mortally offending your hostess. Miss Manners offers her congratulations, and can only assume that you came to her for help because you believe your escape was a narrow one, and are having retroactive anxiety attacks about what might have happened had the hostess discovered your ploy and renewed her attack.

In that case, you need only have renewed your defense. If again urged to sign without reading, you should repeat —with a deprecating laugh, as if it were a failing—your habit of signing only what you understand and support. If asked to read a petition on the spot, crank yourself up to an actual laugh and reply that you are having such a good time that you can't concentrate on anything serious, but would be glad to take home any written explanations of the cause. In the light of day, free from immediate social obligations, it is easier to say, "I have weighed this, but I'm afraid I am unable to sign it," without further explanation.

Reciprocating Neighborliness

DEAR MISS MANNERS:

I am, almost alone in my neighborhood, a mother at home. Every once in a while, one of my children's friends' parents needs a favor—babysitting, rides for their children, or some such small help that I can readily deliver. I do not consider this a big deal, and no one has ever tried to take advantage of me in a steady or obnoxious way. On the contrary—and here is my problem. At times, some of the parents have offered me money for services rendered, and I just do not feel comfortable accepting it. It is true that my decision not to work has caused some financial hardship at home, but my husband does support us all. We are not poor. I understand that these good people are concerned about not being able to reciprocate, but I still don't want their money. I have felt more comfortable when people have given me something from their kitchens or a small gift to my child, whose friend I helped. Even so, nothing is necessary.

I have said, "No, thank you, it was a pleasure to have Angelina in the house" until I was blue in the face, but I have had money slipped into my pocket when my defenseless arms were full of hungry children, have had money left in the hands of children who were taught not to contradict grown-ups, and have felt bad when saying shortly, "Please! I would feel insulted." Should I just gracefully accept the money and take everyone off the hook? Or do you have a suggestion for a remark that would solve the problem?

GENTLE READER:

A lady of Miss Manners' acquaintance who has done endless service in accepting other people's packages and caring for their children explained that she wouldn't mind being asked for such favors "if they didn't always preface it with the remark 'You have nothing to do, so...'" Those who are home and try to be helpful could have their neighborly generosity more amply reciprocated.

The most tactful remark of all is, "I'm sure you would help me out if I needed it," occasionally followed by a practical suggestion. Nice people can't stand always being on the receiving end, which is why these parents are desperately trying to get you to accept money. However, unless you want to set yourself up professionally as the neighborhood manager, who takes in the children and the packages for a stipend—not a bad idea, by the way—you are right not to accept cash, in Miss Manners' opinion. Intended or not, tipping friends for being obliging is insulting. Except for the few who have given the appropriate tokens of thanks you describe, these people seem unable to imagine how they could help you. So, tell them. After saying firmly, "I couldn't dream of taking your money," you could add, "but there's a movie Greg and I are dying to see. If there's a night during the next week or two that you're going to be home anyway, could we leave Daniel with you?" or "This makes it easier for me to ask you if you would mind dropping off my library books on your way to work." Even if they cannot comply with the specific requests, this should establish the idea that the proper reward for kindness should be kindness.

The Neighborhood Handyman

DEAR MISS MANNERS:

I am handy with most household repair tasks and often help family and friends with them. When offered money, I generally refuse. However, I find that some acquaintances take advantage of this, calling me to help them with all sorts of things. Would it be proper to accept money when it is offered, or agree on a price before starting a job, or simply to refuse to help altogether?

GENTLE READER:

"Okay, but it will cost you" is not a nice thing to say to family or friends. You are apt to find bills presented to you on your dessert plate when you visit them. This does not suggest that you should allow people who are not genuinely participating in an exchange of favors to take advantage of you. It's all in how you say it. If you want to go for the money, say, "I'm doing this professionally now, on the side. I hate to charge you, but if I don't, I'll be in trouble with friends who really ask me to do an awful lot and are paying for it." To avoid the work, say, "I'm so stacked up now with repairs I've promised to do for other people that it might be a while before I get to it. You might be better off just getting a professional to do it." The definition, in this usage, of "a while" is "never."

Unsolicited Assistance

DEAR MISS MANNERS:

My friend and I are new occupants of a house. Because of our work schedules, we have not had much opportunity to meet our neighbors over the fence, so to speak. We have noticed that the people on one side are very accomplished in the grass mowing and car-waxing departments, and we are in awe of their dedication. We have had an uphill battle with the grass in our front yard, but we have prevailed and now present a proper suburban appearance.

Imagine our surprise one day to observe our tidy neighbors in our yard with a mower, trimming the edges we had missed. Our astonishment quickly turned to outrage. What is the proper solution to this unwelcome invasion? Do we offer them a (nonremunerative) contract? Do we ask them to trim our borders as they go about their own mowing? Do we say "thank you" and forget it? Do we buy a nervous dog?

GENTLE READER:

The outrage potential in modern living never ceases to astonish Miss Manners. You have managed to find insult in an activity once known as neighborliness. Rather than imagining that your neighbor thought, "Oh, while I'm at it, why don't I help out those nice people next door," you have decided that the act was the result of vicious thinking along the lines of "I'll show the filthy intruders what standards we expect around here." With your schedules, you really don't have time to conduct neighborhood warfare. Why don't you just send a nice letter of thanks, accompanied, perhaps, by a neighborly gesture of your own, such as some homemade food or a bottle of wine?

Dogs

DEAR MISS MANNERS:

What does one do in the case of a neighbor who constantly curbs his dog in one's front yard? This continues almost daily, unabashedly, despite our glances and scowling. One would think that he would somehow get the nonverbal message that we do not appreciate little dog droppings all over our yard. Some friends have suggested that we gather all these droppings and redeposit them on the doggie owner's front doorstep. This seems a rather rash and childish thing to do, but I fear that if I confront him verbally, my temper might get out of hand. We actually like dogs and have several ourselves, but we would never ever curb them outside of their own back yard. How about a temporary "No dog curbing—please" placard in the front yard, or a letter of concern signed "Neighbor"?

GENTLE READER:

If your nonverbal vocabulary contains nothing between a scowl and dumping a load of droppings on somebody's doorstep, you should certainly take up the use of words. The sign is fine. Miss Manners does not approve of anonymous letters, which rapidly lead to ones telling neighbors about the comings and goings of their spouses (for everybody's own good, of course). You could sign a general "Dear Neighbor" letter expressing concern about all neighborhood dog behavior and send out only one copy.

Borrowing

DEAR MISS MANNERS:

There seems to be an unstated rule now that when something is borrowed, the borrower is entitled to keep it. Further, when the owner requests that the item be returned, he or she is made to feel rude or greedy. What is one to do? After lending several of my possessions, only to find them damaged or broken (the ones that were returned, that is), I finally decided to stop lending things and found myself called selfish. Is there a polite way of saying no?

GENTLE READER:

Politeness does not require you to lend your belongings or to feel bad about wanting them back. A polite request is "I hate to inconvenience you, but I'm afraid I will need my widget back immediately. Perhaps you forgot you had it." Any insulting replies are to be met with a cold "Oh, I certainly didn't mean to inconvenience you by lending it to you. Please forgive me for having been so thoughtless. I'd like it right away, and then we'll just forget the whole thing, shall we?"

Communications at Home

✿ THE TELEPHONE

Call Waiting

Miss Manners decrees that Call Waiting is rude. It presumes a policy of last come, first served, and that is against all the rules of polite precedence.

Oh, yes, she has heard the arguments—that this service deals with emergencies, that it spares new callers the frustration of hearing a busy signal, that it prevents one from missing important telephone calls. She tries to picture the exciting lives of those to whom telephone calls are so precious that the possibility of having one missed, or even postponed, is frightening. Are they all expecting million-dollar offers, impulsive marriage proposals, or notification of Nobel Prizes and Medals of Honor? Do all of these life-changing possibilities occur on the spur of the moment, so that they will never be repeated?

As far as Miss Manners knows, telephone companies will still break into a conversation in case of fire, crime, or medical emergency. As for what the service's advertising describes as the intolerable frustration experienced by a caller who encounters a busy signal, isn't a busy signal a quick, efficient, and free way of notifying people that one's line is busy? Why anyone would pay extra for the privilege of offending current callers while having to make this explanation oneself, Miss Manners cannot imagine.

Answering Machines

By condemning Call Waiting as inherently rude, Miss Manners has managed to antagonize everyone who enthusiastically endorses the new telephone technology. It was hard work to insult that many people all at once. She will now attempt to finish the job by alienating those who sided with her by endorsing the technology of answering machines. To offset the danger of winning back the adherence of the owners of such equipment, she will condemn them, too, for misusing their machines with their silly recordings.

It does not seem to Miss Manners that the true division is between those who love telephone gadgets, and therefore attach anything they can to their systems, and those who don't, and so stick with the bare telephone. A more natural one, she believes, is between those who consider the telephone an unqualified boon to civilization and those of us who consider it more of a nuisance. The question is whether it is rude to refuse to be on twenty-four-hour-a-day call to whoever wishes to break electronically into your house, with a blithe disregard for whatever you may happen to be doing. Is that an unbiased way of putting it?

In the days before the telephone, people sent notes and visited. There were regular visiting hours—"morning visits" were understood to take place in the afternoon (don't ask Miss Manners why)—and even then, there was a convention of "not being at home" which was neither said nor interpreted literally. No one was expected to keep constant open house. Allowance was made for those who wished the privacy of their own homes to eat, sleep, work, or make love without interruption.

An idea whose time has come back is that of the formal call. Modern people who are told of the intricacies of the formal call love to laugh at such hilarious conventions as pretending that one was not home when one obviously was, and leaving cards all over town instead of actually succeeding in seeing those called upon. When not making fun of their progenitors, these people are busy instructing their employees to claim that they are in perpetual meetings and causing the world to be papered with small pink forms headed "While You Were Out." Obviously, people have never been able to hold themselves perpetually available to all callers, in either their business or their social lives, so screening devices are necessary. (A lot of people seem to have trouble with this and stumble into such vivid, if true, explanations as "He's in the bathroom right now." The all-purpose excuse was "He's engaged at the moment." Nowadays, this might elicit the response, "When's he getting married?" but Miss Manners would prefer even that to the obvious question following the bathroom explanation.) To prevent the irrational resentment that calls are screened at all, we might go back to the custom of calling hours.

Rather than "I'm at home on alternate Tuesdays," the instruction to telephone visitors could be "You can generally catch me between eight and nine in the morning."

The telephone has no such sense of appropriate timing, and Miss Manners admires those who refuse to let it run wild. It is not rude to turn off your telephone by switching it on to an answering machine, which is cheaper and less disruptive than ripping it out of the wall. Those who are offended because they cannot always get through when they seek, at their own convenience, to barge in on people are suffering from a rude expectation.

It is also rude to waste the time of callers with stale entertainment. The necessity of recording instructions on the answering machine seems to bring out the owners' worst show business ambitions. The best joke in the world would be tedious to anyone who called more than once, and Miss Manners has not noticed a high standard of humor in this particular medium. Nor does having such a machine make one an impresario with a mandate to inflict his musical taste on callers. All that is required is that one repeat the number that has been reached, in order to dismiss misdialers, and give succinct instructions on how a message may be left. You don't need to give your name unless you want to. You certainly don't need to offer an excuse for not answering the telephone. The caller already knows that you are "unavailable" and need not be told why. Isn't Miss Manners teaching you that you have a right to be unavailable?

You do not, however, have a right to be indignant if callers do not use the machine as instructed. People who dislike answering machines have the right of refusal, as do people who dislike being on call. Hanging up on an answering machine is not the same as hanging up on a person, any more than ignoring a telephone ring is the same as ignoring a person who is standing in front of you. There. Miss Manners hopes now that she has reached, or shall we say gotten to, everyone. She will not take calls on the subject.

Telephone Solicitation

DEAR MISS MANNERS:

I have been a telephone solicitor for nearly seven months. Please, we are human just like everyone else. We do not purposely set out to disturb people just as they are sitting down to dinner. It is purely accidental. I do not use hard-sell tactics or attempt to embarrass or inconvenience people. Although sometimes the solicitor may appear to be rude over the telephone, it is more frequently the customer who is twice as rude, and shows his anger by slamming the receiver down.

Phone solicitation is a fact of life. Sending literature through the mail is undoubtedly an excellent idea, but we deal with so many clients that we cannot possibly afford to send information to everyone. Anyway, one can get a point across much more easily when on the telephone, and it saves quite a bit of money. As long as there are things to be sold, there will always be phone solicitors.

GENTLE READER:

Perhaps not. Perhaps eventually, every single one of those potential customers will be driven to using machines, answering services, and other protective devices to prevent unwanted calls from breaking in on their lives—as many people have done already, at some expense and trouble to themselves. Then that will be that.

Oh, dear. Now Miss Manners has hurt your feelings again. You must try to separate yourself as a human-being-just-like-everyone-else from your job, which, judging from the rest of Miss Manners' mail, seems to annoy just-about-everyone-else. Without condemning a legal method of earning a living, Miss Manners asks you to consider why this is so and how you can minimize the offensiveness of what you do. As you are no doubt aware, doing so would be good business. Those people who slam the telephone down are of no use to your employers.

The fact that businesses may save money and sell more by making unsolicited telephone calls is hardly an argument to soften the hearts of people who do not wish to receive such calls. Everyone has a right to control who enters his or her home, through the telephone lines as well as through the doors. This is not to say that there are no potential customers who might consider your service a convenience. You should recognize that it is more of an accident to encounter such a person than it is to find that people who are at home minding their own business are delighted to be distracted by your call.

Miss Manners wishes to emphasize the fact that it is their choice. You therefore do well to solicit their attention rather than seem to demand it. By opening with an apology and a quick request for a hearing, you will at least minimize the intrusion by acknowledging that that is what it is. A proper refusal is "No, thank you, I'm not interested; please remove my number from your files"; Miss Manners does not excuse rudeness. Just please remember that someone who barges into other people's homes has no grounds to complain about the quality of the welcome.

Using Others' Telephones

DEAR MISS MANNERS:

I am sick of business associates and friends running up my phone bill! "Can I use your phone?" they ask, and I foolishly say, "Sure," only to discover that I'm paying local and long-distance toll charges. What a rip! Do I say "Local calls only, please"? Everyone always assumes that their call is local unless they are calling out of state. Do I put up a sign and a jar for money? Pay phones are out.

GENTLE READER:

Just because Miss Manners will not allow you to rig up a pay telephone in your house doesn't mean that she won't help. As you graciously point out the telephone, inquire, in a helpful, hostessy tone of voice, "Do you need to call out of the city?" If the answer is "No," you needn't explain why you asked. If it is "yes," let us hope that the caller will be reminded to mumble, "Is it okay if I put it on my credit card?" If not, you can still say kindly, "Why don't you just jot it down on that pad, then? I've had terrible fights with the telephone company when they bill calls I haven't made, and was embarrassed later to find out that they really were made here."

Calling Hours

DEAR MISS MANNERS:

What are the proper hours for making phone calls to friends? I called a friend at 9:30 P.M.. and was informed that that was socially improper. Please tell me who was in the wrong.

GENTLE READER:

As a general rule, one does not call before 9:00 A.M. or after 9:00 P.M., or during the dinner hour. Aha, you say, but what time is dinner? The answer is that it is best to know the habits of one's friends (for example, people on the night shift may be happy to get calls at midnight but frightfully upset at noon) and to be prepared to get off the line quickly at any time that may, for any reason, be inconvenient for the person called.

"Who's This?"

DEAR MISS MANNERS:

When someone calls me on the telephone at home and says "Who is this?" after I have said "Hello," it annoys me. Someone who dials my number should know who it is, and if not, should say, "Hi, this is Jane; is Kim there?" My response to this rude question is not to give my name but to say, "Well, who is this?" I can control the problem that way in my house. But what about at my place of employment? I often receive "Who's this?" calls and reply, "This is Kim; who's this?" but this response just doesn't feel right. I want to let them know how rude they actually sound, while at the same time not sounding rude myself. I am sure that there are hundreds of secretaries out there who would love to know how to respond.

GENTLE READER:

Miss Manners would like to know how to tell you how rude people sound when they use only first names, especially in business telephoning, but since you use your first name to refer to yourself, she can't without seeming rude. However, that was not your question, was it? Actually, you have two questions, because home usage and office usage are different.

A person telephoning a household should ask for the person whom he is calling, not inquire whom he has reached. There are reasons besides those of etiquette that you do not give out your name to anyone who happens to dial your home number. The answer to the question "Who is this?" is another question: "Whom are you calling?" If you wish to teach your own callers to identify themselves to you, that is another matter. The method of polite instruction is to say, "I'm so sorry, but I'm terrible at guessing voices. Who is this, please?"

Proper office manners require answering the telephone with some sort of identification, however, rather than the deliberately uninformative "Hello" that one uses at home. Announcing what office has been reached, or which individual, or both, as in "Ms. Workman's office" or "Ms. Workman's office, Ms. Arken speaking," will save everyone time and confusion. The latter version is particularly apt when the secretary or another assistant can handle people's inquiries without having to pass on the call.

Electronic Eavesdropping

DEAR MISS MANNERS:

Last night, while tuning my AM radio, I accidentally overheard my neighbor using her cordless telephone. As Miss Manners knows, that is easy to do, at least with some radios. You just tune in and listen to both parties, as I did last night. Anyway, three possibilities occur to me: My neighbor knew she could be overheard but didn't care; she knew but forgot; she didn't know. Similarly, there are three options open to me: Tell her the truth; tell her indirectly ("Speaking of cordless phones, I understand that ..."); forget the whole thing and say nothing. What do you advise? Notice that I'm not inquiring about the ethics of eavesdropping. That's another question, one I may get around to asking later, after the thrill of hearing my neighbor's private conversations wears off.

GENTLE READER:

Actually, Miss Manners did not know how to tune in on her neighbors and doesn't care to know now. She will have to advise you on the etiquette of the situation without ruling on the ethics. The moral position would be to tell the person immediately; the immoral position, to listen and say nothing. Therefore, the polite thing to do is to act as if you have done one or the other. That is to say, you either warn your neighbor that you could hear her conversation, pretending that you changed the radio setting as soon as you realized the fact and therefore actually overheard nothing; or you go on eavesdropping without letting on that you are doing so. What you cannot do is to tease her until she frantically tries to recall what you might have heard. That is plain rude.

Plain Eavesdropping

DEAR MISS MANNERS:

Sometimes when someone in my family answers the phone, and the conversation is obviously about something that concerns me, I attempt to say something or wave my hand to indicate that I want to. I think that my relatives should excuse themselves on the phone and ask me what I want to say. They say this would be rude.

GENTLE READER:

No, the rudeness is your showing that you know enough about their conversation to want to chime in. This is called eavesdropping.

Interruptions

DEAR MISS MANNERS:

I have a very good friend who lives at home with her parents and children. When I am talking to her on the telephone and one of them has something to say to her, they don't wait for her to get off the phone and she doesn't usually ask me to hold. They just start talking to each other, and I am left "in the air." It's usually something trivial that could have waited until the call was finished. How do I tactfully handle this situation? I don't want to hurt my friend's easily bruised feelings, but I think it is very rude.

GENTLE READER:

The phrase you need is "Hello? Hello? Hello?" When your friend asks what the matter is, you say, puzzled, "I heard other voices. Is there someone else on the line?"

"No," she says, "I'm just talking to my mother."

"Oh," you reply. "Then why don't you call me back when you're finished?"

This is an example of the convenience of not always understanding what is going on. By politely assuming that there is something wrong or she would not treat you in what would otherwise be a rude manner, you force her to return to politeness.

Miss Manners requests you to attempt a deeper understanding of what is going on. You concede that emergencies warrant interruptions. But it is possible that your telephone visits are themselves an interruption in the household's life, and that the problem would be solved even more satisfactorily if you either agreed beforehand when would be a good time to talk or held your conversation on actual visits, where you could also occasionally include your friend's family in the conversation.

❧ THE MAIL

Private Correspondence

Assembling a so-called stationery wardrobe, once a major topic for etiquette deliberation, is no longer a problem for many people. They simply steal whatever is in the office. Miss Manners will not attempt to argue the moral issue involved, although she feels it strongly. She trusts you to imagine what someone who never takes home the tiny shampoo bottle from the hotel room, believing that it is intended to be used only on the premises, thinks of those who regard their offices as stationers' supply stores.

However, she has not the slightest hesitation about denouncing, from the viewpoint of etiquette, the practice of using business paper for private purposes. When Miss Manners sees a private letter written on business paper—Joshua's excuse for being late to school written on his mamma's law firm letterhead, thus implying that he is prepared to take legal action if necessary—her immediate conclusion is that the writer is a pilferer, and probably also a show-off. When she hears of people being advised to take business cards with them when they go out at night, just in case opportunities arise that might lead to making a buck, she knows what parties to avoid. (Anyone using a business card to give information to a prospective friend—for lack of a social card or from wariness about giving out a home address that early—should apologize with "I'm terribly sorry, a business card is all I have" and draw a line through the company name.)

Word-Processed Letters

DEAR MISS MANNERS:
   Is it tacky to use the merge capability on my word processor to write all of my friends at once? Please consider that my friends already put up with the tackiness of a typed letter, instead of one that is handwritten. The problem is that they almost never receive letters from me, handwritten or otherwise, because I simply don't have time to write everyone with any regularity. Isn't it better for them to at least receive a letter, even if everyone is getting the same one? After all, it's not exactly like photocopying. I can add things to individual letters and make changes that will personalize each one. Will I be playing fast and loose with the rules of etiquette?

GENTLE READER:
   This is the old mimeographed Christmas letter argument brought up to date, and Miss Manners feels obliged to warn you that for every person who defends mass mailings, more people are offended by them.
   It was not only the smudged purple ink that gave away the mimeographed letters, but the depersonalized writing style. The information included, and the writing style used, are bound to be a compromise to be appropriate to everyone on the list, and are therefore usually inappropriate to any one recipient. Relatives are addressed as friends, people are informed of the news about family members they don't even know, anecdotes are included that were already related to certain people, and so on.
   Personalizing these letters would therefore consist of something more than inserting the name occasionally, as do salespeople. We do tend to repeat certain stories to all our acquaintances, even if we have to copy them out many times by hand.

So, if you can truly write an all-purpose paragraph or two, insert it into a letter otherwise tailored for each individual.

A Gentleman's Letters

DEAR MISS MANNERS:
   Our son, being a computer whiz, would like to create his own thank-you message for Bar Mitzvah presents on the computer. Each one would have an individualized message and would be folded like a greeting card, with graphics on the front. What do you think of his plan?

GENTLE READER:
Your son is about to become a man. This is an excellent occasion for seeing to it that he also becomes a gentleman. Gentlemen write their social letters with their own sweet hands. They do not show off their wizardry in order to invent supposedly new social forms that violate the established ones. They do not send "greeting cards" of any kind, but actual letters, in which they express appreciation for the thoughtfulness of others. If they wish to make their friends presents of their artistic achievements, they may do so—but that does not excuse them from writing letters.

A Lady's Letters

DEAR MISS MANNERS:
   I bought all this beautiful doublefold paper to use for my handwritten wedding invitations and have some left over. If I want to use it to write longer letters, is it okay to fill up all the pages? In what order, and should I number them? Then how should I fold them? (I also bought a fountain pen for the invitations, and now doubt that I'll ever write with anything else.)

GENTLE READER:
   Welcome to the wonderful world of letter writing, featuring not only the fun of fountain pens but the crispness of good paper, the sense of accomplishment when you drop your work into the postbox, and the happy anticipation that someone else in the world also still practices this lovely art, so you might even get a reply.
   What you have is proper ladies' writing paper (gentlemen's is a larger single sheet), and Miss Manners hopes that you will want to keep replenishing the supply. By all means, write on all the pages. There are two correct methods of filling the inside: turning the paper sideways and writing the full length, or using the third page as page two and the second as page three. As this system is not conspicuous for its logic, you may, if you wish, number the pages for people who can't understand why the letter doesn't make any sense when read as one would a book. Fold the finished letter in half and put the fold at the bottom of the envelope, with the salutation facing the back of the envelope. By coincidence, this does make

some sense. When one slits the letter across the flap, the insides come out facing the reader.

Who Writes?

DEAR MISS MANNERS:

I am my husband's second wife and was never made to feel part of the family. I have observed that traditionally the wife keeps up the letter writing to the husband's family, but I have no desire to do this. Should I tell my husband that I am not comfortable with it, and that, since it is his family, not mine, he should take over the responsibility?

GENTLE READER:

It has always seemed reasonable to Miss Manners that people should write their own letters to their own parents, and rather odd to have this job removed by the convention of considering all social letter writing to be the wife's duty. She will therefore join you in wishing good riddance to such a convention if you will oblige her on two small points.

The first is that you refrain from stating your grievances about how the family treats you when you pass the duty on to your husband. Their being his parents is reason enough. The second is that if he, in fact, does not perform this duty, you generously undertake to send them major family news. Miss Manners is not asking for regular letter writing—just letting them know when someone in your household has been promoted, has a more than a routine illness, or is having a baby.

Sending Regards

DEAR MISS MANNERS:

When a friend of mine gets married, do I now address letters to "Dear Bob and Sue," or do I just write to Bob and tell him to say "Hi" to Sue? In this case, Bob is an old friend, but I don't know Sue all that well. In some other cases, I know them both well, but I really want to write to just one of them.

GENTLE READER:

Write to Bob, and send your regards to Sue. Marriage does not nullify the right to engage in private correspondence.

Personal Business Correspondence

DEAR MISS MANNERS:

Since being divorced, I have had much correspondence with lawyers, bankers, and retail merchants, as well as government agencies. I do not have access to a typewriter, and most of my letters have been handwritten.

I am anxious that my future business correspondence appear correct and businesslike, so I have obtained plain white paper of the size commonly sold as typewriter paper. When using this for business correspondence, is it appropriate to affix a return address label as a letterhead? If not, should I print my title and name above my address? Should this be written in the center or to the left, over the date?

GENTLE READER:

A lady writing from home does not try to simulate the efforts of a professional office staff. She may type if she likes, and her paper, if marked, is marked with her formal name and address. Plain paper and legible handwriting, such as yours, are correct for all categories of letters.

You must, however, indicate how and where the recipient may address you. The address may go in the upper center or the upper right corner above the date (in which case the formal name goes under the signature), or in the lower left corner (which Miss Manners prefers, because then the formal name may appear just above it). A woman whose signature is Samantha Jones Rusk may wish to be addressed as Mrs. Jones Rusk (the traditional form for a divorcée), or Mrs. Samuel Rusk (the traditional form for a widow), or Ms. Samantha Jones Rusk (the modern, all-purpose form). Most women let their correspondents guess which they prefer and then get angry if they guess wrong. That is not nice.

Closings

DEAR MISS MANNERS:

Are you and I on a social footing? Are we on a business footing? How shall I sign off this letter? "Very truly yours" is such a convenient business expression, but I haven't read it recently. "Sincerely" used to be a sign-off for friends, but it has now been adopted by business, and "Love" remains appropriate only for family and close friends. "Fondly" seems to have replaced "Sincerely" as between casual friends; for some reason, "Fondly" makes me bristle.

Recently, I wrote to the adult son of longtime friends of ours who are coming to our house for dinner. I said we would be pleased if he would come as well. How to conclude my note? "Sincerely"? No. "Love"? No way. "All the best"? Stow it.

GENTLE READER:

Stow it? Madam, please.

"Respectfully yours" is used for august personages, but Miss Manners is far too modest to suggest it.

As Miss Manners does not have the honor of knowing you, and as you approach her in her professional capacity, there should be no doubt that we are on a business footing, for which the appropriate closing is "Yours very truly" or, just to put the spice of variety into it, "Very truly yours." Strictly speaking, letters to unknown recipients (i.e., "Dear Madam or Sir") should close, "Yours faithfully."

"Sincerely yours" is the conventional social closing where "Love and Kisses" is not warranted. The standard hedge, which seems to be what you are looking for is to write "Yours" alone, allowing the recipient to imagine in what way you are his.

The Thank-You-for-Your-Life Letter

DEAR MISS MANNERS:

A friend told me that one of our mutual and close friends has been given six months to live, due to an inoperable brain tumor. I would like to write my friend a letter, to tell her how much I appreciate her and to thank her for all her kind deeds. Is this a proper thing to do, considering the circumstances? How would I go about starting the letter and keeping it tactful? This person means a great deal to me, and I was terribly shocked to hear this terrible news.

GENTLE READER:

Miss Manners appreciates your sentiments and believes that telling a friend how much she means to you is always proper. However, the first thing you should appreciate about your friend is that she is still alive. Any obituary-like tone in your letter—summing up the memories as if everything is over—is bound to depress her. Write to her as someone who is ill, going on to tell her how much you care for her, as if that were something long overdue, as indeed it probably is. It is not for you to conclude, much less to inform her, that she is dying.

Sealing Wax

DEAR MISS MANNERS:

I want to use sealing wax on some of my letters. Is it appropriate to use it on both business and personal letters? The various colors of wax have different meanings, which I have forgotten. Can you remind me? And lastly, what type of design is acceptable to press into the wax?

GENTLE READER:

Miss Manners gathers that you are thinking of something along the lines of the code for flowers or positions in which a fan is held (e.g., the foxglove meaning insincerity and the fan carried in the right hand meaning "You are too willing"). No one has ever been able to memorize all of these, so people who attempt to use such complicated codes are unfortunately left talking to themselves. Anyway, among purists, only dark red sealing wax will do, except that black is, of course, used during mourning.

A crest, cipher, initials, or motto may be used. There was once quite a vogue for noble ladies to use personal mottoes; the Comtesse de Mortal's *"Et puis apres?"* ("And what then?") is one of Miss Manners' favorites. Perhaps you could use this space instead of your automobile bumper. Miss Manners does not advise you to frighten businesses with such seals. Your friends will be startled enough. Besides, there is no wax color that means "Your computer is in error."

Greeting Cards

DEAR MISS MANNERS:

Is it very poor taste to add a few extra words on a birthday card or sympathy card? At times, I feel the urge to add a few additional or more personal words, but I reconsider.

GENTLE READER:

Miss Manners feels the urge to add a few teardrops to your letter but is trying to be brave. Has it come to this —that writing personal words of congratulation or sympathy is suspected of being in poor taste? Allow Miss Manners to tell you what is in poor taste. Sympathy cards of any kind are in poor taste. Rotten taste. Only personal messages (a.k.a. real letters) are acceptable for conveying such a personal sentiment as sympathy with the bereaved. Birthday cards are all right, but better if individually annotated. Miss Manners would prefer a scrawled "Thinking of you on your birthday" to some printed jingle. Miss Manners has the old-fashioned idea that the personal touch is not misplaced in the personal relationship.

Calligraphy

DEAR MISS MANNERS:

We have been close friends for many years with a particular couple, and several years ago the wife took up the art of calligraphy. Now our anniversary, birthday, and Christmas cards are addressed in calligraphy, which is quite attractive. But somehow, seeing her name and the name of her husband and children signed in calligraphy leaves me cold! It is as if it's more important for us to admire her calligraphy than for her to send us a warm message of love and caring with a normal signature. The words "love" and "sincerely" are never written, just bold, black calligraphy names. I almost feel resentful when opening the cards. How can I tactfully let her know that a plain "Love, Mary, John, and the kids" in her own real handwriting would be more appreciated.

GENTLE READER:

Sorry, but Miss Manners is too busy fielding requests from people who want to do their social correspondence on their computers to chastise someone for taking an extra effort with the pen. Your real complaint is with the content, not the form, anyway. The only tactful way to encourage someone to sign herself with love is to do so yourself when writing to her.

Who Comes First?

DEAR MISS MANNERS:

Last week I was making out a list of couples my new husband would be meeting at a party that weekend. He was watching over my shoulder and casually mentioned that I was putting the woman's name first for each, suggesting that the man's should be first. I looked at him in complete amazement. He rationalized that letters are addressed "Mr. and Mrs. Jones," so a list of couples should follow the same format. What is correct? When I went to high school and college, way back in the thirties, I'm sure the nuns taught us that hand-signed Christmas cards and letters to couples were always addressed "Dear Mary and John" and signed "Mary and John Jones." All the letters we received from his children this past year were addressed "Dear Dad and Mary."

GENTLE READER:

Miss Manners tries to discourage people from using rationality to figure out etiquette rules. It seldom works. Transposing rules for similar situations isn't always useful either. On this wee, simple little matter of which name of a couple goes first, there are actually four different rules:

1. The "Mr. and Mrs." format puts the gentleman first unless the lady is higher in rank: "The Honorable/ The American Ambassador/ and Mr. Quince," for example.

2. When a couple is addressed by first names, the lady's is first: "Dear Mary and John."

3. The same couple signing a card puts the writer's name second: If Mary writes the Christmas cards, she signs "John and Mary Jones"; if John does, he reverses it.

4. A child who acquires a stepparent after the main child rearing has been done (as opposed to one who has received mothering or fathering from a stepparent) may want to add that person's name to his or her salutations as a courtesy (although he could still write to "Dad," adding at the end, "Give my love to Mary"), but the letter is obviously addressed chiefly to the parent: thus, "Dear Dad and Mary."

Extending Greetings

DEAR MISS MANNERS:

Is it proper to put "Mr. and Mrs. J. Doe & Family" or "Mr. and Mrs. J. Doe & Families" on the envelope when only Mr. and Mrs. live at the address? I like to include the family, which is the married daughter or son, when I send a greeting, but not a separate card, due to the expense of cards and postage.

GENTLE READER:

It is never proper to substitute a general category for the actual names of individuals with whom you are supposedly on friendly terms. It is still less so (such distinctions make sense in real life, if not in grammar) when they don't even live at the same address. There is no additional charge for writing "Please remember me to Marcia and Tom" on the card.

Unknown Addressee

DEAR MISS MANNERS:

Would you please tell me the correct way to address the envelope of a Christmas card to a couple who are not married but live together? I don't know the young woman's last name.

GENTLE READER:

It is impossible to address an envelope to someone whose name you don't know without making that fact clear. (If you had her full name, it would be simple: "Ms. Kimberly Allen/Mr. Erich Wendell.") Send the card to the man and write inside "Merry Christmas to you and Kimberly."

"Nontraditional" Households

DEAR MISS MANNERS:

What is the proper mailing address for the nontraditional household? There is John Jones and Mary Smith, elderly widowed brother and sister, who now make their home together. Then there is Betty Brown, widow, and her daughter, Greta Green, divorcée, and Greta's daughter by her first marriage, Whitney White, college student. And the list goes on. We considered wedding invitations addressed to "Occupant" or "To Whom It May Concern" but decided that this would be in poor taste. What about a gift that is meant for the whole family, such as a basket of fruit or flowers? Do we send an orange to Betty, an apple to Greta, and so on, or the basket to one with a note admonishing her to share like a nice girl?

GENTLE READER:

Pardon Miss Manners' titter, but do you consider blood relatives living together to be nontraditional households? My, my.

Whether they are traditional, unconventional, or positively weird, households of unmarried adults are addressed with the individual names, ladies' names appearing before gentlemen's, and ladies of different generations in order of seniority. When you list all the names in that fashion, you needn't specify who gets which grape in the fruit basket.

Original Cards

DEAR MISS MANNERS:

Our entire family was left speechless again this Christmas when we once again received a Christmas greeting from a relative, a professional man (an optometrist), on which his fourteen-year-old daughter did the artwork. The entire family agrees that we have all seen lovelier scribblings and fingerpaint smears rendered by preschoolers. The girl's father photocopied this abhorrent drawing of a girl standing by a Christmas tree and fireplace hung with stockings on his office machine, wrote "Merry Christmas," and signed the family names on the bottom, using his worst handwriting. He mailed a copy of this garbage to all the people on his Christmas card list, in used envelopes, crossing out the previous sender's return address and sticking on his own "Dr. and Mrs." return label.

This relative can afford to send out the most expensive Christmas card available, with all the engravings and embellishments; however, he has mailed out trash like this for the past several years. I think the man is under the mistaken impression that his daughter is a brilliant artist and is trying to show off her work. I agree that sending hand-painted or hand-drawn cards would be thoughtful and individualized; however, his photocopied greetings done by such an untalented artist do not fall into this category. All who receive them are disgusted, insulted, and infuriated by such gauche greetings, yet are unsure of how to tell the sender. Do you think it would be best to advise him that he is cheapening the custom of greetings and delete him from our lists, or should we write "Refused" and "Return to Sender" on the envelopes?

GENTLE READER:

Whose family are you—Raphael's? Miss Manners cannot think of another explanation for the bizarre notion that only fine artwork may be sent through the mail at Christmas time and that failure to meet the family's taste level should be met with a declaration of war. As a matter of fact, the taste scale of Christmas greetings always places family drawings above purchased cards. Artistic talent is considered irrelevant; family feeling is supposed to replace cold aesthetic judgment. Try that on your branch of the family. And while Miss Manners is at it, she might point out that the expense of "engravings and embellishments," the saving on photocopying or old envelopes, and what others can afford above what they spend are not proper topics for Christmas time speculation.

Hanukkah Cards

DEAR MISS MANNERS:

I am a nonpracticing Christian married to a nonpracticing Jew. During the holidays, I send my in-laws a Hanukkah card (because they expect one from their son), a Christmas card (because we have them made with photographs of the family), and a Christmas present, although I don't expect one in return. Now that I've worked out that ritual to my satisfaction, my mother wants to know what kind of card—Hanukkah or Christmas—she should send my in-laws. Does one send a card according to the holiday observed by the sender or the receiver of the card?

GENTLE READER:

As your ecumenical customs seem to work, Miss Manners does not oppose them. You could simply ask your in-laws which they would prefer, but you should be aware that you are dealing here in nonpracticing customs, as it were. The reason Miss Manners cannot give you a firm answer is that there is no all-purpose standard.

There is no one Jewish way of dealing with the fact that a Christian holiday is celebrated as a national holiday in America. There are Jews who ignore it entirely and Jews who treat it as a nonreligious winter holiday, the origins of which are, in fact, older than Christianity. There is also a range of practices in between in regard to specific folk customs of Christmas, such as presents, cards, and trees.

In addition, there is a difference of opinion about whether Hanukkah is observed traditionally or made into the equivalent of Christmas, with corresponding trappings. A Jew who might consider it inappropriate for a Christian to send him a Christmas card may quite possibly care even less for Hanukkah cards on the grounds that they are not a Jewish custom but an obvious adaptation of a Christian one.

Miss Manners cannot understand why one does not simply sidestep the issue and send New Year greetings to those who do not celebrate Christmas. This cannot possibly offend anyone, as there is a general agreement that at the end of December the calendar year is over.

Trimming the List

DEAR MISS MANNERS:
Is there a gentle way to disengage from the slow and stately Christmas dance? I would like to stop sending cards to those people who include no notes and those whose cards conjure up no mental image. This is a propitious time for me, since I only answered Christmas notes last year, following my wife's death, and since I don't like to reveal the shakiness of my handwriting.

GENTLE READER:
Never mind your handwriting. It should not deprive those who are pleased to hear from you of your annual greeting.

Those who have also been trying in vain all these years to conjure up your image, and those to whom the custom is a mere exchange of names, may be relieved if you drop them. A few may give you a year's grace, but the rules of what you describe as the dance are that two years' silence must be respected, so Miss Manners suggests that you sit this one out.

Old Lovers

DEAR MISS MANNERS:
What are the rules on sending Christmas cards to old lovers or their families? After two and a half years, my girlfriend left me. I never had the chance to say good-bye or to thank her parents for their kindness and generosity to me. Should I

send them something? Or her? Or will it only remind them of things they'd rather forget? It seems sad when the people you may know and love the most must be forgotten.

GENTLE READER:

Miss Manners is a great believer in thank-you notes, but not to the extent of thanking your girlfriend for leaving you. Christmas cards are customarily sent to old lovers only if you are (1) still friends, (2) not cured and hoping to rekindle the romance, or (3) trying to point out that you are better off for being rid of them in order to make them sorry. None of these attempts have a success rate worth the cost of the stamp. Miss Manners agrees that it is sad, but warns you that even a polite note thanking her parents for their kindness will be interpreted as an indirect attempt at one of the above.

The Deceased

DEAR MISS MANNERS:

Each year, I have bought some lovely engraved Christmas cards with my husband's and my name. My darling husband died last year, so I didn't send any cards last Christmas. I have a few cards left from previous years, and I should like to use them. I would not like to cross off "and Bill." If I use them, I would leave Bill's name on, because our dear friends would know that he was looking down from Heaven and wishing everyone well.

GENTLE READER:

This is not the first time that Miss Manners has had the sad task of informing the bereaved that retaining social conventions as if the deceased were alive is not the way to invoke that person's spirit in the minds of others. Unfortunately, the reaction of anyone who sees such a card will not be "How nice to hear from Bill" but "Bill? I thought he was dead." Crossing off his name is not pleasant, either. It suggests the opposite of what you intend, as if you had easily crossed off his existence. The way to accomplish what you wish is exactly the way you did it in writing to Miss Manners. Have your own name engraved on new cards or, better yet, just sign your name on some and add something like "I know Bill would wish you well, too."

The Workplace

Businesslike Behavior

Why is it never the employees who speak of a company as "one big happy family"? Having observed the covert exchange of looks among staff members whenever a boss—any boss, no matter how benevolent—uses that phrase, Miss Manners suggests that the workers-as-family simile be dropped. It seems to compel assent only when it brings to mind money squabbles, territorial battles, bitter rivalries, and easy divorce.

One would therefore think it not necessary to squelch an even more laughable simile: work-as-party. Far from articulating such an idea, everyone understands that the correct way to speak of any job is as demanding. Miss Manners hopes that the days are over when women who were pleased with their situations would say, "I can't believe I'm being paid to do what I love; I'd gladly pay them." When these happy employees were taken at their word and, if not actually charged, at least allowed to remain underpaid, it had a dampening effect on their enthusiasm.

Yet both ladies and gentlemen persist in using the informal manners of friendship toward their colleagues, as if they were bound only by the easy and tolerant forms of good fellowship. Bosses often mandate this, and subordinates revel in it. Everyone is on a first-name basis. Formality of dress is an individual choice. Personal life is out in the open through confessions and, if they are not forthcoming, interrogation. Celebrations of special events—a marriage, a birthday, a nationally recognized business holiday such as Friday—are part of the office routine.

In such an atmosphere, punctiliousness about rules and schedules seems unrea-

301

sonable, if not neurotic. Excuses, casually offered, contain the assumption of gracious acceptance. What fun, day in and day out, to have so many pals cheerfully laboring for the common good. Why does Miss Manners wish to spoil it all with her stuffy notions of proper business manners?

If only such behavior really did lead to merry productivity, Miss Manners would refrain from airing what would then be a purely personal prejudice in favor of businesslike behavior. If the relaxed manners of leisure could be used successfully in the office without anyone's being fooled about the realities hidden underneath, Miss Manners could argue against them only on aesthetic grounds.

At the upper echelons, this does seem to be the case. The venerable corporate officer who urges his secretary to use his first name because it makes him glow with assumed youth and fairness is not blinded into equalizing salaries. The upcoming young professional who gives out daily bulletins on her wedding plans has no hesitation about keeping quiet about information that would help her beat out her confidants for promotion. For them, office friendliness is a posture that does not obscure the true structure of the workplace. They dress in a businesslike way themselves, but wouldn't dream of chastising those who dress only for comfort or self-expression. They just don't let them into the executive suites.

For a lot of workers the pretense of equality and sociability does obscure the realities. They may fail to understand that although loyalty in a family means sticking by everyone through thick and thin, loyalty in business means doing your best to honor your commitments but dissolving them—quitting a job or firing an employee—for practical reasons. They don't realize that while true friendship means accepting and helping without regard to reward, office friendliness refers only to a dignified and pleasant demeanor that is not incompatible with fair competition or paying as little as one can get away with.

Some hard-working people are seduced into putting their faith in the kindness and generosity of supervisors who act like friends. Less dedicated people may be lulled into thinking that their apparent buddies should be tolerant about their lapses. For both, the discovery that they may be held to strict account, or not rewarded as they deserve, is disillusioning. If they encountered a different atmosphere at work than at their social gatherings, they would not be so confused.

Isn't that old-fashioned, pretentious, and stuffy ask those who have never been exposed to legitimate office manners? No, actually, there are some people who have been practicing office manners successfully, without your realizing it, right under your eye, for an important and ever more common reason. Suitable office manners are exactly those a responsible worker uses toward his or her own family or potential family member while on the job.

If you were having a romance with someone in the company, or if your spouse or child were working in the same office, how would you behave toward that person in front of the other employees? If you were smart, you would observe formal courtesies in a pleasantly aloof manner, while strictly avoiding any suggestion of personal feelings or activities outside of the office. You would be meticulous about treating that person with a degree of distance suggesting that your manner was uninfluenced by any consideration but that of fairness based on job performance.

The Workplace

That is the proper tone for business. What happens after hours, among the same people, is not the business's business.

Being Nice

DEAR MISS MANNERS:

I recently accepted a job that offers reasonable pay, ample opportunity for growth, and new challenges. During the interview, I informed my prospective employers that I was a nice person—"nice" meaning congenial, agreeable, not prone to losing my temper. Because of, or in spite of, that, I got the job. My new co-workers are just the opposite. It is a small company, and never have I experienced such backbiting and sarcasm. They unabashedly thrash one another in their absence. When together, there is very thinly veiled sarcasm. These people have never heard of politeness. So, I continue smiling and offering unreciprocated "Good mornings" and "Thank yous" to the point where they sound hollow and insincere. I am not a persnickety person. Nor do I require an atmosphere of excessive formality. I simply find it very hard to do my job while constantly ducking flying daggers and looking over my shoulders. Do I change jobs, attempt somehow to ameliorate the situation, or continue smiling and ducking? The profession I am in is fast-paced, tension filled, and highly competitive. As you well know, because you, too, are a journalist.

GENTLE READER:

People are not being nice to one another in the newsroom; is that it? Journalists are Miss Manners' dear colleagues, and she has often been called upon to defend them against charges of rudeness. Oh, perhaps curiosity about the doings of others might run a bit higher among them than one would tolerate among the neighbors, and there might be a style of sporty roughness that you would not want your children to pick up. But Miss Manners promises you that journalists are all good at heart and merely need a bit of kindness to bring out their natural benevolence. It sounds as if you have been supplying this. Miss Manners begs you not to be discouraged from continuing to do so. She humbly offers herself as evidence that life in a newsroom need not have a damaging effect upon the spirits or the manners.

❧ WOMEN IN THE WORKPLACE

When is it proper to notice another person's gender? In the old days, the answer to that would have been a ringing "I beg your pardon!" Ah, they had wonderful expressions in the old days, as Miss Manners is fond of recalling. The old attitudes were not always as good. In this case, the real answer to the question, beneath that splendid remark, was that one noticed a gentleman's gender socially but regarded him by his professional identification in the working world. One noticed a lady's gender always.

Let Miss Manners explain what she means. She has the uneasy idea that this is beginning to sound ever so slightly soiled. She is not talking about office romance, or sexual harassment, or anything quite that intriguing. It is only a matter of manners as symbolism, and knowing what is appropriate for work and what for play. The old system was based on the idea that primary business was done by gentlemen, and the ladies were there only in an auxiliary capacity. (Miss Manners' quaint habit of always saying "ladies and gentlemen" where the modern usage would be "men and women" is going to get her into trouble in this little argument. Please bear with her.)

Among businessmen, precedence was clear. The boss outranked the employees, and everybody knew exactly what the hierarchy was, all the way down the line. Certain courtesies were shown in each direction: One let one's superior go through the door first, and one also let one's superior pay for lunch. Businesswomen, however, were seen in a quasi-social light. No matter how hard they worked, that social identity clung to them, as hostesses, belles, matrons, or old maids. Even well-meaning male colleagues saw and reacted to gender rather than rank.

That is what all those fights were about in the offices of the seventies as the businesswomen increased in number and identified their problems. When they objected to being asked to make coffee, given personal compliments, deferred to at doorways, or prevented from paying expenses, they seemed to be condemning manners. Not at all. Miss Manners, who wouldn't stand by when anyone of any gender attacked manners, assures you that the objections were valid (provided they were as politely made as other legitimate complaints about office procedure). The offense was, properly speaking, not about having manners in the office but about applying social manners to some workers and business manners to others. When this happens, there is a clear implication that when the ladies are around, serious business is suspended. This is not helpful to the careers of businesswomen.

Miss Manners insists that business be performed courteously, but the courtesy standards of the social realm do not necessarily apply. It is rude to discuss money socially, for example, and somewhat difficult to do business without doing so. Competitiveness, calling attention to one's achievements, and taking serious objection to other people's views are all social errors which are mainstays of the business world.

The Ladies First system of precedence never belonged in the work world. Miss Manners also trusts that the idea that the businesswomen were responsible for all quasi-social hospitality is disappearing.

None of these problems would arise if everyone refrained from noticing gender on the job. You are supposed to look at someone and think "Vice President," "plumber," "driver," "balloon restorer," not Boy or Girl. And what if you can't help noticing? Well, office hours are not around the clock, you know.

Difficulties in Not Noticing

DEAR MISS MANNERS:

After a meeting I attended in a nearby city, the woman who conducted it invited another gentleman and me to lunch. The day was warm, sunny, and extremely windy. I must point out that the lady was appropriately dressed for business in a conservative blue print dress. In the almost gale force wind, it was apparent that she was having an impossible time keeping her dress down while carrying a purse and briefcase. I felt sorry for her and decided that it was best simply not to react.

The third member of our party was not so sympathetic. He was quite amused at her embarrassment and joked with her in a way which bordered on harassment. During lunch, this continued. He remarked that his wife didn't wear a slip, either, and even commented about the type of pantyhose she was wearing. Should I have offered to carry her briefcase so that she could better hold the folds of her dress, or would that have been insulting? Should I have brought up the fact that I thought the third party was rude with his remarks? She was such a good sport about the whole episode. Am I overreacting?

GENTLE READER:

Ladies' Choice now often means having to choose between being a good sport and claiming sexual harassment. As it is difficult to conduct business while doing the latter, a lady's choosing the former does not mean that she is happy with it. Probably she would—and Miss Manners certainly does—commend you for your kind attention to her difficult situation. You might have offered to carry her brief-case without showing undue excitement about the nature of the problem, but ignoring the difficulty was also a polite solution. The way to end the other person's unsavory talk would have been to say to him coolly, "I really don't think we came here to discuss Mrs. Trefoil's underwear," and then immediately to turn to her with a business question.

The Woman Driver

DEAR MISS MANNERS:

I am a female college student recently hired as limousine driver. I am familiar with the courtesies that male drivers extend to passengers, such as assisting a bride by the hand or merely shaking hands with a gentleman. However, should I assist ladies? If so, how? Should I assist gentlemen? Is it proper for a lady to shake hands with either ladies or gentlemen? In these times of supposed equality, proper formal etiquette is terribly confusing.

GENTLE READER:

Miss Manners is aware of the history of scandal between rich ladies and their chauffeurs, but people are not supposed to notice the gender of their limousine drivers. You must think of yourself on the job as a driver, whose gender during working hours is irrelevant because you are doing what used to be considered a man's job. If you neglect its traditional functions, such as opening doors for all passengers and assisting ladies to alight, you will fuel prejudice against women performing this job. Scandalous doings aside, faking friendship between drivers and passengers lowers the dignity of the employee, who should be offering for sale only his or her professional services, not social ones; and it is a nuisance and intrusion on whatever social life may be conducted in the back seat. There is therefore no reason for any driver, male or female, to be shaking hands with the passengers.

The Businesslike Lady

DEAR MISS MANNERS:

I am a technical professional woman working in a rather aggressive field, often greatly outnumbered by men. In many instances, the men lay claim to my work (if it is good or creative); or I am totally blamed for some problem for which I am only partly, if at all, to blame. What is a polite and effective way to combat this problem? Also, all too often, someone is mouthing baloney. You may say that I should just let it go, but either my own credibility is at stake (as in "Why didn't you say anything?") or the company will have more problems if it acts according to these misstatements. What is a polite and effective way to correct these people? If possible, I would like not to alienate anyone. Keep in mind that I don't always have the luxury of talking to the people involved afterward, one at a time.

GENTLE READER:

It is no accident that a woman is asking this question. Whether men realize it or not, they have always known that the sort of good manners you describe—refusing to brag, allowing misstatements to pass uncorrected, giving away credit—are for social use only and will not do in the marketplace.

Unlike proper social life, business is naturally competitive, and its goal is to get things done rather than to spread charm. Miss Manners expects you to treat others with unfailing courtesy and respect in all aspects of your life, and does not want to hear any workplace screams of "You're full of baloney." It is perfectly good business manners to say such things as "Yes, I'm glad this worked out the way I envisioned; that's why I fought so hard to do it this way," or "It's too bad it failed, but you know I opposed this all along," or "Now just a minute—let's go over this again clearly, because I don't think you've considered the possible consequences."

Household Tasks at the Office

DEAR MISS MANNERS:

I've had it! I came to work today and found dirty dishes left over from Friday's lunch on my desk. I spoke to my secretary about it. Her response sounded like some crazy idea out of an Equal Rights Amendment dictionary. I couldn't believe it! Here my employee was telling me, her boss, what her job responsibilities were. I had to laugh right in her face. Thank God, most women in Virginia still know their place. Naturally, I pointed out the fact that I hired her and that I could just as easily replace her. She said that I didn't have that right. Maybe if you would tell her that I do have the right to expect any employee to do what I tell them, she will come to her senses and I won't have to get rid of an otherwise excellent worker.

GENTLE READER:
Miss Manners would hate to see such an otherwise happy working relationship marred by a trivial dispute. She feels obliged to point out to you, however, that while you may be able to get away with firing the secretary, you will have great difficulty replacing her. A cleaning woman who is also able to take dictation, type, file, run an office, and handle telephone calls and visitors is hard to find these days.

The Company Hostess

DEAR MISS MANNERS:
I am a woman who holds a vice presidency in a male-dominated company. An executive vice president's position is currently being filled, and I am a candidate, as are all the male vice presidents. Yesterday, the president's secretary called to ask me to chauffeur around town, on Sunday, the wife of a visiting candidate for this same position. In the meantime, her husband would be meeting with other executives in the company. I was informed that the reason I was asked, rather than a company wife, was that this woman is a "professional lady." (What her profession is, is not clear.)

This time, I was caught off guard, not knowing how politely, but firmly, to decline a request which I felt was unprofessional and in bad taste. How can I handle a similar request in the future? Is there something I can do immediately to ensure that this won't happen again? Needless to say, I am not sure of what to wear on Sunday—my "success" suit or my usual Sunday attire of casual slacks and sweater. I have tentatively decided on the latter.

GENTLE READER:
The general weekend business clothing rule is to wear sports clothes in order to emphasize the fact that one is contributing one's own time to the company. Miss Manners trusts that, being stuck this time, you will be gracious, perhaps using the opportunity to draw out the lady in a casual, conversational way in order to discover her husband's (and your rival's) weaknesses. Naturally, you would be too nice to use any such information in an underhanded way. Monday morning, you will march into the president's office and say, "I really don't think you want me to be company hostess, as it were. I don't feel businesslike about hearing the confessions of a wife who thinks she's talking privately. I could never tell you what she said. He's after the same position I am, and that would give me an unfair advan-

tage. From now on, I think it would be best if my duties were the same as all the other vice presidents'. That way, no one need worry. After all, you wouldn't want me taking advantage of being a woman to pump *your* wife, would you?"

Compliments

DEAR MISS MANNERS:

Is it proper for a man to compliment a woman on the beauty of her dress or the attractiveness of her jewelry? I recently heard it implied that a man's comments about a woman's attire could be construed as harassment. I have also heard some people say that even a compliment may be construed as too personal. Please enlighten me on this touchy subject.

GENTLE READER:

It is a delicate subject, and Miss Manners asks you to listen carefully. She does not want you to retain the impression that it is the nice habit of complimenting—giving well-intentioned praise—that is now backfiring. What can be an insult—although it may be worded the same way as a genuine compliment—is the implication that a lady in a business situation exists for your aesthetic pleasure. Complimenting the appearance of a lady you do not know (for example, saying something on the street) is such an insult. So is diverting a business situation to discuss a lady's appearance (such as saying "I love your blouse" to a colleague in the midst of a professional argument). The same remark addressed to a lady with whom you have a social relationship would be a true compliment, and most welcome. A gentleman need only ask himself in what circumstances he would be pleased, and when disconcerted, to be told, "I love your suit."

Expletives

DEAR MISS MANNERS:

I am in low-level management at a medium-sized corporation, one of two females in management in my division. Usually, I am the only female present at meetings I attend. My problem is profanity. When there are heated discussions during meetings, it is not unusual for someone to utter an occasional expletive, and I am sure that the men do this freely when no females are present. However, when I am present, the men are reluctant to use profanity, and I am quite uncomfortable with the way some of them handle this situation.

One man swears, then turns to me and says, "Sorry" or "Excuse my French." Another man very obviously substitutes milder phrases for common profane phrases, then turns to me and says, "I would have said something else, but I didn't want to offend you." How should I respond in these situations? I have been responding with a slight nod or brief weak smile, but I would like to be able to tell them in an unobtrusive manner to stop singling me out. It seems to me that if they deliberately choose to use profanity despite the belief that I would be offended, an apology becomes a mockery; and if they choose not to use profanity, it is certainly unnecessary to call attention to that fact.

GENTLE READER:

You would think that these men would realize that the tantalizing possibility of shocking women with words has been gone for some time now. Even Miss Manners, who dislikes such language, cannot pretend to be so unfamiliar with it as to pass out cold if profanity reaches her dainty ears.

Nevertheless, men who don't hesitate to curse at home, or who would be profoundly shocked if their own wives objected to vulgar language in films or books, often do this coy slip-and-apologize number at the office. The most common way that women disabuse them of this idea is to swear back, only worse. Miss Manners asks you to forgo this satisfaction. It hurts her to see anyone purposely meet the lowest prevailing standards. Anyway, she believes it would be more effective to take a businesslike approach, singling out the next offender, say, in a gentle tone (that the entire room can hear): "I think we would save time if you decide either to swear or not to swear, but not take up valuable meetings with your apologies." If you want to be even meaner, you could brush aside the next apology with "Never mind. I don't think any of us have time right now to work on either your social graces or your grammar." Miss Manners guarantees that the mention of a slip that he would not consider dashing will devastate him—even if he never made a grammatical error.

Insinuations

DEAR MISS MANNERS:

As a young, single female and a recent college graduate, I find that much of the business world assumes (erroneously) that I have a vested interest in all young, single males with whom I interact. At a recent promotional event for my company, a female employee of the host location probed for my opinion of Bill, also an employee of the host location, by loudly asking, "Don'tcha think Bill is cute?" Angered at the pubescent nature of her question, yet not wanting to hurt Bill's ego, my response was, "When?"

This sent my female co-worker into gales of laughter, and earned a glowering look and forced smile from Bill. Had I said "yes," a proclamation of my attraction to Bill (and I had none) would have been made; had I said "no," Bill would have been mortally offended. As it was, I spent the rest of the evening working with Bill at arm's length, due to his newfound suspicion of me because of this offhand question.

GENTLE READER:

Nobody asked Miss Manners' opinion of Bill, but she thinks he's a dud. Your response to an impossible question was both ingenious and funny, and she fails to see how any sensible person could be offended, rather than amused, by it. However, she understands that it is not a good business policy to allow anyone, however humorous, to go away disgruntled. The tactful thing to say when you observed this (and which you may still put in a note) was, "I hope I didn't embarrass you by my little joke. The fact is, I was put on the spot, and was only defending myself from the embarrassment of being asked to pass judgment on a businessman who I believe deserves to be treated with more dignity."

Conventions

DEAR MISS MANNERS:

On one issue at least, I am either an old-fashioned prude or sensible. My wife thinks the former. The issue is the dinner arrangements of a married person traveling alone and staying at a hotel for a conference or trade show. I think it is improper, except when schedules prevent important business from being dealt with during the day, for one married person to have dinner solely with another conference attendee of the opposite sex. My wife thinks I am overly concerned with appearances, as well as unmodern. We don't fight about this, and she doesn't "sneak" dates. However, we would appreciate your opinion. I contend that a hotel where both people are staying is not a proper setting for such a twosome to have their evening meal and drinks. I say that there is a full day to arrange group dinners and further the same casual business contacts. Finally, I never have dinner with one woman in such situations, though I have been asked. When pressed, I say why I feel I cannot. My wife says that most of her business at such meetings is with men. If asked, she will neither turn down such an invitation nor insist on having additional companions. She sees nothing wrong with such dinners, since they do not lead to less public contact. My wife seems to be of the I-am-in-charge-of-this-situation-and-so-what school, and I of the it-is-best-to-avoid-potentially-awkward-situations one. Our question is whether Miss Manners thinks I am too rigid and old-fashioned—a thirty-six-year-old fogey.

GENTLE READER:

Miss Manners is having great trouble with your characterizations of the two sides. Given the choice, she would prefer to think of herself as old-fashioned, rigid, prudish, and concerned with appearances, rather than modern and sensible, but the fact is that she sides with your wife.

Conventions such as you describe are really full-time working situations. We are not, Miss Manners trusts, talking about the kind of recreational convention that serves as an excuse to go looking for out-of-town sin. It is perfectly respectable for working people to continue having discussions or cementing professional contacts over dinner, either in the convention hotel or local restaurants. Pairings or larger subgroups for this purpose are formed by interests rather than by gender. It is not as though one can go home to one's family in the evening. Your system merely deprives you and your wife of using all the business hours that others will be taking advantage of and may confine you to dreary hotel room isolation.

❧ PROFESSIONAL STANDARDS

Power

Have you ever fantasized about being in a position so powerful that you could deal with people exactly as you feel they deserve, without worrying about retaliation? You would be so strong and safe that you need not bother with etiquette; you would be strictly on the receiving end of manners, not to mention obeisance, without having to dispense any yourself.

Miss Manners is sorry to report that there is no such position. If there were, she would be the first to dangle the possibility, in exchange for a promise of good behavior en route. If you were president of the United States, you would be continually worried—except in those moments when your mind wandered off to the economy or the national defense—about whether people liked you. If you were a monarch or a dictator who knew even a smidgeon of history, you would do well to do the same.

Ultimately, a boss, no matter how exalted, is dependent for his position on his workers; a star, no matter how brilliant, on his fans. One can defy them, scourge them, mock them only to a point—and those who yield to the temptation rarely notice that point as it goes by. That is why we are able to have so many moral tales in which wicked people come to a satisfactorily bad end.

Miss Manners does not believe that people are ever as pliant out of fear as they are from affection. Whether what one wants them to do is work harder, acknowledge one's near-divinity, or just hand over their money, it is always safest to make them want to do so.

Don't bother asking Miss Manners how one does this on a large scale. If she knew, would she be sitting here on the porch fanning herself, instead of having someone else do it for her? On an everyday scale, it means that courtesy, and the appearance of respect and consideration for others, are needed in direct proportion to the number of people over whom one has power. Being beloved is the chief job requirement of the most exalted positions in existence, and it is not acknowledgment of superiority but appreciation of graciousness that prompts the sentiment.

Miss Manners is sorry if she spoiled your fantasy. She will try to compensate by assuring you that if you aim for a position in which you never need people to vote for you, to support your policies, to do any work for you, to buy tickets to your shows, to defend your life and property, to make you look good in the eyes of your own superiors or constituents, to treat you with respect, to come to your aid when you need it, to admire you, to contribute money in the form of taxes or patronage of one sort or another, to refrain from ridiculing you, to abstain from plotting ways of getting you out of your position, to support you in rising even further, or to shed a tear when you are dead—then you can probably trample on the feelings of others in relative safety. It is still only relative safety, because some offended person may get you yet with a sideswipe. But then, if your wildest dreams are that paltry, that might not make much difference.

Unpaid Professionalism

DEAR MISS MANNERS:

Could you offer some guidelines on the proper way to treat volunteers? I have contributed my services to several organizations since I was a teenager. Some treat me as though they were doing me a favor by letting me work there. Quite a few think a certificate and a tea party adequate compensation for a year of aggravation and frustration. But I have also had the distinct pleasure of working for someone who always appreciates good work and is tactful about ineptitude.

GENTLE READER:

It will come as no surprise to you that Miss Manners sides with appreciation and tact, as against grudging surliness. Volunteer workers especially should be rewarded with gratitude, as well as by the satisfaction of what they are giving.

That matter of ineptitude raises another question. Organizations to which volunteers donate their time are presumably doing worthwhile work. It is up to the volunteers to make sure that they enhance rather than interfere with the tasks at hand. They should therefore maintain the same work standards as if they were being paid: keeping faithfully whatever hours they have agreed upon; using work time to work, not to socialize; and recognizing legitimate lines of command, rather than using their independence to thwart the paid workers. It is not enough to volunteer in order to win the respect and appreciation of the organization's professionals. One must also work.

Candy from a Receptionist

DEAR MISS MANNERS:

Please explain the protocol of candy dishes on office desks, especially receptionists' desks. If she doesn't offer, may I take?

GENTLE READER:

If the candy dish is on the receptionist's side of the desk, it may be her lunch. If it is on the visitor's side, it is for visitors. Generally, however, some sort of comment is offered in order to acknowledge this arrangement. If the receptionist does not say, "Have a jelly bean," the visitor may prompt this: "Oh, jelly beans!" to which the receptionist will say, "Have some."

The Office Pest

DEAR MISS MANNERS:

I have run out of responses to the office pest, and I still cannot stop him. He fancies himself brilliant, witty, and politically neutral, and he is none of the above. His stupid interruptions include opinions that he forces down everyone's throats. I know more about his politics, which I find offensive, than those of my friends.

Others vent their spleen by insulting the pest as directly as they dare, still without stopping him. Meanwhile, my temper is getting short. I'm the new person in the office, and I don't want to offend my friends or my bosses. I thought I would get used to him, but my polite attempts to tell him that I've heard enough are useless. I dislike getting distracted from my work, especially when I'm working on fixing up a mess left by the pest. Please, is there some way I can politely tell the pest to shut up before I lose my temper? My boss, who doesn't work in the same room with us, seems to grin and bear it.

GENTLE READER:

The last excuse anyone seems to think of at the office is, "I'm sorry but I have work to do." If telling the pest that doesn't stop him, Miss Manners is afraid you must tell the boss that you really can't get any work done under those circumstances. That generally wipes the grin from bosses' faces.

Names and Titles

DEAR MISS MANNERS:

This is serious: I just called my architect. I identified myself as Leonora Rogers. The (new) secretary said, "Leonora, he's in a meeting right now. Could I have him call you?" Was I wrong? Should I have said "Mrs. Rogers"? I know that she was wrong, but I am sure that nothing will change. About a year and a half ago, I was seeking mortgage money. A man from the company called me by my first name! I made sure they did not handle my loan. Two weeks ago, a bus driver practiced the same effrontery. It was a tour, and he saw my name on the contract. I work in a government office where the use of first names is the practice, but I know these people. Yet it is unsettling. Please attack again.

GENTLE READER:

Miss Manners will offer you a bargain. She will attack again, and keep on attacking until this dreadful problem is solved, provided that you help out, at least by refraining from conceding that "nothing will change."

Please take the care to correct these people gently. You identified yourself correctly to the architect's secretary, but you could have then told her, "Be sure to tell him that it was Mrs. Rogers who called." The mortgage company representative and the bus driver should have been informed pleasantly that "No, Leonora is my first name. My last name is Rogers. Mrs. Rogers." You do your part, and Miss Manners will promise to go on doing hers.

Terms of Endearment

DEAR MISS MANNERS:

We work in a twenty-five-person text processing department under a female department head who seldom calls us by our given names. Instead, she uses diminutive "endearments" like "babe," "dolly," and "hon," although she obviously has neither the friendly feelings nor the close relationship with most of us that these forms imply. None of us is fooled by this false jocularity. We all find her salutations anything from mildly annoying to absolutely infuriating.

Now her particular favorites and assistants are beginning to pick up the habit, calling the rest of us (although they are younger than many of us) "hon," "dear," and so on. How can we, emphatically but without incurring her (easily aroused) professional wrath, tell "babe" that we have had it with her phoniness and that we like our names?

GENTLE READER:

You have no idea how relieved Miss Manners is that the boss in question is a female, addressing other females, rather than a male. So relieved, in fact, that she was just about to sink back and rest, forgetting that there is still a question to be answered.

There are, in fact, several questions:

1. Are endearments suitable for office use? No.

2. Do employees have a right to be addressed in a dignified fashion by their boss? Yes.

3. How do you correct a boss's offensive habit? This is the hard one. You cannot correct a boss's mannerism when you cannot also indicate that there is a question of civil rights lurking behind it.

However, don't move: Miss Manners is not giving up. You may attack a general office problem. In this case, the habit has, as you pointed out, spread. What you may properly and inoffensively do is to issue a memorandum, signed by as many people as possible, stating something like: "We have noticed a general tendency in the office lately toward sloppy, pseudosocial language, which seems out of keeping with the efficiency and professionalism of this department. In the interests of keeping a dignified working atmosphere, we would like to suggest that we all get into the habit of addressing one another formally, rather than by nicknames or slang phrases ('sweetie,' or whatever)." Miss Manners believes that it would be wise to suggest honorifics and surnames, as a stand against the general but pseudofriendly habit of using first names in offices. She has, you may notice, selected an example that you do not mention as being specifically used by your boss. She would not blame you for maintaining that you were not thinking especially of the boss, or deprive you of the satisfaction of knowing that this would then implicate those who have been imitating her.

🌹 APPROPRIATE ATTIRE

The two words most likely to start a fight in this society are "appropriate attire." Miss Manners has never actually heard anyone come out for the right to wear inappropriate attire, but a great many people are prepared to fight to the death against the stultifying idea of appropriate attire. Most offices have therefore abandoned the effort of requesting anything better. When some institution does make a feeble attempt to mandate clothing more formal than that worn for the messier active sports, there are cries of violation of individual rights such as used to be reserved for political revolutions.

The United States Treasury Department once suggested that its male employees have jackets within reach in which to meet the general public, and that its female employees wear dresses, skirts and blouses or sweaters, suits, or pantsuits. The two traditional objections were immediately voiced:

That employees ought to be treated as adults; and

That people should be permitted to express their individuality through their choice of dress.

What Miss Manners hears unspoken beneath this is the argument that there ought not to be any symbolism connected with dress. If no such interpretations can be made about the choice of clothing, then it stands to reason that each person may be safely left to make his or her choices dictated by individual taste or comfort. Well and good, but she has noticed that the very people who battle clothing standards accept the notion that clothing is symbolic. If anything, it is more of a "statement," not less, to wear sweatpants to the office than it is to dress as expected.

What should work clothing symbolize? That the work is in the hands of responsible adults. By wearing outfits associated with adolescents or with leisure activities, grown-ups signify that they are not seriously committed to their jobs. By stressing what they call individuality, they are distancing themselves from representing the organizations that employ them. Miss Manners does not want to do business with people who signal that they represent only themselves (and couldn't care less whether the company they work for satisfies the customers), and unwillingly at that (because they'd rather be off playing with the rest of the kids).

Dress Codes

DEAR MISS MANNERS:

We need a simple formula to define the dress code for a small office. Expressions such as "pants that are too tight," "revealing necklines," or "loud and garish colors" do not do the job at all. Nor does "proper attire," "good taste," or "businesslike clothing."

GENTLE READER:

Request that all executives and employees who aspire to executive positions dress accordingly, while expressing understanding that people who are satisfied to spend their careers on the lower levels may consider it important to "express themselves" through their clothing rather than their ideas.

Taxi Driver Dress

Miss Manners, who cherishes the notion of being occasionally unpredictable, is not lacking in sympathy for the cause of freedom among taxi drivers. There is a spirit of romance about the job, which is traditionally associated with independence, not only in working conditions but in attitude. One can, after all, also aspire to make a living driving a car by seeking employment as a private driver, where uniforms are standard, along with regular wages and hours. Cab drivers, by contrast, are trading some of those advantages for the flexibility to regulate their own lives, perhaps in connection with other jobs or interests. Shouldn't they also be allowed to escape the trivial conventions that are associated with more routine jobs?

It was in this uncharacteristically wavering frame of mind that Miss Manners braced for the expected arguments from cab drivers against authorities in several cities, where prohibitions are being discussed or enacted against drivers' wearing tank tops, bathing suits, cut-off jeans, open-toed sandals, or other such ultra-casual attire. Customer complaints are cited, along with the idea that cab drivers should convey more of an impression of professionalism. As she expected, their reply was to complain about other types of transgressions on the part of passengers. Passengers in taxis are often unpleasant, sometimes drunk, usually stingy with tips, and occasionally sneaky enough to get off without paying. Their actions can threaten everything from the upholstery to the very life of the driver. Anyone who deals with the public in large numbers will have a range of legitimate complaints, and taxi drivers, because of the solitary nature of their place of business, come in for more than their share. How do taxi drivers judge potential troublemakers? By dress, of course. They get quite adept at using appearance to judge who is likely to be law-abiding, generous, and/or going to the airport.

Miss Manners has not forgotten her initial tolerance in this case. She does not expect taxi drivers to wear business suits. She has no objection to the comfort and informality of open shirts and slacks. Clothes that are, or that closely resemble, beachwear or underwear do not belong on city streets, even inside taxi cabs. That's not independence; it's a blatant disregard for the surroundings and prevailing conditions. And that is not an attribute one wants in a taxi driver.

🌹 BUSINESS COMMUNICATION

The Telephone

DEAR MISS MANNERS:

Extremely involved business people frequently spend days playing phone tag before they actually talk to one another. In the course of this activity, each "player" speaks to the other's main switchboard and/or secretary a number of times, and in each instance, the receptionist or secretary asks for a number where the caller may be reached. Certain self-impressed people peevishly snap, "He *has* it," and slam down the phone.

The receptionist generally does not have a reference volume to consult, has to pass on a message slip without the number, and may be criticized because her precise duty is to furnish the number with the name and time of the call. She may have the number somewhere if she is efficient, but she has to take the time to research it. In a busy office, this petty chore takes up valuable time needed for less mundane things. How much easier and more pleasant if a caller simply gives his phone number when asked, even if he is calling the same person for the umpteenth time; this cannot take any longer than fruitlessly venting his spleen on people who are trying to assist everyone concerned.

My employer, in an effort to keep his seriously overburdened desk free of clutter, will attempt one time to return a call. If he does not reach the intended party, he leaves his name and number and throws out the message slip. He may have hundreds of calls coming and going in any one day, and obviously many incoming calls are not completed. He would need another secretary to keep track of which of his messages needed to be kept and which were completed, so he needs the number new on every incoming message I give him. There is only one larger size of desktop Rolodex than the one I have, so you can imagine how much of my day could be wasted putting numbers on incoming messages if many clients got ugly about giving their phone numbers.

The same overimportant people who cannot stoop to give their numbers courteously often want to hold for my employer, hoping that they will be put through next when he hangs up. This ties up my line so that I cannot make any outgoing calls that I have been instructed to make. However, my employer often has priority calls to make. He can dial and get through to a new call before I realize he has terminated the prior call, so people on hold wind up getting mad and hanging up, with their blood pressure no doubt rising at a rapid and dangerous rate. Their own secretaries probably dare not instruct their bosses about this self-defeating behavior of theirs, and it likewise is not up to people from outside offices to lecture them, but someone needs to shoulder the task for the benefit of all involved parties.

GENTLE READER:

Meaning Miss Manners, she supposes. Oh, all right, but only if you first allow her to vent—not her spleen, which would be unladylike, but a gentle protest. The game of tag that you describe is designed to run people around in circles until they don't know whether they are coming or going. When you conduct business in such a way that you are constantly trying to get the attention of people who are busy trying to get other people's attention, you cannot be surprised when the players exhibit frustration. The behavior you describe is more likely to be a result of that than of egotism.

You are pointing out, as Miss Manners is always doing, that a purpose of etiquette is to superimpose a better form of behavior on those feelings than they would naturally inspire. She agrees, now that you mention it, that providing one's number repeatedly may be a convenience. Perhaps if you said "Do you mind giving me the number again, please, so I can put it in front of him?" you would remind callers of the need. It would also be polite for you to warn them about the difficulties and delays of "holding on" and, if at all possible, to check in occasionally with the holders, to apologize for the delay, give a progress report, and ask if they want to continue to hold: "I'm sorry it's taking so long. I'm afraid he's tracking down legislators before lunch, and likely to be tied up for some time; perhaps it would be better to call at two."

That said, allow Miss Manners to suggest that much office business could be more easily conducted by mail. There is no use saying "No, this is something that can't wait; I have to use the telephone because I have to be in touch immediately" when, as you have shown, immediacy has little to do with current telephone practices.

"Hold" Music

DEAR MISS MANNERS:

Please exert your influence to banish the evil practice of playing music through the telephone for people on hold. Entertainment or assurance that an accidental disconnect has not occurred are puny reasons for such perpetration compared with the gratuitous injury visited upon the helpless "beneficiary." Too often, the victim is already being treated to similar fare, courtesy of his own insensitive employer or colleagues, and would rather not have the battle of the bands raging inside his head. Besides, in our age of superb sound reproduction technology, the telephone receiver execrably distorts even one's favorite musical delights.

Silence, for some of us, enhances concentration. It is surprising how many tasks can be accomplished while one is on hold. Best of all, when the phone is in use, it cannot ring, and people are reluctant to interrupt one's thoughts when they observe one's ear glued purposefully to the instrument. Annoying sounds—even advertising, sometimes—destroy the opportunity to employ holding time effectively. They must be listened to or one may miss the persons called when they do come on the line.

Finally, and most important, we who have developed and refined our precious musical tastes by a lifetime of careful selection of what we choose to hear and not to hear are offended, even insulted, by the mindless, cacophonous drivel that passes in the common mentality for acceptable musical fare. The experience is as foul as having to sit though ethnic jokes or across the dinner table from a smoking cigar.

GENTLE READER:

Miss Manners has spent a lifetime trying to escape the musical drivel of which you complain—hanging up telephones, refusing to patronize stores and restaurants, making herself unpopular with taxi drivers. It doesn't seem to have done much good, but she is cheered by your words, which bring hope that perhaps others will join us. What amazes Miss Manners most is the idea that businesses pay good money to install devices that offend some customers. As far as she knows, peace and quiet never drove anyone away angry.

Writing Paper and Business Cards

American business etiquette has never approved of foisting one's cards on those who are minding their own business. The exchange is supposed to build to the point where it can reasonably be assumed that the other person might like to get in touch. This may not be an explicit request for the card—it could be as minimal as "Well, let me think it over, and I'll let you know"—but there has to be something. A pile of one's cards discarded on the way out of a meeting do not convey that aura of success that might be desired.

Business cards are also used to identify the source of other material sent to business associates. Most politely, one hand-writes a brief explanation on the card—"Thought you'd like to see this" accompanying a brochure; "Congratulations on the new job" with the present of an office plant—and, if on a first-name basis with the recipient, one crosses out the formal name and signs the given name. The cards can also be used for very brief messages, although it is always more courteous, as it is socially, to stretch such information into two lines to make it constitute a real letter on full-sized paper. If one's new employer is not going to send out a third-person announcement of one's arrival, cards or letters saying "I'm here at Wallman's now" take care of it.

In both cards and letterhead, business identification should be simple and clear. Few people need to know, on first acquaintance, where to reach you day, night, and in all your branch offices by all electronic means invented. Except for certain fields in which titles are used both socially and professionally—the military, high reaches of government—honorifics are not used about oneself. A social card should read "Mr. Herbert Tell," but a business card just "Herbert Tell" with his position, company name, and its address and telephone number. The position appears below the name, which is beneath and to the right of the company's name and address on the letterhead, should the company care to pay for it. A company logo may be affixed at the top of the paper or card, and Miss Manners prefers that it be blind stamped, which means that is raised, white on white. But, then, Miss Manners has a prejudice against attention-getting devices, not only on taste grounds but because all business paper seems to be screaming for attention and she, for one, pays attention to the ones that are unusual because they are correct.

Frank business invitations—staff parties, press parties, celebrations of anniversaries or new ventures—are issued in the name of the business, with or without its chief officers as hosts, and therefore carry the company name and logo. For truly insidious business entertaining, when you want to suggest that you are inviting the person for charm, not power—thus creating a false obligation that your hospitality should be returned in terms of professional advantages—private paper should be used. It is much more flattering to identify yourself as an individual, thus suggesting that the business is incidental to the friendship, rather than the other way around. What, you may ask after all these years of raiding the company supply cabinet, is private writing paper? It consists of plain sheets, or paper marked with one's name or initials, and/or one's address. And, oh yes. It is paper you go out and buy.

Computer Copies

DEAR MISS MANNERS:

I am using my personal computer more and more for business correspondence. I can not only produce correspondence with a professional appearance in very little time; I also get a permanent copy, a copy that does not clutter my desk or fill my filing cabinets.

Often in business, it is necessary to send copies of letters to persons other than those addressed. Standard practice is to type the original and sign it, and then photocopy it to send to others (listing them on the original). Copies of the signature then appear on each sheet. With a personal computer and attached printer, however, the process of photocopying can be eliminated, since the computer can generate multiple "original" documents.

Which copies does one sign? I am not comfortable signing all copies, as it may appear to the recipients of copies that I placed the wrong name and address at the top of the letter. Yet it looks unfinished to simply leave the space for my signature blank. If you will kindly inform me of the proper method for handling this problem, I will rest easier, knowing that I am doing the right thing.

GENTLE READER:

Miss Manners votes for the blank signature space, which is startling enough to alert those who hadn't paid attention to the name and address at the top that the letter is a copy. In addition, to prevent its looking like misaddressed mail, she suggests circling the recipient's name on the "cc" list in ink. Let us retain this quaint abbreviation even though these are no longer carbon copies.

Nonsexist Salutations

DEAR MISS MANNERS:

I am the one-woman publicity department of a small, nonprofit agency, and often receive mail addressed simply to the agency and routed to me. I also receive mail addressed to my position, rather than to me personally—"Information Department," "Publicity," and so on. Almost without exception, such nondiscriminating envelopes contain letters that hail me as "Gentlemen" or "Dear Sir." Assuming that I have a need to answer and that I can swallow my irritation long enough to do so, is there any way at all that I may politely call the attention of my correspondents to the folly of their ways? I have a clearly feminine first name and use it in all my correspondence, so there will be no ambiguity on that count in my reply. But I itch for a way to alert my correspondents more pointedly, and to perhaps create a more hospitable atmosphere for working women.

GENTLE READER:

Come take a look at Miss Manners' mail. You will find mountains of letters from people who realize that the traditional business salutation, which presumed that all workers were male, is now inappropriate, but who cannot figure out what to do. The answer is "Dear Madam or Sir" or "Ladies and gentlemen." It isn't all that hard.

Let us both have some sympathy for the bewildered until the new forms become standard practice. Reemphasize that yours is a feminine name by putting "Miss" or "Ms." in parentheses before your typed name below your signature. Then hope for the best. Taking pointed digs at people does not contribute to a hospitable working atmosphere for anyone.

The Life Cycle of a Job

In the Leftover Etiquette Box, Miss Manners has discovered, tied with faded ribbons, an assortment of attitudes and rules about beginning and ending romances, no longer used because they are not considered businesslike enough. Not caring to throw away something in perfectly good shape (possibly because they were forgotten when most needed), she has found a new job for them as business manners. It happens that they will do very well for beginning and ending jobs.

People briskly considering whether a prospective romantic partner will meet their needs have no patience for making themselves irresistible. Those planning marriage are anxious to ensure that there will be a fair split in concessions and duties. It is deemed an unwise bargaining position to let on that your only desire is to please the other person. Yet a job interview is the perfect time for making someone else feel that he or she cannot live without you and would be foolish to try.

Couples who are splitting up are intent upon placing blame, and then putting out their individual sides of the story, not only for the satisfaction associated with revenge but in order to demonstrate that their marketability has not been impaired. The old official line of civilized divorce, which is that the other is perfectly wonderful but both have decided, without rancor, that they would be happier apart, is exactly right for firing or being fired from a job. Unless extreme provocation is involved, it is incumbent upon the initiator of the split to ease the other's transition. Job comings and goings require the control of manners over natural anxiety and hostility. No one—employer, prospective employee, or about-to-be-

323

former employee—should try to get through such ordeals without a stiff dose of etiquette.

When Miss Manners muses about the old patterns of romance, she is fully aware that practical matters were not neglected. You have to admire the kind of manners that permitted someone to say tearfully "It wouldn't be fair to subject you to the burdens of family life, and I would be in despair because I know I should be no help to you, knowing nothing of the hardships of life" in order to convey "I discovered you're not rich enough for me." Thus, while the job seeker quietly discovers the salary and benefits, he or she articulates, through dress and behavior as well as conversation, only eagerness to please the employer through enthusiasm for the work itself and the style of the working environment. An employer, like a lover, ought to deduce from a pair of shining eyes that daily life is about to improve in ways that can only be imagined.

If hiring involves each party feeling unable to live without the other, firing must demonstrate, in a dignified way, that both can. If Miss Manners continues the divorce comparison, she is bound to run into trouble when it comes to suggestions such as finding a new position while still occupying the old one. The basics do apply, however. The person engineering the split doesn't make sudden announcements, but regularly displays warning signs that things are not going right. If possible, the idea of parting should be planted in the other person's mind, who should be helped to maintain the public posture that the departure was voluntary. Reasonable concern about the future welfare of the other should be shown. In divorce, it is not expected that the initiator must help find the other a new situation, but in business it is a virtue.

Being rejected requires less concrete responsibility but even more restrained behavior. You don't start grabbing property that doesn't belong to you. You make it discreetly known that you are again available but display no unseemly anxiety about it. You are gracious to your successor if you happen to be thrown together. Above all, this is the time for everyone to use those forgotten phrases "Nobody could be nicer; it's just that we weren't right for each other"—just as the beginning is the time for each to insinuate that "Nobody will ever be as good to you as I will."

Requesting a Raise

DEAR MISS MANNERS:
I am sixteen and have a babysitting job for a family with two children. I'm often there until midnight. They don't pay much, but I never specified what I wanted. Is it the custom to pay more for later hours? If so, what is a tactful way of asking for this? I don't want to sound greedy.

GENTLE READER:
No, but you want to sound businesslike. It is by no means the same thing. The businesslike thing to do is to fix a reasonable fee and state it unapologetically, with the assumption that fair-minded people expect to pay the going rate (includ-

ing, if you wish, somewhat higher rates for late hours) but cannot be expected to guess what it is. This is easier to do when beginning a job, but you can certainly tell this family, "I'm going to be charging (whatever an hour) now. I hope you think me worth it. I'm fond of the children, and I've tried to do my best."

Discussing Dismissals

DEAR MISS MANNERS:

How does one cope in a job interview with the question of why one was dismissed from a previous position?

GENTLE READER:

The only reason for having been dismissed by an employer is that the two of you were unable to agree upon your future in the organization. It is perfectly proper, and even thoughtful, to refuse to elaborate on this on the grounds that you had some happy years at that place of employment and do not wish to discuss anything unpleasant concerning anyone there. Should the employer who dismissed you choose to disclose the fact that he fired you for charging your secret lunches with his wife to the company expense account, he will at least not have marked you as a liar with your prospective employer.

Resignations

DEAR MISS MANNERS:

I'm planning to resign soon from a company I've worked at for several years. I've had long-standing disagreements with the management, but principally I simply feel that it's time to move on. Would you discuss the proper approach for announcing a resignation? When is a letter of resignation called for, as opposed to simply telling the boss that I'm quitting? How should such a letter be phrased? My work for the company is often valuable, and I won't be easily replaced. I suspect that my resignation will come as something of a surprise to management, so I wonder if some kind of explanation is in order. It is, of course, not my intention to put down management or the company.

GENTLE READER:

Absolutely, you should write a letter, if only because it is easier, on paper, to control the satisfaction you feel in knowing how you will be missed. Of course, you will tell your boss, too, as a courtesy, but handing him the letter will underscore the fact that you are really leaving, and not just threatening in order to renegotiate your position there. Unless one is resigning under protest, a letter of resignation omits any dissatisfactions with the company and states formal (that is, restrained, not emotional) regret at leaving. It is customary to say how rewarding your years there were, implying as delicately as possible that they were rewarding for the company as well ("I had the great satisfaction of participating in the development of . . ."). You close by wishing the organization and everyone in it well.

Now the antihypocrisy squad will leap at Miss Manners, demanding to know why this cannot be the occasion for screaming how much an employee has always hated the place and how delighted he is to walk out that door forever. You obviously understand this, but let Miss Manners just run through the two reasons anyway, one of courtesy and one practical. The first is that manners demand the convention of stressing the positive when leaving. You do not tell your hostess that you found the crown roast of lamb more interesting than your dinner partner. The second is that you are dealing with a company, not an individual; individuals come and go, but the files remain. That letter could remain in it long after anyone who caused you dissatisfaction has also left and someone with whom you may want to have dealings is there.

Commiserating with Co-Workers

DEAR MISS MANNERS:

What is the proper etiquette in dealing with a friend and co-worker who has been (or is in the process of being) fired? And what do you do afterward, when there is often an extended period of unemployment? Is any inquiry appropriate (How are you? What's new?)? On the one hand, it seems cruel to withdraw from a friend during a difficult time. On the other hand, it seems inappropriate to be bubbling with anecdotes, information, and gossip about your work and job activities.

GENTLE READER:

You are quite right that it is cruel to shun a friend and colleague who has been fired and rude to bubble about one's own job. What you have here is a perfect opportunity for airing all your accumulated job dissatisfactions. Remember all that grumbling that bores people in the office cafeteria? Now's your chance.

Retirement

DEAR MISS MANNERS:

On my retirement, I am being honored at a dinner during the annual meeting of a professional association with which I have worked. I have never attended such an affair and have no model of how I should behave. Will I be called on to make a speech or respond to a toast? What do I say?

GENTLE READER:

You will undoubtedly have to say something, but unless you can get one of the planners to tip you off about the nature of the tribute, you cannot be sure whether you will be offered a toast, a present, a capsule history of your career (serious or humorous), or some combination of these. So, you should have a few remarks prepared to use in some form—bearing in mind that dinner remarks should always be brief, and that it is charming for a guest of honor to be somewhat emotionally overwhelmed, to the extent of being incapable of recounting the history of his or her life even if urged. However, that brief statement must include thanks to everyone within sight, a catchall statement of gratitude that will include anyone you may have missed, the confession that you owe any success you may have had to those with whom you worked, praise for your successor, and a quick description of at least one pleasant memory you will retain, in addition to that of the dinner. If you are not called upon to say all this to everyone at once, you must keep repeating it to individuals.

A Day Worker's Retirement

DEAR MISS MANNERS:

My cleaning lady, who has been working for me for twenty-seven years, coming in twice a month, is retiring. Could you please tell me what would be an appropriate gift? If I give her money, how much should I give her? Money would probably be best, as she is difficult to buy for.

GENTLE READER:

If you don't know what would please her after twenty-seven years as her employer, how should Miss Manners know, who never met her? That is why, in the business world, we use money. Certainly, a monetary contribution to her retirement would be highly appropriate. Miss Manners would consider six months' wages a minimum, and would really like you to consult with her other employers to produce among you an amount she could live on. Even though this is a business relationship, it is a very long one, and it would be nice if you gave her some small memento in addition to money. Please try to think about what type of thing you have that she may have admired. Bear in mind that those who clean your good things are apt to recognize what you consider quality.

4

Business and the Public

Dealing with the Public

Ah, yes. Miss Manners remembers—oh, way, way back, children—when claiming that a particular form of improvement that would result in making one more romantically attractive was considered enough of an incentive to get everyone busy. Apparently such a result would now be considered hardly worth any effort. The question is: Will it increase one's income?

Miss Manners thought that etiquette would have been the last field to indulge in such vulgar hucksterism. Become a lady or gentleman in order to make money? Why, the whole idea of making money used to be in order to secure the leisure to become a lady or gentleman.

Miss Manners never cared for the juxtaposition of politeness and money, in whichever direction the formula was supposed to work. It seems to her that politeness is a highly desirable end in itself, practiced because we all want to lead pleasant and proper lives. Pleasant, anyway.

Miss Manners does not utterly deny that good manners are also good business. She just believes it to be against the ethics of her own business to claim more for etiquette than it can deliver and beneath contempt to offer financial incentives for decent behavior. In the interests of the good reputation of the etiquette business, she would like to sort out what truth there actually is in such claims.

Yes, all things being equal, sensible people prefer to do business in a pleasantly polite atmosphere. Businesses that demand that their employees treat the public with unfailing courtesy have Miss Manners' warmest wishes for success. Courtesy is a powerful attraction, but it cannot disguise the lack of efficient service or reliable goods. Miss Manners hates to see etiquette degraded as still another attempt to use image to disguise the absence of substance.

It is also unfortunately true that there are some decidedly nonsensible people who believe that when they are treated arrogantly, they must be privileged to be among their betters. Miss Manners says nothing of the businesses that live off such pitiful, self-deprecating snobbery; she simply takes care to avoid them. Less reprehensible but also offensive is exaggerated warmth, which amounts to an unauthorized assumption of personal friendship with the client. The hope that such a demeanor will confuse the recipient into thinking that he owes this pseudofriend his full support is, of course, the oldest business trick in the world. She would like to point out that the technique is regularly carried to its most absurd form and has come to alienate more people than it fools.

Not surprisingly, the most attractive business manners in all professions, whether dealing with the public or within the organization, are businesslike ones—cheerful and accommodating, but also workmanlike and responsible. This not only attracts people by making them assume that doing business will be agreeable and efficient but, to a reasonable extent, makes up for temporary business deficiencies. Such phrases as "I'll be with you in just a moment" and "I'm terribly sorry you've had trouble" may prevent a customer's walking out or denouncing the place in front of other customers. Damaged feelings probably inspire many more lawsuits than the actual damaged pocketbooks that are cited.

Miss Manners has no objection to anyone's getting materially ahead through the practice of good manners. She just refuses to allow good manners to push ahead with the claim that etiquette will make people rich. Isn't it enough that it does promise to make people polite?

Inappropriate Friendliness

Perhaps you believe that people are always more comfortable in an atmosphere of friendship. Let us consider some particular cases.

1. You are having a physical examination or treatment in a doctor's office or a hospital. The medical staff, some of whom you never saw before in your life and some of whom are perhaps half your age, address you by your first name. You know that they, at least, are only trying to be friendly, but you feel uncomfortable without knowing why. Miss Manners will tell you why. It is because, if you were among friends, you wouldn't be exposed while they were dressed. Which you would all be, Miss Manners does not presume to say. The convention of the impersonal situation, which makes it respectable for others to see you unclothed, has been violated, leaving you feeling—well, naked.

2. You are a woman (Miss Manners could make this situation unisex, but it is not worth the trouble) who has ordered breakfast served in your hotel room, and have put on a robe to receive the table and sign the bill. The waiter admires your looks, or perhaps just asks you where you are from or how long you plan to be in

town. Although you do not suspect him of criminal intentions, you feel frightened. Again, a tacit agreement has been destroyed. By the customs of hotel keeping, a woman may wear nightclothes in her room because room service and cleaning people observe the convention of being rigidly unobservant. A friendly remark shatters this delusion and leaves the woman realizing that she is wearing her negligee in a hotel room with a strange man.

3. You are on the telephone, and a stranger addresses you familiarly and makes personal inquiries. Misled into believing that this is someone you know so well that you are expected to recognize the voice, you reply in a friendly fashion. Then you find that it is someone who wants to sell you something or to extract some favor you do not care to grant. Feeling like a fool puts you at a great disadvantage.

4. A colleague, an employee, or your boss takes you into his or her confidence, repeatedly informing you of personal troubles ranging from emotional crises to transportation breakdowns. Your sympathies for a fellow human being are aroused, and you try to dissociate your compassion from an increasing irritation that you are also asked by this person to do extra work, lend money, overlook late checks, or otherwise compensate for those troubles. Yet they are related. The work contract carries the assumption that everyone can manage to meet his or her obligations except in rare emergencies. But friendship means making allowances for the failings and troubles of friends without counting whether the favors are strictly reciprocal. By enlisting your friendly interest in his or her troubles, a business associate confers on you the social obligation of tolerance.

All this is well-meant friendliness, designed to make strangers feel that they are among friends, but the effect is to make them feel worse.

❧ THE STAFF AND THE
PRACTITIONER

Office Visits

"Someone will be out to get you right away. Have a seat." Why is it Miss Manners' heart, rather than the rest of her body, which sinks upon hearing these words spoken by an office receptionist? Because she knows why she's being asked to take a seat. It is because nothing is going to happen right away.

It is an etiquette hardship nowadays to visit anyone's office, no matter how earnestly and graciously requested to do so. The manners that ought to be associated with the office visit have been abandoned for an unpleasant routine suspiciously more suitable for showing off one's importance on one's own turf than for performing the duties of a business-world host. In Miss Manners' experience, the fancier the company, the worse the manners. Law firms whose reception areas look like the saloons of old luxury liners are among the worst offenders. Authentic reproduction antique wing chairs, corporate art, corporate coffee, and polished tables featuring magazines in five languages do not take the onus off putting someone with a proper appointment on in-person hold.

Miss Manners is aware that offices require some screening process for visitors, for security reasons or just to stop the leisured public from dropping in to chat. However, even if the business in question is so intriguing that crowds of the curious would overrun the place if not prevented, it is polite to make the presumption that a visitor who properly presents himself is legitimate. "Let me see if he's expecting you" is not a polite statement. One can always declare, after checking, that "there seems to be some mistake," because he's not. "Mrs. Amtram is here" is the proper announcement—not "What did you say your name was again?" or "There's a Mrs. Amtram"—unless, of course, the other Mrs. Amtram is already in the office discussing the bigamy suit.

Miss Manners does not want to place the major blame on receptionists, who, being in that vulnerable position of visibility, are already the focus of glares inspired by the faults of their employers. Many have the grace to be embarrassed when time passes and nothing follows the announcement, and the more conscientious ones even make apologies or do voluntary prodding.

Not receiving an expected visitor immediately is as rude in an office as it is at home. The excuse that a secretary, busy with other tasks, must be sent out to fetch the visitor does not help. That would be like assigning a butler to open the door but letting the guests stand on the front porch because he is polishing the silver. Miss Manners understands that there is other work going on in the office and that people are in the middle of it when the visitor arrives. One can also find something useful to do at home, she dares say, and yet one does not finish paying the bills while guests are left listlessly turning the pages of coffee-table books.

It is not the social model that seems to be used for the office visit, but rather the outpatient medical model. This is the one that invokes the lifesaving activity of the doctor in order to explain why those whose time is less valuable, which is to say everyone else, must arrive punctually for office visits but then can be kept waiting almost indefinitely. This routine is not as popular as it once was. Patients have begun to ask themselves if their doctors are, in fact, constantly engaged in unforeseen emergency lifesaving, and whether their own working time, at whatever it is they do, is really so significantly less important. Miss Manners does not goad people to revolution, but she would not be sorry to see a quiet revolt in which patients demanded to be called and warned if their appointments have in fact been postponed.

This procedure simply won't do for office visits in general. We must have some polite rules that recognize the value of everyone's time, not just the host's. Miss Manners supposes that she will just have to dictate them:

People who don't have time for visitors shouldn't schedule visitors. Visits should be scheduled at times when other business is not likely to interfere, making interruptions unnecessary. Always barring genuine emergencies, there should be no telephone calls or other infringements on the visitor's time. A visitor who arrives early should still be announced immediately, but may then be told, "I'm so sorry, she wasn't expecting you until three," and asked to take a seat until then, but he or she must be received at the appointed time.

There should also be an appointed time at which the visit ends. If the visitor does not observe it, he may be told how kind of him it was to stop by and courteously shown the door. Now there is a routine people might want to learn for polite home use.

Physicians

Time was when they didn't have any etiquette studies in the *Journal of the American Medical Association*. Poor Miss Manners used to go about alone, prescribing politeness to people who claimed that rudeness made them feel robust, thank you, and please go away with your old-fashioned remedies.

Now there is an *AMA Journal* study, "Patient and House Officer Attitudes on Physician Attire and Etiquette," showing that patients appreciate being treated with polite formality. This should come as quite a shock to the First Person Plural Brigade ("Now, we're going to be cooperative, aren't we?"). As a matter of fact, it seems to have come as a shock to the sneaker-wearing physicians-in-training whom the authors of the study queried. Patients seem to want their doctors to be full-fledged grown-ups who wear shoes. The report found that "72 percent of house officers did not always wear a white coat when seeing patients, and 43 percent wore sneakers or tennis shoes when seeing patients. It is not clear whether these trends reflect trainee ambivalence about new career roles or whether they simply reflect the pursuit of comfort.

"Nevertheless, 65 percent of patients believed that physicians should wear white coats during patient encounters, and 27 percent believed that sneakers were inappropriate, suggesting that the white coat remains a powerful symbol and that physicians should adopt formal standards in attire as well as speech to avoid alienating these large subsets of patients."

The question of forms of address was also taken up in the study: what the doctor should call the patient and what the patient should call the doctor. Almost all the doctors and a majority of the patients acknowledged what the authors call "the imbalance of the physician—patient relationship," in which doctors should be addressed by title and surname while more freedom is allowed in using the patient's first name. "Do these data indicate that physicians should address patients by their first names, since a majority of patients would not object?" the authors questioned.

"Investigations in the psychiatric literature indicate that first names are used to address children and to establish informality, familiarity and closeness, while last names are used to address older people and superiors and to convey formality, respect, and distance. . . . Our data also raise the possibility that patients who come from disadvantaged social classes may feel a greater need for formality and the respect it implies. . . . Although only 18 percent of patients indicated a specific wish always to be addressed by their last names, inadvertently addressing such patients by their first names might interfere with the development of a working relationship. . . . Physicians may wish to dress more formally for all patient encounters. . . . The physician may prefer to adopt conservative habits to avoid displeasing a substantial segment of the patient population."

Well, yes. The physician may want to listen to Miss Manners' diagnosis of the problem and take her advice. That "imbalance" is unhealthy. People who are sick are not looking for pals, but for those who appear to be competent professionals. Oh, yes, and one more scientific observation: That people from the "disadvantaged social classes" understand such concepts may not indicate that they need more respect. It may just show that brains are not necessarily connected with the possession of material advantages.

Personal versus Professional Questions

DEAR MISS MANNERS:

I agree with you that personal conversations have no place in a professional situation. However, how does one handle such questions when they are initiated by a professional (such as a doctor to a patient, in my case)? I am in my early twenties and am subjected to questions such as why I married so young, why I have a baby already, and various comments about my appearance. These are meant as compliments, but they make me feel uncomfortable. How should I respond? I was even propositioned by my former optometrist.

GENTLE READER:

No one has a professional privilege to proposition. Nor does job status excuse anyone's taking liberties in a nonsocial situation. This is not to suggest that your social acquaintances may freely proposition or interrogate you, but the definition of what constitutes a liberty socially is one you must make in the light of each relationship.

Of course, a little judgment is also required in distinguishing irrelevant social talk from legitimate questions on the part of your doctor. Miss Manners presumes that you can tell the difference between "Has anyone told you what beautiful eyes you have?" and "Are you aware that you have a rash on your back?" or between "Why did you marry young?" and "What did your father die of?" If in doubt, ask, "Is this for my medical history?" Come to think of it, you should ask that when you are not in doubt about a question's being inappropriate. Just pronounce it more coldly, and follow it, if necessary, with the statement, "I don't care to answer irrelevant questions."

Professional Courtesy

DEAR MISS MANNERS:

My husband is a physician practicing in a town ten miles from where we live. On the few occasions on which I have gone to a doctor for my own needs or those of our children, the doctors have graciously extended "professional courtesy." They have not charged me at all. While I appreciate this generosity, I feel very uncomfortable, particularly if I need to go back. It's almost like saying, "Here I am for my free visit." Since the area my husband practices in is a low-income one, it is extremely unlikely that he could extend the same courtesy to other physicians' wives or families. I would appreciate your advice on how to handle this situation.

GENTLE READER:

Professional courtesy, a charming custom that is unfortunately being eroded, along with all the other courtesies, is not the same as bartering. It is, rather, an acknowledgment that each member of the profession is contributing to its objectives in his or her own way, as, indeed, your husband seems to be doing. So, you need not regard it as if your husband owed free treatments to these particular doctors' wives. However, an occasional present to demonstrate your gratitude would certainly be in order.

"Esquire" for Lawyers

DEAR MISS MANNERS:

I am a legal secretary for a very fine mid-sized law firm. There has been some discussion among the secretaries lately on what the proper and courteous form of address is for women attorneys. It is my belief that the term "esquire" is a masculine one, and I do not wish to insult any lady.

Webster's New Twentieth Century Dictionary, second edition, defines "esquire" as:

"1. formerly, a candidate for knighthood, acting as a shield-bearer and attendant for a knight.

"2. in England, a member of the gentry next in degree below a knight, given to the younger sons of noblemen.

"3. a title of courtesy placed after a man's surname and corresponding, more ceremoniously, to Mr.

"4. a landed country gentleman.

"5. a man who attends or escorts a woman in public; escort."

I must admit to avoiding the problem altogether by simply leaving off all titles, beginning or ending, when having to list both men and women. However, this bothers me, too. There are certainly some less than perfect apples in this particular barrel, as in other barrels, but for the most part, I believe that attorneys are due the small indication of esteem of having a title following their names. My question is: What is the title?

GENTLE READER:

The use of "esquire" among American lawyers is (1) silly and (2) customary. The second argument carries more weight than the first in matters of etiquette, and therefore you should use it for all lawyers.

Miss Manners would consider it wrong for women lawyers to be offended on the grounds that the designation was originally intended for males only. The term has come a long way from its historical usage, even in Great Britain, where it is much more generally used than here. You never heard of male lawyers being offended by being so addressed on the grounds that they were not, in fact, landed or perhaps not even gentlemen.

Authors

The cry of the stung author can be read in the letters section of almost any journal of criticism. It constitutes a separate art form, one which Miss Manners has long followed with interest. So alike are these epistles in tone and form that one would think that they had been copied from a letter writers' guide, of the sort that used to be published to illustrate the proper forms for correspondence. This one remaining modern example of the art of conventional letter writing is most often produced by writers of books, but dramatists, and film makers and their loyalists have also made notable contributions.

"I don't know what book Mr. Blenheim has read, but it certainly wasn't mine," the letter opens. "Of course, he is entitled to his opinion. But I think your readers have the right to know some of the facts."

These facts are as follows:

Mr. Blenheim is known to be constitutionally ill-natured. It is widely recognized that he takes a disgruntled view of the arts in general, and in particular of the genre this work represents. Only slightly less certain is the fact that he obviously had a quarrel with his wife and an indigestible dinner immediately before approaching the work he was to review.

Mr. Blenheim was totally unqualified to evaluate something he knows nothing whatever about. It is also a blatant conflict of interest, as Mr. Blenheim has produced his own work on the same subject, and is known to have odd prejudices and personal disappointments within the field.

The petty errors that Mr. Blenheim caught with unwarranted nastiness are isolated details unrelated to the important point being made, which Mr. Blenheim seems to have missed altogether.

After a few phrases such as "totally incapable of understanding," "unbelievably shallow," "completely out of context," "one shudders to think how he would have reviewed Hamlet," and "never in my career have I been subjected to," the letter writer concludes with the selfless hope that in the future, the journal will give others the benefit of more intelligent and disinterested reviews.

The new form letter is not a good one. Miss Manners is sorry to have to point out that it merely serves to repeat the fact of the original offense for readers who may have missed it, to alert everyone that the criticism made its mark, and to identify the author as a spoilsport who can dish it out but not take it. That is not to say that Miss Manners disapproves of the impulse to write such a letter. She has not flinched from taking on powerful opponents, but to oppose such a force of nature as that would be foolhardy. Let it be understood that Miss Manners disapproves only of actually sending such a letter.

It seems to her that the etiquette obligation in such cases is on the friends and supporters of the wounded author. There are times when one's loved ones have an obligation to threaten to hold one's head under water in the bathtub until an irresistible urge that must be resisted has passed. In their further obligations, study of the form letter itself will be of great use. In times of public criticism, it is always proper for one's immediate circle to assure one that any attacker is stupid, uninformed, prejudiced, disgruntled, and totally alienated from the tastes and judgments of the vast majority of intelligent people.

Everyone's a Critic

DEAR MISS MANNERS:

I need a polite but firm response to a friend's refrain whenever the subject of the book I wrote comes up. She says, "Well, you know I read the first draft of one of your stories. Frankly, it wasn't any good." Her opinion was never asked, though she has given it at least six times. I don't want to match one rudeness with another. However, I don't like her to think that I want to hear this pointless critique. The last time I said, "Well, the publisher obviously thought it was." I haven't been around her since, but I want a polite way to close the topic before she goes on when next we meet.

Why do people do that? If someone wants to know my opinion of their work, I give it carefully and I make it as constructive as possible. But I always make sure that my opinion is desired, and I determine why it is being sought. It is more important to support the effort to create than to put down the end product.

GENTLE READER:

Why do people do that? Because everyone is a critic nowadays and feels privileged to offer everyone else formulae for improvement in all business and personal matters. Aside from the deficiency of humility, it certainly does make social life hazardous, as you describe. Socially, one does not deliver such judgments, only admiration or the nearest possible equivalent. When one actually seeks the opinion of a friend, one says, "I really want your help with this; tell me the truth," and then accepts it. Your answer, confessing that one cannot hope to please everyone, was fine. By now, you may switch to saying, "So you keep telling me."

Letters to the Editor

DEAR MISS MANNERS:

I recently wrote an article criticizing the electric utility for the editorial page of the local paper. A few weeks later, I was castigated in a letter to the editor by a customer of the utility who deplored my lack of knowledge. I felt personally attacked.

I now find that his relationship to the utility is more than simply business. His son is employed by the utility.

I would like to know if there is a proper way to react to this situation.

GENTLE READER:

With equanimity. In common parlance, this is known as: "Don't dish it out if you can't take it." Why should you feel "personally" attacked any more than the electric utility does? You have attacked its performance, and someone else has attacked yours. Each of you is on record for the readers to judge.

Your real question is how you can make a personal attack on the letter writer, charging that his argument is influenced by his son's employment. You can call that to the attention of the editor, of course, but Miss Manners would be inclined to let it go.

The Attitude Problem

The Service Economy

"How do you get there?" asks the taxi driver when given an address.

"Look over there. If it isn't on the shelf, we don't have it," replies the store clerk when asked about the stock.

"We can't say when the truck will arrive," says the delivery service, "but if you're not there, we can't leave it. You'll have to come out and pick it up."

For years, Miss Manners had naively assumed that it was part of the job of a taxi driver to know how to get around the city, of the store clerk to know what the store had in stock, and of the delivery service to arrange deliveries so that people could receive them. Silly Miss Manners. The prevailing rule now seems to be that if you don't know how to instruct the service person, help do his job, and await his convenience, you don't deserve to have his cooperation at all in performing the task. The attitude is by no means limited to the situations mentioned, but it seems to prevail in most of the so-called service jobs. Miss Manners is not even counting the commercial establishments that admit that they do not provide service, although she considers them honor bound to keep their prices low in consequence.

The rule now is that the onus is on the customer. If the customer is not able to do what is required, the driver, clerk, delivery man, or such heaps scorn on him and may refuse to serve him altogether. If the issue at hand is correcting a mistake of the company providing service, this goes double. Calls to higher authorities in these places usually produce a recital of the company's difficulties—how many needed people are off, how hard it is to get parts, how overburdened the authority is, and so on.

Whatever happened to the pretense of customer convenience? Miss Manners is calling it a pretense because she is trying very hard to stick to the etiquette aspects of this situation. Although she has heard that unemployment problems and technology put an emphasis on service jobs that machinery cannot do, she can still believe the new versions of that old refrain, "It's so hard to get good help."

It is not hard to teach people to pretend that they are giving good service. The apology, the expression of concern for the customer, and the statement of efforts to help will go a long way toward appeasing the poorly served customer. The driver who says, "That's one street I don't know—that's terrible; let me look it up"; the clerk who runs out and says, "Unless they're all gone, they're here; let me find one"; and the delivery scheduler who says, "What time would be convenient for you?" and then negotiates until one fits the truck's schedule are probably going to get the very cooperation which, when demanded as a right, is so offensive to the customer who thinks he has paid for the service.

Excuses

"There are times when I can't cope, and this is one of them, so you're going to have to be patient."

"There've been so many people out that I've even had to postpone my own vacation."

"I'm going through a very difficult personal situation, and I really can't concentrate on this."

"I have exams coming up, and the job is just going to have to wait."

In each of these cases, Miss Manners was overcome with the desire to cluck her tongue and say, "There, there."

Of course, people have duties, illnesses, and commitments that sometimes make it difficult for them to work. They get frazzled, tired, and helpless from time to time, and the job naturally suffers.

"Now, now," Miss Manners wants to reply. (Why she must say everything twice on such occasions, she does not know; she simply does not know.) "You run along and get things done, and then get some rest." Miss Manners manages to suppress such urges. Instead, she says a cold and formal "I'm very sorry," and then goes right back to inquiring why they are not doing what they are supposed to do, cutting off any repeated bids for sympathy.

How, you may wonder, can she be so heartless? Miss Manners wonders at it herself because she does not find it easy. However, none of these statements were made to her by her relatives, friends, acquaintances, neighbors, or colleagues. Should any of those people be in need of understanding or assistance, Miss Manners trusts that they would not find her wanting. The explanations came from strangers with whom Miss Manners had brief business dealings. Typically, she would ask why an item or a task for which she had contracted, and perhaps paid, had not been produced or performed.

Miss Manners is not sure when this country ceased to be known as a place where things got done and became a place where people specialize in explaining why things haven't been done. Perhaps it is our sympathetic natures combined with the reluctance to judge others, or perhaps it is the influence of therapeutic methods that stress motivations and handicaps rather than results. From the smallest children to those in the most authoritative positions, the explanation has come to take the place of the achievement—or even the apology that used to accompany an admission of failure. Telling one's troubles has become an art form, no longer limited to one's intimates, and our biggest heroes are those—hostages and other victims—with the greatest claims on our sympathy. We have become a nation of wounded birds.

That being the case, Miss Manners had better set some standards for throwing oneself on the mercy of others:

The truly sympathetic and considerate person never asks sympathy of those to whom he does not offer it. Thus recitals of troubles, other than those made to professionals in a position to help, such as doctors, teachers, and bartenders, are confined to family and close friends, whose troubles one also shares.

The need to do one's duty, whether it is a moral, personal, or professional duty, cannot be satisfied by explaining why one hasn't done it. The explanation needed, at times of failure, is how one plans to make up for it.

Sympathy, when someone has failed to do what was required, is due not to the person who failed but to the person whose expectations he has failed. Instead of asking for understanding or pity with the confession of error, one apologizes for the inconvenience it has caused.

Miss Manners does not doubt the veracity of these excuses or condemn human frailty. As a rule, she believes that the workplace ought to make more allowance, not less, for employees' total lives, which means that they need leave for their children's illnesses as well as their own, as well as pregnancy leaves that are at least half that of the old two-year military leaves, and with the same safeguards.

Be that as it may, the customer should not be expected to suffer because of perfectly ordinary personnel problems; those are between employer and employee. A good boss knows when excuses are reasonable. How on earth is the customer supposed to know whether his or her sympathies are being requested by a conscientious worker caught in a temporary bind or a chronic shirker?

Instead, Miss Manners requests that customers be notified when a business is unable to live up to its promise, so that they have the choice between being patient or making other arrangements. Then there could be a ban on all individual pleas or demands to outsiders for sympathetic tolerance. As a society, we have come to have such unbounded faith in excuses, explanations, and mitigating circumstances that more work may be put into presenting them than into the task at hand. In the end, she thinks, this would mean less work for everyone. It would certainly be easier on easy emotional touches such as herself.

April 1, 1999

The Brookdale Opera
Brookdale Center for the Performing Arts
Brookdale, Connecticut 01010

Dear Madam or Sir:

In my entire life, I have never encountered such a
combination of incompetence and insolence as greeted me
when I attempted to exchange my subscription seats to
your slapdash season for something within commuting
distance of the stage. I do not entertain much hope that
this complaint will receive the dignity of a response,
since my previous ones have not.

I am aware that my having been a faithful subscriber
for many years means nothing to you. I do not expect to
have any influence as a result of my annual donation which,
although a sizeable portion of my disposable income, is
no doubt trifling to you. I am not even surprisedto be
told that if I wish to see your Ring Cycle, I must also
once again take tickets to your loathsome production of
"Hansel and Gretel," which has been part of your subscription package for as long as I have the misfortune to
remember.

But when your representative meets my legitimate complaints with the words, "Chill out, Alex-- there're lots
bigger donors ahead of you," I can no longer bear it. No
amount of beautiful music can compensate me for the sound
of the unauthorized use of a mangled version of my first
name and such a dismissal.

Yours very truly,

A. G. Perfect-Awful-Fright

A.G. Perfect-Awful-Fright
Vice President for Corporate Gifts

A CRANK LETTER. *This is a typically unpleasant personal letter of complaint, and the writer
has no business using her business paper, especially as she has left the business and the title she
assumes is in the nature of voluntary consulting. A history of correct but unanswered letters
had driven her over the brink.*

The Brookdale Opera
BROOKDALE CENTER FOR THE PERFORMING ARTS
BROOKDALE, CONNECTICUT 01010

Seiglinde Soave
GENERAL MANAGER

April 4, 1999

Ms. A. G. Perfect-Awful-Fright
127 Primrose Path
Brookdale, Connecticut

Dear Ms. Perfect-Awful-Fright:

I was deeply shocked to hear of your unfortunate experience with one of our spring vacation interns, who mistakenly assumed that it would be "friendly" to address you in the highly informal manner customary in his peer group. You have our profoundest apologies, and you may be sure that such a thing will never happen again.

In checking your subscription records, I find that you have, indeed, seen your share of our "Hansel and Gretel," which has been popular with our outreach program to introduce school children to the wonders of opera. I am pleased that we were able to find eighth row seats for you for the Ring Cycle, and would be honored to have you and your guest join me at our Bayreuth Buffet during the first intermission of "Valkyrie" to discuss any ideas you may have on how we might better please valued patrons such as yourself. Although we are deeply appreciative of your donations--indeed, it is the support of people like you that make opera in Brookdale possible--we cherish you even more as a faithful subscriber.

Very truly yours,

Seiglinde Soave

Seiglinde Soave

AN APOLOGY. *Although the Brookdale Opera has had six general managers in its last three seasons, proper paper goes with the job. The local engraver is a member of the board.*

Interruptions

DEAR MISS MANNERS:

What does one do, when one has finally gained the attention of a clerk for a retail transaction, about the person who butts in with his own questions or concerns? Most clerks seem to welcome the interruption, as if anything is preferable to completing the business at hand. A mild objection, such as "Just a moment, please," has no effect on these intruders. A growl of "Wait your turn" would surely not meet with your approval. Surely you can offer something to rescue your readers from this temptation. Only once have I seen a clerk wave off such an interloper, and she is probably not a clerk anymore. She has no doubt disappeared into the ranks of management.

GENTLE READER:

There is such a thing as a legitimate interruption, and the clerk is the best person to judge if that is what it is. Customers should not have to wait in line to ask such questions as "Is this the right line for credit purchases?" or "Could you please tell me where the rest room is?" or "Do you carry shirts here?" or "Where do I find someone to demonstrate the washing machine?"

A competent clerk ought to be able to answer such questions without suspending the mechanics of making a sale. He or she should also be able to say firmly when customers are actually trying to barge ahead, "I'll be with you as soon as I'm free." If not, or if the question is "Would you write this up now for me because I'm in a hurry?", you, as the immediate customer, should say to the clerk, "I'm sorry, but I would appreciate your finishing helping me before you get involved with helping another customer."

Unwarranted Sympathy

If a gentleman accompanies a lady when she shops for her clothing, the saleswomen feel sorry for him and treat him with consideration tinged with amusement. If a lady accompanies a gentleman when he shops for his clothing, the salesmen feel sorry for him and treat her with coolness tinged with rudeness. Miss Manners believes that the latter are making a mistake.

If you were to ask men's clothing salesmen why so many of them ignore inquiries from the lady accompanying a customer, curtly refute opinions she expresses, request confirmation from the gentleman before honoring her instructions, and generally shoot him sympathetic, sometimes sarcastic, looks for being burdened by her company, they would probably answer compassionately.

"The poor slob," they might say, although perhaps more circumspectly. "She can't even let him pick his own clothes. I was just trying to help and give him some dignity by treating him like an adult who is free to do what he wants." A noble impulse. The mistake is that they think they know what he wants better than he has clearly demonstrated. How did the lady get there at all, unless the gentleman asked her to accompany him? And why would he do that unless he wanted her advice, opinions, and company—the very things for which he is being pitied for having to endure?

Gentlemen's clothiers often seem to have been unduly affected by the spectacle of little boys being put by their mothers into suits they didn't want to wear. No doubt this is dreadful torture to be forced to watch, and Miss Manners will refrain from mentioning the fact that the salesmen naturally side on such occasions with the mammas. And so they should. The fact that children do not easily take to the conventions of their society is cause for sympathy but not for letting them escape being civilized. Besides, an equal number of little girls are marched into stores by parents who offer such unabashed lies in their daughters' names as "She wants a navy blue coat big enough to last two or three winters." Yet ladies accompanying other ladies shopping are presumed by the sales staff to be trusted counselors whose opinions will be a crucial factor in any decision.

The point about grown gentlemen, however, is that they are grown. And that means that they have certainly figured out how to slip out, unaccompanied, on excursions for whatever purpose they wish to pursue alone. A gentleman not under house arrest can always manage to shop without a lady in attendance, no matter how closely they are otherwise connected. It is therefore a reasonable assumption that a gentleman brings a lady shopping with him because he wants her along.

Some gentlemen have no interest in learning to judge quality in clothing and prefer to use the expertise of ladies who are knowledgeable about such things. Some gentlemen dress to please certain ladies and want to be sure of producing that effect before making purchases. Some gentlemen hate shopping and find it pleasanter when in feminine company. Some gentlemen are color blind and know that if they go out alone, they will come home with green suits. And some gentlemen even have a certain nostalgic affection for that mother–son ritual, and feel happy and fussed over and even a little wicked when performing it with ladies who are not their mothers.

When the ladies with any of these gentlemen are treated gruffly, the gentlemen tend to be annoyed. Not only are their gentlemanly instincts to protect their ladies affronted, but a slur has been cast on their autonomy, and their purpose of benefiting from the lady's taste, knowledgeability, or company is being thwarted.

Miss Manners recommends to the salesmen a gallant posture of sharing with the lady her concern that the gentleman be attired in all the splendor she undoubtedly believes he deserves. Bringing her a chair, inviting her judgment and offering theirs to her, and generally treating her as an honored expert will, she promises, be extremely rewarding.

Superfluous Thanks

DEAR MISS MANNERS:

I have received a brief, handwritten letter personally thanking me for patronizing a particular women's clothing store and expressing the hope that I will enjoy wearing the dress I purchased there. Although I am touched that the shop in question appreciated my patronage to this extent, I am baffled as to what to do. Do I drop them a line advising them of my social triumphs while wearing the dress? Should I stop by the store next time I'm out shopping and pay a visit on the particular salesperson who wrote me? What if she's not there?

GENTLE READER:

It drives Miss Manners crazy that in a period when social obligations are more often shirked than met, commercial establishments have taken over social forms as a way of advertising. It's not that she minds superfluous politeness. The clerk's hope is that you will remember her name when you are ready to shop again, and perhaps it works in some cases—but how many thank-you letters have you gotten from people to whom you sent presents or gave dinners? Anyway, it shouldn't be all that hard to realize that a thank-you letter from a sales clerk for shopping does not require you to write back, send her a birthday present, or invite her to dinner.

Mail-Order Shopping

Shopping by mail is one transaction that does not require much etiquette, Miss Manners naively believed before she tried it. Silly Miss Manners.

Perhaps shopping by mail is etiquette free when everything goes as scheduled. Miss Manners wouldn't know. Since she is not a priestess of consumerism, it is not her place to question why a commercial establishment would send out a catalogue for the purpose of responding to prompt orders by notification that the item is unavailable. There seems to be a lot of that going around.

What concerns her is the rudeness built into methods of dealing with the out-of-stock or not-yet-in-stock item, the wrong item that is delivered and the right one that isn't, or is damaged, the erroneous billings, and other such commonplaces of shopping by mail. This is the assumption that the customer's time and trouble are not factors, and, what is more, that the time and resources—long-distance telephone calls, copying machines—of his or her employer are available for these personal transactions as well.

Let us say that the customer has ordered two chair covers, a saucepan, and a toothbrush. A month later, feeling mealymouthed and seeing the toothbrush advertised more cheaply in a local store, the customer calls, asking if the order may be canceled. No, she is told; it is already on its way. Ten days later, a package comes with the saucepan, slipcovers, and a notice that the toothbrush is unavailable. The customer calls again (and by the way, the ordering line is toll free, but the complaint one isn't), and is told to photocopy the company's own notice and mail it back so that the account can be credited.

She is also asked for a daytime telephone number. By setting things up so that adjusters must return customers' calls, they ensure that the customer's work time, whether at the office or at home, will be interrupted.

About the bills and the finance charges that aren't removed even when the original amount is, let us say only that a great deal of photocopying is involved. Someone who does not work in an office, or who refuses to use company equipment for personal business, would have to make a special trip to have this done.

Miss Manners does not doubt that a customer who is available by telephone, oblivious of long-distance telephone bills or untroubled about using the company line, and cheerful about running around getting things copied will, with a little patience, be able to settle an altercation that develops when shopping by mail goes wrong. She just doesn't understand why the term "convenience" is used in connection with such transactions.

The Careful Consumer

DEAR MISS MANNERS:

Please let your readers know that it is in good taste to request a detailed contract or sales slip and that it is not underhanded to check out a firm with the local consumer assistance department. A trusting "perfect" lady, I didn't do these things. Now I am out many dollars and owner of a down quilt through which one can see daylight. I hope that others will benefit by my being too genteel.

GENTLE READER:

As it is one of Miss Manners' missions in life to dispel the unfortunate notion that being a perfect lady or gentleman requires being a sucker, she thanks you for this opportunity. The technique to use is the polite, firm complaint. You should have made as strong a one as possible. Incidentally, the reason for keeping protests polite is not only that one should do everything politely, which indeed one should. It is also that ultimately, when people of authority review the problem, the reasonable-sounding complaint is treated more seriously than the burst of outrage, whatever the respective justifications for each.

Assuming the Worst

DEAR MISS MANNERS:

Recently, I received from a film-processing company two fifty-foot reels of Super Eight movie film that were not mine. Their customer relations department told me to send them in so that they could find the owners, and said that they would let me know if anyone reported receiving mine by mistake. To this date, no one has, so why should I turn in theirs? I feel like a heel keeping them; one is of a birthday party and the other seems to be of children looking for Easter eggs. But one would hope that the people who received my film by mistake would report it or, if they like my film, would duplicate it and send the originals back to the film company. If they are not decent enough to do that, why should I give them back their film and never see mine?

GENTLE READER:

Because you do not belong in the business of judging crime and making punishments. Miss Manners does not know, or want to now, how interesting your own film was. But as you point out, if they only wanted to be dishonest, they could always duplicate it. Therefore, they must be malicious as well, harboring evil intent toward you and relishing the thought of defrauding you. You've got to watch out for such people. For years, they've been waiting to pull just such a trick, when they weren't doing other mean things like hiding Easter eggs for the children, and you played right into their hands.

Actually, Miss Manners can think of one or two other possible explanations. Maybe the film company made two mistakes, not just one. Maybe they lost your film or sent it to someone else, so that the people whose film you have received have nothing to exchange for their lost film. Or perhaps they did get it but decided to put aside these sweet records of their children to look at when the children themselves weren't quite so underfoot, and therefore are unaware that they have the wrong film. Miss Manners' advice to you is to stop quarreling with some unknown people harboring imaginary evil intent toward you and demand of the film-processing company that they find your film or compensate you for the loss.

Real Estate Agents

DEAR MISS MANNERS:

As a new real estate agent, I have been encouraged to prospect for clients, but I am uncomfortable with this. I have not yet presented myself unannounced (or otherwise) at someone's front door, although I have made phone calls. When calling strangers, I feel as though I am intruding upon whatever they're doing. They're quite nice about it, but I'd appreciate any suggestions or insight you have to offer. In the future, I can depend upon referrals. However, at the moment, the only way the public will know that I am there to serve them is if I tell them. I'm caught between the need for survival and my respect for people's privacy.

GENTLE READER:

Miss Manners wishes you a successful career and is confident that retaining your present attitude will help you achieve it. She has received a number of letters from people who complain that real estate agents regard their own working hours as a period when those in the housing market also ought to be devoting themselves exclusively to this business. Telephone calls, surprise visits to prospective buyers, and demands that both sellers and prospective purchasers be ready at all hours are the subject of such complaints. Agents who are careful to call first and to ask "Is this a convenient time for you?" have a distinct advantage. They also get better cooperation. People are much more likely to put themselves out wholeheartedly when respect has been paid to their wishes.

The Travel Industry

On two different occasions, Miss Manners was aboard an airplane that was stuck on the runway for more than four hours, during which there were periodic announcements about when it would take off, followed, after some delay, by announcements that it wouldn't; and repeated instructions about not disembarking because of the continuing uncertainty. Fortunately, however, there was an etiquette lesson to be learned. Not everybody feels that that saves the day, but Miss Manners does.

One of the airplanes in limbo was filled with increasingly angry passengers, whose mumblings crescendoed into shouted threats. The other consisted of people whose exasperation took the form of exchanging condolences with one another and the crew and recommending philosophical resignation. The passengers who did finally desert the first flight left promising to have their lawyers corner all the airlines personnel, both present and absent, presumably to beat them up in the schoolyard during recess. On the second flight, several people who finally picked up their belongings (known in the technical language of aviation as "personal belongings") and left were heard to murmur "Oh, it's not your fault; good luck to you" as they left. What made the difference was manners. Miss Manners' own manners were, of course, the same in both cases, which is to say, perfect. While she finds it inexcusable that people usually do express their frustrations in rudeness, she noticed that the striking difference in manners among other passengers was directly attributable to the way in which the two crews handled the situation.

In neither case were the crews responsible for the thunderstorms and the resulting unpredictable delays. The first group found that their own irritation with the matter was compounded by passengers asking unanswerable questions, making special requests, and complaining about their own inconvenience. They didn't actually say so, but it was apparent in the weariness with which they fended people off for as much time, and with as little exertion and information, as possible.

The second crew took a less logical position. They apologized repeatedly, as if the weather were, in fact, their fault. Yet they treated the situation as one in which we're-all-in-this-together, offering crisp information with the assurance that "We're telling you everything about this that we know"; complied with reasonable requests to make things more comfortable, such as turning off the background music because some people wanted to work and others to sleep; and offered empathy and advice on individuals' scheduling problems.

Thus one crew offered passengers a more tangible target for their wrath than the weather. It is easier to threaten to sue, boycott, and kill an airline than to shake a fist at an unruly sky. The other crew volunteered to take that wrath on behalf of their employer, thereby reminding people how unreasonable it is to blame an airline for the weather. At the same time, they treated the passengers as reasonable people whose complaints and requests commanded attention.

Miss Manners did notice that neither crew was able to do what she and the passengers really wanted, which was to fly them to their destination. She is grateful that the second one was able, through manners, to give her her second choice, which was to be allowed to read peacefully on the stranded airplane without a lot of fomerly decent citizens making terrorist declarations.

The Passenger's Part

In airplane travel, small infringements can easily have a wide effect on the well-being of many. This is an excellent argument against being sick on an airplane or allowing one's children to be sick. Being sick is the classic case of something that, while not actually rude, causes great discomfort to others. Failing the ability to exercise such control, one should at least be neat about it.

Other forms of helpful behavior include:

- Organizing one's hand baggage before boarding in such a way as to make it possible to slip into one's seat with it and then distribute it overhead and underfoot, rather than standing in the aisle to do so while several hundred people pile up behind you.
- Taking no more than one's share of the amenities—pillows, blankets—and of storage space, and less of that, if possible.
- Cooperating in exchanging seats with people who want to sit together, see the film (if you don't and they can't from their assigned places), or be farther from or closer to the smoking sections (if you don't care).
- Spending as little time in the bathrooms as possible, for which Miss Manners will give special dispensation to do moderate grooming at one's seat.

- Staying out of the aisles and out of the way of moving service carts.
- Not begrudging moving to let those in one's row out when they deem it necessary for whatever reason.
- Controlling one's children so that they refrain from such voluntary actions as kicking the backs of the seats in front of them and endowing them with strong constitutions so that they do not indulge in involuntary unpleasant actions, as referred to above.

The Lone Lady

DEAR MISS MANNERS:

I love to travel alone but find myself prey, inevitably, to males seeking to flirt with me. A quiet, peaceful meal or walk is often intruded upon. I do not wish to hurt anyone's feelings but find that if I am not very curt (rude!), the person persists in making friendly overtures. These encounters put a damper on my entire vacation, as I am very sensitive and brood over having injured someone's pride. Doesn't a woman traveling alone have a right to her privacy? I am plain in appearance and endeavor to appear even more so when traveling in order to discourage such encounters. How might I handle these situations tactfully?

GENTLE READER:

Your request is so polite and humble that Miss Manners can hardly stand it. Do you really believe that you have to efface your own appearance and fret over damage to others' feelings in order to be allowed to walk about without being molested by strangers? It is an intrusion, which may well border on the illegal if it gets persistent, for a man to attempt to force his attentions on a woman who doesn't know him and doesn't want to. That other women may respond to such advances does not make it a social convention that you must apologize for not wanting to follow. The proper responses to these advances are (in order of severity, as necessary if the man persists): (1) ignore him; (2) say "Please leave me alone" and walk away; or (3) say "Please leave me alone or I'll call for help" and walk away.

❧ HOTELS

The word "luxury," when used to modify "hotel," has no more to do with pampering than "adult" has to do with maturity when it is used in connection with "movie" or "bookstore."

Miss Manners, whose days of student-style traveling are over, came by this information the hard way. If you are skeptical that there could be anything difficult about patronizing pretentious hotels, you are probably paying more or less reasonable rates at no-frills inns while cherishing the notion that you would not be treated so rudely if you were paying through the nose. It may be a comfort to hear that you are wrong.

There are indeed novelties available at the higher price, but courtesy, efficiency, and helpfulness are not generally among them, in Miss Manners' experience. Your standard luxury hotel now offers:

- The entire stock of a dollhouse drug store, consisting of items that you would probably not stop to take if they were being given out as samples on the street, but that are intended to give the hotel customer the guilty thrill of making off with something for nothing.
- Bathrobes with tags euphemistically explaining that condoned pilfering does not apply to them.
- A warning that it is unreasonable to leave anything of your own in the room and expect to find it there again, with the advice that anything you care to retain should be locked in the hotel safe during your stay.
- Two chocolates a night, sometimes accompanied by a wee bottle on a paper doily, and snack-and-liquor vending machines disguised as hospitably stocked refrigerators.
- Morning newspapers, although rarely the local one.
- Fancifully done up characters, such as a concierge at an oversized, antiquey-looking French desk, or a person who identifies himself or herself as a butler, to bring you a morning cup of coffee.

The luxury hotel also offers:

- Curt announcements to the weary early morning traveler that rooms are not available before late afternoon—and to the weary late traveler that reservations are not honored after late afternoon.
- A shrug from the reservations clerk when the customer who is not allowed to enter his room wants to make telephone calls, receive messages, hang up clothes, send them to be pressed, or otherwise use basic hotel conveniences and a finger pointed toward the pay phone and baggage claim, which the homeless customer must then negotiate individually for himself, paying out of pocket as he goes.
- The same procedure in reverse when he checks out, so that requests for such related services as luggage transportation, bill, and taxi require individual requests with no time coordination.
- Message taking as a specialized function, unrelated to the original unanswered call and requiring a second telephone call.

In other words, frills and little snobbish embellishments are offered aplenty in luxury hotels, but the basics—service and politeness—are not.

What, pray, does any of this have to do with etiquette? It is not Miss Manners' place to suggest that even though most rooms may be occupied until checkout time, there could still be an attempt to match the ones that are vacated early with the early arrivals, or that related services could be anticipated and performed as a package for the convenience of the customer. It is only her function to explain the very concept of service, which traditionally has to do with making life easier for the client, rather than trying to make up for built-in snubs and frustrations by tipping him or her with small novelty items.

True service can be provided only by thinking people, who have the imagination to put themselves in the place of the customer, figuring out what he or she needs and how it can be most easily done, and who have the largesse and grace to be pleasant about it. Any surly fool can slap chocolates on pillows and serve up self-help advice to people who are desperately in need of being helped by others. Flexibility to meet each need as it arises is the key to good service, rather than mindlessly programmed routines, fancy or not. Only inventive people of good will can, in Miss Manners' opinion, provide true luxury. When she finds them, she is going to send them the chocolates.

Checking Out

DEAR MISS MANNERS:

What is the proper way to leave a room at a hotel? Where do you put used towels, and so on, and is there a difference depending on whether you are staying or leaving that day?

GENTLE READER:

If Miss Manners trusted the ordinary standards of hotel guests, she would point out that service is provided there, and one need not do housekeeping oneself. As the linens are changed every day, there is no need to indicate in the placement of them that one is departing. However, she is afraid that that might be taken as license to use the towels to shine shoes, flood the bathroom, and make off with the ashtrays. The rule is to leave the room as one would leave a room at home if there were a valued maid who would quit if pushed too far.

Traveling with a Television Addict

DEAR MISS MANNERS:

I am going on a cross-country trip with a dear friend who is, unfortunately, a television addict, which I am not. The set goes on as soon as we enter the motel room and stays on as long as we are awake, whether we're watching the program or not. This affects me like a third person babbling away in a corner while one is trying to conduct a conversation or read or write. It's distracting. I turn on the set when there is a program I want to see; I watch it, sans conversation; and then I turn it off. I treat a television program as I would a movie or play. I love my friend, and I am looking forward to the trip—except for the "entertainment." Can you suggest a tactful way (I don't want to start off with an aggravation) in which I could alleviate this situation? We are both middle-aged females.

GENTLE READER:

Television, like smoking and exercise, seems to be one of those emotionally laden subjects on which the most neutral statement can provoke a fight. If one merely confesses that one doesn't watch television, for example, or watches less than other people, one is treated as if one has launched an attack on them. Within such a dear friendship as you describe, you ought to be able to state your preference mildly without seeming to condemn your friend's. Indeed, you must, or you will be driven mad in a situation with which Miss Manners fully sympathizes. (She hates that dreadful drone, but please don't tell anyone lest she give offence to those who like it.) Try saying, "Maybe we'd better get separate hotel rooms, because the television gives me a headache." Either she will respond, "That's silly; it will cost us double, and besides, the fun of the trip is being able to talk," and agree to turn it off, or perhaps you had really better get separate rooms because of what that noise will cost your nerves.

Improving Service

Miss Manners is sadly aware that being rude often gets results from offending institutions when being polite does not. Several people of her acquaintance have explained to her how to get a hotel room when, as only too commonly happens, you arrive late at night, when there is nowhere else to go, and are told by an indifferent clerk that your reservation has been lost or given away. "Tell him, 'All right, then, I'll sleep in the lobby,' and start taking off your clothes," Miss Manners has been told. "Funny thing, they always manage then to find you a room."

Somehow, Miss Manners has never managed to follow these directions. Therefore, she has been several times stranded because no one has bothered to listen to insistence and indignation when it was politely, if firmly, delivered.

Speaking of delivery, Miss Manners spent nearly a week calling to complain that her morning newspaper was not being delivered, without getting any results. A kind-hearted circulation department employee finally took pity on her and explained that the system was set up so that little action was taken until the complainer had called several times and could be characterized as irate. "Do you mean to say," Miss Manners inquired in her wee, ladylike voice, "that the people who are driven berserk by this system and start screaming are the ones whose problems get solved?" Indeed, that was what he regretfully meant to say. So, Miss Manners asked timidly if he would be so kind as to put her down as having been loud and obscene, and he gallantly promised to do this.

Miss Manners has read of a recommendation for getting out of bureaucratic tangles in departing from foreign countries; that one stand in the airport and scream until allowed, or perhaps even encouraged, to leave. She has heard countless stories of people yelling so much in stores that they received service—not because service was due, but because the stores felt that the presence of screaming customers was undesirable.

Much as all this shocks and saddens Miss Manners, it will never lead her to employ rudeness in the cause of combatting rudeness. Satisfaction from behaving well does mean something, and she is not willing to give it up. She wishes, instead, to appeal to the better feelings of those who establish the rules in institutions for handling complaints:

Please, do not teach your public to be rude by ignoring legitimately stated complaints and providing redress only for those who behave outrageously. The more you reward rudeness in this way, the more rudeness you will get. Those people Miss Manners described were not congenitally rude; they admitted to seeming out of control sometimes as an act, when they were not really angry, because they knew that that was the only way to get results. Soon all your customers will be behaving that way because those few who refuse to do so will have gone sadly away emptyhanded.

The formula for soothing complaining customers is:

(1) an apology; (2) a promise to do something; (3) an acknowledgment that mistakes should not happen. (Skip 4: bitter laughter. That is best done privately.)

Employees don't think of this because they are thinking of themselves. They know that they are not at fault, they know that there is no such thing as perfect service, and they also know that customers are equally likely to commit faults—failing to pay on time, for example, or exceeding the bounds of politeness when making their complaints. All these things are undoubtedly true. Where, then, may a customer direct his dissatisfaction? Who is qualified to answer for the company, other than its president, reached at home at midnight, should you be clever enough to discover his or her telephone number?

A proper employee should be taught not to think of himself or herself, when on the job, as an innocent individual under attack, but as the representative of the company, who is therefore able to accept the company's responsibility, express its regret, and pledge its renewed effort. As an impersonal spokesperson, the employee could then state official shock that less than perfect service ever occurs, accept any auxiliary comments to be passed on to those responsible, and even tolerate anger, knowing that it was directed toward the business, not himself.

🌹 RESTAURANTS

The right to use the word "fine" in connection with dining is hereby revoked for all commercial establishments. Miss Manners finds that there is an inexplicable amount of public awe of expensive restaurants and remarkably little knowledge in them of the basics of proper service. In what we shall call the "slow-food restaurants," the use by the staff of intentional rudeness—designed to have the same effect on patrons that cruelty on the part of teenagers has on those who have crushes on them—has blinded people to their ineptness. People would not dare be that arrogant, the customers seem to figure, if they were ignorant. Oh, no?

Do you know a single restaurant that is free of all the following travesties?

- Failing to provide the proper eating utensils, such as dessert spoons, and fish knives for fish instead of meat knives.
- Using improper terms. "High tea" is not scones, cucumber sandwiches, and meringue cookies; that is just "tea." "High tea" is a simple supper, with soft-boiled eggs and cold meats, nothing fancy intended.

- Checking with the lady after being told what she wants to eat, as if the gentleman who reported this were unauthorized to speak for her and there will be a terrible fuss and perhaps a lawsuit unless she confirms the order. (This is a new one, undoubtedly associated with the obsolescence of the custom by which a lady gives her order to a gentleman,, who places it with the waiter. Miss Manners is not defending this odd tradition but only asking that those who still practice it not be cross-examined. You may be sure that no gentleman today would have the nerve to announce that "Madam will have the steak" if Madam had not instructed him to do so.)
- Serving filled plates from the kitchen. (Miss Manners does not expect food to be transferred from serving dishes to individual ones by the table unless the restaurant has pretensions to grandeur and prices that pay the dishwashers. Only restaurants that make a silly show of table-side preparation, expecting the attention of the diners as if they were at a sideshow, seem to do this any more.)
- Making an even sillier sideshow of serving the wine. Miss Manners, who has a weakness for a bit of champagne, is tired of watching gentlemen who know better obliging waiters by going along with the ritual of tasting it. (This is not properly done with sparkling wines, as they go obviously flat if they have turned. Even if the ritual is done correctly, it is rarely done properly, which is to say inconspicuously.)
- Serving any which way. (Food should be served from the left; if there is a crest on the top of the plate, that goes at the top.)

All right, Miss Manners feels better after getting all this out. She does not want to be accused, however, of expecting this sort of service from informal restaurants. She doesn't even really expect it any more in so-called luxury restaurants. Her intention was merely to wipe the smug looks from the faces of those who run such establishments.

Restaurant Service

Miss Manners has lived her life, and plans to go on living it, under the following assumptions:
- that a restaurant is a commercial establishment that sells cooked food to orderly patrons who pay for the service.
- that customers are welcomed by business establishments on a first come, first served basis, and that while many restaurants take reservations for the convenience of both clients and themselves, these, too, are secured in the order they are requested.
- that the United States is a republic, and that being rich or famous does not mean that one is in a different class of citizenship, entitled to preferential treatment.

If there are restaurants that do not subscribe to these ideas, but think that either publicity or bribery is the proper route to special treatment, Miss Manners wants neither to hear about them nor to dine in them. That is not to say that she does not sympathize with people who grow impatient with the service they receive as ordinary citizens, which tends, even in public accommodations without these pseudoaristocratic notions, to be routinely rough and rude. It may interest the sufferers to know, however, that the so-called V.I.P. treatment is, if anything, even worse.

In restaurants, special treatment requires that the object of it devote a good deal of time to socializing with the higher-ranking help. The restaurant owner or manager not only introduces himself or herself, but pauses periodically at the table to chat. Waiters, headwaiters, and wine stewards habitually address the customers in tones loud enough to cover and interrupt the conversation that is going on at the table in order to request or give orders, to require that their memories be refreshed about who is having what, or to beg for reassurance with that new rhetorical commonplace: "Is everything all right?" (Well, it was until you spoiled the mood.) That is when they are trying to be pleasant.

Miss Manners would like to see established a new sort of Business Class, in which the client is neither flattered nor insulted, but merely allotted, in his or her turn, the service for which he has paid.

Asian Restaurants

Having heard that slurping and burping are permitted, getting into other people's food is expected, and tooth picking is encouraged—or why would the picks come with the chopsticks?—many Americans have gotten the idea that eating in a Chinese or Japanese restaurant is an etiquette holiday.

Miss Manners invites such people to visit the homelands of these fine cuisines. They will come crawling back to her, full of appreciation for her permissiveness in manners. The East is Etiquette Central, compared with which America's behavioral demands are child's play.

Neither Miss Manners nor American-based restaurateurs expect Americans in their own homeland to have mastered the manners of all foreign-cuisine establishments they patronize. Even when traveling abroad, one is given leeway in retaining American habits in noncrucial matters. Indeed, it is sometimes more polite to appear as a bewildered American than to risk botching courtesies because one doesn't understand important nuances.

While using a visit to a restaurant to practice foreign customs can be instructive and entertaining, patrons are expected to go along with the adaptations that have been made in the service to meet American sensibilities. But the spectacles that the staffs and other diners are often forced to watch are the worst of both sides of the world. Abandoning one's native manners without acquiring those of another culture does not count as one-worldism.

What Miss Manners is suggesting, as a minimal standard of etiquette for Chinese and Japanese restaurants in America, is a compromise. She encourages practicing foreign customs as long as they are properly performed and are of a nature that does not affront Americans.

As a motto, she proposes "Slurping But Not Burping," meaning that yes, you can help shovel noodles into the mouth at close range by means of mild intakes of air, but the pleasurable expelling of air, no matter how culturally documented, is not accepted in America.

Although using chopsticks has become an expected American social skill for people who partake of dishes designed to be eaten with them, it is not shameful for an American to call for a fork. (Knives are not necessary; they have been amply applied to the food in the kitchen.) Those who do use chopsticks should handle them correctly.

Miss Manners is not going to give a lesson here in how to hold chopsticks in order to pin one's dinner morsels in them. She has noticed that such explanations always turn out to be unintelligible, if not nonsensical, even—or especially—when accompanied by drawings with arrow-driven half-circles all over them. But just as an incorrect grip on a fork is not as noticeable as an offensively parked fork (grabbing it with the fist would not be as conspicuous as sticking it in the water glass), the question of where the chopsticks should be placed when not in use is important.

Chopsticks should never be left in a bowl, in a crossed position, pointing across the table, or splat on the table with nothing underneath. They go horizontally across the top of a bowl, on a chopstick rest, if one is provided, or, in Japanese restaurants where they appear in a paper holder, parallel to the edge of the table just in front of the diner, on top of the paper.

Chinese manners permit using one's chopsticks in a communal dish (the modern health prejudice against this has resulted in the appearance of serving spoons), but Japanese manners require reversing one's chopsticks to use the clean end for serving if other serving utensils are not provided.

Lids on bowls should be carefully removed (the really careful technique for a lacquer bowl of hot soup being to squeeze the bottom), the one on the left by the left hand, that on the right by the right hand, and they should be replaced at the end of the meal.

A Japanese meal is properly eaten by alternating foods (except the dessert pickles, but including the soup), with rice first and then between bites from other dishes. Chinese meals are properly eaten course by course.

While the rice bowl is lifted to the mouth, it is not supposed to have other parts of the meal in it, but rice only. The bowl is placed on the table after being filled, before a bite is taken, and eating the last kernel signifies that one has had enough.

Bones that must be removed from the mouth go via the chopsticks, and fish bones left on the plate must end up in the same order they had when served. Japanese soup is sipped from the hand-held cup, with any solid food in it eaten with chopsticks; Chinese soup is taken from a porcelain spoon.

And oh, yes, there is one thing all the cultures agree upon: Picking the teeth at the table is considered disgusting.

Surf and Turf

DEAR MISS MANNERS:

With a surf-and-turf dinner, the waitress brings a tiny fork with a wedge of lemon pierced on the prongs. This is on the plate; the dinner fork is already in place on the table. How should the tiny fork be used? I use it to remove the lobster tail from the shell and then set it on the plate, proceeding to use my dinner fork for eating the lobster, potato, and beef. Others eat their lobster tail with this tiny fork, and also their baked potato, and then continue to eat with it if they take a piece of meat.

I think this looks silly. I was told that I am wrong and that I should eat my lobster tail with this bitty fork. What is correct?

GENTLE READER:

You are correct. It sure does look silly to eat big pieces of food, surf or turf, with a bitty fork. As a matter of fact, the item is an oyster fork, also sometimes known as a "seafood fork." Basically designed for a first course of oysters, clams, or mussels, it could also be partially useful for extracting hidden morsels from whole lobster, where the chief technique is to tear the thing limb from limb.

For large globs of seafood, lobster tails as well as fish, the proper instrument is a fish fork, to be used with a fish knife. One hardly ever sees such things in American restaurants, more's the pity.

Given the limited choice, Miss Manners would select the dinner fork for eating this entire meal. Life is not long enough to spend the amount of time it would take to eat a potato with an oyster fork.

Fish and Chips

DEAR MISS MANNERS:

Recently, my family discovered a wonderful fish and chip restaurant in a neighboring town. The food and atmosphere are classic English. We have only one complaint: The food is served on paper plates with plastic utensils. My father objects to the uselessness of the knife and fork. He feels that the next time we visit the restaurant, we should bring our own metal utensils. Is this acceptable? How would one go about doing it?

GENTLE READER:

Actually, this is not classic English fish and (like you, Miss Manners is incapable of writing " 'n' ") chips service. The classic way of serving this treat is to wrap it in newspaper. However you may feel about digesting the news, it does make it easier to get fish to mouth. Miss Manners totally agrees with your father that no human being should be expected to eat anything with plastic utensils. Bringing your own flatware to a restaurant is not classic behavior, although you might try to pull it off by merrily unpacking your forks and plates from a wicker basket, as if you believed that the establishment was a picnic supplier rather than a restaurant. It would be safer to ask to use the place as a takeout and simply take the food to your forks.

The Maitre d' and the Hostess

DEAR MISS MANNERS:

When I go to a restaurant with a gentleman friend and we are seated by a hostess instead of the maitre d', when she pulls out a chair and stands behind it, is she seating me or indicating that my friend should seat me in the opposite chair?

GENTLE READER:

We are trying very hard to rid ourselves of meaningless gender distinctions in the working world, and Miss Manners would appreciate it if you would help. It was once believed that formal table service required that men do the job, while less formal service could be done by women. What that meant was that women could get only the lower-paying jobs. "Hostess" is a silly job title, but then so is "maitre d'." A restaurant captain of any kind who pulls out a chair for you means for you to sit in it. An alert person might wonder why, then, the chair is pulled out for the lady. The answer is that in social life the anachronistic but charming system of ladies first still prevails.

Friendly Service

DEAR MISS MANNERS:

In my eighteen years, I have had two jobs—waiting tables and delivering pizzas—and in both have encountered two problems. The first is my name. Both employers require me to introduce myself to customers ("Hi, I'm Jennifer"), probably believing that this sounds friendly. I think it sounds dumb. This practice arms customers with my name. I seethe when these strangers call me by name many, many times in one sitting, as if to prove that they know it. I would like to know if you think my annoyance justified, and what you think of businesses that require their employees to hand out their first names for the abuse of strangers.

My second problem is more serious. I need to know how I can tactfully avoid unwanted flirting and personal questions from customers. I would like to appear as friendly as possible, but I do not think that it is a customer's business where I went to school, where I live, or what time I get off work. How can I not answer these questions? How can I indicate that comments about my personal appearance, even if positive, are not appreciated? Such intrusive behavior on the part of customers makes me feel threatened and unsafe. Do you think that I can still get a tip if I brush off someone's flirting?

GENTLE READER:

Your two problems are related and stem from the national confusion between friendliness, in the sense of offering oneself for social acquaintance, and a pleasant, cheerful, courteous, and mutually respectful demeanor for doing business.

"Hi, I'm Jennifer" is an opening (such as one would properly make at a party, although Miss Manners wishes that even then it would be accompanied by a surname) that suggests social availability. Yes, in a business context, the implication and sometimes, alas, the reality is that you will get tipped more for acting as if you would be pleased to be courted, so to speak, by the customer, a.k.a. flirting.

That is not a dignified position or even a particularly safe one when you are off on your own, for example, ringing people's doorbells to give them their pizzas. Miss Manners asks your employers to revoke such a foolish and counterproductive policy. Hungry people would rather receive food than senseless introductions. Until you or she can get the policy changed, she recommends that you say briskly, "I'm Ms. Renssalaer; please let me know if you need anything."

Special Requests

DEAR MISS MANNERS:

My fiancé and I cannot agree on the proper procedure for dining in a restaurant. If you do not like where you are seated, do you ask to sit elsewhere and suggest a table you would like, or sit where indicated and not say anything? What about asking for alterations in items on the menu? Is this acceptable in a nice restaurant? When a waiter recites specials, is it all right to ask their prices?

GENTLE READER:

While there is no reason not to make such reasonable and polite requests as "If that table isn't reserved, we'd like to have it" or "May I have salad instead of the potatoes?", it is possible that your requests may not be within the restaurant's policy. Therefore you would do better making your requests along with your reservations. Waiters who recite specials without prices need to be gently reminded that they are in the business of selling food. No sensible person wants to order a pig in a poke.

The Napkin

DEAR MISS MANNERS:

After being shown to our table at an elegant restaurant, my husband, son, and I removed the pleated napkins from our plates and placed them on our laps. But my daughter-in-law sat stone-faced and very proper until a waiter arrived and removed her napkin from her plate and placed it on her lap. I have had dinner in many elegant restaurants, and in some the waiter removed the napkin, but in others he didn't. I was under the impression that either was correct. Was my daughter-in-law correct in making it so obvious that we appeared to be ignorant of this procedure? I have no problem with table manners and the social graces, but she has such a superior attitude toward many things and feels that she is correct in everything she does.

GENTLE READER:

There are two different etiquette questions here:

1. The Napkin Question.
2. The Stony-Faced Daughter-in-Law Question.

The Napkin Question doesn't seem to interest you much, but it interests Miss Manners. She has long thought it a ridiculous nuisance, amounting to a minor insult, to have waiters assume the task of putting people's napkins on their laps. Soon they'll be dabbing our chins for us and saying, "One more bite for Kevin-Your-Waiter." If a waiter sees that he will be unable to serve a dish of food because the customer has neglected to move the napkin from service plate to lap, this custom is justified. Otherwise, people who go to restaurants should be trusted to feed themselves.

If your daughter-in-law is really making a show of distinguishing her behavior from yours, and the "stony face" is a conspicuous dramatization of disapproval of the rest of the family, then, yes, she has been rude.

The Order for Orders

DEAR MISS MANNERS:

Please tell me the proper way to order when dining in a restaurant. Do you tell the waiter your choice of entree first, followed by the choice of soup and appetizer, or do you order the way the food appears on the menu: appetizer, soup, and then main course? Or does it matter at all what the order is, as long as you pay the bill?

GENTLE READER:

If you don't pay the bill, nothing else matters, does it?

You see, Miss Manners dealt with the last part of your question first, and not very sensibly at that. But you, like your waiter, can probably sort things out. It is slightly easier on your waiter if you order in order. But most people decide the main course before choosing what they plan to eat first, and all waiters are smart enough to allow for that by leaving space to write in the earlier courses.

Elaborate Place Settings

DEAR MISS MANNERS:

We just returned from a cruise where there were eleven pieces of flatware on the table for dinner: three knives and a soup spoon to the right of the plate, four forks to the left, and a cocktail fork, teaspoon, and demitasse spoon above the plate. Could you please explain the function of each? Coffee was served in a regular cup, so I see no reason for the demitasse spoon.

GENTLE READER:

What you describe is a place setting that is not only incorrect but ridiculous. It was not designed by any standard of correct service, but in order to impress the customers and save the staff work by placing implements for all possible courses you may order on the table at once.

In true formal service, the meal can be fully planned in advance. You do not have to worry about letting people make choices, and then cooking and supplying what they want. Ten would be the maximum number of complements that could be on the table at the same time: a seafood (or "cocktail") fork (nestling in the soup spoon); the soup spoon; sets of forks and knives for three courses (usually fish, meat, and salad and/or cheese; if more are needed for additional courses, they should be brought in separately); and a dessert spoon and fork above the plate. A teaspoon has no place at a formal table because tea and coffee are not served during the meal; after-dinner coffee, formally served in a drawing room in a demitasse cup, requires the small spoon.

Public dining rooms, even lavish ones such as are found on ships, cannot operate in this fashion. Miss Manners thinks that they would do well to put out a basic place serving and then bring in proper implements for eating whatever has been ordered. (If people do wish to drink coffee at the table, for example, the appropriate spoon should be put on the saucer.) Surely that would save on the dishwashing, as well as the self-confidence of the diners.

Only the Food Need Be Warm

DEAR MISS MANNERS:

When dining out and giving my order as well as my guest's to the waiter, how should I indicate what my guest will be having? To say "She will have the Peking duck" seems a bit cold or stilted. But we don't know the waiter, and he doesn't know us well enough to call us Dick and Jane.

GENTLE READER:

In a restaurant, the qualities of warmth and coldness apply to food, but not to the customers' relationship with the waiter. Of course, you must speak in a businesslike manner, not pretend that you are confiding your wishes to a friend. Miss Manners supposes that you do not wish to use the old formula "Madam will have the duck." But surely you can say, "The lady will have the duck." If you can't, well, then, you'll just have to eat duck yourself, so that you can say, "We'll have the Peking duck."

Foreign Language Menus

DEAR MISS MANNERS:

Many restaurants, striving for a certain sophistication or wishing to give their patrons an opportunity to savor a few hours in France, Italy, or some other country, have menus printed in the language of the country represented, often without English translations. No doubt this serves to cow the uninitiated and to prevent uncomfortable questions about the service, the freshness of the food, or the authenticity of its preparation.

I have recently been subjected to mild embarrassment by trying to comply with the demands of atmosphere and placing my order as it appears on the menu unless there is an English translation—for instance, saying, "I will have the *canard á l'orange,* with the *saumon fumé* as an appetizer." While not fluent in French or Italian, I have studied these languages and feel competent to understand and pronounce such common menu terms. However, I was taken aback on several such occasions by waiters who showed, with unnecessary facial contortions, that they hadn't the slightest idea what I was talking about or, equally disturbing, translated my selection aloud into English for the rest of the party to speculate on the unforgivable errors in accent or pronunciation I must have committed.

One such event took place in the company of my boss. As the only woman present, I had to place my order first, and I chose to place it in French. The waiter's reaction not only convinced the remaining diners to make their requests in English but served to make me look as though I were trying to show off in a foreign language, which is certainly not the case. In fact, I would much rather have ordered in English, except that the menu did not contain a single word of that language. I understand that many waiters at this time barely speak English, let alone French or Italian, even if they represent an establishment that pretends to operate exclusively in those languages. Is it correct and even expected, therefore, to translate one's choice into English? Or does one make a valiant stab at the intended language and suffer eyebrow raising and shoulder shrugging as part of the inevitable rudeness of modern times?

GENTLE READER:

Miss Manners is not willing to concede that the unquestionably pervasive rudeness of modern times is inevitable. Do not cooperate in this exercise. Miss Manners does believe in ordering in English. By saying, "I'll have the duck, with the smoked salmon to start," you make it clear that you managed to translate the menu. By the way, she does not think that anyone need be embarrassed to ask a waiter what something on the menu is. If you want to order in French or Italian and the waiter behaves as if he does not understand, call over the headwaiter and say, "I'm afraid this person does not understand my order. Would you be kind enough to take it or to send someone who can?"

The Middle of the Menu Rule

DEAR MISS MANNERS:

When a host is treating several guests to lunch, does he order first and the guests afterward, and do they order the equivalent in price of what the host ordered? Or do the guests order first? In this case, it was a small group and the host ordered first, having soup and nothing else. We felt embarrassed to order a sandwich or dessert; this was supposed to be a treat.

GENTLE READER:

There is a little game that must be played at a restaurant, when one person is acting as host:

1. The host urges the others to order first.

2. They either order something moderately priced (remember the old rule: A lady always orders from the middle of the menu?) or hedge by saying, "Oh, I don't know. What's good here?" or "What are you having?"

3. The host then states his choice or makes a recommendation. They may order either of these or something in about the same price range.

However, if the host's choices are moderately priced and he is willing to spend more, he adds something along the lines of "But of course, the steak is excellent." If he is having something less than a full meal, he is obliged to urge the guests to do otherwise: "I'm afraid I'm on a strict diet, but please don't let me inhibit you. The food is marvelous here, and I hope you enjoy it." As your host seems to have omitted this speech, the guests were obliged to stick with the middle of the menu. Guests are not allowed to go hog wild unless urged to do so but politeness does not require them to have less than a full meal when invited out.

Salad Bars

DEAR MISS MANNERS:

Is it permissible to get your salad bar goodies in a restaurant and start to eat before the others of your party return with theirs? I have seen it done, but at other times, guests have waited. We have been to a number of select supper clubs, and it is crucial to me to feel that I'm doing it in the correct way. Right is right—right?

GENTLE READER:

Right. Wait. Your salad is not going to get cold.

Sharing

DEAR MISS MANNERS:

Often at a good restaurant, I will encounter a dish so delightful that I cannot help wanting to share a taste with my wife. Is this simply Not Done? If it is done, what is the polite way of doing it? Can I feed her off my fork, like a baby bird? Just hand her my fork? Should I cut off a morsel and put it on her bread plate? Should we switch plates? Switch seats? There doesn't seem to be a graceful way of doing this, but depriving her of something I am enjoying so greatly seems the most impolite of all.

GENTLE READER:

As long as the sharing is agreeable to you, your wife, and the tablecloth, it may be Done. The graceful method is to tell the waiter that you plan to share a particular course, so that he can bring an extra plate and fork. This is known as splitting an order.

For spontaneous sharing, use the bread plate method for anything dripping sauce, but the fork is all right for nonmessy items. One way is to offer your plate so that your wife may take something with her own fork. The baby bird version is vaguely romantic. However, the main consideration in choosing which way to do it is not your feeling about your dinner partner but respect for the linens.

Trash on Tables

DEAR MISS MANNERS:

The restaurant my family and friends and I can afford almost always serves baked potatoes wrapped in foil. I never know if I should unwrap the potato completely or just fold back the foil. If I unwrap it, what do I do with the foil? Recently, I had dinner with seven other adults and was embarrassed to find that I was the only one who had removed the foil.

GENTLE READER:

The issue of trash on the restaurant table—sugar packages, cellophane from crackers, potato foil—puzzles people because they assume that it has a right to be there. They also assume that restaurants meet the social standards of correct service, so there must be a correct way of dealing with this rubbish. Oh, Miss Manners knows all about health regulations and all that. She is not trying to ban the little papers but is only cautioning you that they are outside the dictates of proper service. Therefore you must deal with them in the simplest, most practical way, which is to remove them, crumple them to reduce the volume, and place them out of the way on the side of the table.

Telephones at the Table

DEAR MISS MANNERS:

Twice recently I have had the unpleasant experience of dining next to a table where a portable telephone was in use.

Overhearing portions of the conversation was unavoidable because of my proximity to the call and the volume of the conversation. I trust that Miss Manners will not chide me for eavesdropping, as in neither instance was there a vacant table to which I could move, nor do I feel it polite or, for that matter, feasible to attempt to eat with my fingers in my ears.

I deduced from the loud laughter accompanying each call that the conversations were not related to an emergency or to serious business. In both cases, there was one other diner at the offending table who was completely ignored during the phone call.

With this latest technological intrusion upon us, must we diners who appreciate our peace and quiet ask for a separate "no portable phones" section in restaurants? Perhaps Miss Manners would shed some light on how one should deal with this latest distressing battle in the technology-versus-etiquette war.

GENTLE READER:
Your etiquette problem is nothing compared with that of the dining partners of the telephoners. Had Miss Manners been one of them, she might have been tempted to excuse herself politely from the table in order to ring the person up for conversation.

In your case, it is not the technology that interfered with your meal, but the noise. You should merely have asked the waiter for a quieter table.

"Is Everything All Right?"

DEAR MISS MANNERS:
When the waiter or waitress comes by and asks, "Is everything all right?", is this a question of pure courtesy, like "How are you?" Should you always answer "Just fine, thank you," unless you or your dining companion are already suffering from an attack of botulism? If everything is not entirely "fine," should one answer honestly?

1. My husband and I had a meal at a charming, moderately expensive French restaurant. Most of the meal was delicious, but my rice was too salty. I did not eat it, but said nothing to the waitress. On the other hand, when my husband found a ceramic potsherd embedded in his frozen dessert, he gently pointed it out to the waitress. She apologized and told the chef, returning later to say that he had no idea how it got there.

2. At another quite nice restaurant, my steamed mussels tasted strong, almost gamey, and rather unpleasant. I frequently order mussels, so I know how they usually taste. I was hungry and did not think that they were spoiled, so I ate them anyway, but I can't say I enjoyed them. I did not say anything. Later that evening I had an attack of nausea, but since I am in the early weeks of pregnancy, I put it down to that rather than the mussels.

Should I have said something about the salty rice in the interests of helping the restaurant improve its cooking? Should I have sent the mussels back, or is a diner stuck with the dish she orders unless she suspects that the food is actually spoiled? Should I have asked the waiter to taste the mussels to see if that is how they usually taste?

GENTLE READER:
Ordinarily, Miss Manners has a high tolerance for useless courtesies, but this innovation happens to annoy her. It's not just that "Is everything all right?" is superfluous, because a properly run restaurant can assume that everything is going well if the patrons do not complain. One does not generally wait to be asked if one

is suffering from botulism. What irritates Miss Manners is that pretentious restaurants have steadily increased the intrusive interruptions of patrons' conversations, while the standards of actual service have declined. However, if they are going to do this, let us make use of it.

It is not for serious criticism. Such complaints—legitimate complaints are about food that is spoiled, that is seriously misprepared, or that contains foreign elements—should be volunteered as soon as the problem is discovered. A good restaurant will prefer receiving such a complaint to losing a customer, and will correctly respond by apologizing profusely, replacing the dish, and, as an extra courtesy, adjusting the bill to compensate for the problem.

Thus, your husband was definitely right about the ceramic and should have complained about the chef's reaction as well. If your mussels could have been spoiled or your rice was truly inedible, you should have complained about that, too. If those foods were just not as skillfully cooked as you would have liked, you can't send them back. Ordinarily, you can only resolve not to return. But if the waiter is going to ask you, Miss Manners hereby gives you leave to say politely, "Everything else is fine, but I find the rice a bit salty," or "I'm a little disappointed in the mussels; they were so much better here before."

Monitoring Others

DEAR MISS MANNERS:
I took a lady to dinner recently. Before I finished my meal, she excused herself to go to the rest room. It did not seem urgent. That did not seem proper.

GENTLE READER:
It did not seem urgent to whom? What seems improper to Miss Manners is for a gentleman to presume to monitor a lady's private needs.

Clearing Courses

DEAR MISS MANNERS:
At restaurants, is it correct to remove the plates of each person as he or she finishes, while the others are still eating? I find myself being more and more upset by this, especially when I am the hostess. I am embarrassed to see others hurry to finish once the first plate is removed. I have been requesting in advance that dinner plates not be removed until everyone is finished. I have discussed this with others at our club and find mixed opinions. Some people say that they want empty plates removed immediately. I think it is rude.

GENTLE READER:
Interestingly enough, formal service at different periods has also been subjected to this disagreement about whether plates should be removed as each guest signals he or she has finished by placing the fork and knife at the 10:20 P.M. position.

Of course, in formal service, the plate is always replaced immediately by a clean, empty one, not, as in restaurants, by the next course, already on its own plate, or simply by leaving a tableful of crumbs. But even in formal service, Miss Manners is squarely on the side of the wait-till-everyone's-done school. Sitting in front of one's own emptied plate cannot be as offensive as feeling that one must hurry to catch up or attending a dinner where the courses get all out of whack. She congratulates you for informing the club of the service you want, rather than submitting to its choice of practices.

Cockroaches

DEAR MISS MANNERS:

Recently, I entertained a gentleman friend at a social club where I belong. We were enjoying cocktails at the bar when my guest noticed a cockroach near the base of his glass. He quickly killed the intruder and expressed his intention to inform the bartender. I prevailed upon him to dispose of the insect and dismiss the incident. I felt it better to remain silent out of respect to the caliber of the establishment. My guest was of the opinion that although the sighting of one insect was relatively inconsequential, the bartender should be summoned, for he would want to know. I don't want to sound like a snob, but do you agree that given the surroundings, it was better not to cause a stir?

GENTLE READER:

A stir? You mean by screaming, "Eeeeeww! There's a cockroach! Yuck!"? Yes. But a discreetly made remark to someone in charge does not reflect adversely on the caliber of the establishment. To imagine that the club staff either already knows of the presence of insects or doesn't care is to reflect badly on the place.

The proper statement from the staff is, "How terrible! Why, this has never happened before in the history of this restaurant!" The proper action is to refuse to allow you to pay a bill, which inhibits most people from reporting the incident to the health department. Miss Manners is afraid that to encourage this little scenario, you must seem actively repulsed by the cockroach, whether or not you murder it. Save your tolerance for your friends' roach-infested houses.

Coupons

DEAR MISS MANNERS:

A mature, educated, cosmopolitan, above-average-income man frequently invites a similarly situated lady to dinner at various nice restaurants—occasionally the most expensive, but usually the class just below that. Sometimes a coupon is available to the man ("Fifty percent off on second dinner" or "Order two, second is free"). I'm sure you've seen them. Lady objects, "Don't use a coupon when you are with me. Save them for your chintzy friends." And so on. Is it demeaning to be the guest at an unannounced "coupon" dinner? Should the guest be informed beforehand so that she can accept or decline the coupon situation? Or is it not her concern whether the check is paid in dollars, plastic, coupons, rubles, rupees, or whatever satisfies the restaurateur?

GENTLE READER:

Exactly so. A lady does not even notice how the bill is paid (unless she is the hostess, in which case the gentleman becomes unaware of how the bill paying is accomplished), so how can she possibly prefer one method over another?

Fighting for the Check

DEAR MISS MANNERS:

When my husband and I invited two family members and their spouses to dinner at a nice restaurant, our intention was to reciprocate, in a small way, for the many times we had been entertained at their homes at holiday time. When the waiter took the order, my husband asked that it all be put on one check and given to him. During the dinner, one of our guests left the table and made arrangements with the waiter to have the check put on his credit card. No bill was brought to my husband. When he inquired, the waiter said that it had been taken care of. My husband and I were hurt and angry, but made no comment other than to thank him. What do you think of this behavior?

GENTLE READER:

Up to a point, the sport of Fighting for the Check is a good-natured one. One person grabs, another grabs back, and everyone looks robustly generous. But sportsmanship includes the ability to lose gracefully. The sneaky maneuver you describe, designed to defraud you and your husband of your chance to be hosts, was wrong. Miss Manners understands that the waiter was caught in the middle, but he should not have allowed your instructions to be overturned. She suggests that when next you entertain these persons in a restaurant, you instruct the waiter beforehand that he is not to accept their payment.

It is hard to believe that a generous act could be rude, and Miss Manners trusts that your relative did not intend this to be so. Nevertheless, that is its effect. There are occasions when check squabbling is permissible, even expected, among relatives. For example, a young person with limited income ought to attempt to pay checks for older relatives, even though they both know that the older people should not allow it. Never to allow reciprocity is offensive.

Taking It Home

DEAR MISS MANNERS:

What is your opinion of the practice of asking for a container to take home from a restaurant the remainder of the prime rib or the fettuccini or the immense baked potato? It bothers my husband and me to leave good food to be thrown away, yet we do not want to appear gauche by asking for a doggie bag.

GENTLE READER:

The custom of taking home extra food is an ancient one—Roman hosts distributed the remains of dinner parties to parting guests—although today it is applied only to commercial establishments, and not to people's homes. The term "doggie bag" has become a well-understood euphemism. If it is too cute for you, you may simply say, with dignity, "Would you mind wrapping this? We'd like to enjoy it later."

Tipping

Until the beginning of this century, since which time so many things have gone wrong, the custom of tipping was considered highly un-American. To accept a bit of money as an optional handout from the beneficiary of one's honest labor was recognized as a quintessential example of Old World servility, unsuitable to a free and dignified people for whom honest work, of whatever kind, involved regular compensation.

Miss Manners abhors the custom of tipping as a way of completing anyone's wages, since it has long ceased to be a matter of expressing a financial opinion of services rendered. All it means now is that part of the expected wages for certain jobs are paid only at the discretion of the client. It is all very well to imagine that clients exercise this privilege by rewarding hard workers and penalizing poor ones. In practice, it is all too common that those bearing the ridiculous title of "maitre d'" get slipped huge fees for doing nothing scornfully and harried waitresses get nothing for running their feet off.

When this anachronistic arrangement exists—as in the case of waiters, taxi drivers, and hairdressers—one cannot fairly withhold a tip unless under extreme provocation. If one is so provoked, it is courteous and sensible to make the problem known to the person's supervisor. An average tip is now 15 percent; 20 percent is a good tip. The exception is that one does not leave less than a quarter, even if that is a huge percentage, as it might be if one ordered only coffee.

These rules hold regardless of the type of service, even that which consists only in pointing out the route to the salad bar. Service people are on full working duty during the meal. Worrying about how hard they actually work or exactly who should get tipped for what only upsets one's digestion. One need only add the appropriate amount to the bill and give the restaurant the problem of distributing it fairly among the various personnel. When entertaining others in a restaurant, the host pays the tip, thereby avoiding a general discussion of the bill. In a bar or restaurant, it is proper to offer a musician a tip and, if it is unwelcome, the musician may say graciously that it is his or her pleasure to play for you. One need not tip strolling musicians if one would rather they strolled elsewhere, but if one makes requests, one offers one, three, or five dollars, depending on the expense of the establishment.

Other jobs, such as bus driver, pilot, or tree trimmer, are not associated with tipping. There is no logic to the question but merely a crazy quilt of folk custom. Tipping when it is unexpected is sometimes taken as an insult.

So, whatever happened to that grand old American sentiment that tipping is demeaning? Perhaps the anxious people who confide to Miss Manners their worries about correct percentages, the labor force dependent on whimsical generosity, and, most important of all, the employers who believe that an opportunity to collect tips is a substitute for wages could get together and work out a sensible system for full compensation to people who provide needed services. It would be a lovely gratuity for Miss Manners, not to mention the nation.

Tipping Procedures

DEAR MISS MANNERS:

When my husband was alive, he handled everything, so I never thought about tiny details such as how to tip at restaurants. Now many single friends and I eat out together, and sometimes we are confused. It seems each restaurant is different. Fast-food places are no problem. But sometimes a waiter will bring a little tray for our money. We take the tray with our bill and money to the counter. Do we leave the tip behind on the table? In other places, they bring us the tray and we put our money on it; then they return with our change. If the tray is left, do we leave our tips on it? Sometimes, when paying with a credit card, the receipt is left on the table or tray. Are we always expected to tear out our copy and leave theirs? It is embarrassing to take our bill up to the counter and have them tell us that the waiter will handle it from our table. How does one know? It's the pits not having a man around to do the little extras!

GENTLE READER:

Now, now. Ladies can manage tipping just as easily as gentlemen, whose memories we want to treasure for larger contributions to happiness than this.

You pay bills at the table unless told otherwise. Sometimes there are instructions on the bill to pay as you leave, or you could watch what others do, but you should not be embarrassed if the waiter informs you of this practice. Patrons are not expected to know each restaurant's policy. In any case, the tips (unless they are included on the credit slip) and trays are left on the table. In fact, the tips are left in the trays. If you pay at the counter, you take only the bill with you and leave the tip behind. If the waiter does not give you your copy of the credit slip (and, in these sad times, your carbons), you may either ask for them or take them yourself.

The Christmas "Tip"

Once a year, all sorts of unlikely people show up to play—with more or less grace—the otherwise defunct role of the old family retainer. From the person who delivers the newspaper out front to the gang who comes around the back later to pick it up, a varied cast acts out this peculiarly old-fashioned drama. The idea is to suggest to its audience of one the role of generous patron of the working classes.

Miss Manners is not against the custom of Christmas bonuses. Appreciation for good work done is a fine thing, and the most sincere language of the business world is money.

However, the Christmas time "tip" from individual householders to service people whom they do not voluntarily employ, but who are in a position to make their lives more or less comfortable as they see fit, is something in between these two. Miss Manners is not unaware that such tipping often comes less from the overflow of bountiful Christmas feelings than from a hope of not finding the alley's worth of garbage on one's lawn.

The jobs of people who serve blocks or apartment buildings full of householders are not actually designed so that part of the expected fee comes directly from the customer. Nor is it exactly like the end-of-the-year bonus, in which a business encourages merit or heightens motivation among its own longtime employees by monetary awards.

The householder is, however unwillingly, in the position of being a fraction of an employer to someone—or perhaps a series of people—who are assigned to do tasks in or against his or her dwelling. It is, indeed, the custom to tip such people at Christmas time, provided that their real employers do not have a policy against this practice.

Therefore, yes, you must now hand out a few nice round bills this time of year when your door is rattled. (Amounts vary by region and even by the poshness of the neighborhood, but the average is $5 or $10 for ordinary services and more for extraordinary ones.) Miss Manners prefers that the bills be in envelopes, inside cards with a few words of thanks, but knows that the recipients are often willing to overlook the absence of that nicety.

The little bonus itself should be in cash, because that is something we know everyone can use; the rule of showing interest by selecting some appropriate object applies only in the social, not the business, world. If there is a team of people involved, the amount is handed to one of them with the request, clearly within the hearing of the others, that it be divided.

Because such tips are customary, one cannot be overcome with the sense of one's own largesse. One can withhold them if the function that was supposed to be performed all year wasn't done or if the applicant for Christmas tips was not the year-round worker. In such cases, Miss Manners permits the householder to say, "Super? I didn't know there was a super in the building. I asked about it only recently, when my toilet was stopped up, and was told that I should call a plumber." Or, "Hello. I don't believe I know you. When is the regular carrier coming back? I'd like to give him a little something in appreciation for what he's done all year."

Miss Manners hopes that this clears up the immediate problem or befogs it enough so that you will resolve to pretend that you didn't hear the crashing of lids that announces the Christmas season. She is aware that it does nothing to solve the deeper cultural problem. That is that Americans have never been happy with the idea of having servants.

Nevertheless, the fiction leaves a lot of people looking silly. Which is sillier, the surly chap on the front porch pretending that he depends on your generosity for his welfare, or the embarrassed householder who suspects blackmail and fears retaliation, it is hard to say.

Miss Manners' Tipping Guide

General Rules: One tips 15 to 20 percent of the bill in restaurants, hair salons, and taxicabs and appropriate amounts for special services. The minimum tip for small services is a rapidly increasing 50 cents. The greater the service and/or the more expensive the establishment, the larger the tip. In very pretentious establishments, dollar bills are used the way quarters are elsewhere.

Catering: As at a restaurant, 15 to 20 percent to service people.

Clubs: Most prohibit tipping; some have holiday collections. Check with the management.

Coat Checking: 50 cents to $1 per coat, depending on the luxuriousness of the establishment rather than of the coat.

Cruises: Overall, count on spending 15 percent of the cost of the cruise. On short cruises, tip the night before going ashore; on long cruises, tip weekly. Some cruise lines provide tipping guidelines, or one can inquire at the purser's office on board.

Groceries: Delivery, $1.

Hairdressers and Nail Sculptors: 15 to 20 percent, to be distributed among appropriate employees by the management. The owner, even if he or she does your hair or nails, is not tipped.

Hotels: Bellhops (if one can find them): 50 cents to $1 per bag, but $1 minimum.

Concierge (only for special services, such as obtaining hard-to-get theater tickets): $5 to $10.

Doorman: 25 cents to $1 for hailing a taxi, depending on the effort expended and the nastiness of the weather. For help with baggage, same as bellhops.

Maids: The rule, rarely observed, is: For stays of more than one night, $1 a day (can be placed in an envelope in the room before checking out).

Room service: 15 percent of the bill. Double check to see if this has already been added as a "service charge."

Parking: Valet parking at a restaurant, $1. Commercial parking garage, no tip required if you were planning to have body work done on your car anyway.

Pizza Delivery: $1 per pizza.

Resorts: If there is no service charge added to the bill, tip as in a hotel. For meals on the American plan (breakfast and dinner), $1.50 a day for the waiter.

Golf caddies: $4 to $5 per bag or 15 percent of the greens fee.

Laundry or valet service: 15 to 20 percent.

Masseurs and masseuses: 15 to 20 percent.

Pool attendant: 50 cents per day except in Los Angeles, where you are expected to offer a movie rôle.

Restaurants: 15 to 20 percent of the bill before taxes, to be divided among the appropriate employees by the restaurant. If a form has spaces for several people, one may write the all-inclusive tip in large letters to cover several such spaces. Buffet-style service requires full tipping for those who serve the food and provide drinks.

Specific service people need be tipped separately only for extra services:

Headwaiter (or maitre d'): If he must be bribed, $5 to $10 is standard.

Captain: Add 5 percent if he carves the pheasant or flambés the crepes.

Wine steward: Up to 15 percent of the cost of the wine if he makes a special effort.

Restroom Attendants: In America, only if a service is performed. Handing out towels is considered a service; tip 50 cents minimum in such cases.

Shoeshine: 50 cents.

Skycaps (airport baggage porters):   The same as bellhops.

Staff in a private house: Ask the hostess.

Taxis: 25 cent minimum, 15 percent on fares over $1. Drivers in large cities expect 20 percent.

Trains: Dining car staff: As in a restaurant.

Pullman attendants: $1 per night

Redcaps (train station porters): $1 per bag (35 cents of this is a fee levied by the railroad).

Do Not Tip:

Airline attendents.

Bus drivers.

Elevator operators.

Government employees (e.g., police, senators).

Owners of bed and breakfast inns.

Train conductors.

Ships' officers (unless one is borrowing a friend's yacht, in which case one tips the captain).

Your parents.

5

When Business Gets Personal

How to Tell Business from Social Life

Many people cannot distinguish their business lives from their social lives anymore. The people are the same; the conversation is the same; the only difference is in how the groceries are billed. You know it's a business occasion if you can put it on the expense account; if you have to go to the trouble of paying for it and then trying to justify deducting it from your taxes as a necessary professional expenditure, it's considered your social life.

This is awful. Miss Manners sees great progress in the fact that ladies and gentlemen can pursue many different occupations, not just the traditional ones of exploiting serfs and marrying money, but it dismays her that they have forgotten how to act like ladies and gentlemen.

Here are some reminders:

You do not use your own house or that of a friend to make business contacts, collect free advice, or publicize your achievements. Social occasions are for making romantic contacts, offering free advice to people not present, such as the President on what to do about the economy, and publicizing your children's achievements. You do not hand out business cards at social events. There is such a thing as a social card, which may be used, but it carries only your name, and not your Telex, logo, slogan, and the address of your London office. You do not quiz other people, beyond the few pleasantries that help you pick a topic of conversation, on the subject of their occupations or employers, even if you are willing to put in "How fascinating!" at regular intervals. Well-bred people go about socially for recreation, not to seek opportunities to complain or brag about their jobs.

✿ SOCIAL HARASSMENT

Could we please do something about social harassment in the workplace? Unlike the truly sinister problem of sexual harassment, social harassment is intended to be kind, generally disinterested, and often generous. It is directed impartially at ladies and gentlemen, young and old, employees, bosses, and the families of both. It is not a crime, but it can be a nuisance.

Social harassment is the pressure, in big and small ways, to engage in simulated friendship with everyone with whom one does business or hopes to do business. It requires that time, energy, and privacy be surrendered to acts of sociability with people with whom one is thrown together involuntarily during the course of work, rather than through the pure freedom of social choice. It affects the waiter who is expected to engage in flirtatious banter with the customer and the executive who is expected to take important people home with her. It may be dictated by the service person who inquires whether you are married and what you paid for your house when he comes to repair your appliance or by the co-worker who regularly organizes office parties to which you are expected to contribute money as well as time.

Uh-oh. Now Miss Manners has done it. She can just hear the indignant protests: Why, that is simply American friendliness! We recognize that we are all human beings, on the job as well as anywhere else. If politeness requires that we treat one another like robots, then it is just another word for snobbery.

No, not quite. Miss Manners will attempt to explain the difference. Just as sexual harassment has nothing to do with a freely contracted office romance, social harassment is unconnected with extraoffice socializing among people who meet over business. Curmudgeon though she may be, Miss Manners is not against your striking up friendships wherever you may find them. Nor is she for a moment suggesting that one should abandon the cheerful and helpful demeanor that is the proper tone for business as well as private life. Friendliness becomes social harassment only when it is an intrusion:

- Social harassment is having to engage in irrelevant chatter with a customer, co-worker, employer, or employee even when this significantly prolongs the task at hand or keeps other people waiting.
- It is the presumption that you are open to intimate questions or unsolicited personal advice from people you never chose as friends.
- It is being asked to celebrate the personal milestones of people you may hardly know, because they come and go with the normal rate of personnel turnover, but all seem to get married during their stay.
- It is having to commiserate with people about personal problems, when it seems churlish to protest that they translate into your needing to do extra work.
- It is surrendering leisure time, and the right to choose how to spend it and with whom, in favor of such activities as business entertaining or staff retreats.

Miss Manners maintains that none of this is genuine American friendliness,

```
┌─────────────────────────────────────────────────┐
│                                                 │
│                                                 │
│                                                 │
│                  LISA AWFUL                     │
│                                                 │
│                                                 │
│                                                 │
│                          18 COMMERCE STREET     │
│   VICE PRESIDENT FOR IMAGES   BROOKDALE, CONNECTICUT │
│   PERFECT PRODUCTS            (203) 555-1212     │
│                                                 │
└─────────────────────────────────────────────────┘
```

```
                    ┌──────────────────────────────────┐
                    │                                  │
                    │                                  │
                    │                                  │
                    │                                  │
                    │      Mrs. Sean Shame             │
                    │                                  │
                    │                                  │
                    │                                  │
                    │                  131 Primrose Path │
                    │                                  │
                    └──────────────────────────────────┘
```

Two cards for the same lady in her professional and personal identities. The business card could also have read "Ms. Lisa Awful-Shame," but she decided to use the conservative style in order to shock her friends. Honorifics are used on social cards, but not on business cards.

which traditionally recognized the freedom of workers from non-work-related tasks and resisted allowing their job rankings to carry over into private life. It goes against recent American rebellions at the intrusion of the personal—the employee being asked to make coffee or do personal shopping for the boss—into business life.

We have created a phony social world that Miss Manners believes to be a serious threat to our real private domain. She also happens to have noticed that it is a world where work is done at a decidedly leisurely pace.

Payroll Deductions

DEAR MISS MANNERS:

Our company has an Employee Association which collects money weekly through payroll deductions to buy gifts for weddings, new babies, hospital flowers, and funeral flowers. This deduction is voluntary and private, and the rate varies among different employees. The company contributes $200 yearly, and the association has always had plenty of funds. Officers, voted annually, take care of buying the gifts, for which the amount is preset. The problem is this: When people send wedding invitations to the bosses at their homes, should the bosses buy additional gifts even though they do not attend the weddings? The bosses' wives generally don't know the employees. Are they expected to give to anyone who sends an invitation? Is the invitation to the wedding the key to receiving a gift?

GENTLE READER:

Having such a sensible way of dealing with a burdensome problem, you should not sabotage the system. If this were an ideal world, which is to say, if everyone behaved the way Miss Manners knows is best, offices would not perform social duties. (The exception is the funeral, where the boss should make an official appearance and write a letter informing the bereaved of the value of the employee and the esteem in which he or she was held.)

Most offices have frequent collections in which employees are coerced into giving money whether they care about the people or not. Your solution is the next best thing to Miss Manners'. It is not in keeping with this system to make the bosses attend weddings and give presents to people whom they obviously don't know socially (because then the wives would be part of the friendship, too). One is never obligated to send a present to a wedding one does not attend. Friends who care still do, of course, but invitations that are refused because one does not feel close enough to the couple require only a formal refusal and, if one especially wants to be gracious, a separate letter wishing them well. Miss Manners advises your executives to make it a policy to do this until the employees realize that they need not invite them.

Professional Pranksters

DEAR MISS MANNERS:

As a male nurse in a busy hospital, I tend to rush about on my many errands of mercy. One evening, during a mild emergency, I went out to the nurses' station to obtain much needed medications and, to my horror, I was confronted by a mime with a painted-on smile and the obstinacy of a trained professional. I was presented with a rose, which I really appreciated, but the catch was I had to play Twenty Questions, my misfortune being that I was the only one who could speak (mimes aren't allowed to). I quickly explained that I was in a great hurry and couldn't play the game, and this creature mimed crocodile tears and disappointment, as I only got to questions three or four. I blew my professional cool and told the mime that I had to leave, tears or not. Later, I had twinges of guilt. The times being what they are, this may happen again.

GENTLE READER:

Miss Manners doesn't know about the rest of you, but she believes that the charm of surprising and embarrassing people in their places of business, by way of expressing gratitude or congratulations, is worn out. Not everyone is as secretly thrilled at being singled out to be made a spectacle of as the perpetrators of such pranks imagine. In any case, it is an interruption of work that could range from annoying others to (as in your case) creating a serious hazard. Until this dreary fad has played itself out, Miss Manners can only bolster the victims by promising them that politeness does not oblige them to play the good sport if their inclinations are otherwise. It is the premise of the professional interrupter that is rude, not the refusal to play along with it. You were quite right to accept the rose with a word of thanks and then firmly return to work. How the professional prankster deals with this failure is not your problem. At least in this instance, it was in silence.

Compulsory Partying

DEAR MISS MANNERS:

A senior staff member of our organization has adopted the practice of hosting a pool party at his home every summer. These parties are deadly dull, with neither conversations nor activities of general interest. However, the majority feel obligated to attend. Each summer, more and more staff members offer polite excuses for being unable to participate. Alarmed by the high number of negative responses, the host has announced that this summer he will circulate a list of possible party dates, so that each staff member can indicate when he or she is available, and then schedule the party on the date convenient for the majority. Obviously, we cannot all be busy every weekend from now until September. If we are truthful and admit to being free on a particular date, what excuse can we give? No one wants to hurt this man's feelings, but everyone wants to avoid going to this party!

GENTLE READER:

Here is a pitiful example of what is wrong with the idea that businesses should be staffed by friends. The American tradition of entertaining, or being entertained by, the boss has resulted in very little pleasure or productivity compared with the amount of anxiety, boredom, or remorse it produces. Your poor old boss probably doesn't enjoy this any more than the staff does. He thinks he is doing it as a favor to all of you, and while you people are trying to spare his feelings, he is saying to his wife, "I know you hate it, but I can't disappoint the staff; they'd be so hurt."

Let us get everyone off the hook. So that no individual appears surly, send the boss a memo from the entire staff, thanking him for his generous hospitality but explaining that family and other personal commitments make it impossible for you to be sure of keeping clear your off-hours recreation time. End on a note of thanks for the offer, with the deep regret that this results in insurmountable scheduling problems that make it impossible for you to take advantage of his kindness. Miss Manners guarantees that your relief will be nothing compared with that of the boss's family.

Ersatz Entertaining

DEAR MISS MANNERS:

Living in a middle-class suburb, I am subjected to suburban blackmail several times a year. People are no longer satisfied with Tupperware parties—they have diversified into crystal, cosmetics, jewelry, toys, baskets, home decorating, and so on. I think you have the idea. I have had enough!

Are we dependent on these companies for social events? Whatever people's motives might be, I feel more like a dollar sign than a friend walking through their door. Even though the hostess assures me that I don't have to buy, I almost always feel obligated so that the hostess can meet her quota for a free prize. Deep down inside, the whole thing makes me feel tacky. I would like a gracious reply to these overtures in which I can gracefully refuse while letting these people know how I stand on this matter. It's not that I don't want their friendship, but I feel that they are putting a price tag on it.

GENTLE READER:

Miss Manners shares your indignation but disagrees with your analysis. Her question to your ersatz hostesses would be not "Can't you find another way to entertain?" but "Can't you find another way to make money?" It is a tremendous advantage to commercial companies to get people to use social connections and pressures to make sales. Exactly the embarrassment you describe, when one feels obliged to write a check for a friend when one would have no trouble turning down an unknown salesperson, is what they are counting on.

Miss Manners is not lacking in sympathy for those in need of an opportunity to make money at home. She believes that your hostesses, too, would prefer to enjoy genuine social life, and are doing this in the belief that they can combine this with a job in order to make work agreeable and social life profitable. As your reaction testifies, this cannot be done. Even if customers don't mind being treated as friends, friends are bound to resent being treated as customers. Respectable people do not offer their social graces for sale, no matter how hard up they are.

You may certainly refuse to participate in this exploitation, saying, "I'd love to see you some time when you're free, but I'm afraid I just don't like shopping parties"; if you find yourself at one without warning, you may leave as soon as the wares appear, telling your hostess, "Thank you; I was so glad to see you, but if everybody's going to be shopping now, I think I'd better run along." It would be particularly gracious if you then invited the same people to a real neighborhood social gathering.

PRESENTS AND BONUSES

Rewarding the Boss

DEAR MISS MANNERS:

Together with another doctor, I own a medical practice and employ ten people. Each holiday season, my partner and I give each employee a bonus of approximately one week's salary. I regard this as a bonus, not a gift. It is, of course, paid out of our corporate funds and is subject to taxes and other provisions of the Internal Revenue Code.

My employees have chosen to reciprocate and buy a collective gift for me, but I declined in advance because I felt that it was not proper. I think that any such collective gift is really not voluntary but somewhat obligatory. Also, the contributions come out of the individual employees' personal spendable income.

I have tried to distinguish the employees' salary bonus at Christmas time, which is really not a gift, from the collective gift to me, which is something completely different. This has left a lot of ill will on both sides, and my employees were insulted that I declined the gift. Your comments on this matter would be appreciated.

GENTLE READER:

Miss Manners thoroughly applauds you and wishes to encourage you to make your very sensible attitude understood by your employees so that, far from taking offense, they will understand that it is to their benefit. She believes that the poor reaction you received was the result of poor timing.

In the case of employees buying a present for the boss, there is, as you are aware, a coercive element, no matter how much they may genuinely like you. Even if nine of the employees are lifelong associates, overcome at Christmas time with warmth and gratitude toward you that is crying out for tangible expression, the tenth is bound to be a new employee, or one who is in the middle of an office dispute with you, or one who is miffed at being asked to contribute $10 for you when his family is feeling the pinch and has put a $5 limit on presents for relatives. You cannot allow them to go through all that, only to reject the present. Declining in advance means before they do any work.

For next year, begin calling the Christmas bonus a "year-end" bonus and announcing that if the employees are going to give a collective Christmas present again, you'd like to contribute to something you and they can all enjoy at the office, such as a plant or a new coffee machine.

Gender Bias

DEAR MISS MANNERS:

I would like your opinion on how to show appreciation for services rendered by the very helpful staff—two secretaries, a head maintenance man, and two or three maintenance men under him—at the fairly large complex in which I rent an apartment. The custom of the few people I know is to give something at holiday time. They give $10 each to the men and cookies to the women. I wonder how many cookies the women can eat! And why the sex difference? One person said that he gave money to the men and gift certificates to the women.

GENTLE READER:

Money for men and cookies for women? And where are the smelling salts for poor Miss Manners, who has just fallen over in a heap? She thought that the overt practice of treating workers according to their gender had been stamped out by now. But your horrifying example illustrates how deeply ingrained is the misunderstanding on which this is based. It may even be that the gift certificates one person gave the women were equal in value to the cash he gave the men. That still wouldn't make it right.

The distinction is based on the idea that it is not quite nice to give women money. And why is that? Because people have long held the myth, in the face of overwhelming evidence to the contrary, that women properly belong only in the social realm (where there is plenty of work, but without wages), while men divide their lives between that and the workaday world (where money is the chief measure of achievement). The fact that poor women worked for whatever money they could get since the world began did not interfere with this idea, but Miss Manners thought that the influx into the market of women from all levels might have done so.

In the social world, money is a crass present. It means that you have no idea what your friend would enjoy. In the business world, it is inappropriate to try to guess how an employee would enjoy having the money spent; one gives it to him or her to spend. Even a gift certificate is limiting. Miss Manners urges you to give cash bonuses to all of these valued workers. If you can't bear to hand money to a woman, by all means put it in an envelope.

ANNOYANCE IN THE WORKPLACE

The Office Philanderer

DEAR MISS MANNERS:

My employee, a friend and also a most productive salesman, is having an affair, unbeknownst to his wife and four children (with another on the way). My secretary is aware of his philandering, since she must take messages and proffer excuses to clients and family. She is very distraught and allows her angry feelings to show. This is also a frustrating situation for me. Without firing either person, how should I deal with this delicate subject?

GENTLE READER:

Whose problem are you planning to deal with? Your secretary's or the sales-man's wife's? Miss Manners suggests choosing the former. In your capacity as boss, you may, and in fact should, rule that no employee be required to perform any personal service for any other, especially one so morally distasteful as lying. Your secretary should confine herself to saying that the salesman is out of the of-fice and, if queried, that she doesn't know where he is (as she should make it her business not to know where he is off philandering). The salesman must be told firmly to keep his personal affairs, as it were, out of the office.

Since he is also a friend, you are obviously tempted also to deal with the person-al problem. Miss Manners advises you not to do so overtly, either by confronting the man or by informing his wife. The reason that this man is philandering is not that no one has troubled to point out to him that there is anything wrong with it. Nor is it helpful to a woman pregnant with her fifth child to be informed that oth-ers find her in a position that they expect her to consider intolerable. If you wish to show your disapproval, withdraw your friendship while maintaining the formal business relationship. It is more cutting to show that you consider a cad not worth your friendship than it is to express disapproval in terms that will be interpreted as envious.

Unbusinesslike Attentions

DEAR MISS MANNERS:

A young woman member of a professional organization my husband belongs to is blatantly interested in married men. I became aware of this one evening when my husband called to say that he would drop by her house to check it out for a cocktail party for the group and would be home at 7:00 or 7:30. He arrived home around midnight. He was accompanied by another officer of the group, so I was not too worried, but I was a little.

While driving the other gentleman's wife to the ensuing social gathering to join our husbands, I voiced some concern about the morals of this young woman. At the gathering, my suspicions were borne out; however, her attentions were direct-ed toward my friend's husband, and not mine. Despite the gentleman's repeatedly introducing his wife to the young person, she ignored the wife and continually hung on his words, rubbed his back, massaged his neck, and several times ap-proached him from behind and hugged him. He did ask her politely to stop.

I resorted to humor and remarked that I did not want to say that she was cheap, but I had noticed a parking meter next to her bed and a condom machine in the bathroom. Since then, my husband and the other gentleman have quoted this quite a bit, laughing hysterically. Normally, Miss Manners, I do not say such vulgar things, but I really felt provoked.

Now I understand that I am to encounter her at a small brunch next Sunday. Must I speak to her, or may I ignore her? She has turned her attentions to another married man, a good friend, who has several small children. Is there any point in suggesting to her that she turn her attentions to unmarried men? My husband wants to have a party for the group at our home. I do not see how we could avoid having her. May I ignore her then? Nothing overtly rude, you understand; I just don't want to welcome her to my home.

GENTLE READER:

Whatever success this person has in luring married gentlemen into sin, she certainly is succeeding in ruining your behavior. By your own admission, you have already succumbed to vulgarity, and now you are considering cutting your husband's colleague at a party and snubbing your own guest in your own house. If she is as bad as you say, you are also probably amusing and encouraging her.

A lady cannot police her husband's party behavior, much less that of anybody else's husband, however numerous and small his children. She will only make a fool of herself, while alerting others, including the husband and whatever predators he attracts, that he cannot be trusted to behave himself without strict supervision. A great many people, male and female, take that as a challenge.

You can, however, act as your husband's confidential adviser and tell him, in a spirit of trust, how to control distasteful overtures. That he may not have known how distasteful he found them until you cheerfully assumed so is irrelevant. Suggest that he, perhaps with other gentlemen in the organization, remind her that these little gatherings are more professional than social and inform her that they find the atmosphere spoiled by her unprofessional behavior. However much she enjoys threatening other people's marriages, she will not care to threaten her own career.

Friends' Services

DEAR MISS MANNERS:

When one has friends whose husbands are professionals (doctors, lawyers, hairdressers, etc.), what is one's obligation to use their services? I have more than once been coerced into making appointments with friends' spouses with a promise that I will receive discounts or other benefits. I feel very uncomfortable doing this and prefer to continue going to my own dentist, manicurist, and so on, but do not quite know how to go about this without insulting my friends. They are all more than acquaintances, and I have struggled along with them during their husbands' rise to glory. Must I now become their customer?

GENTLE READER:

If you are uncomfortable now, how will you feel if you take on one of these practitioners as a favor and find yourself dissatisfied with his services? Or if one of them absentmindedly asks you at a party if your rash has cleared up? Miss Manners would prefer to handle this problem now. For many reasons she is strongly against mixing business and social life. Fortunately, she is also very good at finding polite ways of stubbornly refusing to be coerced into doing something she doesn't want to do. The one for this occasion is "Oh, dear, I know Judson is a genius, but I can't be disloyal to my Dr. Sprakling, whom I've been going to for years."

Protecting Private Time

DEAR MISS MANNERS:

I find myself constantly being approached by both friends and strangers who want me to make commitments (without my calendar or engagement book to check), answer questions, give advice, and so on while I am innocently going about my personal business on weekends. I'm a reporter for a small weekly newspaper. I work sixty-plus hours per week, days and most nights, and highly value my private time. It is possible, in a busy shopping mall, to pretend I haven't heard my name called amid the hustle and bustle. However, I've been approached while on a date, at the theater, playing sports, even vacationing far from my town. It is frustrating to find oneself without nonbusiness time. I've even been called very early on Sunday mornings to "come to our breakfast in fifteen minutes." How does one politely deal with this menace?

GENTLE READER:

One develops an inability to concentrate on anything else while relaxing. See if you can learn these basic social phrases:

"I'm so sorry, I don't have my calendar with me. Why don't you call me at the office?"

"I'm so sorry, but I've got to finish my errands. Why don't you call me at the office?"

"I'm so sorry, but I'm concentrating on the game (or the play). Why don't you call me at the office?"

"I'm so sorry, but I don't want to bore this young lady with our business. Why don't you call me at the office?"

"I'm so sorry, but I really empty my mind when I'm on vacation. Why don't you call me at the office when I get back?"

"I'm so sorry, but I was asleep and I'm a bit foggy. Why don't you call me at the office?"

Miss Manners also recommends acting surprised if the call does come and making the other person state his or her whole point all over again from the beginning. Once you discover how useful absentmindedness can be, Miss Manners promises that you will never again wish to be taken for someone who is always in full working order.

Performing

DEAR MISS MANNERS:

At a recent dinner with my father's family and other guests, a lady who knows that I am a professional singer asked me to sing. I politely refused, stating that I didn't feel right singing at a dinner where I was a guest. I explained that singing was my profession and that I would prefer to keep work and play separate. When she asked me again, I told her that I had a cold and didn't want to hurt my voice. Again she asked, and I said no, because there was no piano. She kept asking me all through dinner and for about two hours afterward. I finally said (rudely, I'm afraid), "Absolutely not." I had to promise to make her a tape just to shut her up and let me enjoy the evening.

Was I wrong? No one asked my father to do accounting or my mother to type. These are their professions, and I do not see any difference in my refusing to work at a dinner. My mother said that I should have sung because they were flattering me. What they all do not know is that at every party, bar mitzvah, or other social event that any entertainer goes to as a guest, he is expected to perform. I think that if you want an entertainer, you should hire him and not invite him expecting him to "sing for his supper." All of my entertainer friends feel the same way. Are we wrong, or do these other people have bad manners? Help! Everyone still thinks I'm horrible.

GENTLE READER:

Miss Manners would like to invite your parents to dinner. Your father could do her taxes while your mother typed her new book. You don't happen to have a cousin who's an electrician, do you? We could eat by candlelight while he rewires the chandelier. Miss Manners would be happy to flatter these people while they worked.

So much for who was rude. You, in Miss Manners' opinion, were admirably patient. Just keep declining. If you were to give in merely because rude people were insistent, you would only be proving that such techniques worked. You need not have offered to give this person a tape. It would have served just as well to say, "I'm so flattered that you want to hear me. I'll be sure and let you know the next time I'm performing."

"Let's Have Lunch"

DEAR MISS MANNERS:

One of the most frequently heard phrases now is "Let's have lunch sometime," but what this phrase often means is "I actually have no intention whatsoever of having lunch with you." When I was gullible, I thought that people meant what they said, and I responded by suggesting a date and place for lunch. Then my troubles began. I found out, painfully, that the seemingly simple procedure of arranging lunch can be an extraordinarily difficult and humiliating experience. I hereby suggest a lunch scheduling etiquette. Those who violate it do so at their peril. The principles apply to the average professional who has the time and money and is roughly equal in position—with no ulterior business or personal motives.

The first rule is that once you've got past the "Let's have lunch" stage, you should arrange for a reasonably immediate date. I've had friends actually tell me, "Call me in three months; I'm actually crashing on some work right now." That's rude. No job is that busy. I'm not talking about lunch every day—just one day.

Second, if you must cancel a lunch, reschedule it. That seems like the most elementary form of politeness, but on several occasions I've had friends call up an hour before lunch to cancel, saying they were too busy at work and promising to call back to reschedule later—and never doing so.

A third principle is to make every effort to attend a rescheduled lunch. I once had someone reschedule five or six times in two months. No one is that busy.

A fourth principle is to be willing to go over to the other person's place for lunch. I have friends who frequently invite me over for lunch, but when I suggest lunch at my place of work, they are reluctant.

I can't think of a more inexcusable insult than breaking a lunch commitment. I remember such insults; I can't help it. For example, recently I was asked to provide a reference for the person who rescheduled five or six times, and I told the questioner, quite honestly, I believe, that this person was undependable and seemed to have little political sense. So, the next time you encounter someone in the hallway and find yourself saying, "Let's have lunch," do it. That someone might be me.

GENTLE READER:
Who is that person who put business obligations ahead of a social lunch in the middle of the work day? That is the kind of employee Miss Manners would like to have. Had you made this whole eloquent case on behalf of dinner, Miss Manners would have been the first to endorse it. People who treat off-duty social obligations cavalierly are rude.

Lunch time occurs during the working day. It is lovely to have a social break if one can and to take the time to run across town to see a friend. It is also a wonderful time to see people whose spouses one can't stand. All this is filled in around one's professional obligations. The one rule Miss Manners suggests is that those who cannot expect to have guaranteed free time during the day—and although you don't believe it, a great many jobs do require the flexibility of tossing in one's lunch hour—should not make social appointments without warning that they might have to be canceled.

No Obligation Incurred

DEAR MISS MANNERS:
I wish to know what is the correct response to a new and increasingly prevalent form of impoliteness—people refusing to notice one's existence. Examples of this sort of thing include potential employers who never answer or even acknowledge job applications and inquiries, people who promise to phone back and never do,

messages to be forwarded that never get forwarded, or dates who stand up their partners without a word of explanation or a trace of embarrassment. Is there anything to be done about such amnesia, or is it wise to ignore it as best one can?

GENTLE READER:

As long as you are open to the occasional convincing explanation—"I was having emergency surgery, and tried to call you first but passed out during the attempt"—you may make the general assumption that people who ignore you want to avoid you. But you have lumped together some quite different situations, requiring reactions that range from a philosophical shrug to taking high insult.

If you have sent an application to a movie studio asking if there is an opening for a star, you cannot expect the consideration you should get from someone who asked you out to a movie. If you are ignored by a store from which you planned to buy something, the best response is to go elsewhere; if you are ignored by the store's credit department when you attempt to correct a wrong bill for which you are being dunned, you might want to go to a lawyer instead.

The key factor is whether the noncaller, corporate or personal, had an obligation toward you. Anyone attempting to avoid a business responsibility should be coldly pursued, and anyone avoiding a social contract (an overly fancy way of saying breaking a date) in this manner should be coldly dropped. The philosophical shrug is for those who use silence to tell you that your unsolicited professional or personal hopes are doomed. Miss Manners assures you that the comfort of being able to blame them for not replying is greater than that of listening to them spell out why they don't want you.

Mixing Professional and Private Life

Family Visits

Under the traditional system, the rules of etiquette concerning families in the workplace were simple. Rotten at the core, of course, but simple and sweet on the surface. The children visited the office once a year to see where Papa worked. All but the most curmudgeonly co-workers stopped what they were doing in order to teach toddlers to make paper clip chains and let the older children play with the typewriters. "Wouldn't you like to come to work every day, like Daddy?" they would ask. The boss was required to emerge from his office long enough to tell the children that the business simply could not function without the valuable services of their very own father.

Mamma was even luckier. She got to go to all the evening and weekend functions, such as the annual holiday party or summer picnic. The social highlight of her existence was the opportunity to entertain the boss at home, a subject of tre-

397

mendous consternation and elaborate preparations. The outcome of this meal, she was led to believe, was a major factor in her husband's career. Who would want to promote a man whose wife was not much of a cook? Should the husband's career be in the armed forces, diplomatic service, or higher reaches of corporate life, the wife would have a full load of auxiliary duties, the reward of which consisted of the assurance that the institution simply could not function without her valuable services.

Indeed, no business could function without the support and cooperation of the worker's family. For performing the necessary duties of life that work left little time for—running a household and rearing children—to submerging individual preferences when the job called for a move, to supplying the pseudosocial life that gives work a humanistic veneer, a family was required. Although allowances were made for the poor bachelor (with sympathy still never accorded a spinster), he was at a disadvantage.

Now, of course, the worker is as likely to be Mamma as Papa. The children are not asked whether they would like to come to work every day because some of them have to do so. The auxiliary jobs have not been dropped just because there is no one available to perform them. Employers still expect their workers to move about the country and to do evening social duty, and don't particularly want to hear about the conflicts created when there are two workers in the family and no full-time support person.

Miss Manners would like to correct this dreadful situation in a once-and-for-all sweep by restructuring the workplace. By removing the assumption that geographical mobility is important to most jobs, the ugly necessity of weighing crucial interests of family members against one another will be reduced. By ceasing all that business partying so that everyone agrees to compete on the basis of regular workday activities alone, valuable time will be returned to workers for their private lives. The establishment of day-care centers at all workplaces will enable the needs of small children, including emergency access to parents, to be met without unduly disrupting business.

Before Miss Manners can manage to talk everyone into this, she must acknowledge that the strain of coping with the unworkable workplace is a strain on etiquette. Etiquette always gets stuck with putting a good face on inadequate situations. The interim rules are:

Parents who are forced to bring their children to work are responsible for protecting colleagues from possible resulting interruptions. Even the kindly folk who love children and adore bouncing a baby around once in a while can be driven crazy when this becomes a normal part of the job.

No spouse should be either required at or barred from evening business entertaining. However, those who attend should know how to take a turn at playing the supportive role gracefully. They should neither expect special attention nor try to obtain it (especially by announcing, "I'm a person, too").

If ceremonial functions are deemed essential to the business, professional people must be found to perform them. Claiming that family participation is purely voluntary isn't enough when no other arrangements are made. What happens then is that the highest ranking wife, or the one who seems to be most available, or the one most easily made to feel guilty ends up doing the job alone. Appreciation should be shown for true volunteers by giving them whatever professional support is needed. By now, you must see how much easier it would be merely to rearrange the national workplace.

Being Kind to Associates

In complicated events of a professional nature that also had gracious pseudosocial overtones, the gentleman was doing everything to make himself useful and agreeable. One could see, as he calmly and charmingly accomplished the myriad small and large tasks necessary to smooth everyone's way, why he was the trusted favorite of the top executive who employed him and of the company's special visitors. He provided fascinating conversation as easily as quick results when the most trivial services were requested.

The visitor who reported this not only came away in a glow about the event and the company that sponsored it, but wondering whether that particular person might be hired away. It was only when she returned to her own office that she was disillusioned and retrospectively angry.

Another person was engaging a prospective client in a practiced presentation that was going over extremely well. The appeal consisted not only of the expertise that was displayed, but the realization that one couldn't help feeling how delightful it would be to work with such a gentleman. Telling the client to go home and make up his mind was just one of those soft-sell formalities. Obviously, he was already sold. Only what happened when he did that was that he abruptly changed his mind and decided not to go through with it because he no longer wanted to deal with such a person.

In a third case, the lady had no immediate business to perform but was pleased to discover, among the guests at a party, a couple whose financial resources and political connections could enhance any number of projects in which she was involved. Far from showing any excitement over their potential, she merely made a point of being particularly charming to both husband and wife as the ebb and flow of the party seemed to bring each accidentally her way. If she happened to mention some activities of hers that would benefit from their interest, it was only in response to their polite questions and out of an excess of her own enthusiasm for the causes.

As they went to their car, husband and wife exchanged favorable impressions and the desire to see her again, perhaps to hear more about her work. It was only in the car that they crossed her off their list of people they ever wanted to see again.

What happened? In the first case, the visitor returned to her own office to be told by two secretaries that the method of smoothing out difficulties used by the helpful host had been to call them repeatedly, lacing various demands with unpleasant language about their abilities and personalities. In the second case, the professional had directed his entire presentation, and all his charm, to the gentleman member of the couple who were presenting themselves as potential clients, and the lady complained bitterly afterward that her questions and contributions had been ignored. In the third case, the couple had both been courted, but it happened that their teenage son was at the event also, and had been the object of scornful remarks and instructions by the lady.

In societies where rank is based on birth, every courtier knows not to neglect the feelings of consorts, princelings, and ladies- and gentlemen-in-waiting, not to mention mistresses and the masculine equivalent, generally called "favorites." Those close to the throne are crucial in influencing the monarch. We prefer a meritocracy, where individuals rise on their own and are not able to bring others along with them quite so blatantly. Therefore, the family has no professional position, and subordinates have only their own job rankings.

Nevertheless, each person has others—employees, family, friends—who are not there accidentally but because he or she wants them there. To neglect or antagonize such people is tantamount to attacking their protector's honor and judgment.

Business Motives in Social Life

Here are two sad stories with a social moral from Miss Manners.

Sad Story One: Eloise and "Mac" Druffin, a popular couple with a knack for fitting in anywhere, were delighted with their new assignment. Not only was it a significant promotion for him, but everyone in the new town seemed so eager to welcome them. As president of the company, Mr. Druffin naturally had a great many social obligations, but Eloise Druffin was a great planner with a flair for both large parties and small dinners. They were entertained constantly by people in equivalent positions. Although they both put in a good day's work, they were still fresh practically every night for the cocktail parties, dinners, usually in restaurants or clubs, and occasional company trips, which gave them a rich social life. The company paid all the bills, but Mac Druffin had enough polish to get his business exchanges done quietly and to keep the talk pleasantly general. Mainly, anyway, the value was for the contacts.

"Everybody's so friendly here," Mrs. Druffin was fond of exclaiming. "Why, they hardly let us have a night to ourselves."

That was one reason, after the shock of Mr. Druffin's being forced out of his job, that the couple decided to stay in their beautiful new house. The "retirement" had been done gracefully, so there were no financial problems. But there was another shock in store. The invitations dropped off suddenly and have now almost ceased.

"People are so fickle here," says Mrs. Druffin bitterly. "They only cared about us for the job, not for ourselves."

Sad Story Two: For forty-three years, Lois Quiggle had toiled faithfully in the same office, gaining respect, if not promotions. During that time, she had also served as counselor, tear wiper, professional advisor, and romantic confidant to generations of younger people who had come and gone. Occasionally, she still gets a postcard or marriage or birth announcement and tries to put that together with one of those bygone office faces.

Her husband and children knew these people as characters in the anecdotes, sometimes funny, sometimes not, that she told at the dinner table. But her husband has been dead for some time now, and her grown children are living in other cities, so even the names of those who attended Mrs. Quiggle's retirement party would not have been known to them. It was one of the company's better parties, with flowers and presents for the guest of honor, and both funny and sentimental speeches, even though her boss, who had only been there a year, got a few of the stories, which he had asked his secretary to collect from old-timers, somewhat wrong. There were multiple promises about getting together for lunch, but after one trip to the office, when everyone greeted her heartily, but when it happened to be a busy day and they were eagerly discussing new projects she didn't know about, she gave up asking. No one has asked her, either, although several noted on Christmas cards that they planned to in the indefinite future. All those years (she writes to her children), and she has been dropped by her friends as if she had died.

Miss Manners does not dispute that these stories are sad, although she knows that her gentle readers are finding the latter story more sympathetic than the former. Nevertheless, the moral she has to deliver is the same for both, and it is a harsh one. The reason these people do not have friends later in life is that they never did have friends. What they had, however graciously they were treated, were colleagues, and colleagues do not remain with one when one leaves a job unless one has taken the trouble to make friends out of them. Friends are people you invite to your house on your own time (and at your own expense) for the pleasure of enjoying their company. They are people with whom you share deeper interests than the gossip of the workplace and in whose lives you have an emotional stake, as they do in yours. You do not get any professional advantage out of them, nor do you confine your bond to sharing a particular experience—having children at the same time, for instance, or divorces—and seek other friends when you have passed to another stage. Instead, you make yourself interested in stages you might not share, simply because they are occupying your friends.

The Druffins might have spent time preserving their friendships with the couple who introduced them at college, or pursued a new one with their neighbors, if they hadn't been so caught up in a pseudosocial life with people who indeed valued them for his position—as, for that matter, the Druffins judged others. Mrs. Quiggle might have developed the office acquaintanceships into friendships by bringing those people into her life, taking them home, finding interests in common outside of the workplace, and sharing more than the crisis points in their lives. Miss

Manners is sorry for these lonely and embittered people, but she blames it on the illusion that mistakes business contacts for friends.

Barring Dates

DEAR MISS MANNERS:

I am planning to have an open house at my office, to which many women business acquaintances will be invited. It will be on a Sunday, and I do not mind if husbands appear, but I do not wish to encourage dates. I do not know who is married or what their husbands' names are. Is it possible to indicate that spouses are welcome? How?

GENTLE READER:

You are asking for trouble. Miss Manners does not want to be around when you explain that someone's live-in true love (or even a candidate for same, met last week in a bar) cannot attend because your guest is not legally married. The cause of the trouble is not today's romantic mores so much as the hybrid business-social occasion.

If you knew these people socially, you would know the husbands and could invite them by name, omitting the temporary dates of others. If this is truly a business occasion, it should not be held on a Sunday, and not even spouses should be present. Allow Miss Manners to suggest that you hold "open office" in the late afternoon after work. You could then suggest that any woman's husband who cared to stop by to pick her up on the way home would be welcome to join.

The Semibusiness Dinner

DEAR MISS MANNERS:

My husband was recently invited for dinner at the home of a client, a single gentleman who has hosted us both at business affairs in the past. The other guests were an employee of my husband's, another business contact, and his girlfriend. Because my husband did not want to impose on his client, I spent the evening at home with a book. In similar situations, I have assumed that exclusions of one's spouse were an oversight and, when I have been invited to similar events, have asked if I could include my husband. Perhaps I assume too much.

GENTLE READER:

The semi-business dinner, in which it is considered a treat to bring along a private partner for a free meal at the expense of his or her being bored by business talk, is something no one agrees upon. Some people simply refuse to participate in order to have a truly private life; others, like your husband, meticulously treat it as a business event; and still others, the majority, try to extract what social pleasure they can from it.

The only solution is to ask. It may be assuming too much to believe that not inviting a spouse is an oversight, but there is nothing wrong with saying, "Is this strictly business, or is my husband (wife, spouse equivalent) invited also?"

Escorts

DEAR MISS MANNERS:

I am a woman bank vice president, age thirty-five. There is no man in my life at present, nor am I particularly anxious to find one. This is not a problem in my social circle, as I am quite comfortable attending parties, the theater, outdoor activities, and so on with groups of friends, married couples, or single woman friends.

However, my work involves a lot of formal entertaining and socializing, including luncheons, dinners, theater parties, company parties, ball games, and picnics. My problem concerns those events to which spouses are invited. Keeping in mind that I am quite capable of enjoying myself without a partner, and that the problem is strictly one of etiquette, please explain which of the above events requires an escort and which may be attended as a single member of a group, possibly escorted by a married couple.

Does the size of the group, location (private home or restaurant), or time of day make a difference? When I receive an invitation to a company party, how may I determine whether an escort is required, and, if so, how do I gracefully decline the invitation? Please don't dismiss this problem lightly, as single sociable men are hard to find and, when found, are rarely willing to attend more than one of these sometimes boring gatherings.

GENTLE READER:

Dismiss this lightly? Why, you have hit on two of Miss Manners' favorite examples of what is wrong with modern business and social life. The first (which, she notes gratefully, you have been too clever to endure) is the idea that people must go about their social lives in tandem. Refusing to go out without a date of some sort has deprived many people of pleasures ranging from attending the theater to being free to flirt with someone new and has alienated countless hosts who hate being asked to entertain the unknown guests of guests.

The second, on which you seem to be vacillating, is the even sillier notion that one should bring innocent people to one's business functions, even when they are misleadingly designed and labeled to pass for fun. Miss Manners is surprised that so many spouses sit still for these events, which are bound to bore anyone not on the office staff—and a great many who are—and would certainly not subject to them anyone whose company she was planning to save for better things.

Appropriate Thanks

DEAR MISS MANNERS:

My husband and I attended a conference connected with his job. While we were there, we were wined and dined. Is it correct to write thank-you notes for the dinners, or does it suffice for my husband to thank the hosts verbally the next time he sees them? The wining and dining was sales directed, and we thanked our hosts as we left.

GENTLE READER:

What you describe is a pseudosocial event, to which business, not social, practices apply. Thank-you letters are not required. However, for the same reason that your hosts wished to soften you up by giving social airs to their pitch, you, on behalf of your husband, may also wish to charm them by treating the events as if they were social. It is never incorrect to write a thank-you letter.

The Successful Business Party

Using the same crystalline reasoning that has convinced Miss Manners that business parties are cruel, cynical, and—watch out, business world, here comes the insult—inefficient exploiters of time and money, she will now tell you how to give a successful one. Please spare the remarks about who is calling whom cynical. Noting how many others toil in their columns to improve your morals, Miss Manners tries to confine herself strictly to dictating how things should be done, rather than debating whether.

Businessmen already realize that the more luxurious this type of partying is, the more successful it is. If people are entertained more richly by businesses than they would ever be by friends, they are grateful for opportunities to enjoy what they might never experience in private life. What the host businesses often fail to realize is that the more social the occasion looks and feels, the better this whole charade works.

Therefore, you should begin by making your invitations look social. Formal ones not only have the advantage of promising luxury but also create more of a feeling of social obligation than the logo-covered, machine-addressed, frankly business types. Address them to people's houses, if possible, rather than their offices, always using correct names, and those of spouses or whatever the equivalent is in that person's life on the date of the party. Invitations that look transferable don't flatter anyone.

Making people dress up for evening occasions helps fool them into believing that these events are unrelated to the day's business dealings. The site, food and drink, and manner of service should be chosen to resemble those of an individual (with a party budget the size of a corporation's) entertaining his or her friends for the sheer pleasure of it.

Rather than trying to lessen the guest's share of social duties—showing that you don't expect a correct response to your invitation, allowing a guest to be represented by someone else, or failing to have some sort of receiving line to greet people and hosts obviously available to be thanked upon departure—you should have the clear expectation that amenities will be performed. For example, a host-to-guest call, saying, "I don't know whether you received my dinner invitation, but I very much hope that you and your husband will join my wife and me," warns people that you are not to be treated like—well, like some big, impersonal business that is to be exploited with no return.

Far too many people now use their own friends that way, and will attend parties bringing their own guests without permission, failing to greet or thank their hosts, and feeling utterly lacking in an obligation to return the hospitality. That Miss Manners considers truly shocking. If a business goes to all the trouble and expense of entertaining people, and does it in such as way as to allow them to feel no particular indebtedness, that is bad business.

The Promotional Party

DEAR MISS MANNERS:

I will be opening a children's clothing store and am unfamiliar with the protocol for store openings. I have no difficulty with the planning of the retail opening, with some fun promotional-type things for the first day, but should I have a little reception prior to this? Perhaps a wine and cheese party the evening before? I am a little uncomfortable with the fact that all the merchandise will be priced, and I wouldn't want people to feel uncomfortable about that.

GENTLE READER:

Well, Miss Manners would feel mighty uncomfortable inspecting a new store without knowing what its merchandise costs. Do not make the mistake of confusing a promotional party, because of its pseudosocial veneer, with a recreational gathering, even if the second party is for your friends. The purpose is obviously to let people know what kind of store you have, and they can hardly find out if you withhold the most relevant information.

Invitations and Replies

DEAR MISS MANNERS:

We live in an age of junk. We started with junk mail and have gone on to junk telephone calls, junk meetings, and junk social functions. I am on many charitable and political lists for these junk social functions and meetings. I recognize that every civilized person responds to an invitation he intends to accept (except for the "regrets only" invitation, which I do not understand). But when one does not intend to attend (and one could not possibly attend every such function and fulfill any other calling on this earth), is one obligated to communicate that fact? Does every human being have the right to have me communicate with him in some way by inviting me to an event or requesting a meeting?

What I have done, and will do unless you say otherwise, is this: I have instructed my secretary that all invitations to and requests for junk meetings are automatically turned down the second time they are communicated to my office. As for requests for personal meetings and lunches, I have had to give my staff the courage to say, "Mr. Doe will not be able to meet with you at any time. Could you send the information in writing?" or something like that, just as a young lady must deal with the pimply-faced, ugly boy who asks, "May I see you on the first available Saturday night?"

GENTLE READER:

Oh, dear. Miss Manners was so thoroughly with you, probably against all expectations, until you came up with the pimply-faced boy. He must be refused politely, no matter how many times this needs to be done before he understands the hopelessness of it all.

The key distinction, you see, is not how attractive you find the person issuing the invitation, but whether you are in fact dealing with a social obligation at all. We must respond politely to all social invitations. Miss Manners will brook no exception to that rule. As you were pointing out before that unfortunate illustration, the invitations you are describing have nothing to do with social life. They are, in fact, business solicitations, no matter how many drinks are to be served or how often these people try to slap you on the back and call you by your nickname. Miss Manners presumes that you do a certain amount of this pseudosocializing, as nearly everyone does, and observe the niceties of business etiquette with the other people concerned. You keep the appointments you make, for example, and answer invitations to gatherings where your presence might reasonably be expected.

What you so aptly characterize as junk invitations seem to be attempts to lure you into business associations you consider worthless and have done nothing to encourage. Those you may treat as a young lady should a mash note from a stranger, no matter how clear his complexion.

Substitutions

DEAR MISS MANNERS:

My clients host business luncheons and dinners to which executives are invited. I address the invitation directly to the individual and follow with his title, company name, and address. Often these executives cannot attend the function and send their assistants. (How do you suppose these executives became such with these deplorable manners?) My problem is that my clients don't want the assistants. Is there any way of indicating on the envelope that the invitation is for the addressee only? I have been grappling with "Nontransferable" on the lower left-hand corner of the envelope, but it seems a bit harsh. Please help me out.

GENTLE READER:

What you are attempting to do here is to issue business invitations to people whom you have chosen solely on the basis of their current jobs, and then claim that these people refuse to honor them according to social manners, when one is invited only for one's pretty blue eyes. Miss Manners is not saying that you cannot accomplish your objective—only that you must first understand what it is.

Those you invite are not to be blamed for believing that, in requesting the presence of a top representative of the company, you would be satisfied with that of one enjoying the professional confidence of such a person. Indeed, you may want to reconsider barring those who are so obviously on their way to the top. They, too, could confuse the personal with business and believe, when they are themselves presidents of companies, that you unaccountably failed to appreciate them as individuals. However, you may politely keep them out by requiring telephoned answers to your invitations (the most common practice in business anyway) and replying to the proposal of a substitute by saying kindly, "I'm so sorry, but if Mr. Bigg cannot accept, we shall just have to invite him on another occasion."

Reciprocation

DEAR MISS MANNERS:

My husband and I are occasionally invited to social events at the homes of hosts far above our social status—his boss, for example. Typically, these are intimate dinner parties attended by a sprinkling of Big Names—a member of Congress, an ambassador and wife, you get the picture—and we are the youngest people present by a decade.

We'd like to reciprocate, especially for those hosts who invited us more than once. However, we're not sure that the limited facilities in our small basement apartment (we even have folding dining room chairs) would be suitable to entertain guests accustomed to oak dining tables, cocktails by the pool, and cognac by the fireplace. Is it rude not to invite our hosts over, or is discretion the better part of valor?

GENTLE READER:

In polite society, people are supposed to socialize for the sake of being with other people, rather than with oak dining tables or even by or in swimming pools. Youth and poverty are therefore no excuse for failing to reciprocate. For that matter, ambassadors are always professing to be anxious to see how the real people of the country live; by "real," they mean the sort of people who don't entertain ambassadors.

In a democracy, there are few people of exalted rank who have never been personally familiar with modest circumstances. Therefore, you entertain as nicely as you can, given your facilities and resources. The only essential point to remember is never to apologize for the way you live.

Notice, however, that Miss Manners mentioned polite society, which is something different from—well, not rude society, but business society. That is because you described some of these events as being given by your boss, at which your position may well be slightly different. Those who do large-scale business entertaining often draft presentable junior staff members for social duty. Although technically you attend such a party as an equal with the other guests, the fact is that you may be treated with less formality—invited to fill in at the last minute, for example—and expected to do social duty, such as amusing a difficult guest rather than anyone who happens to appeal to you. If such is your position at your boss's parties, you must thank him as any other guest would, but you need not reciprocate.

The Business of Charity

Philanthropic Souls

For a really sour evaluation of the human spirit, listen in on any high-powered fund-raising committee as it plans its year-end "phone-a-thon" or grand charity ball:

"She's always pleading poverty, but all you have to do is to look at what's on her back. That crocodile belt alone! And did you see the coat? We're not going to let her get away with that."

"I notice they only took four tickets. I bet we can get them to take a table if we give them some V.I.P. guest to be at it. Suggest what a good way that would be to impress their clients. I heard they're not doing too well this year, and that could be a real boost."

"One of his partners is a neighbor of mine, and I'll get him to call. He'll be embarrassed not to give big when it's someone from his own firm who earns the same salary he does."

"Let them know that we all know what they paid for that house, and we should decide what percentage we expect them to give."

"She's been made a vice president; try telling her that a hefty donation has always gone with that kind of position."

"They have a lot of rich friends. If one of them won't serve on the committee, at least make them give us a list of names and make calls for us."

"Sure, he's a boor, but you can stand him for one evening. Keep pouring and telling him how great he is, and watch what he does when the auction starts."

"They're new in town. You're going to have to make it clear that if they want to have the right connections, they've got to do better than that."

Mind you, these things are being said by people who have volunteered substantial amounts of their time and energy to raise money for such excellent causes as health, education, and culture. Can you imagine what mean and selfish people might say? Moreover, they are not discussing the presumed callousness of strangers, but what they believe to be the vulnerability of their own friends, colleagues, and acquaintances—emotions that these philanthropic souls are probably projecting from self-knowledge.

Miss Manners is appalled. She doesn't claim that it mightn't be true, but she is appalled. Even if the human impulse to help others and better the world is ludicrously feeble next to that all-powerful urge to seek social status (a vice that seems to have preempted such old-fashioned sins as lust and sloth), Miss Manners would object to this use of it. Yes, she knows that the causes are good. But bludgeoning people with the tools of social embarrassment and toying with their hope of gaining personal advantage are, however effective, also dangerous.

For one thing, this kind of thinking is contagious. Miss Manners assures all you committee members that the minute one of you leaves the room, the others all start talking about what you paid for your furnishings and what you ought to pay for what you think of as friendship or respect. For another, those who think this way demean the very people whose donations ought to purchase them some moral satisfaction. It must be hard to convince yourself that you are contributing to the welfare of others by impressing your own social set or the one to which you aspire. Miss Manners is not naive about the difficulty of raising money by raising people's sense of obligation to others when their sense of obligation to themselves already provides such an effective motivation. Only if those who resist unpleasant tactics also do their share will we be able to afford to wipe out the rudeness.

She suggests that those who are the recipients of these methods rebuff any discussion of their personal finances, ignore suggestions of social or business advantages, and ask instead about the charitable organization—how monies are distributed, what hope there is of alleviating problems, what percentage of the money given actually goes to the problem, and so on. This is a much more dignified conversation for both parties, and you might even learn what your money can do, which ought to be gratifying.

In any case, it is not necessary to let your acquaintances know the extent of your contribution; merely thank them for calling the need to your attention and send in your money directly.

However, if snobbery is really necessary to make the sacrifice palatable, Miss Manners has a super-snobbish suggestion. If enough people said, "Oh, dear, yes, I certainly want to help if money would be enough, but I wonder if the cause could excuse me from dressing up and going out. I do that only for purely private, selfish reasons," a great many charities could be saved a great deal of money. And those who give generously of their time could work on the problems of the poor rather than those of the rich.

Telephone Solicitations

DEAR MISS MANNERS:

Kindly give me your views on and solutions to the outrageous practice of charitable solicitations by telephone at night—often at mealtime, and sometimes very late to out-of-state contributors. These are good causes, but the abuse of privacy and the crass telephone solicitation by absolute strangers have gone too far. My reaction has been to say that I do not accept telephone solicitation and to ask for any requests to be mailed. Perhaps these people should be told to remove my name from the calling list and informed that any future call will end my support of the cause for all time. It is time even for people of good will to tell some charities that they have gone too far in aggressive, insensitive solicitation.

GENTLE READER:

Miss Manners is sadly aware that hard-sell tactics, including attempts at embarrassing people as well as inconveniencing them, are now considered an indispensable part of fund-raising for good causes. People of good will, who are unselfishly donating their own time to such events as "phone-a-thons," will certainly argue that the effectiveness of such methods outweighs their unpleasantness. These techniques will continue to be used unless people such as you make it clear that they are counterproductive.

Miss Manners supports you in this. By all means, you have a right to control your time and to require that solicitations be made in writing, so that you can study them at your leisure. May she, however, discourage you from penalizing the very idea of philanthropy because of this abuse? When you announce your intention of ending your support because of the rude tactics, she asks you to inform the annoying caller that you will donate the same amount of money to an equally worthy cause that has not so offended you. Should you omit doing this and keep the money, you would merely be confirming the notion that no one gives without being bullied.

Public Meetings

Clubs, schools, and civic organizations hold meetings because they want to
1. Collect new ideas and air differences of opinion.
2. Accomplish business.
3. Go home.
Miss Manners has not actually seen this list on any organization's agenda. That irresistible come-on, "We want to hear *your* ideas," is scrawled on the flyer or pronounced breathlessly over the telephone, only by those whose task it is to round up

a quorum. The unscrupulous have even been known to add, "And we promise to get you home early." But the actual agenda contains only item 2.

Nevertheless, Miss Manners has noticed that accomplishing business is of secondary interest to people who attend meetings. In the first half of the event, their priorities are as listed above. In the second half, the order is reversed. When the number of people who are looking at their watches and simultaneously murmuring "What time is it?" overwhelmingly outnumbers the number of people giving their opinions, the meeting is over, whether the person running it realizes this or not.

Let it be noted that Miss Manners is speaking of meetings of more or less worthy organizations, in which participation is voluntary. Business meetings, when participants are being paid for their time and professional reputations may be at stake, have their own problems.

When everyone is volunteering, you would think that the joint cause would be more important than individual egos. That is, you might think that if you had never done volunteer work. Why otherwise efficient and temperate people, many of them demonstrably capable of running the world, should get long-winded and emotional in their extracurricular activities Miss Manners does not pretend to explain. Perhaps it is exactly because their livelihoods are not involved.

In the interests of the hapless functionaries who run such events, Miss Manners will suggest a bit of etiquette to keep meetings bearable.

The lady or gentleman occupying The Chair has, of course, a separate agenda with only one item: Get everyone to rubber stamp decisions already made by those who have bothered to find out what is involved. This is known as Guided Democracy.

But since administering it involves calming down some of the members and making the rest feel that they have contributed to the cause, Miss Manners' item 1 is also on the schedule. And since it is necessary to have the meeting last long enough for the members to feel that attending was worthwhile, but not so long that they resolve never to do so again, item 3 is there as well.

It is item 1 that causes the trouble. Robert has kindly set rules for item 2, and motions for adjournment are not difficult to inspire.

Miss Manners does not eliminate the possibility that people who have not been doing behind-the-scenes work may suddenly come forth at meetings with excellent ideas and valid objections, presented politely and succinctly. She merely notes that unruly and repetitive participants are not unknown, either.

A chairman's first line of defense is to thank the speaker. "Thank you," perhaps accompanied by "I believe that you have made yourself clear," is said crisply to an abrasive speaker. If the object is only to inform a rambling speaker that his time is up, "Thank you!" is called out gaily and loudly, but with a pleasant smile.

Experienced chairmen do not need to pause for breath before calling on someone else. Some use the opportunity to bring in reinforcements—an assertive speaker who will help to squelch reluctance or relapses on the part of the yielding speaker.

A kinder ploy is practiced by a gentleman of Miss Manners' acquaintance, who believes in calling on the inarticulate by saying, "You haven't said anything. What's your opinion?"

Miss Manners rather likes this method, because it draws on a residual sense of fairness in the membership, and everyone has a chance to calm down while the embarrassed object generally voices agreement with both sides.

Her own contribution to getting everyone home is to tell well-meaning people who keep vehemently restating their views what her own mamma used to say to dear Uncle Henry when he did that. "The trouble with our discussions," dear Mamma would say, "is that you think that if I disagree with you, it must be because I don't understand your position."

~6~

Genuine Social Life

Friendship

It is nonsense to think that only your best friend will tell you that you are obviously—desperately—in need of psychotherapy, a redesign job on your face, a new wardrobe to disguise your body, and a stronger bath soap. Strangers on the street will gladly tell you all these things and more. You can hardly stop them.

The need for that best friend you can trust is greater than ever; it is just that the services such a person can provide have changed. Your best friend still tells you things for your own good, but they are things you will not hear from those who are devoted to improving you, rather than devoted to you. Only your best friend will tell you that your party was a tremendous success, that the people who were screaming at each other were having a stimulating discussion, and the reason it broke up so early was probably that everyone had to get to early services on Sunday morning. The person who explains that you should have planned your guest list better and the reason so much meat was left over was that it had been cooked senseless is not your best friend.

Nor is the person who says that you should stick to clothing with vertical lines and not go swimming when anybody is looking until you have put in two or three years at a health club. Your best friend is the one who shrugs when you moan about your physical condition and says, "Well, all I can say is, it certainly doesn't show." According to your best friend, your baby is perfect. Your best friend therefore sees no need to inform you of the corrective procedures available if the child still looks that way when he reaches adolescence.

The person who sees both sides when you confess how a parent or in-law is driving you crazy, and suggests how you can stage a showdown with that person, is not your best friend. Your best friend is the one who agrees how exasperating the situation is, but manages to persuade you that it is bearable because it is also funny. If the problem is with a child, the best friend does not trace it to your child-rearing methods; he tells you that the difficulty is a normal stage, which will pass.

A best friend never admits to having heard one of your stories before. If you realize in mid-sentence that he has, he says that he had forgotten, or that it is his favorite, and he wants to hear it again. Nor does he admit having told your secret. Human nature being what it is, he probably did, but at least he saves you the anguish of remorse for not having been able to keep your own secret yourself.

Does all this mean that you have a liar for a best friend? Someone who will not take the same interest in helping you that the merest acquaintances are willing to provide? Not exactly. It means that your best friend is someone who likes you the way you are, notices your strong points rather than your weak ones, thinks reassurance is a greater gift than criticism, and does not pretend to possess a formula for perfection of which you badly need to be made aware. If you have such a friend, Miss Manners begs you not try to improve him. Cherish him.

Friends' Success

DEAR MISS MANNERS:

How does one handle longtime friends when their fortunes improve and yours remain the same, and who now treat you in a condescending and superior manner because you are still poor, single, working for a living, and so on? This has been my experience on several occasions with old friends to whom I had been loyal and supportive in their times of trouble, and who now have no time for me because of their improved financial or social status.

GENTLE READER:

Miss Manners begs you to make sure that you are not looking for insults. Are they really behaving snidely toward you?

Isn't it possible that your friends' rise was accompanied by time-consuming new responsibilities or interests? True friends understand and sympathize with the new claims without demanding that the pattern of their friendship remain exactly the same.

Can you rejoice in their success without feeling affronted? Can you accept any stylistic changes they may make without considering these symbolic of a wish to reject their past? If you can truly say that you are innocent of reverse snobbery, and that these are people who believe that, being rich, they can afford to throw away old friends, then drop them without remorse. They too foolish to be worth anyone's friendship.

Making Friends

DEAR MISS MANNERS:

I am fifty-eight years old and don't drink or smoke. I am not in the best of health, so I have kept to myself a lot. I don't make friends easily, but I would like a few. Can you tell me what to do?

GENTLE READER:

Miss Manners supposes that if you had it in mind to run an advertisement saying, "Fifty-eight-year-old nonsmoker, nondrinker, nevertheless not in the best of health, wishes to meet same who is also slim, gourmet cook, independent, intelligent, with good sense of humor, fond of old movies and walks in the woods, for discreet, kinky afternoons," you would not be coming to her for advice. Her suggested method for meeting people is a pokier one, but it seems to work better. It is to find a way to be kind to others, and allow the rest to happen as a by-product.

There is no one who cannot find someone less fortunate than himself, or who cannot find some way, within whatever limitations health creates, to be useful. Miss Manners suggests that you inquire around until you find a civic or philanthropic project that is suitable to your capacities and get to know other volunteers.

The advantages this has over the more direct method of finding friends are that once you plunge into work, you will be too busy to think about whatever prevents you from making friends; you will be more attractive to others than all those dreary people who are thinking of their loneliness, because you will be shining with purpose and good will; and the other people you meet doing this will be, as they say in those advertisements, "same."

Apologies

DEAR MISS MANNERS:

My best friend and neighbor accused my son of making annoying phone calls to her, and I am afraid that I lost my temper and used some harsh and insulting language. She remained cool during my outburst, even suggesting that my son seek some kind of counseling. We later found out that my son did, in fact, do these things. He apologized and she forgave him, but she never visits or calls me, and I think I've lost my friend forever. I haven't approached her, either. Who should make the first move?

GENTLE READER:

Your son seems to have done so, and it was successful. The best thing you can do is to follow his example, not by making funny phone calls but by apologizing. If he can plead youth, you can plead an excess of maternal blind loyalty.

Dissolving Friendships

Dear Miss Manners:

Kindly advise me on the subject of how one terminates old friendships. I have a number of friends from past years who have relocated to other parts of the country. My lifestyle and values have come to be different from theirs, so when they moved away, I assumed that our friendships would fade. To my surprise, these folks (three of them, all unrelated) seem determined to cling to our former friendships. During the last three or four years, I have never written or called, and I assumed (wrongly) that they would take the hint! When they call, I am polite but not effusive. When holidays roll around, one of them invariably wants to visit for a week or two. I find their visits exhausting and expensive. Miss Manners, I have no desire to hurt these former friends, but I am close to desperation. How can I extricate myself without being unkind?

Gentle Reader:

Miss Manners urges you not to be too thorough about divesting yourself of old friendships. Lifestyle tastes come and go, but people who stood up for you on the grade school playground or listened to the hopes of your teens become increasingly precious over the years. That is not to say that Miss Manners feels you need to have them in the house with you now. It is your inadvertent good fortune, Miss Manners believes, that your hints enabled you to wind down the friendship, omitting the usual correspondence and calls, without convincing your friends that your true intention is never to have to set eyes on them again. Do the same in regard to visiting. Even the closest friends should understand that having houseguests requires a commitment of time and energy that even people of good will may not be able to make. To avoid opening your door now, you need not slam it in anyone's face or nail it permanently shut.

Enemies

Dear Miss Manners:

I'm unavoidably thrown into occasional business and social gatherings with a person I consider to be utterly corrupt and unprincipled. We have been in eight court battles against each other so far (I won them all), and each of us is assiduously trying to end the other's career. All this is publicly known to everyone at these gatherings. Do I shake hands with this man, make pleasant small talk, and thus behave as an out-and-out hypocrite? Are social lies necessary? Or do I refuse to shake hands with him or associate with him on these occasions? It seems to be a no-win situation.

Gentle Reader:

Etiquette recognizes the category of "enemy" (although only among equals; someone for whom you can routinely make life miserable, such as an employee, cannot be treated as an enemy). As your enmity is public, feigning friendship would be as pointless as it is distasteful, and almost as conspicuous.

Being inconspicuous is what proper enemies owe to their hosts and other bystanders. The skill you need is the ability to miss seeing your enemy, so that you need neither socialize with him nor make a scene. This is called a "cut." You should be able to look past him, so that you need not greet him, and to mumble a sudden general "Excuse me," as if called away, when you would otherwise need to talk to him. A lesser form is to bow stiffly to him without a smile or a word. A severer form is to say, "Sir, I do not know you."

Let us hope that your enemy also retains his manners, which are all the more important when other civilizing forces are in jeopardy.

☙ FINANCING FRIENDSHIP

The old-fashioned way for people to entertain in a style beyond their means was to go into debt or to take up embezzlement. Miss Manners is not recommending either course, but she doesn't care for the new methods either. Nowadays, hosts with grander ideas than budgets look to their employers, their fellow citizens, or finally, their guests to make up the difference. If they can't put the cost on the office expense account or deduct it from their taxes, they ask the guests for contributions.

Miss Manners has long been appalled by people who announce, at strictly social restaurant meals, "Oh, don't worry, my office is paying," or who go so far as to collect each person's share of the bill in order to put the entire sum on their own credit cards and claim it for tax purposes.

Lately, however, she has been hearing about a more honest, but hardly more palatable, device of charging guests for dispensing what used to be called hospitality.

Invitations to wedding anniversary parties, showers, grown-ups' birthdays, retirement parties, and even weddings and religious ceremonial dinners, carry a notation stating how much money each guest should contribute for the honor of attending. She saw one such invitation on which it was charmingly noted that one could pay by check, cash, or credit card. The style used for these invitations is that of the charity function—a quasi-social event at which efforts are made to establish the idea that guests are chosen, as if it were a real social occasion, but for which tickets are sold. At least the motivation for charity events is to raise money for others. The soul of true socializing is sharing—extending hospitality. Whether that happens to be luxurious or humble is beside the point and is usually unrelated to how successful the event may be.

The new motivation for charging guests is, Miss Manners keeps hearing from the people who plan these things, to be able to do something "really fancy" that the host could not otherwise afford. The sheer greed of such an idea is sometimes disguised by the claim of doing it to please the guest of honor—the "special" trappings that children propose to give their parents for their wedding anniversary or that parents propose for their children's weddings. However softened, this idea still is a perversion of hospitality. One does not charge guests. The idea that the style of the party is more important than allowing hosts to exercise their generosity—and perhaps their ingenuity in finding cheap but pleasant ways to entertain—is horrible.

One of the most delightful forms of entertainment, afternoon tea, is also one of the least expensive. Breakfast parties can be as lavish as dinner parties at a fraction of the cost. You can avoid mealtimes altogether and entertain people when they're not hungry, at late morning coffee or after dinner. There are also legitimate forms of entertainment in which everyone contributes part of the food or drink—pot luck suppers or bring-your-own-bottle parties—but these are very informal events, practiced in circles where everyone is hard pressed for either the time or the money to do the full job of being host to all the others. One can also have a club in which funds are collected and members take turns being nominal hosts.

The unilateral declaration that you want to entertain in a more lavish way than you are willing or able to pay for, along with the demand that your guests support this practice, cannot be considered hospitality at all. The person who offers it is not a host but an unlicensed food vendor.

Splitting the Bill

DEAR MISS MANNERS:
If I say, "Let's go to lunch," can the other person assume that I'm paying for her? If so, how do I ask and let her know that it is "dutch" without sounding rude? We are retired females who have worked together.

GENTLE READER:
"Let's go to lunch" does mean a split bill. "I would be very pleased if you would have lunch with me," followed by a suggested date, means that the inviter is willing to pay.

Collecting

DEAR MISS MANNERS:
We asked out-of-town friends, whom we see about once a month, if they wanted to join us for a concert. They didn't offer to pay for their tickets. Should we ask? We feel awkward asking for money from friends. We did invite them, but in our social circle, we often include one another in evenings of entertainment and expect that each will pay his or her own way. On principle, we think we should say something, but we don't want to cause hard feelings over $22.

GENTLE READER:

Consider that you paid $22 to learn how to issue such an invitation, which is not "Would you like to go to the concert?" but "We're going to the concert Thursday. Why don't you get tickets, too, and we'll go together?" If they can't charge the tickets by telephone, you can then graciously offer to pick them up for them.

Ducking the Bill

DEAR MISS MANNERS:

I have been dating a man who, when the restaurant bill comes, will excuse himself and go to the men's room. The last time, when he returned, he stared at the check still on the table and gave me an exasperated look. I realized that his excusing himself at check time was his way of permitting me to pay the bill, and he was upset when I did not. The gentleman makes two or three times as much as I do.

Is it now customary for a gentleman to invite a lady out, choose the entertainment himself, and then manipulate the lady into picking up the check from time to time? I have been under the impression that when a gentleman asks for a date, he pays, unless stated otherwise. I have reciprocated by buying theater tickets, inviting the gentleman home for dinner, and so on. Should I also whip out my wallet?

GENTLE READER:

So that it will be safe for such a gentleman to come out of the men's room? Miss Manners is not sure she wants him out. The gentleman seems to be suffering from confusion about how to apply the new egalitarian principles to old customs. Miss Manners does not blame him for that. It is confusing, even chaotic, but she does not care for his solution.

It is still customary for a gentleman who invites a lady out to pay the bill, unless they both clearly understand in advance that they are paying separately. That is more usually practiced by students, by nonromantic friends, and by business associates than by mature people who are, in some degree or another, courting.

What has changed is that the lady may now reciprocate more openly by doing some inviting herself and paying that bill. (Who makes more money has nothing to do with the principle of reciprocity, although it may have to do with the host's or hostess's choice of restaurant.) What offends Miss Manners, and obviously you, is the assumption that one can divide the host's duties by having one person do the inviting and the other person the paying.

False Obligations

DEAR MISS MANNERS:

How can I avoid buying useless things when a friend's child or another friend's grandchild comes around to sell anything from candy to novelty items? I wouldn't mind if I had the extra money, but I'm pinching pennies to buy things for my own family. I do buy so that I don't hurt friends' feelings and don't lose their friendship.

GENTLE READER:

Just as friendship is not for sale, neither does it require periodic payments. There is no social requirement to buy things from one's friends or their relations, and doing so when this creates financial difficulties is foolhardy. Miss Manners cannot imagine that any friend worth the name will hold a polite refusal against you.

Miss Manners suspects that your problem is that you don't want to disappoint children. Consider, however, how much better it is for them to learn from this experience now, than to grow up ruining parties by hustling. "I am so sorry, but I don't believe I'll take any. But it was nice to see you" is more kindly than an exasperated "Oh, all right" with an order.

Organizing Social Life

"The husband accepted one day, and the wife declined on the next," reported a gentleman of Miss Manners' acquaintance who was trying to perform the impossible modern social task of finding out who was coming to his party. "What worries me is that they're always saying that they never have time to talk to each other. Is she declining for both? I forgot to ask. I suspect that he doesn't even know I talked to her. Then there was the office secretary who promised to give her boss the message, but when I called back a few days before the party because he hadn't replied, she could only tell me that she'd given him the message."

For goodness' sake. Who is in charge of keeping people's social records nowadays? Can't anyone give an authoritative yes or no?

Apparently not. When an answer is given, it often turns out later not to have been authoritative. Supposedly organized people are forever professing ignorance and surprise that the regular social expectations that they failed to meet were really upon them. "I forgot, I have to be out of town that night," they say, or "We're going to something else, too, but we'll try to stop by," or "If I don't need to work, I'll be there." Worse, they simply don't show up and report these excuses afterward, or say they forgot, or say nothing at all.

Miss Manners has heard of the modern malady called fear of commitment, but she hadn't known it was so far gone as to prevent people from committing themselves to dinner a week from Friday, or to terrorize them into immobility when they realize that they are actually expected at brunch. No one is more aware than she of the part played in this by the general decline of manners and the failure to honor the simplest social contracts, no matter how much trouble one thereby causes people whom one claims as friends. She is not unsympathetic about the universal problem of lack of time to perform professional and domestic duties, let alone social ones, but the same people's business schedules seem to work, and those who are too busy to socialize need only decline invitations promptly.

Miss Manners does not fail to consider that superficial problems are sometimes more significant than deep ones. In this case, she suspects it is that nobody is keeping the social records, as married ladies used to do for their families. As a result, nobody feels responsible to the extent of considering social pledges binding.

Once upon a time, the lady of the house could answer invitations because she knew when everyone was free; and she kept track of when they needed to reciprocate, when there were occasions that required buying presents, and when letters of congratulations, sympathy, or thanks should be sent. That was a lot of work, especially as she did a great deal more of it than she delegated. The lady is no longer likely to be in the house, and Miss Manners does not contest the wrongness of assigning this task by gender alone. The work can be divided, but someone has to know when to issue instructions: "Tell them no, we're away that week." "Don't forget to pick up something for Cousin Annabelle's wedding." "Find a free Saturday; we owe everybody."

The every-person-for-himself method of social record keeping isn't working, no matter how many inserts people buy for their notebook agendas. It works only when the individual assumes responsibility for coordinating all aspects of his schedule, and stops trying to claim that his social life fell between the cracks of home and office or husband's schedule and wife's.

A secretary may keep the office schedule, including so-called business entertaining, but with the understanding that bosses are responsible for their private schedules. Those are best kept by one member of a couple, provided that the other has learned to say, "I'm sure we'd love to, but let me check with Clint and call you back," and does so; and that Clint has the authority to say firmly, after checking the family's social records, "Last week, you asked me to accept going beagling with the Pickerings on Saturday. You have to go; we're committed. And don't forget to congratulate her on making partner, unless you've already written the letter I asked you to last week."

The Family Calendar

DEAR MISS MANNERS:

My parents frequently accept invitations to dinners, picnics, barbecues, and so on for the three of us without even asking if I am free to go. So I have to rearrange my calendar for what my mother says is a "social responsibility." Are they being inconsiderate, or am I being ignorant?

GENTLE READER:

What does your family have a refrigerator for? Why aren't appointments posted on its door, so that anyone who seeks to make an engagement for anyone else knows if that person already has something scheduled?

On principle, Miss Manners tries not to call anyone's parents inconsiderate. Shall we say that they are thoughtlessly forgetting that you are old enough to have your own social calendar? Even grown-up children must respond to the call of social responsibility, but that should only be invoked on grand occasions—yes, you must attend Cousin Betsy's wedding even though you hate her, and no, you may not skip visiting Grandpa in the hospital—and with as much warning given as possible.

CONTROLLING SOCIAL LIFE

Let others weep over Little Dorrit or Little Nell. In Miss Manners' opinion, the most poignant scene in all of dear Mr. Dickens' writing occurs in *The Pickwick Papers* after a merry evening: "There was a glorious supper down-stairs, notwithstanding, and a good long sitting after it; when Mr. Pickwick awoke, late the next morning, he had a confused recollection of having, severally and confidentially, invited somewhere about five-and-forty people to dine with him at the George and Vulture, the very first time they came to London; which Mr. Pickwick rightly considered a pretty certain indication of his having taken something besides exercise, on the previous night."

Whatever Mr. Pickwick took—and Miss Manners has always believed the Pickwickian day-after explanation that "It was the salmon" that made gentlemen ill, and not whatever was necessary to wash the salmon downstream—his malady is a common one that needs no outside stimulant. Many unfortunate people suffer from Excessive Fits of Hospitality.

Miss Manners believes that hospitality is a wonderful, indeed a sacred, thing. She is all for joviality and largesse, the open hearth, the lavish larder, and that sort of thing. However, she advocates nothing in excess, not even salmon. Excessive hospitality is the impulse to entertain people who one does not want to entertain or who do not want to be so entertained, or the impulse to entertain people to an extent one does not really want to or they do not really want.

An excessive fit of hospitality may be something as small as refusing to hear of dinner guests' departing, even though the evening has run its course for everyone, or as large as suddenly insisting that new acquaintances become houseguests or casual friends sign on as vacation partners. The open-ended invitation—"Feel free to use our pool (ski lodge, lawn mower, services as a baby-sitter) whenever you like"—is a sure sign of it. The fact is that people generally do not want those outside their intimate circles to "feel free" to partake of what they should retain the right to offer as they see fit, and to have regarded as generosity each time, not as a standing obligation.

Chances are that the people you dread inviting because you have nothing to say to them also dread the invitation because they have nothing to say to you. They may feel as obliged to accept as you feel to issue the invitation, and then they owe you, issue another invitation, and you feel obliged to accept. The result is either misspent time or the vague misery of social guilt. Those subject to Pickwickian fits already know that, not only from sad experience but because their spouses, forced to participate in the results, keep telling them. What they don't know is how to stop. Miss Manners will have to instruct them.

The first step is to examine ruthlessly duties to people whose company one does not really enjoy. If they are relatives or outgrown friends, there are obligations, but these should be kept within reasonable bounds, such as holiday visits or the occasional letter. Cutting back on hospitality may mean the difference between preserving amicability and engendering irritation. Other apparent duties may, under scrutiny, disappear. Two evenings with the neighbors are adequate to establish that you would be happier smiling across the fence than across a dinner table. Somebody should call a halt by not issuing or not accepting that third invitation.

Those who suffer from spontaneous fits, such as Mr. Pickwick's, must force themselves to learn two techniques.

1. Never skip a stage in the development of a friendship. Dinner invitations must come before weekend invitations, and weekend invitations must come before offers to buy a holiday house together.

2. Never carry a datebook. By knowing that you are not fully authorized to make engagements until you check with your spouse, office, or private calendar, you may curb your dangerous tendency. At the least, it will give you something to blame the next day, when you have to call back and cancel.

Declining

If you are home with nothing much to do, you may be surprised to hear that there are legions of people who are indignantly offended to receive social invitations. How dare certain people ask for the pleasure of their company? Oh, perhaps the popular ones wouldn't complain if they were invited to cruise the Aegean during the proper season. They do complain when they receive invitations to showers for ladies at the office they hardly know, invitations to dinner parties from people whose menus they know they won't like, invitations to weddings that are too far away, invitations to office parties when they'd like to go home, invitations from hopeful suitors who are unattractive, or birthday party invitations from neighbors they don't like. The motives behind these invitations, according to their analysis, are social climbing, hope for business advantage, or greed. No one would bother to ask them over if not in the expectation of payment in some form, whether it is prestige or a present.

Miss Manners is thinking of starting a national drive to train the socially besieged to cope with this onslaught of unwelcome hospitality. The campaign will be called "Just Say No, Thank You." An invitation, unless it is to go to another realm, is not an insult and cannot be treated as such. If the inviter's expectation that the receiver would be pleased to attend is wrong, that does not mean that the would-be host must have known that and therefore harbored another reason for offering hospitality.

An invitation is not a summons. People who don't want to attend events to which they are invited have the very simple option of declining these invitations. Provided that they do so promptly and politely, they have no further obligations. They are not required to supply presents (although those who genuinely regret having to decline welcome invitations may want to).

Just Say No, Thank You merely requires that all social invitations (not unsolicited pseudosocial invitations that require payment with acceptance) be answered upon receipt in the form in which the invitation was issued.

To decline a telephone invitation, say, "Oh, dear, I'm so sorry, but I won't be able to attend; thank you for asking me." To decline an informal written invitation, write the same statement. Declining a formal invitation requires using the third person formula used on the invitation:

Dr. Arabella Carmel

Mr. Ivan Johns

regret that they are unable to accept

the extremely kind invitation of

Mr. and Mrs. Simon Nathernal

for Wednesday, the second of September.

Please note that in none of these cases does the invited person flounder about, trying to explain that he would have attended but for overwhelming circumstances. When no excuse is offered, it is assumed that the person would love to attend the event if only it were humanly possible. It is when he or she babbles uncontrollably that doubts arise. Just Say No, Thank You.

Types of Excuses

There is not a lot to be said for the Lame Excuse, but there is something. How is that for a half-hearted endorsement? A Lame Excuse is not the same thing as a False Excuse, a treacherous piece of work with which Miss Manners refuses to associate. In a False Excuse, you make up a series of reasons, which any fool can tell are lies, explaining why you cannot do what you can do but do not want to do.

There are subdivisions of the False Excuse: blatant ("I twisted my funny bone and am lying here in traction") and the more devious theoretical ("I may have to have my appendix out that night"). Miss Manners is unalterably opposed to both. Inevitably, someone will ask you to go dancing that night, and you will run smack into your would-be hosts. This will lead to further False Excuses ("My doctor ordered me to get some exercise, and this was all I could think of at this hour"), each more idiotic than the one before. In these cases, she believes in No Excuse. "I'm terribly sorry, but that night is impossible for me" can mean that you had already planned to be making a public fool of yourself for all to see, so you need have nothing (else) to be ashamed of if caught.

The Lame Excuse is a different matter, because it is designed to let people know that you are not really enthusiastic about what they propose in the hope of discouraging them from proposing it again. It is also an impeccable way of indicating anger without bringing on a direct confrontation. In this way, it is akin to the great art of sulking, because the recipient knows that something is wrong but cannot corner the aggrieved person into admitting it. This is masterfully maddening. There are also subdivisions of Lame Excuses: Literal and Inexplicable. Both, if used properly, are allowable.

Let us suppose that you have been asked to dinner by the very people you saw out gallivanting the night they said they were too sick to attend your dinner, which you then canceled for lack of interest. The classic Literal Lame Excuse, hallowed by its use by junior high school girls of six generations on what they quaintly termed "creeps," is "Oh, dear, that is the night I wash my hair." A more adult version might be little better than "I'm so sorry, but that's the night I always play solitaire" or "No, we promised ourselves to organize the travel slides that night." Miss Manners will permit this only if you do not then allow yourself to be caught. You must actually stay home, although not necessarily pursuing the announced pastime. If the unfortunate who is told this argues ("Can't you do that another night?"), you are not allowed to break down and state your anger, but must continue politely to insist on its validity. For that reason, the Inexplicable Lame Excuse is easier. "It would just make things too complicated" is one version; "I'm afraid I'm just not up to it, but thank you anyway," is another.

Once you get the hang of it, you will find that the Lame Excuse has it all over such retorts as "I wouldn't have dinner with you if you were the last person on earth." It is a social law that evasiveness is infinitely more damaging than the direct insult.

House Rules

DEAR MISS MANNERS:

I am a newlywed and new homeowner, and my husband's and my single friends occasionally visit us, not only on the weekend but also during the week. I am an early riser and need eight hours of sleep to function efficiently at my job. My husband, his friends, and my friends have desk jobs and bankers' hours. When his friends visit and the hour becomes late, I politely excuse myself and retire, leaving my husband to entertain them. Is this proper? When my friends call and say that they are stopping by for a visit during the week, I make it a point to say that I need my sleep and plan on retiring around ten. This has not done any good; they still stay past 11:00, sometimes 12:00—even until 2:00 or 3:00 A.M. on weekends. How can I politely get them to leave without sticking my husband with the task of entertaining them? I am starting to dread their visits. We have tried to explain that we need our rest and also time alone on weekends.

GENTLE READER:

What you need, to go with your new marriage and your new house, is a new policy on entertaining. The old singles crowd informality of dropping in at will and sitting around all night is not working. As hospitable as you may be, as much as you may love all of these dear people, it is your house. You get to set the rules. When someone offers to drop by, reply, "Oh, dear, we'd love to see you, but tonight is out of the question. We're exhausted." (Note that the excuse of tiredness is more socially acceptable than the one of wanting to spend time alone, which, while understandable, not only suggests that friends are intruders but leads to newlywed jokes of questionable taste.) Your method of leaving your husband up with his friends is also acceptable, provided that you make a gracious departure. To speed guests on their way, begin your parties early, and serve the food and drink early. If you find that you really must dislodge people who have no intention of budging, learn to wait for a silence, stand up (this is important—you must both stand up), and say, "It's been wonderful having you. We do so hope you'll come soon again."

Warnings Posted

DEAR MISS MANNERS:

We were recently invited to an open house party occasioned by the hostess' desire to show off her newly decorated apartment. We were astounded to find that the decor included little lettered signs in strategic locations warning the guests "Do not bring food or drink to the living room," "Please do not sit on the bed," and "No drinks or ash trays on the piano." We understand that one invitation was given on condition that the couple's five-year-old child was not to come. Needless to say, most of these guests were put off, feeling that their intelligence had been insulted. I sincerely doubt that future invitations to this particular museum will find acceptance.

GENTLE READER:

Hospitality requires that one trust one's guests to behave themselves. Miss Manners is aware that some of them betray such trust but finds no excuse for treating them all as potential violators. She agrees that the kindest thing these people can do for their hostess is to leave her to enjoy her premises without fear.

Visiting the Sick

DEAR MISS MANNERS:

Recently, my wife and I visited a casual friend who had just come home from a stay in the hospital. After forty-five minutes, she got up and put on the television to watch "Divorce Court." I told her, when she asked if I watched the show, that I am not a television watcher, and, needless to say, we made an excuse and a fast retreat. What is the proper attitude to take in this situation?

GENTLE READER:

Miss Manners is very good at waxing indignant about people who are so rude as to drown out their visitors' conversation with television, and approves of any such visitors making an immediate departure. But just a minute here. You spent forty-five minutes visiting a casual friend just home from the hospital?

While it is an act of kindness to visit the sick, this is not done at the instigation and convenience of the visitee. The hostess, as it were, is sick. Visitors have an obligation not to tax the energies of the convalescent. More than half an hour for a casual friend is excessive; twenty minutes should be the maximum unless you saw that you were visibly cheering and entertaining someone who had recovered to the point where her chief remaining problem was boredom. Miss Manners is not at all sure that this poor lady simply couldn't think of any polite way to drive you away.

Dropping In

DEAR MISS MANNERS:

I belong to a group of lady friends from the old country. We meet once a month, and some of us also visit in between if we happen to be in someone's neighborhood. I have noticed that no one ever calls on me. When asked, I was told that they don't like to make an appointment to see me. Was it wrong of me to ask for a short call before they wanted to visit? I love having someone visit me, but I like to know it in advance so that I can arrange things and make the visit more pleasant.

GENTLE READER:

Miss Manners finds it unfortunate that your friends consider your request a lack of hospitality. To contradict that impression, you should make a habit of saying that you hope they will give you a ring when they are coming to your neighborhood, because you would hate to miss such a visit.

Dinnertime Guests

DEAR MISS MANNERS:

Occasionally, my husband's best friend drops by (no notice) with his young girlfriend, who repeatedly announces that she's hungry. What is the proper response in order to avoid feeding her?

GENTLE READER:

There is no reason on earth that you should make a connection between a visitor's problem of being hungry and the possibility of your providing a solution. A polite response to this rude announcement would be, "Well, then, I won't keep you. You'll be wanting to get home to dinner. So nice to have seen you."

Dogs and Children

DEAR MISS MANNERS:

How can I extend an invitation to my sister in-law and her husband and not include their dog, whom they consider a family member? If there is not a tactful way, how can I limit the territory of the pet while visiting? Miss Manners, I cannot feign allergies. My husband is relying on me to find a solution to this delicate problem, as we both want family harmony.

GENTLE READER:

It's not easy to argue over the definition of family and harmonize with it at the same time. A warning, disguised as an apology, which can also be adapted for children, is, "Our house is just not set up for pets, and I'm afraid it would be unfair to have to be after him all the time." Notice that this establishes the idea that the dog will be confined if they do bring him. In that case, you can establish your good intentions by repeating "What a shame that we can't let him run loose" while standing by your refusal to do so.

Social Obligations for Hosts and Guests

The Extra Person

A most peculiar character used to occupy a curiously privileged position in the literature of etiquette. While other mortals were severely admonished to follow all rules under pain of pitiless scorn from the civilized world, this personage was treated with gentle toleration. It was understood that he would never perform more than the minimal civilities, the omission of which would have condemned anyone else, and he was deluged with gratitude if he deigned to do them. Cajoled to show even basic decency, he was fawned upon in any case. Miss Manners' predecessors were obviously afraid of scaring him away altogether, and it was believed that society could not function without him.

He was the Extra Man. Because he did not have a regular household, because he was presumed to be lonely, and, most of all, because there were more widows than

432

widowers in society and its goal was the Balanced Table, the Extra Man got a free ride. He went to all the best parties but never dreamed of reciprocating. If he actually showed up when expected, properly dressed and sober, he was considered a paragon of politeness; if he sent a note or flowers afterward, he was extolled for his graciousness. The boldest etiquetteers hardly dared more than suggest that he should show "polite attention" to his hostesses when he encountered them elsewhere, as if he might otherwise pass those whose food he had eaten the night before without troubling to speak.

Whatever happened to this popular fellow with the carefree life?

Miss Manners killed him. He wasn't worth his feed.

Society was not immediately ruined in the way that had been supposed. It turned out that dinner partners chosen for anticipated compatibility, rather than gender alone, got along just as well. The Extra Man, under the lax standards he enjoyed, had invariably been declared "frightfully amusing" if he was capable of saying "How d'do" without spitting, but he hadn't really added to the fun.

At first, Miss Manners and her accomplices were pleased with themselves. Part of the settlement was that Extra Women, previously treated as nuisances, should be judged as guests on their personal merits. Unfortunately, as with many attempts to promote equality, the standard adopted for everyone was not the better but the worse of the two that were in effect before. Instead of Extra Men being forced to do their social share, everyone—male, female, married, single, and whatever you call the in-between state—assumed the privileges of being an Extra Man.

Suddenly, there was no one around who led a regular enough life to do a proper share of the entertaining and to perform other niceties. In addition to the plea of being unmarried, the excuses included being overworked, having an overworked spouse, traveling, having a spouse who was away a lot, having children, being in a state of emotional crisis, being young, being old, or having a middle-age crisis. We became a nation of Extra People.

Who is going to play the thankless part of keeping society going for all these people? Those who did not at first take advantage of the ability to declare themselves unsettled—and who except Miss Manners has a perfectly ordered life and is still alive?—soon got fed up serving all these irresponsible and ungrateful people.

Miss Manners would like simply to declare that Extra-social behavior is wrong. But since that doesn't frighten anyone anymore (how Miss Manners longs for the days when it did!), she must argue that its natural consequences are both unhealthy and impractical. The decline of reciprocal social interaction means that more people are going without the genuine relaxation of seeing friends in a nonworking situation. Lack of employment, whether it is through choice, being fired, or retirement, leaves them stranded. It also means that the skills involved are missing when they are needed, as anyone who has tried to give a nonbusiness function, such as a wedding or a children's birthday party, has discovered. It seems that Extra Men and Extra Women, who feel no responsibility to those who would entertain them, are producing a crop of Extra Children.

The Hosts versus the Guests

There are two distinct types of people on the party circuit, whose customs and ideas are so much at variance that misunderstandings are inevitable and bitter clashes frequent. One group is called "Hosts" and the other "Guests." Miss Manners often wonders, considering how little these groups have in common, why they socialize at all. Hosts are by far the more fastidious lot, and she is sure that if they knew anyone else to invite to their parties besides Guests, they would never let those thoughtless people in the house.

For example, Guests firmly believe that the rule about having to let Hosts know whether you are accepting their invitations has been repealed. "Nowadays"—the term to designate a generally lawless state—they explain, "no one expects anyone to answer invitations." Except Hosts, of course. Hosts have never for a moment wavered from the absolute rule that all invitations require quick responses and can cite impressive reasons: They need to know how much food to cook, how many places to set, what sort of a group they will have and therefore who would go well with it, and so on. Guests believe that the bigger the function, the less it matters whether they signify a desire to attend. Hosts are sufficiently intimidated that they prefer to pretend that it is not they who are so petty as to care to know who is coming to their weddings, but a perfect stranger, such as the caterer.

Guests are confident that they are warmly welcome if they show up at something that they did not accept, but also that Hosts will not notice if they fail to show up at all. However, Hosts always notice who attends their functions, no matter how large. Even those who are sincerely overcome with bereavement notice who has attended a funeral and who has not. Even though Guests feel free to enter parties without greeting their Hosts or to depart without saying good-bye, Hosts always notice who has been there, when they left, and what duties they skipped. Paradoxically, the same Guests who believe that Hosts don't notice or care if they attend believe that Hosts are always radiant with pleasure at the additional opportunity for hospitality provided when strangers show up on their doorsteps. Guests therefore feel free to invite their own Guests, all of whom have been assured that Hosts are infinitely flexible about the number of Guests they can accommodate.

These rifts are so serious that even Miss Manners is in despair of persuading such different people to adopt a common code of behavior that will satisfy them both. Perhaps the only solution is for Hosts to entertain only other Hosts and for Guests to confine their visiting to the homes of other Guests.

Remembrance of Things Past

Not having any motivation to pick up self-improvement books, Miss Manners is free to spend her reading time meandering about in the emotional landscape with those writers who are her old friends.

Unfortunately, the majority of Miss Manners' writer friends have been dead for upward of fifty years. They seldom surprise her by bringing out new books. This melancholy circumstance ought to enable her to view their personal troubles with a degree of detachment. Right now, however, she is distraught over an account of the social difficulties of a friend—a whiny friend, it is true, but a valued one nevertheless—who was only trying to entertain a few congenial souls at dinner.

Here is Miss Manners' friend's predicament: Although he didn't feel well, in fact had hardly felt well for a day in his life, and his apartment was as disarranged as the day he had moved into it, he said casually to an editor friend that he would like to have him to dinner some day. The day he had in mind, he later confided to another friend, was years off, but the editor immediately got out his engagement book and mentioned which days he was free. So Miss Manners' friend, cornered, resigned himself to hoping that he would be able to engage a public room secluded enough so that he could survive the evening without choking to death. (Miss Manners warned you he was whiny.) In mid-June, he invited some friends to dinner on July first at 7 P.M., with a recital of music to follow. He planned to have about twenty people. Here are some of the responses:

Mme. Lemaire couldn't give him a definite answer because she didn't know whether she would be back from London by then. Mme. de Brantes apparently had an ill cousin, and she reserved the right to cancel should the cousin die. Mme. d'Eyragues said that she didn't know if she would be spending that time on the banks of the Loire or not. Mme. de Noailles said she probably wouldn't be back from London until July second. Mme. de Chimay said she didn't know whether she would be back from Holland before July third. M. Hahn said he would be in London. Mme. de Chevigne said to be sure to keep a place for her, but later said she wouldn't attend after all. Then she arrived after dinner. Mme. Straus said she would be going to the theater and might stop in afterward, but then said she probably wouldn't. In any case, M. Straus, who was known to dislike the other prospective guests, would certainly be too tired. M. Dufeuille, who wanted to know if Mme. Straus would be attending, said he wouldn't know until the last minute whether or not he would be free. It depended on whether or not some friends of his who were away would have returned. Mme. de La Rochefoucauld, after hearing that Mme. Straus would not attend the dinner, said she was not free. Mme. d'Haussonville said she would definitely come, but without her husband. Mme. de Clermont-Tonnerre said she would come with her husband, but M. de Clermont-Tonnerre's political opinions were such that it was imprudent to invite M. Reinach, who represented the opposite views. M. Reinach's views were acceptable to the host, and M. de Clermont-Tonnerre's were not, but the host owed M. de Clermont-Tonnerre, and not M. Reinach.

The poor host was in despair. Suppose that none of the people who said they might come did? But suppose that he invited others to fill their places, and then they all showed up? Couldn't anyone give him the least idea of what they would feel like doing, he begged.

It was July 1, 1907, and the host was Marcel Proust. All these years later, Miss Manners is joining him in despair. Rather than taking comfort from the fact that guests' manners then were just as bad as they are now, she is desolate about the thought that nothing will ever change.

Issuing and Honoring Invitations

"Reply early and win a prize!" This exhortation was reported to Miss Manners by a gentleman of her acquaintance who found it not on the back of a cereal box, but on an otherwise conventionally engraved and worded wedding invitation from respectable friends. Oh. A new social form. A new version of "The favour of a reply is requested" or "Répondez s'il vous plaît." No doubt, it will soon catch on and be abbreviated as "R.e.w.p."

A whiff of smelling salts soon restored Miss Manners, and she was kindly helped up from the floor and into a chair. When she was feeling quite herself again, she reflected that such is the logical outcome of a situation she has long been following with dismay.

Traditionally, social invitations contained no instructions whatsoever about replying. Common sense and common decency so obviously required allowing party givers to know who would attend that it would have been insulting to point this out. How much humanity does it require to recognize the callousness of friends' ignoring your hospitable overtures? However, it has gotten harder and harder to insult people by assuming that they have no manners or consideration, and so the "R.s.v.p." was born—the discreet reminder in the corner of the invitation that yes, we really do care this time.

This conceded that it was not worth the effort to get replies for certain types of parties, and so hosts would concentrate their forces on the important ones. The trade-off was a willingness to pay for wasted cocktail party hors d'oeuvres if they could get a head count for expensive dinners. It wasn't successful, and even more coercion was attempted. The horrible preprinted "R.s.v.p." card, already stamped, was included so that the guest wouldn't be taxed with the job of writing. Telephone numbers were supplied. Then there was "Regrets only," an oddity that puts the host in the amusing position of assuming that everyone who refuses regrets having to do so.

None of these ploys works, as Miss Manners is constantly hearing from desperate hosts. All she can advise them to do is to telephone the people they invited and politely state, "We do hope we'll have the pleasure of seeing you next Saturday." Miss Manners' confidence that this would produce shame, or at least results, in the delinquent guests seems to have been unfounded. People who have tried it report that the supposedly cornered guests reply airily, "Well, we'll try to make it."

That bribery is now being attempted in order to force people to answer wedding invitations should not be a surprise. Miss Manners is only waiting to hear about lawsuits in which hosts will attempt to recover from prospective guests the expense of providing for those who refuse to indicate whether they will attend.

Teaching Children

DEAR MISS MANNERS:

I enjoy creating special occasions, inviting people whom I like and respect to have Sunday afternoon lunch in my home. I have sit-down, planned meals. Children are treated with the same courtesy as all other guests. Having the parents and children mix is part of my pleasure. I invited four friends who have little girls between eight and ten, all of whom are intelligent, attractive, and active. All of the guests accepted by telephone.

On the morning of the day for which the luncheon was planned, one of the guests called to say that a friend had asked her to do something else, and that she and her daughter would come to see me on the following Sunday. I thanked her for calling but explained that I would not be at home the following Sunday, as I have work commitments on many Sundays. She said that her daughter would be very disappointed because the little girl remembered visiting me when she was eight.

My problem is that I feel guilty. Should I include them next year with the eleven- to thirteen-year-olds and their mothers?

GENTLE READER:

You feel guilty? It seems to Miss Manners that you have given an event of rare charm and reacted with restraint when your hospitality was shamefully abused. She only asks that you try not to take the mother's bad manners out on the daughter. Would you consider inviting the daughter out alone? Then you can gently say to the mother, "Please tell Melissa that this is a firm date now; I'm going to make plans, and I will count on her being there."

Vague Invitations

For examples of the comparative social contract in different cultures, Miss Manners is indebted to Mr. Edward Hall and his interesting book, *The Silent Language.* Writing in 1959, he noted, for example, that in American social life, "a girl feels insulted when she is asked for a date at the last minute by someone whom she doesn't know very well, and the person who extends an invitation to a dinner party with only three or four days' notice has to apologize. How different from the people of the Middle East, with whom it is pointless to make an appointment too far in advance, because the informal structure of their time system places everything beyond a week into a single category of 'future,' in which plans tend to 'slip off, their minds.''

In view of the fact that quite a few Americans—whom Miss Manners is too discreet to name—now accept last-minute dates from people they don't know at all, perhaps it is time to state the system which is in current use in America:

An invitation issued and accepted by people attending a cocktail party is binding only if (1) it is to take place within the next hour or (2) both parties take out their pocket engagement books and write it down.

"You must come to dinner with us" is not an invitation at all, but only a statement of genial intent. "Let's get together," "Come by and see us some evening," and "We must do something" are merely indications that an actual invitation will be made or welcomed in the future. A genuine invitation, issued by voice or by mail, includes a date and a time: "You must come to dinner with us! How about Saturday the seventh at seven-thirty?"

Written invitations should be addressed by name to the people expected to attend, even if that means doing a little research to find out whether that awful person your friend seems to be living with has a name. Miss Manners also advises stocking up on "to remind" cards or reviving the custom of the hosts writing those words on their own cards, now that most invitations are issued by telephone. Such invitations, issued up to three weeks in advance, are strictly binding according to the terms stated. That means that one arrives in the social unit in which one was invited (romances occurring in the interval between invitation and event are not excuses for substitutions), with no reneging permitted (death, preferably one's own, being the exception).

Invitations to stay in other peoples' houses are enforceable only when the hosts mention the date and preferred time of arrival. If the house to be visited is in a choice resort area or a foreign country, the invitation must be in writing. However, "Drop in on us if you're ever in Switzerland and want to ski" is not a serious invitation. To make it so, a prospective guest must apply in writing: "We're going to be in Switzerland next spring and would love to see you," and hope to elicit the necessary written specifics.

Invitations to weddings are serious if they are issued on paper or orally within two weeks before the wedding. Those issued before the marriage proposal ("If Bertrand and I finally get hitched, I want you to be a bridesmaid") are not.

Interpreting Awkward Phrases

DEAR MISS MANNERS:

1. After inviting someone to my home, I hear: "Who else is coming?" or "Did you invite anyone else?"

2. Not having heard from someone in a while, I call and hear, "I hesitate to call you because I figure you must be very busy." This is similar to "When did you stop beating your wife?" I can either protest that I'm really not busy or agree.

3. The person I haven't heard from says, "I never call anyone." A mutual friend said to me, "That's the way she is; she never calls anyone. You have to call her." Is my ego too fragile for this one-sided relationship, or do I lack sympathy for another's idiosyncrasy?

4. The person who never initiates anything says, "When am I going to see you?" or "When are we going to get together?", putting the onus on me to plan something.

GENTLE READER:

1. If the inquiry about other guests is made before accepting an invitation, it means "Will this be worth my while?" and is rude. A proper answer is a sweet "Why, you're the first person I thought of." After accepting, it really means "Is this a dressy occasion, or is it just us for an informal evening?" and should be answered accordingly.

2. "I hesitate to call because I figure you must be busy, is properly said only to someone who has refused many invitations (in which case it means "If you really

want to see me, it's up to you") or who is obviously doing something time-consuming, such as running for President (and means "Let me know when you're finished"). Any other use of it should be countered with a pleasant "Well, I'm never too busy to see you."

3. There is no nice construction one can put on "I never call anyone." It means either "Don't bother me" or "I don't give socially; I just take." It is a mistake to sympathize with this position. The correct reply is, "Oh."

4. You can either accept the challenge of "When am I going to see you?" or return it. An example of the former is "How about Thursday?"; of the latter, "When would be convenient for you?"

"Whatcha Doin'?"

DEAR MISS MANNERS:

Among those of my generation (I am twenty), the phrase "Whatcha doin' tonight?" (along with such clever variations as "Whatcha doin' tomorrow?") has become unfortunately rampant. It translates as "I think I maybe might want to ask you to do something tonight (tomorrow, etc.), but I don't want to take a risk and come out and ask you to go out with me." Miss Manners, how does one respond? I find it offensive, not only because it's so wishy-washy, but also because I don't think it's anybody's business what I'm doin' or not doin' tonight. Furthermore, does the response depend on how close a relationship the inquirer has with the inquiree? Is it an acceptable question for a spouse/close friend but not for an acquaintance?

GENTLE READER:

Yes. When a spouse says, "Whatcha doin'?", it means (aside from the fact that he is too lazy to open his mouth wide enough to pronounce the words) either "Do you have anything on the schedule that I need to know about?" or "Do you have any ideas about how we should amuse ourselves?" Those who have no right to assume that you will be spending the time together, or that your schedule will automatically affect theirs, should not ask such a question. How does one know whether one wants to accept an invitation until that invitation, with relevant particulars, has been offered? One can only defend oneself by answering in the style of the question. By saying, "Oh, I dunno. Coupla things I oughta do. Wha 'bout you?", you leave room to declare that you will either postpone the unspecified "coupla things" to accept an invitation to go out to dinner, or that you will be too occupied with them to accept an invitation to help paint someone else's house.

Special Requests

DEAR MISS MANNERS:

I have a severe hearing impairment but pursue a social life. Many times, I have dinner invitations, including some formal ones. The seat I am assigned to is of the utmost importance. If I am in a position where I cannot carry on a conversation, I feel dead inside and cut off from the world, and would rather stay home and do something constructive instead of indulging in self-pity. I never know in advance what the seating arrangements are, and I must respect the hierarchy. Would it be permissible to ask politely for another seat, perhaps one rank up or down? I love meeting people, but I am unwilling to occupy an unsuitable seat.

GENTLE READER:

Your problem is the opposite of the dinner guest question that Miss Manners usually gets. She is constantly being importuned by people who wish to notify the hosts of their menu requirements—diet restrictions, idealistic objections, or simple preferences—in order to enjoy themselves more fully. To them she must reply that eating is only an incidental part of a dinner party and that it is not fair to expect hosts to provide custom meals for a variety of guests; that one eats what one can, perhaps fortifying oneself against starvation beforehand.

What, then, is the main feature of the dinner party? Why, conversation, of course. If, therefore, a guest has a special requirement in order to be able to participate in the conversation, he should say so. It would be considerate to mention this to your hosts at the time of the invitation, as Miss Manners gathers that your friends are in the habit of doing serious seating arrangements.

Although dinner table ranking is done less precisely than it used to be (it is more than a quarter of a century now since round tables were introduced at the White House to avoid the sort of strict ranking that might result in incompatible dinner partners), a health consideration such as yours always took precedence over form.

Meal Bargaining

DEAR MISS MANNERS:

I was uninvited for dessert, and I'm angry. Please give me some perspective. The invitation to dinner was issued. I wanted to go to an A.A. meeting and said I'd like to stop by afterward. My partner was able to go to the dinner. One of the hosts said this would be fine. I've done this before at their suggestion, since the one host is also in A.A. The following evening, I was disinvited, along with my partner. "This is going to be a formal dinner, and we just can't have people coming in late. It'll throw the setting off." I need a lesson in good manners. Perhaps I should have just said that I couldn't come for dinner.

GENTLE READER:

You and everybody else need that lesson. Miss Manners is so glad that you asked.

There seems to be an impression now that an invitation to dinner is merely the opening suggestion in a bargaining session, to be continued until a compromise about the evening is achieved. Those honored with invitations feel free to negotiate the time, dress, and menu, and often to wangle an additional invitation for someone who is a stranger to the host. All of this is rude. If an invitation cannot be accepted as offered, it must be refused. The host may then amend it if he wishes— "Oh, then stop by afterward," "We'll understand if you don't have time to change," "I didn't realize you were seeing someone regularly; please bring her"— but the guest cannot.

An Improper Response

DEAR MISS MANNERS:

Perhaps you might say a word about people who reply by telephone to R.s.v.p.s on invitations on which no telephone number is listed. We have a friend who even telephones to say she can't come, and then goes on at length to say why not! And then there are those who wait until the time of the party to telephone and ask directions.

GENTLE READER:

The word (said twice) is "Tsk."

Miss Manners knows of several otherwise intelligent people who, faced with an invitation requiring an answer but no telephone number, couldn't figure out how to respond. (Hint: The hosts had supplied their address, which was where the party was taking place.)

Rules for Breaking Engagements

DEAR MISS MANNERS:

Could you offer some guidelines for breaking social appointments? I am a married woman, and my close friend is divorced. We quite often meet for lunch or arrange to go out for the evening. My friend frequently breaks engagements at the last minute because a man has just invited her out. When I finally expressed my annoyance, she seemed genuinely surprised and implied that friends were expected to bow out graciously at such times.

She has also canceled appointments on the grounds that her teenage daughter was feeling "depressed" and needed "cheering up." The first few times that happened, I was sympathetic, but her daughter's bad moods come so often that I have a difficult time taking them seriously, especially when expensive concert tickets are involved. Am I too rigid? This woman is remarkably considerate in other ways. Are friends supposed to step aside for lovers and family members, as she implies?

GENTLE READER:

The assumption that any social opportunity offered by a gentleman automatically takes precedence over one between two ladies was always unpleasant and is now obsolete.

That is not to say that all engagements are equally binding. Highly casual arrangements between old friends, such as evenings of talk in one or the other's house, may, with the formality of the other's permission, be postponed when more formal invitations are issued. When concert tickets or other complicated arrangements are involved, your engagement is not a casual one, and it takes precedence over any subsequent one. Emergencies cancel all engagements, but they had better be emergencies. A depressed daughter who needs to be taken to a hospital is an emergency; a depressed daughter who is bored or sulky is not.

As you seem to wish to retain the friendship, you need to establish ground rules. Make her get the concert tickets. She will not be so cavalier when she has to return them or suffer the financial loss. Incidentally, what was to stop you from suggesting that you—good friend that you are—cheer up the daughter by taking her to the concert while your friend stayed home?

Specifying Dress and Time

"This is Liberty Hall!" Victorian hosts used to announce jovially upon welcoming visitors. This was intended to convey that their hospitality was so unstructured as to permit guests the choice of either taking a walk or writing letters between the end of tea and the moment everyone was expected to go upstairs to dress for dinner.

It strikes Miss Manners as rash nowadays to suggest that guests do whatever they feel like doing. You never know what bizarre activities they might be able to think up and what shape your furniture will be in when they finish. Yet hosts do this more than ever, and guests are enjoying it less.

There are few festivities more discouraging than those in which the guests are led to believe that they must decide everything for themselves. People who are told in advance that it doesn't matter what they wear and are given vague evening hours as an arrival time—but not warned whether a full meal will be served—generally find themselves in sports clothes at a dress-up party or vice versa, with everyone either sitting around grumpily waiting for them so that dinner can start or happily ensconced with pre-filled tummies. How other guests seem to be able to guess correctly on these issues has always been a mystery to Miss Manners; but there are never enough other wrong guessers around to keep the inappropriately dressed or fed guest psychological company.

Miss Manners believes it to be the sacred duty of hosts to organize their parties and to guide their guests through them. Guests hate to improvise. A guest who is forced to dig for basic information by asking questions, and then is told for his trouble that "It doesn't matter" understandably concludes that the whole evening probably won't matter much. Minimum orders for hosts to issue to their guests are as follows:

• What time really to get there. We all more or less understand that "6:00 to 8:00" means "6:45 to 9:15," but there are some 8:00 invitations to have one drink and then eat dinner at 8:40, and other 8:00 invitations to get drunk and stuff oneself with tiny bits of junk, and then eat dinner at 11:15. The latter is unfortunately more usual, so if the party is to be of the former kind, the host should say, "We'll be sitting down fairly promptly." The guest then knows that if he's not there by 8:20, the host will grill his baby-sitter about what time he left home.

- How much one can expect to be given to eat. All entertainment scheduled to begin between 6:00 and 8:00, except those labeled "6:00 to 8:00" (puzzled readers should reread the previous paragraph), include dinner. This may be indicated as "dinner" (you will be issued table space, as well as a chair), or "buffet dinner" (chair only). A 9:00 P.M. invitation should include the word "reception" or "party" or "dance" if people need to be warned to seek full nourishment elsewhere.
- How to dress. Hosts cannot be coy about telling people what to wear. "Oh, anything," means even less than "We're very informal," which has no meaning at all, unless there are such strong regional or group customs that everyone invited knows whether "informal" means "Change into something smashing after work" or "Whatever you jog in." Just below "White tie" and "Black tie" is "Oh, we thought we'd dress just a little." If the hosts don't state their terms, the guests must demand to know what they are wearing.
- What to drink. The correct offer of a drink mentions a choice of specifics ("Let's see: I have gin and scotch, and there's wine if you like, or tomato juice"). The host who asks "What do you want?" and claims to have "everything" deserves to spend an hour making Singapore Slings and Bellinis.
- When to eat dinner. "Please come in to dinner" must not only be said, but must be accompanied by the host's grabbing a key guest and forcibly walking that person in while insisting that everyone else follow. Miss Manners doesn't know why people think it polite to accept a dinner invitation and then pretend that they are reluctant to eat, but most do.
- Where to sit. People who are told to "sit anywhere" generally end up next to their own spouses or ex-spouses, suddenly unable to think of any topic other than car pools or custody schedules. The thoughtful host not only assigns each person a place but shoos them away from their dinner partners before dinner, so they don't use up all conversation before they sit down.
- Finally, when to go home. This is—more's the pity—the only instruction that the host cannot put into words, and for which he requires some initiative on the part of the guest. It seems to be very difficult, even for exhausted or bored hosts, to refrain from saying, "Oh, come on, it's still early," but replacing this urge with a silent smile is, Miss Manners assures them, the most valuable party rule of all.

Cocktail Hours

DEAR MISS MANNERS:

I would like to have a small cocktail party for about sixteen people in my immediate neighborhood, casual friends, from, say, about 5:00 to 7:00 P.M. How would you suggest I word the invitation to indicate that those are the only hours—no staying over, as some people like to do, and hanging around drinking for hours. In other words, what would be the right wording to let people know that the party is over at 7:00 P.M.?

GENTLE READER:
"Cocktails, 4:00 to 6:00 P.M."

Reciprocity

DEAR MISS MANNERS:
I consider myself a thoughtful hostess, and I instinctively look for potential guests wherever I happen to be. The week before having people over, I work hard and make elegant dishes. Everybody, including myself, has a good time. So what's the problem? That hardly anybody reciprocates, that's what. In fact, the doctor and his wife are the only ones who extend to us lovely invitations, either at their home or their country club.

My husband, who is twenty-one years older than I, blames himself for the lack of invitations. He says that people probably say to themselves, "That old fogy doesn't need to get out; he is fine at home." He also says that if I were married to a man my age, we would be the most popular couple in town. We are both bookworms and have a great time just reading. Once in a blue moon, however, I do feel like hearing the phone ring or an excited voice say, "Come over to a great party." No such luck.

GENTLE READER:
Let's deal with the emergency first and then get to the party problem. Even in the etiquette trade, where we like to take things calmly, we bestir ourselves when we smell real trouble. Your husband is being gallant by seeking to take the blame on himself in order to comfort you in your disappointment. The danger is that he believes what he says; even if he doesn't, he will if he keeps hearing himself repeat it.

There isn't a chance in the world that people are talking about your husband's age. What they are actually saying is, "We really must have some people over—the Goodhearts have had us several times now—but the house looks awful and we might as well wait until we can afford to get it painted."

"Mrs. Goodheart always does everything so beautifully. I'm embarrassed to have her taste my cooking."

"Well, of course, it's easy for the Goodhearts. It would take me a week to turn out a dinner like that."

Miss Manners will not allow you to conclude from this that you should lower your standard of entertaining or drop all lazy people. In the first instance, you would only decrease the amount of enjoyment in the world; and in the second, you would be hard put to find guests.

Go on entertaining, as it gives everyone a good time, and occasionally tell someone you like, "We often feel sociable when I just don't feel like cooking. Give us a call sometime if you feel like doing something with us." You may not, Miss Man-ers must tell you, continue to seek consolation from your husband. At most, you may complain to him, "Isn't it awful that no one seems to know how to entertain anymore? They're all anxious to come and see us—you notice they jump at the chance—but nobody's willing to bother and give a party themselves." It would be no more than the truth.

The Widow's Return

Widows and widowers seem to have different social problems. Miss Manners does not think that quite fair and would appreciate hearing, just now and then for a change, from widowed ladies of advanced age who are suffocating from the relentless romantic attentions of too many eligible suitors. In the meantime, she would like to offer some less exciting, but perhaps more useful, advice to bereaved ladies who are prepared to take up social life again. Divorcées are welcome to pay attention, too, but Miss Manners has noticed that many of them, perhaps because they had some say in arranging their new status, tend to show more spunk than those who have been emotionally felled by the sudden termination of a happy marriage.

A lady who has led a pleasant social life in connection with her husband will find that she has many offers of sympathy and assistance upon his death. They come, however, at a time when she does not have much of an inclination to participate in the normal festivities of life. Mourning customs require that her friends adapt themselves to this fact by calling on her and supplying, in her house and on her terms, such items of hospitality—food, drink, reassuring and loving words—as are normally dispensed by the lady of the house.

Unfortunately, by the time the grief has eased enough for the lady to contemplate a return to society, she has, in many instances, accustomed herself to this special, if doleful, treatment. Feeling free to pour out her own sorrows without concern for the lesser problems of others, and expecting others to manage all of the mechanics of social life without her assistance, are the privileges of the new widow. In a person making the conventional social rounds or expecting to do so, they are selfish, dreary, and unbearable.

Miss Manners does not wish to seem callous. But life must go on, as many a shallow philosopher has observed, and when it does, people are expected to carry their own social weight. A widow who dines out with friends may not have noticed that when she did so as part of a married couple, her husband made sure to pick up their fair share of the bill. She may have forgotten that she herself kept loose social accounts of who had invited them out and made sure that they kept up with their reciprocal obligations. Like it or not, those rules still apply, but she must obey them alone without asking for the charity of pity.

Miss Manners does not accuse these ladies of wishing to free-load. She is aware that this behavior is often a result of sadness and of an unfortunate belief that they are not as desirable socially as they were when their husbands accompanied them.

Nonsense. It is a cruel world for people of all ages and genders, and a kind and generous woman, with a motherly aspect and long experience at daily loving and caring, has all the ingredients to be a smashing social success if only she will pull herself together and make the effort.

✿ THE GUEST LIST

Social Lions

A hostess of Miss Manners' acquaintance was attempting to entice her into one of those tsk-tsk conversations about how rude guests are nowadays. This is not difficult to do; Miss Manners has been going on for so long about the rudeness of people who don't answer invitations, show up late, bring extra guests, and don't write thank-you notes that she can do so on automatic pilot while engaged in writing her own sprightly thank-you letters.

This time something caught her attention. While the hostess was condemning her errant guests, she nevertheless also seemed to be making their excuses for them by bragging about how busy they were. "Really, it's disgraceful," the hostess was saying. "You'd think they would know better. After all, these are incredibly important people. You know, I always like to have people who are involved in whatever the big issue of the day is. Yet they know so little about manners that sometimes they come hours late, or even fail to show up altogether."

Miss Manners ventured the timid opinion that big issues of the day aren't always tidied up by dinner time. "Why don't you invite them when they're less busy?" she suggested mildly. Oh-oh; now she'd done it. The hostess gave Miss Manners a haughty look. Obviously, she did not want to be taken for the sort of person to have at her dinner table people who had nothing better to do than go out to dinner. By snagging guests while they were in the thick of things and then demanding that they drop the very exploits for which she prized them in order to behave as if they were entirely at leisure, the hostess had set up a contest she was bound to lose.

Miss Manners is not recounting this story just to provide you with a snicker on the dangers of social lion hunting. She believes there is a greater point here about the risks of forgetting that socializing, whether it is grand scale dining or beer and the ball game, is supposed to be a purely recreational activity based on good will alone. The cynicism that sets in when one knows one is sought for one's position is not entirely unjustified. Once you know that you bestow on your hosts something more valuable than merely your charm, you no longer feel quite like a guest. Gratitude disappears.

Miss Manners expects those who accept invitations to go along with the idea that they are there for their personal qualities only and to observe the forms. They may, with the agreement of the hostess, accept provisionally: "As long as you understand that if the session runs late, I won't be able to get away. Don't hold dinner for me." The guest is therefore excused in advance for anticipated violations, and the hostess has almost as much fun telling the other guests who would have been there and why he is absent as she would get from his presence.

Mixing the List

DEAR MISS MANNERS:
   My husband is a medical resident. Around laymen, he is quite witty, but as soon as other residents come near, he, like them, becomes unable to discuss anything but medicine. At social events involving residents and their spouses, it is impossible to wrest the conversation away from medicine or money. I usually take refuge with the age fifty-and-above group, who are discussing literature, art, or music—subjects on which I can contribute something. Is there anything I can do short of forsaking my own generation? I was brought up to believe that one didn't discuss money or one's job, beyond certain general comments, in social situations.

GENTLE READER:
   The best way to avoid special interest groups at social functions is to mix the guest list. Too many people with too much in common—the same profession or employer; the same background, such as having gone to school together; the same personal milestone, such as having a new baby—always produce single-topic conversation. You can't prevent it. The solution is either to have no nonparticipants at all, or to have enough of them—such as all the residents' spouses—to conduct separate conversations. These are really two types of office parties. Miss Manners suggests that you tolerate some shop talk occasions in exchange for an agreement to participate in genuine general-interest parties. She begs you not to consider age to be one of those categories that binds people in a single-interest group.

Singles and Couples

As Miss Manners' dear grandmamma used to say to one of her younger sisters, it wasn't that she minded her living in a ménage à trois. If Sister and her husband were both satisfied with the arrangement, and the other gentleman was, too, she supposed it was their business. But when such goings on threw off the seating arrangements at other people's dinner parties, it became other people's business, Miss Manners' grandmother pointed out in a tone of voice that indicated that "other people's" meant her own.
   A, ahem, couple consisting of a lady and two gentlemen is extremely difficult to seat at a formal table, where the other ladies have exhibited more restraint about taking seconds. Miss Manners' grandmother was of neither the era nor the inclination to say, "Sure, bring whomever you want at whatever time is convenient;

we're real casual." That attitude does prevail today, and perhaps you think it has solved the problem. Not a bit. The difficulty and indignation hosts experience in accommodating odd living arrangements are worse than ever.

For one thing, "odd" no longer means only such conventional and old-fashioned forms as the three-person household or the same gender couple. Arrangements other than single people who socialize alone and married couples who socialize together, which is what used to pass for normal, include single people who socialize in couples and married couples who socialize alone. There is still a vague assumption that a romantic bond between people also serves to make them a social unit, but how can one tell whether a bond is romantic?

It's all very confusing, and many hosts have long since despaired of doing any kind of orderly entertaining. It is not just the alternate-seating formal dinner party that has gone by the wayside, but anything requiring knowing in advance exactly how many people will be present. Hosts who try the oh-who-cares approach may go so far as to pretend indifference to the prerogative of controlling the guest list, but they seethe when guests take them at their word.

In a time when the personal question and the personal confession have left nothing unsaid, one would think that it would be easy enough to find out who goes about socially with whom. Although the facts to which acquaintances carelessly make one privy may be astounding, the essential one is rarely told. "Natasha is here only on alternate weekends, but I'd love to see you." "Now that the kids are gone, we have a dear friend staying with us, and I'd like to have him meet our friends." "Josh and I are no longer together." "Justine and I are entertaining together now." Miss Manners does not suggest that a simple statement suffices to require any specific invitation to expand to meet changed circumstances. (Shrinking is another matter: The availability of half a couple is a partial acceptance, not an attempt to renegotiate an invitation.) General notice about stable social clusters would help hosts to plan their parties.

Even Miss Manners' great-aunt was able to make the point that an orderly group consisting of a lady, a gentleman, and an Extra Man (she was offering her husband in this guise) had its place in society. Or at least she would have been able to get away with it had she not pushed her luck by adding an occasional third gentleman to the group.

Uncertain Couples

Dear Miss Manners:

What's a person to do these days about social invitations to longtime friends who are separating, divorcing, and making everyone uncomfortable? Do we issue invitations separately, upon the first notice that one or the other has moved out? Is she Mrs. Horrible Hubert until the divorce decree has been granted? Do we always invite both persons, or do we have to decide which one to ask? What do we do when she says, "Is he coming? If so, I'm not"?

GENTLE READER:

The fact is that warring couples should not be invited to the same parties, not only for their sakes but for those of the hosts, furniture, and other guests. Occasionally a separated couple will continue to go out together, but unless you know that to be the case, you should ask them on separate occasions or, at the very least, warn each that the other might be there.

Expanding Invitations

DEAR MISS MANNERS:

I invited the members of our department for refreshments. One person asked me if spouses were included. I explained that I can comfortably have twelve people, but not twenty-four, and therefore it was for staff members only. He replied that he would not go where his wife was not invited and stayed away. Another time, my husband and I invited a couple to be our guests at a restaurant. The wife phoned me and asked whether her daughter was invited also saying the daughter was quite fond of me, and so on. I was too embarrassed to refuse. My husband was annoyed at me and at the bill. I invited a friend to come and spend some time with us. She replied that she never goes anywhere without her husband and would not come unless he was included. I have no reason to expect my husband to tune in with her husband. Are these liberties considered appropriate behavior?

GENTLE READER:

You are a little ahead of changes on the social scene and bound to run into more problems of this nature unless you slow down. Miss Manners gathers that you wish her to put these people in the same category as those who insist on bringing dates wherever they go, which is to say, using your invitation to entertain their own guests. She is always ready to chastise such people, but your guests are not talking about prospects they picked up last night; they are talking about their own immediate families. It is understandable that working spouses resent being asked to evening engagements that again separate them from each other, and from the children as well. If you care about such people, Miss Manners urges you to be open to knowing their families as well. If it is merely an extension of the work-time coffee hour relationship, then confine it to weekday lunch time, when they are separated anyway.

Uninvited Guests

DEAR MISS MANNERS:

A friend invited my family to a cookout given by a friend of hers. I declined, saying that although she and I were used to bringing uninvited guests to each other's big feasts, it was not the same thing. My friend pressed me, saying that her other friend was as casual as we were and would welcome us. We went, against my better judgment, bringing something for the grill. Needless to say, the first words my husband heard were "Oh, look, uninvited guests!" delivered in a totally dead voice by our unwilling host.

My husband neglected to tell me of this remark until we were home. I became deeply embarrassed and wrote a note of apology, and by way of apology (not as an excuse for my bad manners) told of the custom with our friend and how she pressed us. Then I thanked the host and hostess for their generosity and hospitality in spite of everything. Later the hostess appeared at my friend's door, saying how deeply hurt she was by my implication that she was not as open as my friends. This ridiculous saga is only what I deserve for not adhering to good manners, regardless of reasons not to do so. Manners help to save everyone from hurt feelings and embarrassment. So, if a trusted friend should press you one day, please remember my note.

Gentle Reader:

Your point is well taken, and Miss Manners is only sorry that the hosts were unable to accept graciously your fine apology. (Miss Manners is assuming that it was a full apology, containing no hints about their lack of "openness.") By belatedly claiming openness, they are not only sacrificing your feelings, but condoning and encouraging the practice that offended them.

Social Occasions

🌹 NEW AND OLD FORMS

The Open Party

You have done a wonderful job of teaching the children to be warm, open, and hospitable, and Miss Manners congratulates you. Now you must teach them to shut the door firmly in people's faces. How sad that this is necessary, but the truth is that the teenaged invention, the Open Party, is not, Miss Manners regrets to say, a good idea for a new social form.

She is willing to admit that the impulse for inventing the Open Party was, in part, sweet. Not wishing to appear exclusive and run the risk of hurting people's feelings, teenagers have taken simply to announcing parties, with the understanding that anyone who shows up is welcome. The innocent parent who inquires about such antique conventions as invitations is told that one isn't "invited" to such events; one "hears about" them.

What one hears about them after they have taken place is not quite so sweet. One hears about wrecked and looted living rooms, slashed tires, neighbors bringing in the police, drunken or otherwise damaged guests emerging to do wider damage to themselves and to others, and shocked young hosts trying to explain how things got out of their control. That last result could have been anticipated. A characteristic of the Open Party is that the parents of the host are unaware that it is taking place, usually because they are out of town. The confidence of the younger hosts that they are fully in charge is misplaced.

The fact is that an Open Party can never be under anyone's control. Opening it, with whatever hospitable intention, means relinquishing the traditional control hosts exercise over who enters their homes and how they are expected to behave. That control is based on obligations of friendship, in which gratitude for being entertained, along with concern for reputation, creates the desire to please. It does not exist among strangers. Even those who are not complete villains naturally have laxer standards among those they don't know and are not likely to see again. An unknown house, filled with strangers one does not have to encounter again, is free territory where lawlessness can be presumed to go unpunished.

At all levels, hosts have to reassert their right to control their own parties. Rather than being an act of tyranny, choosing one's guests should be looked at as an opportunity to confer honor. It is also a duty, rather than a curb on freedom, to orchestrate the entertainment, including what is to be eaten and drunk. However, it takes some confidence and experience to exercise such control. That is why parents have the obligation to assume the role of the heavy, who says, "I'm sorry, but we were not expecting you," while the teenaged host is allowed to look as if he would be running a permanent open house if only those people were not at home. As, indeed, we know he would.

Daytime Parties

It seems years since Miss Manners was invited to a kettle drum. Why do you suppose that is? It is not that Miss Manners used to hang around with the boys in the band and reformed or fell out with them.

The kettle drum was a late Victorian form of daytime entertainment that seems to have passed out of fashion. In one way, it is probably just as well. The instrument for which this social event was named was, indeed, present (in miniature), so that a lady in funny dress could bang on it at odd intervals, probably just when Miss Manners was in the middle of a delicate witticism. A kettle drum was not a soothing way for those who had had too much fun the night before to pass the afternoon.

Still, Miss Manners sees a need now for more forms of informal daylight socializing. Too many people have either overbooked their nights, feel odd about going about unpaired in the evening, or are reluctant to leave their children during their rare off hours. Easily put together events, at which people need not dress up and the ages can be mixed—with perhaps a separate area for young children, so that the adults can talk and still watch them play—would be useful.

The kettle drum was invented to occupy a place between the simple afternoon call, at which tea was served to whoever showed up, and the elaborate afternoon reception. (It is a great concession for Miss Manners to keep sticking the word "afternoon" in there. Actually, all daytime events were properly referred to as "morning" ones, regardless of the time; morning calls, for example, always took place in the afternoon. "Morning" simply meant any time before evening; any party that wasn't a "soirée" was a "matinée." The word, from the French for morning, survives in America to designate an afternoon theatrical performance. Don't ever say that Miss Manners never taught you anything.) As calls were replaced by telephone calls, and receptions by cocktail parties and buffet suppers, the tea party got more formal and more infrequent, and the even more formal reception was left for weddings and other ceremonial occasions.

That's where the kettle drum should now come in. It was invented in India by English officers and their wives who didn't have their good china and silver with them. In the spirit of camp life, the drumhead was used as a table. Refreshments and dress were practical rather than dainty. Guests dropped in for a half hour or more. If there was any entertainment other than conversation, it was more likely to be amateur music from the guests than a professional performer.

Miss Manners is not crazy to hear that drum being banged again, and in no way wants to discourage a revival she has happily noticed of the tea party requiring lace tablecloths and hats. She only wishes to point out that the idea of an unfancy afternoon gathering without alcohol would be particularly useful now.

If you don't like the kettle drum, she has another suggestion for you from her vast knowledge of obsolete social forms: the chocolataire. A chocolataire is similar to a tea party, except that everything is loaded with chocolate. Hot chocolate is the drink offered in winter and chocolate lemonade in summer, and the food consists of chocolate cake, chocolate ice cream, chocolate wafers, chocolate bonbons, chocolate pastries, and chocolate candies. Oh, you like that one a little better than the drum, do you? Miss Manners has just noticed that the condescending facial expressions of those who thought that quaint old forms were not for them has changed. Please use your tea napkins to wipe your mouths.

The Luncheon

Traditionally, a luncheon is a lunch that takes an eon. Perhaps that is why this particular form of entertainment has fallen into second-class status in recent decades. That, and the ugly necessity of working for a living, and perhaps also the way people look at six o'clock who have had three wines at midday. The luncheon party used to be something quite jolly, and Miss Manners is seeing signs of its becoming so again. She is not talking about restaurant lunches, whether they are knee to knee or the kind where the guests go home afterward with the floral centerpieces, but the formal, or approximately so, lunch given by private individuals at home for purely social reasons.

By definition, this sort of luncheon, if given on a weekday, must be given by and for people who can wander off in the middle of the day from their jobs, and whose work will not suffer from any lapses of attention should they happen to wander back afterward. That is why, when gainful employment became a universally desirable hobby, luncheons first evolved into "ladies' luncheons" and then virtually disappeared. They can be given on weekends, of course, but the guests will then treat them as brunches, wearing sports clothes and demanding Bloody Marys.

At lunchtime, as opposed to entertaining at dinner, you can invite the people you want without having to have the people they want. The food is simpler, three light courses being considered sufficient, and egg and salad dishes being quite respectable as the main course. Anyway, everyone gets to fill up on bread and butter, which do not appear together at formal dinner parties. Damask tablecloths and flag-sized napkins are not needed. Even the most formal luncheons are served on place mats with square napkins. There are no candles to dribble on your bare table.

The custom of gentlemen wearing cutaways to Sunday luncheons and sack coats to Saturday ones having died out, formal dress for a luncheon is within anyone's reach. Hats, regrettably are, no longer required for ladies, but luncheons are an excellent opportunity for anyone who has one to take it out for a treat.

Best of all, people usually arrive on time for luncheons, and they eventually leave, which cannot always be said of the same people at dinner time. The reason is that they have the odd notion that one needs an excuse to depart from the scene of hospitality, and while "I guess I'd better be getting back to work" suffices in the daytime, they can't rack their brains for any reason for going home at night.

In short, the luncheon is a fine way to get around the modern problems that have made the dinner so difficult to give properly. What would be compromises at dinner are correct procedures at lunch. A formal luncheon solves all the problems one encounters at dinners, except one: the problem of what to say to your boss at 4:30.

Picnicking and Tailgating

There is nothing quite so pleasant in summertime as a bird and a bottle, shared with merry friends on the grass, in the shade of an old tree, with the sunlight filtering though the leaves and the chirpings of wildlife all about. Unless it is the same meal, properly served, at the dining room table.

The urge to picnic is nearly universal, which means that it annually seizes people who know better. They have discovered, in previous years, that Nature, along with her undeniable charms, also has ants, poison ivy, damp ground, and things falling out of trees. Yet they persist in confronting these dangers with no better protection than paper—paper tablecloths, paper napkins, paper plates. To attack the forces of the universe armed only with a plastic fork is, in Miss Manners' opinion, quixotic at best. It is possible to have a reasonably civilized meal on the lap of Nature, but, like the simple pleasure of bouncing a baby on one's own lap, it is foolhardy to attempt such a thing without adequate protection.

The handiest thing to take along on a picnic is a butler. This has more uses than a Swiss army knife. A butler can, for instance, direct the footmen where to place the tables and chairs, and supervise their setting out the linens, silverware, and stemmed glasses before unpacking the food hampers. (Now is the time for letter writers to inform Miss Manners, with some indignation, that many people nowadays have neither butlers nor footmen. Ah, well, children will do just as well for carrying hampers and adequately for fetching. Why it is that people who cannot afford footmen think they can afford children, Miss Manners does not know. In the long run, they are a great deal more expensive.)

Whoever carries them, the hampers must be hampers, not paper shopping bags. A proper hamper may be wicker, wood, or the baby's old car bed, and some excellent ones work off season in the laundry room. The paper bag theory is that there will be nothing to carry on the way back, but when the bag soaks though, one can also travel light *to* the picnic spot.

Besides, you need something to carry home the flatware, the glasses, and the tablecloth and napkins. It is strange reasoning that makes people associate barbecue sauce with paper plates, grilled steaks with plastic knives, and greasy finger food with paper napkins. It is not only Miss Manners' natural elegance that makes her insist on proper tableware through the rigors of rusticity. The open air brings out the natural aggressiveness of food, and the ill-equipped picnicker has little chance of surviving intact.

An autumn variation is the tailgate picnic. There's nothing quite as smug and happy-looking as someone lounging indolently on a folding chair at a charming little table in the middle of a parking lot, who is peering over a long-stemmed wine glass at people eating out of paper wrappings and drinking from bottles.

There must be more food and drink available than are necessary for the number of expected guests. Small picnic groups do not have to share with those having picnics nearby, making this one of the few situations where one is actually allowed to enjoy the contrast of the superiority of one's own dinner to that of one's neighbors. Acquaintances who stop by, trying to make conversation with watering mouths, need not be invited for the full meal, but it is customary to offer a drink and a small snack.

Other decencies must be strictly observed. Setting up a grill so as to choke other picnickers with smoke or strewing trash around is not allowed. It seems to Miss Manners that showing off one's food and service is quite enough naughty fun for one afternoon without having to resort to the cruder methods of annoying one's neighbors.

Ceremonial Pouring

DEAR MISS MANNERS:

I recently attended an elegant affair where punch was served and several ladies of the community had been asked to pour. I was appalled that some of them, while serving, proceeded to eat cookies and drink punch. Please discuss the etiquette of punch or coffee pouring for guidance in future similar affairs.

GENTLE READER:

Miss Manners does not want to disappoint you by failing to bristle over this, preparatory to going around knocking the cookies out of these ladies' hands. Ceremonial pouring, being done by honored guests rather than by servants, is not incompatible with taking a wee sip or bite when business is slow. That is not to say that Miss Manners would condone having the pourers slurp and chomp away while others clamor for attention. To have a cup of one's own delicately parked to the side is not a crime. Incidentally, the ritual was developed for the pouring of tea and, by extension, coffee or chocolate. Punch, being naturally kept in a punch bowl rather than a pot, does not lend itself to this method. If the punch is not professionally ladled, cups should be decoratively arranged around the bowl so that the guests can help themselves or one another.

Buffet Dinner

How people can expect to navigate modern parties without the skill of being able to hold a drink, carry a plate, and shake hands simultaneously, Miss Manners cannot imagine. Personally, she can do all three while also fanning herself, jotting down a telephone number, and holding a nosegay, but she understands that there are people who, not being so perfectly trained, react with dismay when given a filled plate, knife, fork, napkin, and wineglass—and no table.

She therefore believes that the buffet meal is a form that should be used sparingly and carefully. Just because she is able to juggle, that does not mean she likes being required to demonstrate her talent, especially at mealtime. She long ago made a wise decision to control the amount of carousing she does by skipping all social functions at which she would be expected to stand.

This need not rule out buffet meals entirely. The buffet meal is always a compromise—the presumption is that if you could serve all eighty-three guests at the dining room table, you would—but, then, few aspects of socializing do not leave something or someone compromised. Let us at least set the standard that every guest invited to a full meal is provided with a chair. Half of them will sit on the rug, but that does not excuse inviting people to your house for the purpose of eating dinner from your floor.

The buffet table is properly set so that it would form an attractive pattern if viewed by a guest hanging from the chandelier. Miss Manners prefers diagonal rows of forks across the front left corner, with a row of overlapping napkins at the same angle, closer to the edge, but tolerates those who are partial to circular formations and such whimsey. Plates are stacked at the back corner, not too high, and platters are set at rhythmic intervals.

A long buffet table is set with two supplies of everything in a mirror image. This is so that two squadrons of guests can approach from opposite ends and meet just after the middle, where every one of them will exclaim, "Oh, that's the same salad! I already took some of that." The brighter guests will then depart from the table.

The less swift-minded will continue down against the tide, exclaiming, "Oh, that's the same rice," and so on.

Centerpieces are not absolutely required, but if one is used, it had better look like a centerpiece. People will eat anything on a buffet table. The same guests who would never take seconds from a passed platter go back for fourths when they see all that food laid out like sale merchandise in a shop.

Buffet food should not require the use of a knife by the eater, and it should taste almost as good lukewarm as hot. A host who does not use large plates and huge napkins for a buffet meal deserves what he eventually finds on the rug. Dessert should not be on the table with the main course, or at least three people will say, of the triumphant result of your having beaten egg whites until your arm was about to fall off, "Eeeeew! This is sweet! I thought it was potatoes."

It is customary to offer some service, even if it is only going around saying, "Here, let me take that," to stop guests from marching into the kitchen and dumping their garbage in all the wrong places. If there are enough authorized hands to do so, it is sensible to hand out extra courses and to bring around the platters from the table for seconds. The fewer times your guests get up, the less you have to reupholster.

The ideal buffet meal is one at which the guests, having taken their plates, are shown to a set table or a variety of small tables and allowed to eat on something more reliably horizontal than their laps. From there, it is but one short step to a truly civilized meal.

Off-Color Entertainment

DEAR MISS MANNERS:

I get extremely uncomfortable and embarrassed whenever someone starts telling off-color jokes in mixed company. The same goes for watching "adult" scenes on video machines at people's houses. When my husband is present, as he usually is, it is quite mortifying for me. I feel like such an old prude, even though I'm only in my early thirties. Isn't it bad manners to invite people over to your house and then turn on a movie, whether or not they care to watch? Most of the time, we are not told of the movie plans in advance. I've tried making conversation to distract attention, but it never works.

My husband understands how I feel but doesn't get upset over things like this. He works at a job where such off-color humor is very common. As far as the movies are concerned, he agrees that it is rude to make people feel obliged to watch, but I believe that if it weren't for me, he would be content to go along with the crowd.

GENTLE READER:

There seems to be a social law now in effect—the reverse of the traditional one—whereby the lowest forms of behavior take precedence over better ones. Under this rule, the person who objects to being made to watch dirty movies takes the social disapproval, rather than the one who is showing them. Similarly, people who want to listen to loud or continuous background music intimidate those who are offended by it.

Miss Manners is working to repeal this law, but she is not getting a ground swell of support. Those who ought to help are too busy trying to stop the offenders from doing what they are doing, instead of making them contain it so that it doesn't annoy others. With the risk of sounding tolerant and reasonable, Miss Manners must say that she really doesn't care how people enjoy themselves as long as they don't scare the horses on the street. Yes, it is bad manners to show pornographic movies to guests who expected conversation, but it is also bad manners to talk over the dialogue. Just say a pleasant good-bye and leave. Not laughing at dirty jokes puts a damper on them, but if the entire conversation is offensive, you should also leave.

Unless you are running about scolding others, drop the term "prude" from your thinking. This presumes that dirty movies are polite and that you are strange for thinking otherwise. However, your social life is not going to straighten out until you and your husband agree on either mutually enjoyable or mutually exclusive forms of entertainment.

———

BALLS AND DANCES

Reports are that proper ballroom dancing is returning. This being a country where people will go in for anything, provided that it is new enough or old enough, young people who thought dancing meant gyrating into solitary trances are now setting about finding out what they missed.

Along with learning the ballroom steps, Miss Manners would like to request that neo-dancers practice ballroom manners. This will require learning a new attitude, or rather an old, wicked one. The old-fashioned combination of dutifulness and permissible naughtiness is hardly imagined by the present age. It was the strictures imposed by ballroom manners that created the license for a substructure of intrigue, flirtation, and other pleasures and dangers associated with romantic excitement. One could not simply attend a dance with a favorite person and spend the evening leaning together and swaying. The program was made up of a series of clearly separated dances, and manners required that each person dance with a large number of partners.

A gentleman always had his duty dances with the hostess, any daughter of the house, and the guest of honor, and he was expected to do his share of rescuing wallflowers, especially sisters of friends who could be induced to do the same for his sister.

A lady was obliged to dance with whoever asked her, unless she could plead a previous promise or fatigue, which she was not allowed to contradict with subsequent action. This rule saved many a young girl who submitted to it the subsequent heartbreak of finding out that a gentleman's attractiveness was not necessarily obvious at the age that he entered his first ballroom and that the snubbed

Black Tie

This traditionally meant dinner dresses with sleeves and narrow long skirts, but ladies can go all out for grand black-tie occasions. Gentlemen exhibit their taste by the exquisiteness of their tailoring, rather than by wearing ruffles or funny colors.

White Tie

Now you can legitimately wear the wing-collared shirts or eighteen-button gloves you mistakenly think look so spiffy on lesser occasions. Ladies properly wear huge skirts and plunging necklines, and gentlemen strive to look more like orchestra conductors than headwaiters.

Dress Optional

This is what you deserve when you refuse to tell the guests what to wear, and each of them shows up dressed for a different party. When each of the guests are all secretly convinced that they are the ones who are incorrectly dressed, it throws a damper on the festivities.

Dressing Up

had long memories. A lady was expected to find a pretext to excuse herself when she believed a gentleman to be stranded with her; that was one of the chief uses of powder rooms.

The key phrases of the ballroom were "May I have this dance?", to which the answer was something like, "Why, yes, with pleasure," or "I'm so sorry, I've promised it," or "Oh, dear, I've danced so much, I really must sit down now."

The American custom of "cutting in," allegedly a frontier solution to the shortage of ladies, had its own rules: A gentleman could not cut back in on someone who had cut in on him, and a lady could not make come-on gestures behind the back of her partner, although nothing could stop her from shooting a meaningful look at someone else across the room.

The special dances were the first, the last, and the last before supper, because one would then be the supper partner of the person with whom one was dancing. Romance was not an excuse for dancing plastered together, but was expressed in such invisible gestures as pressing hands and accidental momentary brushings together of faces.

If anyone complains that this sounds stilted and dull, Miss Manners will lodge a countercomplaint of a lack of imagination. The dance floor was, under those circumstances, wild with romantic tension. Would the right person ask one to dance or accept one's offer? Was it plausible that that person was dancing with a certain other person only out of polite pity? Did the pressure of a hand against a waist or shoulder mean anything? Was that redness of cheek a rush of passion from her hair brushing faintly across his cheek, or was that an accident and the high color from the heat of the ballroom? Miss Manners would remind skeptics that when dancing in couples first began to replace group dancing, with lots of room between, nobody thought it was a turn for the quaint.

The "Semiformal" Ball

DEAR MISS MANNERS:

My husband and I are planning to attend a "semiformal ball." Please define the phrase "semiformal attire" for me. Is my husband's suit appropriate? Is a short evening dress considered semiformal? Would a long, casual dress do? I enjoy dressing up but seldom get the opportunity.

GENTLE READER:

"Semiformal" means that the hosts want to give a formal ball but are intimidated by people who say that they hate formality, don't own evening clothes, think formality is elitist, and so on. They are therefore going to settle for a hodgepodge effect, believing it impossible to persuade everyone to dress properly. A ball ought to mean that gentlemen wear at least black tie, unless white tie is specified, and that ladies wear balldresses, which are long, wide, low-cut, and anything but casual. Since you asked Miss Manners, she is going to tell you to dress properly. However, should you prefer to make less of an effort, you could seek a second opinion from your hosts or the host committee. They will undoubtedly reply wimpily, "Oh, anything you feel comfortable in," which authorizes you to wear your tennis clothes if you like.

Dance Cards

DEAR MISS MANNERS:

One of my professionally delegated responsibilities is the coordination of our annual awards banquet and dinner dance. I am unable to find any record of dance cards at previous functions. Since there is no tradition to follow, I am free to design and distribute dance cards in an appropriate fashion. Is it appropriate to have the logo of the society on the card? Please provide guidelines for distributing dance cards as well.

GENTLE READER:

The custom of the dance program enabled a lady to order her evening and to keep a souvenir of it afterward, and Miss Manners is delighted to hear of your reviving it. You may distribute the cards from a silver tray near the door or put them at the table places. The program consists of a tiny, gilt-edged card, folded to look like a miniature book, with a silk cord that can be tied around the wrist, and a pretty, match-sized pencil. It often has a sketch on the front cover or a bit of poetry; go ahead and put your logo there, provided that there is no accompanying material to make it look like an advertisement.

Inside the program are numbered lines on which gentlemen can write their names. The honor system requires that a gentleman put himself down no more than two times—or possibly three, if he is consumed with passion and the lady is willing—and the lady may occasionally claim, "Oh, dear, I've already promised the fifth dance" without being put on oath. This system requires that the dance numbers be announced, so that each gentlemen knows when to collect the lady to whom he is engaged for that dance. Cutting in and secret erasures are not allowed.

Strange Partners

DEAR MISS MANNERS:

Last Saturday night, I took out my lady friend with her sister and brother-in-law to a nice eating place and then dancing. After only one dance they started playing polkas. I don't dance polkas, but a total stranger sitting at the bar came and asked me for permission to dance with my lady friend. I said that it was up to her, so he asked her and she said, "Do you mind?" I replied that it was up to her, and she said, "You don't polka," and got up and danced. She was back in two minutes because he didn't, either. You notice that I didn't say yes or no. I wanted to know what kind of lady I was out with. I thought it was a cheap trick, and got up and went home. Did she do wrong or was I wrong? I have broken up with her. We are senior citizens.

GENTLE READER:

Speaking of cheap tricks, do you think it is proper for gentlemen to set traps for ladies? Miss Manners cannot claim it proper for ladies to dance with strangers who saunter over from bars. The manner in which this happened—each of them asking your permission—demonstrates that they had confused the manners of private dances, where a lady may indeed accept other partners, with manners appropriate to commercial establishments, such as night clubs or discos. You are therefore wrong to shun her as if she had behaved like a tramp.

Sharing Partners

DEAR MISS MANNERS:

We have been taking dance lessons, for something to do together. We are almost seventy years old and have been enjoying this new hobby and exercise so very much. When we go to dances, we see so many widows and divorcées without partners. Is my husband expected to dance with them? I realize that would be the gracious thing to do, but I don't want to dance with any other men, even if asked. So, what started as a lot of fun has become a source of friction, and after fifty years of marriage, we don't need that. We have almost decided to give up dancing.

GENTLE READER:

That would be a shame. Perhaps you should give up going to dances where you know other people and confine your hobby to nightclubs, where you will be among strangers. Among friends, it is customary to exchange a number of dances. That is, you and your husband may have most of the dances together, but he should also ask, and you should accept, other partners.

Miss Manners wonders if the friction occurs because there are more unattached ladies than gentlemen at these events, and his socializing means that you are left without a partner more often than you like. She would still ask you graciously to socialize with the others—to be friendly to them while your husband takes an occasional turn with one of the unescorted ladies. Surely it must occur to you that there but for the grace of God go you.

When One Doesn't Dance

DEAR MISS MANNERS:

What can a woman say when asked to dance if she cannot, because of sheer lack of physical coordination and rhythm, possibly oblige? The excuse is not always accepted gracefully. I have been physically hauled out onto the dance floor, only to have my partner discover, to his dismay, that I was telling the truth. Now that I am older, it is even more embarrassing, since I get sympathy invitations ("Tom, why don't you ask Miss Smith to dance?" and he dutifully does). Or I go to the office party and the head of the department asks me as a signal honor.

The worst was a distinguished foreign gentleman who didn't know enough English to comprehend any joking excuse. Fortunately, I saw him coming and escaped through the ladies' room to an icy alley, where I sprained my ankle before finding a taxi to take me home. I was overjoyed: the perfect excuse. If anyone asked what happened to me, I could pretend that I had sprained my ankle on the way to the banquet and had endured the pain as long as I could. I stayed home two days just to make the story better, and the foreign gentleman sent me a charming bouquet and a farewell note.

GENTLE READER:
You are really a martyr to etiquette, aren't you? Even Miss Manners has never heard of anyone's describing a sprained ankle as a source of joy because it alleviated social awkwardness. The words you want are "I'm sorry, but I don't dance." If they are not respected, you must follow them with "No, I really don't dance." A gentleman may then either be encouraged to move on by your adding "But I enjoy watching; do find a partner, and I'll watch from here" or, if the overture seems more of a quest for your company than for a dancing partner, you may say, "But if you would like to rest for a minute, I'd be delighted if you sat this one out with me."

Proms

Assuming that practically nothing comes naturally, Miss Manners will now explain to girls and boys how to be girls and boys during their school prom festivities. After that, they are on their own. Miss Manners goes to bed early. Who is the boy and who is the girl have nothing to do with who is the host or hostess. That was presumably settled long before prom time. The current confusion seems to have to do with changing patterns within the adult world based on increased financial independence among ladies and a resulting increase in frankness about their providing and reciprocating hospitality. Very young ladies are not the only ones to combine the new with the old tradition in the worst possible way by issuing invitations to gentlemen and then presenting them with the bills.

Miss Manners does not suspect teenage girls of trickery when they invite boys to their dances and then inform them, in advance or on the spot—not a good idea when you are dealing with gentlemen too young to carry credit cards—that they are responsible for related dinners and incidental expenses. Rather, she thinks that when they do the inviting, the girls are dressed in their jeans and their fathers' shirts, and think of themselves as using the same behavior patterns as boys. Then, when they get into the prom dresses that Miss Manners is so pleased to see come back into fashion, they switch to the pattern of being a girl that they believe to have been in use the last time such dresses were worn.

Since that may have been slightly before their mothers' day, they are not getting accurate guidance. They imagine that a girl who wore pretty dresses never lifted a finger, certainly not to put it into her own wallet.

That's not exactly true. A great many girls, including your own ladylike Miss

Manners, attended girls' schools, for all of whose dances they issued the invitations to the young gentlemen they wished to escort them. For school weekend invitations, the guest provided his own transportation and lodging costs, while the hostess planned and provided tickets for the chief events.

Paying the bills for an evening's entertainment she has initiated does not make a girl into a boy. She does not have to mimic the boy's pattern by calling for her date, for example; nor does she have to start making him pay the bills in order to retain the role of girl. Paying the bills simply makes her the hostess. The hostess for a prom night makes the arrangements for the evening and pays for dance tickets, meals, and any extras she may wish, such as having professional photographs taken. She neither assumes herself nor demands from her date such male functions as sending flowers, opening doors, giving the dinner order to the waiter or checking the coats.

A note to young ladies who have never heard of such strange practices and who may be alarmed by them: These are merely little superficial social customs, graced by tradition and pleasant to practice. They go with your pretty dress, which also, you may notice, bears a significant gender distinction from your young man's formal clothing, and are not to be overanalyzed for sociological content. Equality in essentials does not require total sameness; there is nothing whatever contradictory about allowing a gentleman to hand you out of a car and then smashing him one on the volleyball field or at the debating society's meeting. The rewards of being a hostess are the same as those of being a host. You get to choose whom you want to invite, you get to submerge your feelings of outraged disappointment when politely turned down, and you get the satisfaction of having devised an evening of entertainment that provides as much pleasure to yourself as to your guest. And who knows? You may even get a goodnight kiss.

Shifting Roles

DEAR MISS MANNERS:

My fifteen-year-old daughter will soon be going to a high school dance with a young man she has asked to be her date. Both attend gender-segregated private schools, and neither drives at this time. Since my daughter issued the invitation, my wife or I will drive for the occasion. When we arrive at the young man's home, is it proper for her to go to his door alone and walk with him back to the car, or should this duty be delegated to the driver, leaving our daughter alone in the car? Should she be escorted to the door and the three of us return to the car together? We do not know the young man's parents but are aware that they are responsible people. I assume that the good-byes will be said in the car and he will return to his door unescorted.

GENTLE READER:

Interestingly enough, you and your daughter have similar problems in this situation. (She probably doesn't think so. She probably thinks her problem is you—but never mind.) Each of you must adapt an accustomed set of manners to an office not usually associated with them. She, as a girl, will be acting as host of the date, which the boy generally does; you (or your wife), as a parent, will be acting as a functionary excluded from social participation, which is what a professional driver is supposed to be. It would be as foolish for her to act like an honorary boy as for you to pretend to be their employee. Yet she cannot ignore her duty as hostess, and you cannot join in on the date. You must both adapt your manners to the requirements of the occasion without sacrificing the basic behavior suitable to your identity.

For example, you should obviously not have the young man sit up front with you while your daughter is in the back seat, as would be gracious if she were merely entertaining a friend. The two of them should sit together in the back, and you must restrain yourself from entering the conversation, no matter how tempting it is. Yet you will greet the boy with a few friendly words, as befits the father of his hostess, and wish them a pleasant evening when you drop them off at the dance. Parents should not pretend to be impersonal and invisible.

It will take some talking to convince your daughter that you should accompany her to her date's door to pick him up, but Miss Manners believes you should. It makes her look less as if she were a gentleman caller, as it were, and it will reassure the young man's parents that there is a responsible driver. However, if she feels that this would humiliate her to the extent of blighting her life, you might allow her to go in by herself and announce, "My father is outside; he can't park the car" or "My mother dropped me off and went to get gas; she'll be right back."

As you say, neither of you need accompany him to his door afterward. You will, of course, wait in the car until he is safely inside, as you would for any guest of any age. Miss Manners thinks it would also be nice if you said, as the boy was getting out, "Patty, why don't you sit up front with me?" That way, the young people will both have to emerge from the car, which will give them a chance to say a private word, if they wish, while you look for your glove on the floor.

Improper Prom Clothes

DEAR MISS MANNERS:

As the prom season approaches, I find myself drowning in a sea of etiquette questions. What exactly is tea length? From what I understand, it is longer than knee length and shorter than floor length.

Recently, a bridal salon brought their prom collection to my school. I noticed several styles of garters. Can I assume that garters are an optional accessory? The other thing the collection included was hats. I was under the impression that hats were to be worn during the day. My final question pertains to shawls. The style the salon carried was pre-tied. I have also seen shawls that were very long, wide, lightweight scarves. No good way to wear them sprang to mind.

GENTLE READER:

Garters? What sort of prom activity do they imagine would indicate whether the ladies were wearing garters? What Miss Manners imagines is that in looking for other commercial outlets for their bridal finery, this establishment would just as soon pass off inappropriate artifacts on innocent students. The ancient and risqué custom of the bridal garter has nothing whatever to do with evening clothes such as are worn to a prom. Hats may be worn with long dresses by brides and brides-maids at daytime weddings, but since they are not worn at night, as you know, they also are unrelated to prom clothes.

A pretied shawl seems rather strange, too, as one would have to put one's head through it. The advantage of any sort of shawl, scarf, or other wrap is—in addition to the fact that it is an easy way for ladies who do not have evening coats to avoid having to wear their school raincoats over their evening dresses—that it covers the shoulders without messing the dress.

Tea length is indeed those wide skirts of midcalf length that are associated with tea dancing, while evening clothes are traditionally floor length. Miss Manners is aware that there is such a thing now as the hip-length strapless dance dress but prefers not to think about it.

❧ PARTIES WITH A POINT

Giving Parties for Oneself

Suppose that you want to toss a party for the person whom you love the most, and who you have always felt deserves to be showered with a great deal more attention than has been forthcoming. Should the wording on the invitation be "In honor of me"?

A great many people do seem moved to give parties for themselves or for their next of kin, and Miss Manners does not want to condemn their generosity. She just wants to make sure that they don't find themselves honored by a chorus of guests grumbling "I notice she never remembers *my* birthday" or "They never miss an excuse for presents, do they?"

Before giving your own birthday, graduation, or anniversary party, or one for your parents, spouse, or children, it is prudent to consider whether feeling for the honored person runs high enough to bring out the guests in an affectionately cele-bratory mood. Mind you, the alternative need not be toasting yourself in the bath-room mirror. Miss Manners will explain how it is still possible to mark the occasion with a party that will please your guests, or at least all but your great-uncle, who believes that your very birth was an excuse to extract from him the price of a pair of booties.

Parties for oneself or members of the family are always permissible when they are confined to a group in which each person is honored in turn. Sometimes that means keeping the celebration in the family—each family having its own customs about the distance of the relationship or for how long the relatives are to be remembered in this fashion (as far as first cousins, perhaps, or up to the age of twenty-one). The society, in general, recognizes children's birthday parties up to the age of sixteen, and then again at age twenty-one, provided that the parties are planned with special attention to the pleasure of their guests. That is to say, the main entertainment at that age cannot be watching the host opening presents.

At the other end of the scale, birthday parties for anyone ninety or up are attended enthusiastically, if somewhat patronizingly. The celebrants may get tired of being asked their "secret" for not being dead yet. Otherwise, friends will generally sit still for two birthdays: fifty and seventy-five or sixty-five and eighty. It is not advisable to ask the same guests to appear for fifty and sixty-five or for seventy-five and eighty.

An earlier adult birthday, at thirty or forty, is popular among those who want to mope about how ancient they are, or among their relatives who want to distract them from doing so. It is wise, however, to confine the guest list for such an ocassion to those who are the same age or slightly younger. Mature people are not amused by thirty-year-olds moaning about how life has passed them by.

Anniversary parties outside of the immediate family should also be widely spaced. You could do the twenty-fifth, fiftieth, and seventy-fifth, or another series consisting of the thirtieth or thirty-fifth, the sixtieth, and the seventy-fifth. One way to beat these odds is to honor other guests as well. Couples who were married at about the same time will be happy to celebrate any number of anniversaries if their own are included; people with the same birthdays may celebrate cooperatively; and a graduation party is infinitely more appealing if it honors classmates as well as the host or the hosts' child.

The sticking point for other guests is the idea of presents. Presents are a central part of children's birthday parties and of showers, which is why the former have an age limit and the latter are never properly given by a relative or a prospective relative, much less the person honored. If you eliminate that issue, people will be only too glad to honor you and yours. This is best done by a sort of reverse surprise party: You surprise the guests by telling them only at the party itself that this is your birthday, your parents' anniversary, or whatever. A surprising number of people will forget, from year to year, why you choose this date for the party. This enables them to say, "I wish you'd told me! I would have liked to get you something."

Nevertheless, some people will bring presents, and Miss Manners hopes, even if you don't, that they know that small, symbolic, or amusing presents, rather than substantial ones, are appropriate for an adult's birthday. Sneak a quick look, if you can, just after they are handed to you but do not make an event of opening them, as children do. Otherwise, you will spend the evening listening to the blubbering apologies of those who didn't bring anything.

If all else fails, you might consider sacrificing yourself to a grateful nation. Your birthday will then be declared a national holiday, and citizens all over the country will use it (or the nearest Monday, for their greater convenience) to go out and buy things (on sale) for themselves. The gratitude will probably not show itself until after your death, but so be it.

The Spinster Shower

DEAR MISS MANNERS:

A friend of mine invited me to a spinster party, offering suggestions for gifts and stating that considering her "patience and generosity in having attended and/or participated in all your weddings, she has decided that this is her chance to get even!!! Bring Presents!!!" Many of my single friends have joked that it would be appropriate for us to have a shower; we also need help in setting up a household. I had mixed reactions. Although I did bring "a tacky birthday gift," as the invitation suggested "for those still single," the "spinster" called to assure me that she was registered at the best stores. Is this becoming a common practice? Should I have given a traditional shower or wedding gift?

GENTLE READER:

Miss Manners was not aware that people got married for the purpose of extracting household artifacts from their friends. Oh, yes, she was—how could she help but be, with the mail she gets?—but she is trying to rise above it.

The concept of "getting even" for having given presents to friends out of a desire to symbolize the pleasure one takes in their weddings does not strike Miss Manners as amusing. If it passes for wit in your circles, she has no objection, provided that it is treated as a joke; a serious request for presents is not funny. If your friend really wants to mark the establishment of her household, she should give a housewarming party.

The Sweet Sixteen Party

DEAR MISS MANNERS:

I will soon be sixteen, and although my parents are on a tight budget, I want a sweet sixteen party. Should it be formal, with dresses and all, or just a casual party? If dresses, what color? This is really special to me, but I don't want to put anyone in debt. Should we rent a place to have it, or use my backyard?

GENTLE READER:

Miss Manners is all in favor of your having a dressy party, provided that you learn to eschew those aspects of it that drive up the price. Renting a place to give a party is expensive. All you have to do to make your backyard formal is to call it a garden. Setting a clothing color means asking your guests to buy something to wear. Asking them to wear dresses or suits sets a standard of formality without special expense. "Not informal" might be the way you put it on the invitation.

The Housewarming

DEAR MISS MANNERS:

My husband and I are purchasing our first home, and we are planning on having a housewarming. When sending out the invitations, is it proper to include the colors of the rooms (for example, "kitchen: yellow; restroom: blue; bedroom: mauve," etc.)? If it is not proper, I would appreciate any suggestions.

GENTLE READER:

Miss Manners is not sure that you will appreciate the suggestion that you learn to think of the party as a way of welcoming your friends to your new home, not a way of extracting decorating elements from them. If they want to know what colors your rooms are, they can just look when they get there. Should they be so gracious as to bring you tokens of the good will they feel for you on this occasion, put the yellow ones in the kitchen, the mauve ones in the bedroom, and the blue ones in what are called bathrooms when they are in people's houses, rather than at highway rest stops.

The Autograph Party

DEAR MISS MANNERS:

I have spent the last four years writing an autobiography, and I waited six months to enter it in a first book contest. When (if) I win, can I give myself an autograph party? Or should I wait for someone else to give me one?

GENTLE READER:

It is a bit difficult to ask yourself for your own autograph, except, of course, on those checks Miss Manners and you hope will be arriving any day now. Book parties are given by someone else—a friend, a bookstore, a publisher. The author can then look appropriately modest and surprised that anyone would think his or her signature worth having.

Children's Parties

DEAR MISS MANNERS:

My five-year-old daughter attends kindergarten, and I have become concerned about the manner in which birthday party invitations have been distributed in her class. Believe me, Miss Manners, I have better things to do than sit around and try to decipher which children are having birthday parties and who is being invited (five-year-olds are not always accurate in their information). I am also in no way suggesting that a parent invite an entire class of twenty-one children to a child's party.

However, I do object to the parent's sending the child to school with party invitations to pass out in front of other children who are not invited. After the third such episode, I confronted my daughter's teacher. She confirmed that she allows the birthday child to distribute invitations at the end of class before dismissal, and that sometimes there are invitations for all of the children, and sometimes for a smaller number.

When I told her that my daughter was hurt and confused by this, she told me she was sorry but that "after all, this is life." I was shocked and told her that I felt this was not "life," and if the invitations did not include the entire class, they should not be passed out in class and could be mailed. She agreed that it was tacky and said she would discuss this with the principal. However, I understand that this has occurred in other classes, and I am the only mother who has complained. Therefore I am uncertain as to whether anything can be done to prevent this practice.

GENTLE READER:

The dynamics of parental intervention in school are that most people go along with anything until one person turns conspicuously active. In other words, few people want to initiate change, but lots of people will join someone who does.

Miss Manners believes your point worth making but would like to modify the way you present it. Yes, it is "life" that not everyone gets invited everywhere, and also that everyone in a class will find out what parties take place no matter how the invitations are issued. The concerned parent explains the vicissitudes of social life, reminds the child of them when that child is acting as host, and offers comfort when it is needed. That is no reason for permitting two lessons in bad manners to be conducted in the classroom. It is bad manners to issue social invitations in any formal group that has been brought together for another purpose. Children who are allowed to pass out birthday invitations during class time will grow up to put their wedding invitations on company bulletin boards. If a child wants to seek out his or her prospective guests during lunch hour or recess, or to put the invitations in their cubby holes or lockers, that would be acceptable. It is incredibly bad manners to issue any social invitation at all in front of people who are not being invited.

Miss Manners has long defended teachers from parents' demands that they teach the children good manners. That is a parental job, and well-meaning teachers who try to make up for the parents' omissions are adding to their already heavy loads a burden they will not be able to carry. But she will not countenance the teaching of bad manners in the classroom.

The Theme Party

DEAR MISS MANNERS:

I am planning to have a party for my daughter's third birthday. Is there a polite way to tell the guests, if they are planning to bring a gift, to bring a book for her? She has a closet full of stuffed animals that she never plays with.

GENTLE READER:

There is a way to do this, but Miss Manners won't tell you what it is unless you promise not to allow this child to grow up with the idea that she can demand cash payments on graduations and anniversaries on the grounds that she doesn't want all that junk that people might think of themselves to give her. Is that agreed? For childhood birthday use only, you may declare a literary theme party. Send out invitations with pictures of books or characters from children's books and call it something cute, such as "a little Great Books party." That should give them the idea. In return, Miss Manners requests you to teach your daughter that she must welcome all presents with equal warmth.

❧ PARTY PROCEDURE

Extra Duty for Guests

Are there party guests out there willing to do extra duty? They are sure to be treasured by their hosts, and Miss Manners offers them a special commendation for services above the minimum requirements.

Let us first assume that everyone else who has been invited out does perform the basic routines expected of a party guest. Let us assume that Miss Manners got into the Madeira and is picturing a better world than has existed for some time. Here are the opportunities for extra points:

If you arrive at a large party ten minutes after the actually stated hour, just when the hosts have forgotten that they themselves, when guests, always come a good half hour into such parties and they are sensing disaster—not to mention dreading having to eat party food well into the next month—you get one extra point.

If you begin eating when first asked to, rather than thinking that it is more chic to stand around ignoring the attempts of the hosts to get you to help yourself or go to the dinner table, you get two extra points. If another guest says, "This looks too good to cut into" when presented with a prettily made offering, you get double for saying, "Yes, it looks marvelous; I'll have some."

Asking "May I help?" does not count in itself, but asking and then actually following instructions, whether they are to perform a small task or not to help, merits three points.

Seeking out guests who seem momentarily isolated is worth eight points; doing that to stranded members of the hosts' family who are not of the same generation as the other guests—their children or parents—is the same, but only if you succeed in engaging them in conversation. A mere "What grade are you in?" or "How long are you in town for?" doesn't count unless you use it to get to conversation.

The grand prize, twenty points, goes to the guest who is the first to realize that the party is over and to go home. If he or she does so in such a way as to encourage the other guests to do so as well—a loud, cheery, "Oh, my, I hadn't realized how late it is!"—it's worth fifty.

The Infectious Guest

DEAR MISS MANNERS:

My wife caught a severe cold a few days before we were due to go out to dinner with friends. Since her symptoms included frequent and loud coughing, which I felt would be offensive and disturbing to other diners, I suggested that we postpone the dinner until a later date. She reacted by accusing me of allowing my perception of other people's opinions to dominate my life. She felt everyone would understand that a cold is a natural and common occurrence and that no one would be bothered by a few coughs. Besides, she had already made all of the necessary arrangements and was reluctant to cancel them.

GENTLE READER:

Please keep your wife away from Miss Manners. Not only does Miss Manners not want to catch her illness, but she doesn't want to catch her attitude—admittedly as common as her cold—that naturalness is an all-purpose excuse, that consideration of others is allowing them to dominate your life, and that suiting your own convenience, at the risk even of other people's health, is in itself healthy.

Filling the Gap

DEAR MISS MANNERS:

My husband and I were invited to my friend's house to eat at five, but my husband came home from work at four, starving. He wanted me to call her and see if we could come over then, but I wouldn't. How would you have handled this?

GENTLE READER:

With a sandwich.

Party Hopping

DEAR MISS MANNERS:

My acquaintances are of the opinion that during the holidays, it is permissible to accept more than one invitation for the same evening. They go "cocktail hopping," imbibing here and there and leaving halfway through each festivity, informing the unfortunate hostess, upon accepting, that they won't be staying long because of another engagement.

Last year, one such group was brash enough to arrive at an informal party in black tie, so that they made the gathering a ridiculous mix of game birds and penguins. I thought it a rude and flashy social gambit, enticing the other guests to inquire where they were heading. An ostentatious departure leads the others to worry that they are overstaying their welcome.

My real complaint deals specifically with dinner parties. I recently was hostess to a simple weekend affair with a limited guest list. I was flabbergasted when one

The Late Arrivals With an Extra Guest

Taking Orders

The Five-Year-Old at the Cocktail Party

Party Disasters

couple calmly informed me that they couldn't stay for drinks afterwards because they were going on to a cocktail party. I had prepared the menu myself, set the table days in advance, and was anticipating the end of the meal when I could relax with my friends over coffee or liqueur.

GENTLE READER:

You have apples and oranges here, as well as game birds and penguins. A cocktail party is designed to be dropped in and out of; a dinner party is not. The custom of dropping into many large holiday parties is a sanctioned one. Indeed, there is a sort of community spirit in visiting eggnog bowls all about town, and as long as you are a good guest there for an hour, how many you are able to cram in is a matter of logistics and depends on whether you have someone to drive you home. You are also allowed to attend cocktail parties before you are due at a dinner party, even though the dinner clothes may be provocative to guests who are filling themselves for the night at the cocktail buffet. Dinner is sacred. Once there, you must stay. Only after the full evening has passed and all the guests duly leave may the tireless ones among them stop on the sidewalk to say, "Okay, where shall we go now?"

Early Arrivals

DEAR MISS MANNERS:

I maintain that under no circumstances should dinner party guests arrive even a few minutes early, but rather at the appointed hour or preferably a few minutes later. My spouse is of the opinion that it is acceptable for guests to arrive slightly before or on the hour. Your advice, please.

GENTLE READER:

A great many hosts would like to have guests with your problem. Their guests show up hours late, and since they haven't even answered the invitations, the hosts don't know when to sit down and eat or even when to give up and go to bed. But yes, it is better to arrive a few minutes after the hour than before. Eight minutes past the appointed hour is ideal. Twelve will also do.

If guests should happen to arrive before the time specified and you are not quite ready, you may apologetically finish whatever you need to do, provided you insist that you are especially pleased to have a chance to talk to them alone before the others arrive. You do not actually have to sit and talk with them you understand. It is perfectly all right to say, "How wonderful that we shall have a few minutes alone together" before returning upstairs to change out of your bathrobe. Do not have any fear that this will encourage them to pull this trick again.

Greeting Hosts

DEAR MISS MANNERS:

We've been invited to several open houses, cocktail parties, and coffees this week. Are guests required to ring the doorbell or knock on the door, or is it proper just to walk into the social gathering and not disrupt the host or hostess from the party?

GENTLE READER:

It is improper not to distract the host and hostess upon entering their party. It only calls to everyone's attention that they were neglecting their duty of greeting new guests, even though they may have been occupied in performing other social duties for other guests. Even if the door has been left open, the bell, or the knock, summons the hosts. If it does not, or if you slither in undetected, you must seek them out to allow them to welcome you.

A Vintage Present

DEAR MISS MANNERS:

As an elderly bachelor who is sometimes invited to people's houses for dinner, I have the lifelong custom of taking along a bottle of wine to present to the hostess. In former decades, the hostess would invariably serve that wine at dinner, usually exclaiming on its excellent flavor. But I have observed in recent years that the hostess usually does not serve the wine I have brought, but rather some other wine off her own rack, laying my offering aside, presumably for future consumption.

GENTLE READER:

What has happened is that you, your friends, and presumably the wine have all aged—for the better, Miss Manners trusts. When a young guest brings wine to the dinner party of young hosts, it is to make a contribution to that evening's dinner. Students and others in temporarily straitened circumstances often do this. When an elderly bachelor brings wine to hosts of his generation, he may expect them already to have chosen a wine appropriate to their dinner menu. Therefore, his contribution is not to defray the burden of giving a party, but merely to show his appreciation with a present for them to enjoy later.

Showing the House

DEAR MISS MANNERS:

Recently, when the choir was here, someone who is interested in antiques announced that she wanted to "see the house," and a friend offered to show her around. My husband uses one bedroom for his volunteer tax consultant work, and my sewing machine is in another. We have family pictures in our bedroom that we sometimes show, and a special piece of furniture or two, but there is nothing remarkable. The living room, den, kitchen, and master bath were prepared for guests and my bedroom for coats.

The friend who conducted the tour stayed later to help after everyone else had gone, and when I mentioned to her that I disliked having people dragged into what I consider red places that were none of their concern, she and my husband assured me that "nobody else feels that way." She added, "If I had what you have, I'd want to flaunt it." Am I a strange sort of person, rather selfish and much too sensitive, as they suggest, for not asking visitors immediately, "Do you want to see the house?" Frankly, I find it tacky. But I promise not to be totally crushed if you come down on the other side. Only a little bruised and ruffled.

GENTLE READER:

Miss Manners is certainly not going to come down on any side that condones "flaunting it." So that puts at least two of us in the category of "nobody" who feels that the admittedly widespread habit of examining other people's possessions—food, clothing, real estate, furniture—with unabashed curiosity is rude and vulgar. Aside from deliberate housewarming parties, one properly only asks to see a house, or offers to show one's own (certainly not anybody else's), only with a specific excuse such as "I know you like old houses" or "You're such a marvelous decorator; I wonder if I could see the rest of the house?" One can always say, "Oh, some other time, perhaps." People will assume that you didn't make your bed, but never mind.

Multiple Conversations

DEAR MISS MANNERS:

Is there a gracious way of circulating at a cocktail party? I always feel awkward and unsure of how to move from one group of people to another without seeming rude.

GENTLE READER:

The cocktail party is designed for multiple, quick social encounters rather than prolonged conversation. It may be argued—and Miss Manners would be glad to undertake the task—that that makes the event rude by nature. Nevertheless, one must learn, if one attends cocktail parties, to end conversations. Elaborate excuses are a poor idea because everyone can see perfectly well that you have left only to talk to someone else. The standard excuse is "I'm going to get another drink," but even that is hardly necessary. Just wait for a pause and announce, "Well, it was lovely to talk to you," and move on.

Guest Towels

DEAR MISS MANNERS:

I suppose I will date myself by asking about guest towels, but what is one to do when the only towel available is a family affair? We enjoy visiting these people, but they are all prone to have many problems with infections. I doubt if just soap and water kills germs.

GENTLE READER:

Why should you date yourself by asking about guest towels? Would anyone else want to date someone who didn't wash up? The official solution to the problem is to call cheerily from the bathroom, "Excuse me, but may I trouble you for a towel?" Since no one wants to do this, the usual solution is the unofficial one of using toilet paper to dry the hands.

Rummaging

DEAR MISS MANNERS:

At a high school reunion party, while guests were viewing slides of past glories, we heard a loud crash from the bathroom. A young lady emerged, red-faced. The hostess then announced that she had booby-trapped the medicine cabinet by placing several hundred marbles inside in case any of her guests decided to snoop. Is it horribly unmannerly to look in a medicine cabinet for an aspirin or a Band-Aid, rather than disturbing a hostess who is entertaining forty guests? Is it thoughtful for a hostess to leave items such as these in plain view for guests?

GENTLE READER:

Towels, soap, and tissues are the only required items in a guest bathroom. Extra supplies, including not only first-aid items but also hairpins and sewing materials, are thoughtful additions, but one is not required to run a pharmacy or to allow guests to rummage around. Suppose that the young lady had torn her stockings. Should she have gone through her hostess' bureau looking for replacements?

Nevertheless, this hostess was rude. She has a right to store her marbles in her medicine cabinet, but not, when she catches a victim, to explain why. Miss Manners assures her that the lesson had been learned and that she could afford to say graciously, "Oh, dear, I'd forgotten, that's where I store my marble collection."

🌹 DINNER PARTIES

A Substitute Host

DEAR MISS MANNERS:

My husband is frequently out of the country on business. Is it proper for me to have a male friend sit at the head of the table at a formal dinner party, or must I leave the head of the table empty? This assumes that it is proper for me to host dinner parties when my husband is absent.

GENTLE READER:

Miss Manners trusts that you do not expect her to say that no, you ought to be home alone, knitting socks for your husband and building up grudges against him for preventing you from having friends. Certainly, you may give dinner parties while your husband is out of town. If you leave the place at the head of the table empty, all the guests will stare at it until his absence gives them the creeps.

However, you don't want to make seating arrangements the source of too much amusement for them, either. The way to neutralize the symbolism of having someone "replace" your husband is to assign that seat to another lady, or to a gentleman who is a relative or an obviously respectably intimate friend of the family, or to choose someone apparently on the inspiration of the moment ("Bill, why don't you sit at the end, next to Maxine," or "Roland, I'm going to put you opposite me and ask you to pour the wine, if you don't mind").

Place Cards

DEAR MISS MANNERS:

When the place card is on one's carefully rolled napkin on the service plate, it must be removed before the napkin can be placed on one's lap. What should one do with it? My husband suggests eating it. Should one put it in one's pocket as a souvenir or on the table so that there will be no uncertainty as to who spilled their wine on the tablecloth?

How formal should the identifying name on the place card be? I would expect that when the service is à la Russe, the place card would be as formal as possible. What does one do at formal family occasions such as Thanksgiving, when one wants to ensure that my mother does not sit too close to my husband's mother? Surely "Grandma" is incorrect or too informal and "Mrs. Irene Klutz" and "Mrs. John Ornery" would be too formal for family. May they be labeled "Irene" and "Josephine"?

My husband and I recently attended a charity ball put on by our church. The people there were all friends or acquaintances (at least on the roof-constitutes-an-introduction principle), and I certainly don't feel that my place card should have said "Mrs. Primand Very Proper." Shouldn't it have said "Prissy Proper" if my husband's card said "Prim Proper"? I found being called "Mrs. Primand Proper" irritating. It is not my name, nor does it convey the propriety of my husband's and my relationship.

GENTLE READER:

Do not allow your husband to eat his place card. Repeat: not. No matter how much wine he has soaked it in.

The place card has uses other than the obvious one of showing people where to sit. If you put it above your plate, the person next to you will be able to glance at it surreptitiously and pretend to have remembered you from the last ten times you met. If things are really going well, one uses it to write down one's telephone number for one's dinner partner.

It is not the formality of the table service but that on which the guests stand that determines how the names are written. On an occasion such as a charity ball, when the guests are not assumed to be on intimate terms, the formal form is used, but it is not "Mrs. Primand Proper"; only the title and surname are used, as in "Mrs. Proper" or "Ms. Correct." If guests are all family or close friends, it is lovely to get out the service plates and little pasteboard place cards but absurd to pretend to be on formal terms with them. If your mother has become universally known in your house as "Grandma," then "Grandma" it is, but if the grown-ups call her "Mother" or "Irene," then that designation is used rather than the children's. Tell your husband not to imagine that we all don't know who spilled the wine.

The Signal to Begin

DEAR MISS MANNERS:

Is it true that when guests are invited to one's house for dinner, nobody is supposed to eat until the first bite has been taken by the hostess, or by both the host and hostess? Is this true of buffet dinners, as well as dinners which the hostess serves at the table? Is it also true when guests are invited to a picnic? What if the host and hostess expect the guests to take the first bite? Is this a breach of etiquette? Is it appropriate for me, as a guest at a buffet dinner, to mention that I am waiting for the host and hostess to start eating so that I can eat?

GENTLE READER:

The rule about waiting for the hostess to eat the first bite applies only to the dinner table. Buffet guests and picnickers may begin as soon as they have found a place to sit and have mopped up whatever they spilled while putting their plates on their laps. At the dinner table, the hostess starts things by lifting her own fork or, if the first food served is congealing while others are still empty-plated, by saying, "Oh, please go ahead and begin." Derelict hosts may be prompted by a guest's staring woefully at his filled plate and saying, "Oh, this looks delicious."

"Some More"

DEAR MISS MANNERS:

I don't like anyone to ask me if I will have "some more" of anything. "Will you have some more potatoes?" "Will you have some more wine?" and so on. Isn't it proper to say, "Will you have some——?"

GENTLE READER:

Indeed, it is. Miss Manners especially wishes to draw this to the attention of the many people who consider that a gracious offer consists of "Oh, do have a third piece of pie" or "Come on, a fifth glass won't hurt you."

Turning the Table

DEAR MISS MANNERS:

What should I do at a large, round table when the person on either side of me gets into a prolonged conversation with his other neighbor? It hardly seems polite to catch up on my reading or correspondence.

GENTLE READER:

Dinner party isolation is indeed awkward and is a justification for the unfortunately obsolescent custom of the hostess' "turning the table" by speaking to the gentleman on one side of her for half the dinner and the other for the rest, thus creating a domino effect around the table. (That is not exactly what Miss Manners means, is it? But the picture of all those people in black and white falling on top of one another is too delicious to correct.) Without that, you must simply insist upon entering one conversation or the other. Not doing so is unpleasant not only for you but for anyone helplessly observing your predicament. This is done by leaning into one of those two conversations until you can catch enough of the drift to make a comment. Failing that, you simply tap someone and say with a timid smile, "May I join in?"

Toasting

DEAR MISS MANNERS:

How should a toastee behave when standing and when sitting? Should he or she pick up their (excuse the grammar—we need a neuter singular pronoun in English) own glass? When? If so, should one just hold it while the toast is offered? Does the toastee drink when the toasters do, and if sitting, does he or she remain seated, though toasters stand?

GENTLE READER:

The toastee (we need a better word for that; one wonders where is the marmala-dee) does not pick up a glass at all until the toast is over. Too many people make the silly mistake of drinking to themselves so no proper person would run the risk of even touching that glass. He or she should remain seated, with a modest, and inevitably rather foolish, smile. Only after the "Thank you," which can be two words or twenty, does that person get a drink.

Cleaning Up

DEAR MISS MANNERS:

It is difficult to understand why a hostess, whose guest I am rarely more than twice a year, and then at her strong insistence, ignores me prior to dinner because she is cooking; during dinner because she is serving; and after dinner because she is spit-shining the dishes, pots and pans, appliances, serving trays, ash trays, countertop, kitchen floor, and anything else not moving. In my home, no one is permitted to clean while visiting. After guests leave, it takes about fifteen minutes to do the dishes and put things in order. I enjoy this period while I reflect on the delightful conversation and events which transpired.

Yesterday, I visited a home as a consultant. The hostess, whom I met for the first time, cleaned the whole hour I was present. I had to converse with her by the kitchen sink, competing with running water and ammonia fumes. Is it possible that these people have a communication problem? I have observed people hiding behind their children, pets, home movies, photo albums, telephone calls, and taped comedians to avoid conversation. Could cleaning be another cover-up? My mother never allowed guests to participate in cleaning chores, but she had servants.

GENTLE READER:

Just about everything is defined as a communication problem these days, but it sounds to Miss Manners as if what these people have is a servant problem. Unlike your mother, they don't have any. Unlike you, they have not learned how graciously to be both hostess and cook-server-and-cleaner. (Even Miss Manners, who is pretty efficient herself, is impressed with your being able to clean up a dinner party in fifteen minutes.) What a shame that the duties they chose to sacrifice were those of the hostess: to entertain and be entertained by her guests. Since these happen to be the reason for having company at all, it seems an odd choice.

Perhaps they do not realize that they could serve simpler meals, dished up from platters at the table during the conversation, to avoid last minute cooking and mealtime commuting. If one removes plates (after everyone is finished) and holds them for an instant under a running faucet, one can put them directly into the dishwasher or stack them neatly for later washing in hardly any more time than it takes to pile them haphazardly on the counters and let them get gummy and hard to clean.

Heavy-duty cleaning should certainly not be done in front of guests. Miss Manners was expecting to hear that your hosts started beating the rugs. (However, if the client you visited had not expected you, it may well be that continuing her housework in front of you was necessary for dealing with the unscheduled demand you made on her time.) This does not answer the question of what to do when they engage in it. Disapproval of the practice does not entitle one to continue the party alone, even if that were any fun. Lighting out of there, an understandable impulse, as you were invited to dinner, not to spring cleaning, is unattractive.

It is required to ask, "May I help?", no matter how listlessly and whether or not one actually does. At family dinners, clean-up time is often quasi-social time, and you would do well to pitch in. Miss Manners trusts that you would also assist a hard-pressed friend. But even if the hostess is merely choosing to do her routine cleaning up rather than socializing, you must pick up a dishcloth in the hand that is not holding your drink. The most you can do is to try to distract the hostess. "Please, we haven't had a chance to talk. Couldn't we sit down together just for a minute?"

Who Cleans?

DEAR MISS MANNERS:

In two recent situations, at the end of an informal dinner where I did not know the host/hostess well, all the women stood up at the end of dinner to clear the table. In each case all the women were there because the men were friends with one another; the women were not well acquainted. The men just sat there and talked. I was quite torn between graciously offering to help and sitting with the men, feeling ungracious. Needless to say, the men should have helped, but were not about to do so. How can contemporary, well-mannered women free themselves in polite society from being relegated to the unshared responsibility of a cook-housekeeper?

GENTLE READER:

By acknowledging that help may be necessary without acknowledging that only ladies may provide it. Spring up, declare, "Oh, we must help," and then put a friendly hand on your gentleman friend's shoulder and say, "You men are just gossiping, anyway. Why don't you chat in the kitchen, while we women sit down and really talk?" Then sit down.

Knowing When to Go

It is a widespread and firm belief among guests that their departure is always a matter of distress to their hosts, and that in order to indicate that they have been pleasantly entertained, they must demonstrate an extreme unwillingness to allow the entertainment to conclude. This is not necessarily true. If a guest rises suddenly in the middle of the fish course and vanishes without a word, the host may well worry that something is amiss. When a guest settles in comfortably, two hours after dinner, for a conversation in which the phrase "Did I ever tell you about . . ." is conspicuous, the host knows that something is wrong.

Miss Manners assures you that most hosts are quite resigned to the fact that their guests are theirs only for a defined amount of time, and accept philosophically the idea that they have homes of their own to go to. One needn't, therefore, worry about the rudeness of admitting to this or apologize for departing in ways that suggest that if overwhelming reasons for going did not exist, one would gladly remain until the end of time. "I hate to leave, but we have a new baby-sitter who's only ten, and her mother made us promise to have her home on time, and she lives clear across the city, and we'll probably have to stop for gas, and Mirabelle has a working breakfast tomorrow, and I've got a big meeting—actually, not till afternoon, but I've got to prepare for it, and Benjamin doesn't really sleep well until he knows we're home" is not the way to take leave of one's hosts. It is the very people who babble like this who fail to understand that the reply of "Must you?" is a conventional, unliteral, rhetorical question, and who then plop down again, saying, "Oh, all right, we'll just have one more quick drink," to accompany the sound of the host's heart sinking.

The way to go is to go. "What a charming evening; I'm afraid we must go now" is the proper announcement. One can only reply "Must you?" to those who understand its use; sometimes it is safer to say, "If you must—well, it was delightful to have you here." The only protest from a host to be taken seriously is a whispered "Let them all go; I need to talk to you," and then only at one's own risk. Departure times are:

Half an hour after the last opening offer of service (coffee, after-dinner drinks), not counting offers of refills. Offers to scramble eggs for guests who were originally invited to (and fed) dinner do not count; neither does "Shall I make a fresh pot of coffee?"

Two minutes after the first couple has sent each other exasperated looks, if you are the guest of honor, or, when you are the recipient of one of those looks, if there is no guest of honor.

One minute after the host stands up and says, "We're so glad you could come."

Not even half a minute after you have been given your coat and are standing in the hallway with your hosts—no matter how many clever, complimentary, and explanatory remarks have just occurred to you.

A Victorian gentleman would have known, however, how to encourage the departure of a guest by saying, "Oh, dear, I suppose you want me to order your carriage." It works just as well if there is valet parking or with the substitution of the word "taxi."

Time of Departure

DEAR MISS MANNERS:

Could you please advise me if there is any way on this earth to leave a party politely when, after only a few moments, you find that it is a big, crashing bore?

GENTLE READER:

To leave after a few moments requires an emergency, and Miss Manners does not advise inventing these on the spot. Faking appendicitis or suddenly remembering a funeral only lead to embarrassing inquiries later. However, if it is a large party, you may leave after twenty minutes to half an hour, provided that you do not offer a specific excuse. Clasp the host by both hands and say, "This is a fabulous party, and I hate to have to tear myself away. But it was either that or not coming at all, and I couldn't resist stopping by, even knowing that it had to be brief." Exit.

The Obligation Remains

DEAR MISS MANNERS:

If one accepts a dinner invitation from a person whom one heartily dislikes but does not wish to offend, how soon after the completion of the meal can one tactfully leave?

GENTLE READER:

Half an hour, which is to say, neither sooner nor later than from a dinner given by a person whom one is crazy about but wouldn't mind offending. Etiquette does not recognize a distinction based on the emotions one has for or against one's host. Once you accept a person's hospitality, you incur the obligations of a guest. Perhaps this is why people usually do not run around having dinner at the homes of those they cannot abide.

❧ FOOD

Mixed Messages

DEAR MISS MANNERS:

What do you think of a dinner hostess, skeletally thin, who, immediately after serving the main course, passes around cute little diet buttons that read "He who indulges, bulges" and "Taste makes waist"? As the only fat person at the table, I felt terribly humiliated and self-conscious. As it happens, I have a serious medical problem, but I shouldn't have to announce this in order to get a little courtesy and relief from endless comments about weight, diet, etc., and so on.

GENTLE READER:
It is a new one, even to Miss Manners, that a hostess could first feed her guests and then insult them for having eaten. If she were you, she would have arisen from the table at that point, apologized for having assumed that the hostess had provided food with the intention of your eating it, and departed.

Special Diets

DEAR MISS MANNERS:
If the hostess is obliged to follow a diet for medical reasons, is it considered proper for her to oblige her invited guests, who are in perfect health, to eat foods required by her diet?

GENTLE READER:
Not if they notice. Anything she can pass off as a treat is all right, but if she's on a pitiful diet, she is obliged to excuse herself as briefly and lightly as possible from joining them in the hearty fare that she has provided and which would (she says) give her so much pleasure to see them enjoy.

Allergies

DEAR MISS MANNERS:
I have had, since childhood, an allergy to mustard. As I've gotten older, it has become more and more severe, so that now I carry an adrenaline kit at all times. I was told by the doctor when I had my last taste of mustard, five years ago, that the next time could be my last. You can easily imagine that since mustard is often one of the "spices" on the label of packaged food products, I must be vigilant when I eat out.
How do I politely ask the hostess to tell me every ingredient she has used when I am invited out to eat? I always apologize and explain my problem. People are very understanding, but are often put in the position of feeling that they should cook me a separate dinner if they have, by mistake, used mustard. I can always find enough to eat at parties and want to put my hosts at ease.

GENTLE READER:
No host is going to be at ease while being grilled about all the ingredients used in dinner. Perhaps he secretly ordered carry-out food and has no idea what is in it. Even if he made it, he will be aware that forgetting a mere culinary detail could lead to your demise at his table. Those with extremely complicated food problems are advised to eat before social events, so that they may survive if nothing is avail-

able that is beyond suspicion. In your case, you could also request from people you know fairly well that a piece of plain meat, fish, or whatever be put aside for you without any sauce whatsoever.

Apologies

DEAR MISS MANNERS:

Last night, my husband and I had a dinner guest, an employee in my husband's business who is a sweet lady and very important to the business. My husband chose the menu. I did all the cooking. I was unhappy at the way the pork chops turned out. I said so, and I apologized to our guest for the less than pretty chops. She smiled and said, "Don't worry about it." Again, during dinner, I remarked that I did hope that the pork chops tasted better than they looked.

Later on, when we were in bed, my husband brought up the pork chops and belligerently told me two or three things I should have done when I saw that they were not up to par. He says that I should say "I am sorry" over and over and over again for serving an inferior meal. We have been married thirty-six years, and this is a common scene. Please tell me, how would you handle such a situation?

GENTLE READER:

By saying, "For heaven's sake, darling, it's after midnight. Next time, I promise, I'll let you make the pork chops. Good night." However, Miss Manners admits that after thirty-six years, the strain would probably get to her. Criticizing one another's behavior after social events is not her idea of the recipe for a good marriage.

The best way to ruin a dinner, no matter how good or bad the cooking, is to keep apologizing for it. People who turn out perfect fare have been known to leave a bad taste in everyone's mouth by claiming that it could have been better. Even if the meal is dreadful, the polite thing to do is to laugh it off once and then forget it. To do otherwise suggests that the guest must have come only for the food and informs her that her hostess is more interested in her own showing as a cook than in enjoying the guest's company. Both ideas are insulting.

Secret Recipes

DEAR MISS MANNERS:

What is a polite way to decline giving away a recipe to a friend or even a relative? I have worked awfully hard, and searched high and low, to learn the few recipes I have. There are ten years' worth, and I am proud of them. It has never failed that when I have had guests over for a meal, they have repeatedly complimented me on my dishes. I'm sorry to say that I am not as pleased about their compliments as I should be, because what always follows is the dreaded question, "Can I have your recipe?"

My main reason for declining is that then I would run out of recipes I could comfortably cook for them. My dishes would become everyday to them and no longer special. The situation has gotten so bad that I am very reluctant to invite guests home for a meal or even pot luck. I would very much like to get back into the mainstream of family and social gatherings without that dread. If only I knew how to decline in a friendly manner, so as not to offend.

GENTLE READER:

It's a good thing for you that Miss Manners' concern is etiquette. That way, she is not tempted—or at least is able to resist the temptation—to explore the values of someone who believes that her social worth is connected with the originality of her recipes, and allows fear of forfeiting that to come between her and her relatives and friends. Were Miss Manners to stray from her mandate, she would take you severely to task, forcing you to understand that human relationships are based on something deeper than menus.

She will now do her proper job. The way to refuse to give out a recipe is to say, pleasantly, "Oh, no, that's a secret. I want you to keep coming back here for that." Please do this with a merry twinkle that conveys the idea that you do not truly accuse these people of trying to "steal" your recipes. Miss Manners hopes that if you do this often enough, you will come to believe it.

Store-Bought Food

DEAR MISS MANNERS:

I complimented a friend several times on a vegetable salad she served at a dinner party. When I called to thank her for the lovely evening, I asked her for the recipe. She admitted, without embarrassment, that she had bought it at a well-known gourmet shop. I, however, was very embarrassed at having put her in the position of having to admit this. Do you think it is proper to ask for recipes, especially in these times, when women work and are often too busy to prepare an entire meal by themselves?

GENTLE READER:

Like your friend, Miss Manners sees nothing embarrassing in a lady's admitting that she didn't cook the dinner she serves her guests. There was a time, in some circles, when it was considered rude to assume that she did: One didn't compliment the hostess on the food because it was supposed to have been provided by her cook. More recently, it became conspicuous when a guest did not discuss the food because hosts had presumably put so much work into preparing it. Even aside from the fact that, as you say, more people are serving precooked food, extensive quizzing or explaining about the food is enough to send many of the faces around the dinner table drifting down to rest quietly in that food until the conversation picks up. To request a recipe privately, as you did, is perfectly acceptable; so is your hostess' answer.

Reserved Wines

DEAR MISS MANNERS:

At a company party my spouse and I attended, there was a menu beside each place setting stating the foods and wines to be served. Three wines were included. We were served a rosé with the meal, and my spouse asked for a glass of the burgundy. Our server thereupon informed the table that the chablis and burgundy were for "V.I.P.s." We were all rather taken aback. The man who plans this annual party is usually unerringly correct. I would not dream of questioning him about it but am curious to know if this practice is acceptable. Surely if some wines were reserved for V.I.P.s, they should not have appeared on the menu.

GENTLE READER:

The concept of the V.I.P. does not exist in the annals of etiquette. All guests are important, and while there may be a guest of honor, there are no menus of honor. Your unerring host erred at least three times: by serving different wines to different guests, by putting a clue to this disreputable behavior on the menu, and by employing an indiscreet waiter.

Caffeine

DEAR MISS MANNERS:

Can you suggest a tactful way to learn whether a host is serving decaffeinated coffee? When it is on the tip of my tongue to inquire, I suddenly think that if the answer is "no," the host will feel obligated to rush to the kitchen to prepare it. I love coffee with dessert but am not willing to pay the price of a sleepless night, and I certainly do not want to inconvenience the host.

GENTLE READER:

Reply to the offer, "No, thank you, I love coffee, but I can't drink it at night." If the host then turns to the next guest, it's caffeinated; if it is decaffeinated, he will say so.

If he offers to make decaffeinated coffee, you might want to pause just a bit before protesting that he should not go to the trouble. During that pause, Miss Manners promises you, six other guests will jump in with "Oh, then I'll have some, too," and they, not you, will have persuaded him to make some.

The Food Pilferer

DEAR MISS MANNERS:

Over the Christmas holiday, I had thirty people in for dessert. In addition to things I had made, I ordered a medium-sized array of chocolate-dipped strawberries and orange sections. One of my guests left early, preparing a "doggy bag" for her four children of the chocolate dipped fruits. She didn't ask, but as my husband saw her wrapping up the chocolates, she nervously asked if it was all right. When he told me about it, I was shocked and felt that this woman showed very poor manners. My husband said that other guests went to the table to try the fruits and were disappointed that they were already finished.

GENTLE READER:

Bad manners? You're lucky that this woman didn't sweep your lace tablecloth and silver forks into her bag to give her doggy-children the treat in its proper setting. Miss Manners hardly blames your husband for being too stunned at the spectacle of an invited guest turning into a thief to say anything. Had he managed, however, the thing to say would have been "I'm so sorry, but this is for our guests. Had I known your children would be hungry, I certainly would have arranged to send them food. Please allow me to do so tomorrow." What is more, Miss Manners would have then sent them a package—not of candies but of basic groceries. This is a form of polite sarcasm that she admits would probably not faze your brazen guest, but it would make Miss Manners feel better.

Social Disasters

It is not that most people cannot be trusted to make fools of themselves upon occasion without Miss Manners' help. But they do not seem to know what to do next.

One need not take the trouble to be drunk and imaginative to disgrace oneself. Any one of the following situations will do:

- Breaking an obviously unique and treasured item in someone's house.
- Looking a dear old friend in the eye and addressing him or her by a wrong name, preferably that of someone your friend does not particularly admire.
- Making an innocent remark that seems to have an obscene meaning—so obscene, in fact, that one does not want to acknowledge, in order to stop the titters, that one is aware of what it means.
- Stating a prejudice without realizing that it directly affects someone present. Miss Manners is not talking about true bigotry, which she has no desire to defend from such punishment, because the lesson that it is never safe to make such statements should be forcibly taught. She means such things as saying, "I'm so sick of gravlaax, everybody who wants to be chic is serving it these days," just before the gravlaax is served at dinner.
- Spilling one's food or drink all over oneself, or better yet, making an extravagant gesture that spills it over one's dinner partner.
- Showing up at a social occasion so wrongly dressed that one is automatically isolated by the other guests.
- Getting the calendar confused and therefore not showing up at an event

where one's absence will be conspicuous, such as a small dinner party where the others have been growing progressively surlier by being kept waiting, or showing up on the wrong night to find the host and hostess in bathrobes.

• Arguing a point vigorously, only to be told, after one has thoroughly stated and defended one's position, that one's opponent in the conversation is a leading authority on the subject.

The solution that appears most helpful to anyone in this position is to disappear from the face of the earth. Miss Manners does not deny that it would best solve the problem, but there are some other techniques one might try first. Miss Manners hardly dares hope that they will erase the searing memory of shame with which these events leave one, but only that they will banish the worst symptoms, such as the need to hide under the blankets weeks later when there is no one else present. There are no guarantees that any of these will work; she is only offering a possibility of comfort in situations that are basically hopeless.

1. Denying it. "Roderick? I didn't say Roderick, I said Herman. How could I get your name wrong? Haven't we been best friends for eight years? At least, I've always thought so, Herman. I don't know how you feel."

2. Rising above it. "Did I say something funny? Oh. Well, obviously what I meant to say was . . . "

3. Claiming to be understood out of context, as it were. "No, no, I didn't mean gravlaax. I love gravlaax. This is delicious. I meant what people try to palm off as gravlaax, which isn't anything like this."

4. Making a joke of it on the spot. The best such example of which Miss Manners has heard was Franklin P. Adams' reaction when George S. Kaufman's wife broke someone's antique chair, which fell on the floor in a pile of expensive splinters. "Beatrice," he said, "how many times do I have to tell you that's not funny?"

5. Making a joke of it later. "Then, after I had expounded my whole theory of Renaissance art, guess who I found out I was talking to?"

6. Apologizing. "How could I have gotten the date wrong? Good heavens, I can't believe I did something so awful. Why, you must be furious—but no more furious than I am at myself. This is unforgivable."

7. Groveling. "No, no, please, you must let me pay for it, or I will never be able to live with myself. I ought to be shot. No one so clumsy ought to be allowed to walk around free. Please, I can't stand it; I hate myself." This is a form of number 6 so exaggerated that the recipient will do anything to put a stop to it. If it doesn't work, it at least airs the subject's feelings, thus taking the edge off his own conversations with himself.

Don't Let it Happen Again

DEAR MISS MANNERS:

A discussion of unforgivable accidents prompts me to reveal a dark secret of my life. Thirty years ago, I found myself in an old building in Paris, one of those antiquities in which a communal toilet in a closet under the staircase survived as a relic of the seventeenth century. Miss Manners is probably familiar with those ancient public conveniences where a hole in the floor serves as the outlet of human endeavor. As I pushed the door open, I saw a flaking ceiling and flaking walls lit by a fifteen-watt bulb. No sooner had I ascertained the wattage of the bulb than a horrible scream from the lower regions of the closet drew my astonished eyes to a squatting female form. Always the perfect gentleman, as Miss Manners would have me, I did not run away, but stood my ground and delivered a lengthy apology in halting French, but to no avail. My speech was met by a string of curses and the lady's attempt to push the door shut with much force. I pushed the door open again to continue my expression of regret, but she simply pushed the door back, most unladylike. This inconsiderate behavior led me to wait outside until she appeared, upon conclusion of her business transaction, when I asked if she could ever find the heart to pardon my unpardonable conduct. To this she replied that she could not, as long as she lived. I never returned to Paris to verify whether she survived the ordeal, but this disastrous experience taught me to be moderate in my excesses and never to apologize too profusely. What is Miss Manners' advice for these occasions?

GENTLE READER:
Miss Manners is highly amused by your story, but resents the attempt to associate her with the conduct of a gentleman who would insist on holding open the door of a water closet while a lady was using it—would, indeed, barge in on her a second time—under any pretext whatsoever. If you really want Miss Manners' advice, it would be to continue to stay out of Paris. Your use of the term "these occasions" worries her. How many of them do you plan to have? Miss Manners would think that one of them would be enough.

The Disastrous Dinner

DEAR MISS MANNERS:
In an abortive attempt to impress the various dignitaries of local "society," and thereby to gain access to their circle, a lady of my acquaintance invited them all to a splendid formal dinner party. Her setting was superb; the lighting, delicate; the wine, perfectly coordinated. Everything was moving briskly along, according to the stuffiest standards, through the aperitif. It was at that moment, with all her guests eagerly anticipating the main dish, that the hostess suddenly realized that cooking a main course had somehow, in the heat of all the other preparations, slipped her mind. Dinner ended with the appetizers: There was no main course.

Time and distance render us callous. When I heard later about her fiasco, although I knew I should have kept a straight and, if possible, sorrowful face in the presence of such suffering, I confess to bursting out in uproarious laughter. Never mind the lecture on my rudeness. Karmic laws being what they are, my heartless mirth has undoubtedly ensured that I, at some future time, will be forced to reenact the scene. And with each succeeding guffaw, it becomes increasingly likely that I shall have to do so as the hostess. It is against this impending cosmic retribution that I am wondering if you might tell me just what, in the face of a dinnerless dinner party, is the appropriate behavior of (1) the guests and (2) the hosts. P.S. Use my name and you, too, shall sustain karmic penalties.

Gentle Reader:

Don't threaten Miss Manners. She doesn't take to it well. However, she does appreciate being amused. Without knowing how eventful social life is in the circles you describe, she can tell you that this incident would have enlivened any society she frequents. Do not worry about having laughed at it; laughter is the essential ingredient of social disaster. The hostess should have led the laughter, and it would have been rude of her guests not to join in. There is nothing more embarrassing than having people treat you as if they were not greatly surprised when you did something spectacularly awful.

Should this happen at your table, let out an exclamation of some sort (the kind that means shock, not anger) to get the attention of everyone. Then say: "You'll never believe what's happened! I spent so much time trying to make everything perfect, and working on the appetizer (murmurs from guests: "It's delicious"), that I forgot to make a main course! Good grief! There's nothing for dinner! Wait! Everybody have some more wine, and I'll go scramble some eggs" or "send out for something" or "make a restaurant reservation."

By this time, the hostess should be doubled up in laughter, and the guests, reassured that they will not starve, should join in with merriment and offers of help in the kitchen or emergency measures. Their final obligation is to assure the hostess, when they leave, that the improvised evening turned out to be more delightful than any uneventful one could have been.

Extraordinary Embarrassment

Dear Miss Manners:

When I was purchasing some gardening items at the local supply store, I placed my selections on the counter while the prior customer was placing her change in her purse. I didn't notice that my rake had become caught on the hem of her very full dress. While searching for the price to show the cashier, I lifted the head of the rake, which brought her hem up with it. She suddenly shrieked, and I looked forward and saw that her hem was almost waist high, and she was quite clearly uncovered. Before I could utter an apology, she began a barrage of insults directed toward me, which lasted long after her dress came back down and I had said that I was sorry about the accident. I could understand her being upset; she probably felt that I had intentionally lifted her skirt, which I had not. But wasn't it rude of her to carry on in such a manner? I feel that this only added to everyone's embarrassment.

Gentle Reader:

You are quite right that when an embarrassing accident occurs, with no one's intentional misbehavior to blame, the usual polite thing to do is to subtract from the embarrassment, rather than add to it, after apologies have been made. However, every once in a while an accident may occur that is so awful, so grotesque, and so conspicuous that the only thing to do is to go with it, so to speak. The consolation comes later, when the acute embarrassment has subsided and both parties are left with a funny anecdote to tell.

This is such a case. The lady's shrieking, although dreadful for you, was the inevitable result of your unfortunate action. For her calmly to assess the fact that she was uncovered in public, quietly remove her dress from the raised rake, and nod pleasantly in acknowledgment of your protestations would have been too much to expect. Besides, it would have implied that she was not greatly surprised at finding her hem around her shoulders in public. The only thing you could have done, in addition to apologizing, was to rival her expressions of embarrassment by your own, calling out "How horrible! How could I have been so clumsy? I'll never forgive myself," and so on (always wording it so that it was clearly an accident), until it was the lady who became anxious to shut you up, rather than the other way around.

Drunken Guests

All over America, after entertainments, there are people suddenly seized by a sense of politeness that inhibits them from telling their cherished friends that they are too drunk to drive. These paragons of manners therefore stand politely by and watch others hit the road, or miss it, as the case may be. Miss Manners is naturally only interested in the etiquette aspects of this situation. Her worry is that those frozen with politeness may subsequently find themselves with apologetic feelings towards the families or victims of their friends that will be impossible to express in the normal social vocabulary. Let us therefore do what we can to prevent the greater etiquette problem, while not violating the delicate feelings that make one reluctant to express disapproval of the conduct of one's friends.

Miss Manners has asked herself whether this dangerous confusion of duties and priorities is part of the Guest Towel Principle of Social Education. That is the principle by which people who were told 632,598,347 times during the course of their childhood to pick up their clothes never learn to do so, but the same people, having been told only once not to use the guest towels in the downstairs powder room, never touch a guest towel in their entire lives. Not even when they are guests.

Is the problem, then, that attempted socialization does work, after all, but only on all the wrong occasions? Miss Manners is inclined to think so. She cherishes the belief that there is an urge to politeness in everyone, battered as it may be by the urges more generally given free expression, and that if it doesn't get used in the proper channels, it will come out inappropriately elsewhere.

Etiquette is rigorous, but it never requires stifling cries of danger. Admittedly, one applies different standards when this occurs within the true social network, where it is desirable to season the warnings with tact—but if that is not possible, the alarm takes precedence.

The rule about stopping one's drunken friends from driving is absolute. Politeness is then added when the person is fit to receive it. By definition, one's friends are never drunk; they are "obviously not well." The way to caution a slightly inebriated person is to say, "You must be on some medicine. I didn't see you drinking anything much, but you may not realize that you're having a funny reaction. Let me drive you home. You know, with some of those medicines, even a glass of wine will do it." To a person not in a fit state to understand such subtleties, one merely takes charge at the time. A version of that tactful speech about the effect of medicines is made the next day. You didn't think Miss Manners was going to advise you to perform a completely tact-free action, did you?

Houseguests

The Guest Room

The ideal guest room does not have a guest in it. It is thus the ideal place to store books that nobody wants but nobody can bear to throw out, spouses who snore, and knickknacks of tremendous sentimental but absolutely no aesthetic value.

If you do not put a guest in your guest room, you also need not put in it the standard essentials: extra blankets and pillows, current magazines, a reading light, towels in a range of sizes never used by people in their own homes, padded hangers, mirrors, empty drawer space, wastebaskets, a key to the house, and a clock; or the considerate extras: writing paper and stamps, flowers, ice water, sewing kit, and fresh miniature toiletries.

Surprisingly, it is easier to stock your guest room with all these things than it is to keep it empty. Even people who are scrupulous about never issuing invitations to anyone not within easy commuting distance have relatives or friends who take vacations in their cities, need shelter from domestic quarrels or painters, dispatch their own friends and children on vicarious visits, or misinterpret such ordinary pleasantries as "Let us know if you're in town." Miss Manners does not deny that there are times when it is a pleasure to have houseguests and people who are delightful to see around the clock. There is a question, however, of control. Hosts

495

who abdicate control at the beginning are likely to go to pieces at a time when the other members of the family have to keep saying, "Shhh, they'll hear you."

The first rule is: Never issue an invitation that you do not want to issue. The way to refuse a houseguest who proposes himself by saying, for example, "I thought I'd come down for a week or two," or "Can I stay with you until my furniture comes?" is to reply, "Oh, let me make a hotel reservation for you, and be sure to keep an evening open for dinner," or "Oh, dear, that's a bad time for us." One does not say, "I'll probably be out of town then" ("Okay, fine, I'll house-sit for you") or "I'm expecting my in-laws at about that time" ("Love to see them—and I can just plop down on the couch").

The second rule, for those who have violated the first or for those issuing any invitation, however genuinely, is: Never propose an open-ended visit. "Come on Friday and stay though Sunday" is better than "Come for the weekend," because people tend to interpret "weekend" as they wish their employers did. It can be "We'd love to have you spend the summer—say, the Fourth of July until Labor Day," if you must, as long as the departure date is stated.

The third rule is: Yes, you may throw out people who ignore the departure date. The polite method is to say, "We've had such a marvelous time having you. I'm afraid we're going to need the room by Tuesday." Then the guest room may be put to its most enjoyable use, as sprawling space for a family happily spreading out again after even the most beloved of guests has gone.

Time Apart

DEAR MISS MANNERS:

I am a college student who will be bringing a friend home for ten days at spring vacation. Naturally, I want to spend a lot of time with Jane, but my best friend at home, Susan, will also be there, and I want to see a lot of her, too. Some of the time, the three of us could do things together. Quite frankly, though, Susan and I will want some time to ourselves. I want to do what is correct, but the prospect of being Jane's twin for ten days rather daunts me. How can I tactfully explain that I want to go off for several hours and leave her to her own devices? What provisions should I make for her entertainment while I am gone?

GENTLE READER:

Hosts and guests both need some time off during a ten-day visit, and Miss Manners will help you have some, but she warns you that the laws of hospitality do not permit you to import someone into a strange home in a strange city and then expect her to improvise independent activities, as she would at home.

Jane must be included in all your social plans while she is visiting, but you can have quasi-social activities if you have provided for her first. If she sleeps late, for instance, you could announce that you are running out in the morning and will be back by the time she gets up. Or you could pounce on something she said she wanted to see and suggest, "Why don't I drop you at the museum and take care of a few things, and then pick you up?"

Trials of a Troubled Host and Hostess

The Modern Houseguest

The rules of etiquette for houseguests were developed with people in mind who are so overwhelmed at the honor of actually being encouraged to use the lace-edged guest towels that their only desperate wish is to be worthy. Dear friends of their hosts though these people may be, confident as they undoubtedly are in their ordinary pursuits of life, they only want to be told how best to avoid making trouble. Should they arise at dawn and spend the whole morning, if necessary, listening for the first creak so that they may pretend to arise at the identical hour the family does? How can they insist that they adore eating out, so as to carry a portion of the meal costs, without seeming to slight the cuisine of the house? What, oh what, do they do about the shameful fact that they cannot leave their sheets as laundered as they found them? Miss Manners does not wish to discourage such houseguests from showing sensitivity to their hosts, much as one is occasionally tempted to tell them, "Oh, lighten up," because they may be making more trouble fretting than they do just by existing.

Communal arrangements, promiscuously offered hospitality, and the general decay of civilization have created a new sort of creature calling itself a houseguest. This is the person whose invitation was never authorized by whoever runs the house; who feels less obligation to the owners than he would to a public accommodation, where he at least understands that he has to pay bills and be responsible for damage; and who is confident that questions of reciprocation, consideration, and gratitude have nothing whatever to do with his situation.

The chief difference between such people and squatters is that somebody connected with the house did invite them. There is no question of ejecting them unceremoniously, although it sometimes comes to that. One or more residents want them there, and the others—whether they are co-renters or parents—recognize the legitimacy of allowing visitors.

They could even turn into pleasant additions if they were required to abide by rules of behavior protecting the hosts from undue imposition. For that, one needs a house policy about how invitations may be issued, expectations about guest behavior that the inviter must convey to his or her guests, and perhaps even a clear definition of a houseguest. A houseguest is a person who stays for a defined and limited amount of time, as opposed to an unanticipated resident, who may be the result of a sudden attack of romance or insanity on the part of one of the residents. (Overnight guests who leave before breakfast don't officially exist.)

In a house in which parents preside, the policy should be that all prospects and the timing of their visits must be cleared in advance. These houseguests do not incur expenses, but they do incur obligations—the minimal normal courtesies being acknowledging the presence of the parents, observing the amenities of the house, and thanking them afterward in a letter. Households of peers may recognize each person's right to entertain separate guests without providing character references, but the houseguest should nevertheless be introduced to all residents, so that he or she recognizes that this is a household and not a rest station. The object is to make the houseguest sensible of a position which may be flattering, convenient, and pleasant, but should never be comfortably free of that awareness that one is, in fact, living at the pleasure, if not the sufferance, of the hosts.

Setting the Terms

DEAR MISS MANNERS:

We enjoy vacationing visitors, but the visits are very expensive. If I'm showing my guests around town, who is supposed to pay for lunch? Occasionally, we will take our company to another town on an all-day outing. Once, when my husband and I and our guests were having an expensive lunch out, the gentleman looked at us when the check came and asked if we wanted to pay for lunch or dinner that night. Since we had already made reservations, we were obligated for at least one. We wouldn't have eaten out if we didn't have company.

Both my husband and I work. I work at home, providing most of the money. When my guests awake, I leave my work to make breakfast. One friend visited us for two weeks, and each day she waited for me to stop working so that we could go out for the day. I suggested that she take my car and go herself, but she said she didn't mind waiting. When she didn't reach for the lunch check, I had to. She is very wealthy, and we are not. How do I get out of playing cook or social director? We love our family and friends and certainly don't want to hurt their feelings, but we really can't afford this. How can we make them realize that they are on vacation, but we are not?

GENTLE READER:

The time to establish the terms is when the invitation is issued or, more likely, when the visitors' request to visit is approved by the hosts. While Miss Manners is not exonerating your guests, or excusing them from sensitivity to your requirements and attempts to lighten your load as host, she believes that you have inadvertently misled them. A simple and gracious "Why, of course, we'd love to have you" only suggests that you are free to make holiday with them, and considerately planning excursions plants the idea that you wish to be hosts on those occasions as well.

It would be no less charming to write, "We'd love to see you, of course, and you are most welcome to stay here, but I'm afraid we'll be working most of that time, so you'll be on your own all day." You can suggest side trips, but if you assume that they will take them alone, and they then coax you to come along (which you can also decline, of course), they will be more likely to understand that that part was their idea, and therefore their treat.

Houseguests "Au Naturel"

DEAR MISS MANNERS:

We are fortunate enough to have a lakeside second home. Our bedroom opens directly into the den, where my husband's cousin was sleeping on the sofa bed during a recent weekend visit. He is about our age, early thirties. I'm an early riser, and one morning I emerged from our room and froze in my tracks. Our guest was flat on his back and fully displayed. His covers had evidently slipped off, leaving him *au naturel.*

I paused for a long moment, not knowing how to proceed. The internal debate went something like this: If I went over to cover him, he might wake up while I was doing so, resulting in a great deal of embarrassment for both of us. Even worse, he might wake up as I walked toward him. If I passed through the room to the bathroom and on to the kitchen, he might be awakened by the sounds from either place. Then he'd be embarrassed, knowing that I had been in the room while he was exposed. I also thought of going back into our room and making enough noise to rouse our guest before I opened the door. He would then cover himself before I entered the den. This idea was passed over because the appropriate noise would also awaken my husband.

Finally, I decided to return to my room and go back to bed, to wait for our guest to wake up on his own. Presumably, he would cover himself, even if he rolled over to sleep some more. The problem resolved itself an hour later, when I heard him moving about the den. After waiting a few minutes, I entered the den to find him fully dressed and in the process of folding up the sofabed. He never knew I'd been in the room earlier.

What about the future? May I be so bold as to ask our houseguests to wear nightclothes? If that is not allowed, how should I handle another scene like this? Do you think I did the right thing this time?

GENTLE READER:

It seems to Miss Manners that you have given an awful lot of thought to what is essentially a nonproblem; she only hopes you have enjoyed doing so. Had you merely passed through the room while the gentleman was asleep, he would never have known when he had shed the covers, and therefore whether you had observed him. He might even have re-covered himself later in his sleep.

The proper way to warn him or future guests would be to say, "I'm afraid there isn't a great deal of privacy in the den. I'm generally up early, and I have to pass through in order to get to the kitchen. I'll try to be very quiet and not wake you, but you might want to bear this in mind."

Separate Rooms

DEAR MISS MANNERS:

My husband and I are both thirty-eight, have been married for ten years, and have no children. Three years ago, my father-in-law died. I liked him, and to this day, I still feel the loss. I did not expect Eva, my mother-in-law, to become involved in a sexual relationship, because she is religious and talked degradingly of her friends who engaged in this. However, she became involved in a sexual relationship with Jim, based on "enjoying each other's company." The three of us were invited to the house of my father-in-law's nephew for Thanksgiving, and Eva took Jim along. For Christmas, Eva wanted to stay at our house and to bring Jim.

To be truthful, I like Jim a lot, but I felt intruded upon and uncomfortable having an outsider who I had just met once sleeping in the bed that my in-laws had slept in for so many holidays. Knowing this, my husband asked his mother to come alone, but she refused. So we went to Eva's and the four of us had a wonderful time. Now Eva is asking to visit again. This time, I asked her to come alone, but she refuses to visit without her lover. I feel I would be betraying my father-in-law by having them sleep here.

My husband has had no problem accepting this relationship, but he plans on having them sleep in separate rooms if I insist. I think I would be more comfortable if I were introduced to Jim over a period of a year, so that I could ease into accepting him and having them sleep at my house.

GENTLE READER:

If you want to take a moral position about what goes on in your household, as you are entitled to do, please keep it clean. It is one thing to refuse to put unmarried people in the same guest room, and quite another to picture what they might do there and how the lady's deceased husband might feel if he were watching. Your speculation along these lines is unseemly.

Besides, this is a bogus issue. If Eva and Jim were married, you could not refuse to include him at family gatherings or to house them together. As it is, you can insist upon putting up unmarried guests in separate quarters, in respect for your own moral stance—but not if you muddy the matter by declaring that you could get used to immorality in a year's time. As for including him at family events, why not, if it pleases your mother-in-law? Serious suitors are generally asked to such events. Miss Manners cannot believe that you would prefer her to remain miserable in her widowhood. Aside from how it affects your household arrangements, your mother-in-law's morality is for her to decide. If your husband is thirty-eight years old, his mother is—wait a minute; Miss Manners has to get out her calculator—a grown-up.

Service

DEAR MISS MANNERS:

My parents, my three brothers, and I were invited by friends to use the guest house of their estate at the Cape for a week. The morning of our departure, I stripped the beds, replaced the spreads, collected the towels, and prepared to wash them in the washer/dryer in the pantry of the guest house.

My mother rebuked me for doing so, saying that she would not expect her guests to launder their own linen. I realize that our hosts have a staff, as do my parents, and would not be doing the wash personally. However, as I pointed out to Mama, her guest house does not have a washer/dryer, so she could hardly expect her houseguests to lug their linen up to the back door and chat with the cook while waiting for the dryer cycle to finish. Neither was I planning to remake the beds or scrub the bath. Common sense and the availability of the washer/dryer led me to believe that the simple task of washing the towels and sheets we used was a nice gesture. My mother remained adamant about my being incorrect, but as the sheets were off, I washed them and stacked them in the linen closet.

GENTLE READER:

Miss Manners wishes that she could just whisper to you that no, it was not really necessary to do the wash, although it was hardly the social crime your mother seems to think. The reason she hesitates to make a public statement is that people will soon be using this as an excuse to leave messes in households where there are no staffs which, at that last census, seemed to be a more common arrangement than the one you describe. One tries to save one's hosts trouble by leaving the dirty laundry in a neat pile and replacing the bedspreads; and one does not make extra trouble for their employees. Routine household work, including laundering the bedclothes of visitors, is what they are paid to do. If you think about it, the washer/
dryer is there so that they will not have to lug the linens around either.

Suspicions

DEAR MISS MANNERS:

We traded homes for part of our summer vacation with some acquaintances and then had a friend stay in our house. When we returned, we could not find our antique hallmarked silver spoons in the silver drawer. I have searched the entire house and can find no trace of them. I feel awkward about asking any of the people who stayed in the house if they know the spoons' whereabouts, as I am certain that the spoons are no longer here. What could I do in order to get my spoons back?

GENTLE READER:

It depends on whether you want friends, as well as spoons. If not, you could try reporting all these people to the police. Allow Miss Manners to advise extreme caution. When one has lost or misplaced something, the first temptation is to accuse others. It is notorious that people who are frantically looking for something often overlook the obvious. If you determine that your spoons really are gone, the most you can do, short of making legal accusations (in which case you are bound to be accusing at least one person unjustly), is to write politely to your guests, reporting the loss and asking whether they put the spoons away for safekeeping and forgot to tell you.

The Guest's Pet

DEAR MISS MANNERS:

I am a young, single, working-class male, owner of two dogs. These dogs are my friends, and I enjoy traveling with them. Some relatives are not dog fans and object to my visits with the dogs, but I do not wish to leave them in a kennel. I understand that this is a diverse world, and that some people own cats or just don't like dogs. I'm not a fanatic; I just want to take care of my friends.

In visits of over two or three days, is it impolite to suggest, volunteer, or usurp household chores? I back off if the host declines, and I won't offer to clean the bathroom, but I will gladly cook or mow the lawn.

GENTLE READER:

As your attitude seems reasonable, Miss Manners has decided to allow you to get away with the idea of classifying your pets as full-fledged friends. One does not, however, bring along any uninvited friends when making visits. One does not even request to be allowed to do so. What one does, to cadge such an invitation, is to say, "No, I'm sorry, I can't stay with you because I'll be traveling with my dogs," and then fall silent, so that the prospective host may, if he wishes, reply, "Oh, for heaven's sake, that's no problem. Bring them along."

The question of compensating hosts for their hospitality is a separate problem. The correct methods of compensation are:

1. Being helpful. This mean that you not only clean up after yourself (and your friends) but cheerfully offer to help around the house. You can't go so far as to usurp chores, but you may say with conviction, "I'd love to cook for you tonight" or "Let me mow the lawn. I need the exercise, and I would really enjoy it."

2. Asking them out (and insisting on paying for it). "Oh, come on, let's go out tonight. Show me a restaurant that you like."

3. Sending a present. This can either be a luxury item of food or drink or anything that you feel, after staying in the house, would be accepted with pleasure. Miss Manners only asks that if you decide it should be a dog, you check with the hosts first. Not everybody wants a live-in friend.

A Bread-and-Butter Check

DEAR MISS MANNERS:

A few months ago, an elderly friend of my husband's asked to stay at our house while he recuperated from the loss of his dear wife. Of course, we said yes. This gentleman and his wife were like a second set of parents to my husband, never having had children of their own. Yesterday we received a lovely note thanking us for the hospitality of our home. We also received a check for a very large amount of money. Miss Manners, we don't know what to do. We did not ask him to stay to derive any financial benefit from the situation. And we don't want him to think that the reason we ask him to return is to receive similar reimbursement. My husband and I want nothing to do with that check, yet we fear insulting the gentleman by returning it.

GENTLE READER:

This is what comes of the increasingly common practice of giving money instead of presents, a custom that Miss Manners considers unfortunate, although she has heard a thousand times the arguments in its favor (too hard to shop, can't think of the right thing to buy, etc.). Had the friend sent you a present, any present, you would have understood the gesture. Even presuming that that was what was intended, Miss Manners agrees that you cannot allow your sympathetic hospitality to be recompensed as if you were running nothing more personal than a hotel.

One solution would be to donate the money to charity and so inform your friend. You may also return the check with a letter saying that you appreciate the gesture but cannot possibly accept reimbursement for the privilege of being such a intimate friend; that you were honored by his visit at such a difficult time in his life, and consider that it is you who are indebted to him for a lifetime of kindness. Yes, this will probably embarrass him into going out and spending the money to buy you something. This does not worry Miss Manners, as it was something he ought to have done in the first place. Besides, it will do him good to get out of the house, and to be forced to leave off dwelling on his sorrow by having to think of what might please you.

Absent Hosts

One could say that the best host is an absent host—the one whose invitation is, "I'm going to be away all summer. Why don't you use my beach cottage (city apartment, mountain camp, weekend retreat, boat, townhouse) whenever you feel like it?" One could, but one wouldn't. What one would say, Miss Manners prefers to believe, is, "But do you mean to say you're not going to be there? It's a charming place, but we'd really hoped to spend some time with you. That's incredibly sweet of you, but are you going to be gone all summer? What an awful shame. Well, perhaps we might run up once or twice if you're sure that would be all right. But it just won't be the same without you. Let us know when you'll be back, so that we can have you here." Only later, and well out of earshot, may one add, "Wow."

The absence of the host does not mean an absence of obligations on the part of the guest. It just means that these are suspended until the host returns. In other words, anything you can clean up or replace without subsequent detection doesn't count.

Thus it is not technically improper for the houseguests of an absent host to hop about the house, saying, "Did you ever see anything so tasteless in your whole life?," and "I bet this cost him a bundle," and "Look what's behind the stove." Miss Manners devoutly hopes that a civilized guest would not be able to do this, being used to a lifetime of waiting until getting home from any social event before saying, "I'd forgotten how tedious they can be; could you keep a straight face when they asked how we liked that new picture? I hope we have something in the refrigerator, because there really wasn't anything edible there." This is not license for snooping.

It is polite to remove evidence of having pursued even legitimate activities. If there is time, one has the sheets cleaned, instead of just folding them, as one would if the hosts were present. Trash should be removed. One wants to avoid what a lady of Miss Manners' acquaintance calls the Eue! Effect of having some-one come home to a supposedly clean house and, upon finding hairballs in the wastebasket, exclaim "Eue!"

Not only should food supplies consumed by the guests be replaced, which requires careful attention to exactly what the items were, but extra treats should be left for the returning hosts—imperishables if they are not returning immediately, or, if they are, fresh food for preparing the first meal or two after their return. This is the equivalent of taking one's hosts out to dinner, which you would do if they had been there entertaining you.

Oh, yes, you would, unless they actually cried and stamped their feet when protesting that they didn't want to go out. Protests by hosts that they would rather cook all their houseguests' meals, or attempts by them to pay the resulting restaurant bills, are polite conventions not to be taken seriously.

None of this excuses the houseguest from providing a proper present in gratitude for having been entertained overnight, and in proportion to the number of nights. Miss Manners is not going to help you out by suggesting what would be an appropriate present for you to get. You know your hosts better than she does and ought to be able to guess at their taste. You know what they could use. Oh, yes, you do. Miss Manners saw you peeping around when you thought she wasn't there.

Presents

The Person Who Always Remembers ought to be a joy to the world, and receive a special commendation and lots of brisk pats on the head from Miss Manners. So, why do we feel so lukewarm about the acquaintance who never fails to send a card for each birthday, anniversary, and holiday? What makes the office staff groan when another supply of home-baked goodies is distributed by the one person who always thinks of it, and who promotes all the office gatherings and celebrations? Why is the visitor who never, ever comes empty-handed, but always with a little special present to offer, not always greeted with open arms? Is it possible that thoughtfulness can get to be a nuisance?

Unfortunately, it is possible. Miss Manners is not crazy about thoughtlessness, either, and does not mean to suggest that there is any comparison between the consequences that these opposite attitudes produce. Thoughtlessness can be anything from annoying to heartbreaking. Thoughtfulness is nearly always heartwarming—and even when it is annoying, it is frankly not that much of a trial.

Not in order to strengthen the victims of thoughtfulness in resisting further abuse does Miss Manners bring the matter up. Anyone who would go so far as to demonstrate offense at what are obviously kindly intentioned actions will find no protection from her. Rather, she wishes to explain the problem to those who have extended themselves in order to be agreeable to others and have been disheartened by the results, and perhaps discouraged from practicing optional courtesies altogether.

506

"I always call people on their birthdays. Do you think anyone ever calls me?"

"They hardly bother to thank me anymore; they just expect me to do everything as a matter of course."

"Wouldn't you think it would occur to anyone that maybe I have feelings, too?"

Those are the secret dark thoughts of the Person Who Always Remembers. When they eventually burst out, they produce some uneasiness in the recipients of all that thoughtfulness. But not for long. Nowadays, these people are soon able to comfort themselves with such callous observations as "It's different for him; he's got nothing much else to do," "She's just trying to lay a guilt trip on me," and "All that attention he lavishes on everyone is just a sign of his low self-esteem." Worse, they assert, "She shouldn't be doing it for thanks, anyway," as if hope for acknowledgment tainted good deeds. Miss Manners will endorse no such cheap excuses for people who insult kindness. Yet, she does understand why the recipients of constant small attentions may become a mite edgy instead of purely grateful.

The problem has to to with proportion and appropriateness. Does the gesture exaggerate the degree of intimacy? Would reciprocation be a chore because it is unsuitable to the relationship? It's one thing to have your mother remember your birthday; you are supposed to remember hers anyway. It is a delight to be surprised by an occasional fuss made by an old friend or a promising new one. It is quite another thing to have to keep track of the former neighbors' family milestones solely because they fire off automatic remembrances of yours. If an occasional treat is unilaterally institutionalized, without the enthusiastic cooperation of others, is it as much fun? Colleagues may not want always to be taking without giving, but they may not be willing, either, to commit themselves to regularly catering for the office. A rare, lavish present in return for an exceptional favor is a pleasure; escalating the exchange in frequency or value makes it a burden.

Miss Manners is not trying to dampen the generosity of those who want to do something extra to add to the charm of life. She is only saying that this effort will be more appreciated if it is done cautiously, with the individual situation in mind, and due attention to whether reciprocity will be appropriate and manageable. Being thoughtful requires some thought.

Joint Presents

DEAR MISS MANNERS:

If my daughter is living with a man but not married to him, and they give gifts at Christmas time, is it proper to say that they're from her and her live-in boyfriend? I'm not particularly happy that they are not married.

GENTLE READER:

Whether you are worried about how the card should be signed or how the item should be identified when showing it to others, you have not made clear to Miss Manners. You have made your chief worry clear, but that is not a question of etiquette. In any case, a present from two people is associated with both of their names: "Love, Kelly and Clint" or "Kelly and Clint sent me this lovely doily." Etiquette does not recognize the term "live-in boyfriend" to use in this connection, as, for example, a card might be signed "Merry Christmas from Aunt Karen" or "this is from my Great-Uncle Lloyd."

Hints

DEAR MISS MANNERS:

What, if any, is the correct and proper way to let people know that one has a birthday coming up and would like to be remembered? I'm not talking about expensive presents, but just a card or warm greeting or small remembrance so that the day won't be a total waste. I must tell you that I'm usually the one to bake the birthday cakes, send the cards, buy the gifts, and so on, since my mind is like a steel file cabinet of calendar dates. I don't expect everyone else to have this phenomenal memory, but why is it that they usually forget my birthday? There must be a polite way to bring it up in conversation without making it sound like a broad hint. I'm not a kid or a teenager, just a recycled one living in prime time.

GENTLE READER:

Miss Manners appreciates your recognizing that your expectation is both unreasonable and childish. We are presumably not talking about your mother, but about more or less casual friends who neither have your sort of memory nor especially expect you to celebrate their birthdays. As long as that is understood, and you don't use the occasion to mope and pout and draw tragic conclusions about the failure of your life and the callousness of the world, she is willing to help you. Oddly enough, the solution is a mild version of this, something along the lines of "Wow, I can't believe I'm going to be thirty-three on Wednesday. Really makes you stop and think, doesn't it?"

The Task of Shopping

DEAR MISS MANNERS:

Every year, I receive Christmas and birthday gifts from my parents, in-laws, and others, that I know have been thought of, shopped for, often paid for and mailed by the female half of the couple. I am beginning to question addressing my thank-yous and letters to both parties when it is the woman who is doing all the extending. I continue to do so for fear of hurting or offending either party or both. The women involved obviously want their mates included, so perhaps it is none of my business what part, if any, the male species played.

I think that men and women should be responsible for signing their own names to their own gifts and letters, but I do not wish to impose my way of thinking on others, especially those of an older generation. Yet I do feel pretty strongly about men "checking out" of certain duties. Am I just being peevish?

GENTLE READER:

Not only peevish, but foolish, Miss Manners is afraid. In the name of justice, you are condemning cooperation. One of the advantages of being part of a couple is the ability to divide the work. It would be ridiculous to have two people living together—whatever their gender or relationship—each cook an individual dinner, for example, or do laundry separately. Families generally send joint presents. How they assign the tasks is their business. You don't care for the traditional way of doing so by gender, with correspondence falling to the wife while car maintenance may fall to the husband; it would be better if each person chose the tasks he or she preferred.

Miss Manners, who gives you credit for refraining from insulting people who only want to give you presents, and from imposing your wishes on others, especially your elders, doesn't believe you are being as fair as you imagine. You would not feel the same way if it were the gentlemen who were doing the joint correspondence or present-giving. Not only is it not for you to criticize these divisions in someone else's marriage, but how do you know that the aunts wouldn't rather do the shopping and writing?

"No Gifts"

DEAR MISS MANNERS:

When one receives an invitation to an anniversary dinner party stating "No gifts, please," do most people generally disregard that? I do not like to go empty-handed if everyone else, or almost everyone else, will be bringing a gift.

GENTLE READER:

Miss Manners stands firm against the practice of stating "No gifts" on an invitation. One is not supposed to be thinking, when giving a party, of collecting presents—even thinking of them to the extent of warding them off. She has always disliked having to do this, because the motivation behind "No gifts" is a kind one.

Now you, and no doubt others, are making this unattractive ploy useless as well as incorrect. Well, so be it. If people ignore the offensive phrase, perhaps hosts will drop it and Miss Manners will no longer have that conflict. However, she cannot in good conscience advise you to go against the expressly stated wishes of your hosts. What others do is never an argument against doing what is right.

Pricing Presents

DEAR MISS MANNERS:

Every Christmas my father's feelings are hurt because I buy him a nice present and buy my stepmother a small, inexpensive gift. Neither of my brothers acknowledges her, not even verbally, and my sister mails one small gift for both of them. I am buying something only to pacify my father, not because she is my favorite stepmother. I buy small gifts for my stepfather and my husband's stepfather, whom I like. My father says, "We spend the same on you as on your husband, and you should do that for us." I am ready to stop exchanging gifts altogether!

GENTLE READER:

It is not quite nice of you to price your presents according to whether people are relatives or steprelatives, but, then, it's not quite nice of them to notice how much the presents are worth, so you are even. Your sister seems to have an effective solution in getting them a joint present, so that the unevenness of outlay on each of them is not apparent.

Multigenerational Presents

DEAR MISS MANNERS:

It has been my custom through the years to give gifts to all my grandchildren at Christmas and birthdays. Now, being on a fixed income, I find it harder and harder to buy gifts and was wondering about omitting gifts to the parents and giving only to the little ones. But of the five grandchildren, one couple has no children, and it seems cruel to cut them out entirely.

GENTLE READER:

Indeed, it does. What about a present, for each household, of something they can all enjoy? The edible comes to mind, as it always seems to during holiday time, but perhaps something like a family photograph album or a copy of a very old family picture could be enjoyed by both generations.

Using Presents

DEAR MISS MANNERS:

I made a wedding gift for a very dear friend and her husband, who have been married one year, and I have yet to see it displayed in their home. This hurts me, since I spent many hours working on it, always with their colors and tastes (so I thought) in mind. Many people complimented me on it, and a few even hinted that they would have liked it. Is there a tactful way of asking for the gift back, possibly suggesting that they might like another gift in exchange for the one I made them? I ask this only because so much of my time went into it. A store-bought gift would never make me ask this.

GENTLE READER:

You have no control over a present once it is given, however much care, thought, money, or work you put into it. That is what it means to give something. Not only can you not ask for it back, you cannot inquire about why it is not on display. Anyway, Miss Manners is sure that they are so crazy about it that they are saving it for a special place or time.

Inappropriate Presents

DEAR MISS MANNERS:

Every year, I get the urge to write to my friends and relatives, telling them what not to send me for Christmas. I never do, of course. I just smile and thank them and stuff their gifts into the back of my closet. All anyone has ever seen me wear is silver jewelry, but everyone buys me gold jewelry. I never wear it, but that doesn't stop them. One boyfriend decided to surprise me with a gold and diamond engagement ring. He's the one who got the surprise: How could I marry someone who paid that little attention to me? The guy I married was smarter; we went shopping together.

The message I'd like to send is:

If your friends are vegetarians, find out why. If it's for their health, don't buy them chocolates or cakes; a fruit basket is more appropriate. If it's because they don't like killing animals, then leather, fur, and ivory are inappropriate.

In my first year of marriage, I appreciated kitchen stuff. By the second year, my cabinets were full, but it still comes.

Most people know not to send a *Playboy* subscription to their minister, but they don't think about the political and/or religious views of others before sending subscriptions.

Don't send Tootsie Rolls for people without teeth.

Obviously, to tell people what not to send me would be to criticize past gifts, and I can't do that. But I'm expecting my first child, and I'd like to know if I can prevent toy guns, robots that turn into guns, camouflage diapers, toddler army suits, and junk food from coming into my house. I guess I can intercept packages, trash the gifts, and buy replacements, but the grandparents might get suspicious if the kid writes a thank-you letter for a *Speak 'n' Spell* when they sent an M-18.

GENTLE READER:

Oh, merry Christmas to you, too. Miss Manners promises never to send you diamonds or furs. Dear me, that was not at all the attitude Miss Manners intended to take. Indeed, she agrees with you that the most important aspect of a present is the evidence that the giver has put himself in the place of the recipient, and used thought and imagination to discover what might delight that person. An inappropriate present is disappointing not only as a nuisance, but as a sign that this sort of loving observation has not taken place.

There was something about your tone that lost her. People make mistakes with the best of intentions. Miss Manners finds it hard to sneer at a gentleman in love who assumed that a gold and diamond engagement ring would be welcomed even by a lady who was not already demonstrating her taste by wearing one. She also fears for grandparents who may err, or who may even select something that pleases the child, only to find it on the parents' proscribed list. The answer is that one cannot fully control the selection of presents for oneself and one's children. The only proper tool available is the hint, and if that fails, you have to say a falsely enthusiastic thank-you and put aside what is inappropriate.

Fathoming Taste

DEAR MISS MANNERS:

We are proud of the successes of our adult children, but the down side is their attitudes toward presents. Just to receive a gift is not sufficient anymore; the gift must follow exact color schemes, preferred labels, and so on. Can you imagine our concern when a gift of handwoven placemats was opened and held up to the wallpaper to ensure that it was a perfect color match? It was, but our hearts were in our throats.

Should we not feel hurt when we see gifts that we've carefully selected end up in garage sales? What used to be a joy in selecting gifts has become an agonizing situation, as we're on a fixed income, and these "yuppie" habits have destroyed the spirit of giving. Giving cash is out of the question and repulsive to us. They are double-income families, but their gifts are not extravagant. Is this "perfection" a phrase of yuppie success or peer pressure? Is this selfishness a rejection of us or our values? One-upmanship? How do we handle this?

GENTLE READER:

Just as your children are overscrutinizing your presents, you are overanalyzing their scrutiny. This sort of thing can lead to madness. Miss Manners concedes that your children seem a bit finicky, and ought at least to conceal from you even the possibility that your presents might not match their tastes. Yes, it would be nice if they kept them for their sentimental value, but perhaps it would be best if you did not attend their garage sales.

Miss Manners steadfastly refuses to find sociological or psychological significance in this. Your values or theirs are not symbolized by the color of the placemats; they just like the silly things to go with the walls. Miss Manners applauds your disdain for solving the problem by giving money. There must be other kinds of presents—books, food treats, wine—which you could choose with some confidence that your taste coincides with theirs. You could also give family mementos, whose value is beyond the question of mere taste.

Returns

DEAR MISS MANNERS:

A very close friend moved into a new apartment recently, and my husband and I bought a large basket as a gift for her. Saturday night, we were invited to her home for dinner, and in Saturday's mail there was a card from the store saying that we had a credit for a basket that was returned. I jokingly said to her, "Well, that's the last time I get you a gift." She laughed and said, "Well, it just wasn't right. But they weren't supposed to do that." One of the other guests said, "Everything has to pass (the decorator's name)." There was some banter about the ethics of our using the fifty-dollar credit for ourselves, and whether we should buy her another gift. On the way home, we decided to ask your opinion.

GENTLE READER:
Miss Manners' opinion is that you are pretty good friend, able to survive an awkward situation by joking about it. Lots of people would have managed to escalate this into a major fight about taste and rejection, in which the word "values" would have been thrown around until all hope of saving the relationship was gone. The only culprit here is the store. It is acceptable to exchange a present, provided that one does not directly confront the giver with this action, which your friend did not intend to do. You need not send another present, but it would be a nice gesture, just to show that your feelings were not hurt. How about flowers or fruit, nicely arranged in a disposable basket?

Disposing of Worldly Goods

DEAR MISS MANNERS:
People warned me that being poor would be difficult, but no one told me that becoming poor was going to be a problem! In six months, I shall be leaving the United States to become an overseas missionary. I shall be gone for a minimum of four years. My dilemma involves what to do with all of my worldly possessions. Since my parents are nearing retirement age and are in the process of selling their house and moving into an apartment, storing special items with them is not an option. I am twenty-two, and most of my friends are near my age. None of them has the space available where I could store things.

I don't really mind not being able to keep things, since I don't value possessions all that highly. But how do I get rid of them? Since I'll be in a tropical climate, I won't need my heavy wool sweaters and skirts. Would it be improper to give a few of them to friends, or should I donate all of them to the Salvation Army? I have a beautiful red and black sweater that would look much better on a certain friend than it ever did on me. Can I just give it to her, or would that be tacky?

I can't throw away a painting or dishes I've never used. In this case, would it be in poor taste to return them to the giver? Would it be better to give them to someone else? What do I do with an inspirational message addressed to me personally that a friend wrote, copied onto parchment paper in calligraphy, and had framed for me?

I have been very blessed by the amount of love friends have bestowed on me. I know that they'll understand in general that I need to part with many of my material possessions, but I don't think that will translate easily into an understanding that I can't keep the afghan that was crocheted especially for me.

Do you think it would help if I composed a poem thanking them for all they've given me and explaining that it is only because of all the love that each of them has given me that I am able to find the strength to become a missionary? What if I had a small party and allowed close friends to choose any possessions of mine that they would like to have? Those things that no one expresses an interest in but that are of some value could be donated to a worthy organization—or am I in danger of hurting someone's feelings again?

GENTLE READER:

Yours is an unusual problem—refreshing in an age not unduly complicated by the desire to purge oneself of possessions—and, as you realize, it requires unusual tact. Allow Miss Manners to assist you to take your natural sensitivity just one step further.

Your friends, in giving you these presents, treated you as a treasured individual. They will therefore not enjoy being treated in return as a group. Rather than writing one poem and distributing it to everyone, please take the trouble to write each person an individual letter, expressing your friendship and awareness of the symbolic value of the article that particular person gave you, along with an explanation of the strange circumstances in which you are unable to keep it. Be sure to omit any comment about not valuing possessions. To say so would not only deprecate the symbolic meaning of these presents but cast aspersions on the normal worldliness that these people presumably enjoy.

In some cases, you could ask the donor to keep something precious for you and to remember you by. You could suggest to some people one or two things they might want: "I've always thought this sweater would look better on you; tell me frankly if you could use it" or "Do you need any dishes?" A giveaway party would be a mistake. Can you imagine the feelings of someone who sees his own present picked over and rejected by everyone?

Taking Offense

DEAR MISS MANNERS:

My relative read a self-help book that she really liked and said I should read. Then she gave me a copy. I gave her no indication previously that I was interested in such a book, and I am insulted that she thinks I should read it. I resent her trying to "fix" me. How do I refuse this book and the mothering it represents?

GENTLE READER:

It is rude to refuse a present unless you are positive that it was intended as an insult. (A peculiar subdivision of this category is the diamond bracelet from a gentleman one hardly knows; that is an insult one refuses very sweetly. Unfortunately, that is not your problem.) Although you are offended by this ill-chosen offering, the fact that your relative herself used the book indicates that it was not offered as an affront.

Miss Manners does not realize why more people are not aware that presents and advice may easily be accepted without ever being used. Every tot knows instinctively that the way to accept unwanted mothering is to say, "Certainly, Mother," and then do nothing about it. Should your relative make the further mistake of asking if you have read the book or changed your life in accord with its dictates, the polite reply is, "Not yet, but I'm looking forward to it."

The Expensive Insult

DEAR MISS MANNERS:

Throughout the seven years of my marriage, and before, I have been a supporter of animal protection. My views are well known throughout my family and my husband's family. Whenever asked, I have expressed my views on the use of animal pelts for fur garments. I do not approve of it. To be clear, I do not approve of it for myself. My mother has a mink coat, and I certainly would not think to criticize her for buying it. But whenever the coat has been offered to me for special occasions, I have declined.

A couple of years ago, my mother-in-law, knowing full well my feelings, presented me with a lynx coat for Christmas. Every eye in the room was on me, watching for my reaction to this confrontation of my convictions. I said seriously, "You really shouldn't have," and everyone laughed, because they knew exactly what I meant. My mother-in-law said that she expected to see me in the coat often. After all, it had been an expensive gift.

My husband told me that it would be very rude to ask his mother to return the coat, so I sold it and took the money—which I considered to be mine, as the coat was mine—and forwarded sizable donations to various animal protection organizations. Frankly, that was a great Christmas present for me. When I was discovered, the dam broke. I am now the most inconsiderate, ungrateful creature who ever lived. Maybe I am, but wasn't my mother-in-law a little inconsiderate in her actions?

GENTLE READER:

What we have here is a modern etiquette rarity: the expensive present intended as an insult. It seems to be worth a great deal of money to this woman to annoy you.

Do not succumb to the attempt to put the etiquette onus on you. It seems to Miss Manners that by refraining from criticizing the views and practices of others, even though they are in opposition to your morals, and by managing a fairly gracious response to this unpleasant gesture, you have behaved meticulously under trying circumstances.

Pets as Presents

DEAR MISS MANNERS:

Am I correct in thinking that someone should not bring live animals (dog, cat, chicken, duck) as a gift? Is there a polite way to tell someone that you do not want the responsibility of an animal?

GENTLE READER:

Short of leaving a baby in a basket on someone's doorstep, this is about the most inconsiderate present one can give. The polite response is "Oh, how darling, wouldn't we just love to keep him? But our routine is such that we couldn't possibly give him the kind of home he ought to have. It wouldn't be fair to the poor thing. You're sweet to think of us, but I know he'll be happier with you." And then pick up the duck, cat, or baby, and hand him back.

A Poor But Generous Grandmother

DEAR MISS MANNERS:

What's the right way to tell a seventy-seven-year-old grandmother who gets you clothes at thrift stores (cheap-looking, too) that you really don't like them? Most of the time, whatever she gets is not "in," has a tear, or has something missing. If it is okay, it usually breaks or tears, and she blames me for not taking care of it. She can usually tell that I don't like it by my expression. I can say I like it, but still she says, "No, you don't, hon." Should I tell her to give me money instead, or have her bring me along, or what?

GENTLE READER:

There is no right way to tell her. That is not what she needs to know. Miss Manners understands that there is a real problem here, which cannot be ignored, but you have to deepen your understanding of it before you can solve it. There are two things to be learned from this situation, and both of them are way beyond the matter of the actual offensive presents:

1. Your grandmother wants to please you.
2. She is short of money.

The real question, therefore, is not how you can turn clothing you don't want into items you do, but how you can allow your grandmother to feel that she is succeeding in her kind attempts without undue cost. That eliminates your suggestions of her giving you money directly or shopping with you. Because she sees through your attempts to look pleased when you are not, your well-meant policy of accepting with thanks and letting it go at that isn't working, either.

You know your tastes and what might be possible for your grandmother to do; Miss Manners asks for your ingenuity in coming up with solutions. Begin by telling her, sheepishly, "Well, since you asked, it's true that the kids wear all kinds of crazy fashions I wouldn't expect you to keep up with, and I really would prefer—" and then you mention something of little or no cost. Make sure that your gratitude beams on your face. Miss Manners promises you that such an exercise in consideration will be an invaluable addition to your life.

❧ EXPRESSING GRATITUDE

Motivated Thanks

DEAR MISS MANNERS:

For my whole life, I was asked, forced, and coerced into writing thank-you notes for gifts I had received. The habit remained when I moved out on my own, until one day about six years ago. On that day, I realized, while writing a thank-you note, that I didn't have to write these notes anymore if I didn't want to. However, on that same day, I knew why I should write them. I was truly grateful by that point for each and every gift I had received. I knew from my own experience the thought, time, effort, and money that went into a gift purchase. If that did not at least elicit a thank-you, then I was truly an assuming and ungrateful individual.

The years went on, and I sent my own and my daughter's thank-yous, and I never really noticed if anyone else sent them. But now, because of the number of gifts I buy, I realize that I rarely receive thank-yous, and I'm sick of it. With the cost of things nowadays and my valuable time and effort, I cannot understand someone not sending a thank-you note for a gift. What is right nowadays?

GENTLE READER:

Miss Manners would have hated to send you a present during the time after you had decided you were not required to write thank-you letters, just before you concluded that you would do so voluntarily. She would have felt exactly as you do about people who do not trouble to express thanks, which is exactly the way everyone else on the giving end feels. Only those on the receiving end consider it unimportant.

Your manners happen to have worked, because there was no such hiatus between your automatic thanks and your motivated ones, but your rationale doesn't work. Miss Manners would go so far as to say that the reason the whole society doesn't work these days—have you noticed?—is exactly that people take your approach: that they should observe the amenities only if they happen to feel the genuine impulse to do so.

Small children are able to separate their enjoyment of presents from any feeling of gratitude to those who gave them. That is natural behavior. Therefore, they must be taught by rote, as you were, to do the right thing, whether they like it or not. You are doing your daughter no favor by writing her thank-you letters for her. Miss Manners happens to think that it is that very habit of doing the right thing, unnatural as it may be, that suggests to people such as yourself the idea of improving upon their original and natural impulses. Had you never been required to express your thanks, you might well have gone merrily through life without ever having pondered the relationship between gifts and gratitude. Many a grown-up brid-al couple manages this with no trouble at all—except from people such as yourself and everybody else in the world, who resent not being thanked. However, had the philosophical basis never occurred to you, the habit of writing thank-you letters would have served to put a decent veneer of kindness on your natural lack of gratitude.

The Reward of Gratitude

DEAR MISS MANNERS:

Having followed instructions and taught a child to write thank-you notes, I call on Miss Manners for help in dealing with an unexpected side effect. My daughter, now six, writes her own notes and expresses delight in most gifts, even new tooth-brushes, so it is fun to give her presents. Her grandmother and godmother enjoy it so much, that they give her several gifts each month. Even if a child could keep her toys picked up, it is physically impossible to keep forty dolls in our two bedroom townhouse. They are occupying the dining room and scouting the living room. I have tried to remove the least favorite toys, but I feel heartless at best, and she now regularly checks all wastebaskets and bookshelf tops. It must be inappropri-ate to blame family and friends for a domestic problem, but what is the proper perspective?

GENTLE READER:

First, may Miss Manners borrow your child for a short while? She wants to trot her around the country, saying to all the other little children, "You see what hap-pens when you write thank-you letters? Do you begin to understand what an in-vestment that is?" We won't tell them of the other result—your perfectly reason-able desire to end this flow of booty. Miss Manners thinks it admirable; she just doesn't want to sabotage the lesson on greed she is teaching the others.

Let us hope that it won't warp your daughter's attitude if you feel that you can pass on a tactful word to her admirers that token presents and attentions, such as letters, would actually mean more to her than adding to a doll overpopulation. Your daughter is ready for advanced etiquette. You have taught her the joy of re-ceiving, and now you might try teaching her the joy of giving. It is cruel to confis-cate toys she has already become attached to, but before a major influx of presents occurs you could suggest that she have the fun of choosing what she wants to keep and deciding what she can give to other children—say, through a hospital or other institution.

Explaining the Connection

DEAR MISS MANNERS:

For many years now, I have sent gifts to my five grandchildren, whose ages range from eight to sixteen. To date, I have not received so much as a thank-you note or a phone call in acknowledgment. I have discussed this with my two daughters (mothers of the children), with no results. Frankly, I am feeling reluctant to give more because of the children's poor manners.

GENTLE READER:

Your children's manners are now out of your control, but you might try working on your grandchildren's. A kindly talk with each, saying that you had always hoped to please them with your presents but are afraid, from their lack of response, that you failed ought to provoke a protest in which you explain the necessity of feedback to keep generosity going.

Gratitude and Gullibility

DEAR MISS MANNERS:

I think it dreadful to teach children to deceive—to trick—to feign emotions! They will learn that soon enough. Furthermore, who would they think they were fooling? Not a grandmother!

GENTLE READER:

Miss Manners takes it that you are a grandmother who does not want to receive thank-you letters for presents unless the child really adores the present and is spontaneously moved to sit down and express gratitude in writing; your grandchild is not inhibited from asking you to give him what he wants in the way of presents, treats, or cash; you do not want to be asked how you are unless the child is curious about your health; and you wish to hear in honest terms what the child thinks of everything you offer him to eat and what he would prefer to have. In other words, you want the child to remain in the natural, and therefore uncivilized, state in which he was born, which is to say infantilism. Miss Manners congratulates you. The chances of getting your wish are extremely good.

Birthday Thanks

DEAR MISS MANNERS:

My son has attended many birthday parties in his first years of grade school. I buy nice presents, costing between $6 and $10, depending on the child. Should the mother of the birthday child send a thank-you to the parents and/or child in the mail? The birthday child ends up with about thirty presents (what a day!), and I feel it's only polite to thank the parent who drove to the store, purchased the gift, and wrapped it.

GENTLE READER:

The mother of a child who has had thirty children at his birthday party ought to be spending the next day in bed with a cool compress on her forehead, not writing thank-you letters to the guests' mothers. The fiction is that it is the children themselves who give and receive presents, not the mothers. That means that guests' mothers should require their children to help with the selection, while the birthday child must express his own thanks. The parental work in both these matters is considerable, but it is supposed to be a learning experience, as they say in the trade. Written thanks are not required for such presents delivered in person. If a present is sent, the birthday child must write; if preliterate, he must be present at the writing, talking over the wording of the letter.

Published Thanks

DEAR MISS MANNERS:

Is there any redeeming social value to the publication of private thank-you announcements in local newspapers? It has always been my feeling that a thanks expressed in person to the gracious party, and followed by a written note mentioning specifically the gift or service given, was fundamental and efficient. These public announcements in our local papers express thanks to all and sundry and are always followed by the phrase "and anyone we may have forgotten." To forget to thank someone would be the height of neglect, so aren't these public expressions redundant?

GENTLE READER:

People will go to any lengths to get out of writing thank-you notes, won't they? Well, it won't do. The only possible excuse for a newspaper expression of thanks is that one does not know the identity of one's benefactors—if, for example, one was the victim of an accident and was aided by people who disappeared before anyone learned who they were.

Self-Addressed Envelopes

DEAR MISS MANNERS:

What is your opinion of asking guests at a shower to address thank-you card envelopes to themselves so that the bride or mother-to-be will have the correct address? I was appalled by such a request at two recent family showers. When my own daughter was married a year ago, I gave her a variety of thank-you notepapers, an address book, and a roll of stamps.

GENTLE READER:

Why not just ask them to thank themselves? One wouldn't want to overburden someone already gracious enough to receive so many presents with the necessity of showing gratitude. Miss Manners is not only as appalled as you, but curious as to how anyone managed to issue party invitations to all those people whose addresses were unknown.

Recreation

❧ THEATERS AND OTHER
PUBLIC PLACES

Going to the Movies

It is with regret that Miss Manners anticipates the passing of Going to the Movies, an activity rapidly succumbing to a double onslaught of advancing technology and retreating manners. She is aware that the public movie theater has not quite closed yet and that clusters of them are being built in shopping malls every working day. There are people in these theaters, and they must have gotten there by Going to the Movies. Still, the viewing areas keep shrinking to something that may one day approach living-room size; living-room manners are being practiced in them; and, as a result, people whose tolerance is shrinking are retreating from them to their own living rooms.

The problem is that members of the audience, who were never taught the difference between going out and staying home—and the manners appropriate to each—are making the experience unbearable for others and even for one another.

Now that it is possible to show feature films at home, many people are simply giving up the struggle of going out.

Miss Manners thinks that a shame. It is not just the movie itself for which people like to go out, but the occasion. She thinks movie watching at home is a sensible idea, generally cozier, more convenient, and cheaper than going out, but she thinks people ought to have the choice. There is no real choice when the only difference is between being among people who have agreed on how to behave and among those who have not but are prepared to fight it out on the spot.

Home viewing manners are different from audience manners. Miss Manners is not insensible to the fun of supplementing film dialogue with the much wittier (to the ear of the beholder) repartee of family and friends, or to the comfort of lounging and the pleasure of eating. (This must not be taken to negate the firm rule that it is rude and vulgar to watch television while eating a meal. It only means that it can be enjoyable to consume food, and maybe lots of it, while watching lightweight entertainment. Anyone who doesn't see the difference probably believes that manners are just a matter of common sense.) What can be fun among friends is offensive when strangers do it. Their remarks simply interfere with the sound track, rather than elucidating it, and their food always smells terrible.

Being in public has different pleasures to offer. Getting out of the house, savoring the anticipation and specialness of having to plan something, dressing for it, getting there, mixing in crowds, sharing one's reaction with lots of others—these activities were traditionally available at the movies for less money, formality, or preparation than at theaters or concert halls.

The trade-off was forgoing the chatting, the chewing, and the cuddling. These things, like garlic and amateur music, are meant to be enjoyed voluntarily, with everyone participating. Such rules were more lax at movie theaters than in other auditoriums, because attendance is more casual and there are no performers present who might be distracted. So, for decades, there was general agreement in the society that whispers, popcorn, and an arm around the back of someone else's seat (or other mild courtship; the rule was that it shouldn't change the silhouette seen by the person sitting behind) were tolerated.

The new generation is naturally bewildered to find that its viewing manners work fine in one place and arouse fury in others. Such subtleties as the definition of a whisper or the difference between popcorn and pizza are not even suspected. Miss Manners is afraid that these people will soon be the losers. Going out is fun exactly because it is different from being at home, and the most casual public place still requires different behavior. When those differences disappear, there will no longer be any point in having such places to go to.

Entertainment Therapy

DEAR MISS MANNERS:

When a private citizen pays admission to a performance to be entertained, do the performers have a right to change the viewer into a performer himself, without his prior consent? I bought a ticket for what was billed as a performance by duo-organists. Nothing was said about audience participation. During the show, the performers had an audience sing-along. Since I can't carry a tune, I just moved my mouth. But one of the organists could tell I wasn't really singing. He stopped the show, came to the footlights, pointed directly at me, and declared, "Hey, you in the fifth seat of the third row—you're not singing!" Needless to say, this was embarrassing. I felt like telling him off in front of everyone but kept my cool.

Had I interfered with his performance, I could have seen some reason to be injected into the show. Katharine Hepburn reportedly gave an audience member a tongue lashing for popping a flashbulb—against very specific instructions—during a performance. And there are those audience participation shows where everyone knows in advance that they might suddenly be part of the show but, by attending, they consent to it. But what rule do you think should prevail for the quiet member of the audience who does not want to be in the limelight when he is thrust into a humiliating situation? Is this good manners on the part of a performer?

GENTLE READER:

It is only an illusion that there is any entertainment in this society, or education or politics, or anything else one used to recognize as a service to the community. There is only promiscuous emotional therapy.

The show-business subdivision of this activity takes two basic forms. Allegedly serious types of culture want to "shake people up," while light ones seek to "loosen them up." None of this has anything to do with the intellectual, aesthetic, or recreational pleasures that may induce one to purchase a ticket. Embarrassment, to the point of humiliation, is not recognized by the practitioners as the rudeness it is; they regard it as a tool for your emotional development.

In the face of such bullying bad manners, the only thing one can do is to refuse to cooperate. As your object is to avoid being made a public spectacle, it will be poorly served by your telling such a person off. Even departing, which is a great temptation, would only serve as a cue for another needling. Passive resistance—sitting in expressionless silence—is the only recourse. It may not be as satisfying a protest as you wish, but it will demonstrate the failure of the tactics.

Reaching One's Seat

DEAR MISS MANNERS:

Will you please describe the correct way, if there is one, to pass already seated listeners in a crowded theater or concert hall? Contrariwise, is there a correct way to let others pass you when you are already seated? I am always uncertain whether to stand, for example, and whether to pass face-to-face or sideways. No matter how I or others do it, I feel clumsy, but I might feel less so knowing that I am squeezing past people correctly.

GENTLE READER:

Miss Manners is glad that you recognize the distinction between a correct way and a graceful way, and also the suspicion that the latter does not exist. The correct way in this country is to turn the body toward the stage but turn the head toward the approaching seat, which enables the passer to say "excuse me" to each person passed. To be passed, one smiles at the passer apologetically (eyebrows up, mouth closed in a foolish upward tilt) while moving out of the way any hindrances such as coats or skirt overhang. Gentlemen should rise and press back against their folded seats. Ladies may sit back and slant their legs in the direction the passer is moving.

Solemn Silence

DEAR MISS MANNERS:

I recently attended a vocal recital with Malcolm, a friend from my church choir. During one particular rendition, which had a catchy melody, I was moving my head slightly in time to the music without really being aware of it. Malcolm became very annoyed, jabbed me in the side, and whispered, "Are you aware that you are moving your head in time to the music?" It wasn't a question; it was a reprimand. I stopped immediately but felt irritated that he would tell me how to behave, as I felt it was none of his business. In fact, after the recital, the vocalist told me and another lady that she enjoyed seeing our smiling faces in the audience.

Since then, Malcolm has mentioned at least four times that I so embarrassed him by my "ignorant behavior" that he wanted to "crawl underneath the pew"! He has a trained "legitimate" (as he calls it) voice, and attends the opera and recitals regularly, and says that the proper response is attentiveness and no other reaction, lest the performer be distracted. Since the age of five, I have been performing musically myself (piano, dancing, singing, and acting) but am not classically trained. Personally, I don't want a deadpan audience!

However, I do concede that a church recital is fairly formal. Is Malcolm right? Did I behave inappropriately? Should I be careful in the future to keep a blank facial expression and sit very still? I am in my fifties and have attended many recitals and stage plays. Malcolm has made me feel like a country bumpkin. But don't mince words, Miss Manners—give it to me straight!

GENTLE READER:

All right, then, here it is straight. Too bad Malcolm didn't crawl under the pew. He would be better off out of sight, because he committed three serious breaches of etiquette during the recital (whispering, correcting, and jabbing) and, by your count, at least four afterward. Nodding the head slightly is, Miss Manners assures you, nothing whatever in comparison. As an annoyance, it is in a category with small-gestured conducting on one's own lap, which puts it way below foot tapping and snoring. Even those serious errors fall under the general heading of Reactions to Music (Enthusiastic and Less So), rather than Sinning on Purpose, such as making noise with candy wrappers.

Concert manners vary not only according to the program and hall, but by country and century. At the annual Wagner Festival in Bayreuth, Germany, audience breathing is considered disruptive, and passing out, even while wearing evening clothes in temperatures of over 100ºF, a major gaffe. At choice Italian opera houses, failing to deliver a mid-aria critique to a singer is considered to show lamentable lack of interest. So, while it is true that a trance-like state, eyes blank and lips slightly curved in the idiot position, is the safest stance to take, there is no rule applicable to all occasions everywhere. Except that Malcolm is not the person with whom to enjoy music.

Booing

DEAR MISS MANNERS:

I attend the symphony regularly, and I am getting tired of hearing new compositions which do nothing for me except grate on my nerves like a piece of chalk scraped across a blackboard. Is it polite to boo such a piece? I've read that they used to tear up the seats in Paris theaters. Why should we in the United States be so polite and suffer in silence?

GENTLE READER:

Those who tear up seats in this country are not generally music critics. However, Miss Manners is not against the proper expression of displeasure, as well as pleasure, at musical events. Although too timid herself to boo, she does not recognize the need to thank performing artists for their efforts, and therefore interprets applause as a show of approval for the success of those efforts; where there is room for approval, there must also be room for disapproval.

If you boo a piece at its premiere, the disapproval is presumed to be for the composer, and it is those occasions where people had such high old times in Paris and elsewhere. However, tearing up the seats in the auditorium as a sign of aesthetic disapproval usually turned out to have been an historical error, marking one for future generations as a major philistine scorning composers who later turned out to be regarded as immortals. If you boo at a later performance, your comment is taken as critical of the performers.

Shades of Meaning

DEAR MISS MANNERS:

My wife and I (students in the field of communication) were present at a large meeting at which a well-loved leader was accepting responsibility for a problem, one for which the majority of those present would not have blamed him. What is the appropriate way for one hundred people to convey to a public speaker: "We support you, and we do not accept your unfounded self-criticism"? The two standard options, the boo-hiss and the hurrah-clap, would convey the wrong message. The audience intuitively recognized that no alternative open to them would make the necessary distinction and kept silent. Is this just another situation in which silence seems like a compromise but is the wisest course anyway?

GENTLE READER:

As you point out, the vocabulary of audience reaction during a speech is limited to approval and disapproval. The extremes of these reactions are standing up to clap, to show respect as well as appreciation; or walking out, to show disrespect. Depending on the nature of the gathering, an occasional phrase or word may be shouted—for example, "No!" when this speaker announced, "It was all my fault." Generally, though, one saves the audience verdict for the end of the speech. At that point, applause and hurrahs would have signified unqualified support.

Ovations

DEAR MISS MANNERS:

Recently, I was a member of an audience that gave standing ovations constantly during the speaker's speech. It seems to me that because they have become so prevalent, standing ovations have lost much of their significance. Because I personally think that such demonstrations should be reserved for the rarest occasions, I should like your advice on what I should do when I am a member of an audience that seems prone to standing ovations.

GENTLE READER:

Miss Manners shares your opinion about ovation inflation. One should leave some demonstration of enthusiasm in case Demosthenes comes back from the dead to give the speech of his career. During standing ovations given in appreciation of artistic performances or in endorsement of spoken sentiments, a dissenting member of the audience may, with propriety, keep his seat. However, when ovations are given to show respect for an individual's longtime achievements (at the Academy Awards, there are standing ovations for the lifetime contributions of every actor or actress over thirty-five), politeness requires everyone to follow.

Intermittent Applause

DEAR MISS MANNERS:

When is it appropriate to clap at the ballet?

GENTLE READER:

Serious-minded people believe that clapping should be confined to bows at the end of performances and detest any such manifestations while music is being played. By prevailing standards, however, applause is also customary at the ballet for any stage set more elaborate than one painted tree and an oversized mushroom stool; at the appearance of a favorite dancer; and for any three leaps or four turns.

Museums

DEAR MISS MANNERS:

I am repeatedly confronted with a problem in American museums. As I am perusing the world on the walls and trying to concentrate on the works of art, my attention is arrested by loud patrons of the museum. These people insist on informing all around them of their likes and dislikes, not to mention their perceptive opinions on artists and art. One example: "There are as many different ways to look at a figure as there are artists." This will suffice to show that wit and intelligence ordinarily are not aspects of the discourse to which I refer. How does one politely ask others to be quiet? Is there a deferential way of making one's displeasure known, or must one suffer the insipid comments of others as a penalty for visiting museums?

GENTLE READER:

How curious that you specify American museums in your complaint. Do you imagine that foreign museums are peopled only by wits and art historians?

Miss Manners does not share your sneer at the unoriginal remarks of museum goers. The great experiences of life inspire feelings that are no less valid for being shared by the rest of humanity. The commonplace statement "I love you," for example, is neither original nor witty, but it is stirring to those who say or hear it. Miss Manners prefers genuinely felt truisms to pretentious, arty chitchat. In any case, quiet conversation is not banned in a museum, as it is in a concert hall. She must warn you that a person who ventures, in public places, to eavesdrop upon, and then voice criticisms of, other people's conversation is considered a public nuisance.

Dressing for the Occasion

Sensitive about the outrageous but common notion that anything refined must also be snobbish and hypocritical, Miss Manners has never liked the stereotype of Opera Goers. There is the inevitable lady in pearl dog-collar necklace and lorgnette, with a gentleman beside her who is wreathed in white walrus moustache and snores. But where? Where, outside of cartoons, does one actually find this fatuous couple, willing, for the sake of appearance and showing off, to endure any trial, even opera? Not in the opera houses, surely, or the cultural centers, or other school or civic facilities where opera is presented these days.

Opera happens to be Miss Manners' sport (you didn't suppose it was mud wrestling, did you?), and she has never actually seen such people. When she looks at opera audiences—or those at the ballet, concerts, or theater—she sees stern young people wearing blue jeans and critical expressions, and radiant older faces atop office clothing.

This has always pleased Miss Manners. Not only does she take pleasure in seeing people have a good time, but she can hardly imagine anything more ridiculous than submitting to entertainment that one doesn't enjoy. Duty, certainly, and work, if necessary. For people to endure being bored by their own recreation (which is the impression she gets from the listless bodies and blank faces of those who sit around a lot watching television) seems strange to her at a time when so many people shirk their obligations on the grounds that they're not amusing.

It is with some timidity, therefore, that Miss Manners now requests a small extra effort of the satisfied audiences of what are generally acknowledged to be "good" or "high" cultural performances. Might it be possible, if it's not too much trouble or expense, for the audience to help just a little in restoring the sense of occasion to these grand events?

First, she has a confession to make. Imagine this as a short aria. (Miss Manners fancies that she has all the makings of an opera singer except, unfortunately, one.) The secret she must reveal at the top of her lungs is that, truthfully, she has occasionally caught a glimpse of a lady at the opera with pearls and lorgnette—but not in the audience or on the stage. It was in the foyer mirrors.

Miss Manners does not dress for the opera in the hope of showing off. On the contrary, being innocent of any ambition to be visually daring, she is aware that if she is noticed at all, it is probably with some (kind, she hopes) amusement at the maintenance of the old tradition. Nor are those her only clothes, which she also wears to the grocery store, using the lorgnette to compare prices. Formality on the wrong occasion is even worse than misplaced informality. She is hardly asking people to follow her stylistic lead, and will not be the slightest bit difficult about any unwillingness to spend money on clothes when the price of the tickets is already a strain, or any plea about not having the time to change clothes in the rush from office to dinner to opera house. All such excuses will be accepted without question. What is more, she recognizes that a number of different levels of dressing are appropriate, just as there are different levels in the theater. One would not want to dress for standing room as one might for sitting comfortably. Excessive show has always been considered vulgar. At the height of the reign of formality, only on a few nights were evening clothes worn. The young should not be expected to dress as the elderly do (or vice versa, which is more common now).

She only asks for a bit more effort according to each person's capability and circumstances. When most people regularly made such an effort, the clothing style was known as "Sunday best," without prejudice to one person's "best" over another's. Some people will insist on interpreting any such effort as the flaunting of money, but something has changed since the invention of that stereotype about the snobbish life of the rich. No longer does it inspire sneers; nowadays, the reaction is more likely to be "If it's good enough for them, why can't I enjoy it, too?"

Dressing up for the opera conveys the idea that complex art is a treat; that it offers, in return for greater study, greater sensual enjoyment; that those who know what is best do not settle for the commonplace in culture, any more than in objects. Too many people appear to be dissatisfied with lowest-common-denominator culture for it to be wise to dismiss anything else as pretentious. Miss Manners does not want to spoil the ambiance of those varied audiences she has been describing. She only suggests that some effort on their part to restore the idea that high culture is chic might be an incentive to others to discover new pleasures.

Box Seating

DEAR MISS MANNERS:

What are the appropriate arrangements in a four-seat opera-house box? Upon our arrival for the ballet, the other couple had taken the two front seats. This relegated my guest and me to the rear seats. Should the others have taken either the left or right side of the box?

GENTLE READER:

The proper arrangement of box seating is ladies in front and gentlemen behind. Miss Manners supposes that this is based on the presumption that ladies are (1) shorter and (2) more interestingly dressed than gentlemen. Miss Manners does not want to hear the obvious but irrelevant information that there are some ladies who are taller than their gentlemen and less interesting for the rest of the audience to look at. If there is not that convenient social pattern to follow—if all people are of the same gender, for example—couples should still divide the box from side to side, rather than front to back.

❧ PARTICIPATORY SPORTS

Tennis

When the first poison-yellow tennis ball was lobbed, Miss Manners ducked. She had an idea of what else might be hurled across the net after it: obscenities and insults, no longer muttered but frankly shouted; clothing that was claimed to express the individual inside, which is to say that it declared the person's shopping affiliations or more lucrative commercial ties; rackets tossed angrily on the ground or at other people; backtalk to umpires; demands for special treatment; and goodness knows what else. An orderly, aesthetically pleasing sport, known for the purity of its conventions, including the ritualistic enactment of respect between winner and loser, has turned into something very much resembling the rest of modern life.

Miss Manners also anticipated correctly that these changes would be accompanied by arguments that this deplorable package of uncontrolled and rude behavior represented:

1. The democratization of a previously elitist game.
2. A flowering of individualism and self-expression.
3. The necessities of the age of television.
4. An inevitable accompaniment of the glorification of champions, whose requirements, grandly called their lifestyles, must be met if they are to agree to be our sports heroes and heroines.

As you can imagine, poor Miss Manners was feeling flushed and exhausted without having lifted an arm. Her reply, as she picked up her parasol to stroll as far away from the nasty court as possible, was, "Pooh." Bad behavior and poor sportsmanship serve no such causes. The concept of sport, like that of other forms of civilized behavior, is based on the idea that everyone acknowledges certain arbitrary rules and forms, and then tries to shine individually within that context. Not even sweet little ladies like Miss Manners need to be as exacting about conventions of dress, equipment, and behavior as do athletes. A proper baseball team is composed of gentlemen who remember to wear their hats outdoors and observe traditional patterns, such as taking turns and spitting on their hands.

Let us examine the arguments in favor of debasing (oh, let's have a quick pretense of fairness here and call it changing) tennis. Tennis can be said to be elitist in that it does require space and equipment that cost money. Nearly all sports do, which is why athletic facilities at schools and public buildings are desirable so that everybody can participate. You cannot tell Miss Manners that requiring a white T-shirt in place of bright and/or obscene ones is a financial drain on the players. As for behavior, Miss Manners considers it antidemocratic to suggest that only bad behavior is possible to the poor and, therefore, that lowering standards to fit all those slobs is a tribute to democracy. Losing gracefully comes just as unnaturally to the rich as to the poor. Overcoming that and behaving well is one of the rare status symbols that are free and available to all.

Individual achievement is one of the things that sport measures. When each person tries to individualize the costume and rules of a game, the result is that the true area of competition, which is athletic prowess, is muddied. The glorification of people who can simultaneously excel in sport and brattiness debases the athletic part, in Miss Manners' opinion.

Nor does she understand why the concept of tennis as a television show, in which the task of distinguishing between two small figures is accomplished by all kinds of crude effects, should be allowed to change the fundamentals of the sport. If they wish to put on a drama with unruly characters, fashion competitions, and other such antics, it is perfectly all right with Miss Manners, provided that no one seriously mistakes it for the fine sport of tennis.

Board Games

DEAR MISS MANNERS:

Is there an etiquette rule regarding that games require one to give intelligent answers in order to win? Should players be able to label other players "stupid" in the name of the game? How may I continue a social relationship but bow out of certain games that are a natural part of an evening? Here is what happened: It was my turn. I had already answered several times (both correctly and incorrectly). The person asking the question stated, "Now here's one you will know the answer to." Of course, you can guess that I did not know the answer. Saying so only prompted my tormentor to say, "Oh, come on. Think. Of course, you know the answer to this. Everyone knows the answer to this. You can't be that stupid." My stomach was beginning to roll, a flush came over me, and I was horrified to find myself close to tears. I answered again that I did not know, and then, pressed, gave an answer, any answer, the wrong answer, and was immediately met with a look of astonishment, raised eyebrows, and a clear "cluk" of the teeth as if to say, "Well . . . she really *is* that stupid."

The game continued. I was extremely nervous. The entire episode was repeating itself when a woman in the group interrupted, saying, "Stop. Don't present the question in that manner. It's demeaning and it's degrading. Just state the question and don't make any remarks of that type." I was grateful for the defense but embarrassed at the situation that caused her to feel a need to defend me. To all of this, my tormentor replied, "It's just a game."

Before you say it, I know that the name of the game is Trivial Pursuit, but that doesn't seem to help. I don't seem to be good at it. I don't enjoy it. How may I continue to see these people and refuse to play? I certainly wouldn't dream of asking them not to play it. (Would I?) Unless you can offer some perfect sentence that I can deliver, I'm doomed to not sticking around for that part of the evening, which is often followed by things I really would like to do.

GENTLE READER:

The sentence is, "Oh, dear, I'm not good at games; let me just watch." Miss Manners assures you that in some circles not being good at games is something to brag about. This does not excuse the extreme rudeness of your friend, which already seems to be annoying others and will probably soon have him thrown out of the game. Game playing, like driving, is an activity that brings out the worst in some people.

Serious Bridge

DEAR MISS MANNERS:

I am a retired senior citizen, male, and I often play duplicate bridge. Although duplicate bridge is not supposed to be a social activity, but rather a battle of wits and knowledge, I often encounter opponents who ask me my age and address, and inquire about conditions and past tragedies in my life. How can I, in a courteous way, tell them that these matters are none of their business?

GENTLE READER:

In these days, when any occasion that groups people together, including waiting for a traffic light to change, is considered a social opportunity, Miss Manners cannot scold those who make social overtures over bridge, even duplicate bridge. That is far from saying that you need socialize with the other players or answer personal questions. What you must learn to do is to look up blankly after any such question and reply, "Excuse me. I'm still thinking about that last hand. I think there's another way it could have been played." You are then free to return your gaze firmly to your cards.

Whistling

DEAR MISS MANNERS:

We are a group of women who play cards weekly. In the middle of a game, one of the women begins to whistle. I find this disturbing and ill-mannered. When I mentioned this, I was told that there is nothing wrong with a woman whistling.

GENTLE READER:

Traditionally, whistling during card games is not a matter of gender so much as survival. Miss Manners prefers that such people be silenced with a glare, but has heard of its being done with a bullet.

~7~

Courtship

and

Romance

Methods of Meeting

The New Arranged Marriage

Nobody could be more surprised than Miss Manners at the return, in a slightly modernized form, of the institution of arranged marriages. It was once widely believed, at least by parents, that the major ingredients of a successful marriage were similarity of financial resources, social status, and living habits. That elusive ingredient called love was, mammas and papas would explain, something that was bound eventually to grace an appropriate union, but hardly substantive enough to serve as the sole foundation for a social structure as important as marriage. Parents were naturally more qualified to judge, and to check out the family and personal qualities of candidates, than were the inexperienced and emotionally befuddled young themselves.

The adults were never really able to persuade the young to accept this system, and even tyrannical Victorian papas knew that it was hopeless to impose their choices on their docile-looking daughters, who knew a thing or two about wearing down parents at their own hearths. After a period in which parents limited their interference to providing ample opportunities for suitable candidates to meet, and attempting to discourage or ratify their children's romantic choices on practical grounds, parental participation became an empty formality. Love, which only the couple themselves could judge, was finally acknowledged to be the essential ingredient of a successful marriage. It might have been desirable to have other common grounds, but love was supposed to be able to transcend differences, while a loveless marriage was considered doomed, no matter what the objective advantages.

Now look at what has happened. With parents no longer allowed to provide the social life from which prospects are drawn, young people must find their own mates according to their own qualifications. The classified advertisements, or the longingly stated requirements of the single person, refer to career status, stability of personality, physical presentableness, and such details of living arrangements as no ancient matchmaker would have deigned to notice—eating and smoking habits, choice of sports, and how one feels about Humphrey Bogart movies. If these requirements are matched, the current theory goes, love ought to follow. We are back to the premise of the arranged marriage, with the difference that the candidates have the unseemly task of conducting their own searches.

You would think that Miss Manners would be pleased. Although not quite the period piece that she sometimes finds it convenient to pretend to be, she does have a sentimental attachment to the graceful forms of the past. Not in this case. Miss Manners has always subscribed to the romantic notion that love is erratic and inexplicable, and that the most sensible matching of requirements is no more likely to produce it than differences are to discourage it. The concept of romance as something for which one can organize a reasoned search, as opposed to something that knocks one senseless while one is trying to go about the ordinary activities of life, repulses her. The funny thing is that when love was not openly pursued, it always seemed to arrive anyway, with remarkable frequency and force.

Turning love into a business, in which goals are frankly declared, practical advantages are shamelessly sought, and techniques are scrutinized for the efficiency with which they are likely to achieve quick results, strikes her as vulgar.

She also notices, from the flood of loneliness and unhappiness in modern society, that it does not seem to work. While her sympathies were always quickly engaged on behalf of the lovers of olden times who fought for the spirit of romantic love against the materialistic cynicism of their parents, she can hardly figure out how to comfort those who inflict such tyranny upon themselves.

Classified Advertisements

DEAR MISS MANNERS:

My engagement was mutually broken off almost three years to the day after we met. We had met through a newspaper ad and were very serious about our relationship. There were differences that could not be resolved, but that is life. Now, as a single man approaching his thirty-fifth birthday, I have gone back to the ads. Now that I have been receiving phone calls in response to the letters I had mailed to blind box numbers, I need to ask some questions regarding quasi-blind date etiquette.

If the parties decide to meet for a drink or Sunday brunch, is there any established pattern as to who is expected to pay for it? When I have the opportunity to speak with the ladies who have decided to call me (so that they can be confident that I'm not going to sell them into white slavery), I'm told tales of rudeness and "cheapness."

Remember, it is the lady who put the ad in the paper. If a fellow responds and she calls, the fellow may be on the hook if she decides that she would like to meet him, but has difficulty thinking of a place and the fellow suggests one. Conversely, if the fellow places the ad and would like to meet a lady who responds, he is on the hook again for the meeting.

GENTLE READER:

Miss Manners can think of two reasons for this problem, and she doesn't care for either.

1. That ladies claim the right to be aggressors in initiating courtships, and then refuse to take the responsibilities of planning them and paying the bills;

2. That you are being auditioned for financial generosity by those who consider bill paying a prerequisite for romance.

Miss Manners' objections to these concepts are related to a deep distaste for advertising for romance, however much she hears about the lack of alternatives in modern society. The traditional alternative was, one way or another, to get involved in the society as much as possible, so that ineligible people one liked would supply similar but eligible ones. Miss Manners still considers that not only more respectable and safer, but actually more discriminating than setting out heartless criteria such as "not being cheap."

Now that Miss Manners has gotten that off her heaving chest, let her apply herself to your problem. Such first meetings as you describe ought to be brief, cheap, and public. (If further acquaintance seems desirable, you can work out other arrangements.) If asked for a suggestion, you should propose coffee or tea. That should be reassuring to anyone afraid of sinister possibilities. If this discourages someone who interprets it as an unwillingness to invest in her—sight unseen, at that—all the better. Miss Manners would think that self-respecting people of both genders would not want to incur obligations at that point. In any case, the bill will be small enough to allow you to pick it up if you sense that the lady seems unable to follow through on her convictions of independence.

The New Début

Always on the lookout for new social forms, Miss Manners was fascinated to read of the solution reached by a group of parents on Long Island who banded together to do something about their grown-up children's problems in meeting eligible people. It seems that the offsprings' own attempts to find suitable suitors were failing. As hard-working "professionals" (a term that is beginning to tire Miss Manners, who has always preferred to socialize with amateurs), these young people found no proper facilities for meeting those equal in status but opposite in gender.

The current social form of the singles gathering, at bars or under more respectable roofs, did not serve the purpose to their satisfaction. As Miss Manners has often heard, this event is populated exclusively by undesirables, with the sole exception of the complainant. An even more insidious criticism is that videotaped exchanges, classified advertisements, and other such devices for matching people attract only those who are (1) not matched and (2) eager to be matched. Indubitably. At any rate, the available forms, collectively known by the erstwhile participants as "meat markets," were not working. More drastic social action seemed to be called for.

Taking matters into their own hands, the parents organized themselves under the name of PUNCH, for Parents of Unmarried Children, and began throwing their own social events. Culling a guest list of some 500 children, ages twenty to forty, of 200 couples, they took turns scheduling Sunday afternoon parties of thirty to forty young people of approximately the same social level. (Miss Manners prefers not to go into the unseemly matter of which careers qualified and which did not.) Providing the pleasant, normal social environment of their own homes, the host parents stayed quietly in the background, intervening only to rescue stranded guests. The guests themselves seem to have taken the social posture of reluctant but gracious compliance with their parents' plans. Relieved of the onus of obviously voluntary participation, they were apparently able to exhibit the attractive posture of interrupting their satisfactory lives out of filial obligation.

In sum, the project seemed to be a success, and one of the parental organizers reported encouragement from other parents and the likelihood of the practice's becoming widespread. You will have to forgive Miss Manners for laughing herself silly (in a subdued, ladylike way, of course). If one has been observing the social scene as long as she has, one is occasionally rewarded with the hilarity of watching people taking pride in laboriously producing the obvious. These people have simply reinvented the débutante party.

Just as those who rejected marriage as an artificial and constricting form have gradually refined the custom of living together by specifying emotional, household, financial, and other legal obligations until they have now pretty much reinvented marriage, the Long Island parents have discovered what parents have always known: If you want your children to find suitable mates, you must provide them with a pool of such people from whom to choose. Not only does this allow you to use your own judgment, but it saves face for the children by permitting them to deride your matchmaking instincts instead of having to acknowledge their own.

In our time, the form of the début has become so encumbered with obsolete practices as to have pretty much outlived its usefulness. Débutantes are supposed to be eighteen and innocent, but nobody, especially not Miss Manners, checks them at the door. As the purpose of a début is to present a girl just coming of age to adult society, the event was given by her parents or other close adult relatives. It was generally a tea, or a small home or club dance, in addition to which several families might have combined to give their daughters a ball.

Miss Manners speaks of this in the past tense because today's mass events, run by hired specialists, bear little resemblance to a début. They "present" to strangers a girl who has been running freely since she was twelve. Commercially run balls often require that the young women have one or several "escorts" (thus forcing supposedly innocent young women to dredge up young men for a party whose ostensible purpose is for them to meet young men for the first time), in order to provide extra dancing partners or to populate those sideline groups of young men who drink too much and make unpleasant comments about the débutantes. The enormous expense of all this and its association with limited groups (who even then often have difficulty mastering the traditional social practices) make it unsuitable for most people; the specified age is now wrong, because the eighteen-year-olds do have sufficient social opportunities when they are in school but are not yet ready to marry; and the ludicrous custom of presenting débutantes to people their parents don't even know, sometimes in strange cities, defeats the original purpose.

This new type of party strikes Miss Manners as a sensible adaptation of the purpose of the début, suitable to the age group that really is ready to marry. By lessening the expense and formality, one is able to prolong the "season" and remove the pressure. Miss Manners only advises more subtlety about the name and stated purpose. The success of the début, or of any such event, depends on the subjects' being able to eschew any interest except that of placating their unreasonable parents.

Matchmakers

DEAR MISS MANNERS:

I am a single, middle-aged male who recently moved to a new city where some close relatives reside. A friend of one of them, in the presence of the relative, provided me with the name and telephone number of an unattached woman whom I was strongly urged to call. For some years, I have steadfastly avoided such situations. This way of meeting people is invariably uncomfortable and tense, often culminating in a hurtful rejection—expressed or implied—by one party of the other. Here, the go-between knew I was unattached, so I could not plead the existence of an ongoing relationship elsewhere. I accepted the name and number, promising to call but intending not to, anticipating that the go-between would ultimately accept my inaction as a demurral. However, the go-between persisted, and my relative is chagrined. What should I have said to the go-between? What can I now say to my relative to restore her confidence in my etiquette?

GENTLE READER:

What you say to your relative is, "Really, I know your friend means well, so I didn't have the heart to tell her that I'm not interested. Would you be a dear and break it to her in whatever way you think would be least offensive?" The general thing to say to a would-be go-between is, "Thank you, but I'm afraid it will be a long while before I have a chance to call her, so perhaps you'd better not mention it to her."

This is less firm a refusal than Miss Manners generally advises for things one does not want. Before the invention of singles and thus of a singles problem, it was just such attempts, more or less subtly made, that matched people without resort to videotapes. She is not asking you to accept such an offer, you understand— only not to think scornfully of someone whose motive is to make at least one, and probably two people, happy.

On the Job

DEAR MISS MANNERS:

I am twenty-six, male, and single. I am a recent graduate of an optometry school, now practicing with my father in a small Southern town. Since I graduated from school and moved back here, I have had dates or multiple dates with at least seven or eight women, but none of them has been the right one. Consequently, I am still looking around for eligible young women to date and, if right, marry. I have come in contact with several such women within my practice; they are my patients. Is it proper for me to call and ask one of my patients out for a date, or is this unprofessional?

GENTLE READER:

Compared with some of the ways people meet nowadays, it is positively restrained. Miss Manners was recently astonished to read a newspaper article attributing the popularity of paid advertisements about one's availability to its safety over the "traditional method" of meeting in singles bars. My, my. Another sweet, old-fashioned tradition gone.

Miss Manners will move only so far with the times. In any unorthodox meeting—and the orthodox one is still being introduced by a mutual acquaintance or meeting under the "roof" of a respectable organization, such as a school or church—she insists upon some acknowledgment that one is breaking the rules. Among other things, it is effective, being more flattering to the person approached than the assumption that the initiator habitually approaches people wherever he finds them.

When you call a patient for social purposes, appear to have been so overwhelmed by her that you are acting against your own sense of propriety and anxious not to offend hers. "I hope you won't consider this terrible of me, but I so enjoyed our chat when you were in the office that—I don't actually mix my business life with social, but—" and so on. An "other thing" in "among other things" that Miss Manners wants to protect you against is having word get around in your small town to "watch out for the junior one in the office there. If you don't want to get more checked than your teeth, ask for the father to help you."

Relevant Information

DEAR MISS MANNERS:

I am interested in a young man, but I am not certain of his sexual preference. How may one tactfully inquire about this delicate matter?

GENTLE READER:

One may not. What one can attempt to find out, more through observation than questioning, is whether the young man is romantically interested in oneself. That, rather than the broader question, is what is your business. Anyway, a positive answer to that question should make the more general question unnecessary, while a negative answer makes it irrelevant.

Singles Bars

DEAR MISS MANNERS:

I am a married woman who enjoys going to singles bars. I live in a small city where all the entertainment that I enjoy is predominantly frequented by singles. I enjoy music, dancing, and meeting new people as much as any single person does, but I have experienced some problems regarding this. I have met some wonderful men and women while out, and I make no distinction as to whether one is male or female, attractive or unattractive, when I am socializing. I think that accepting dancing invitations only implies that I want to dance. If I accept an invitation, how can I let the person know that I am not available but would love to dance with him? Is there a difference in the answer if I am out with my husband or not, or if I am at a private party, having conversations, or dancing?

GENTLE READER:

Miss Manners never expected to live to see the day when she would be defending singles bars from the invasions of respectable married people. Nevertheless, house rules are house rules, and it seems to Miss Manners that singles bars frequenters have a right to expect everyone there to be single. You are proposing making yourself a nuisance to those who are spending their time and money for a particular purpose that you do not share.

Flirtation, which is what you seek, is a different activity from the clearly declared search for partners that goes on at singles bars. By definition harmless because it doesn't lead to anything, flirtation is a gentle amusement now seriously threatened by the goal-oriented activities of those very people among whom you hope to practice it. Tasteful flirting is done in ordinary social settings—the more conventional the better. This is part of the tact and restraint it requires, so as not to imply that one's appreciation of others reflects on one's loyalty to one's spouse. Miss Manners suggests that you start giving or organizing parties with dancing. Then you can dance to your heart's content, with both single and married partners, without suggesting that you are prepared to entertain your dance partners in other ways.

Age Suitability

DEAR MISS MANNERS:

I am a retired professional gentleman of fifty-nine, and since my divorce several years ago, I have found that I enjoy the companionship of bright professional women in their thirties. Some of my friends, mostly women of about my age, are quite critical of me for choosing "kids" instead of ladies in my own age group. Recently, my current companion (thirty-nine) told me that she had been lectured by two of her friends for "wasting her time with an old man" and had been given pop-psychology analyses involving father images.

Is there, in American society, a social norm which holds that there is something incorrect, even improper, about a romantic attachment between a man of fifty-nine and a woman of thirty-nine, or, for that matter, twenty-nine? Is it only correct for an older man to date women within, say, five years of his age? I believe that ladies who choose younger men suffer even more from explicit and implied criticism. Do you see any rationale for this?

GENTLE READER:
The actual source of your older friends' complaints could range from annoyance, when the next generation fails to understand their references and jokes, to the grievance that they are not as likely to find romance with the young as gentlemen are. The young lady's friends could also be smarting from a sense of competition.

None of this is etiquette's business. What is etiquette's business is that unsolicited curiosity and advice about other people's choices are rude. So is all that emphasis on age. We are supposed to judge people as individuals, not as representatives of their age groups.

If you want to discourage this, you yourself had better stop regarding your romantic possibilities as representatives of a decade rather than as individuals. The position that you prefer "women in their thirties" is offensive, even, perhaps especially, to the ladies themselves, who won't always be in their thirties. Saying, "I can't understand why you don't like Lisa; she's really an interesting woman, and she told me she'd love to get to know you better" would silence any friend who attempts to classify the lady merely as a thirty-nine-year-old.

Props for Flirtation

In the social symbolism of the late Victorian era, it was understood that a lady who held her fan in her left hand while apparently accidentally exchanging glances with a strange gentleman in, for example, a public ballroom was desirous of making his acquaintance, and that efforts on his part to nab someone who could introduce them properly would not be unrewarded. Nowadays, of course, one can achieve the same effect by running around town in a T-shirt with "Try Me—I'm Terrific" written across the front.

Perhaps it is not exactly the same. Miss Manners is vaguely aware that something has been lost in the translation. It is true that a button that says "Kiss Me!" is clearer than a fan with the tip held to the lips, which meant the same thing, but Miss Manners is not sure that she likes living in a world where everything is quite that clear.

The value of social props was their ambiguity. In a matter as serious as flirtation, it was considered essential to be able to make a complete denial if things did not turn out as hoped. Carrying the fan in front of the face with the right hand meant "Follow me," but if the fan-shielded lady happened to walk smack into her husband while her instructions were being obeyed, nobody could prove a thing.

Now that ambiguity is an endangered species, we have abandoned most of our props. The gloves that could be smacked across the offender's face to say "You want to make something of it?", the gentleman's hat that could be tipped to say "Why, hello there," the severe hat that a young lady could use to say "Take me seriously," and the outrageous hat that a matron could use to say "I still have a girlish heart" are all gone. The message of a lace handkerchief floating to a gentleman's feet is not the same as that of a wad of Kleenex thudding to the floor.

Still, we do have a prop in modern life for purposes of modern flirtation, such as it is, and Miss Manners had better explain its use. One day these nuances will be as forgotten as the differences between the wide-open fan ("Wait for me"), a shut one ("You have changed"), and one that is being snapped open and shut ("You are cruel").

Our prop is the book. In a public place, such as an airplane or a museum, an open book being intently read means "I am not available." An open book on the lap, when the head is tilted upward and there is a dreamy expression in the eyes, means "I am willing to listen to what you have to offer before I make up my mind whether I want to know you."

If the hands are folded over the exposed pages, so that the subject of the book cannot be seen, an interested party may open with "What are you reading?" Allowing the title or a representative page to be seen saves misunderstandings because the nature of the book carries a message, too.

- Literary classic or scholarly work: "Don't bother me unless you have an education."
- Current world affairs: "You must be someone who is concerned about serious matters."
- Current fiction: "You must be *au courant* but soulful."
- Guidebook to a place at the current location or destination: "I am a stranger open to suggestions."
- Guidebook to remote place: "Go away; I'm planning my honeymoon or family vacation."
- Material related to a particular occupation: "I am a substantial person."
- Psychology or self-improvement book: "One kind word and I'm yours."
- Erotic literature: "Kind words are not necessary."

Ploys

DEAR MISS MANNERS:

A while ago, a beautiful gal with her mom dropped a doughnut on the floor beside me as I was turning to walk out of a snack shop in a shopping mall. I have been puzzled about the meaning of that—if it was an accident, or if I missed the chance to meet her. How should I respond so that I don't miss the next opportunity like that?

GENTLE READER:

If there is a standard flirtation maneuver called the Doughnut Ploy, Miss Manners is blessedly ignorant of it. Frankly, she does not think that was much of an opportunity you missed. A doughnut cannot be scooped up gracefully, like a dropped handkerchief and presented to the lady with a deep, meaningful look and an ingratiating "Excuse me, but I believe this is yours."

Gender Roles

Leap year is not quite the etiquette giggle it used to be. It is some time now since Miss Manners has heard anyone die laughing over the idea that a lady could ask a gentleman for a dance, a date, or his life. While the right of the lady to pursue the gentleman openly has been established and exercised, the manners involved in doing this decorously, and receiving such attentions, both when they are welcome and when they are not, could use some work.

Invitations and replies alike are often characterized by a perhaps related harshness. Miss Manners always considers it a danger signal when people speak of having "just as much right" as others to make a social move. When last she checked, the Constitution did not deal with the delicacies of courtship, and society prefers to treat such matters as privileges. One is at others' sufferance when pressing attentions, and the rule for the object of such attentions is to cause as little suffering as possible. (This does not preclude the fact that one must make rejections when necessary. False hope can be a cause of severe suffering, and never saying no to anyone leads to a life of sin.)

The difficulty that ladies seem to have in finding the right tone for taking romantic initiatives, and that others have in responding to them, probably shows that the participants themselves are not as indifferent to the customs of their past as they would like to be. They may believe with all their minds that it doesn't make any difference who begins—and why should it?—but they have secret prejudices. The lady who claims to be confident enough may harbor the hope that she will not have to, and the gentleman who claims to be flattered may also wonder why the lady is resorting to this. Such ambivalence leads to the attempt to engage in displays of admiration and interest while sounding as if one doesn't care in the least whether or not they succeed. This is neither polite nor attractive.

Miss Manners is willing to accept the idea that the increasing ease in seeking one another's society that young ladies and gentlemen show in their nonromantic attachments will eventually extend to potentially romantic ones. For the moment, she only begs both ladies and gentlemen to recognize the weight of tradition that has them both secretly feeling that there is something not quite right about such egalitarianism. Understanding that ought to eliminate the need to sabotage the grace that should characterize all such encounters. They should then recognize that the proper forms for issuing and replying to overtures of courtship are the same, whichever side one finds oneself practicing.

A lady, as well as a gentleman, can say, "I enjoyed meeting you, and I'd love to see more of you. If you're free next Saturday, may I take you out to dinner?" Having been the receiver of invitations, she should know not to make one so subtly that the other person doesn't know it has been made at all ("If you ever decide that you want to hear more about the tax law, you can reach me at my office"), or with such an open end ("Let's get together sometime") that it is impossible to accept or refuse.

Ladies may know about polite refusals, but gentlemen often don't. One can refuse the specific date with or without refusing the idea. "I'm so sorry, I can't on Saturday, but I would love to some other time" is entirely different from "I'm terribly sorry, I won't be able to make it. My schedule is really overcrowded these days. But thank you for asking me." A lady ought to be able to understand them as being different and to take no for an answer. Miss Manners hears tell of inquiries, coaxing, and repeated invitations that, if a gentleman made them, would be called harassment. A proper acceptance is "Thank you, I'd love to," not "Okay" or "Well, I don't know, sure, let me see, what was the date?" or "Hey, why don't you come over to my place?"

The rule is, and always was, that the person issuing the invitation pays the bills. If you subscribe to the belief that a gentleman must initiate all engagements with a lady, it follows that he pays for their entertainment. However, if you believe that either the lady or the gentleman may take the lead, you have to accept the fact that being hostess entails the same responsibilities as being host. Having begun a successful courtship, a lady who reverts to the older system and demands retroactive sponsorship of her own activities is not ladylike.

Taking the Initiative

DEAR MISS MANNERS:

My dilemma is that I have found Mr. Right, but he doesn't know it! I met him at a seminar over a year ago and haven't gotten him out of my mind since! He told me he was sorry that we hadn't been able to spend more time getting to know each other, because he found me very attractive, and asked if we could keep in touch.

Since then, neither of us kept in touch, but not a day goes by that I don't think about him! I know it is ridiculous to continue to think about him without doing something about it. However, being the old-fashioned girl I am, I have always waited for the man to take the initiative. This has gone on long enough. But now what do I do?

Since we work for the same employer, I could probably get enrolled in a seminar at his location. Or should I go to his city for some other reason, call and let him know that I will be in town, and ask if he would like to get together for a drink? Would it be construed as coming on too strong? Then I could ruin my chances forever! But I suppose it is better than spending the rest of my life wondering what could have happened had I taken the chance! I would give almost anything to come up with a foolproof way to approach him that would rekindle his interest!

Please don't think I am crazy! I am twenty-eight years old and a college-educated professional with a responsible marketing position. I have never had trouble getting dates with men. I want you to know that I'm not an eighteen-year-old with a schoolgirl crush! I realize you probably still believe that women should be courted by men (so do I), but if I approached him, I wouldn't actually be asking him out for a date; it would be less formal than that.

GENTLE READER:

Something about all those exclamation points touches Miss Manners, and she hopes that the next question from you will concern wedding etiquette. She still has to tell you that nothing in romance is foolproof. Also, a year is a long time, and one tends to forget that other people's lives do move on.

Now, let's get down to tactics. Of course, you should make some sort of business excuse to get in touch with him. Just be sure that your excuse is good enough, and your tone noncommittal enough, so you that can appear to be delighted if he tells you that he has just gotten engaged. If he is still interested, it will be easy enough to warm up your comradely friendliness, but you need to be able to retreat gracefully if he is not.

By the way, Miss Manners is constantly amazed that so many people seem to believe that nice, old-fashioned girls just sat around waiting for something to happen. No one was ever expected to believe that except love-befuddled gentlemen. Those young ladies didn't have your advantage of being able to put forth business pretexts, but, Miss Manners can assure you, they did the best they could.

Married Men

DEAR MISS MANNERS:

How does one go about informing a certain gentleman that his advances would not be unwelcome? A year ago, I was hired as a secretary to a manager of a stock brokerage firm. The moment I met him, I felt that pleasant rush that poets try so vainly to describe. I also noticed the wedding ring on his finger. Being somewhat of a realist, I decided to act calmly and sensibly, treating him with the respect and civility due one's employer. However, lately, I have reason to suspect that my em-

548 COURTSHIP AND ROMANCE

ployer not only returns those pleasant feelings but is suffering severe torment because of it. I share his anguish because not only is he married, he has two young children whom he adores and a sweet wife whom, I am certain, he would not willingly hurt, despite his lack of special feelings for her. Am I being too polite?

GENTLE READER:

Are you being too what? Oh. Well, no. Just polite enough, Miss Manners would say. Don't move, or you'll spoil it.

The problem, as Miss Manners understands it, is not exactly what you state. What you wish to do is not so much to announce your availability as to enter into the battle this gentleman is having with his conscience in the hope of influencing the outcome.

That is not nice. Nor is it wise. You must let him conduct this alone. Should he lose the battle (or win, depending on your point of view), you will find it more plausible for you to continue saying the sympathetic things you are saying about his family if he knows that you did not help persuade him to leave them.

"... Buy Me a Drink"

DEAR MISS MANNERS:

I have a female friend who continually and consistently asks her male friends to buy her a drink when she encounters them in nightclubs. Is this proper? I think it's out of line. Can you think of any remark that could be made to her?

GENTLE READER:

Miss Manners was under the impression that hanging around nightclubs asking males to purchase drinks for one was a professional maneuver rather than a social one. In either case, it may certainly be declined. The least objectionable way for a gentleman to do so to someone already of his acquaintance would be to say, "And here I was hoping you'd buy me one."

Flowers for Gentlemen

DEAR MISS MANNERS:

I recently became taken with a man of my acquaintance, and his actions led me to believe that my attentions would not be unwelcome. I tried unsuccessfully to reach him by telephone. Undaunted, I had flowers delivered to him, along with a card bearing my name and telephone number. There has been no response whatsoever.

I am not so much hurt at his failure to return my feelings as appalled at his total lack of response. What should I do the next time I encounter him? I shall probably be able to resist the temptation to present him with the florist's bill, but I would like to be able to (properly) make him feel like the cad he is. Or is it incorrect for ladies to send flowers to gentlemen they do not know well in the hope that a mere acquaintance may become something more?

GENTLE READER:

To your claim that it was not the failure of interest that upset you, but only the question of etiquette, Miss Manners says: Piffle. Had the gentleman refused your flowers with the explanation that he wished to refuse you, you would not, Miss Manners dares say, have been less likely to call him a cad. Where did you get the idea that a romantic overture to a new acquaintance confers an obligation on that person? Not from your own experience as the object of such attentions.

As every lady knows, one must discourage unwanted attentions firmly. One does not want to spell things out rudely, but the aroused heart will take almost anything else as encouragement. Silence is therefore often used as a way of saying something too harsh for words, namely, "I really have no interest in you and never will, so leave me alone." That, Miss Manners is sorry to tell you, is what the gentleman has said. It does not give you the right to behave as if he had ordered flowers and attention, for which he is now refusing to pay.

Instant Intimacy

Dear, dear. One should not venture into a rough trade like the etiquette business if one is going to be squeamish. You would have been proud of your Miss Manners for her game smile when two young ladies descended on her with detailed questions about the subject they assure her is in every sweet young thing's thoughts these days: disease.

Actually, she has encountered the subject before, to the extent of being asked whether it is polite to ask someone with whom one is about to become intimately acquainted whether such an acquaintance is likely to be unusually memorable. The answer is that while Miss Manners thoroughly believes that one should be prepared to suffer in the name of politeness, receiving an incurable disease because one does not want to risk offending someone with a question seems excessive.

These young ladies wanted to know when a health question should be posed. That is a matter for etiquette arbitration. One does not ask personal questions about the afflictions of others until it becomes apparent that the question is not an idle one and that, personal as it is, it is about to affect the person of the person, so to speak, who is doing the asking.

Miss Manners has always made it a rule to keep out of other people's bedrooms, except when she is directed to leave her coat there. You have other advice available on the subject, if you care to pay attention to it, and Miss Manners has quite enough to do trying to mind your manners. However, there is a point to be made that has to do with the workings of society, which are a part of Miss Manners' business. That is that you cannot eliminate risk from the practice of consorting with strangers. Miss Manners will allow you to decide whether you wish to consort with strangers, but even she cannot tell you how to remove the danger of your being stricken, robbed, murdered, or otherwise damaged. Polite society is not being snobbish when it insists on introductions and knowing who people are before becoming even socially intimate with them.

This does not totally erase risk. Victorian gossip is full of stories about innocent brides receiving unpleasant diseases from their parent-chosen bridegrooms. It is nevertheless a general rule of human nature that people are more fastidious about the welfare of others when their behavior is a part of their permanent social records.

The One-Night Stand

DEAR MISS MANNERS:

If a respectable woman meets a respectable man in a respectable manner (a book in itself), and the two find toward the end of an evening that their romantic interests have been stirred and they succumb to these interests, what is the proper behavior that should follow, for example, the next day or the next week? I've recently found that an annoying habit of some male members of society is to do nothing at all! Of course, such an encounter is not cause for a formal engagement, but it does merit some reaction. I liken it to the dreadful rudeness of a dinner guest who neither calls nor writes to tell the hostess that her company was enjoyed.

GENTLE READER:

You wouldn't care to lend Miss Manners the book-in-itself, would you? There is nothing like a nice story about passion run amok to while away a lazy afternoon. As a rule of living, it has its disadvantages. The trouble with strangers is that one doesn't know anything about them. It is not just that one doesn't know if their manners include thank-you calls, but one doesn't even know their definitions of what should make them grateful.

You have charmingly described such encounters as succumbing—presumably to rare and uncontrollable passions. It is perfectly possible that to the strange gentleman, these are routine incidents, devoid of romance, in the category that Miss Manners believes is known as the "one-night stand." The one-night stand is characterized by the time limit stated and by its lack of obligations. That is why respectability has that tedious requirement of checking out emotions and manners before intimacy.

Drawn-Out Courtship

"Why, Mr. Whiffle!" says the heroine with a wide-eyed look. "I didn't know you cared." She then lowers those eyes demurely. "I'm afraid you will have to give me time to get used to the idea."

While Mr. Whiffle suffers, waiting for his answer, Modern Reader gets sick. This is the kind of thing, she declares, that makes old novels unreadable. How can anyone be so hypocritically coy? Of course, the musty old heroine knew Mr. Whiffle cared. She has no intention of not accepting him. She just wants to indulge herself in this dishonest charade to make him miserable.

The modern heroine stoops to no such thing. Immediately upon meeting Mr. Whiffle's grandson, the gourmet lifestyle consultant, she tells him frankly that she, being fully independent but lonely, finds him acceptable and invites him to share her life. In other words, she loves him. He need not suffer any suspense. And he doesn't. He accepts her provisionally. Then he makes her suffer.

Why, modern heroines want to know, are gentlemen so rude as to refrain from the attentions of courtship, such as regular telephone calls and appointments, let alone sending flowers, notes, or presents? Why do they treat these relationships as being of little consequence and end them with no ceremony? Etiquette aside, the real question is, why do single gentlemen seem less committed when ladies are frank about their enthusiasm? Or shall we ask—to take the unfashionable gender distinction out of this—why the openly and instantly committed person, male or female, is likely to be slighted by the object of his or her immediately declared attentions?

Miss Manners could dismiss this as a prolongation of the adolescent concept of romance as sport, in which winning a heart only inspires one to look for a more challenging one. Indeed, that is her usual diagnosis when she hears people complain that the lack of uncertainty in marriage eliminates the pleasure.

Skipping the stages of courtship is another matter. It leads, Miss Manners believes, to skepticism about the value of the love being offered. It actually curtails the development of reciprocal love and the courtesies it should inspire.

The Victorian heroine kept a check on expressing her feelings not only to torture her suitor but to give him, as well as herself, time to let that first excitement of romantic attraction develop into serious longing. The looking-forward period, as any child knows who has had to wait until a birthday for something he wanted instead of having all whims satisfied on request, increases the pleasure. She was also guarding against the humiliation of offering herself to someone who had not yet decided whether he really wanted her. That risk was considered a gentleman's burden in those days, but there is no escaping the fact that whoever makes the first overt declaration, as someone has to, runs the risk of rejection. In truth, the Victorian heroine had a much greater need to find someone than the modern one. Marriage was to be not just emotional sustenance, but usually the source of her livelihood.

The funny thing is that the modern heroine knows this procedure in her career behavior. Rather than declare that she needs a job desperately and will settle immediately, without investigating the situation, she hesitates, allowing the prospective employer to woo her and grow anxious to win her. Only after she accepts the job does she put herself wholeheartedly at the disposal of the company's welfare. She doesn't call these tactics coyness or hypocrisy, but simply putting a high value on herself. That is also what her Victorian ancestor called it.

Being Talked About

DEAR MISS MANNERS:

I'm a woman twenty-one years of age and still a virgin. In this day and age, I have found it rare. My boyfriend is sometimes rude in telling people about his "strikes" with me, and my face turns beet red. It's not just that; they always come out with jokes about it. As far as I'm concerned, I think it's good that I've still got my virginity, because I have never been accused of cheating and doubt that I would be. But what should I say to people, or my boyfriend for that matter, about their embarrassing virgin jokes?

GENTLE READER:

This may come as a shock, but one of the traditional advantages of chastity was that a lady could not be safely "talked about" in the fashion you describe. Any gentleman, but particularly one who cared about her, would make short work of anyone who dared mention her name disrespectfully. Now you tell Miss Manners that virtue is ruining your reputation, and that the chief offender is the very person who ought to have been your chief defender. The sound you hear is her profound sigh.

Do not be embarrassed to employ the manners of respectability. This includes warning the young man that anybody who discusses a personal relationship with you is not going to have any. Inform tasteless jokers that they may expect to be horsewhipped by him if they don't stop—a remark that, incidentally, has the effect of making him sound more masculine than he does as an unsuccessful seducer.

The Stages of Courtship

🌹 SOCIAL PROMISCUITY

The secret adults have best kept from the young is that it is perfectly proper and respectable for single people to date as many other single people as they wish. You may not think that the lust for propriety and respectability races through the blood of teenagers, but Miss Manners knows better. The unfortunate convention at high school and colleges now is heavily on the side of narrow fidelity, even if that is of short duration. Dating around, as it were, is discouraged.

You can perhaps imagine how surprised Miss Manners is to find herself in the position of advocating promiscuity, even a mild, social form of promiscuity. (As she is not in the habit of peeking into parked cars or dormitory rooms, she is blithely unaware of any other kinds of behavior that may be so labeled.) However, she believes that youth would be better off if this secret got out, and young people discovered that there is nothing immoral or disloyal about simultaneous courtships. She will endeavor to show that this stand is actually on the side of morality, rather than against it.

Traditionally, etiquette has never recognized any tie between a lady and a gentleman not otherwise related other than that of being friends, engaged, or married. In modern society, a submarital category has been added in which reside couples who actually reside together, but, as the youth problem is one of people who "go out together," rather than of those who stay home together.

Among them, the common pattern is to have a series of exclusive arrangements, taking care to break one off just as another takes its place. As Miss Manners is delicately given to understand it, the terms are that romantic privileges are exchanged for the even more coveted license to complain ad infinitum about one's terrible parents, rough childhood, unfair teachers, and so on. Such bonds may, of course, be dissolved, and they frequently are, but not without a great deal of explanation, recrimination, and hurt feelings. The breaking up is often treated more seriously than the original romance, and a lot of teenagers are pitifully bruised at this time by being subjected to hearing how objectionable they are from the very people they most trusted and admired. The standard is, in other words, a rather dreary form of serial monogamy, followed by the pain of a simulated divorce.

Miss Manners believes that such a form is both unsuitably restrictive and unnecessarily hurtful. If no obligation to exclusivity is acknowledged, many of these disadvantages would disappear. She believes that much unhappiness could be spared—not all, of course; what would courtship be without suffering?—by barring any such arrangements. Historically, "going steady" or "being pinned" served various purposes:

1. People who were freer with their favors than they had been brought up to consider proper salvaged their conscience with public recognition that they were involved in reciprocated True Love.

2. Implicit in the terms was the assurance of a standing date when it would be most needed—holiday parties, proms, and such. (In Miss Manners' day, things were so bad that an articulated reason for getting married was "I'll never have to worry again about getting a date for New Year's Eve.")

3. When early marriage was common, lesser arrangements were a way of getting used to monogamy in stages.

These unfortunate circumstances are less common now, and the only advantage supposedly left in tying someone up with preengagement declarations never did work. The decent person will never try to hold to a promise someone who is no longer in love, and the decent or indecent person who wants out will get out.

Miss Manners' chief reason for opposing the custom is a moral one: At some time in life, everyone makes the astounding discovery that half the world's population is of the opposite gender. This is always received as amazing news—which, indeed, it is—and gives rise to all kinds of exciting ideas. Miss Manners favors allowing people in their teens or twenties to make this discovery unfettered by the responsibilities of exclusivity. To dash from one person to another, reveling in the wicked pleasure of infinite possibility, is best accomplished, it seems to her, during youth. Miss Manners is tired of listening to the pathetic tales of those abandoned in middle life by overgrown boys or girls who have only just made that discovery.

Multiple Beaux

DEAR MISS MANNERS:

I have the good fortune to be dating several gentlemen simultaneously, two of whom are friends with each other. Miss Manners will recall the problems this otherwise pleasant glut can entail, even if she is not currently having them herself. Can you suggest a gracious way of informing Mr. B that Friday is taken without resorting to the overused term "busy" (femalese for "not interested")? What can be done to prevent Mr. A, Mr. B, and Mr. C from running into each other coincidentally while making informal visits to my residence, and what can be done to make each comfortable when it does happen? My mother, who is a strong believer in the male competitive drive, thinks that these situations are to my advantage, but so far I feel inept at the jungle etiquette, having been on the other side before and not feeling the least urge to compete.

GENTLE READER:

"Competition" is such a strong term. So is "jungle etiquette," for that matter. Let us just say—your mother and Miss Manners—that a gentleman is supposed to have to make an important effort if he wishes to secure exclusive rights to a lady's company. Otherwise, he is going to experience discomfort in finding that she is not always available to be with him and has other gentleman friends. This is not a disgrace and should not be so treated.

One way to prevent them from running into one another is to let it be known that you do not entertain unannounced visitors. "Do call if you're thinking of coming over. I'd like it to be at a time I can receive you properly" is femalese for "I don't really plan to account to you for my time." You are right about too much busyness meaning "Go away," but "Oh, I'm devastated that I'm not free then. Some other time, I hope," means "Keep trying."

Rivals

DEAR MISS MANNERS:

I am living with a man whom I love and who loves me, but he has had affairs with other women. He is presently seeing a woman and has had sexual intercourse with her. She gave him a shirt and tie for his birthday. I felt it was pretty nervy of her to do this, and I wanted her to know that I knew all about her relationship with my boyfriend, so I called her up and invited her to a birthday dinner I was planning for my boyfriend and, at the same time, I thanked her for the birthday present. She got terribly upset and called my boyfriend, and he was terribly upset with me, and we broke up for about a week over this. Don't you believe it was perfectly correct for me to invite her to dinner with my boyfriend and me? I feel that if a woman is having sex with another woman's man, she has no rights and should not be treated with courtesy.

GENTLE READER:

We need a bit of clarification over the terms of possession here. Although you are living with the gentleman, he seems to consider himself a free agent, which makes your complaints about the other parties to his activities inappropriate. Whose boyfriend he is at a given time is not so clear.

On the other hand, you are doing an impressive job of handling the situation. In spite of your declaration that you need not treat the other lady with courtesy, you did. In fact, you have anticipated Miss Manners' advice by treating her with an excess of courtesy. Provided that this was politely done, she can hardly see how either one could object to your thanking a friend of the gentleman's and inviting her to his birthday party. Miss Manners fears that you may have undermined this excellent strategy by telling one or both of them your motive and feelings. It is not otherwise possible to be attacked for one's subtext when the text itself is impeccable.

The Stages Defined

DEAR MISS MANNERS:

I have become involved with a wonderful but somewhat commitment-phobic young man. He is in his late thirties and has never been married, although he professes a great desire to have a wife and family eventually. Our relationship is not yet a year old. About two weeks ago, this charming gentleman, who I now believe I am in love with, professed similar feelings for me, and as I waited for the ultimate proposal, he said, "Let's go steady." Feeling that half a loaf was better than nothing, and that this was at least a step in the right direction, I said okay. Now I wonder what I have actually agreed to.

In your estimation, outside of high school, where I assume—never having done it—that going steady entitled one to a goodnight kiss and maybe a bit more for the boy, and a regular date each Friday and Saturday for the girl, what are adult parameters for "going steady"? Have I agreed to premarriage, or just not to jump into the sack with any Tom, Dick, or Harry who happens to catch my fancy? Also, how do I find out what he thinks this means without having to come right out and appear too eager by saying, "So are we looking at marriage here, or is this just your way of keeping me exclusively until you make up your mind?" Today's relationships seem to come and go so quickly. I'd like this one to last, but I'm not getting any younger myself, and if this man isn't inclined toward marriage, I want to cast my net elsewhere.

GENTLE READER:

There are, indeed, different stages of courtship for teenagers and for adults, the difference being that grown-ups can get married if they want to. That is why they put so much effort into claiming they can't—because they can't afford it, can't break someone else's heart by severing the previous bond, can't manage it emotionally, and so on.

Miss Manners is sorry to tell you that going steady is strictly a teenage category. The stages of teenaged relationships are:

Liking someone. This means that the two people have no direct relationship whatsoever, but at least one of them confides the state of his or her heart to all mutual acquaintances, who then use the information to make life miserable for the object of this affection.

Going out together. This can consist of merely one date, or even as little as one evening spent paying attention to each other. Because it becomes public knowledge, the participants must "break up" in order to have a date with someone else.

Going steadily. This means either that one party is hedging because he or she likes the status of going steady but not the other person, and hopes to do better, or it means that one person's parents have forbidden going steady.

Going steady. As you say, this is a standing date with certain privileges. A token of some kind is exchanged.

Being engaged to be engaged. Same thing, except more privileges and a better token.

Secret engagement. There is only a secret to a secret engagement if one of the partners declares it without the other one's knowledge. It can also be declared for the purpose of annoying parents.

The adult stages are simpler:

Friendship. Although this term is used to describe opposite relationships—an asexual one or one of high passion—it always means that the couple has nothing romantic that it wants known.

Courtship. In its serious manifestations, this is a theoretically nonexclusive arrangement—one or both may have no emotional interest in going out with anyone else, but neither can demand it of the other—which is understood to lead either to a lot of heartbreak, accusations, and other depressing late-night conversation or to one or more of the following states.

Engagement. This is a public announcement and usually means that the couple plans to marry sooner or later. The leeway of "later" allows fastidious people to use it instead of the alternative announcement of:

Living together. Formerly known as "trial marriage" and only announced by people who were hoping to give their parents heart attacks, this is now a common arrangement between one person who believes it to be an unbinding temporary state and another person who believes that it is a preliminary to marriage.

Marriage.   As an adult going steady, you have the disadvantages of the teenage rules (no looking at anyone else) while subscribing to the concept that going steady is as far as you can go, marriage not being considered as a practical possibility. That is Miss Manners' guess. To find out exactly what the gentleman means, say coyly, "Oh, I don't know. Do you really think we're ready yet to be practically engaged?" If the reply is "Engaged? Who ever said anything about being engaged?", you might want to look elsewhere.

The Preengagement Ring

DEAR MISS MANNERS:
Ever since I received a gorgeous pearl preengagement or promise ring from my boyfriend, I have been researching and racking my and everybody else's brain, trying to find out something—anything—about the ring, the symbolism, and the etiquette. I have had conflicting reports about which hand to wear it on, which finger, and especially what to tell my parents and friends. Is there another name for this sort of gift? I will wear the ring anyway, but I would rather do it properly.

GENTLE READER:
In the absence of tradition, what you call this ring and where you wear it depend on both your taste and your assessment of what would annoy your parents the least. If your parents are really conservative, you should wear it on a chain out of sight, because they will take the position that a young lady cannot accept jewelry from someone to whom she is not engaged. Most parents would be satisfied merely to sigh and give you a lecture about not tying yourself down. Miss Manners dares say they would prefer that you wear it on the right hand and call it a "friendship ring."

Illicit Romance

Conventional society, once considered the ruthless enemy of unsanctioned romance, has grown tolerant and even genial toward renegade lovers. Most of the violations for which illicit couples used to be condemned have been removed from the books. So you would think—or rather, Miss Manners would, since her mind tends to wander towards matters of etiquette while everyone else is concentrating on the merely salacious—that such lovers would, in gratitude, show extra respect for the few remaining conventions.

The proper rules of conduct for improperly paired lovers (sin being no excuse for bad manners) toward others are:
• Make as few confidences as possible, and only to people who seem receptive. The natural desire of all lovers to have everyone in the world know about them—based on the assumption that everyone is envying them rather than

thinking "What on earth do they see in each other?"—leads to reckless show-ing off. We tolerate this in approved lovers, holding back snickers only for the inevitable time when they voluntarily stop cooing in public; in illicit ones, it is embarrassing to many people.

- Do not ask others to lie for you. We are all responsible for our own morals, and to ask people to compromise theirs without the advantage you enjoy of being compromised, as it were, is unethical.
- Do not put others into situations of dramatic irony, in which they are aware of double meanings in behavior of which others, usually the spouses of the lovers, are innocently oblivious.
- Leave borrowed quarters as they were found. Bread-and-butter presents are appropriate from all houseguests, even those who did not actually stay overnight.
- Each of the lovers is as bound by discretion, loyalty, and secrecy about any privileged information about the other lover's spouse and family as the person who told it was supposed to be.

Miss Manners recognizes that frail humanity is often subject to chaotic emo-tions and uncontrollable passions. She refuses to acknowledge that the careless or willful desire to violate the rules of etiquette is one of them.

POLITE REJECTION

"How can I tell my lover that it's all over without making him feel rejected?"

"This woman keeps calling me. I don't want to reject her, but I'm really not interested."

"What's a polite way to get rid of someone without rejecting him?"

Miss Manners receives letters with questions like this all the time. She stares at them, gets up and walks aimlessly around the room, goes out and makes herself a pot of tea, returns to her desk, looks at them again, and sighs. Then she folds them up neatly, puts them back into her desk, and turns her attention to letters with sensible questions, such as what to say when a friend falls down the stairs ("Did you trip?").

The desk is acquiring that overstuffed look. The belief that it is a sin to reject anyone for any reason, or even to allow a person to feel rejected, is widespread. It ought to follow that there are a great number of people who sacrifice their own in-terests to the desires of others, but that, as the questions indicate, is not what they had in mind.

When she continues to read the letters, however, having retrieved them and smoothed them out nicely, she finds another contradiction. After requesting a nonrejecting way of ridding themselves of pests, these people often specify that they want to be open and honest about it. They suggest that all of these objectives may be accomplished by informing the unwanted person, with all frankness, just what it is about him that is unbearable.

Now just a minute here. Miss Manners has only managed to get this far by translating the idea of not rejecting to mean not doing so cruelly. She can hardly think of anything more cruel than presenting someone with an irrefutable argument stating why one would have to be out of one's mind to have dinner, or spend one's life, with him or her.

The greatest comfort, when one is rejected, is to believe that the other person is making a mistake, which will be bitterly regretted sooner or later. Such thinking is most easily achieved when one is rejected on vague and flimsy grounds. It is easy to understand that the person who is always too busy to go out with you, or suddenly in need of solitude to reassess life, or just not ready to settle down with anyone is a fool. Anyone with a grain of sense would see how much more important it was to seize the opportunity of being with you.

Suppose, however, that the one you love admits that those things would not matter if the right person came along, but that you, given your personality, looks, conversation, and personal habits, will never be that person. Or suppose you are told that you seemed, for a while, to qualify but on better acquaintance have proved hopeless. At best, you must then try to go on, knowing that a person you value has pronounced you unworthy. At worst, you make a pitiful effort to change what that person doesn't like about you and find that even if it is something you can change and do, it doesn't help.

While one can hardly get through life without ever rejecting anyone, it is important to be able to do so without attempting to destroy that person. Checking the temptation to justify the rejection with honest and open arguments, and allowing oneself to be considered capricious and foolhardy, is the humane thing to do. Finally, Miss Manners fears that she must both reassure and disappoint those who do the rejecting by informing them that most rejected people get over their rejections and go on to live perfectly good lives, sometimes made happier by remembering what might have been.

Declining an Engagement

DEAR MISS MANNERS:

In past years, a gentleman would ask me if I would like to go out, and I might decline and thank him for asking. That would be the end of it. Now I find that many men will not take "no" for an answer. I am referring to intelligent and otherwise well-mannered businessmen, stockbrokers, and so on. After what I believe is a polite refusal, they inquire into my reason for the refusal, often asking if it was something they did wrong.

Although I consider the fact that they ask such a question to be quite rude, since it makes for an awkward situation, I do not wish to reply in kind. Therefore, when I am sure that I will not be found out, I indicate that I already have a beau. But even when assured that it is fairly serious, they often continue to pursue me by calling at my place of business. I have a management position at a local firm and do not see how I can avoid mentioning the firm's name in conversation. I have not encouraged these requests through flirtation, nor do I give out my unlisted home phone number.

I do not wish to imply that I am deluged with such requests; however, the problem I have described is becoming more frequent. Several women friends have also experienced the same stressful situations. With men who are aware that I do not have a beau, I am at a loss. Suggestions that we have little in common open up debate, while excuses that professional and other obligations leave me with virtually no free time only prolong the agony by encouraging more attempts.

GENTLE READER:

A lady does not give reasons for not being accessible to a particular gentleman. She doesn't explain why she won't go out with him, she doesn't explain why she won't marry him, and she doesn't explain why she won't do anything in between. The very notion that every lady would yield, if she didn't have a compelling reason not to, is insulting. Gentlemen may think that they want to hear why a particular lady is turning them down, but they are mighty unhappy when they do. It is, of course, true that declining one date leaves a gentleman ignorant of whether you are simply not free or intend to decline all his attentions. The third try is supposed to tell him that.

However, as you point out, such subtlety eludes some of them. Therefore, you must master the all-purpose refusal. Do not make up stories about boyfriends or, worse, tell them truthfully that you have nothing in common. If they track you down at work, you may certainly say curtly, "I'm sorry, I don't take personal calls at the office."

Asking for One's Letters Back

DEAR MISS MANNERS:

A few months ago, a delightful young lady and I parted company. It was her decision, because she could not return my feelings with equal intensity, but we went our divergent ways cordially and courteously. During the more incandescent phase of our involvement, I had expressed my sentiments in a series of letters. Now I am uncomfortable with the idea of so much personal and closely held material being in the possession of one who rejects its premise. Would it be churlish of me to request the return of those letters? I realize that gifts are normally not returnable except for engagement rings, and I cherish the farewell gift she gave me—accompanied by the only letter I ever got from her, informing me that there was not a place for me in her life. The entire issue may be moot, as she may have discarded my letters, but is it correct even to ask?

GENTLE READER:

In a society where nobody knows how to break up properly anymore, you have excellent instincts. All that remains is that you be informed about the proper traditions of breaking up. "Asking for one's letters back" was not only correct, but so common as to be a euphemism for discontinuing a romance.

Returning Jewelry

DEAR MISS MANNERS:

What is the proper thing for a lady to do with jewelry that has been given to her by an admirer whom she no longer sees? Is it appropriate to continue to wear it, or should it be given away, possibly to a charity?

GENTLE READER:

Just one moment, please. Miss Manners is straining herself to refrain from asking why a lady has accumulated jewelry from an admirer to whom she is not married. All right, she has that under control. This is not the first time Miss Manners has had to skip the part about whether one should have the problem and proceed to solving it.

Return all jewelry. If the breakup was an unpleasant one, you may throw it in the gentleman's face. However, if you merely got bored with him, or found a better source, wrap it all up prettily and attach a note saying that you wouldn't feel right keeping it.

Avoiding the Postmortem

DEAR MISS MANNERS:

My younger sister and I, both college students, have each recently ended serious dating relationships that lasted more than one year. My sister's was ended because of an unfaithful suitor, and mine because of a long and painful realization that the man I loved and I were not right for each other. Each of us has an extensive list of friends and relatives who ask, upon chance meetings, "How are you and Humphrey doing?" or "So, when do you and Poindexter plan to be married?" I have been in this position before and know that when these well-meaning individuals are informed that the relationship has been terminated, they become round-eyed and exclaim, "Really? What happened?" It is none of their business, of course, but "I would prefer not to discuss it" seems to have no effect on them. Could you propose a proper response, other than bursting into tears, which is messy and generally impractical?

GENTLE READER:

You already have the proper response: "I prefer not to discuss it." Why are you searching for something that might suit rude people better? One reason rudeness prospers so nowadays is that the victims feel they must keep negotiating until their tormentors acknowledge that they have been trounced. Just keep repeating what you said until they give up.

The only proper public reason for the parting of two people who were once a publicly declared couple is the one you gave about yourself. It applies to your sister equally well, if you think about it. Infidelity is a common way of discovering that someone is "not right" for oneself. Not only is any explanation other than a parting by mutual consent not anyone else's business, but it reflects badly on the teller, no matter who was at fault. Miss Manners promises you that if your sister said, "The cad deceived me," these people would only murmur among themselves, "She probably drove him to it."

Recovering from Rejection

DEAR MISS MANNERS:
For the past three years, I've enjoyed a lovely platonic relationship with a gentle man. Since I am happily married, I made it clear that our deep relationship must remain platonic. Alas, I fell in love with him. Now he has found a wealthy woman and is planning to marry. He called to tell me the news. I acted happy, but deep down, I am very hurt and pained. I have just received the wedding invitation. Would it be permissible not to attend? What excuse can I give besides a broken heart? Do I still send a gift? He wants to be friends, but I feel so depressed. I would rather never see him or speak to him again. Intellectually, I realize I'm a fool, but my heart refuses to stop bleeding.

GENTLE READER:
One of the greatest arguments for manners is that they prevent people who are being fools from looking like fools. Miss Manners cannot heal your bleeding heart, but she can help you keep the wound from showing and promise you that, oddly enough, this speeds the recovery.

Your outward behavior must convince everyone—beginning, in order of importance, with your husband, the gentleman, and his bride—that you are delighted about the marriage. One must always seem to be delighted when one's friends get married. Later, you can taper off the friendship, and everyone will understand that you simply didn't find the spouse as interesting as the original friend. It happens all the time under innocent circumstances.

The quickest way to accomplish the task would be to put on an act at the wedding, but Miss Manners doesn't quite trust you to do so. Look at that crack that slipped out about his having "found a wealthy woman." A disinterested person would say that he "fell in love—and by the way, she happens to be rich." So stay away, with a convincing excuse and an expression of regret, and send them a lovely present. That way, if the bride suggests that you seem jealous, the gentleman will protest, "Oh, no, she's very happily married," which will make the lady's remark seem in slightly bad taste. He may even confess that you had rejected him. This leaves you in the position of being one of his regrets—the lady who declined what she, the bride, was only too glad to take. As you will recall when you begin to feel better, this is indeed the case.

Ceremonies and Celebrations

Engagements

The Premature Engagement

DEAR MISS MANNERS:

A close friend of mine has announced her intention of marrying a nice young man. He agrees to this prospect. Unfortunately, as is all too often the case these days, the young man in question must first sever his legal connection with a spouse. Thus, firm arrangements cannot be made for the nuptials.

Can I, as a friend of the betrothed, give her a shower without there being a set wedding day? Is she, in fact, betrothed, since her fiancé is technically wed to another? Should I call the party by some other name? Should I, for heaven's sake, not give a party at all? The last seems a bit mean-spirited. But one wishes, after all, to do the Right Thing.

GENTLE READER:

Civilized people recognize that a married person cannot be engaged. It was one thing for your friend to inform you that she intends to marry; it would be quite another for her or you to indulge in the customs and trappings of an engagement. The right thing is to give your shower between the young man's divorce and the wedding. That period, even if it is only an hour, is the time of engagement.

The Traditional Proposal

DEAR MISS MANNERS:

Well, my heart goes thumpity-thump whenever she's near, so this longtime bachelor is contemplating the purchase of a ring with which to make my intentions

567

clear to my lady. Diamond rings are sold not only in jewelry shops and in the jewelry sections of quality department stores, but also at the discount variety shop and catalog store, and even via television shopping networks. I want to make the proper impression, but I also have a prudent and thrifty nature. Just what are the advantages and disadvantages of buying an engagement ring at such establishments?

Not that such a question should come into play at this moment, I suppose. Alas, it seems that my imagined scene—the gentleman drops down on one knee, proffers the lady a ring in a velvet box, and then "pops the question"—is but a myth. It would seem that with the credit systems and merchandising practices of today, a ring obtained in advance can always be exchanged later to more closely match the lady's preference or returned should the offer be declined, no? Even worse, from this traditionalist's point of view, is the "courtship form" revealed to us by television and film. The modern way to propose is by concealing the ring in an object, a piece of cooked food (a dinner roll?), or even a dressing robe pocket. What's a fellow to do nowadays?

GENTLE READER:

Well, Miss Manners wouldn't advise a fellow to bake a metal and mineral object into anything he planned to serve as dinner to a lady he professes to care about. Perhaps that is what comes of getting your manners from the entertainment industry. It would be equally inappropriate to get your consumer advice from an etiquette adviser, so Miss Manners presumes that your question about where to buy the ring has to do with whether you need a box proving that you paid full price for it. Certainly not. Your fiancée may approve of your thrift—Miss Manners presumes you know her better than she does—or you could simply dispense with the box and slip the ring on her finger after her acceptance.

That is still a charming and memorable gesture, although the more practical-minded keep pointing out that the lady may prefer a ring to her own taste. Indeed, and she may be prohibited by the sentiment of the occasion from exercising it to exchange the ring. Still, Miss Manners thinks that the delightful fact that you want to make a full ceremony of the occasion, ring and all, makes it worth the risk. You ought to be able to handle the practical matters, too, by saying after (and in spite of) her exclamations of delight, "Of course, I chose this as a symbol. Let's go back to have it sized and see if there is a ring you might like better." Manners require her to say, "No, I never want any ring but this" three times before she says, "Of course, I always did like sapphires better than diamonds."

Financing the Ring

DEAR MISS MANNERS:

I am in the process of getting engaged. What I mean is that all the formalities are over except picking out the ring. The man I am engaged to is twenty-three. His parents and immediate family are a bit more refined than I. I don't know if this is due to breeding or my age (I am twenty-one), but some members of his family like to remind me of this occasionally in subtle ways.

My fiancé and I have decided that the ring we will get will cost about $1,000. John is not rich, but he has a good job and a bit of money in the bank. We decided on this amount after figuring the money we would need for wedding expenses, honeymoon, house, and so on. I also have a bit of money in the bank, and I asked John if it would be all right if I put $1,000 towards the ring along with his, so that I can get one I had seen that is a bit more elaborate. He wholeheartedly agreed, thinking the same as I: that I will probably never have the chance to buy a diamond ring again, so I might as well get one I really want and for once not be so practical. Is it wrong for John to let me pay half? The reason I asked him is because I didn't want him to feel that what he would buy would not be good enough—$1,000 will buy a beautiful ring. Is he wrong for accepting my offer? Is this something that is not done in the cultural society? I don't want to show his family anymore how unsophisticated I am compared to them.

GENTLE READER:

What is not done in polite society is to allow anyone to know how one chooses to spend one's money. Näiveté is not the charge you will face if you and John do not keep this particular private arrangement to yourselves. Since you mention sophistication, allow Miss Manners to say that the more sophisticated way to accomplish what you wish would have been to suggest that John splurge on the ring you want, and that you put more of your savings toward the house you will buy together.

What Constitutes an Engagement

DEAR MISS MANNERS:

Several months ago, my beau and I decided that we would like to spend the rest of our lives together. To that end, we plan to buy a house, move into it, and marry—in that order. While we made no formal announcements of any kind, we told friends and family about our plans when the subject came up.

The unresolved matter of etiquette is this: The young man believes that we are not formally engaged to be married unless and until we have a date for the ceremony. It is my understanding that, on the contrary, in times gone by, long engagements without a set date for the wedding were quite common. My feeling is that we are engaged to be married simply by virtue of our public intention to marry, and that no further announcements or signs (such as a ring) are required. I hasten to add that this is a very proper young man who organizes his life according to Miss Manners' dictates. We would both appreciate it if you would let us know if he is, in fact, my fiancé.

GENTLE READER:

Please give the gentleman Miss Manners' congratulations on his engagement. The public declaration of an intention to marry is an engagement. (The private declaration is a secret engagement.) Rings, parties, check-off lists of tasks and prospective guests, and a relationship with a caterer are optional. Besides, the gentleman ought to be grateful that this arrangement provides him with a proper and practical term, "fiancé," by which he can be easily identified. If he can think of a term that would equally well describe the preengaged or unengaged state of householding, Miss Manners would very much like to hear it.

Insinuations

DEAR MISS MANNERS:

I am a foreign citizen, a student in your country, and I have recently become engaged to an American whom I have known for two years. I am very much in love with my fiancé, and he with me, so it troubles us greatly when the insinuation arises that I am marrying him "to obtain a Green Card" or "to get to stay in the country." Ever since our engagement, people whom we considered friends, and even members of my fiancé's family, have repeatedly implied that our decision to marry was made purely on the basis of expediency, and that any notion of our being in love is simply a front. I can't understand why this view prevails with so many people, because I assure you that our feelings are genuine and deep, and that we dated for a long time before arriving at this stage. Often the accuser claims to be "teasing," but I am tired of putting up with these slurs.

GENTLE READER:

Miss Manners never ceases to be amazed at the inventiveness of people who believe that communicating everything that comes into their ungenerous minds is the way to spread happiness in the world. "How lovely; I wish you both happiness" is too tame for these people, who prefer such forms as "It's about time," "What's your hurry?" "Are you sure you know what you're doing?", "Are you expecting?" and now the remarks that you report. Miss Manners would prefer that you limit yourself to saying, with shining eyes, "I knew you'd be pleased for us." But if that is too subtle for them, she will look the other way while you say, "Oh, I hope that's not the custom here. Where I come from, we only marry for love."

Impertinent Questions

DEAR MISS MANNERS:

I am a recently engaged college student. As my fiancé cannot afford a diamond ring, I am wearing a look-alike substitute, but we will be purchasing a diamond ring after marriage, when we are more financially stable. Unfortunately, I do not know how to reply to the question "Is it real?" How can I answer ambiguously without giving personal details or outright lying?

GENTLE READER:

Give them your brightest, bridelike smile and say, "Yes" (they didn't ask real *what*). You might add, "Our love is real—yes."

The Bridegroom's Ring

DEAR MISS MANNERS:

I inquired of my fiancé as to the style of wedding band he might prefer. I refer, of course, to the gold ring, and not to a musical group. I was somewhat rudely shocked when he replied that he wasn't sure he would buy one. He stated that for a construction engineer, it can be dangerous to wear one to work, and furthermore, that rings do not fit him well. Regardless of how often one wears it, what is the proper approach to the purchase of a man's wedding ring?

GENTLE READER:

As much as Miss Manners likes symbolism, she would consider it foolish to require a gentleman to wear a ring that might annoy or handicap him. Should he wish to own one, please tell him he cannot skip the symbolism of having his bride give it to him. Obviously, anyone wants to have a say about the style of ring he or she is to wear, but the little fiction that one is only helping to choose a present from the other person is worth maintaining.

Broken Engagements

DEAR MISS MANNERS:

I am writing to you on behalf of my best friend, Cathy, who is engaged to be married. She recently postponed the wedding date indefinitely for financial reasons. Since then, she has had some doubt about the relationship, and has contemplated breaking off the engagement until certain things are worked out. She and her fiancé have received several engagement presents from friends and relatives. What should Cathy do with these gifts in the event that she breaks off her engagement temporarily? Or permanently? If it makes a difference, Cathy and her fiancé are not cohabiting.

GENTLE READER:

It probably makes a difference to Cathy and her fiancé, but not to Miss Manners. Anyway, Miss Manners is occupied trying to figure out the time element. Postponing a wedding "indefinitely" is a euphemism for canceling it forever. (Incidentally, it is odd to hear of someone's doing that for "financial reasons." In Victorian times, that would have been a prime reason, but nowadays, whether the couple has anything to live on is not supposed to be a factor.) If, indeed, this is or becomes a permanent break, the presents should be returned.

Breaking an engagement temporarily sounds to Miss Manners like what used to be called a "lovers' quarrel." In that case, they should hold on to things until they make up their minds for good. To bounce the presents back and forth to their hapless donors while that is going on would be a nuisance to all concerned.

Punitive Measures

DEAR MISS MANNERS:

You stated that if a woman breaks her engagement, she should give the ring back. What if a man breaks it off? I've been engaged for about six weeks. My dad came down with lung cancer and had to have around-the-clock care. My mother works, and I have an eleven-year-old daughter. The other kids are out of town, so it was up to me to help all I could. This guy said I had too many duties to my parents and Tammy, so he wanted his ring back. I'm not going to give it back. He says he's going to take me to court. That's the only way I'm going to give it back.

GENTLE READER:

Going to court is the only chance you may have of keeping it. Miss Manners is not a lawyer, but she is not going to let you keep it on social grounds. The laws of etiquette absolutely require you to return an engagement ring when the engagement is broken, for whatever reason, and by however nasty a fiancé.

Splitting Expenses

DEAR MISS MANNERS:

What is the proper financial arrangement when an engagement is broken? Three weeks before our wedding, my former fiancé decided that he didn't want to get married. Besides being in shock, I was out of a lot of money, since a nonreturnable deposit had been made on the reception hall, photographer, cake, and flowers, all of which I had paid for myself. I made a list of expenses and gave it to my former fiancé, and he agreed to pay one-half, and gave me a check. Some of my friends said that he should have paid for all of it, since he was the one who called it off.

GENTLE READER:

You are within the realm of tradition when you wish to translate emotional disappointment into punitive financial action, but suing for breach of promise has gone out of fashion. It was an idea Miss Manners is not sorry to see go. Legally or emotionally, one can never be truly compensated for the failure of love, and in an instance such as this, where the damage is so much less than it would have been in a failed marriage, your self-respect would be best served by letting it go. A no-fault settlement may cost you more, but it affords you more dignity. Just consider what the financial mess would have been had the gentleman changed his mind about you after the wedding.

Showers

For the Bridal Couple

DEAR MISS MANNERS:

In recent years, the prospective bridegroom has been present at all bridal showers that I have attended. Lavish as these affairs have become, am I wrong in assuming that they still should be considered "girl parties," with all the appropriate gushing, giggling, and gossiping? The man must be bored to tears. Is this an omen of things to come? Will the bride-to-be soon be expected to pop out of a cake at the stag party and have to listen to raunchy jokes told over a few steins of beer? If one, why not the other? Do I sense a double standard here, and if so, why? Are all the traditional bastions of etiquette crumbling like a house of cards?

GENTLE READER:

Cards don't crumble. However, Miss Manners does not mind if some customs do. The gender-separated wedding party, based on the idea that the bride and the bridegroom have opposite notions of social fun and are bored senseless by each other's friends, is not a tradition that Miss Manners is going to go to a lot of trouble to rescue from oblivion.

Not that she objects to it. Giggliness and raunchiness are all right in their place, and sharing a session of one or the other with compatible souls of one's own gender is all very well. The specific bridal customs you mention often overdo

573

things, with an unpleasant emphasis on materialism for the ladies and unacceptable forms of entertainment (such as ones that end in the bridegroom's being arrested) for the gentlemen. For this reason, and because of the increasing tendency for friendships to be formed on the basis of common interests regardless of gender, the sort of divided party you mention is becoming less and less popular. So be it.

The Basic Rules

DEAR MISS MANNERS:

Is it appropriate for a bride-to-be of an affluent family to have a shower in her honor? Is it proper for owners of gift shops to be hostesses for showers? When invited to a shower, must one always send a present? Is is proper to send the wedding present to the shower? Please bring us up-to-date on the etiquette of bridal showers.

GENTLE READER:

Quaint as it may seem, whether or not the bride is rich is not supposed to determine what bridal honors are done her. You are not even supposed to notice, my dear. If the bridegroom's family wishes to ask her whether she is able to support the young man in the style to which he wishes to become accustomed, that is another matter.

Bridal showers are given by friends of the bride's (not her relatives). Owners of gift shops may certainly give showers, as may people in any other line of work, provided that they do not intrude their commercial interests on such purely social occasions.

Shower presents are supposed to be "small." Naturally, no well-bred person notices how much was paid for a present (that's the same well-bred person who refused to notice whether or not the bride was rich). Shower presents are generally trousseau or household items (often on some theme suggested by the hostess), whereas wedding presents, whatever their cost, are more "serious" items of decorative value. If you go to a shower, you take a shower present, not the wedding present, which is sent directly.

🌹 BABY SHOWERS

Unwed Mothers

DEAR MISS MANNERS:

With the fast pace of this ever-changing world, has society accepted baby showers given for unwed mothers? I've been invited to several and would like to know your views on this situation.

GENTLE READER:

When Miss Manners last checked, the purpose of a baby shower was still simply to celebrate an anticipated birth. She does not recall any sweet, old-fashioned custom of first investigating the circumstances of the conception.

It's a Girl

DEAR MISS MANNERS:

We are planning to give a baby shower. The mother-to-be will be having an ultrasound test to determine the sex of the baby prior to the shower. How do we let our guests know the outcome on the invitations without sounding crass?

GENTLE READER:

You will sound crass only if you dwell on how this information was discovered. There is nothing wrong with inviting people to a shower with an invitation in honor of "Megan Bass, who is expecting a daughter."

Subsequent Showers

DEAR MISS MANNERS:

My good friend is about to have her second child, and I would like to have a baby shower for her. She says that she had a shower with her first child, and she is not sure it is proper to have another. I say that the baby shower is for her new baby and has nothing to do with her other shower.

GENTLE READER:

No, it's for the mother. The new baby will, ahem, be there, but not as a full-fledged guest. Second baby showers are discouraged because the mother, although equally excited about the new baby, is no longer so thrilled by seeing tiny garments and baby equipment, with which she is now supplied, as well as only too familiar. Her friends, although equally pleased for her, may also enjoy a rerun less. Rather than run the risk of being either tiresome to the guests of the previous shower by inviting them or offensive by not inviting them, why don't you just gather a few intimate friends for a luncheon or tea without calling it a shower?

Twins

DEAR MISS MANNERS:

I've been invited to a baby shower for a woman who is expecting twins. Is it customary and/or expected for one to give two of whatever gift is selected? I've asked several people, but no one seems to know the answer.

GENTLE READER:

This is one of these rare cases in which custom may be tempered by common sense. While one must acknowledge both babies, it is perfectly possible to do so with one present. You wouldn't give two booties when four feet are expected, but you could find something they could use together—a mobile, a music box, or a double picture frame, for example.

The Noninvited Guest

DEAR MISS MANNERS:

A neighbor of mine received a standard invitation to a bridal shower for the future daughter-in-law of her best friend, but written on the side of it was the message, "I regret space does not permit your attendance." My neighbor was justifiably hurt but said that she still sent a nice gift. Myself, they would have had a long wait for a present without my presence.

GENTLE READER:

Miss Manners, they would have had to track down at the emergency room of the hospital, from the shock of the very idea of inviting someone not to attend a party. The rule against allowing anyone even to hear of a social event to which he or she is not invited is such an important one that polite people go to great lengths to avoid any allusions that might hint at such a thing. What this person invented was a written version of the school playground taunt, "Nyah, nyah! I'm having a party, and you can't come!"

Proper Unwrapping Procedure

DEAR MISS MANNERS:

I have been present at wedding and baby showers and have observed that the honoree, when opening gifts while the whole company watches, is seldom at ease in removing the gift wrappings. These wrappings frequently show that a great deal of care has been taken by the giver to present the gift beautifully. What is the proper way to remove the ribbon and paper, and extract the gift so that those present may exclaim? Does one carefully and slowly remove the tape, avoiding tearing the gift paper, fold it neatly, and then take the present from the box? When this is done several times, it seems to make the occasion more tedious than it would otherwise be, to say nothing of creating embarrassing silence while all eyes are on the guest. Yet to recklessly tear off all decorations and toss them aside in the haste to see what gift is inside does not seem a gracious way to treat presents carefully selected by others. If you could outline the proper procedure, I am sure that other Gentle Readers besides myself would be most grateful.

GENTLE READER:

Neither of the ones you describe, the This Is Too Good to Throw Away method and the Lemme at It method, is actually incorrect, although they each lack something in audience appeal. The answer is a short burst of admiration. Exclaim "Oh, how beautiful!" or "Why, this is a work of art in itself," and then get on with the business at hand.

Weddings: An Overview

Just because Miss Manners happens to be fond of tradition, that doesn't mean she isn't willing to fool around with it. On the contrary. After all, you're fond of—no, skip that. All that wedding champagne must be making Miss Manners giddy. Wedding tradition has always been evolving, and Miss Manners does not oppose graceful adjustments that reflect basic social changes.

The set-piece wedding that is fixed in most impressionable minds—something between a Broadway musical and an honor-yourself beauty pageant—is neither old enough to be considered sacred nor appropriate enough to modern marriages to be adopted without a bit of customizing, as it were. In Miss Manners' opinion, one best honors tradition by examining it carefully and subtly adjusting what obviously doesn't fit. A pattern designed for very young couples, where the bride leaves her father's protection for her husband's, is going to require a bit of letting out to be used for a bride who was, for example, brought up solely by her mother, has been living independently for some years, and may have children from a previous marriage or be acquiring stepchildren.

Does that mean she can't have the traditional wedding? No. Miss Manners is not one of those old crabs who runs around complaining that certain brides are "not entitled" to white dresses and wedding formality because of courtship details that these crabs, if properly behaved themselves, would not know or speculate about.

A few changes would personalize that wedding tradition in a way that silly paper goods stamped "Melissa and Curt" do not. Here are a few developments of which Miss Manners approves. Some have already become part of the wedding pattern to such an extent that it will surprise you to hear that they are relatively new; others are ones that Miss Manners is simply hoping will be adopted.

Children of the bridal couple should be at the wedding unless there are emotional factors of divided loyalty that make this undesirable. Arranging day care for the children of guests is a generous gesture for those who are willing to undertake it, but excluding those children is not a social offense. Absolutely to be excluded are the bridal couple's former spouses. Former suitors may be invited because they are picturesque when they look a tad disappointed, but that is an expression impossible to ex-spouses, who are apt to look either sullen or relieved.

Alert observers have noticed, in recent years, that bridegrooms are just as likely as brides are to have parents. There is some feeling that this discovery ought to be reflected in wedding customs, hitherto designed around the idea that the bridegroom was an accessory to that dazzling creature, The Bride—greater in importance than, say, the penny in the shoe, but not nearly as interesting as the trousseau. The bridegroom's parents, who had nothing to do between calling on the bride's family after the proposal and enjoying their hospitality at the wedding, may be allowed to—but not assigned to—participate more fully. Having them give the rehearsal dinner is not a traditional custom, but it is a sensible one if feasible. (As hosts, they get to decide how to do it and how much to spend on it.) Although Miss Manners does not believe that the bridegroom's provenance belongs on the wedding invitation—his parents are named only if they, rather than hers, are issuing the invitations—she sympathizes somewhat with the need to remind his side of the guest list why they are invited. She hereby announces that this may be done by the inclusion of the bridegroom's parents' visiting card with the wedding invitation.

The "giving away" of the bride can be omitted altogether, as an anachronism, but if it is retained, it should be fitting. One does not seek out a male to do the job, however remote he may have been from the household. If the bride does not have a father, stepfather, or other male relative who has helped rear her, she could certainly have her mother give her away. There is nothing startling about a mother's giving away the bride. Dear Edith Wharton has a passage in her novel *The Mother Recompense* in which the mother of a fashionable bride is severely reminded that, the father being dead, custom demands that she give the bride away. (The mother is reluctant because the bridegroom is her own secret former lover. Never mind that now. This is just a sweet, old-fashioned novel from the twenties.)

Miss Manners is heartily in favor of allowing both sets of parents, mothers as well as fathers, in that inner circle at the altar. Parents need not be fitted into such roles as best man, matron of honor, or donor of the bride—there is far too much emphasis on these titles anyway—although they may be. The Jewish custom of having both sets of parents at the altar ought to be more widely adopted.

As it is more or less admitted that some couples already have households, Miss Manners permits giving their address under the "R.s.v.p." line on the invitation, so that presents, as well as responses, will be sent to their home. There is no reason that a bridegroom as well as a bride, cannot write thank-you letters. It is helpful to friends if the couple finds a way of indicating how they wished to be addressed; at-home cards, with their new name, are an excellent way of doing this.

Miss Manners also likes, but by no means requires, some stylistic changes that are not as radical as they may seem. Truly old-fashioned weddings did not have special, one-time-use uniforms; the wedding party was outfitted in good clothes to be used afterward. It is practical and, Miss Manners believes, attractive to have bridesmaids in harmonizing dresses that suit them individually, rather than to force them into one style. Nor does she disapprove of pastel wedding dresses (silver is actually as venerable a tradition as white), colored flowers, or chocolate wedding cakes.

You will perhaps be relieved to hear that there are some current ideas that Miss Manners absolutely can't stand:
- The assumption by either guests or hosts that wedding invitations may be casually distributed or regarded.
- The show-business mentality of issuing programs with cast lists and applauding the ceremony, which came into vogue when the society decided that the highest and most important form of activity it could imagine was entertainment. Miss Manners is not against joyous enthusiasm at weddings, but believes that it should be expressed (although not with applause) at the reception after a dignified service.
- Black wedding-party dresses, preprinted thank-you cards, R.s.v.p. cards, showers given by relatives, and bridal couples hanging around their own weddings so late that the guests want to sneak out before they do.
- Any idea connected with channeling the potential generosity of wedding guests, whether it is billing them for wedding reception food or drinks, asking for cash donations rather than presents, circulating the list of received presents among other potential donors, or otherwise reminding people that they haven't yet come across. Equally offensive is a guest's asking to count his transportation to the wedding as a present.
- Other bad ideas include engaging professional masters of ceremonies; abolishing receiving lines at receptions or postponing them for extended photography sessions; and guests' bringing their presents to the wedding or reception, rather than sending them to the home. Don't even try to think up a new scheme, such as preprinted cards or postal cards from the wedding trip, for lessening the chore of writing thank-you letters. The very thought is rude.

Multiple Weddings

DEAR MISS MANNERS:

My fiancé lives on the East Coast and I on the West Coast. We plan to have a small church wedding in California, with handwritten invitations to those who can attend and engraved announcements to friends and relatives in the Midwest and

East. Immediately afterward, we will move back East, and my fiancé would like to have another wedding in Maryland that his family and friends can attend later, after we are settled and have time to plan it. I would prefer a reception only, but this is very important to him. Should these people receive announcements and then later invitations to the second ceremony or reception? Should a reception card be enclosed with the announcements so that they know there will be some sort of gathering? How should it be worded?

GENTLE READER:

Going to take your show on the road, are you? When Miss Manners began noticing people choosing their wedding attendants for uniformity of looks, like a chorus line, and looking for backers, she suspected that the next thing would be touring companies. Indeed, someone has sent her what looks like a travel bureau form—a notice from a bridal couple offering four shows at different locations, from which prospective guests can choose the most convenient time and place, and even style, because two are black tie and two not.

Miss Manners urges you, as does your own instinct, to have one wedding, and have only a reception at the other location. A wedding is a solemn ceremony. It may be repeated for serious reasons—one religious and one civil ceremony, for example, or a sentimental renewal of vows years later—but not simply because the entertainment is popular with audiences.

Send wedding invitations to those closest to you emotionally, ignoring geographical limitations. It is up to them, not you, to decide whether they want to make the trip. (Others receive announcements.) Separately and at the appropriate time, invite both sets of people who live on the East Coast to the East Coast reception. As that one is especially for the bridegroom's family and friends, his parents could give it in your honor, with a formal invitation (Mr. and Mrs. Ashley Arundel request the pleasure of your company/at a reception, etc., with "in honor of Mr. and Mrs. Bowie Arundel" or "Bowie and Anne Arundel" written above).

The Pregnant Bride

DEAR MISS MANNERS:

My daughter, who is getting married soon, has informed me that she is with child. I have had a long list of disappointments and am fighting my own emotional battles, but I feel that acceptance is my only choice. I love my daughter, am otherwise proud of her character, and do not want to risk losing our closeness. I will continue to help her plan the traditional wedding she wants. She is not planning to announce her pregnancy prior to the wedding, because she doesn't want people to think that they're getting married merely because of the pregnancy. I feel that it is her responsibility to inform whomever she wants, whenever she wants, and to suffer the consequences of her decisions.

I am disturbed, however, because a very dear relative is involved in the wedding planning, both emotionally and financially. I feel confident that this person will be morally outraged at all the implications of a white wedding and a pregnant bride—she is etiquette personified—and will feel taken advantage of if she is not told and given the chance to back out. How can my husband and I honor our promise of confidentiality and still respect our dear and enduring relationship with this relative? How may I honor my various obligations without us all being hurt? I realize that this issue is as old as fertility, but it's in my family now, and I'm perplexed.

GENTLE READER:

That's funny. Miss Manners was under the impression that *she* was Etiquette Personified. As such, she believes that bridal pregnancy is a reason for encouraging, not discouraging, a wedding. Miss Manners is not disputing that your relative has other ideas—only that those represent the Voice of Etiquette.

The secret is not yours to tell. Your daughter is now a grown-up. You can no longer make her decisions for her—she is about to be a mother, making parental decisions herself—but can only strongly advise her of your feelings and opinions in the matter. Should she elect not to tell the relative, the consequences to the relationship will fall upon her. You are free to tell the lady afterward that you disagreed with your daughter's decision. No lady who even aspires to personify etiquette could blame a parent for refusing to violate the confidence of a grown daughter.

When the Bridal Couple Gives the Wedding

It has not escaped Miss Manners' attention that not all modern brides emerge blushing from their parents' protection to entrust themselves to bridgegrooms they have known only during publicly observed and regulated courtships.

Some bridal couples must have had more extensive acquaintance or they would not be asking Miss Manners what the proper role in the wedding is for their own children. Miss Manners has always delicately trod that fine line between respect for tradition and recognition of the no longer appropriate. She therefore understands that mature and independent couples might reasonably want to alter a wedding pattern designed for the young and dependent. Giving one's own wedding is certainly a proper alternative, providing that it is properly done.

The trepidation in Miss Manners' tone, on an occasion that ought to prompt unrestrained enthusiasm, comes from sad experience. All too often she has seen the twin motivations of money and power destroy the family considerations that ought to dominate any wedding planning. Couples who give their own weddings are not always prompted by the desire to assume the responsibility of pleasing their families and friends.

That Miss Manners is afraid, is what it means to give one's own wedding. Paying the bills is not enough. Doing the planning is not enough. These are both behind-the-scenes functions. A couple can do all that themselves and still, if they wish, have their parents give the wedding. Giving the wedding means being out-front as hosts.

When wedding invitations are issued in the name of the bride's parents (or the bridegroom's), those people are the hosts. Miss Manners never believed the polite fiction that the bride's mother chose everything, with perhaps a few allowances graciously made for the bride's own taste, but she prefers that fantasy to the reali-ty of parents cravenly suspending their judgment because it's "their day."

Hosts are supposed to take into consideration the comfort and happiness of their guests. And if the bridal couple are hosts for any reason other than that they are orphans or disowned—if it is because they are older and/or live far away—it is their parents whose interests should be looked after first. Some questions to con-sider are: Will they be able to attend without undue hardship? Which of the other relatives and their own friends do they believe ought to be invited? Are there any questions of religious observance (such as dietary restrictions) or social practice (such as very loud music) that are likely to offend the parents or others of their generation?

Couples who issue their own invitations, like those whose parents are giving their weddings, can follow either the formal or the informal form for invitations and announcements.

The engraved invitation is worded: "the honor of your presence/is requested at the marriage of," followed by the bride's name and then the bridegroom's. The in-formal version is a letter from one or the other: "Stephanie and I are being mar-ried on Sunday, April third, and would be so pleased to have you there." The for-mal announcement is: "Ms. Stephanie Insbrook/and/Mr. Jason Kingsley/an-nounce their marriage . . . "

The assumption of this function should not be looked upon as an opportunity to brag. No wedding invitation properly has a way of indicating the joy involved; among civilized people, that is taken for granted.

The part about the bride's being given away is omitted, being inappropriate for the same reasons that made the couple decide to give their own wedding.

What is not omitted is the duty of considering the feelings of others. Miss Man-ners is sorry if any couple had the illusion that doing it themselves allowed them to behave immaturely.

Premature Marriage

DEAR MISS MANNERS:

In a couple of months, my husband and I will be attending the wedding of my friend and a man who was married before. My friend started her wedding plans at the same time her future husband started his divorce proceedings. She says that if he is not divorced by the time they are to be married, she will go on as planned with her reception and get married at a later date.

Do I put in the envelope the same amount of money as I normally would, or just a down payment, with the rest to be paid in full when they get married? What if she does not exchange vows? Should she give the presents and money back? What do you say to the happy couple upon arrival at the reception? "Congratulations"? For what?

GENTLE READER:
Not knowing—or wanting to know—your wedding pay scale, Miss Manners cannot advise you on the rates. The only etiquette counseling that may be useful to you is the information that it is just as proper to send wedding presents after the wedding as before. In such a precarious situation as the one you describe, it seems imprudent not to take advantage of this option.

As for the rest, there are no rules of propriety because the entire situation is improper. This man was not married "before"; he is married now. Society does not recognize that married people may participate in engagement festivities, much less celebrate wedding receptions. Mind you, society is not so naïve as to be ignorant of the fact that people make marriage plans before the termination of existing marriages. It is even dimly aware that there may be causal relationships between the two. It does not interfere in whatever contingency plans couples wish to make in private or care how long a single person has been single before the wedding. It makes a huge distinction between knowing something and allowing it official recognition.

The law also makes that distinction between being married and not being married, and is no more likely to be gotten around with pleas of "Yes, but that isn't really a marriage anymore, and we all know that Tish and Tommy live together and are getting married the day the divorce comes through."

It is perfectly proper for you, as a friend, to commiserate with this couple about the delays, and to wish them well in overcoming these so that they may be free to celebrate their engagement and marriage. If you congratulate them now, it can only be on flouting society's laws and rules.

A Marriage of Convenience

DEAR MISS MANNERS:
Out of the blue, a friend sent me a wedding invitation and then informed me that it was a marriage of convenience, for her citizenship, and that the man was the gay lover of her gay friend. I am confused by their intention of having a party to celebrate their non- (but yet legal) marriage. I did not attend, but I bought a gift that I don't know if I want or need to give to her. They are not living together.

I did mention to mutual friends her "unusual" marriage, and that got back to her. She phoned to ask if I had told people, and I said that a written invitation made it public knowledge. She said she had only invited the people she wanted to know, and even denied it to everyone else, being worried that the information might hinder her single dating status. What's her problem?

GENTLE READER:

Her problem, aside from the legal and moral one of fraud, is that she wants to have it all ways at once. She wants to tell her secret, yet have it kept; she wants to be treated as a bride by friends such as yourself, but retain her single status for others.

None of this is your problem. A wedding is a legal public event, which goes on the public record and cannot therefore be kept secret. You have no obligation to keep a secret that the person most concerned is telling. It is one of the duties of a friend to celebrate a new marriage with good wishes and symbolic tokens of pleasure in the joy of the bridal couple. Almost any marriage should qualify— but not one that the bride herself has declared to be a temporary technicality.

Blessing a Nonlegal Union

DEAR MISS MANNERS:

I have a wonderful daughter who is gay. It was a number of years before our immediate family began to understand or accept this difference in lifestyle. Without dwelling further on that specific issue, here's the debate:

She will be getting married within the next year. Although it is not recognized by this state, it is recognized in a very prominent church nearby. My children will all be attending.

Do I send out invitations? Do I hand-pick those who might be understanding?

Since the topic of being gay is uncomfortable for many people to even discuss, I do not want to hurt any relative or close friend who might want to be there. And yet, I do not want to hurt my daughter by not attempting to invite a few special friends. There are several persons who have met her future partner, and everyone seems to agree that she's a wonderful person.

My daughter plans on having a reception afterward. Although their friends will be attending, it is my hope that cheerful support will also be there from other directions.

GENTLE READER:

Wedding guests are always hand-picked; you don't get them wholesale. It's too bad, because then you could order the attitudes you want.

What everyone has to do instead is to try to collect people who, because of their ties to the couple, wish them well—only too often in spite of reservations. (Heterosexual couples typically encounter disapproval because of religious or racial differences, the pregnancy of the bride, or objections to one of the individuals.) The proper response to those who refuse to condone the wedding with their presence is "I'm sorry you feel that way" and an expression of hope that they will come around when they see how wonderful the particular person is.

In this case, Miss Manners feels compelled to point out that there might be two levels of objections, one of which you could soften with tact.

Social and legal change rarely move in tandem; one almost always lags behind the other. Laws are supposed to be reasonable; customs have more emotional than ideological content. Your daughter may argue that she cares nothing for convention—but she does, or she wouldn't yearn for the society's wedding conventions.

Therefore, people who may not be offended by your daughter's living arrangement may still disapprove of her using traditional forms for what is not actually a wedding (surely what the church does is to bless the union, not perform an illegal marriage).

You can, of course, write off those people, too. Miss Manners is merely suggesting that you might be able to draw on their good will if your invitations and discussions refer to the event as a church blessing and a union, rather than as a wedding and marriage.

A Glossary of Bridal Expressions

In sweeter, more innocent times, everyone knew the proper thing to say in connection with weddings. The parents said, "What's your hurry? You might meet someone you like better," and all the other well-wishers dabbed away at misty eyes and said, "They probably had to get married." If the bridal couple said anything at all, no one paid any attention, because it was obvious that they were too young to have much sense. Now it has been demonstrated all too graphically that there is no event in the life cycle that makes people believe they have to get married, unless they are expecting a tax break, and parents tend to limit themselves to "Well, finally!"

Brides and bridegrooms, of all people, are speaking up. Miss Manners is not at all sure that this is appropriate, no matter what age they are, and is quite sure that much of what they say is unseemly. Here is a glossary of common bridal expressions. Miss Manners never wants to hear any of them again.

After all it's our wedding.   This is the basic refrain, used to justify offending family members, friends, and local customs on matters both large and small. Variations include "After all, we're paying for it" and "After all we're paying for the liquor."

How can we make formal invitations seem more friendly?   The opposite of formal is informal, not friendly; the opposite of friendly is hostile. Formality, an acceptable style for life's most serious events, is not considered hostile. Either keep those formal invitations unchanged or get rid of them altogether and have an informal wedding.

How can we personalize our wedding?   With the possible exception of the Princess of Wales, who mistook her bridegroom's name during the wedding ceremony, those involved in weddings usually have enough sense of the identity of the participants to make distinguishing gimmicks unnecessary.

What should the bridegroom wear to distinguish him from the groomsmen?
Men's clothes vary according to the time and degree of formality of the wedding,
but whatever is proper is proper for them all. If the bride can't tell the bridegroom
from among a small group of identically dressed gentlemen, the problem is not a
sartorial one.

*How can I tell my best friend, who is too (tall, short, fat, pregnant) that I don't
want her as a bridesmaid?* The time to establish the criteria for best friendhood
is at the inception of the relationship. Deciding retroactively that anyone aspiring
to the position must meet certain height or weight standards is not nice. Expecting her to resume the position of being your friend after this has been done is
unrealistic.

*Why do I have to invite (cousin Bert, my father's wife—who's younger than I am,
that horrible man that Grandma lives with) whom I can't stand?* (See "After
all, it's my wedding.") Because a wedding is not a priceless opportunity to start a
feud that the rest of your family will have to live with.

*I am having a big wedding and expect to receive hundreds of gifts, so I simply
will not be able to write personal letters; what else can I do?* You are in luck. You
can, simply by doing nothing, make it perfectly clear to all of your original and
newly acquired relations and friends that the planning, shopping, and spending
each has done on your account do not justify a two-minute effort and a stamp from
you.

*We already have everything we need, so how can we inform people that we want
cash?* The idea of a wedding as a fund-raising event is so widespread that Miss
Manners is besieged with versions of this question, including "How do we tell people that we want them to contribute to sending us to Europe for our honeymoon?"
People seem so disgruntled when she tells them that there is no proper way to
charge admission to a wedding, that she feels obliged to add that there is nothing
to stop them later from giving a charity ball in their own honor. Just, please, don't
come to Miss Manners for advice on how to plan it. By the way, best wishes to you
all.

Bridal Control

DEAR MISS MANNERS:
   My wedding dinner reception last November was for seventy people, as I did
not want a big wedding and preferred a more personal one. A friend offered to do
a video for us. My sister's husband offered to use his good camera for pictures to
put in albums for my husband's family and my family. A sister from out of town
took pictures with her camera and offered them to us if we wanted to include them
in our wedding albums. Two of my nieces also took pictures and offered them. A

third niece took pictures of my wedding and decided to give them to my family for Christmas.

The first person she gave these enlarged pictures to (including an enlarged, framed picture of my husband and me) was my mother (her grandmother). I was upset that she took it upon herself to do this. I immediately called and asked her not to give the rest of the pictures to my family, as it was my wedding and I was preparing albums for them. She haughtily replied that she was doing me a favor and that I had no reason to be upset. I have over a hundred pictures of my wedding to choose from for these albums. Although it has been time-consuming to choose the best shots of each member of the family, we found pleasure in doing this. If she gave pictures of her wedding to my family, I'd say that she had the right. But to give pictures of my wedding to my family without consulting me or asking my permission was not right or any of her business. I am not an expert on etiquette, but I feel she had no right to do this.

GENTLE READER:

Please get control of yourself, Madam; you are frothing all over your bridal lace. The bride does not have a copyright on her wedding, which, by the way, she could more properly refer to as "our wedding." No doubt, your family will be as glad to receive your albums as her pictures—unless, of course, all this squabbling has made them heartily sick of the whole event.

Breaking the News

DEAR MISS MANNERS:

My husband and I, who are both twenty, were recently married and are very happy, but there is just one problem. Our parents don't know about it. They discouraged us from marrying because we are still attending college. Right now, even though we are married, each of us lives with our own parents. I hope we will soon be moving into a home of our own. How do we break the news of our wedding to our families without breaking their hearts? Do we have a reception and tell them then?

GENTLE READER:

Miss Manners loves a party, and especially a wedding party, but she can hardly think of a worse way to spring the fact of your marriage on your families than to do it in a social situation with all their friends looking on. There they will be, expected to throw their arms around you and say, "How wonderful!" while inwardly trying to deal gracefully with the *fait accompli* that went against their express wishes. If you hope to squelch their objections by forcing them into swallowing them for the sake of not making a social scene, you are taking a terrible risk. They might not be able to manage it, and even if they do, will have a second grievance to match the submerged one.

The way to do this is to set up private meetings with the two families separately, and break the news to them by saying how sorry you were to disappoint their hopes, but how much you believe they will understand your impatience and make the best of it. When everyone is reconciled, you should have the party. Miss Manners promises you it will be a lot jollier.

Subsequent Weddings

DEAR MISS MANNERS:

When my husband and I were married the first time, it was by a justice of the peace, with a big, informal type reception at a nearby club, with a band and a buffet. This was fine with everyone except my grandmother. Dear Grandma was not settled in her mind, believing that we were living in sin if not married by a priest. So a year later, we were once again married, along with my father and mother. (Grandma had been pressuring Dad for years to do this.) I wore the same dress as the first time—a regular dress, off-white, with ruffles and lace. It was a very simple, three-minute type blessing of the marriage, and afterwards the four of us invited close family and friends, about fifteen to twenty people, to a party at my parents' home.

Here is where I need your help: About a year ago, my husband and I split up for a few months, during which he lived (and did everything else) with another woman (and her children). It was a truly difficult time, but love did indeed conquer all, and we worked out our differences and learned to love each other in other ways, too. Miss Manners, I truly want another religious wedding. I know God put us together and brought us back together. Since the original vows were broken, I feel strongly we must partake in it again.

I always wanted to wear a wedding gown and pass it on to my daughter some day. If I did have another ceremony, I plan to wear a plain, simple, off-white gown (now I can afford it) and have the priest come to our new house. As for guests, I intend to have my parents and siblings, and my husband's parents. Am I asking too much? Should I just see the priest at his residence and have no witnesses, or forget the whole idea?

GENTLE READER:

You have here an interesting mixture of religious and secular desires. Please understand that invoking God's blessing, and indulging your desire to wear an expensive dress that you envision as an heirloom are two different impulses, although many brides manage successfully to combine them.

You have had wedding festivities twice now for the same marriage, and that is enough. Perhaps your immediate family will stand still for another round, but Miss Manners doubts even that. What if you have another fight with your husband, after which you can afford a still more grand dress? Forgive Miss Manners. She didn't mean to say anything so discouraging. She is only giving you a sample of how others will feel if you continue to involve them formally in what should now be a private matter between husband, wife and, if you like, a priest invoking God's blessing and helping you renew your vows.

Marriage and Mourning

DEAR MISS MANNERS:

Nine months ago, my mother was killed instantly in an automobile accident. She and Dad had been happily married for over fifty years. Now Dad, seventy-six years old, plans, in another two months, to marry a nice seventy-year-old widow from their church, whom he has known for many years. She wants to have a large church wedding with about sixty friends and relatives, followed by a full catered reception, including dinner.

My sisters and I are glad Dad is remarrying, but, out of respect for our mother, we really do not want to attend this kind of wedding. Is such a wedding appropriate under the circumstances? Would it be improper for us to stay away? Should we have to attend any wedding within a year of our mother's tragic death?

GENTLE READER:

You are considering boycotting your own father's wedding on the grounds that the style of the wedding should reflect that the bridegroom is in mourning. Technically, that is an etiquette impossibility. The minimalist wedding during mourning was designed for those bereaved by the loss of a parent or sibling, not a spouse. Obviously, what that means is that one does not marry while mourning a spouse. It will be nearly a year since your mother's death by Miss Manners' calculation, which would cover conservative current standards of mourning, even if they were not sympathetically abbreviated—which Miss Manners agrees that they should be—in the case of the elderly.

In any case, Miss Manners does not find the style of the wedding inappropriate. We do not seem to be talking bridesmaids and garter throwing here. That the couple wish to be married in church, among their friends, and to celebrate with a dinner, is not unreasonable. Miss Manners urges you to attend this wedding. You do not disapprove of the bride or the marriage, and you do not have sufficient grounds for absenting yourself for violations of form.

A Second Wedding

DEAR MISS MANNERS:

My niece was married about two years ago—a church wedding with all the trimmings. In less than six months, the marriage was annulled. I traveled 2,000 miles, sent a nice monetary gift, and had motel and other expenses. Now she is going to be married again, a church wedding again, with all the trimmings. Must I make this trip again? How do I handle another wedding gift? I do not wish to cause any hard feelings in the family.

GENTLE READER:

You are probably wondering how long the young lady is planning to keep this up. No doubt, so are others on the repeat guest list. That is why etiquette rations such weddings—one to a bride. (That is not to say that second, or fifth, weddings cannot be festive; only that they should not repeat that first wedding pattern you probably mean by "all the trimmings"—great numbers of attendants and yards of veiling.)

People who disregard this rule do so either in spite of their intended guests' feelings, or in the security of knowing that their intimates are fond and indulgent enough to enjoy a second round. As you are not in the latter category, you may fulfill your obligations by a warm letter wishing your niece happiness, from which you will please tactfully omit any reference to your previous investments in her matrimonial ventures, and the words "this time."

Planning the Wedding

Nonexistent Rules

Those who are hitting the etiquette books for the only time in their lives, believing that a wedding is the sole occasion at which people should be polite, may be alarmed to find that all the answers they seek cannot be found there.

Can this be Etiquette's fault? Not likely. The problem is not, Miss Manners hastens to explain, that we in the etiquette business do not know everything. Nor that we are keeping anything from you. When there are no answers in the realm of etiquette, you may be sure that the reason is that there are no such questions as the ones being asked.

In every other event of life, Miss Manners is well aware, people harbor the suspicion that etiquette experts too often have answers to questions no sensible person would ask. "I just want to be able to be myself," they argue when about to do something sure to disgust others. At wedding time, they are willing to turn over every second and every breath to regimentation presumably hallowed by tradition. When is the bride supposed to dance with her mother's ex-husband?, they ask. Who is supposed to sit in the eleventh pew?

The answer is: We don't care. How do you like that?

We care that you are polite and considerate, and that you work out solutions that are dignified and agreeable to all concerned. But we don't care to do it for you, and the soft-hearted etiquetteers who break down and do so are only making up solutions that are neither conventional nor universally satisfactory. They mean well, but their hearts aren't in it.

Weddings should, of course, follow the appropriate cultural and social patterns. Miss Manners will not give you an argument on that, but many situations that come up in connection with weddings simply have no special protocol. Nor should they, as they involve practical or festive matters that should be tailored to the group of individuals concerned. Here are some common aspects of weddings that are not sanctified by the careful scrutiny of etiquette:

We don't much care where people who are not participating in the actual wedding party sit during the ceremony. If Mamma wants to avoid Papa's second wife or sit next to her own new beau, that is not a matter for Miss Manners to decide. The people themselves must work out an arrangement. Yes, the parents and grandparents usually sit in the front rows, and the mother of the bride generally arrives last, but there is no official seating chart or a ceremony called The Mother's Entrance. By custom, the mothers and the fathers (except for parents who are in the wedding procession) are seated just before the ceremony, which is the same time that seating stops, so as not to disrupt the ceremony. The idea is to keep latecomers from cluttering the aisle, rather than to give the mothers last entrance privileges. (The ceremony itself begins at the hour stated with the processional. Weddings should start on time. If they are delayed even a little, the guests begin speculating about whether it is the bride or the bridegroom who is balking.)

There is no special costume for any ladies involved in the wedding, other than the bride and bridesmaids. This means mothers, grandmothers, and stepmothers: They have no exemptions from the normal dress rule that long dresses are not worn during the day or hats at night. Whether any of them are to be sent flowers to wear must be decided by those ordering the flowers, not Miss Manners.

The principals will also have to figure out who they want in which posed wedding pictures. The ridiculous concept that etiquette requires that the original family pose together, even if the parents can't stand to be that close anymore, or that rules other people out or in, has given rise to a great many battles that Miss Manners refuses to settle. The only rule etiquette has about wedding photography is that it not make a nuisance of itself.

There is no special guest etiquette that requires the hosts to pay transportation or accommodation costs. Thoughtful hosts try to help out by suggesting convenient hotels or picking up those who might have trouble managing, but these are matters of hospitality, not wedding etiquette.

Although there are many customs relating to parties the night before the wedding, etiquette doesn't care which one you draw upon. The bride's parents can give a dinner; the bridegroom's family can; there can be a party for the wedding party, out-of-town guests can be entertained with the wedding party or at a separate function or left to amuse themselves; the bridegroom's friends can give him a tasteless party and the bride's friends a gooey one for her, or vice versa; or any combination the participants would like.

Finally, we don't care in the least who catches the wedding bouquet, provided that no one gets elbowed in the stomach. Let us leave something to chance. Anyway, what's the matter—can't you people handle spontaneity?

A Nonexistent Problem

DEAR MISS MANNERS:

We spent a lot of money on our daughter's wedding and were glad to do so. Everything was very elegant. But on the day of the wedding, I forgot to stand up when my daughter came down the aisle of the church. I can't believe I did such a terrible thing. I haven't been able to eat or sleep for days. Is there anything I can do to make this up to my daughter? Does the mother of the bride always stand when her daughter comes down the aisle?

GENTLE READER:

No, and please get a grip on yourself. Miss Manners happens to dislike this recent habit of people standing for the bride's entrance. The idea of a mother's rising for her daughter, as if she were royalty, seems particularly unfitting. Be that as it may, Miss Manners is appalled by the idea that such a trivial point could be described as a "terrible thing" that should disturb a mother's well being. If you gave your daughter a charming wedding, it seems to Miss Manners that the debt is on her side.

Tragedy Takes Precedence

DEAR MISS MANNERS:

My brother-in-law and his wife left our city to attend the out-of-state wedding of their daughter. The day before the wedding, I received a wire from the wife's mother in Europe, advising us that her son (the wife's brother) had just died. She asked me to get in touch with the wife and tell her the news. I called my brother-in-law, and he advised his wife. The wedding went on as scheduled. I have received some criticism from the family. They said I spoiled the wedding by passing on the bad news. My thought was that the wife should know, because she might have been able to catch a plane right after the wedding to attend the funeral, or she might have wanted to leave immediately to be with her mother. What do you think?

GENTLE READER:

That these people are trying to stick you with the blame for their own inexcusable behavior. There is no doubt that it is a nuisance to have tragedy interfere with gala occasions. That is why people who refuse to acknowledge that the decent thing to do is to give the tragedy precedence, no matter what the inconvenience, are given to announcing piously that the victim of the tragedy "would have wanted us to go on" merrily pretending that nothing had happened. Had you withheld the news, they could have had their celebrations and afterward maintained, with a clear conscience, that of course, they would have done the right thing had you not criminally kept them in ignorance.

The Private Wedding

DEAR MISS MANNERS:

Please advise me regarding the best (and most proper) way to conduct a church wedding with the following strictures. I will wear my mother's white silk velvet formal wedding gown. There are three bridesmaids, and my younger sister will be the maid of honor. There will be no best man, no groomsmen, and no ring bearer or flower girl.

Can this be conducted just as a formal church wedding would be? A friend's remark that mine would be a "weird" wedding was my motivation for double-checking this with you before proceeding. When one leaves out all groomsmen, does it have to be a "private wedding"? What are the distinctive features of a private wedding?

GENTLE READER:

The style of a wedding, formal, private, or weird, is not determined by the cast of characters. However usual it may be, it is not required that the bridegroom supply exactly enough friends to match up all the bride's friends who are serving as bridesmaids. The point here is to be surrounded by your close friends.

The formality of a wedding is determined by the clothes and the procedure. A private wedding is one at which you want to avoid asking people you think you should ask, so you tell them that practically no one is invited. Go ahead and have your formal wedding. There will be nothing weird about it, unless you invite that funny friend of yours.

Giving Away the Bride

DEAR MISS MANNERS:

I have been asked to give away a bride whose father is dead. This is my first opportunity to march down the aisle with a bride. Outside of the ceremony itself, is there anything traditionally expected of me and/or my wife? We are both very fond of the young lady.

GENTLE READER:

Unlike the position of godparent, which means assuming duties for the future, that of giving away the bride is a recognition of past performance. The bride presumably chose you because she feels that you have been like a father to her. You need only continue to offer her that special friendship, in which your wife no doubt also participates, and which you will extend to include the bridegroom.

During the wedding planning, you should make yourself available if fatherly counsel is needed, and you and your wife might want to give a party for the couple before or after the wedding. This is not required, but it would be a way of showing that she is as important to you as you are to her.

As a member of the wedding party, you may be asked to stand in the receiving line. Fathers are often allowed to do minor host duty in the room instead, accepting compliments and good wishes, introducing guests who seem to be stranded, and so on. If there is dancing, they are active partners, not only with the bride, but with mothers, grandmothers, six-year-old flower girls, and just about everyone else, in reverse order of their popularity.

In your particular situation, you should be careful not to seem to be rejecting the role. Honesty will keep prompting you to go around explaining, "I'm not really her father, you know," but don't. Everybody knows that, and a gentleman honored by a bride as you are is justified in beaming with paternal pride, which is what the occasion demands. The phrase you want is "Yes, isn't she lovely?"

When the Bride Has Two Fathers

DEAR MISS MANNERS:

My husband would have been happy to hear that his oldest daughter is getting married, but he was waiting for her to ask him if he would give her away. He and her mother were divorced many years ago and her mother remarried, but she is divorced again now.

My husband's job takes him out of state two weeks each month, and his daughter set a date for the wedding without bothering to find out whether he would be in town. She did ask for a list of our friends to be invited. We have had her and her fiancé to dinner a couple of times, but there is never any mention of the wedding unless I bring it up. Miss Manners, maybe I'm wrong, but it seems to me that most young ladies are bubbling over with information about their weddings.

When I finally asked if she planned on having her father give her away, she stammered a little and then replied that she was going to have both her stepfather and her father give her away. When I told my husband this, he said he would not have anything to do with the wedding. He was very hurt, and he cried.

Finally, his daughter asked if he was going to be in town for the wedding and if he would give her away with Ben (her stepfather). He told her very gently that he couldn't do that. He feels that two men just don't give one bride away. He informed me that he would not go to the wedding.

I called his daughter and told her how he feels, and she raised her voice to me and told me that it was her wedding and she should be able to do what she wanted. I repeated that her father would not be there and that he was very hurt. She replied, "My stepfather is willing to do it this way, and I can't see why my dad can't agree also."

My husband feels that he was asked as an afterthought. I feel bad about the whole situation and asked my husband if maybe we were wrong to feel that way. Maybe he should agree to his daughter's wishes, even if it was handled a little tactlessly.

Times seem to have changed a lot when it comes to morals and etiquette, so maybe we should come out of the Dark Ages, tuck our tails under, and join the rest of the crowd.

GENTLE READER:

Although Miss Manners hardly approves of a bride's making her father cry (particularly under the vulgar banner of "It's my wedding"), she cannot acknowledge that etiquette is a fault here. The society changed first, in a way with which your husband acquiesced, and etiquette is only trying to catch up.

The change is that society has recognized, in a much more routine fashion than it did a generation ago, the legitimacy of divorce and stepparenting. Presumably your husband accepted the fact that his former wife's second husband also acted in the role of father to the daughter. That this bond was successful in evident from the girl's filial devotion to her stepfather having outlasted his marriage to her mother.

This is not the time to challenge him on his position in her life. Yes, it may look peculiar to have two fathers give a bride away, but this merely reflects the circumstance of the bride's having had two fathers, which is no less peculiar.

The Former Husband

DEAR MISS MANNERS:

A friend is getting married for the second time, and I don't approve of what she's doing. I know I should mind my own business, but I'm not the only one who feels this way. She and her ex-husband are good friends, and they have a young daughter. She has asked her ex-husband to give her away, and she will wear a white gown and veil with all the trimmings. I'm glad that she and her ex-husband are good friends, but having him give her away is another thing. His present wife doesn't object, as they are all friends. Next thing you know, his wife will be part of the wedding party.

GENTLE READER:

Well, now, isn't that nice. Miss Manners trusts that they will round out the symbolism by having the gentleman instruct his successor to pass her along to someone else if she turns out not to suit him, either.

The Classic Elopement

DEAR MISS MANNERS:

I can't decide if I am a selfish beast or eminently sensible and good-natured. My constant companion of the last five years and I have decided to be married. My problem is that I would prefer to get married outside of our home town, on vacation, and announce the *fait accompli* to our families upon our return. I greatly wish to avoid the fuss that would accompany even the quietest ceremony involving our parents. Before you dismiss me as an insensitive young pup who would spoil all the fun, allow me to state what I think are some good reasons for my attitude.

My companion and I have lived together in contentment and ease for three years. Marriage is a personal confirmation for us, and we feel that a traditional ceremony would be inappropriate. Also, our families are devoutly Catholic, and we are not, and we would rather avoid the conflicts and hurt feelings that would necessarily be the result of any ceremony. Our respective parents do not get along, and our mothers are conspicuously unsuited to each other temperamentally. Wouldn't it be kinder to all parties if we made every effort to maintain the equilibrium by marrying privately? We would also avoid stealing the thunder from a younger sister who is planning an orange blossom and limousine wedding soon. We assume that if we elope, while they will still grumble, it will be behind our backs and we won't be bothered. I don't know my own conscience on this one.

GENTLE READER:

Miss Manners knows she is always carrying on about the necessity for a bridal couple to realize that the wedding is not just "theirs" but their families' as well, but one needs an escape clause when the troubles would outweigh the pleasures. That is the classic justification for an elopement. In return for justifying your plan, she asks that you look favorably on any suggestions either side may have about giving receptions in your honor to commemorate the marriage.

A Traditional Setting

DEAR MISS MANNERS:

My fiancé and I want a very traditional, formal wedding in keeping with our means. However, the church we attend does not lend itself to this. Although it is a striking example of modern architecture, the interior has no windows to speak of and no center aisle. Further complicating the situation are the orange carpet and upholstery, which would create a rather nauseating clash with the color scheme we have our hearts set on.

We have found a smaller church with stained glass windows, a center aisle, and an impeccably carved marble and wood apse that would be perfect, but we would rather change our colors to mauve and melon than commit a breach of etiquette. Miss Manners, would Susan and I be eternally banished to Bogeyland if we chose to be married in a church other than the one we attend? If not, how can we ask our minister to perform the ceremony without insulting his taste in architecture?

GENTLE READER:

Miss Manners is wrenched by your question. She knows that she should remind you that a church is supposed to be a house of God, not a stage setting.

The truth is, however, that her heart is on your side. The church you attend sounds to her as if it were not designed to express piety at all, but to keep up with whatever dreadful stylistic trends were going around when it was built. Let us hope that it does not, in fact, express the feelings of your minister, but was foisted on him by some hapless building committee long since disbanded.

Knowing that she ought to tell you that your church is your church, and that it is more important to be married there than to have a pleasant background, she will nevertheless supply you with a tactful protest for your minister. Do not use such secular terms as "color scheme." Ask him instead if he would consider arranging for you the use of the other church "because we are simple, traditional people, and the plain setting seems to us to be more in keeping with our beliefs."

A Shipboard Wedding

DEAR MISS MANNERS:

My fiancé and I are going to be married on a cruise ship, paying for the sixteen people in our wedding party to come along. Some other friends have shown interest in coming, and we would like to give everyone the opportunity to celebrate with us, but we cannot pay for more than our close friends and relatives. We would like to send out announcements and then a second card, telling them of our plans and advising them to call us for group rates if they're interested. We would much prefer their company to a wedding present. But we are concerned about people being offended at the idea of having to pay to go to a wedding.

GENTLE READER:

Miss Manners promises you that they will be. You cannot divide your friends into first class and second class even on a cruise ship. While it is nice that you prefer your friends' company to wedding presents, the real decision is whether you prefer their company in a place where you can afford to entertain them to the glamor of being married on shipboard. Miss Manners is not saying that this should be an easy choice, only that you must make it.

The Bridegroom's Duties

DEAR MISS MANNERS:

I am a blushing bridegroom seeking clarification concerning expenses incurred for a wedding. For several years, I have ranted about couples who refuse to pay for their own weddings (e.g., tuxedo rentals being paid by the individual groomsmen and dresses being purchased by the bridal maidens themselves). This behavior has annoyed and offended me, and now that it is my turn to consecrate my vows with my bride, I wish my friends to know that I will not welsh on my previous opinions.

Several old and dear friends have been asked to share my joy on this day, even though they live far away from where the wedding will take place. I feel that it is my responsibility to provide my groomsmen with transportation, regardless of their economic condition. If this is in fact proper, should I purchase the tickets and book their flights, or allow them to do it and reimburse them? Bear in mind that my best man is destitute and cannot afford the expense of an airline ticket.

Also, I plan to reserve the rooms but do not know how many nights I should pay for. My bride and I will be going to Europe the evening of the wedding, but the wedding party may wish to remain overnight. Please feel free to expound on other expenses the groom should be aware of.

GENTLE READER:

It is the chief duty of the bridegroom, at the wedding and throughout his life from then on, to be aware of his rantings and to soften them with a bit of kindness and humility. Miss Manners approves of your attempt to begin by making good on the extravagant demands you have previously made of others. If not for your past, she would have told you that a bridegroom is not responsible for all expenses his groomsmen entail by participating—clothing, transportation, hotels. It is not incorrect; it is just not required. But it is for you—they all remember what you said—and Miss Manners is proud of you for accepting that gracefully. She will make it as easy on you as possible by suggesting that you pay the hotel bills for only two nights—that preceding and that following the wedding—and let them make their own arrangements if they want to stay on.

As for booking airline tickets, you naturally need to allow people to plan their own trips, yet you want to spare them the embarrassment of having to supply you with a bill. Perhaps you could have your travel agent call each groomsman, or merely ask them to choose the flights but to give you the information so that you may do the booking. Miss Manners foresees a happy marriage for someone who so well understands the balance of expectations and obligations.

The Experienced Bride

DEAR MISS MANNERS:

My oldest daughter has been on her own for over twenty years. During that time, she has had several live-in boyfriends but has never married. She is engaged now, for the first time, and plans to get married in June. She is uncertain as to the size and type of wedding, but has asked if I would help out financially should she decide on a large wedding. She also would like the reception at my home. I live alone, since my wife died a year and a half ago. All things considered, I have doubts as to the appropriateness of a large wedding with me as the "sponsor." Are there any ground rules for such a situation? I no longer work, and although I can handle the financial aspects, my retirement plans did not include an outlay for this purpose.

GENTLE READER:

By one of her rapid-fire calculations, Miss Manners has figured out that your daughter, having lived independently for over twenty years, is not in her twenties. By a large wedding, she must therefore mean that she would like to invite a lot of people, rather than that she plans to have eight bridesmaids, wear a cathedral train, and blush while you give her away. Of the two remaining statistics, one is relevant and one is not. It has long been a source of amazement to Miss Manners that people believe that the lady's romantic history is a factor in planning the wedding, but that the parents' financial capabilities need not be considered.

The opposite is true. No parent is ever required to overstrain his resources for a wedding, no matter how virginal the bride; and no bride, no matter how (oh, never mind), is barred from having a jolly wedding. Miss Manners thinks it a lovely idea for any wedding to be held in the parental home and does not limit the number of guests according to the age or premarital experience of the bride. You must tell your daughter frankly how much or how little you wish to spend, and allow her to adjust either her plans or her own contribution accordingly.

Financing the Wedding

DEAR MISS MANNERS:

I find the custom of the bride's family paying for the wedding anachronistic in today's world. Presumably, the historic rationale is that the family of the bride is "unloading" a financial liability—that is, a member who will not be contributing financially—and must therefore absorb all of the wedding expenses as a way of compensating. These days, however, women are prepared for careers and expected to work just as much as men; indeed, I see many instances where wives today earn more than their husbands. Adding to this their roles as child bearers and primary housekeepers, women these days make far greater contributions to marriage than men. In sum, all of the expenses—and planning—of weddings should be shared equally by both sets of parents. This is not only more democratic, but it also enables couples to have the weddings they want—weddings that are often beyond the financial reach of one family.

GENTLE READER:

Miss Manners has nothing against families getting together to give their children's weddings if they so wish, and would be happy to discuss the issue of adjusting financial arrangements to modern conditions. She has a great deal against the pseudohistorical analysis in which you indulge. While post-Industrial Revolution parents sponsored the weddings of their daughters to wage earners, the custom was also practiced by aristocrats who married their heiresses to the idle rich (or idle poor but enterprising) and by peasants whose daughters were expected to toil alongside their bridegrooms. That brides are liabilities unless they earn salaries is an idea that does not bear scrutiny.

Worse is your assumption that social custom is primarily dictated by money.

This one had to do with a lady's being a member of her parents' social domain until she was ready to establish one of her own. (Young gentlemen tended to marry at a later age and to have bachelor households if they could so afford.) A proper poor lady who was marrying a tycoon who knew he'd have to support her entire clan from that moment on would still have a wedding in the style of her parents.

The biggest change nowadays is that both bride and bridegroom are unlikely to emerge directly from their parents' dwellings into their joint one. For this reason, some couples now give their own weddings, although many brides cling to the charming, traditional, and still emotionally valid form of returning to their parents' jurisdiction for the occasion. If finances were the only consideration, why should the parents be involved at all? (Oh, stop cheering, parents; you don't really want to be excluded.) Neither set is likely to have received a penny from a child, or ever to expect one, barring emergencies.

Miss Manners favors using family considerations to make the decision about who will give the wedding, among them the closeness of the ties, the appropriateness—in age or attitude—of the bride's assuming the forms of being her parents' dependent, and the selection of a location convenient to those least able to travel. Offers to help the selected hosts with the bills should be discreetly made, with the understanding that this does not buy nonhosts voting shares in the occasion. Generosity, especially in preventing well-meaning people from taking on financial hardships, is a lovely impulse. The desire to assess everyone possible in order to have a more showy wedding than family circumstances permit is not.

❧ THE GUEST LIST

Bulletin Board Invitations

DEAR MISS MANNERS:

A young woman in our office recently posted on our lunchroom bulletin board her wedding invitation and a map giving directions to her reception. I do not know the young woman personally, although we do experience some contact through our work. In any case, I do not know her well enough to wish to attend her wedding. What is the proper response to her public invitation? Am I obligated to send a gift? And am I wrong to think it slightly vulgar to post one's wedding invitation among the job-opening announcements on a public bulletin board?

GENTLE READER:

You're wrong about the "slightly." That does not prevent Miss Manners from a burst of admiration, not to say affection, for you. In an age when few of those who receive proper invitations bother to answer them, you have qualms about not responding to a bulletin board. Miss Manners assures you that you are free. You need not do anything at all about this wedding. Please don't walk by any recruiting posters for organizations you do not wish to join.

Public Invitations

DEAR MISS MANNERS:

A family in a small rural church verbally invited members of the church to their daughter's wedding. Some, who were close friends, also received written invitations. Some people said you could attend the reception following it only if you received a written invitation. Others thought as long as you brought a gift, it didn't matter.

GENTLE READER:

The Y'All Be Sure and Come invitation may sound friendly, but it is, in Miss Manners opinion, a disaster. No one feels flattered by it because there was no indication that he or she, as an individual, was wanted. There is no telling how many strangers may show up. As some invitations are often made to individuals as well, it becomes clear that there are two classes of guests, a rude notion.

In this case, Miss Manners guesses that the family was inviting people to the ceremony, but not the reception. Technically, all church ceremonies may be attended by any church member anyway, although it is not considered polite to take advantage of this definition of marrying before the entire congregation. She would not blame any potential guest who misunderstood and, interpreting "wedding" as meaning all connected events, felt invited to the reception.

No, wait, she does blame some—the ones who thought that a present would serve to buy their way in. If one cares enough about a bridal couple to attend their reception, one is supposed to send them a material expression of this affection, but wedding presents, Miss Manners keeps telling both bridal couples and their guests, cannot be considered tickets of admission.

Reciprocation

DEAR MISS MANNERS:

I am a twenty-eight-year-old bride-to-be. In the years immediately following college graduation, I was invited to several college buddies' weddings. Now I am in sporadic contact with these friends but see them rarely, especially since we have all moved to different regions. Am I obligated by etiquette to return the favor of an invitation to my wedding?

GENTLE READER:

Technically speaking, you do not need to invite to your wedding everyone whose wedding you attended. The excuse is that yours is "small." Fortunately, the National Institute of Standards and Technology has not defined wedding sizes.

Miss Manners urges you not to throw over your old buddies simply because you have grown out of touch. That is all the more reason for gathering them together again on this occasion. They still used to be your friends, and those who shared youthful experiences with you will become increasingly dear to you.

Legitimate Extras

DEAR MISS MANNERS:

Weddings are not always happy occasions. We are the groom's parents and have a limited guest list. People call and ask if their fiancé or live-in friend may attend —total strangers to the other guests, as well as to the bride and groom. I resent the inference that because people live together, it is an automatic invitation. What is the best solution? Stick by our guns, call them clods for having the nerve to ask if they can bring "extras," or give in to keep peace and hate ourselves for being intimidated?

GENTLE READER:

Now, now. Weddings are happy occasions, if complicated ones, and we're not going to let this spoil your son's. No, guests should not be allowed to invite their own guests to weddings, but there are "extras" and extras. Miss Manners would back you in refusing requests on behalf of friends, dates, and perfectly divine people whom one met in a health club last week.

You do not invite one member of a socially recognized couple to a purely social function, such as a wedding, without inviting the other. You know yourself that you can't stand Uncle Horace but that you could not possibly invite Aunt Flora to come without him. The difficulty, of course, is defining such a couple. Traditionally, fiancés, as well as spouses, have always qualified. By general consensus, like it or not, people who have set up housekeeping together, declaring themselves to be a social unit, are also recognized.

The Bride's Boyfriend

DEAR MISS MANNERS:

I am preparing the guest list for my wedding. My fiancé and my boyfriend are close friends, and each is comfortable with my relationship with the other. My fiancé does not mind if I invite my boyfriend to the wedding, but some of the other guests do. Should I risk losing him because of the objections of these few guests? I need your help!

GENTLE READER:

Would you mind not referring to the gentleman to whom you are not engaged as "my boyfriend"? Thank you. Your fiancé may not mind, but Miss Manners does. If you mean that you plan not to let the mere matter of a wedding interfere with another ongoing romance, for heaven's sake, warn Miss Manners so that she can fetch a cold compress for her head before she tackles the etiquette involved. If not, the phrase "a former beau of mine" or "an old friend with whom I once had a romance" will do nicely. Perhaps that is what is worrying your guests. They may not wish to be present for more drama than they can handle. If that is not in fact the situation, it is hardly the business of your guests to judge which of your friends you should be allowed to invite to your wedding.

Partners

DEAR MISS MANNERS:

My daughter would like to invite to her wedding a friend, who happens to be homosexual, and his live-in friend. But his parents, who do not condone his lifestyle, will also attend the wedding, and I am concerned that tension may result and spoil the atmosphere. Am I wrong to suggest that my daughter invite her friend without his partner? Should I give in and hope for the best?

GENTLE READER:

Let us certainly hope that no guests consider your daughter's wedding to be a proper arena for either condoning or condemning anyone's living arrangements. It is not nice for people to speculate on the bridal couple's private behavior, much less the wedding guests'. Surely the gentleman's parents have other occasions for expressing their attitude. Anyone concerned who feels in danger of spoiling the wedding should decline the invitation. In any case, the hosts should assume that guests will behave themselves. If your daughter otherwise sees the gentleman and his partner as a social couple, she should treat them as one on this occasion.

Invitations and Announcements

Bridal Forms of Address

The most insidious wedding battles with the most lasting repercussions have to do with names. Wouldn't you think that getting everyone's name right would be a simple matter when dealing with a presumably close circle of relatives and friends?

Yet the following situations are now typical:

The bride may not decide until after the wedding whether she is going to keep her maiden surname, assume her husband's, or use both, and whether she wishes to be styled "Miss," "Ms." or "Mrs." Or she may announce from the start what she wants, only to find it ignored by those who don't approve of her choice.

The bridegroom's family hands in a guest list with initials on it in place of first names, no honorifics, and the notation "and family" to designate children or other resident relatives.

The bride's family succumbs to pressure to allow their friends to bring their own long- or short-term romantic partners and writes "and guest" or "and escort" on the invitations to single people.

The bridal couple demands to have their nicknames on the formal invitations, or their parents think it's too stuffy for them, as hosts, to be "Mr. and Mrs." and want their first names used.

All of this is justified as the simplest, friendliest, or most common current solution. That's what people often say when they violate rules of etiquette, and they always get into trouble for it. In this case, the bride feels insulted by everyone who misaddresses her, assuming that the reason is never ignorance of her preference but the desire to express disapproval of it.

Guests feel insulted because their names are not written as they prefer, and either they use "and family" as license to bring their extended acquaintances or they boycott the wedding because they do not consider that any members of their household not listed by name are invited. Guests with proper fiancés or other stable partners are insulted that no one has bothered to learn the names of their loved ones. Those without such arrangements invite someone, who then either feels pressured because the invitation seems to be a hint that the inviting partner wants his or her own wedding or feels unobligated to the unknown hosts and therefore free from any present-giving or other conventions of wedding guest etiquette. Or the original guest can't find someone to invite and feels depressed and unwanted as a single person.

That is a great deal of ill feeling for the lack of a few basic rules. Here, then, since it is back-to-basics time in the etiquette department, are a few simple rules:

It is now a bride's duty to let people know what she prefers to be called after the wedding. (If possible, she should refrain from telling them why, as in "I don't intend to lose my identity.") She can tell everyone personally, or she can use the old at-home card formula:

Dr. Daniela Tribble-Atkins
Mr. Kevin Atkins

with the new address in the lower right corner and the date from which they will be there on the left. (Two lines are used for addressing two people, married or not, who live at the same address but do not fit into the "Mr. and Mrs." form.)

Guest lists must be accurate. If you don't know the people well enough to find out what their actual names are, and whether they prefer "Ms.," "Mrs.," " Doctor," or "Baron," they don't belong at your wedding. Children as well as adults have names, and so do romantic partners. The tactful thing, if you really want to be so liberal as to permit unknown guests, is to say, "Dora, I know you've been seeing someone; would you like to bring him? Just give me his name and address, and I'll send him an invitation."

Dear bridal couples: If you are not going to bother to get things right now, when are you going to start?

The Deceased Host

DEAR MISS MANNERS:
I am getting married in October. My father gave me my wedding money in September of last year and passed away a month later. My fiancé and I feel very

strongly about my father's name being on the invitations. He is paying for the wedding, deceased or not. We want to word it to say that "The late Mr.———— requests the honor of your presence at his daughter's wedding," and so on. My parents were divorced in 1981, and my mother and I are not on good terms. I do not want her name even to be mentioned on the invitation. I am thirty and quite capable of issuing my own invitations but really want my dad to be acknowledged.

GENTLE READER:

Miss Manners appreciates your sentiments, but you must find some other way to honor your father. (For example, she knew a bridal couple who went off privately and quietly, after their wedding reception, to leave the wedding bouquet on her father's grave.) The person who issues the invitations is the one who will serve as host. This billing is not intended to announce the name of the financial sponsor. Miss Manners urges you to issue your own invitations if you do not want your mother involved. Unfortunately, your father cannot be the host at your wedding. It would be undignified to his memory to chill the guests by suggesting that he will do so from beyond the grave. You really do not want to use his name to give them the creeps.

The Ill Host

DEAR MISS MANNERS:

My brother-in-law is in a nursing home with Alzheimer's disease. He will never come out; he knows nothing and recognizes no one. My niece is planning her wedding. Does my sister put "Mr. and Mrs. John Doe request the pleasure," and so on, on the invitations because he is still technically alive? Or does she put "Mrs. Jane Doe" because he really isn't a father or husband anymore?

GENTLE READER:

Can we soften this question just a little before Miss Manners can bring herself to answer it? A father is a father, no matter how incapacitated. For that matter, he will not cease to be your niece's father even after he is dead.

That does not mean that he is issuing invitations, however. The hostess of this wedding seems to be "Mrs. John Doe" (*Not* "Mrs. Jane Doe"; even widows retain the same form they used throughout the marriage, and your sister is not a widow), although while he is alive, she could continue to act socially in both their names if she prefers.

Crediting Contributors

DEAR MISS MANNERS:

My fiancé's parents are contributing $6,000 toward our wedding, while my parents can only afford to give $3,000. My fiancé and I will pay for anything over

$9,000. My problem is with the wording of the wedding invitations. I feel it is proper etiquette to have my parents' names first, even though they are contributing less. My mother-in-law-to-be, the groom's mother, says "etiquette dictates" that the people who pay most get their names first on the invitations. Thus, she feels that the groom's parents should be named first. I think this will embarrass my parents.

GENTLE READER:

Your prospective mother-in-law is confusing the wedding invitation with the list of donors in symphony orchestra programs. It is true that such recipients of philanthropy print their benefactors' names in groups by the amount of the donation, although the subtler ones disguise this by giving them different names: so much for a patron, so much for a sponsor, a donor, a friend, and so on. Families do not do so on their social invitations, which are issued by the hosts, regardless of the size of their contributions. The bride's parents are usually the primary, and indeed, the only, hosts of a wedding. So there.

A Question of Timing

DEAR MISS MANNERS:

How far in advance of the wedding is it appropriate to send out invitations? My fiancée would like them mailed three or four weeks before the wedding. I feel that because of air fares requiring 30 days' advance purchase, the appropriate time is at least five or six weeks before the wedding, and even sooner if there are guests invited from abroad.

GENTLE READER:

Three or four weeks was sufficient notice of a wedding when it was presumed that both families and their guests lived in the same town, and already knew the date anyway, because the bride had been talking of nothing else since her engagement eight months previously. Miss Manners supports your contention that more planning is now necessary to attend a wedding, and that the invitations should therefore go out earlier. Let us say four to six weeks. (Did either of you realize that it is also possible, even before the invitations are ready, to write actual letters to very distant guests asking them to reserve the date?)

Handwritten Invitations

DEAR MISS MANNERS:

I have received an invitation to a wedding reception, written very formally in longhand, and wonder if this is something new in these days of so many changes.

The bride's mother wrote the invitations, and I know it must have been quite a chore. I am sure it was not done for economic reasons. The parents left for Bermuda after the wedding, and the bridal couple went to Hawaii. I am not asking this to be critical, but am curious, as this is new to me.

GENTLE READER:
It's not new to Miss Manners. Once upon a time, people dashed off formal third-person invitations to one another all the time. And, of course, the equally formal third-person replies to these invitations have always been handwritten.

In these days of imitation engraving and grotesque variations on the forms of formality, Miss Manners almost hesitates to point out that engraving itself is a compromise. One has an invitation engraved, which is, after all, a mass distribution version of handwriting, because one needs too many to be able to write out each one. If the bride's mother was willing to undertake this chore, Miss Manners, for one, applauds her.

To the Reception Only

DEAR MISS MANNERS:
Due to extreme circumstances, there are some people I cannot invite to my wedding ceremony, although I would like to have them at the reception. Would it be appropriate to state on their invitations that a private ceremony will be held, and state on a reception card that they are invited to the reception? For the guests who are invited to both the ceremony and the reception, should I have the usual type of invitation? Am I at certain risk to offend those not invited to the ceremony? I do so want these people to share this special day with me, and I would like to make it special for them as well.

GENTLE READER:
One of the lovely things about tradition is that it anticipates common problems and offers polite ways to deal with them. It has always been correct to invite more people to the reception than the ceremony. The large formal invitation is then worded so as to invite everyone to "the wedding reception of" the couple, rather than "the marriage of," and a small ceremony card is included for those who are invited to both:

Mr. and Mrs. David Augustus Millen
request the honour of your presence
at the marriage ceremony
at four o'clock
Memorial Chapel

Mr. and Mrs. Theodore Bishop Right

request the honour of your presence

at the marriage of her daughter

Victorine Eustacia Awful

to

Mr. Christopher Boniface Wrong

on Saturday, the second of June

at three o'clock

Our Lady of Propriety Church

Brookdale, Connecticut

Mrs. Right's choice.

Shown here and on the two pages following are three correct wedding invitations (and a selection of enclosed cards) depending on the outcome of a small difference of opinion between the bride's mother and father, and a few minor disputes about arrangements.

Reception

immediately following the ceremony

129 Primrose Path

Brookdale

The favour of a reply is requested

Mrs. Theodore Bishop Right

and

Mr. Jonathan Rhinehart Awful

request the pleasure of your company

at the wedding reception of their daughter

Victorine Eustacia

and

Mr. Christopher Boniface Wrong

on Saturday, the second of June

at half after five o'clock

129 Primrose Path

Brookdale, Connecticut

R.s.v.p.

Mr. Awful's compromise. He would have preferred abolishing all rights, so to speak, and billing his current wife as "Ms. Kimberly Awful."

The honour of your presence

is requested at the marriage ceremony

at three o'clock

Our Lady of Propriety Church

Brookdale

The honour of your presence

is requested at the marriage of

Victorine Eustacia Awful

to

Mr. Christopher Boniface Wrong

on Saturday, the second of June

at three o'clock

Our Lady of Propriety Church

and at a reception

following the ceremony

The Bideawhile Hotel

Brookdale, Connecticut

Please respond

212 Trackside Road

Bay Ridge, Connecticut 01010

Victorine's and Christopher's suggestion when they are fed up with parental squabbling. Had they chucked the
whole idea of a formal wedding at this
point, the invitations would have been
in the form of individual letters.

Christopher's parents conclude that
their guests won't be able to figure out
why they are being invited, so they enclose a card.

Ms. Nicole Worse

Mr. Hiram Harold Wrong

Postponement

DEAR MISS MANNERS:

I was forced, on very short notice, to postpone our long-planned wedding when the groom came down with infectious mononucleosis just three days before the wedding. Upon notice by the doctor that he was effectively quarantined for the next two weeks, my family and his immediately called all of the guests who were expected and dropped notes to those we were not absolutely certain we could reach by phone. Fortunately, on our wedding day, no one arrived at the church.

Now that the groom is recovering, we have rescheduled the wedding for next month. What is the wording for a second invitation? Is it appropriate to send a second formal invitation and response card? Or would it be more appropriate to simply call those who were expected to attend the first ceremony and invite them? Should we bother sending invitations to those simply "protocol" guests invited to the first wedding who were never expected and did not intend to come? What about asking additional guests to the second ceremony, who were not invited to the first because of space limitations or oversight?

GENTLE READER:

No, you may not take advantage of this accident to revise your guest list. No, there is no formal invitation that includes the wording "Due to the recovery of the bridegroom." You must therefore write brief letters to all the guests on the original list (or send them second copies of the first invitation with the new date inked in), including those who declined originally and that category which can never be given official recognition—people-we-counted-on-not-to-come. You may be sure that the postponement will be a major topic of discussion at your wedding reception, and you cannot therefore have guests who will learn from the conversation that they were afterthoughts.

Replies

DEAR MISS MANNERS:

A new bride told me her horror story as I was planning my daughter's wedding. Everyone who was coming to that wedding sent a reply. Unfortunately, twelve of these people did not attend the wedding, and did not call to express their regrets, and the caterer presented the bride with a bill for twelve dinners at $21 each. To forget an invitation to something as important as a wedding, when the costs must be absorbed by the bride and/or her family, is coarse, ill-bred, and uncouth. Is there any way that some of this can be avoided? I understand that last-minute emergencies arise and that it may not be possible to reach the wedding party. A neighbor and her husband were in an automobile accident on the way to a wedding and could not call. But I believe that twelve rude people are too many. And weddings today are so costly. I would appreciate your thoughts on this matter.

GENTLE READER:

Miss Manners agrees that a dozen people are too many to be run over on the way to a wedding, and perhaps you should have the highway authorities check out that route. Lesser excuses for missing a wedding are not acceptable. But why must you (and everyone else) feel that financial damage is the only acceptable grounds for complaint? Paying $252 for uneaten food is dreadful, but it is not as serious as finding out that one's wedding is considered, by the intimates chosen to share it, to be an insignificant and easily ignored event.

Menu Selections

DEAR MISS MANNERS:

Would it be acceptable and proper on the response card of a wedding invitation to ask an invitee to select one of two main dishes?

GENTLE READER:

Miss Manners understands that you mean only to please the guests, and that the advance information would enable you to inform the caterer of what was required. However, she begs you instead to choose a menu from which people could satisfy a reasonable range of tastes or requirements. Treating a wedding dinner like a restaurant outing is a poor idea. What would you do if someone crossed out the choices and submitted a menu of his own?

Responding to Response Cards

DEAR MISS MANNERS:

I have been annoyed and baffled for several years by the response cards which are now routinely included with wedding invitations. While I understand that they began as a reaction to people's failure to respond to invitations, I feel, as you do, that they are a tacky concession to bad manners. Whenever I find one with an invitation, I am insulted to realize that someone has assumed that my manners are so bad that I must be prodded to respond.

Would I appear to be ill-mannered if I ignored the response card and sent my personal, handwritten acceptance or regrets? If I do use the response card, would it be considered proper to include a short phrase to the effect that I look forward with pleasure to attending or that I regret that I will be unable to attend? Those little cards seem so cold-blooded and impersonal that I shrink from using them. Two of them are on my desk now awaiting my attention.

GENTLE READER:

As you feel as Miss Manners does, you may do as Miss Manners does, which is to ignore the horrid card (no fair picking off the "Love" stamp and using it to pay your bills) and answer the invitation properly:

Miss Helena Calligraphos
accepts with pleasure
or
regrets that she is unable to accept
the kind invitation of
(substitute "very kind" if declining)
Mr. and Mrs. Cardly
for
Saturday, the fourteenth of May
at twelve o'clock noon

You mustn't let on, except to Miss Manners, who will keep your confidence, that you think response cards vulgar. Your defense, should you need one, is that you simply couldn't imagine what the card was for.

Replying in Kind

DEAR MISS MANNERS:
We live in a small town and receive the usual formal wedding invitations, to which I know I should respond with a formal reply. However, knowing these people, I feel that that kind of response would be considered "uppity" and they would say, "Who does she think she is?" Consequently, I resort to writing an informal note in reply.

GENTLE READER:
What they would have to have been saying was, "Who does she think she is, using the same formal style we're using?" If Miss Manners were you, she would be wondering why people who are presumed to subscribe to the absurd notion that formality is uppity don't issue informal wedding invitations.

"Number Attending"

DEAR MISS MANNERS:
I wanted to have a very nice wedding, but to manage it financially, I had to limit the guest list. I am now faced with replies from several people who have filled for "number of persons attending" more people than were invited. If I receive many more of these types of replies, I will have to change my menu to accommodate people who were never invited. Can I in some tactful manner inform these people that they are not at liberty to invite whomever they please?

GENTLE READER:

Now do you understand why Miss Manners hates those little cards with what appear to be restaurant reservation requests? If you ask how many people your guests want to bring, they are going to tell you. She is afraid that you now have the choice of throwing a wedding for the friends of friends, or calling the original friends and apologizing for having seemed to have been able to accommodate more than those whose names were actually on the invitation: "You know I love your children, but we've simply had to limit the party to adults" or "I'd adore to meet your new friend, but we just can't manage it at the wedding; you must bring him around as soon as we're settled."

Substitutions

DEAR MISS MANNERS:

My husband and I were invited to a wedding and reception dinner, and replied yes to the R.s.v.p., as we were planning to go. Two days before the event, my husband was called out of town. I was still planning to go. Would it have been proper for me to invite someone else in his place, since it was too late to cancel the dinner reservation count? If so, should I have first gotten permission from the bride, and second, would it have mattered who it would be—a single male friend or a girlfriend?

GENTLE READER:

Being invited to a wedding is not like having a theater ticket. Your husband was invited, as were you and all the other guests, because the family wanted you present on this special occasion. Miss Manners hopes that your husband has a pretty good excuse for allowing being "called out of town" to keep him from honoring his acceptance of the invitation. A death in the family, and maybe a major job emergency might pass, but engagements for such solemn occasions should be treated seriously. In any case, the invitation is not transferable.

Nonattendance

DEAR MISS MANNERS:

My only sister will not be able to attend our daughter's wedding because she cannot take leave from her job. Her only daughter, who will be on vacation from college then, will not be attending because her mother cannot come. The fact that my niece will not be here to represent her family saddens me and hurts my feelings. All of us have always been on the most loving terms, and I feel that honor is being taken away from us. Am I too emotional or incorrect?

GENTLE READER:

Yes. While it is an honor to be invited to a wedding, it is an honor that may have

"GUNPOINT HAVEN"
FIRST MANASSAS, VIRGINIA

Vice Admiral Stacy Awful-Nuisance
and
General Trevor Nuisance
accept with pleasure
the kind invitation of
Mrs. Right and Mr. Awful
to the wedding reception of their daughter
Victorine Eustacia
and
Mr. Christopher Boniface Wrong
on Saturday, the second of June
at half after five o'clock
129 Primrose Path

TWO RESPONSES TO A WEDDING INVITATION. *Above, Admiral Awful-Nuisance could have omitted the bridal couple's names, but she does not believe in saving herself trouble. A subtle point is that one accepts the invitation to the reception, not to the ceremony: One can neither invite nor exclude people from God's house, which is why reception lines should not be formed at a house of worship.*

125 PRIMROSE PATH

Dr. Alicia Cecilia Wise
and
Mr. Alexander Wise
regret exceedingly
that they are unable to accept
the very kind invitation
of
Mr. and Mrs. Right
for Saturday, the second of June

Declining an invitation does not require repeating the time and place to show you have gotten it right. It doesn't even require sending a present, but the Wises were feeling generous. Both responses were written on the writer's "house paper," suitable for use by anyone in the house, even the guests, but they could also be written on plain white or ecru paper. Using one's street address on house paper, while omitting the city and state, is a point of old-fashioned pride, dating from the time when one stayed put, and could expect an envelope, on which merely "City" followed the street address, to be delivered. Not being foolish, Mrs. Wise has her envelopes marked with the full address, including the zip code.

to be declined for any number of legitimate reasons. Anyone who considers nonattendance an insult is too sensitive to issue invitations. Unless you have good reason to think that this family—or any other guest—wishes to boycott the wedding, you may not take insult. It would be far more gracious to write the family about how sorry you are and how you will be thinking of them at the event.

Boycotting

DEAR MISS MANNERS:

My sister was married three months ago to a man who has a history of abusing her physically. My family did not approve of the marriage, and only my brother and his wife attended the ceremony, which was in a town one hundred miles away. There had been numerous occasions when the groom and his family had been insulting and abusive to my family, and there was no love lost between us.

Was it incorrect for the bride's family to be noticeably absent? The purpose of the absence was explained to the bride and groom and his family. My sister, however, has found this an unforgivable offense and has not spoken to any of us since. Would it be even more rude not to send a present, or would sending one appear to be hypocritical?

GENTLE READER:

It is possible to miss a sister's wedding because of travel difficulties, misunderstandings about receiving invitations, or a variety of other pleas, and then to argue that the bride has no right to be offended. It is not possible to boycott the wedding of a member of one's immediate family without getting her angry. When you refuse to go, and then explain that you have refused out of disapproval of the bridegroom or his family—rather than pretending that you mixed up the date— that is a boycott, and you must take the consequences.

Mind you, Miss Manners is not disputing your right to boycott the wedding of a wife beater. She is only warning you that you must expect that the woman who decides to marry such a person obviously feels a strong tie to him, and it is not surprising that loyalty is among them.

Sending a present could possibly soften your stance, but it could also further anger your sister. It would not be unreasonable for her to take the position that an object is no substitute for your presence. Your choice now is to undo the symbolic statement of your boycott by apologizing and claiming to be taking an open attitude toward your brother in-law, or to stand by your previous opinion, but attempt to maintain as close a relationship to your sister as her loyalties permit her to accept. The blanket invitation "Our house is always open to you," may be ignored for now but appreciated later.

The Wedding Party

The Best Person

DEAR MISS MANNERS:

My husband-to-be will be having a woman as his best man. We've been referring to her as the "best person." She has been his closest friend for many years, and there is no doubt in his mind that she is the only person fit for the honor. I support him completely in this decision; that is not the issue. The issue is: What should she wear?

It's going to be a morning wedding, and the groom and my father will wear morning suits. The matron of honor will be wearing a lavender street-length dress. There will also be a flower girl and a ring bearer. The suggestions I've had so far are a dress matching that of the matron of honor (but she shouldn't carry a bouquet) or a feminine suit (skirt and jacket). A man's suit is out of the question—talk about hokey! My main concern is that she not stick out like a sore thumb.

GENTLE READER:

Had your best friend been a gentleman, Miss Manners hopes that there would have been no talk of putting him in a lavender dress with a long bow down the back and a floppy garden hat. Your husband's attendant should be dressed as a lady member of the bridal party, equivalent to your matron of honor. They needn't match exactly, but they should be distinguished slightly from the bridesmaids. If the female attendants carry bouquets, there is no reason why the best person shouldn't.

Friends or Family?

DEAR MISS MANNERS:

Help! My brother is getting married soon, and nothing is going as we (the rest of the family) expected. We have had several weddings, and they were all very family oriented. Future brothers- and sisters-in-law were part of the wedding party, as were all available nieces, nephews, aunts, and uncles. Now my brother has asked a friend to be his best man and my other brother and some friends to usher. His fiancée hasn't asked any of our family (sisters, nieces, aunts) to participate. Her sister will be her maid of honor, and some friends bridesmaids.

Frankly, we were surprised and somewhat hurt. If this were a small wedding with few participants, we would understand, but it will be a fairly large, formal wedding. Supposing that my future sister-in-law runs out of friends to honor and asks one of my sisters or me to pour punch or cut cake or something, should we, and can we, gracefully decline? Yes, this is spiteful, but I feel spiteful. If we aren't important enough to be in the wedding party, we'd rather not be anything other than guests. Can we do this, and if so, how?

GENTLE READER:

Your family wedding customs sounded delightful to Miss Manners—right up to the point where another family's following a different custom made you turn spiteful.

A wedding party nominally consists of the close friends of the bridal couple. That makes it doubly charming when a relative is chosen, meaning that there is a voluntary bond in addition to the family bond, and perhaps even more charming when a new in-law is chosen, because it demonstrates faith that the bond of friendship will be part of the new relationship. However, one's closest friends may actually be only friends, and there may be enough of them to make up a wedding party. That is no cause for relatives to feel insulted. Please behave yourselves, participate in the wedding with open hearts, and welcome your sister-in-law as one who joins your family while still having her own family, friends, and preferences.

Mother as Matron of Honor

DEAR MISS MANNERS:

My mother is my best friend, and I want her to be my matron of honor. Can she, and if so, does that mean that my father (they are still happily married) will have to sit by himself while my mother is at the altar with me? Where would my parents sit at the wedding breakfast if my mother is in the wedding party? My mother was overjoyed that I wanted her to be matron of honor, but she doesn't want to be separated from my father during the ceremony or reception. She knows that my feelings won't be hurt if she decides to just be the "mother of the bride," but we are both curious as to whether this has ever been done before.

GENTLE READER:

Of course, your mother may be matron of honor, just as fathers often serve as best man to bridegrooms. If your father gives you away, he may then step back and join your mother. Or you may be escorted by both parents or simply have them both stand with your attendants during the ceremony. Afterwards, they sit at the parents' table—your mother's primary role is still those of mother and hostess.

The Mother's Beau

DEAR MISS MANNERS:

Here we go: My parents are divorced, and I don't see my father. My mother wants to bring a friend to my wedding. This person has made no effort to get to know me, despite my efforts, and I don't consider him a part of my family. Assuming that I have to let him come to the wedding, how do I address an invitation? Do I give my mother one that says "and guest"? Where do I seat him in the church? At dinner? What's the proper way to introduce him?

GENTLE READER:

"Friend of the bride's mother" is not a recognized rôle at a wedding. All the guests are supposed to be friends of hers in her capacity as hostess. Therefore, she can decree that he be invited, but he should be given the dignity of any other guest, which is to say that he should be sent his own invitation in his own name. Guest seating is not as much a rigid matter of protocol as many people seem to suppose. If your mother wants him by her side, she may put him there without implying that he is related to you.

The Expectant Attendant

DEAR MISS MANNERS:

My cousin, who is like a sister to me, has asked me to be her matron of honor. She was my maid of honor. Although I am several months pregnant and will be quite large at the time of her wedding, my cousin and I both feel that in this day and age, my condition should be no hindrance. However, my aunt (her mother) objects, saying that my appearance will be a blemish on the overall beauty of the ceremony, as well as generally embarrassing to the family from the viewpoint of its being socially incorrect or undignified. I object to the idea that a pregnant woman is inevitably ugly, and as I do not anticipate feeling embarrassed about my condition, I see no reason not to go ahead as my cousin wishes. But I certainly do not want to do anything that would be universally considered ill-mannered.

GENTLE READER:

Rest assured, then, that there is nothing ill-mannered about being pregnant. The rule is that one must begin and end a pregnancy in relative privacy, but that the state itself is perfectly presentable. Therefore, there is no reason, short of any possibility of your own physical discomfort, that you should not be your cousin's matron of honor. It would be nice if your cousin could persuade her mother to accept the choice graciously.

However, Miss Manners does not care for your argument in favor of your participation, any more than she likes your aunt's against it. Whether pregnancy is beautiful or ugly, or whether you or any other members of the bridal party are beautiful or ugly when not pregnant, is not a proper issue for deciding who is to be in a wedding. The appearance of a bride's attendants should be pleasing to her because the people are dear to her, not because they will set off her own looks, and to everyone else as a charming portrait of friendship, rather than a parade of matched beauties.

The Child's Place

DEAR MISS MANNERS:

I'm marrying for the first time, and my husband-to-be will be marrying for the second time. He has a little girl, aged nine, from his first marriage. I plan to have a small wedding party consisting of my sister as maid of honor, my eleven-year-old niece as a junior bridesmaid, and a friend of the groom's as best man. In addition, my nephew, aged thirteen, will be escorting me down the aisle and will exit as the junior bridesmaid's escort.

The problem is that I do not want to have my husband-to-be's daughter in the wedding party. There are several reasons, but a primary one is that I feel that too many children will then be involved. I do plan to have her and two of my remaining sisters bring the offerings up to the altar in the offertory rite.

Will I be looked down upon for not having her in the bridal party, since I have two other children in it? Also, is it cruel of me to have her escorted home from the reception after dinner, before the dancing begins? She will have no supervision at the reception, and I do not wish to impose on my guests to baby-sit. I feel that keeping her there will only lead to her tagging behind her father and me. I have considered asking relatives to watch her, but they are elderly and not very attentive.

GENTLE READER:

Yes, you are being cruel, and Miss Manners begs you to reconsider. You are making it clear that you consider the image of the wedding party—specifically, the number of children in it—to be more important than this child's feelings. You are also being foolish. Perhaps you do not realize how much this child and her attitude toward you will affect your chances of marital happiness. Surely you can manage the more usual and emotionally rewarding modern innovation of including children from previous marriages, whom the union will so seriously affect, as a prominent part of the wedding if they so wish. The kind thing to do would be to give her the choice of being an attendant or simply standing near her father at the altar. You should also allow her to stay up for such an important occasion. There will be no dearth of child-loving people to fuss over her. Should she be content to tag after you, Miss Manners believes that you should consider yourself extremely lucky.

The Bridal Couple's Children

DEAR MISS MANNERS:

What time do the children of the bride and groom walk down the aisle when they are not part of the wedding party but are to be included at the altar with their parents?

GENTLE READER:

Funny, tradition somehow forgot to cover this one. All right, then, Miss Manners will have to make up for that omission.

The children need not march down the aisle. They can sit in the front pew with other relatives and step forward when the wedding party is in place for the ceremony.

Firing a Bridesmaid

DEAR MISS MANNERS:

When I became engaged six months ago, I asked a longtime friend to be a bridesmaid. At that time, we saw each other occasionally and called about once a week. Now, however, our friendship has deteriorated. I haven't seen or talked to her in two months. I called about two weeks ago and, since she wasn't home, left a message with her mother. I still haven't heard from her. I would like to know if it is proper and, if so, is there a tactful way to let her know that I no longer wish her to be a bridesmaid at my wedding?

GENTLE READER:

Two months is an awfully short time to give up on a longtime friend, and the silence that offended you is, after all, unexplained. Miss Manners asks you to reconsider firing a bridesmaid on such grounds. However, the way to do it is to say, "I know you've been preoccupied lately, and I just want you to know that if you're going to find it difficult to keep your promise to me, I'll understand."

🌹 DRESS FOR WEDDINGS

The Time Factor

DEAR MISS MANNERS:

My fiancée and I are being married at 4:30 in the afternoon. She would like the groomsmen to wear morning suits with four-in-hand ties. Is it appropriate to wear this at the wedding and then change into full black tie dress for the reception after 6:00 P.M., or is 4:30 too late in the day to consider a morning suit?

GENTLE READER:

You two have never before been involved in the planning of a wedding, have you? You don't know yet what it's like to get even your closest friends all done up properly in formal clothes once, if you can begin to contemplate making them all change to another set in the same day.

It's not that Miss Manners doesn't appreciate your wanting to be correct at all hours. She herself is scrupulous about removing her afternoon hat when a wedding is followed by an evening reception or dinner. However, a 4:30 ceremony means that the beginning of the reception will probably squeak in before 6:00. Wear the morning clothes. (If it had been a 5:30 wedding, Miss Manners might have been tempted to call it the other way.)

Choosing the Color

DEAR MISS MANNERS:

Help! And soon! Who in the bridal party decides the color of the bridesmaids' and the maid of honor's gowns? Does the bride choose, or all of them, or the maid of honor?

GENTLE READER:

Miss Manners hesitates to say that the bride chooses because there is altogether too much bridal tyranny around already. Let us rather say that the bride should submit her choices, both to the wedding party and to her mother, who is usually the hostess of this event. Only serious objections to this choice should be voiced— but those should be heeded. Forcing one's closest friends to wear clothes they hate is not in the proper nuptial spirit.

The Wrong Color

DEAR MISS MANNERS:

My best friend is getting married and I will be maid of honor. There will be six girls in the wedding. We all went shopping for bridesmaid dresses, and everyone fell in love with the same gown.

The problem is the dress is black. It's very sharp and looked good on everyone. We plan to wear black gloves and satin shoes.

The bride's mother and my mother were shocked that we picked black for a wedding. What do you think?

Second Wedding

Formal Wedding

The purpose of the wedding party is for the bridal couple to be surrounded by their intimates, whoever these happen to be. It is not to fill certain set roles, such as Ten Groomsmen Taller Than the Bridesmaids (even though the bridegroom has only six friends, and they're short) and Male to Give the Bride Away (even though she is an orphan and has to get her baby brother to do it).

In the Second Wedding shown here, the children from the couple's previous marriages are standing at the altar, but not participating in the ceremony. The bride's best friend (who proved it by introducing her to the bridegroom) attends her instead of a Maid of Honor.

In the Formal Wedding, the bridegroom has been accompanied to the altar by both of his parents, and the bride is being given away by her mother, who brought her up single-handedly.

I'm very excited and would like the bride's mom to be excited too. I think it will look like a big cocktail party. The bride loves it.

GENTLE READER:

Miss Manners has been hearing a bit lately about this idea of black wedding clothing. People such as yourself who advance it claim to be doing so solely on aesthetic grounds, refusing to recognize any symbolic content.

Nevertheless, there is a great deal of symbolism in clothing, especially wedding clothing. Have you never heard one of those vulgar arguments about whether a bride is "entitled" to wear a white dress?

For that matter, why hold a formal wedding at all, with coordinated clothing, rather than letting each person wear what she likes best? Perhaps one of the bridesmaids would look better wearing her own wedding dress for the occasion.

In this society, black symbolizes death. Although formal mourning is seldom worn except at funerals, and black has become disassociated with mourning in general wear, a great many people are still shocked to see it at weddings, even on guests, because it gives them tragic associations.

	BRIDE	BRIDESMAIDS	BRIDEGROOM (and groomsmen)
MOST FORMAL	Stately, approximately white, long-sleeved dress with train and long veil (possibly even longer than the train).	Long pastel or jewel-colored dresses in the taste of the bride (but not actually offensive to the bridesmaids), with short veils or headpieces and gloves.	DAYTIME: Dark gray or black morning coat, gray striped trousers, waistcoat, stiff white dress shirt, gray ascot tie. EVENING: (Actually less formal than a high noon wedding, but only Miss Manners knows this.) Black tailcoat and trousers, white bow tie, waistcoat and wing-collared shirt.
FORMAL	Long dress with short or no train, perhaps short sleeves. Veil shorter than dress, or picture hat or flowers in the hair.	Long dresses similar to the above, but somewhat less elaborate, with picture hats or flowers in the hair.	DAYTIME: The sack coat, a.k.a. club or stroller coat, with striped trousers, gray four-in-hand tie, and stiff white fold-collared dress shirt. EVENING: Dinner jacket and trousers, or waistcoat, all strictly black, with bow tie and cummerbund, white pleated shirt.
SEMI-FORMAL	There is nothing in this category because Miss Manners has no idea what it is supposed to mean		
INFORMAL	A smashing street-length dress or suit, in white or any pastel or ladylike print the bride wishes, worn with a hat or flowers in the hair.	(Usually only a maid or matron of honor.) A lovely dress or suit in keeping with that of the bride, with something on the head.	Dark blue business suit with appropriate trimmings.
GENERAL NOTES	Whether the bride has been living with her fiancé for six years, or has merely parked out front with him all night, or has been courted by correspondence, the traditional white dress and veil are customarily associated with a first wedding, and all snickering about prior private activities is forbidden.	All of the above should be worn with an expression of delight at the bride's taste. It is more chic to have bridesmaids in complementary dresses than identical ones.	In no case is it necessary to distinguish the bridegroom from the groomsmen by his clothes. If the bride cannot tell which one he is, the problem is not one of dress.
ONLY OVER MISS MANNERS' DEAD BODY	Cleavage. Any visible suggestion that one feels sexy when getting married is redundant.	A chorus-line effect, down to matching hairstyles, makeup and nail polish.	Anything not black, gray, white, or dark blue—especially "contemporary tuxedos" in colors to complement the bridesmaids' dresses.

Proper Wedding Clothes

MOTHERS	FATHERS	GUESTS	
		FEMALE	MALE
Pale, dressy dresses of their own choosing, that they feel don't make them look fat. Long dresses for evening only. Hats (daytime only) and gloves.	The fathers invariably want to wear business suits, but those participating in the ceremony must dress as the groomsmen dress—although they need not associate with them more than is absolutely necessary.	DAYTIME: Dressy afternoon dresses or suits; hats and gloves. EVENING: Long dinner dresses.	In the evening, male guests may dress as the men in the wedding party do, if they have the proper clothes and don't mind being mistaken for ushers. Unless "black tie" is specified for evening, dark business suits are also appropriate, as they are at any time of day.
Afternoon dresses or suits similar to that worn by the maid of honor, allowing for age and size.	Their favorite dark business suits, but with something more dignified than their favorite shirts or ties.	Afternoon dresses or suits not quite as smashing as the bride's.	Same as fathers.
Distinguishing close female relatives by flower badges is dangerous. Once begun, the process never ends, leaving a step-great-aunt seething at not receiving a corsage. The mothers should not wear white to the wedding whether they are virgins or not.	The bridegroom's father actually has a choice—if he joins his wife in the receiving line he dresses as his son does; otherwise, he may wear a dark suit, but everyone will think he disapproves of the bride.	No female guest should wear black or white to a wedding. Black suggests mourning and white looks as if one is competing with the bride.	Male guests should pay no attention to any assurances from the bridegroom that it is not necessary to "dress up".
Matching or pink and blue mommies' costumes forced on them by the bride.	Glares between parents and stepparents.	Disco clothes intended to contrast ironically with the innocence traditional to weddings.	Scaled-down adult evening clothes for little boys.

As you have already found out, the two mothers have this reaction, and Miss Manners promises you that many of the guest will, also.

Is your friend the bride really willing to ignore the fact that a purely fashion decision may plunge many of those present at her wedding into a mood of sadness and an uneasy feeling that ill fortune lurks beneath the festivity?

Groomsmen

DEAR MISS MANNERS:

My wedding will be quiet, elegant, and simple, and I would like my brother to be in the wedding party. But he is a professional musician, with some of his hair shaved off and some of it spiked, and he would be a sight to behold at our formal candlelight service. He says that he can't and won't change his hair; it's part of his profession. I love my brother, but his appearance would be such a strange sight, really ruining the entire image I would like.

GENTLE READER:

Miss Manners imagines that you didn't expect her to deliver a ringing defense in favor of wearing spiked hair to candlelight weddings, did you?

She is obliged to do so. The rule of etiquette extends to setting the general standard of dress for a social occasion, and if he demanded to wear whatever his stage costume is (Miss Manners would prefer not to imagine that), you would be within your rights to insist that he wear dress proper to a member of the wedding party. It does not extend to the more personal aspects of one's appearance. For instance, you could not reasonably require all your bridesmaids to adopt the same hairstyle, even though you are having them dress alike.

Please try to remember that you want your brother to be part of your wedding because you love him, not for his looks. Besides, every wedding album needs to have one hilarious style for the children of the marriage to laugh themselves sick over years later, and you may be thankful that in yours, it will not be the bride's.

Guest's Clothes

DEAR MISS MANNERS:

My girlfriend and I are invited to a wedding, and we are going to the reception dressed in formal gowns. Will we outshine the bride or bridesmaids by doing this?

GENTLE READER:

In whose eyes? The bridegroom's? Miss Manners tends to doubt it, but you are welcome to try, provided, of course, that it is a formal evening wedding.

The Wedding Reception

Much as we all love weddings, there is one currently fashionable kind to which Miss Manners would just as soon not be subjected. That is the Realistic Wedding. She has no objection to shedding a gentle tear at the ceremony of union, and might even be prevailed upon later to shed another should it be shattered by cold reality. She just objects to being asked to do both at once. The realistic wedding is the one at which everybody makes a special effort to have cold reality blowing right through the festivities, ruffling all the bridesmaids' dresses and Miss Manners' spirits.

The clergyman turns toward the bright faces at the altar and says, "Miranda and Justinian, when you have problems —and you will have problems; every marriage does—when you fight with each other . . ."

The bridal couple exchange vows with escape clauses—"As long as we both shall love," rather than "shall live." They make sly references to the physical side of marriage for the benefit of those present who didn't know there was one, and cheerfully explain their prenuptial arrangements in case the marriage is dissolved.

The parents talk jocularly about how much the wedding is costing them per head and whether they are getting back the investment in the value of the wedding presents. If they're not feeling jocular, they take advantage of the presence of ex-spouses and their subsequent mates to reenact their own divorces for the entertainment of those who don't find wedding festivity enough.

The wedding guests are having a good time, too, exchanging details not only of the bridal couple's courtship, but of all their previous courtships, an exercise made both possible and dramatic by the presence on the scene of some of the participants in those courtships.

You may protest: Is not all this, ahem, reality true? Truth is not necessarily a defense with Miss Manners. Never has been. When she was a mere slip of a girl, the romantic heroine who most took her fancy was the elderly Countess Rosmarin Ostenburg in Christopher Fry's "The Dark Is Light Enough," who said (in blank verse): "I know the true world, and you know I do. But we needn't let it think we all bow down."

Yes, Miss Manners is aware that marriages are often based on compromise, rather than high romance; that courtships are no longer always conducted under chaperoned conditions; and that weddings sometimes lead to unhappily ever after. She knows that being married, being related, or, especially, having once been related is no guarantee of consistently warm feelings. She knows that both weddings and setting up housekeeping cost money, and that those involved are aware of the expense. She knows that there is sometimes a gap between the satisfaction of receiving presents and the desire to express appreciation to those who gave them. She prefers to keep weddings a time to look upward, rather than to bow down to all these truths.

🌹 MINOR CUSTOMS

A Time Gap

DEAR MISS MANNERS:

I am going to be a bridesmaid at a 1:00 P.M. wedding, for which the reception, at a reception hall approximately thirty minutes away, will not be until 6:00 P.M. There will be many out-of-town guests. What type of accommodations, if any, should be provided for the guests and bridal party during this gap in time? Who is responsible for these accommodations? Am I right in assuming that the bridal party should not mingle with the guests before the reception?

GENTLE READER:

What sort of tradition is it that you imagine takes precedence over courtesy to guests? This is an extremely unfortunate arrangement, in which the site of the reception seems to have taken on more importance that the purpose, which is for the bridal party to celebrate after the ceremony with those who have attended it. People are being asked to while away four hours, all dressed up and with no place to go. They are naturally going to perch somewhere, eating, drinking, and socializing, at their own expense and without the people whom they came to congratulate.

Unquestionably, it will take the edge off the reception itself. The least anyone connected with the bridal party can do is to find a way to help entertain these people. It would be nice of you as a bridesmaid to help out, but the chief people who ought to be doing it are the bridal couple and the hosts, who are probably her parents. Yes, that would result in their giving the reception earlier and not at their first-choice place. The sacrifice would be made in order to give guests first-class treatment.

Bouncers

DEAR MISS MANNERS:

Our daughter will have a church wedding, followed by a buffet reception in a private club. We expect about 200 guests. The club has a security guard. We are told that often, people do not respond to an invitation and then show up at the wedding and reception, causing problems for the caterers. Is it proper to include a notation on the invitation that states, under the R.s.v.p. line, "Admittance to the buffet reception will be limited to guests who acknowledge and accept this invitation"?

GENTLE READER:

One does not have bouncers at wedding receptions, or issue threats on wedding invitations. Even people with large-scale security problems, such as presidents, limit themselves to enclosing with the invitation discreet cards to be presented at the door.

Miss Manners sympathizes with your anticipated anger at ill-mannered people who do not have the courtesy to reply to a wedding invitation but reminds you that these people are your friends, not hers. What are you going to say if your bouncer asks you, in front of your old pal, whether he should be admitted? The most you can do to shame these people is to call them a few days before the wedding to say how sorry you are that they will not be present.

Loud Music

DEAR MISS MANNERS:

What do you think of the intensely loud music played at wedding receptions? For several years, my family and I have attended impressive church ceremonies, solemn in the sense of being sacred, followed by receptions where we are subjected to loud—deafening—music, if one can call it music. There should be soft, pleasant background accompaniment to the festivities of the occasion, instead of its being dominated by rock sessions.

GENTLE READER:

What's that again? Miss Manners can't hear you with all the noise. A wedding reception is a party, not part of the ceremony, and one can argue that whatever music the bridal party and guests enjoy may be played—that is, if care is taken that none of the arrangements actually make any of the guests uncomfortable. Young people sometimes fail to appreciate how offensive loud rock is to those of us who still have our hearing. Miss Manners agrees that guests of all generations must be considered, not just the bridal party's contemporaries, and that therefore a quiet zone must be provided for those who cannot take the noise.

Name Tags

DEAR MISS MANNERS:

Most of the guests at my daughter's wedding will be out-of-towners, and the families have never met. Would it be proper to use name tags at the reception?

GENTLE READER:

Is your daughter going to wear one that says "Hi, I'm the bride"? Do you really want her wedding to look like a convention? Do you want to ask ladies to smack gummy tags on their pretty dresses? Do you want to let both families know that you think them incapable of introducing themselves to one another? The answers, Miss Manners dearly hopes, are all "No."

Receiving Lines

DEAR MISS MANNERS:

I do not see why abolishing receiving lines is a "no-no." I have attended many weddings and have waited thirty to forty-five minutes to meet ten to twelve people I did not know, nor would they ever remember 200 strangers. I believe that without receiving lines the bride and groom can socialize with guests, have a quick taste of the food they paid for, and even a special dance. This atmosphere is more relaxing for everyone, and it doesn't feel as though the bridal party is on stage for a political handshaking session.

GENTLE READER:

You have got to stop crashing weddings—you and those 199 other strangers attending weddings where you don't know any of the principals. Naturally, it is an unpleasant ordeal for people who never saw you before to have to shake your hand. However, the usual wedding guests are relatives and dear friends of the bride, bridegroom, or their families. They all want to wish the bridal couple well, and those people invited them precisely because they wanted to see them on that momentous occasion. In a receiving line, the hosts and wedding party welcome every one of their guests and give them the chance to offer their good wishes. In exchange, they thank them and add, when appropriate, such polite remarks as "Oh, Saralinda has told me how much she enjoys working with you," or "We are so delighted to meet Basil's old friends." The receiving line exists so that this can be done in the most orderly and efficient fashion, after which all are free to have further conversation with whomever they choose.

Strangers

DEAR MISS MANNERS:

What do you say at the reception to members of a wedding party you know no better than the man in the moon? It really bothers me to kiss strangers who are not the bride and groom. And I'm sure they don't get all excited about it, either. Therefore, I fumble for something to say to these sometimes total strangers: "Good job as a bridesmaid/groomsman," or "Great weather we're having, isn't it?"

GENTLE READER:

Kissing strangers is never a requirement in polite society. Saying "How do you do?" is, and a well-organized receiving line should not leave one time to do much more than that before moving along. If the line gets stuck, the bit more consists of "What a charming wedding," "Doesn't Samantha look beautiful?" and such harmless pleasantries. Making outrageous test statements to see if anyone is listening ("My grandmother just died," "Oh, thank you") is, as are so many things in the realm of etiquette, unforgivable if one is caught but permissible if one is not.

Photographers

DEAR MISS MANNERS:

I am a lady photographer, and part of my business is to record weddings. I need to know if I should continue to wear dresses or if I would be considered acceptably dressed in a pants suit. Sometimes in pursuit of a pleasing angle, I find myself in a position where a skirt is awkward at best.

Am I correct in assuming that I will be fed at a wedding, or should I brown-bag it in case no one offers me the opportunity? At one wedding they had a sit-down dinner, and the groom informed me that I was there to photograph, not eat. I prefer not to catch people with their mouths full of food.

GENTLE READER:

You are there to photograph, and before you work yourself into hurt feelings with overtones of class discrimination because you are not treated as a guest, let Miss Manners assure you that you don't want to be one. Do you want to make conversation with total strangers who have numerous friends and relations in common and assume that you do, too, and therefore can join in a lot of intimate talk that will bore you to tears? Do you want to go through the receiving line? Do you want to send the couple a present? That's what guests do.

People who are there to work do their jobs instead of mingling and eat before or after their working hours. Miss Manners should not have to tell you that wedding dinners are not unrelieved eating. People wander and visit, and offer kisses and toasts, all of which are suitable opportunities for genuinely candid photographs—as opposed to those strangely named "candids" for which the festivities are arranged according to the photographer's checklist. If Miss Manners wished to be consistent, she would also tell you to wear your most practical working clothes instead of dressing like a guest, but she has never pretended to be consistent. Wear an unconfining dress. You will be able to do your job better for being inconspicuous.

Asking Favors

DEAR MISS MANNERS:

Instead of hiring a photographer for our daughter's wedding, we asked my husband's brother if he would take snapshots. In return, we supplied the film, his hotel room for two nights, his meals, and a car while he was here. We did not supply his air fare, which was $99. Is it our responsibility to pay for and send him reprints of these photos, or should he pay for them? To whom are we required to give enlarged pictures? To date, we have given one each to both sets of grandparents, one each to the wedding party, and one to our son-in-law's parents. Are we required to do more?

GENTLE READER:

Souvenirs are not an obligatory part of wedding etiquette. It is kind of you to give out copies of the photographs, but there is no list of required recipients. In the case of your brother-in-law, you do have an etiquette obligation, because you imposed on him to the extent of requesting a guest to do the task of a hired professional. People often do this without recognizing what a favor it is, and Miss Manners is glad to hear that you thought of helping defray his expenses. Sending him copies of his own work, embellished with grateful inscriptions by the bridal party, would be an appropriate additional courtesy.

Changing Places

DEAR MISS MANNERS:

My wife and I recently attended a buffet style, self-service wedding reception where guests were supposed to sit in designated places at specific tables. They had to go from table to table looking for their place cards. We knew that both the bride's and the groom's parents had given considerable thought to the seating, and had tried their best to disregard family relationships and to place likely compatible couples next to each other.

Unfortunately, there were guests who must have disapproved of this arrangement, as a number of them, on their own, exchanged the place cards of those assigned to their tables with cards of those at other tables whom they already knew. The result was that some guests sat through the reception without anyone with whom they could have a pleasant, stimulating conversation. Do guests have a right to voluntarily rearrange seating and, if not, what steps should the hosts take in advance to prevent it? How do they cope with such behavior if they become aware of it?

GENTLE READER:
Bound by the ethics of her profession to answer your question, Miss Manners must first admit that she is in sympathy with the outlaw guests. Weddings are not like ordinary dinner parties. They serve as family reunions, and it is perfectly natural that various branches of the families want to be together, rather than to meet new people. They should be allowed to do so; indeed, as you discovered, they can hardly be prevented. Social efforts should be concentrated on the single young friends of the bride and bridegroom. They, too, will tend to bunch by previous associations—the college friends in one corner, the high school crowd in another—but it is a traditional function of a wedding to inspire future weddings, so they should be encouraged to mingle.

Now, back to your question. Technically, no, guests do not have the right to undo the seating arrangements. The way to make it hard for them to do so is to have a seating chart on general display—one of those prettily lettered ones that also enable people to find their places without going from napkin to napkin, like cattle searching for fresh grass. The hosts' social function, if the seating arrangement does not succeed, is limited to picking up the strays and finding them companionship.

When to Begin Eating

DEAR MISS MANNERS:
I have observed two different practices in serving food at wedding receptions. The number of guests is well over 200 in each example. Reception A: Guests pass through the receiving line and then proceed to sit or stand around until the bride has been served. Mother A says that no one approaches the table until the bride has eaten. Then everyone is asked to queue. Reception B: Guests move from the receiving line and proceed to be served food and beverage. In this case, the bride has seen the table, but takes the position that the people there are her guests, and therefore the party is as much for them as for her and the groom. Later, she and the bridal party proceed to a table to be served. Which is correct?

GENTLE READER:
Miss Manners is so grateful to hear of a bride's entertaining the possibility that the wishes of anyone besides herself should be considered that she would vote for

B even if the bridal party ended up eating with their toes. The A family has, however, a vague point in believing that the bride is accorded precedence at her wedding. Should the wedding breakfast have been a seated meal for twelve, she would be served first. (The idea that others should wait until she has finished eating is as lacking in tradition as it is in sense.)

To maintain this protocol at a buffet supper for 200 people, an increasing number of whom will be standing around hungry while the bride is receiving the stragglers, is insane. The conversation of disgruntled crowds soon develops a nasty edge. A bride who does not want to allow the comments about how lovely she looks to develop into serious critiques will forgo the privilege of being first at the eats. Surely the day will contain pleasures that will compensate the bride for not having had the thrill of viewing an untouched table.

Bridal Pranks

DEAR MISS MANNERS:

What is it about weddings that turns normal people—one's friends—into vicious pranksters from whom the bridal couple, on top of all their other anxieties, must protect themselves? All too often, the poor bride, who has had nearly all she can take anyway, becomes the victim of her husband's old buddies. Clothes and cars are ruined, rice is flung into eyes, and the bride's nerves are frayed by half-serious threats of what the groom's buddies are going to do to prevent him from getting to the wedding. My very expensive silk going-away suit was ruined by the lipstick used to "decorate" our car, and frankly, I feel pretty unforgiving. Isn't it time someone put a limit on wedding pranks? How can the bride and groom protect themselves from friends suddenly turned malicious?

GENTLE READER:

Have you thought of marrying later, say, in middle age, when your friends are likely to be more mature? Miss Manners hopes you understand that you are asking her to take a rare stand against ancient tradition. Bridal pranks, some of them more revolting than anything your friends could think up now, are about as old as marriage. However, that does not make them funny or justify the annoyance they cause supposedly dear friends on solemn occasions. Miss Manners is prepared to support any bridal couples who appeal to their friends, in the name of friendship, to refrain from any but the mildest forms of teasing.

The Bridegroom's Garter

DEAR MISS MANNERS:

My local gift store sells a wedding groom's garter. It looks like a woman's black lace and elastic garter. I also have a faint memory of hearing about a ritual involving this item. However, I have never seen anyone use the garter in any way. What do they do with it? Thank you for enlightening me.

GENTLE READER:

Miss Manners has no such memory. Perhaps she has blocked it out. She has been hoping for years that people would forget the old but vulgar tradition of throwing the bride's garter. As to uses of a bridegroom's lace garter, Miss Manners would very much appreciate not being enlightened.

Tossing the Bouquet

DEAR MISS MANNERS:

At my youngest sister's wedding, when the phase of the ceremony arrived for the bride to toss her bouquet, the ritual produced an incident which I and a few others thought slightly marred an otherwise elegant and delightful evening. Two women, both widows in their sixties, one a grandmother and the other a great-grandmother, were among those vying to catch the bouquet. As luck would have it, the great-grandmother was the one with the longest arms. Thus an event that normally involves a bevy of young quail had the character of a gaggle of mature geese. The single, pretty, fresh young things, each of whom anticipated being the lucky one, mingled around aghast and speechless, feeling cheated.

I told both women in private that this phase of the ceremony was normally reserved for, and more suitable to, young, single women, and that I thought their behavior was tasteless and unsuitable to their current circumstances. Now that Mom and Pop are gone, I am the senior member of our family. One of my brothers agreed with me, and the other told me that I was out of line and it was none of my business.

Now the fact that a woman does catch the bouquet is no guarantee of a wedding. And I have nothing against women of whatever age or status going that route again. More power to them, *n'est ce pas?* I don't know what the protocol is, or even if there is any. I am, first and foremost, for good taste, class, and decorum. One of the widows was our sister! I've attended forty or fifty weddings in my sixty-six years, and this was a first for me. Maybe I do owe the two an apology, which I am not loath to make.

GENTLE READER:

It is not the duty of the senior member of a family of adults to throw criticisms at the junior members on family occasions. Miss Manners appreciates your willingness to apologize and encourages you to do so in a way that will leave no hard feelings. You owe them that, no matter what the etiquette of bouquet throwing.

Miss Manners paid careful attention to the wording of your letter. She notes that you seem to think that bouquet-throwing is somehow part of the ceremony. Weddings consist of the actual ceremony, which is a solemn event, and whatever lighthearted celebration takes place afterward. It is true that there are customs, some ancient, that are connected with wedding social festivities, but they are not as laden with dignity as those of the ceremony.

Bouquet throwing is not to be taken particularly seriously. For example, it is always considered adorable when the flower girl catches the bouquet, although she is obviously too young to be married. You are right that mature ladies did not generally participate, but then, mature ladies were not generally thought of as eligible. Why shouldn't they be, as you acknowledge?

The big formal wedding used to be considered appropriate only for very young ladies going from their parents' roof to their husbands'. Elderly brides, by which people seemed to mean anyone over thirty, were supposed to have quieter weddings. We have quite properly changed that, acknowledging that a wedding is just as significant when the bride is old enough to know what she is doing. By Miss Manners' calculations, if you are sixty-six, it seems unlikely, even allowing for the complexity of modern families, that your youngest sister is eighteen. If she has the benefit of social changes in age limitations, why can't her older sister enjoy that as well?

The Ceremonial Departure

DEAR MISS MANNERS:

My fiancé and I plan to marry in the house where we now live. Our families live at opposite sides of the country, and several family members have been invited to stay with us. His mother, as well as my sister and her family, have accepted. After the nuptials, I would like to spend the evening alone with my new husband. My fiancé feels that it would be rude to leave a house full of out-of-town guests, even though we plan to return the next morning and resume our roles as hosts. By having houseguests, have we lost our right to even a one-night honeymoon?

GENTLE READER:

Miss Manners can think of no good reason for you to forfeit your right to depart from the wedding, amid the knowing giggles of your guests, for the traditional excitement of your first unchaperoned evening together. Well, yes, she can think of a reason, but she prefers to ignore it. The departure of the bridal couple from the wedding reception, before the other guests and as a signal to them that they, too, can go home, is a standard feature of the event. Newlyweds who hang around forever, thus making it clear that privacy is no great treat to them, rob the occasion of its piquancy.

The full ritual involves the bride's throwing her bouquet, changing from her wedding dress to traveling clothes, dramatically hugging her parents, and rushing off with the bridegroom amid a shower of rice. If you can't bring yourself to enact the entire skit, at least say a dramatic good-bye to all, take your new husband's hand, and rush off. If you treat such a plan as an established fact, no one will be mean enough to say, "Wait a minute. Where are you going? What about us?" Take the precaution of asking your mother-in-law to be hostess in your house until your return.

❧ WEDDING PRESENTS

The Wedding as Fund Raiser

As a relief from the Age of Greed, you might think Miss Manners would approve of a starry-eyed couple's planning their wedding as a charitable event. Isn't it generous of them to designate worthy causes as beneficiaries of whatever largesse wedding guests might have otherwise directed towards themselves?

Modestly styling herself "event chairperson," rather then just "bride," to sound more professional, the central figure in such a spectacle appealed to major corporations for contributions to her wedding. She solicited donations from the tradespeople normally hired for a wedding reception—baker, florist, musicians, caterers, hairdresser, and even a "wedding consultant" who seemed to have a flexible idea of what constitutes a wedding.

In return, there were promises that any resulting philanthropy would be credited in a program, and in press kits to be issued in connection with the event, for which media coverage was importuned.

Guests were informed that they should contribute cash to the specified charities in lieu of wedding presents, and enticed with the reminder that the amount would be tax deductible. The definition of wedding guests had been extended from family and friends to include those whose interest was in the benefiting charities, rather than in the couple, whom they might not know at all.

Instead of calling it a "wedding," the couple are referring to the occasion as "a unique fund-raising event," and emphasizing that it is "nonprofit" and that they expect to contribute $5,000 to $10,000 of their own toward an estimated cost of $20,000. Pointing out that they have lived together for fourteen years, they said that they don't need ordinary wedding presents, which they define as "twenty toasters and blenders."

What is wrong with this?

Why is Miss Manners barely able to recount these plans without sinking back into a stupor from which even a splash of wedding champagne (Courtesy of——) will not revive her? Is she so stuck in tradition that she is unable to appreciate imaginative altruism?

Isn't this better than the all too usual bridal couple's figuring out how much they can dun their friends for in the way of presents, or preferably cash, or contributions to whatever expensive goal they announce for themselves?

Yes and no. The immediate motivation may be better, but the appalling presumption underlying it is the same.

That is that a private, even sacred, event is an "opportunity," in the baldest commercial sense of being a chance to extract money from well-wishers. It is that one puts on a wedding not to make a pretty occasion out of an important event that one wants to share with people one loves, but in the expectation of getting a return.

Whether the money is in presents or cash; whether it goes into the pockets of the participants or is directed by them to be given to others; whether it is counted as compensating them for their wedding costs or enlarging their chance to be philanthropists—none of this changes the vulgar assumption that people owe bridal couples for getting married.

Yes, it is customary to give wedding presents when one cares about the couple. Nowadays, it should be obvious that settled couples do not need the basics, and their dear friends or relations ought to be able to imagine—because they know them so well—what they might prefer. People who really don't know the couple or care about them—and another fact of modern life is that wedding givers often mistake their business associates or other remote acquaintances for friends—needn't worry about wedding presents because they will decline the invitation.

Miss Manners has news for all bridal couples, which she would like to announce loud and clear before this sort of thing catches on:

All weddings are supposed to be "nonprofit" events.

Charitable Presents

DEAR MISS MANNERS:

My fiancé and I are considering doing something a little different when it comes time to send out our wedding announcements. We are both devout Catholics and contribute regularly to several special charities. We have both saved enough money to live comfortably without the usual monetary donations couples receive as wedding gifts. So we would like to include a note with each wedding invitation to this effect: "The couple would sincerely appreciate a donation to the charity of your choice in their name as a possible alternative to a wedding remembrance." I've never heard of this being done before. Is it terribly rude, or should we go through with it?

GENTLE READER:

While duly appreciating your motives, Miss Manners regrets to tell you that what you propose is indeed terribly rude. You can give a charity ball or you can give a wedding, but you cannot give a charity wedding. Acknowledgment of the expectation that people will give you money, or any other present, when you marry is rude. However, it would be perfectly gracious to donate wedding checks to charity and to say in your thank-you notes, "We used your generous present to do something special that makes us very happy," and then explain the cause to which you have given.

Guests as Patrons

DEAR MISS MANNERS:

I am a twenty-five-year-old woman living on my own. I have very little money and a strict budget. A few months ago, some cousins called to ask me why I wasn't at another cousin's wedding, and that's when I found out that there was a wedding and I wasn't invited. The wedding was in town, and I would have gone if I had been invited. A friend of mine said that I wasn't invited because I couldn't give an expensive gift, so it wasn't worthwhile to the hosts. Is this true? Is it a new trend in weddings that only the wealthy are invited? Or were the hosts being thoughtless? In talking to my cousins, I find that I was the only close relative not invited. I thought wedding gifts were to be given if the guest wants to give, not because he has to.

GENTLE READER:

No doubt someone is trying to start a trend whereby credit checks are done on prospective wedding guests to find out if it would be worthwhile to invite them. Nothing would surprise Miss Manners in the way of crassness connected with weddings. Nevertheless, Miss Manners begs you to try to believe that your omission was an accident or the result of some misunderstanding.

The Bridal Registry

DEAR MISS MANNERS:

I was invited to the wedding of a cousin but didn't attend. I had a department store ship an expensive gift to the couple. When I didn't receive a thank-you note or an acknowledgment that it had arrived, I asked the mother of the bride about it. (It was shipped to her address.) She told me that the gift was very out of place, and asked me to return it and purchase something in keeping with the bride's "registered gift list." I hadn't seen this, as I live several thousand miles away.

On the eve of another relative's wedding, the tray I sent was returned to me in a cardboard box. I don't even think that the card I had enclosed was read. They also requested that I obtain their "list" from a certain store and mail them another gift. Am I really responsible for returning the gift and purchasing another? This is turning into a lot of time, money, running around, and postage! What is the procedure you recommend?

GENTLE READER:

Miss Manners recommends that you accept the fact that you cannot please these people, return the present for credit to your own account, and forget the whole thing. Bridal registries exist only so that people who can't think of what to buy can voluntarily obtain information without having to ask the recipients directly. That is because the recipients are supposed to be so surprised and overcome that anyone wants to get them anything that they are unable to provide any useful information. That doesn't exactly describe your relatives.

Blank Thanks

DEAR MISS MANNERS:

I was recently a member of a wedding party. One of the bridesmaids, unable to give a timely gift because of financial circumstances, sent her gift several weeks after the wedding. But before the bride received the gift, she sent a blank thank-you note. She also did this to a few other people. Two days after the delayed gift was received, the bridesmaid did get a thank-you note for her gift. I found this appalling.

GENTLE READER:

Just when Miss Manners thinks that things have hit rock bottom in the etiquette sphere, someone hits her with something like this. She is forced to understand that this monstrous bride has perverted the charming custom by which wedding guests wish to express their joy in a tangible form to an expected business payment, for which overdue-payment notices may be sent.

Miss Manners does not often write off etiquette violators as hopeless. A bride's ignorance of simple wedding manners might have been forgiven, but a violation motivated by malicious greed cannot be. Do you really need such a friend?

The Father's Prerogative

DEAR MISS MANNERS:

After seven months of marriage, my father-in-law has failed to give us a wedding gift. He constantly reminds us of how much he earns but has never come up with anything more than empty promises. I feel that he is at fault, that it is a moral obligation to give a wedding gift to his son, but perhaps I am wrong in presuming that anyone is actually obliged to give any sort of gift at all.

GENTLE READER:

You certainly are. So, you imagine that there is some sort of Marital Revenue Service that levies a heavy tax on the associates of bridal couples, and that terrible moral sanctions are put on those who fail to come through?

As a matter of fact, one of the popular options of new fathers-in-law used to be expunging their sons from their wills, known as "cutting them off without a cent" (Miss Manners has also heard the expression given as "cutting them off *with* a cent,") for marrying the wrong sort. Greedy brides suggest that they are the wrong sort.

The Established Household

DEAR MISS MANNERS:

I would like your opinion on couples who have lived together openly—sometimes for several years—and then decide to get married. Suddenly, she acts like the virgin who needs china, silver, and other gifts. In a recent situation of this nature—the groom's mother made it obvious to friends that she expected them to entertain this couple with many large parties, some showers, and a big church wedding. If a couple chooses to break with tradition, that is their business, but to expect people to treat them as a traditional bride and groom is greedy and distasteful. What do they do that is new on their honeymoon?

GENTLE READER:

Miss Manners was not aware that only virgins needed china and silver. Nor is she in the habit of speculating about what couples do on a honeymoon, but she dares say that all of them think of something.

It is always improper for the bridegroom's mother to announce obligations to others, and that should therefore be steadfastly ignored. People who disapprove of a bridal couple, for whatever reason, need only decline the wedding invitation.

Presents from Previous Wives

DEAR MISS MANNERS:

Help! I have been divorced for twelve years and have a wonderful thirteen-year-old son from this marriage. His father is about to be married for the fifth time and has had large weddings each time. Both my son and I have been invited to the couple shower and the wedding. They even included the name of the store where they are registered. Miss Manners, is it proper to invite a child to the shower and expect him to buy them a gift? How about expecting me to buy them shower and wedding gifts? I feel that this is out of place. Some feel it is a good gesture. Your answer will be framed and given to them as a gift, whatever way you answer.

GENTLE READER:

If this is your husband's fifth marriage, he ought to have the hang of it by now and not create problems that Miss Manners has to clean up. Perhaps he leaves all that to his brides, or perhaps some people just never learn. Miss Manners' guess is that none of this was thought out beyond the vague idea that your son might be happier if you were included and a careless issuing of all related invitations to the family.

It is in your power to act correctly even if they didn't. You need only decline all invitations for yourself and have your son accept his to the wedding itself. As for presents—if your son wants to give an appropriately small present the token gesture would be nice. You need not. Once upon a time, former wives sometimes gave their successors leftover formal cards, a present more than slightly tinged with sarcasm. Since those are hardly used anymore, and since many new brides do not style themselves "Mrs." with the husband's name anyway, the joke is obsolescent. Etiquette has not quite come to the point of demanding that previous brides of the same gentleman make fusses over subsequent ones. In any case, however, a framed reprimand is not a suitable present for anyone.

Opening Presents

DEAR MISS MANNERS:

When is it appropriate to open a wedding gift? Obviously the reception makes opening gifts impossible because the bride and groom cannot take time away from their other guests. When I delivered a wedding gift to the bride's home, I thought she would open it in my presence, but she did not. This was especially disappointing, as I had called to make arrangements for the visit ahead of time. Perhaps some encouragement on my part would have alleviated the awkwardness of our visit. I'm being married soon myself, and I do so want to do the proper thing.

GENTLE READER:

You seem to be doing the proper thing, so let us work on everyone else. For the reason you mention—and the additional one Miss Manners often hears about, of presents getting lost or stolen in the confusion—it is improper to take a wedding present to a wedding. Ordinarily they are delivered, for the bridal couple to open in private. For a prearranged personal delivery, when there is no other guest present who may be embarrassed at not having brought anything, the bride should open the present and exclaim over it (although this does not get her out of writing a letter of thanks). Do so yourself, and encourage others by saying, "Oh, do open it now. I am dying to know if you like it."

In the Case of an Annulment

DEAR MISS MANNERS:

My husband and I recently gave our lovely daughter an elegant wedding, attended by 150 guests. Several weeks after the wedding, the groom changed his mind and ended the marriage, leaving my daughter heartbroken. The marriage has been annulled. Are the bride and groom obliged to return the gifts, as one would do when an engagement is broken? And if my daughter some day remarries, is it proper to have another large wedding, to which the guests might feel obliged to give yet another gift?

GENTLE READER:

Technically speaking, your daughter may keep the wedding presents, as the wedding took place, even if it has been legally erased. However, if Miss Manners were she, she would not be able to get them back in the mail fast enough—of course, accompanied by poignant notes of thanks and the regretful statement that "under the circumstances" she would "not feel right" about keeping them.

This is not only a matter of the unpleasant associations such things must have. (That is assuming that there are other people left in the world besides Miss Manners who do not see objects in terms of their market value alone.) Some day, as you say, your daughter may marry more happily. It will be harder to count that wedding as her first real one if you have traded on the fact of this one. The more prudent of your friends will simply stash away the current presents and give them again at that time.

Expressing Thanks

DEAR MISS MANNERS:

A bride of my acquaintance tells me that she has not yet acknowledged any of her wedding gifts and that Miss Manners gives one year as the time limit. I think you have been misquoted. Common sense tells me that two months should be the absolute limit.

GENTLE READER:

Misquoted? Miss Manners has been slandered. It is a popular Young Brides' Tale (as opposed to an Old Wives' Tale) that one can take up to a year writing thank-you letters for wedding presents. This is not true and never has been. Thank-you notes are due right after presents are received. Ten minutes afterward would be a good time, but the maximum, barring severe illness, divorce, or absence from the planet, is two weeks.

The true one-year rule in connection with wedding presents is one that brides don't seem to care for. It is that these presents may be sent up to a year following the wedding. Efficient people, who have kindly sent presents promptly, only to find that the marriage is in danger by the time they are received, might do well to take advantage of this leeway.

Preprinted Thanks

DEAR MISS MANNERS:

At weddings, showers, and anniversaries I have attended recently, I was given a favor with a thank-you note printed in gold with "We sincerely appreciate and thank you for coming to our anniversary," or "We sincerely thank you for your generous wedding gift," or "Thank you for your lovely wedding gift and for sharing in our happiness." Is this a new way to thank the guests for gifts, or am I old-fashioned in thinking that one has to write a personal thank-you note and mail it?

GENTLE READER:

To issue written thanks to guests for having attended a ceremony or party is unnecessary; to issue preprinted ones is ludicrous. Suppose that they had all gotten raucous and made spectacles of themselves? The need to thank people for presents, in one's own words and one's own hand, remains. Gratitude, and the need to express it personally to those who have demonstrated that they care for one, are not subject to fashion.

Promptness

DEAR MISS MANNERS:

Is it proper for a bride-to-be to send a thank-you note for a wedding gift prior to the actual wedding? Upon receiving her wedding invitation, I selected an appropriate gift and had it sent to the bride's home. Within one week, I had received the thank-you note. The wedding is in two weeks. It seems correct to wait until after the actual ceremony to send these notes, but I am getting conflicting opinions.

GENTLE READER:

You are about to get more than that from Miss Manners. You are going to get a cloudburst of tears. Here poor old Miss Manners has been working so hard to get brides to send any thank-you letters at all, and then to get them out within the lifetimes of the present givers, and you complain that you have gotten one too soon? No, indeed, there is no impropriety in sending out prompt thank-you letters, before or after the ceremony. There is only Miss Manners' undying gratitude.

Tardiness

DEAR MISS MANNERS:

After my wedding three years ago, I started writing thank-you notes to all those nice people who gave us gifts. After a few weeks I stopped, and I never began again. I know this is an unforgivable offense, and somehow I feel I must do penance. Should I swallow all pride, beg forgiveness, and finally write thank-you notes? Or should I just forget it and hope that those nice people will too? Most of them live in my hometown, and I have not been able to go there since without feeling deeply embarrassed. Please do not be too harsh on me. All these months of guilt have been harsh enough, though I do deserve supreme chastisement.

One other factor is that I am afraid that someone receiving my too tardy note will say to my mother, "I had the nicest thank-you note from your daughter the other day." My mother would be horrified: She has no idea that I have been so remiss.

GENTLE READER:

As you are suffering for your great sin and are ready to do penance, it behooves Miss Manners to be merciful. Here is a sample of the kind of letter you must write, immediately, to each person who gave you a present:

Dear Mrs. Featherstone,

Every time Gregory and I use the sugar tongs you sent us when we were married, we take fresh pleasure in how beautiful they are, and in your kindness in giving them to us. I don't believe we ever sufficiently expressed our appreciation to you, or told you how much we continue to value your friendship . . ."

Miss Manners promises you that up to this point, Mrs. Featherstone has been positive that you never wrote to her—people never forget such omissions—but that she will now be less sure that this is not a follow-up to a correctly timed letter. With any luck, your mother will imagine that, too, if anyone mentions the matter to her.

An Intermediate Stage

DEAR MISS MANNERS:

I was married recently and have nearly completed all my thank-you notes. However, I have received notification from a few bridal registries indicating that gifts are forthcoming, with the names of the givers and a description of the gifts. I hesitate to write thank-you notes to these kind people because it has been my unfortunate experience that the registries, computerized or not, sometimes misplace or confuse registry purchases. I do not want to mislead the givers by thanking them for gifts I have not received, but I hesitate to let much more time pass without giving proper thanks.

GENTLE READER:

You are quite right. These people, ignorant of the registries' delay, are passing the time by wondering why you have not written to acknowledge presents they have long since purchased. Yet if you pretend that the presents have arrived, you will have no tactful way of prodding them to trace lost ones. Okay, here goes: "I'm so excited! The Happy Times Bridal Registry has written that they will be sending me a magnificent candle warmer, which you have so thoughtfully selected for me . . ."

An Aggregate Thank-You

DEAR MISS MANNERS:

Several weeks after our marriage, we received a very substantial gift, with an enclosed card reading simply, "From the Partners." It is a gift from the 200 or so partners at the law firm where my husband is an associate and will be considered for partnership within the next year. It is essential to respond in some way, but how? Two hundred thank-you notes? One thank-you to be circulated by the office manager? We have found out that there is an office manager type who is responsible for such niceties at the firm. Do we consult her? Only four colleagues from the firm were invited, as the wedding was a small, close-friends-and-family affair, and my husband has been with the firm for only two years. These people gave us individual gifts. We don't even know if all the partners realize that this gift was made in their names.

GENTLE READER:

All presents should be acknowledged with a letter of thanks as soon after they have been received as is humanly possible. But 200 thank-you letters for one present that the givers probably don't know they sent? In this case, you may write a letter to the office manager, telling her of your appreciation and gratitude for the partners' kindness and asking her to convey this to them on your behalf.

Other Ceremonies

✿ BIRTH CEREMONIES

Ceremonies connected with newborn babies—the christening of a Christian baby, the bris of a Jewish boy, and the formal naming of a Jewish girl—represent the last time a parent will be able to see the child featured at a major occasion without worrying about surprises that will, in the exaggerated parlance of such events, disgrace the family.

Ahead lie the birthday parties at which the child may break through the welcoming routine to grab the present and run—while the presiding parent tries to convey to the guest's parent, through an ingratiatingly hopeless smile, that it wasn't as though he or she hadn't been better taught.

There will be graduations at which parents will anxiously scan the line approaching the stage to receive diplomas with the fervent hope that their child has not decided to be one of those who use the opportunity to make a comic public statement. At weddings, stylistic and procedural differences are likely to have been fought out beforehand, but there is always room for improvisation. Anyway, that is the occasion on which the next youngest child transfers parental fears to himself by getting into the champagne.

It's not that an infant can't behave miserably without half trying. It can give out a high-pitched yelp and make horrid faces and hostile squirming gestures when handed to key relatives. But beginners' courtesy requires that everyone else classify this behavior as "showing spirit" or "having decided opinions" or "trying so hard to be patient, the poor little thing." Never again do we get such a free ride in the etiquette department.

Ceremonies for newborns, like their births, do not call for a visit to the engravers. The children not yet having collected hordes of more or less presentable friends, it is only the intimates of the parents who can be presumed to be interested.

Miss Manners has never liked cutesy birth announcements, including the pseudoformal ones in which a tiny card for the baby is attached to the parents' card with a ribbon. "Lesley and I are delighted to tell you of the birth of our daughter," with the baby's name and date of birth, is really much more chic.

These, and invitations to the ceremonies, can be on the writing paper of whichever parent does the writing (and has the paper left over from wedding thank-you letters) or on the parents' correspondence card (a single card with their formal names centered at the top—the successor of the old folded "informal," now too small for the mails) that they also use for party invitations and notes with presents.

For its christening, a baby wears white, and the parents and guests wear dressy afternoon clothes. At the luncheon or tea following the ceremony, which can be held in church or at home, it is traditional to serve a white cake with the baby's initials in icing, and either champagne or the hot eggnogg punch called "caudle."

The Jewish brith milah or bris, the religious circumcision held on the eighth day following the birth, at home or in the synagogue, is followed by a festive breakfast which also includes hallah, honey and sponge cakes, nuts, cookies, and dried fruits, and wines for toasting. A boy receives his name on that day; a Jewish girl receives hers at the Sabbath services following her birth, which may be celebrated with a reception at the temple or at home. Before these ceremonies, one does not ask what a baby's name "is" but what it "will be."

Although gala occasions, these events are of a religious nature, not to be confused with children's birthday parties. Presents are customary but are not made to seem a central part of the occasion. Many of the guests, being intimates of the family, will already have sent or brought baby presents and need not do so again.

What is obligatory is for the guests to coo over the baby, announce that it is the most perfect creature they have ever seen, shows signs of vast intelligence, and so on. This is also the time to say whom the baby "favors" in appearance, because children who understand such conversations find them immensely tiresome.

Especially tactful guests who are parents themselves will use the occasion to make a fuss over the baby's older siblings, conspicuously refraining from asking them how they feel about having a baby in the family. As the elder child does not enjoy the etiquette immunity of the infant, such inquiries often lead to no good.

A Non-Christening

DEAR MISS MANNERS:

My husband and I are expecting our first child. We would like to have a tea in the child's honor a few weeks later. The intention is to replace the traditional christening and after-christening party, which we do not plan to hold, being hopelessly irreligious. What we had in mind was champagne and white cake, and little sandwiches at 4:00 P.M. on a Sunday. The guest list would be family and close friends.

Can we do it, or do we have to get the local minister to mutter something irreligious over the infant's head before progressing to champagne and debates about whom the child most resembles? P.S. Do I get any credit for planning to write notes to announce the child's birth, instead of sending out those dopey little cards?

GENTLE READER:

You get credit for everything except the crack about getting a clergyman to mutter something irreligious. Giving a reception for your intimates to meet your baby is a beautiful idea, provided that you do not attempt to make it a pseudo-christening. Hopelessly irreligious people should have the courage of their lack of convictions.

The Godparent

DEAR MISS MANNERS:

Does accepting the honor of being a godparent include providing college tuition for said child and extravagant presents throughout the godparent's lifetime? I've been chided repeatedly for failure in these areas and resent the sly digs.

GENTLE READER:

How many chidings and digs would it take to get you to pay college tuition? As Miss Manners understands it, we are talking about thousands of dollars. She cannot understand why, instead of being uneasy, you are not laughing in these outrageous people's faces. Presumably, it would come as a surprise to them to learn that being a godparent is a spiritual rather than a materialistic duty. You are supposed to be interested in the child's soul while allowing the parents the honor of tending to such mundane matters as food and tuition.

Traditionally, the godparents' duties are to hold the baby at the christening; give it a lasting present, traditionally something silver, engravable, and of unknown utility; and act as second-string parents to the child, providing moral and religious instruction, birthday and Christmas presents, and asylum when the child becomes a teenager and quarrels with his parents. The godparent relationship is often connected with the willingness to assume guardianship should the child be orphaned. There is no mandate to do this by any standard other than that which you can manage financially—although there have been parents who have considered wealth when choosing godparents in the hope that these tasks would be performed lavishly. Such ulterior motives need concern you only to the extent of resolving to work extra hard at teaching spirituality to a child from a morally disadvantaged home.

❧ COMING OF AGE

Bar and Bat Mitzvahs

If she could take the liberty of slipping just a few extra requirements into the preparation required of a child who is to have a bar or bat mitzvah, Miss Manners promises that the event, and the life thereafter of the family, would be the better for it.

Surely no one will mind. These additions will be hardly noticeable, as they will be within the general tradition of teaching the ideals and responsibility a thirteen-year-old child must develop to enter even preliminary adulthood. Only the practical applications of Miss Manners' lessons will diverge a bit from strictly religious training.

Lesson: This is an event of significance, not just to yourself but to your family, to whom, as you grow up, you have increasing responsibilities.

Application 1: Cooperate in planning a celebration that your parents can easily afford and which, however festive, is still within the style of entertaining to which they are accustomed.

Application 2: Yes, you have to invite horrid Cousin Ruthie.

Application 3: You must be equally polite to all generations. The older relatives will naturally end up socializing with one another, which will leave you to spend the major part of the evening with your own friends. However, you must greet each guest hospitably, suffer any kisses and compliments, and accept congratulations graciously, even when they are laced with the standard adult jokes about growing up.

Lesson: Learning should produce humility, good fortune, and gratitude.

Application: Write those thank-you letters immediately.

Lesson: You are participating in an ancient ritual, which you are expected to learn and respect, not undercut or attempt to improve upon.

Application: No, you can't send out hilarious or adorable invitations to sabotage the solemnity of the occasion. Your choice of styles is proper formal or proper informal.

A formal invitation, which may conclude with a line about a celebration ("luncheon following the services") or be accompanied by a card for a later party, is engraved in black on white or ecru paper:

> *Mr. and Mrs Stephen Jonathan Frank*
> *request the honour of your presence*
> *when their daughter*
> *Geraldine Alisa*
> *will be called to the Torah as a Bat Mitzvah*
> *on Saturday the seventh of April*
> *at nine o'clock*
> *Brookdale Hebrew Congregation*
> *Brookdale, Connecticut*

The enclosed card reads:

> *Dinner dance*
> *at half after seven o'clock*
> *The Brookdale Club*
> *The favour of a reply is requested*

An informal invitation is a letter:

Our son, Jeremiah Eric, will be called to the Torah as a Bar Mitzvah on Saturday, the fourteenth of April, at Brookdale Hebrew Congregation, at nine o'clock. We would be honored to have you attend, and to join us at seven thirty that evening for a reception at our house.

Lesson: Learning gives one a sense of perspective.
Application: Of course, you're not going to get everything you've always wanted. But someday you'll have a wedding.

A Non-Bar Mitzvah

DEAR MISS MANNERS:
Next month, my adopted son will be thirteen years old. Although we are not Jewish, I would like to give him a non-bar-mitzvah party and invite friends. We have been to many bar mitzvahs involving his friends and plan to invite all of them. I am concerned about how to send the invitation. What should it say? I understand that in bar mitzvahs, money and presents are given. I would like him to have this, too. But mostly what I want is a coming-of-age party for him.

Mr. and Mrs. David Hendin

request the pleasure of your company

at dinner

on Saturday, the twelfth of November

at seven o'clock

The River Club Restaurant

Burd Street at the Hudson River

Nyack, New York

in honor of his son

Benjamin Judah

who will become Bar Mitzvah

at the morning service

at nine-thirty o'clock

New City Jewish Center

Old Schoolhouse Road

New City, New York

R.s.v.p.

A bar mitzvah invitation, two replies, and a letter of thanks from the young man.

Every effort should be made to resist the temptation to make bar or bat mitzvah invitations cute. It is a solemn occasion. The formality should not be undercut by the use of the parents' first names or odd colors of ink or paper; the informal version is an individually written letter.

BJH

January 13, 1989

Dear Dr. Reinisch,

    Hi, how are you? I've been very busy playing the flight simulator you sent me, I think it's great. Thank you very, very much.

                    Love,
                    Ben

Mr. and Mrs. Robert Wiley
regret that they are unable to accept
the kind invitation of
Mr. and Mrs. Hendin
for
Saturday, the twelfth of November

Mr. & Mrs. Gil Park
accept with pleasure
the kind invitation of
Mr. & Mrs. David Hendin
for Saturday, the twelfth of November,
at seven o'clock

GENTLE READER:

Well you may be concerned. A bar mitzvah or, for a girl, a bat mitzvah, is a solemn religious occasion marking the child's coming of age (although accompanied by festive rejoicing), and any attempt to adapt it for secular use would be highly offensive. It would be like a mother's wanting to give her little daughter the opportunity to dress up and therefore staging a mock communion. What you are talking about is a birthday party. Give your son as lavish a birthday party as you wish, and by all means invite those whose bar mitzvahs he has attended.

Communion and Confirmation

First Communion, among Roman Catholics, is usually celebrated when the child is about seven, with confirmation four or five years later. Among Protestants, the two are generally at the same time, at around age thirteen. Both are marked with religious services, followed by a small reception in church, at home, or sometimes in a restaurant. Relatives, godparents, and close friends who attend should give the child a present. The rule about all such presents being strictly religious in nature has been relaxed somewhat, but Miss Manners urges that they be appropriate to the occasion, and not, for example, a doll in a silver jumpsuit who looks as if she could get into church only as a bad example.

Graduations

DEAR MISS MANNERS:

Mom says that the proper thing to do when you receive a graduation announcement is to send a gift or $20. I don't agree with her. I think announcements should be sent to people just to let them know, for their information, that the kid they once knew is finally graduating.

GENTLE READER:

Although Miss Manners is as aware as your mother is that some people think children graduate from school at all only in order to shake others down for presents, she does not advise conceding such an ugly point. She agrees with you. Send your announcements to anyone you think would be genuinely interested to hear of your progress. (That does not include people with whom you are not in touch from one year to the next.) And by the way, a letter of congratulations is just as proper a response to such an announcement as a present.

DEAR MISS MANNERS:

I had spent all of my adult life as a homemaker when my husband of some thirty years abandoned me. I am trying to pick up the pieces from the devastation and sorrow, and build a new life. After much hard work, I am to receive a master's degree. What celebration would be appropriate for a woman in her fifties?

Would I be correct in sending graduation announcements to friends and relatives? My married children live nearby, but all other relatives and several friends live in distant states. Should local friends be sent announcements? Would it be proper for me to have a graduation party? If so, should it be at my home, or would it be better for my children to host it? (I have no suitors.) I would like to have others share in this joy, but I don't wish to have either the announcements or a party appear to be a bid for gifts. How can I make this known? Can you guide me toward a fitting celebration?

GENTLE READER:

There is always a "Wow, I did it!" quality to graduation parties, but Miss Manners would prefer you to soften this just a little bit in one of the following ways:

Have your children give it for you so that you may look charmingly overcome at the attention.

Give it yourself, but share the honors with some of your young classmates.

Give it yourself for yourself, but instead of mentioning the occasion on the invitation, simply say at the party that you are celebrating your graduation.

You may send out graduation announcements with your calling card enclosed, but if you want to soften those, too, you could write letters instead, saying how pleased you are at having done this at last. It is not worth considering that anyone may think you went through all that hard work for the purpose of extracting presents.

Including Former Spouses

DEAR MISS MANNERS:

I am a recently divorced mother of teenage boys after fifteen and a half years of marriage. Within a few months of our divorce, my former husband was remarried for the third time, to a person with whom I believe, he had a relationship, if not a commitment, before he divorced me. I am not able to be very civil to either one of them, because I was not employed at the time of the divorce and only recently found part-time employment as a legal secretary. We are dependent financially on my parents when I cannot make our limited budget cover expenses. How should I handle future graduations and other family events? Am I obligated to invite his wife—if he is still married to her when the occasion arises—to parties after graduations?

GENTLE READER:

By Miss Manners' count, you were a second wife, and perhaps had some occasion to learn that financial and emotional accounts cannot be settled by adding into them violations of etiquette. Miss Manners is sorry that your former husband appears to have been unfaithful during your marriage and that he has apparently not made adequate financial provision for you and your children. These matters will not be solved if you attempt to hold official family events without the legitimate wife of your children's father. All that would do would be to alert everyone concerned to your bitterness, at the expense not only of your children's enjoyment but of your own dignity. However, maybe your wishful thinking will turn out to be correct, and it will be only an unknown fourth wife whom you will need to invite by the time the children finish school.

❧ SPECIAL OCCASIONS

Rediscovery Announcement

DEAR MISS MANNERS:

Twenty-one years ago, I gave birth to a daughter. I was not married and placed the child for adoption. I have gathered my courage to search for my child and have good prospects of locating her. If I succeed, and both she and her adoptive parents are willing, I would like to acknowledge her as my birth daughter to friends and some family members who are completely unaware of her existence. Please advise me on this perplexing and delicate matter.

GENTLE READER:

There are no forms for announcing the birth of an adult and, if there were, your daughter would probably object to your filling in her weight. What would she do with the silver rattles sent by careless readers? Miss Manners' point is that this is not a standard, conventional occasion requiring so little explanation that there is a standard way to announce it. It is something odd and special, which should be shared with friends whose sympathetic interest you can count on. Write them letters.

If, in the course of time, you become close to your daughter, and if she and her parents would find it agreeable, you could give a party for the purpose of introducing her to your friends. Miss Manners hopes that she need not tell you that the social emphasis should not be on her illegitimacy and rediscovery, but on your desire to have your grown-up daughter know your circle.

Family Reunions

DEAR MISS MANNERS:

I have taken on the challenge of organizing our first family reunion. I have a date for late this year, and that is all I have thus far. I am afraid I don't know anything about family reunions, including whom to invite, what to plan, and how to arrange for payment of services and facilities used. But I am determined to have a successful reunion in spite of skepticism on the part of my immediate family.

GENTLE READER:

Miss Manners trusts that the purpose of the family reunion is to strengthen the clan's ties. She mentions this because a reunion is also an excellent opportunity for starting intrafamily feuds that can carry on through the generations, and if you wish to avoid that, you must take certain precautions.

The first is to shape your guest list strictly by degree of relationship, making no allowances for your or anyone else's personal antipathies. In other words, you may decide that fourth cousins twice removed are to be excluded, but you may not decide that Great Uncle Tibbit, who has been housecleaning for years by sending his refuse around as wedding presents, should not be invited. Nor should threats— "If you have her, I certainly won't come, so you'd better choose"—be entertained. The answer must be a firm "That's terrible—we will miss you." However, there must, these days, be some flexibility about the definition of nuclear families. If Cousin Annabelle says that that creature is, in effect, her husband, then he is. You may emphasize the fact that this is a family occasion, not a social one, and that it is for relatives, not prospective relatives one met the night before last, but demanding legal proof of relationships is not worth the emotional effort.

The entertainment at a family reunion consists of seeing who looks like whom, catching up on scandal, and taking comfort in realizing that others share the same heritage of advantages and disadvantages that you do. Most of this must be done by people milling around, saying, "I'd know you anywhere; you must be Maud Monroe's granddaughter" or "My, my, the last time I saw you was twenty-five years ago and you were in a miniskirt then, too," and "Weren't you once married to somebody else?" There is a different standard at family reunions about what kind of remark is offensive. That is to say, these things may still be offensive but, since they are family members who are there to mind one another's business, the threshold for taking offense must be higher.

Being seated for dinner necessarily limits the news-gathering operation, although it should provide an opportunity for deeper explorations with one's neighbors. A family reunion is therefore one event at which it is usually better for people to make their own seating arrangements.

You might take just a bit of that time to have someone who is not long-winded give general, bland news: who is there from where; what births, marriages, and deaths have taken place recently; and any special honors family members have received. How old anyone is now, who has been divorced, and who is out of work and looking for rich relatives to extend opportunities should be left for individuals to volunteer or probe. All you need provide, then, for after-dinner entertainment is a large room.

You should encourage everyone to bring memorabilia. Miss Manners went to a delightful reunion where such things were requested in advance, and the hosts arranged the snapshots to make several family trees for separate branches, as it were. She also heard some amazing stories there that her mother had neglected to tell her.

Whatever the financial arrangements are, they must be made clear from the beginning and seem, on the surface, to be the same for everyone. People are generally expected to pay for their own transportation and accommodations, and a list of hotels with a range of prices should be made available to out-of-towners. The hosts usually provide the food and drink, but if you need contributions, announce in your first letter what amount will be needed from each to meet the expenses. You should not enforce the kind of fairness that would give your cousin who collects racing cars the same obligations as Great-Grandmother, who worked herself to the bone putting two generations through school. Inability to pay should be gracefully ignored, and if you are able to send tickets to those who couldn't otherwise attend, or to put up the frail members of the family in your house, do so, but without opening the matter to discussion.

Tissue Paper with Invitations

DEAR MISS MANNERS:

My son recently asked me why there are thin, translucent papers which come with invitations and/or announcements. I responded that they were the engraver's assurance that the ink wouldn't smear, and that they (the little papers) should be discarded before the sending out of the invitations and/or announcements by the inviter and/or announcer. Did I give him the wrong information?

GENTLE READER:

No, you are right, and no and/or about it. Keeping the tissues is like keeping the cellophane covering on a new lampshade. It suggests a state of timidity in which one is in perpetual waiting for an occasion grand enough to remove the protective wrappings and take one's chances with life.

WEDDING ANNIVERSARIES

The Memory Book

DEAR MISS MANNERS:

When my parents celebrate their fiftieth anniversary, their eleven children want to do something special for them. But the children are married and scattered, and it's hard to get them all together to plan anything. We want to rent a room at the Fire Department for a get-together and have friends in. I would like the friends to write a note or send a favorite picture they might have of my parents, or a special memory they would like to send me to make a memory book. Would something like this be right, or a money tree? They don't need gifts. Do we send out invitations? How should they read?

GENTLE READER:

The memory book is a lovely idea; do not embarrass your parents by opening a charitable financial drive on their behalf. As you must explain what you are doing, you might as well combine your request with your invitation in a brief letter. (You could do a third-person invitation card—"The children of/Mr. and Mrs. Clarence Tyler/request the pleasure of your company . . ." and so on—but, as you would then have to enclose a note with the instructions anyway, this seems unnecessarily complicated.) Eleven people cannot sign a letter, and you probably want to divide up the task anyway. The kind of letter each of you could write is:

Dear Mr. and Mrs. Jenkins,

My brothers and sisters and I are giving a party to celebrate the fiftieth wedding anniversary of our parents, Isabelle and Clarence Tyler, on Saturday, October 25th, at 7:00 P.M. at the Fire Department. We very much hope you can be with us.

We want to give them a Memory Book, and are asking each of their friends to send us a special memory or picture for it [telling them where the things will be collected].

Fund-Raising

DEAR MISS MANNERS:

My wife and I will be observing our thirty-fifth wedding anniversary this year. Since I am a musician and will be producing a cassette tape of my music this year, would it be proper for me to give a concert on that evening, introducing some of the music that will be on the cassette and offering copies for sale? A reception for the people who attend the concert would follow the performance.

GENTLE READER:

How much are you charging for drinks? How about souvenir programs? How nice that you want to share the sentiment of the occasion with friends. Have you thought, however, of simply entertaining them? It could either be in the traditional way, of offering food, drink, and conversation, or you could give a little musicale, preceded or followed by those ingredients—provided that you inform people of the nature of the occasion beforehand. But you cannot use a social event for merchandising purposes.

Anniversary Presents

DEAR MISS MANNERS:

My wife and I are planning a party to celebrate our twenty-fifth wedding anniversary at a local inn with 350 relatives and friends. If guests do bring gifts, what is the proper procedure to register them, and how should thank-yous be handled?

GENTLE READER:

As presumably not all guests will be bringing presents, you do not want to make too much of a fuss over those who do. It would be sensible to have an inconspicuous place where you can easily stash them, taking the time (or assigning someone else) to write the names on the packages. You may open them in private after the party and write your thanks.

Attendants' Duties Years Afterward

DEAR MISS MANNERS:

Thirty-nine years ago, I was maid of honor for a friend, and now my sister and I have been invited to celebrate their fortieth anniversary in Hawaii. We are saving to pay our own way. Do I, as maid of honor, have any duties or obligations for this get-together of family and friends? As rubies are out of the question, what would be an appropriate gift?

GENTLE READER:

Don't worry about those rubies. The concepts of milestones being silver (for twenty-five years) and gold (for fifty) have been carried to the point of absurdity by commercial interests attempting to dictate consumer themes for every step along the way. Your present should simply be something that you believe, out of your friendship and knowledge of them both, they might enjoy. As maid of honor, your chief obligation was to tell the bride how lovely she looked and how great her chances were for happiness. Now you merely tell them both how wonderful they look and how glad you are for their obvious happiness.

~*9*~

Funerals

and

Bereavement

Funerals

"We're not here to mourn a death," someone inevitably announces. "We're here to celebrate a life."

Miss Manners squirms ever so slightly when she hears this new funeral cliché. The squirm is slight because she knows that it is well meant. Still, she does squirm, because the denial of mourning—the natural reaction to the mysterious outrage of death—seems to her to be based on the unreasonable premise that happiness is the only proper emotion and sadness something that ought always to be disguised, even at funerals. She also knows that true mourning inevitably consists of focusing on the life that has ended, as well as enabling the bereaved to vent their feelings of deprivation.

In spite of this reservation, Miss Manners generally approves of what is rapidly becoming a standard format for funerals. She still believes that the traditional funeral, at which the deceased's clergyman speaks knowledgeably of that person's life, in addition to offering religious ritual and comfort, is an excellent one. But this depends on the departed's having spent a good part of his lifetime in the same parish, which is now a rarity. All too often now, the deceased and the clergyman may hardly or never have known each other, either because one of them was a newcomer or because the family sought religious affiliation only at the time of death. The result is a particularly awkward form in which presiding clergymen are wont to cover the gap with such statements as "I never actually had the privilege of knowing her in life, but I have heard so much about her from her family that I wish

I had. She was someone who, above all, loved life''—as if the rest of us don't love life.

In the new format, not without its own religious antecedents, the clergyman does the sacramental part and the person's life is depicted by those who actually did know him. At best, this presents an intimate and vivid picture of the qualities for which the deceased was valued, and can be a moving and memorable tribute. At worst, it is an awkward or even boring program at which one learns more about the vanities of the speakers than about the subject of the funeral.

Planning such an event should be a job of honor for someone close to the deceased but not in the immediate family. In general, the spouse, parents, or children should also be discouraged from speaking, which is apt to be too heavy an emotional burden for them. A few friends and colleagues who can talk about different aspects of the person's life should be selected, briefly interviewed so that the talks are not repetitive, and given a time limit, depending on their number. Sometimes there is a general invitation to those present to come forward to say something. The service, which may also include prayer and music, should last about an hour.

Show-business practices, as if the departed were being "roasted" at a jolly party, are particularly offensive. One person may make brief introductions of the others, but references to a "master of ceremonies," or applause for talks or music, are highly inappropriate. Speakers should be identified by their relationship ("We grew up together," "I was his boss for seventeen years"), not their own achievements. Any temptation to show how important one was to the deceased, rather than the other way around, and any stories of which the speaker turns out to be the hero, should be ruthlessly suppressed. One should talk of the person's laudable qualities, using anecdotes that make these vivid. Throwing in examples of the person's foibles is acceptable if done affectionately, and some humor works, but this should be used judiciously and sparingly. The customary closing is a succinct statement of a general or particular way in which the person will be missed.

A subdued social gathering after the service, which is an adaptation of the old preburial wake, is another innovation of which Miss Manners approves. Participants should remember the occasion, and use it to talk informally about the departed and to comfort one another. General conversation, especially when it is heralded with cries of "Great to see you!", is inappropriate. Don't argue with Miss Manners that you know your departed friend would have liked nothing better than for you to have a jolly time. Sure he would—but only if your thoughts, jolly and otherwise, are focused on him. No one wants to be forgotten at his own memorial service.

The Bereaved Companion

DEAR MISS MANNERS:
I believe a breach of etiquette was committed recently at a funeral for a wonderful man who, the last three years of his life, was dying of prostate cancer and very

crippled. A lovely lady had been his constant companion for twenty years. He was very dependent on her gracious, loving care twenty-four hours a day those last years. They had never married. His only child, a daughter, did not have the minister mention this lady in any way as his loyal friend, nurse, and so on. Her grown children, sister, brother, and her other relatives and friends attended the funeral. Needless to say, all were upset, as all the minister talked about was the man's dead wife. Please let me know the proper etiquette in this case.

GENTLE READER:
  Funeral etiquette has not gotten around to recognizing the "constant companion" of the deceased. Without saying it shouldn't, Miss Manners is merely pointing out that etiquette is going hand in hand with the law in such cases, rather than leaping ahead of it. However lovely the lady was, she is not likely to have legal rights, either.
  Friends who knew and approved the situation should certainly give this lady the courtesy of treating her as an immediate survivor. That is to say, they should warmly sympathize with her in her bereavement. Those who did not know or did not approve of the arrangement cannot be forced to treat her as the widow, any more than they are obliged to share with her an inheritance the deceased did not specify.

Learning Ritual

  In the garden of the house where Miss Manners grew up, there were two plain stones, one marked "General Eisenhower" and the other "General MacArthur." No, Miss Manners was not reared in a military cemetery. These were the names of two honorable family pets, who had lost their lives—well, perhaps not gloriously, but not ignominiously, either, considering that they were goldfish. They had been buried with all due solemnity and honors.
  Miss Manners brings this up now, not for the bathos of it—in due course, she did reconcile herself to the deaths—but to illustrate the importance of easing life's difficulties with rituals. The pet funeral, with its shoebox coffins, lineup of small mourners, taps (if anyone is old enough to be taking music lessons), and home-etched tombstones, was a not uncommon feature of family life when the ritual of the funeral itself was still understood. But ritual has come to be so much eroded by "dealing with" emotions through talk that the comfort of traditional forms, particularly for children, is often slighted.
  Miss Manners has nothing against talk; she practices it herself nearly all the time. Talk has a big place in the ritual of bereavement, it being a great comfort to exchange anecdotes about the departed. It just has its limits. Miss Manners is thinking of the pathetic little modern routine whereby one seeks to console a child by inquiring, "How do you feel about this?"
  "Lousy," says the child.

"I want you to know," says the adult, "that it's okay to feel lousy." That generally doesn't cheer up the child, for some reason. So the adult goes on: "It's okay to feel angry, too. It's okay to feel deserted. It's okay to cry. It's okay to feel that life is unfair." Okay, okay. Then what?

Of course, the impressionable child who hadn't yet thought of that full panoply of negative emotions is out of luck, as is the child who begins secretly to consider, "Well, it's not all that bad." Even the child who may have been troubled by the nature of his grief hasn't been comforted. "Permission" to feel bad may deal with the secondary problem of the person who felt bad about feeling bad, but it doesn't do much for the primary cause.

Part of the function of ceremony is also to legitimize emotion by going public with it. Following formal, dignified ways of doing this, without having to improvise the behavior to go with powerful but tangled feelings, can provide the same type of relief that the permission technique is designed to produce.

Funeral ritual has major additional advantages. The survivor is kept busy at a difficult time, with the motivation and satisfaction doing something for the departed. His attention is focused on the loss itself, rather than on his feelings about the death. He will not later find himself feeling bad about having felt bad instead of just having felt bad about someone.

Someone? Didn't we start out talking about goldfish? Miss Manners was, indeed, thinking of the value of teaching ritual as a method of dealing with life's difficulties when, with any luck, the child has not yet had to deal with the death of a person. Contrary to adult propaganda, children do not know how to behave naturally in frightening situations. The knowledge that there are set ways of facing these things emphasizes the repeating patterns of life, which is somewhat reassuring when they have been cruelly disrupted.

Family Duty

DEAR MISS MANNERS:

My husband's maternal grandmother died recently. She was cremated, and then there was a memorial service. My three-year-old son and I did not attend. Was I wrong? Should I have made my son attend? He only met her once. There was a to-do afterward, and again we did not attend. Neither did my husband.

Should I, as a relative, have sent a letter of condolence to my mother-in-law? Should I have sent letters to the aunts and uncles? My husband has two living grandparents, and I have three. When one of them dies, do we, as relatives, send letters to the surviving spouses?

What about my son? Do I make him attend the funerals? He is close, physically and emotionally, to only one of his great-grandparents. I guess what I need to know is: What roles do in-laws, grandchildren, and great-grandchildren play in the death ceremony?

GENTLE READER:

Relatives take part in such rituals for two reasons: to show respect for the deceased and to sustain one another in bereavement. Because it is a family matter, Miss Manners is tempted to suggest that people tailor their actions to the needs of the individuals concerned, but she dares not do that. Even at the happiest family occasions, people are only too quick to rationalize behaving in ways that are based only on their individual desires; and funerals are so upsetting that the bereaved can be trusted even less to judge what is best for everyone.

A three-year-old is generally too young to derive anything but fear from a funeral. However, there are some instances in which a child should make a limited appearance—if a parent has died, for example, and it will be a comfort to the child later in life to know that he paid full ceremonial respects. Miss Manners does not quarrel with your not having your son attend. When he is older, he should understand that this is a family duty, to be performed whether or not he is emotionally close to his relatives. Unless you had absolutely no one with whom to leave your son, you should have attended the funeral and the wake. Your husband should certainly have been at both.

Condolence letters within a family are written by the more distant members to those more closely affected. Those who are together during the funeral planning, caring for one another, need not also write because they will have already expressed their concern and respect extensively.

Paying Respects

DEAR MISS MANNERS:

I am at the age when a lot of my friends' parents are dying. Is it proper to attend a funeral of a parent I didn't know? My thoughts have been that I go to a funeral to honor the family members, i.e., my friend, who has lost a parent or sibling. I don't want to be improper on such a solemn occasion. But I love my friends dearly and would appreciate it if they came to comfort me and acknowledge a death in my family, even if they didn't know my relative personally.

GENTLE READER:

Miss Manners seldom receives the question and answer in the same letter. Yours don't leave her much to do but congratulate you on your sensitivity and commend your attitude.

Painful Presence

DEAR MISS MANNERS:

A young man was killed by an automobile while riding his motorcycle. Would it be proper for the party that was driving the automobile to attend the boy's funeral, or would it be more appropriate to not attend, to avoid an embarrassing confrontation with the victim's friends and family?

GENTLE READER:

Miss Manners is not nearly so concerned about the embarrassment of the driver as she is about the agony of the bereaved, who would have to add to their burdens the necessity of being civilized to the agent of the boy's death. No, that person does not belong among mourning relatives and friends, but that is not to say that he should not demonstrate evidence of extreme contrition. It is just better to express it in a letter; it will be easier for the family to make a measured response to that than to a direct confrontation.

What to Say

DEAR MISS MANNERS:

What does one say to bereaved relatives standing in expectant lines at funerals and wakes? I recently passed through such a line after a church funeral, feeling my usual tongue-tied self, and was especially stalled when I was passed to the elderly wife of the deceased, who said, "It was so fortunate that John went so quickly. He would have hated living with a stroke!"

I muttered a response, but while getting into the car with my husband, I speculated about whether I could have said, "Oh, that is good, then! You must be very happy." This speculation caused me, to have a laughing fit, which my husband said caused him great embarrassment. I feel that it was your fault, since you have provided nothing proper for me to say.

GENTLE READER:

Miss Manners is sorry about having omitted saying that laughing fits and smart retorts to widows are not permitted at funerals, no matter what the provocation. The all-purpose answer she has given, "I'm so sorry," still applies, even if a non sequitur to the remark of the bereaved. The widow is unlikely to snap back with "If I think it's all for the best, what are you so sorry about?"

Assumptions

DEAR MISS MANNERS:

For years, I kept up a regular correspondence with a classmate who had moved to a distant part of the country; then, suddenly, correspondence from her ceased. Since she had been very ill, I presumed she had died, but I received no notification from her family to verify this. When my mother died, I went through her address book and wrote to everyone listed to let them know what had happened, whether I knew them or not. I believe my friend's family owed me the same courtesy even though I was not personally acquainted with them.

GENTLE READER:

Yes, it is thoughtful and kind to notify friends of a death, but is it either thoughtful or kind to take offense at a guess? Surely you should want to inquire about an ill friend and, if necessary, console her family. It is possible that they omitted a task in their bereavement, but it is also possible that your friend is incapacitated and her family is overwhelmed with care.

Postmortem Messages

DEAR MISS MANNERS:

I recently learned of my terminal illness and impending death. I have been enjoying making necessary plans and arrangements regarding my demise but am stumped on one aspect. I would like to arrange to send death notices (same format as wedding announcements). Recipients would primarily be my Christmas card list, which consists of good friends from the past in distant cities, with whom I am in contact only once or twice a year.

Should the card simply bear my name and dates of birth and death, or an opening line such as "It is with regret that you are informed . . ." ? Should it include information such as the cause of death or the address of parents (I am single and have always lived alone), or perhaps a request for a donation to my favorite charity? I had thought of preaddressing the envelopes myself. After my death, an appointed friend would have the cards printed and send them off. I have never heard of this being done before. If it is indeed beyond the scope of good manners, how does one inform out-of-town friends of a death?

GENTLE READER:

Please allow Miss Manners to redirect your efforts in a way that would be infinitely more kind to your friends and to your own memory. You are alive. Can you not use your time and those envelopes to write to your friends individually, letting them know that you care about them? Such a note, even if it is only a line or two, will, Miss Manners assures you, be treasured forever. In contrast, a pseudo-wedding announcement addressed in your hand would be chilling, if not grotesque. Friends are notified of a death by a relative or friend of the deceased, either by telephone (so that they may arrange to attend the funeral) or note. It would be helpful for you to leave such a person a list of names, addresses, and telephone numbers; information you want supplied to those who ask and to the newspaper for the obituary; and your wishes about charitable donations.

Condolences

"What can I do?" polite people ask when there is a tragedy, such as severe illness or death, among their acquaintance. "Please let me know if there is anything I can do." In subtler times, the extent to which the speaker was actually volunteering to help depended on which words were emphasized.

"What can I do?" or "Please let me know if there is anything I can do" meant, "If you're really desperate, you can call me, but otherwise, I trust you're already in good hands and will be all right." It was the polite way for a fairly distant acquaintance to express concern. The correct answer was "Oh, that's so kind of you, but I'll be fine, really."

People who were actually anxious to pitch in and help knew to say "What can *I* do?" or "Please let me know what I can do." The correct answer (notice the subtle differences) was "Oh, no, that's so kind of you, but I know how busy you are and I'm sure I'll be fine soon." This was followed by "Please, I insist," after a few minutes of which the tragic figure could say, "Well, if it really isn't too much trouble," and then name a small task. The sympathizer would respond immediately with "Yes, yes, of course," and could also negotiate for an additional, larger task.

Most people still seem to know to say "What I can do?" but they all pronounce it the same way, and the exchange about what the person can actually do rarely occurs. This often leaves the recipients of this particular politeness bitterly remarking that "Lots of people asked what they could do, but then nobody did anything."

There is, by the way, still lots to do for someone in the midst of tragedy. What to do in the individual case will vary; different cases may even require opposite actions. For example, some people feel that they need to be alone at such a time, while others wish not to be left alone. So, figuring out whether to offer company or help in fending off company requires subtlety, too.

Let us first get back to learning how to make an opening offer of help that is to be taken literally. People who have done their basic duty (such as making one visit, sending a kind letter, attending a funeral, or whatever is appropriate to the tragedy), and merely wish to signify their sympathy and their availability only for extreme emergencies, can continue using the bland pronunciation of "Let me know if there's anything I can do." Others must insist all the more, to make up for the current lack of understanding. First, one should say, "No, no, I really mean it. It would be a comfort to me, too, to feel that I could be of some help, however trivial," and then make specific suggestions.

Each of the suggestions should be bolstered vehemently. "Do you want me to stay with you? This happens to be a particularly free time for me, and I would like nothing better than to be with you at this time. I won't hear another word; let me get my things." Or "Okay, if you really want to be left alone, let me field your calls for you, and make your excuses. Give me a list of whom to call."

Other services one might offer are baby-sitting, food (conventionally, one brings food for condolence visits anyway, but it can also be useful during other difficult periods), shopping or errand running, answering mail, or supplying distractions in whatever form might take the person's mind off his troubles. We do want particularly to avoid hurting people's feelings while they are down. That is why Miss Manners keeps insisting that the more difficult the situation, the more etiquette is required.

Memorial Contributions

DEAR MISS MANNERS:

I have been a widow for five months and have acknowledged each kindness (flowers, food, gently worded letters) with a personal note, rather than the printed variety supplied by the funeral home. As time has passed, however, I find that many of my letters are now thanks for contributions to institutions, etc., to which neither of us belonged to or had any interest. I made no "in lieu of flowers" request in the newspaper obituary, but my husband's memberships and special interests were sufficiently chronicled. Why do people feel that a monetary tribute is necessary at all? I ask this not in a spirit of complaint, but because I want to clarify my thinking.

I suppose all this began before the days of embalming, when the scent of flowers was needed as a camouflage, and the beauty of flowers *is* uplifting. As the family members from far and near gather, extra food is helpful, as are the hugs and kind words of visiting neighbors. But is a death a reason to make a contribution to XYZ church/institution/college? Please, my thinking and emotions are taxed right now. Help me sort this out so that I may be better able to help when a friend becomes a "survivor."

GENTLE READER:
People affected by a death feel the need to "do something." The tragedy is that anything one does falls pitiably short of satisfying that need. Of course, the best thing to do is to comfort the nearest survivors with the sympathy and practical assistance best suited to each individual. This means visits, letters, and such assistance as bringing food and doing errands. Contributions to causes that were dear to the deceased also fall into that category.

You understand that. One must also understand that many people cannot manage this very well. They sign "sympathy" cards instead of sending letters, or contribute to whatever they think of, rather than inquiring what would be appropriate. Miss Manners is the first to say that they should make the effort to do better. She is also the last to scorn the lesser efforts, because she knows they come from the same feeling of helplessness shared by everyone faced with a loss.

The Memorial Fund

DEAR MISS MANNERS:
Recently, our baby son died of cancer. He was not quite two. Many friends and relatives donated money to organizations or gave money to us. We put that money into his account. My husband and I want to start a yearly fund-raiser in our son's name. Our goal is a laboratory or an intern or a piece of equipment in his name. Is it wrong to ask friends and family again for money? We would send out letters asking for donations on a yearly basis. We are very inexperienced in raising money and do not want our family and friends to become annoyed or feel obligated.

GENTLE READER:
Grieved as Miss Manners is for you, she must stop you before you prepare more heartache for yourselves. By all means, work to memorialize your son. Do so with the money you have been given, anything you are able to add to it, and through volunteer work. Do not attempt to establish the kind of major drive it would take to raise enough money for a laboratory. Such fund-raising, difficult at best to keep up, depends on the memories people have of the deceased person's own contributions to their and others' welfare, which is obviously impossible in this case. You will only succeed in making those who genuinely sympathize with you in your loss feel that they must exaggerate their feelings and contributions inappropriately, which would create an emotional rift between you and the people who care most about you.

The Combined Greeting-Condolence Card

DEAR MISS MANNERS:

A dear friend's wife died tragically just a few days before his birthday. I wanted to include a note of condolence in his birthday card, but my wife claimed that this would be totally inappropriate and that I should send two separate cards.

GENTLE READER:

One reason that Miss Manners despises greeting cards is that they are never, by definition, tailored for the individual situation. No, you cannot send two messages, one saying "Happy birthday!" and the other saying "Sorry your wife died!" either together or in rapid succession.

Surely you care enough about this friend to think about his plight. Once you do, it will occur to you that (1) the death of the wife, occurring only once, is more important than the birthday and (2) he isn't going to have a happy birthday under any circumstances this year, and it would look callous to wish him one. The appropriate sentiment is something like "I am so terribly sorry to hear of your tragic loss. Especially today, on your birthday, my sympathies and thoughts are with you." Please write this out yourself, on a plain sheet of paper. Miss Manners hates to think of your running around town demanding a birthday-sympathy greeting-card combination.

A Mixed Blessing

DEAR MISS MANNERS:

If a married couple is blessed with a multiple birth, but shortly thereafter one of the children dies, how should one acknowledge the events? A simple message of congratulations seems oblivious, while a sympathy card seems lacking. Realizing that one must write his own response, what does one properly say?

GENTLE READER:

Indeed, one must, as one should for any difficult situation. Write a letter in which you first offer your congratulations on the birth of the surviving children. Then, in a separate paragraph, recognize the loss with a few words expressing your sympathy. The important thing is not to attempt to connect the two emotions. The parents will know only too well that it is possible to feel both joy and grief at the same time, without the death's spoiling their pleasure in their living children or their mourning for the one being lessened by the fact that the other children survived.

Condolences for a Murder

DEAR MISS MANNERS:

While reading the paper, I ran across an article about siblings killing other siblings. Two of my close friends were named. Jerry had killed his sister Sharon. I met them six years ago, and when I moved a year ago, we lost contact. I have gotten their mother's phone number, and would like to call and give condolences and visit Sharon's grave, so I need to find out its location. How should I approach their mother, or is it rude of me to do so? I would also like to write to Jerry. This is all very touchy and I don't want to cause anyone any more pain, but I'd like to contact them both.

GENTLE READER:

No doubt, this is a touchy situation. Being the mother of both the murderer and the victim is bound to give rise to complex feelings. When you call her, as Miss Manners admires you for planning to do offer her your sympathy for "the tragedy" without going into any specifics. The bereaved are comforted to know that others appreciate their suffering but seldom, even in less touchy cases, care to hear anyone put a moral to the story.

Belated Condolences

DEAR MISS MANNERS:

My father recently found out about the death of his former boss. The man died six months ago. Dad asked me if he should send a condolence card to the family. I advised him not to send one, since it happened such a long time ago, and it might reopen the family grief.

GENTLE READER:

What do you imagine—that the family has forgotten its loss, and will be devastated to find out that someone else remembers? The opposite is probably true. Six months is likely to be just when the flurry of outside attention and the duties associated with a death have lessened, and the bereaved have the double burden of their own loss and the feeling that others have forgotten.

Please encourage your father not to send a condolence card, but a letter, in which he extolls the virtues of the deceased and relates any incidents he can that reflect well upon him.

A Ghastly Mistake

DEAR MISS MANNERS:

About two years ago, I made the acquaintance of a young man through business contacts and subsequently worked with him in our related professions. Although we did not know each other well, we exchanged brief correspondence, i.e., birthday and Christmas cards, and so on. I had not seen this gentleman for close to a year when I was informed that his lovely young wife was terminally ill. After having received this information, not two weeks had passed, when I was told by another individual that she had died. Although I would have felt awkward involving myself in the events surrounding a funeral, I did not hesitate to send a card and a letter of condolence.

I was informed last week, by yet another individual, that the young woman is not deceased, but still, tragically, most seriously ill with a supposedly fatal disease. Naturally, I am both mortified and furious. Mortified that I have sent a letter of condolence when it was not appropriate, and furious at the rumor monger who could be so callous as to report on someone's death without firsthand knowledge. Feeling that I am already more deeply involved in a passing acquaintance's life than I care to be, what should my next course of action be, if any? Two other friends are in the same boat in regard to this hideous rumor, and we anxiously await your reply.

GENTLE READER:
This is awful. This is so awful that Miss Manners can hardly bear to think about it. There are few innocently committed etiquette crimes for which the best solution is for the perpetrator to disappear from the face of the earth, but this is one of them. Isn't that what you feel like doing?

Nevertheless, Miss Manners feels it her duty to come up with a less drastic alternative. She dares not call it a solution, because whatever you do will cause further pain to this person, to whom you have already inadvertently caused pain. That cannot be avoided. Just hearing your name would cause him pain.

Your own pain might be somewhat relieved by writing him to apologize for what you must describe as a hideous mistake, which you thank God is untrue. Make no statements about the health of his wife, but simply send her your regards to indicate that you again think of her as a functional human being. Do not use that pitiful excuse about the nasty "rumor monger." There is no such thing as a person who goes around falsely announcing deaths for the fun of it.

Omitted Sympathy

DEAR MISS MANNERS:
I lost my mother after a long battle with cancer, which was, of course, a difficult time for my entire family. My husband called my friend, who has been fairly close for several years and has known of my mother's illness from the beginning, and told her of our loss the day after Mom's death. Time went by. Mom's memorial service was in a distant city, and I was away for a week or so. I did not receive a card, phone call, or message from her conveying any sympathy.

At first, I didn't let it bother me. I know that people are busy, and we haven't always been timely. Six weeks have gone by. I have learned that grief does not necessarily have a time limit. I really wasn't keeping track of this friend's lack of response, but when I talked to her on the phone, she still didn't even say so much as "I'm sorry." Furthermore, she even used my mother's death as a reference point for an activity in her own life.

DRL

My dear Lars,

We were all terribly distressed to hear about your dear mother. When Gregory first brought you into our family, your mother was kind enough to begin a correspondence with me, which has afforded me great pleasure. What a lovely lady she was. I have always regretted that geographical distance kept us from visiting each other.

My husband joins me in sending you our deepest sympathy and warmest wishes.

Affectionately yours,

Daffodil Right

Tuesday

A CONDOLENCE LETTER. *This can only be written on Mrs. Right's personal paper because hers is so frightfully restrained. Blue or grey, although correct for most letters, would not have done. Unmarked white or ecru paper is always proper.*

May 17th

Dear Mrs. Right,

Your kind letter is a great comfort to me. My mother thought the world of you, and was as grateful as I am for the warmth that you and Mr. Right have shown me.

With fondest regards,
Lars

THE REPLY. *The black bordered paper is not to show off, but because the bereaved wants to warn friends that he is not up to writing his usual witty letters. Mourning paper is hard to find, however, and plain white paper is just as correct.*

I have been stewing about this and wondering what to do. I understand that I really can't solicit a sympathetic response from her, as that would indeed make it worthless. I would love to be able to simply toss it to the winds, but I just can't. I sent her a little "I'd love to hear from you" card, which is something we've exchanged before when one of us thinks the other has been neglectful. But I haven't had any response. How can I overcome this difficulty?

GENTLE READER:
By understanding how much of a burden is put on people when we dispense with manners in favor of individuals' decisions based on what they "feel comfortable with." No one feels comfortable with the awesome task of trying to comfort the bereaved. Regardless of a friend's true feelings, it is awkward and difficult to attempt to share the grief of the closely bereaved. That is why convention informs people of what to do. A letter saying "I'm so sorry," a simple but solemn visit—those are the forms that tradition demands to demonstrate sympathy.

Just as these forms can be followed by people who don't really care, they can also be avoided by people who do care. Either is reprehensible, but possible. These forms are important because they are a comfort. Your friend has been cowardly and callous by avoiding the subject, and Miss Manners does not defend her. She only suggests that if the friendship is really worth preserving, you might ask her whether she is really so indifferent to your feelings or whether, in fact, she was paralyzed by not knowing what to do.

Restating Sympathy

DEAR MISS MANNERS:
What is the proper response when you've sent a sympathy card to someone and, when you see them later, they say, "Thank you so much for the card; it was sweet of you." Do you say "thank you," or what?

GENTLE READER:
The ordinary response to "Thank you" is "You're welcome." In this case, the courtesy offered—the card—is so slight in comparison with the reason—the death—that one instead reiterates the sentiments: "Oh, I was so sorry to hear of your mother's death; I remember her fondly; you've been very much in my thoughts," and so on.

Acknowledgements

DEAR MISS MANNERS:
My brother died four months ago, and as he did not have a wife or children, most condolences (flowers, money, food, deeds, etc.) were directed to our elderly mother. Now, after all these months, she is still so distressed (and she is also a

procrastinator) that she has not sent out more than ten thank-you notes. She refuses to accept help from anyone or let my other brother or me near the list of those who helped. She keeps saying, "People will understand." I say they won't and feel very bad about the situation. Is it too late to send acknowledgments? Should any reference be made to their tardiness?

GENTLE READER:

You are right that people will not understand. What they are after is not praise for their gestures so much as an acknowledgment that their interest in the deceased was reciprocated to the extent that their condolences really meant something to the bereaved. This should be done now, without excuses. If Miss Manners' explanation does not convince your mother of the importance of doing this, try again to get that list and do it yourself. All of you owe it to your brother to let those who cared about him know that this interest was deemed to be important.

Acknowledging Cards

DEAR MISS MANNERS:

When sending thank-you cards to those who have sent mass cards, flowers, and so on to the family of the deceased, should one also send them to the folks who have sent sympathy cards? My daughter says no; I send them as a courtesy.

GENTLE READER:

Preworded cards are the minimal form of expressing emotion, and thus sympathy cards are not in the category of warm gestures that require letters of thanks. It is, however, always nice to show more courtesy than strict rules require. But it seems that you, too, are sending only cards in thanks, rather than letters. These will do fine in exchange for sympathy cards, but those who have sent letters or flowers deserve a few personal words.

Bereavement

Wearing Mourning

DEAR MISS MANNERS:

My husband of fifty years passed away, and I hope you can help me do the correct thing. I don't know what the rules of mourning are. I'm old-fashioned and want to wear black for a year at least. The way I feel now, it might be forever. Do I have to wear stockings all summer? Around the house and during the day? I would wear them if I went out in the evening with the family.

GENTLE READER:

Do not imagine that Miss Manners is attempting to discourage you from assuming formal mourning when she informs you that it is no longer the custom. It was a good custom, serving to protect the bereaved from ordinary social treatment when they might be unable to handle it emotionally, and Miss Manners is willing to help you adapt it for modern use, but we must understand the spirit. Mourning signifies that one is temporarily withdrawing from normal cheerful society because one does not feel up to it. Using the trappings of mourning to show off one's feelings, or to dampen the spirits or activities of others, was always considered vulgar.

One does not, therefore, wear obvious mourning to an office, or as casual wear, or to any social event. This used not to be a problem, as a woman in mourning simply stayed home and a man's black hatband or black suit was fairly inconspicuous.

A widow wore deep mourning (black clothes with plain, matte finishes, with a widow's bonnet and crepe veil) for a year, and then "second mourning," including black ribbons, jet ornaments, and touches of white, gray, and mauve.

Let us adapt this to modern dress. Veiling should be worn only to shield the widow's face at the funeral itself, where Miss Manners prefers it to the current substitute, sunglasses, which look incongruously jaunty. To an office, or when engaging in the normal business of life, wear plain black clothes, with just enough white so that uninformed people don't jokingly ask who died. Miss Manners would not consider black stockings necessary, any more than you need order black-bordered handkerchiefs. As you do not wear mourning casually, you need not worry about events to which you would go stockingless anyway.

If you do attend social events, do not wear mourning, although you may use black, gray, or mauve to avoid dressing gaily. Around the house, unless you have visitors, it doesn't matter. Remember that the purpose of mourning is not to demonstrate loyalty to your late husband but to remind others of your delicate emotional state. Therefore, Miss Manners begs you not to set a time limit. Society no longer recognizes one. Let us instead hope that the time will soon come when, although still bereaved, you feel up to resuming normal life.

The Widow's Rings

DEAR MISS MANNERS:

How long after a woman is widowed can or should she wear her wedding and engagement rings? I have had people give me different answers. Some say a month, others say as long as she wishes. I am a widow and am still wearing both, but if I go out with friends, I notice everyone looking at my ring finger. Should I take them off? I would feel lost without them. I know several others will be watching for your answer.

GENTLE READER:

Oh, so the Torture the Widows Squad is out again, is it? There is no rule of etiquette about the removal of rings. Some widows remove the rings when they feel that they are ready to be available for courtship; others never remove them.

Marking a House of Mourning

DEAR MISS MANNERS:

Last year, I suffered the loss of my brother and his wife, who were killed in an auto accident on their way to visit me and my family. We managed to escort the caskets home and do what was necessary in the state of adrenaline push and numbing shock. Upon our return home, the whole horror and grief swept over us. Our family doctor counseled us that we were truly ill, and to be especially kind to ourselves.

I was home alone during the day. It seemed as if everyone who pushes doorbells came here in a constant procession: Good causes, bad causes, zealot missionaries, poll takers, and general inquiries kept me running to the door. Often a simple "No, thank you," followed by a firm push on the door, was not enough to get rid of them. My husband suggested a "Do Not Disturb" sign. Although it might have worked, it would also have driven away those I most needed to see—the friends coming to offer their comfort.

In desperation, I pulled some black satin ribbon from my sewing box and tied a tailored, simple black bow to our door. I know I shouldn't have been hurt, but I was, when some people thought I was being "theatrical." It was an impulsive gesture in the hope that the real intent would be understood and respected. Later, I heard others lament the passing of the formal black wreath, to protect them in their time of need. Can't there be some way to indicate the need for privacy at that time in people's lives? One suffers a good bit to avoid being thought of as theatrical, comic, or just plain odd.

GENTLE READER:

It is odd, indeed, that one must fear being considered odd for requiring a period in which to mourn the dead. In Miss Manners' opinion, it is the modern attempt to do without such emotional safeguards that is odd. Mourning signs serve to warn others of one's state, and just because they were used to excess in previous eras is no reason to abandon them all to a pretense that nothing has happened. She urges you not to concede such phoniness to be normal or to worry that your very sensible behavior violates it.

Sharing Grief

DEAR MISS MANNERS:

Neither my family nor the hospital informed me when my uncle died of cancer. I read about it in the newspapers. I put on a black suit, dark shoes and stockings, and my everyday black coat and drove over to his house, where the family was assembled, preparing to drive in procession to the memorial service at church and then to the graveside ceremony. I had never been to a funeral before, nor have I had the occasion to attend very many formal ceremonies of any kind. It never occurred to me to wonder whether I would do or say the "right thing."

My uncle's passing from this world was a great loss to me, although he and I had disagreed about how the world should be run and by whom. Before he became ill, we had some heated discussions, which upset us both, about the meaning and purpose of life. But I loved him. The rest of the family did not know it, but all our differences were reconciled, and we forgave each other, two weeks before he died.

What bothers me now is that my presence at the funeral was resented by his wife and his son. I think, too, that my wearing black clothes was misunderstood. I was, as it turned out, the only one who dressed that way. I cannot repair my mistake, I'm afraid. I feel that even to make reference to the way I dressed at the funeral would be petty, as well as pointless. But perhaps your readers would do well to inquire whether the immediate family intends to wear black. Or should everyone be advised that traditional mourning clothes are not acceptable anymore? I didn't mean to offend anyone. I just didn't know.

GENTLE READER:

Miss Manners will be glad to discuss the proper clothing worn to funerals, but that is not your problem. Your problem—one that can and must be cleared up— has to do with the emotions of bereavement, not its trappings.

Your uncle's widow and son had cause to believe that you were on bad terms with your uncle when he died. In their grief, shunning you was an exaggerated but understandable form of loyalty. If you did not care for him alive, they must have reasoned, you should not pretend to do so at his death. Only you know that this was not the case. You have eloquently convinced Miss Manners that you loved your uncle in spite of your philosophical differences, and that you were even able to let him know this before he died. Tell the rest of the family. It will make an enormous difference.

Mourning clothes are, of course, a symbol of bereavement, and what your relatives resented was your seeming to make a show of what they thought you did not feel. While it is true that people seldom dress properly for funerals anymore— proper dress being black for the family and subdued, dark clothing for friends—it is certainly not inappropriate to do so. Had your relatives believed that you were genuinely grief stricken, they would not have objected.

Family Comfort

DEAR MISS MANNERS:

I am a retiree, sixty-three years of age, from a family of five—two brothers and two sisters. My mother passed away recently, and my wife and I traveled back East to attend the funeral, staying at my unmarried sister's house, where my mother had lived. The night before the funeral, my brothers, their families, and my forty-year-old niece wanted to come to my sister's home for a social gathering. I was in no mood to socialize because of our bereavement and mourning, so I told them I would prefer not to at a time like that.

From this point on, my niece took over as a self-appointed leader, and my brother initiated the rumor that I prefer to be with my sister only, and not with my brothers. This we heard via the grapevine after our return home. Their behavior at the time was sulky and aloof, which my wife and I felt was ill-mannered and uncalled for. It was surprising to us, because our past relationships with them have been amicable. My wife and I "fogged the issue" by ignoring their behavior, but we found it upsetting. After two months, it still bothers me, and I am wondering if I handled the situation properly. Should I have confronted them and asked the reason for their behavior?

GENTLE READER:

What a sad misunderstanding this is. Miss Manners can hardly think of an instance where a misinterpretation of etiquette can do such damage within a family. The mistake is in your thinking of the family gathering as a "social gathering." One does not attend social events during bereavement, and had this been a true party, you would have been quite right in declining. It is the custom for families to do their mourning together, seeking comfort in one another's presence and in the feelings they share. That is what a gathering of your mother's direct descendants, your siblings and niece, would have been, rather than a social event. They were offended not because you didn't want to party, but because you didn't draw close to them in this time of mutual need. So, while their sulking and aloofness are upsetting, they are, you should recognize, the reaction to a perceived snub—and one of a very intimate nature. Miss Manners asks you to be big about it now and write to them, defusing this behavior.

Legacies

Inheritances

The supreme test of family manners occurs when the bereaved gather to dismantle the house of a deceased relative and to distribute all the belongings, no matter how valuable or trivial, that were not mentioned in the will.

Funerals provide opportunities for unpleasantness among those who have a keen eye for seizing them, and are an excellent occasion for relatives who did not participate in making funeral arrangements to declare them to be either vulgarly showy or "not right by" the deceased. The shortage of time and emotional energy usually postpones the worst, however, and most people confine themselves to criticizing one another's clothes, general demeanor, facial expressions, and whether or not they cried. All of these can be pronounced either disrespectful or hypocritical.

These are mere surface matters. It is later, after the constraints of being observed in their mourning by outsiders, that the family members hit their stride. Customary remarks when the residence of a deceased person is being closed include:

"I know Mamma would have wanted me to have this."

"It seems only fair, since he left you the car, that I should get the equivalent."

689

"I'm entitled to more, because I was the one who looked after them."

"Oh, sure, grab everything. You were always the favorite, weren't you? You always got everything you wanted."

"This goes with my things. It would only look strange in your house."

"You're never going to use it, so why take it?"

"Of course, the jewelry goes to me. It always goes to the eldest."

"I have children and you don't, so I should take this to keep it in the family."

"Papa always meant me to have this, but he never got around to putting it in the will."

Miss Manners hates to intrude on such a domestic scene, but would like to suggest that these arguments are as meaningless as they are ugly. Wills exist in order to allow people to express their intentions about the distribution of their belongings after their death. That they generally do not provide for the distribution of everything they own is presumed to mean that they have no strong feelings about what is left over.

Whether their wishes are fair, as judged by the merits or relationships of the survivors, whether carelessness made them overlook some items, or whether they changed their minds but forgot to alter their wills are issues that it is too late to remedy. They are also matters that look remarkably different to different members of the same family.

The proper form for this sad event is, then, to have the immediate heirs gather and take turns choosing what they want, with no arguments, especially from ancient family history, necessary to bolster the choices. More distant relatives are then asked what they would like.

For conversation, Miss Manners suggests exactly reversing all the above remarks. There is nothing wrong with "I know Mamma would have liked you to have this," "It seems only fair, since I got the car, that you should take more now," and "I think that as the one who took such good care of them, you ought to have whatever you like."

Bequeathing Children

DEAR MISS MANNERS:

During a visit with my brothers and sister at my parents' house, the subject came up of what would happen if we died.

Two couples said that their children would all go to the same other couple. My husband and I are basically like this couple in lifestyle, and we all get along pretty well. We have no children and show our love to all of our nieces and nephews. I was offended that the other couples would make this announcement in front of me, with no recognition of how I might feel. Could I have let them know that my feelings were hurt by their not wanting us to care for the children *and* by their openly announcing it in front of me? Was I better off doing what I did—saying nothing except to my husband?

GENTLE READER:

Did it occur to you to say to each couple, "We also want you to know that we love the children dearly, and would be only too ready to do everything we could for them if anything should happen to you"? No? Why not?

Bequeathing the care of one's children is a bit more than a popularity contest, which is the way you are treating it. The emotional and financial responsibility of rearing orphans is an incredible commitment, and any parent would want to know that it would be undertaken gladly, with no reservations whatsoever. Miss Manners does not know (or ask) why you are childless, and does not know whether your siblings know, either. It may be that they skipped you because they believe you do not want children, or, even if you do, that you are not aware of the commitment that having children entails.

She can promise you that, whether or not they might consider making you guardians—and, for that matter, whether or not they die before you—it would be a great joy to them to hear that you are seriously devoted to the welfare of their children and can be depended upon to help them if they need it. That, Miss Manners believes, is what families are for, not for scrutinizing one another for possible slights.

Obituaries

DEAR MISS MANNERS:

I have noticed new trends in the publishing of public notices of engagements, weddings, and deaths. (Since we all get about equal starts, birth notices have so far remained unchanged.) Wedding announcements are now very long, and tend to go on and on about the accomplishments and social pedigrees of—no, not the young couple—but the parents and grandparents. It is as if they now have a legitimate right to brag.

This tell-all trend also is found in one's final public announcement, and the position seems to be that in death, one's life is an open book. I refer particularly to the mentioning of previous marriages and how they ended. Either this has become mandatory, or else everyone is of the opinion that you just have to do it to show what a good sport you are. Or does everyone have grieving ex-spouses who have to be considered survivors? I call it tasteless.

While I am in good health, I do want to be prepared. My personal request is that no mention be made of my first marriage. It is no secret, nor do I feel ashamed, but it simply adds nothing to the story of my life, unless to say that hardship builds character. There is no need to mention my former husband's name in connection with mine anymore. I certainly would mention all my children, with their correct surnames or married names. This is not the "final slight." There is no animosity, only memory. He has accumulated a number of ex-wives.

My darling husband says that he would comply with my wishes, as he knows it would just kill me otherwise. He's fun to live with but too funny to be trusted with this job. Is it true that a chronological ordering of major legal events is the rule?

The next thing we'll see is all manner of public indignities, with even our school grades published. I digress. Anyway, I once thought that only the rich and famous had to contend with having every detail of themselves laid out for public scrutiny.

GENTLE READER:

The newspaper announcement of a birth, marriage, or death is something oddly between the private announcement, by which people tell their immediate circles the news in their lives, and the newspaper story in which information of interest to the community is set forth. In a private announcement, you can delete what you want, but you do not give your genealogical, social, or professional credentials, as the friends to whom you write presumably know them. An obituary gives whatever information the editor thinks will interest the public, and that includes defunct marriages.

One cannot control the printing of material on the public record. The real difference between the rich and famous and more private citizens is that the latter tend to be the only source of information to the newspaper concerning the births, marriages, and deaths of their immediate families. On the one hand, they can pretend that they include what you consider "bragging" information in a newspaper announcement only because the public wants to know it. On the other hand, they need only neglect to mention information they don't want to be available, and the chances are that it will be omitted. Miss Manners regrets to tell you that it is not customary to prepare one's obituary or possible to edit it when the time comes. You will simply have to trust your nearest survivor, sense of humor and all.

~10~

Protocol

The American Way

In a modest burst of patriotism, Miss Manners will speak in defense of American manners. This is the same Miss Manners who generally deplores those manners. Furthermore, she doesn't plan to let up until every citizen is behaving, and she won't take back anything she has ever said about the sad state of American behavior and its influence on that of other countries. Miss Manners has always believed that manners based on equality and dignity are superior to those dependent on rank and subservience. The theory of American manners is splendid. It is the execution with which we have trouble.

Foreigners are only too ready to remind us of our failings by quarreling with the basic premise. As Fanny Trollope wrote in her 1832 bestseller, *Domestic Manners of the Americans*, it will only be when Americans abandon the absurd quest for equality that they will acquire "the graces, the honours, the chivalry of life" that would enable her to welcome us "to European fellowship." Loath as Miss Manners is to criticize a colleague and the mother of a dear friend (although there is no truth to those rumors about Miss Manners and Anthony Trollope—cannot a lady and gentleman be friends without causing talk?), she cannot pretend to admire such rubbish.

What disturbs her a great deal more is finding Americans who assist such foreigners by agreeing that politeness is incompatible with egalitarianism, and that therefore civility is impossible in America. Some of these Americans conclude that foreign (by which they mean well-to-do English and French) ways are better than American ones and ought to be emulated.

This sort of self-sneering snobbery has unfortunately existed since our country was founded, and the bad luck of its practitioners, in being scorned or misled by the very people they admire, is a source of much merriment to the rest of us. The fact is that the founders of America, while not insensible to the appeal of graceful society (Miss Manners refers you to some of the racier biographies of dear Benjamin Franklin), believed, as does Miss Manners, that good manners can be modified from the basic royal court model, which assumes hereditary class differences, to a democratic one in which honors are modestly apportioned, and only to individuals.

Thus we do not bend our knees to our highest officials (much less to foreign ones, such as visiting royalty). Our highest title is "Mr." (or its female equivalent), as in "Mr. President," and it takes the individual some doing to be addressed by it. There are no titles for members of the President's family, and the wife is properly addressed as "Mrs. Bush" only. "First Lady," although sometimes useful as an identification, always seemed to Miss Manners to be a silly title, fully in keeping with referring to a White House pet as the "First Dog."

Other Americans who agree with the premise of democratic manners come to the opposite conclusion. Commendably anti-snobbish, they unfortunately decide that courtesy must be sacrificed because its practice causes the demise of egalitarianism. "Elitism" is the word they currently use to describe any standard above the lowest. Miss Manners sympathizes with those who are anxious to avoid snobbery, but she has watched sadly as the forces against elitism have come to advocate a sort of social Know-Nothingism.

If it were only practices that emphasize distinctions of birth or wealth that the anti-elitist troops wished to abolish, Miss Manners would be their most fervent leader. In fact, Americans hardly take notice of birth, whatever that means. If there is one practice unfortunately common now at every financial level, it is showing off through competitive purchasing. Smeared by the charge of elitism, any other distinctions seem to be suspect. Any manners that acknowledge differences among individuals, including those of age or achievement, or recognize that some occasions are more serious than others, are condemned. Formality, whether it addressing the elderly by respectful titles or giving symbolic solemnity to the ceremonies of life, is smeared as elitism. This is not a solution to the American dream of a meritocracy whereby anyone can rise to a position of honor through personal effort. Keeping everyone down was never meant to be our way of achieving equality.

A Gesture of Respect

DEAR MISS MANNERS:

I am British, and I understand the point you have made about Americans not curtsying to our Queen. But do Americans know that this is a two-way street? On several occasions, I have been loudly and publicly berated by various of your countrymen simply because I have remained seated while the American national anthem was being played. Not long ago, I was unceremoniously yanked to my feet by an unknown American for what he termed my "disrespect." When I tried to explain that it was just another foreign tune to me, he became even angrier. Yet I'm sure you understand that the two situations are analogous. Things which provoke an immediate and emotional response in one nation simply have no meaning for others, and it would be hypocritical to pretend otherwise for the sake of appearances.

GENTLE READER:

No, the two situations are not analogous. Miss Manners is not the one to enlist when denigrating the importance of appearances, especially in ceremonial matters. A more apt comparison would be that of a person attending services in a church when he is not a member of its religion. He does not have to kneel or repeat the prayers, but he does have to remain silent and stand when the congregation does. He has to refrain from mentioning that the service is "just another routine to me."

One does not bow or curtsy to a foreign monarch because the gesture symbolizes recognition of her power over her subjects. One nevertheless treats her with respect. You do not have to sing another country's national anthem, but standing symbolizes respect, which you should demonstrate. Singing demonstrates allegiance, which you do not demonstrate to any country but your own. The crucial difficulty for most Americans occurs when they wish to do both for our national anthem, and can't remember the words or carry the tune.

Musical Protocol

DEAR MISS MANNERS:

An uncertainty about how to respond when our national anthem is played, other than to stand with respect, has plagued me. I always felt that this was the only response necessary, but often I will see a few people place the right hand over the heart, which I know is correct for the pledge of allegiance to the flag.

What is the proper procedure in singing two songs? I say that "The Star Spangled Banner" is always sung first, but some of the people in my organization say that it is correct to sing first the song that pertains to your religious belief. When a meeting is opened with two national anthems, those of the United States and of a foreign country, when, according to protocol, is "The Star-Spangled Banner" sung, first or second?

GENTLE READER:

The custom is that foreign anthems are sung before our own as a courtesy, but religious songs are not. This is not a question of priorities; it is just that God does not have any one theme song.

One stands at attention for a public rendition of "The Star Spangled Banner." In other words, you don't have to jump up at home before the television ball game, knocking your beer from the arm of the chair. People in uniform salute. The hand-over-the-heart gesture is optional for all and mandatory for civilian men wearing hats, which they remove and hold there. Hatless gentlemen and civilian ladies, with or without hats, may keep their hands at their sides.

Applauding the Anthem

DEAR MISS MANNERS:

I remember, when I was in grammar school, being taught not to applaud after the playing of our national anthem. I was always under the impression that one's national anthem is "presented," not "performed," and therefore the response would not be the same as to a performance. Now, it seems, everybody applauds at the conclusion of the national anthem. Can this be correct? Nobody applauds after "God Save the Queen." What is the proper response to the playing of the national anthem? I still prefer to sing and then be seated.

GENTLE READER:

It is a misplaced attempt at politeness to applaud the national anthem or music at religious services under the mistaken notion that these things are being offered up for the listeners' pleasure and judgment. One expects those who do this to next offer God a special television award for outstanding effort in a creative field. You were also taught, back in those days in grammar school, to do what you knew was right, rather than copying other people when you knew they were doing wrong. (However, after a brief pause, a sports audience may properly—a relative term at sports events—applaud the opening of play.)

Being a Dumb Foreigner

DEAR MISS MANNERS:

I'm interested in American tendencies to say or do the wrong things abroad because of our lack of knowledge about other countries' customs and manners. Could you please tell me some of our biggest mistakes when we travel to other nations?

GENTLE READER:

Major Mistake 1: Not inquiring what local customs are for showing respect, tipping, dressing, accepting what one is offered, issuing compliments, initiating social relationships, eating and drinking, showing gratitude to hosts, minding one's own business, and what time to show up in relation to the time stated on an invitation.

Major Mistake 2: Pretending that one is thoroughly acquainted with local customs, and thereby forgoing the advantage of playing the dumb-but-well meaning foreigner, whose inevitable errors of etiquette will be regarded as amusing and forgivable lapses, rather than vulgar violations of known standards.

America Bashing

DEAR MISS MANNERS:

We like to travel and enjoy meeting people from other places. However, not long ago, the simple question "Are you enjoying your stay in the United States?" was answered by an extended treatise on all the things wrong with the United States. The other non-Americans joined in. As the only Americans at the dinner party (which we hosted in our home!), my husband and I had to listen to America bashing for more than an hour, and we were uncertain about what to say. Our feeble attempts to defend our nation's habits didn't end the discussion. How should one respond when one's nation is heavily criticized (often unfairly)? My husband and I are neither flag wavers nor blindly patriotic. We would like to be able to say something in support of our nation, yet answer politely.

GENTLE READER:

This is the reward we Americans get for our reputation for being open-minded. You probably know what these people say at home about Americans who dare to express anything but worshipful admiration of everything when they are traveling abroad. Miss Manners does not believe that your choice is between submitting to national insult and committing the rudeness of chastising your guests. Just enter their conversation with a few gentle questions and observations:

"Oh, dear, I'm sorry you had so much trouble getting through. What is the telephone system like in your country?"

"No, no, we don't consider that our cuisine. It's what we call 'junk food,' and we love it for snacks and fun, but we also have serious cooking and are really very health conscious. But didn't I hear that American fast food places are doing fabulous business in your country?"

"Well, you see, we enjoy the rough and tumble of the democratic process. Perhaps it's like the way your people turn out for bicycle races."

"You mean to say you've missed our high culture? That's a shame. You should talk to your own countrymen who are in opera or painting or dance about what we're doing here. In fact, you'll find a lot of them here in America."

"Television? Oh, I know. Americans are always so amused when we travel to see American programs that we enjoy as trivial being so carefully and seriously watched abroad."

"Oh, I'm sure they didn't intend to be intrusive. Americans are traditionally both curious and affable, and that kind of casual friendliness is not only meant to be hospitable, but to reflect a real interest in other people."

"You have to understand that our young people don't take those fashions seriously; it's meant as a kind of spoof. We rather like giving youth the chance to try lots of things before they have to accept serious responsibilities. I don't suppose your youth ever rebel."

"Well, you know, we're not worried here about rank. We don't expect the same kind of subservience from service people that you do. It wouldn't seem right here."

"I'm sorry you feel that way. You ought to have the American experience while you're here, and that involves a certain attitude of easygoingness and tolerance and openness. I'd hate to have you go home never having really been here."

Official Life

Miss Manners would like to say a kind word on behalf of American diplomats. Nobody else ever does unless they have been kidnapped. Possibly because diplomats are almost the only people Miss Manners knows who don't brag about "not knowing which fork to use," as if incompetence at the dinner table were a sign of goodness of heart, she has always had a fondness for the profession. She gets thoroughly indignant when she hears the Foreign Service spoken of as comically, if not insanely, frivolous just because it follows certain formal patterns of internationally accepted behavior.

Protocol, which many people seem to regard as vaingloriousness translated into action, is merely a specialized form of etiquette. Both are designed to avoid the misunderstandings that are bound to occur when individuals improvise and when insult may therefore be taken when none is intended (or vice versa). It should be obvious that assorted foreigners need a common language of behavior if they are to get along with one another in the civilized atmosphere best suited to solving international problems.

Just when Miss Manners thinks she has managed to get it across that civilization is better than chaos, and coherence better than incoherence, some fool comes along to ask why those who conduct international diplomacy can't just relax and be themselves. Why are state visits and other international rituals so stuffy? they want to know. Must everyone be so stiff and formal? Don't people get along better when they act natural and friendly? ("Natural" and "friendly" are commonly used now to denote blue jeans, first names, and psychobabble, while all other possible styles are condemned as "stiff" and "stuffy," especially those which come naturally to Miss Manners and which she finds relaxing.)

American businessmen and women, with their expertise in accepted business strategies involving the knowledgeable use of turf, power lunches, and dressing to kill, are proud of their ability to use symbolic behavior. They do not tend to relax during negotiations, express their personal emotions at the expense of their business interests, or go wild and free with the fun of it all when entertaining clients or bosses. If they think about it, they do not want the representatives of their country abroad to do so either. Do we really care to be represented by a bunch of mellow souls, each pursing his individuality at, in more ways than one, the national expense?

Then what is all this nonsense about protocol being ridiculous? Miss Manners thinks it comes from the popular idea that, left alone, everyone—countries as much as individuals—naturally behaves kindly, and that trouble and conflict arise from too much, rather than too little, civilization. From this, you get the idea that harmony is best achieved by revealing accurately everything in one's heart and mind (or national agenda), because only lovable things can be found there; that formality is incompatible with charm because spontaneous expressions are more endearing than thoughtful ones; and that people who have opposing goals will drop their selfish interests once they know about the desires of others.

This idea is bad enough in everyday life, where etiquette provides a decent cover for unattractive feelings and an acceptable method of avoiding confrontation or solving conflicts. Among countries with even slightly opposing ideological, territorial, or economic interests, the unfettered expression of these natural but conflicting desires would be disastrous. So, to all those American diplomats on duty abroad, Miss Manners extends her thanks for not relaxing on the job.

Formality in the Foreign Service

DEAR MISS MANNERS:

My husband and I are both officers in the United States Foreign Service, currently stationed overseas. We will soon be transferring to another post, and three close friends expressed a desire to throw a going-away party for us, asking if we would like the party to be formal. This is a very informal post, and we all agreed that a formal dinner would present a nice, unusual chance to dress up and have fun. Soon a sit-down dinner for twenty was planned, with engraved invitations, bartender, and waiter. We were both very touched.

Meanwhile, our boss had been planning a smaller, equally appreciated, but more informal dinner. When we received the invitations, we noticed that they featured a cartoon mocking formal affairs and noted that this party would be "Casual, Black Tie Optional." We were a little nonplussed at what appeared to be a veiled snide comment about the other dinner but decided that we were being oversensitive. Five days before the formal party, our boss called one of the hosts out of a meeting to discuss it. He then gave the host what he said was "advice," calling the dinner "pretentious, juvenile, and collegiate." The boss said in no uncertain terms that the idea of a formal dinner was offensive to him and his wife, and implied that others felt similarly. He said that in all his fifteen years in the Foreign Service he had worn a tuxedo only twice, and none of his acquaintances owned tuxedos. When he discovered that the dinner was to be sit-down, he became still more indignant. After listening to the diatribe, the host coolly informed the boss that there had been no intent to offend anyone, and that if the boss and his wife would not feel comfortable at a formal dinner, they did not need to attend, although they were still welcome.

We could not believe that a seasoned diplomat could be so outrageously rude and unkind. If his intention was truly to teach the newer officers about U.S. Foreign Service usage, would he not have been better served by doing so after the fact? I assure you that the intent of having a formal dinner was an innocent wish to do something out of the ordinary. It was thoughtful and original of our friends, and we included all of our American work colleagues so that no one would feel slighted. We felt responsible for smoothing this over. Since the issue was so emotional, and since the host told us that he never should have discussed the matter with us, we simply pretended that we knew nothing. We are going to the party full of affection for our thoughtful friends, trying to ignore the pall cast on it.

We realize that such an affair is slightly pretentious, but we are playing along with it for the fun of dressing up and eating graciously.

GENTLE READER:
It is a sad day when Americans feel that simple formality is pretentious, or even, as you do, "slightly pretentious," good chiefly for a lark. Miss Manners has never believed that democracy meant that no one could rise to such dignity; she thought it meant that anyone who wanted to could. She is particularly shocked that a "seasoned diplomat" would be unaware of what a valuable tool formality has always been in his trade. It enables people with seriously opposing viewpoints to resolve them in an atmosphere of civilized restraint. That is why professions that deal in conflict—not only diplomacy but the law, the military, and sports—pay close attention to matters of dress and form. Miss Manners only wishes that she could register more genuine shock that an American official considered it proper for him to evaluate the private social lives of his subordinates.

The White House Dinner

Contrary to popular belief and in defiance of the obvious entertainment value, no presidential couple in recent decades has given an improper state dinner. While it is true that Miss Manners has witnessed the odd incident when a President had too much fun or a guest had an amazing sartorial mishap, these are mere accidents to which any social function is liable, no matter how carefully planned.

In her travels, Miss Manners has discovered that it is a national amusement to suppose that the perceived style of any given administration is dramatically demonstrated in its formal functions, and thus to picture one era as hilariously hayseedy and another as stupefyingly glamorous. Such, she feels obliged to report, is not the case. State functions necessarily employ a set routine that any politician can follow. Avoiding nasty surprises by having everyone familiar with the same graceful pattern is one of the aims.

Naturally, this form has been modified over the years, although the reason stated for each change has remained identical. Since the Republic began, politicians have been earning admiration for declaring that they personally hate all royalist trappings. This is a commendable stand of which Miss Manners thoroughly approves, provided that one does not confuse the dignity of formality with aristocratic pretension, and thus condemn all attempts to be serious and ceremonial. Miss Manners doesn't grudge anyone's enjoying state dinners—she good-naturedly hopes everyone will—but she tries hard to believe that her taxes pay for more than simple recreation.

She has no quarrel with the basic form of the modern White House dinner, which is low-key formal. The last major innovations ("major" is a relative term when we're talking dinner parties), which happened in the Kennedy Administration, were sensible, in her opinion. Dinner was cut back to four or five courses from seven (in the good old days, it was closer to thirty) and served on small round tables, where guests could be mixed without violating protocol, rather than at one huge E-shaped table, where they had to be lined up without regard to compatibility. Notice that these are both changes that scale down oppressive formality. Miss Manners is not unreasonable.

There has been a great deal of slippage in the last dozen years, petty changes that were not for the better but were designed to meet sinking standards. White House guests are no longer expected to write answers to invitations; they may use the telephone. They are allowed to bring their own guests—not just spouses or a grown-up child, but anyone they fancy who is not an outright security risk—as a result of which the White House has lost control over who receives the honor of being there. Nor is it always treated as a high honor by guests or hosts. Perhaps because of the comparatively casual way invitations are now made, they have also been casually refused. Only illness, a death in the family, or hardship in making the trip are legitimate excuses for declining such an august invitation, but now one occasionally reads of a celebrity's having airily refused to go to the White House because of rehearsal fatigue or a livelier party elsewhere. That the chosen guests should be exemplary citizens is an ideal not examined too closely, heaven knows, but the presence, now and then, of celebrities who are willful defiers of common American standards cheapens the honor.

Miss Manners' recommendation for how to give a proper White House dinner is: with confidence. If the White House can't set a standard, who, besides poor Miss Manners, can? If guests were invariably chosen for their worth, rather than the kind of fame that does not exclude notoriety, and if they were made to understand that they must take the invitation seriously and attend to the formalities involved, the dignity of the occasion and everyone involved would be enhanced. Who knows, it might even encourage citizens to treat their friends' invitations with careful respect. That would constitute the proper trappings of a democracy.

Questions of Precedence

DEAR MISS MANNERS:

I am planning a dinner party at which my guests will include a retired monsignor of the Catholic Church, a retired colonel of the air force, a retired captain of the infantry, and several other guests. My problem is, who gets precedence in introducing and seating? The monsignor is much older than the colonel. Do I use the colonel's and captain's titles, although they were retired after World War II? They would like it, but I don't know if it is correct.

GENTLE READER:

In unofficial situations, both age and clerical status are given deference. The military go in order of rank, but in cases where two people are of equivalent rank in different services, the order of precedence of the services prevails. One addresses retired officers by their titles unless one knows that they prefer otherwise. Miss Manners threw all this in merely because your party is too easy: (1) the monsignor, (2) the colonel, (3) the captain. Please let her know when you are presiding at an official occasion on which you have invited a young bishop, an elderly, retired Commandant of the marine corps, a foreign vice admiral, and Mother Teresa.

DEAR MISS MANNERS:

I am celebrating my ninetieth birthday. My rabbi and the congressman of the district will be present. Please let me know who should be greeted first.

GENTLE READER:

The one who arrives first. In strict order of precedence, your representative would outrank your rabbi. You could, however, accord the rabbi courtesy precedence. No politician in his right mind would object.

❧ TITLES

She is not "Princess Diana." You perhaps know the lady Miss Manners means—the blonde one, who wears hats so nicely but has not always managed to keep her hair out of her eyes; the one who seems to attract so much attention. Born a commoner, she was styled "Lady Diana" by courtesy because her father is an earl. She is now, having married up, "The Princess of Wales." Only should she become queen consort would a royal title appear before her first name, as "Queen Diana." Is that clear?

Of course not. We Americans decided long ago to reject the idea of classifying some people as, by virtue of birth or marriage, belonging to a higher order of humanity than their fellow citizens. The British do show up on our shores now and again, however, and mild interest is taken in their wardrobes and activities, so one may want to know their usage. Besides, it is difficult to make one's way through nineteenth-century British novels or twentieth-century British television without being able to figure out who is called what and why. The subject is infinitely complicated, and disputes have been known to last for centuries. Miss Manners will concern herself only with the basic outline.

Only the reigning queen and her mother (as the widow of the previous king) are addressed as "Your Majesty," other members of the royal family being addressed as "Your Royal Highness." Children of the sovereign also use the prefix "The," as in "Their Royal Highnesses, The Prince and Princess of Wales."

The peerage has five grades, in descending order: duke (not to be confused with royal dukes), marquess (most use the good old English spelling rather than the French "marquis"), earl, viscount, and baron. The female equivalents, for wives or widows (the latter styled "dowager" if the succeeding peer has a wife) are: duchess, marchioness, countess, viscountess, and baroness. There are also countesses and baronesses in their own right. Except for dukes and duchesses, who are called by those titles, peers and peeresses are addressed as "Lord" or "Lady," with the name of the senior peerage they possess.

Legally, the children of these people are all commoners. However, dukes, marquesses and, earls tend to have other titles as well and, by courtesy, their sons and heirs apparent (as opposed to an heir presumptive, who is heir but not son to someone who is still presumed, sometimes by courtesy, to be able to produce a son) use the next family title down until after, courteously enough, the funerals, not the deaths, of their fathers. Younger sons of dukes and marquesses are styled "Lord" before their given names and family surnames (which are apt to be different from the peerage name), dropping the surname on second reference. Their wives use the husbands' given names, rather than their own, with "Lady."

Daughters of dukes, marquesses, and earls have the courtesy title of "Lady" preceding their given names and surnames, keeping the designation if they marry and change their surnames. The younger sons of an earl, and all sons and daughters of viscounts or barons are styled "The Hon." before their full names, but that designation is never used except on envelopes and by the formidable Mitford girls—when they were girls, rather than writers and duchesses.

Then there are titled commoners: baronets, whose degrees of honor are hereditary, and knights, whose are not. They use "Sir" before their full names, but are addressed with the title and given name only. Their wives use "Lady" with the surname only, never with their given names (a common American error), unless they happen also to be the daughters of dukes, marquesses, or earls.

This is only the beginning. Miss Manners will not bore you with the collateral privileges of the siblings of heirs presumptive who succeed, the rights of duchesses who were divorced in interesting trials, the children of peers who disclaimed their peerages, and so on. She only asks you to stop saying "Princess Diana." Never mind that British newspapers do it all the time. Wherever did you Americans get the notion that the British always behave properly?

Her Royal Highness

DEAR MISS MANNERS:

Several of us who contribute to a sports magazine have had the unexpected pleasure of meeting Princess Anne of Great Britain during equestrian events. Ever since, we've been debating how we should have addressed her. Calling someone "highness" just because of her birth into a certain family didn't appeal to me. I was afraid that she might not like to be called "Mrs." (or "Ms.") Phillips." I considered calling her by her title and first name; that would simply recognize what she is, without implying any status derived from it. However, it seemed somewhat familiar. I wound up not addressing her by name at all, which seemed rude. The problem is unlikely to recur, but I would like to know the proper way for an American to address one holding an hereditary title.

GENTLE READER:

While sympathizing with your interest in democratic symbolism, Miss Manners also believes in humoring people by using the style of address they prefer. While the lady in question is, indeed, "Her Royal Highness, The Princess Royal" she is not addressed as such. The initial correct address to her is "Your Royal Highness," but if you can't stomach that, you may proceed directly to the second correct address, which is "Ma'am."

Past Presidents

DEAR MISS MANNERS:

I am a house interpreter in the Charlottesville home of our fifth president, James Monroe. In my presentation, I refer to the gentleman as "Mr. Monroe." Recently, one of our guests sparked quite a controversy among our staff by suggesting that I was incorrect. He said that the presidency was the highest office the man had held, and that he should be called "President Monroe"; We learned from you that one should not address him as "President Monroe;" however, we weren't sure if we could refer to him as such. We found that, for the most part, his contemporaries called him "Col. Monroe" throughout his life, ignoring the variety of offices that he held. Please tell us what was correct in his lifetime (1758–1831) and what is correct today.

GENTLE READER:

The rule that only one living person holds the title of "President of the United States" was in effect from the beginning of the country, and former presidents who modestly observed it (Miss Manners says nothing of the motivations of contemporary ex-presidents who violate it) used a previous (military or state) title after leaving office. For example, both George Washington and Dwight D. Eisenhower were styled "General" in retirement. Should James Monroe return home, you would be correct to greet him as "Colonel."

The question of proper address does not apply to the deceased. It is customary to refer to historical figures by the titles that best identify them, but not with courtesies you would use face to face. If you refer to any British monarch in your explanation, you do not, Miss Manners trusts, style him "His Majesty." It would be inappropriate for you to refer to the gentleman as "Colonel Monroe" now, as it would imply that you were on speaking terms with him; and it is appropriate for you to refer to him as "President Monroe," the "former" being understood.

Miss Manners does take issue with your critic over his explanation. It is not rude to style an American gentleman "Mr."

Senators

DEAR MISS MANNERS:

I recently wrote to my senator and realized I didn't know the right salutation for him. I recall that you address a senator differently in writing than in person.

GENTLE READER:

No, it is "Senator Loyal" to his face and "Dear Senator Loyal" in a letter. You may be thinking of the envelope, on which his full name is on a line by itself, preceded by "The Honorable." Or you may be thinking of what people call him behind his back.

Dishonorables

DEAR MISS MANNERS:

What is the proper salutation for a former congressman or judge who has been convicted of accepting bribes and is now serving his country in a federal penitentiary? I know that former public officials are normally addressed as "The Honorable John Doe," but does the conviction for acts of moral turpitude serve to revoke the "Honorable"? Where I come from, this is not a theoretical question.

GENTLE READER:

At the rate things are going, we may soon need a set of regulations spelling out exactly which of the many interesting forms of moral turpitude that our public servants seem to enjoy indulging in should result in revoking their privilege of being addressed as "Honorable." Miss Manners will be sorry when that happens. The ironic humor in so addressing an inmate of a federal penitentiary fills her with such glee that she is tempted to find out who your former state officials are for the sheer pleasure of writing out those envelopes.

Index

Index

N

U

V

W

Miss Manners' best friend, almost from the time she was born, is David Hendin, whose brilliance has shone on her every undertaking.

She is also indebted—and very grateful—to Diana L. Drake, Linda Bosson, Jennifer Georgia, Eileen Schlesinger, and Cindy Williams.